Contemporary Research in E-Branding

Subir Bandyopadhyay
Indiana University Northwest, USA

INFORMATION SCIENCE REFERENCE

Hershey · New York

Director of Editorial Content:	Kristin Klinger
Director of Production:	Jennifer Neidig
Managing Editor:	Jamie Snavely
Assistant Managing Editor:	Carole Coulson
Typesetter:	Larissa Vinci
Cover Design:	Lisa Tosheff
Printed at:	Yurchak Printing Inc.

Published in the United States of America by
Information Science Reference (an imprint of IGI Global)
701 E. Chocolate Avenue, Suite 200
Hershey PA 17033
Tel: 717-533-8845
Fax: 717-533-8661
E-mail: cust@igi-global.com
Web site: http://www.igi-global.com

and in the United Kingdom by
Information Science Reference (an imprint of IGI Global)
3 Henrietta Street
Covent Garden
London WC2E 8LU
Tel: 44 20 7240 0856
Fax: 44 20 7379 0609
Web site: http://www.eurospanbookstore.com

Library of Congress Cataloging-in-Publication Data

Contemporary research in e-branding / Subir Bandyopadhyay, editor.

    p. cm.

  Includes bibliographical references and index.

  Summary: "This book presents research on the emergent global issue of the Internet as a central organizing platform for integrating marketing communications"--Provided by publisher.

  ISBN 978-1-59904-813-0 (hardcover) -- ISBN 978-1-59904-815-4 (ebook)

  1. Internet marketing. 2. Branding (Marketing) 3. Communication in marketing. I. Bandyopadhyay, Subir, 1958-

  HF5415.1265.C665 2009

  658.8'72--dc22

                2008014459

British Cataloguing in Publication Data
A Cataloguing in Publication record for this book is available from the British Library.

Dedication

To the memory of my parents

Table of Contents

Detailed Table of Contents

    Subir Bandyopadhyay, Indiana University Northwest, USA
    Rosemary Serjak, University of Ottawa, Canada

In recent years, many online brands (or e-brands) have emerged. For a brick-and-mortar brand to excel in the online environment, the brand manager must appreciate some of the key features of the Internet and make adjustments to the traditional brand management strategy. For example, the control of communication in case of online brand management lies with both the brand manager and the consumer, whereas from the traditional branding perspective, the control by and large rests with the brand manager only. The authors of this chapter highlight the differences between traditional brand management and online brand management. They then focus on several key success factors in building a successful online brand, which they believe will help guide the brand manager through a series of steps leading to successful online branding.

    Luis Casaló, University of Zaragoza, Spain
    Miguel Guinalíu, University of Zaragoza, Spain
    Carlos Flavián, University of Zaragoza, Spain

The Internet is taking on an increasingly major role in political marketing and branding strategies. This is because of the use that the public itself is making of the Internet when taking part in the decisions made by their representatives and in the events of the environment they live in. These digital citizens have found in the Internet, particularly blogs, a new way of forming relationships with politicians, by communicating with them directly, coordinating their activities with other citizens with similar political ideals or even financing electoral campaigns. This chapter describes the use that some political leaders have made of blogs. Therefore, the authors analyze the two cases that represented the beginning of the use of the Internet as a major electoral tool: Howard Dean and Wesley Clark in the Democrat primaries in the USA in the 2003-04 campaign. Thanks to the analysis of these two cases and the theories developed around the concept of social capital and virtual communities, this paper presents the main characteristics of this type of digital citizen and the possible political marketing strategies developed around them. The analysis of these cases provides various implications for better management of these political marketing tools, whose potential is yet to be discovered.

## Chapter III

This study tries to identify the brand personality dimensions that search engine companies create in the minds of Internet users by using past research on brand personality scales as a guide. Furthermore, it is also aimed to determine the distinct brand personality dimensions of Google as the most preferred and used search engine. It is found that Google has been perceived as the most "competent" search engine brand. Furthermore, depending on the MANOVA results, it is shown that all three search engines have statistically significant differences only on the "competence" dimension. "Sincerity" and "excitement" are the other two dimensions which significantly differentiate Google from both MSN and Yahoo.

## Chapter IV

This chapter examines whether classical brand naming concepts are sustainable for entrepreneurial firms in the Net Economy. A prior study of Kohli and LaBahn (1997) covers the formal brand naming process and gives insights into brand name objectives and criteria. To follow the research purpose, their findings have been adapted to entrepreneurial firms in the Net Economy. 319 E-entrepreneurs located in German business incubators were analyzed for their brand naming process. The availability of an appropriate domain name is found to be a basic driver for deciding on a brand name. The domain name influences the course of action during the naming process. Two groups were found that significantly differ in proceeding with the naming process. One group of E-entrepreneurs follows the traditional process of Kohli and LaBahn (1997), whereas the other group follows a new approach giving more emphasis on the domain name. Here, the process shows to be iterative in nature instead of a step by step procedure.

## Chapter V

Consumer-centric organizations recognize customer relationships with brands as a source of sustainable competitive advantage that they can leverage to successfully introduce brand extensions. Marketers seeking to leverage brand equity associated with core offline products to introduce e-brand extensions recognize that success depends on initiating brand relationships with prospective customers, as well as maintaining relationships with existing customers. This research proposes and empirically demonstrates that investment on e-branding relationships with current users generates higher returns for online extensions that have close fit with the core offline product. In contrast, investments on non-users have a higher return on adoption of online brand extensions that have low-fit with core products, compared to current customers and can increase overall profitability. Further, the authors show that website features like personalized email and interactive aids have a significantly higher impact on customer profitability and motivate prospective consumers to move to higher levels of relationship with the firm, than financial incentives like sales promotions. Managerial implications for return on e-branding investments and future research directions are discussed.

Chapter VI

> *Fang Wan, University of Manitoba, Canada*
> *Ning Nan, University of Oklahoma, USA*
> *Malcolm Smith, University of Manitoba, Canada*

Though marketers are aware that online marketing strategies are crucial to attract visitors to Websites and make the website sticky (Hoffman et al., 1995; Morr, 1997; Schwartz, 1996; Tchong, 1998), little is known about the factors that can bring out such a compelling online experience. This chapter examines how specific Web atmospheric features such as dynamic navigation design, together with Web users' surfing goals, can lead to an optimal online experience. In addition, the chapter also examines the consequences of an optimal surfing experience on consumers' attitudes toward commercial websites/brands (promoted on these sites) and purchase intentions. In this chapter, the authors review related research on online consumer experience, identify two key antecedents of the optimal online experience, report an experiment testing the effects of these antecedents and provide insights for future research.

Chapter VII

> *José J. Canals-Cerdá, Federal Reserve Bank of Philadelphia, USA*

Internet markets are usually under the command of a market intermediary that charges fees for its services. Differences in quality across items being sold allow the market intermediary to employ lucrative nonlinear pricing strategies and to offer different levels of service. For several years now, eBay has been using a nonlinear pricing policy that offers sellers the opportunity of having their items listed first when buyers search for specific products in return for an additional fee. A similar pricing strategy is also used in other online markets like Overstock.com and ArtByUs.com, and is also employed by search engines when sponsored links are displayed first. In this paper, the authors analyze this topic from a theoretical and empirical perspective. Results also indicate that the pricing policy implemented by eBay increases revenues significantly for sellers and for the market intermediary when compared with a single-price policy and acts as a coordination mechanism that facilitates the match between buyers and sellers.

## Chapter VIII

Brand positioning is a crucial strategy to any brand's strategy. Given the rapid development of technology and it impact on online strategies, changing lifestyles of consumers and the consumer interaction required as a part of contemporary brand strategy, there may be need for brands to synergize their positioning strategies with online positioning strategies. This would enable brands to adapt to an environment which is increasingly becoming digital. The paper after taking into consideration the published literature on brand positioning, attempts to formulate online positioning strategies using different aspects of brand positioning, price, customer interactivity and consumer community orientation. Implications for marketing managers are provided.

This chapter presents the case study of a successful dot-com venture in India, Naukri.com, in the job search market. The authors begin by providing an overview of job search methods in both general and the specific Indian contexts. The advent and growth of the e-recruitment market is also discussed. The authors then provide background information for Naukri.com by focusing on its business model, growth, organizational structure and human resource management. The product/service offerings of Naukri.com for recruiters and job-seekers are discussed next. Then, a critical analysis of the consumers of the company and their competitors is provided. The chapter concludes by assessing Naukri.com's marketing strategy during initial (1997-2000) and recent (2001-2004) time periods.

## Chapter X

Corporations rely on brands to stimulate consumer awareness and foster an affinity for their products (Spinello 2006). Legal protection against brand infringement comes from trademark law – a subsection of intellectual property law that prevents third parties from benefiting from the vale and goodwill built up in a brand (Gallafent 2006). However such legislation has developed in the offline world. How do its principles and practices transfer to e-commerce? While still a developing subject, this paper examines the ethical and legal position surrounding trademark infringement in a specific area of the electronic arena – within paid search advertising. The paper explains the rationale behind the problem, outlines the current legal situation and offers advice as to how trade name owners can better protect their e-brand.

## Chapter XI

Brands have evolved from signs of property rights to signs of product attributes to signs of consumer attributes. Brands have become an important mode of consumer communication, identifying and distinguishing consumers as social objects within consumer market culture. Virtual communities have evolved from telephonic verbal communication to highly interactive electronic media that provide rich audio-visual sensory detail that gives consumers a sense of being in an environment. As a fundamentally cultural phenomenon, marketing communication reflects shared patterns of consumer thoughts, feelings, emotions and behaviors. Virtual communities are particularly suited for communication in consumer culture because they afford consumers authentic cultural presence. Culture depends on communication. Communication depends symbols. Symbols constitute electronic environments. eBranding affords consumers the necessary tools to communicate their roles and relationships in virtual consumer culture environments for transfer to actual consumer culture environments. Consumption in actual environments results in brand viability and marketing success.

## Chapter XII

As the Internet expands to include individual applications such as banking, shopping, information gathering, and so on, brand managers and marketers have turned to the Internet to utilize it as an effective branding vehicle. Consequently, understanding how the Internet could be used effectively in e-branding becomes imperative. One barrier to a successful utilization of the Internet as a branding tool is the rate at which individuals adopt and use the various e-services made available to them. As will be discussed, adoption depends, in part, on the users' level of Internet self-efficacy. This chapter illustrates a conceptual framework for understanding Internet self-efficacy and presents findings from an exploratory experiment designed to investigate the link between self-efficacy, attitudes toward e-services and individuals' likelihood of using such e-services. Results are presented and managerial implications for e-service providers are drawn.

This study examines Websites created by American multinational corporations (MNCs) in the Czech Republic. Utilizing a content analysis technique, the authors scrutinized (1) the type of brand Website functions, and (2) the similarity ratings between the home (US) sites and Czech sites. Implications are discussed from the Website standardization versus localization perspective.

## Chapter XIV

Limited studies have investigated online consumer loyalty and retention from a relationship orientation in electronic commerce research. It is important to understand the differences in relationship orientations between people who have the propensity to stick to particular web sites ("stayers") and people who have the propensity to switch to alternative web sites ("switchers"). This study proposes a relationship-based classification schema consisting of five dimensions, i.e., commitment, trust, satisfaction, comparison level of the alternatives, and non-retrievable investment. Data were collected from 299 college students who had experience with e-commerce websites. Using discriminant analysis, the authors found that stayers and switchers were significantly different along the five research dimensions. Satisfaction with the current website was the most important discriminant factor, followed by trust, commitment, comparison level of alternative websites, and non-retrievable investment in the current website. Implications of the findings for researchers and practitioners are discussed.

    Piyush Sharma, Nanyang Business School, Singapore
    Rajiv Mathur, Percom Limited, New Delhi, India
    Abhinav Dhawan, team4U Outsourced Staffing Services, New Delhi, India

Offshore outsourcing is a fast-growing aspect of the world economy today and it has drawn attention from policy makers as well as public at large in many developed countries. However, there is hardly any research on how outsourcing of customer services may influence individual consumers, their perceptions, attitudes and behaviors. In this chapter, the authors first review the extant literature in the country-of-origin and services marketing areas to highlight key concepts and theories relevant to this area. Next, they show how offshore outsourcing of customer services may influence consumer perceptions about service quality, brand image and brand loyalty on one hand and impact customer satisfaction, complaint behavior and repurchase intentions on the other. The role of several relevant demographic and psychographic variables is also discussed. Finally, the findings from a survey-based study among customers in three developed countries (US, UK and Australia) are reported along with a discussion of managerial implications and future research directions in this area.

    Edward J. Garrity, Canisius College, USA
    Joseph B. O'Donnell, Canisius College, USA
    Yong Jin Kim, Sogang University, Korea & State University of New York at Binghamton, USA
    G. Lawrence Sanders, State University of New York at Buffalo, USA

This paper contributes to the literature in three ways. Firstly, the proposed model provides a nomological network of success factors that provides a better understanding of how intrinsic and extrinsic motivation factors impact the use of systems in general and websites in particular. Secondly, this paper incorporates two dimensions, Decision Support Satisfaction and Interface Satisfaction, as antecedent variables to expand our understanding of Perceived Usefulness (implemented as Task Support Satisfaction). Thirdly, Decision Support Satisfaction not only provides for enhanced explanatory power in the model, but it can also offer important insights into the decision support provided by consumer shopping-oriented web information systems (Garrity et al., 2005). This is especially important because consumer shopping-oriented web information systems differ from conventional DSS in a number of ways, including and most notably that consumers have an extensive and different decision making process from managers (O'Keefe & McEachern, 1988).

## Chapter XVII

The topic of online consumer behavior has been examined under various contexts over the years. Although researchers from a variety of business disciplines have made significant progress over the past few years, the scope of these studies is rather broad, the studies appear relatively fragmented and no unifying theoretical model is found in this research area. In view of this, the authors provide an exhaustive review of the literature and propose an integrative model of online consumer behavior so as to analyze the online consumer behavior in a systematic way. This proposed framework not only provides us with a cohesive view of online consumer behavior, but also serves as a salient guideline for researchers in this area. The chapter concludes with a research agenda for the study of online consumer behavior.

## Chapter XVIII

Multi-channel retailers that utilize an eCRM approach stand to benefit in multiple arenas - by providing targeted customer service as well as gaining operational and competitive advantages. To that end, it is inherent that multi-channel retailers better understand how satisfaction – a necessary condition for building customer loyalty – influences consumers' decisions to shop in one retail channel or another. The purpose of this study was to examine the influence of shopping experience on customers' future purchase intentions, both for the retailer and for the channel. Using a controlled experimental design, U.S. and European subjects responded to a series of questions regarding the likelihood making a future purchase following either a positive or negative shopping encounter. Results suggest that shopping intentions vary based on the shopping channel as well as cultural differences.

Among the potential determinants of consumers' commitment to on-line shopping site are information features of the web site because on-line shopping consumers have to base their judgment solely on the product or service information presented on the site. When consumers are satisfied with such information features and perceive clear benefits from their relationships with the site, we can expect them to be more committed to the site. This study investigates the relationship between such determinants and consumers' commitment to an on-line shopping site. Results of the on-line survey with 1,278 Korean customers of on-line bookstores and ticketing services indicate that information satisfaction and relational benefit are highly predictable of consumers' commitment to an on-line shopping site. In addition, the authors found that information satisfaction is affected most by product information quality while relational benefit is strongly related to service information quality. These results seem to reflect the consumers' different perceptual weights to different information contents of the web sites in forming their web site perceptions.

Preface

It is indeed a pleasure for me to announce the publication of the book titled, *Contemporary Research in E-Branding*. In recent years, many online brands or e-brands have emerged. Also, most traditional brands or brick and mortar brands have introduced corresponding e-brands. These e-brands, however, have met with varying levels of success. In order to ensure continued success of their e-brands, brand managers must appreciate the strengths and weaknesses of the online environment. It is also important for them to explore relevant theories and study cases of companies that are successful in developing e-brands. This book contains a set of excellent chapters that offer a smorgasbord of research findings on e-branding. These chapters encompass research undertaken in many countries thereby providing a wide coverage of how e-branding is practiced across the world. In order to offer readers with a wide variety of scholarly work on e-branding in one book, we have included five articles published earlier in other IGI publications. At the end, we include five more papers in the "Selected Readings" . These papers are not necessarily on e-branding, but offers the readers a set of valuable reference on related topics such as online consumer behavior, online customer behavior, online shopping experience, and eCRM.

The first chapter by Subir Bandyopadhyay and Rosemary Serjak titled, "Key Success Requirements for Online Brand Management" outlines the difference between traditional branding and e-branding. For example, the control of communication for e-brands rest with both the brand manager and the consumer, whereas for online branding, the control of communication rests largely with the brand manager. Authors go on to outline the critical success factors for an e-brand. According to them, the most critical steps to developing an e-brand is (1) creating name recognition, (2) providing a unique product and/or exceptional customer service, and (3) advertising through a variety of media.

The second chapter discusses an interesting application of virtual communities, particularly blogs, in political branding. In this chapter titled, "The Role of Blogs on a Successful Political Branding Strategy", Luis Casaló, Carlos Flavián and Miguel Guinalíu describe the use that some political leaders have made of blogs. They outline the electoral campaigns of Howard Dean and Wesley Clark in the Democratic Primaries in 2003-2004. It is interesting to note here that almost all candidates in the 2007-2008 campaign have extensively used the blogs to communicate with citizens, provide a forum to supporters to network with one another, and even raise funds for their electoral campaigns.

The next chapter deals with brand personality – a critical property of a brand. In their chapter titled, "Brand Personality of Web Search Engines: Who is the Conqueror of the Digital Age?", Aslihan Nasir and Suphan Nasir compare the brand personality profiles of three major search engines (MSN, Yahoo, and Google) on five dimensions of brand personality: sincerity, excitement, competence, sophistication, and ruggedness. These comparisons reveal an interesting differentiation between the three major search engines.

The importance of corporate e-branding is highlighted in the next chapter titled, "The Naming of Corporate eBrands." Tobias Kollmann and Christina Suckow emphasize that an online company should specify the objectives for the brand name first before prioritizing the brand name criteria. Based on a survey of more than one hundred e-entrepreneurs in Germany, they rank-order a set of brand name criteria in terms of their importance to brand management.

For any off-line brand to venture into e-brand extension, it is important to understand how to leverage brand equity of core off-line products to introduce e-brands. The next chapter titled, "Returns on e-Branding Investment: Linking Pre-Acquisition Marketing Activity to Customer Profitability", the author Patrali Chatterjee addresses the issue. She empirically demonstrates that investment on e-branding relationships with existing users generates higher returns for e-brand extensions that have close fit with the core off-line products.

The next chapter titled, "Consumers' Optimal Experience on Commercial Web Sites: A Congruency Effect of Web Atmospheric Design and Consumers' Surfing Goal" investigates if consumer attitude toward an e-brand is influenced by consumers' online experience. According to the authors Fang Wan, Ning Nan and Malcolm Smith, consumers' optimal online experience depends on the congruence or synergy between Web design features (such as static vs. dynamic navigation design) and Web users' surfing goals (such as information seeking vs. fun seeking). They empirically show that the pairing of a dynamic navigation design with a fun-seeking goal produces a more optimal online experience than the incongruent pairings of dynamic designs with an information-seeking goal, or a static navigation system with a fun-seeking goal.

The success and longevity of e-brands depend largely on their ability to generate sustained revenue. Successful e-brands such as eBay and Amazon achieve this objective through innovative product and pricing strategies. In the next chapter titled, "Nonlinear Pricing in E-Commerce", José Canals-Cerdá outlines one such innovative pricing strategy called "Featured Plus" (FP) pricing developed by eBay. Here, the company (e.g., eBay) offers the sellers the option of having their items listed first, if they pay an extra fee, when buyers search for specific items. Results indicate that the FP policy has an important positive effect on revenues for eBay and for the sellers in the market for arts sold by self representing artists.

Brand positioning is a critical strategy to any branding strategy. In the next chapter titled, "The E-Mode of Brand Positioning: The Need for an Online Positioning Interface", the author S. Ramesh Kumar deals with the brand positioning of e-brands. Based on in-depth study of several examples of successful international as well as Indian e-brands, he outlines a set of implementable positioning strategies for e-brands.

The next chapter comes to us from India. In his paper titled, "Job Search at Naukri.com: Case Study of a Successful Dot-Com Venture in India", Sanjeev Swami outlines how an Indian company has successfully developed an online portal for job seekers in direct competition with the powerful *monster.com* in India.

The following chapter titled, "Trademark Infringement in Pay-Per-Click Advertising" deals with a critical issue faced any brand – how to protect its brand name or the trade mark. This is even more challenging in the online environment because of the practice of paid placement offered by many paid search networks. Here a company can bid for third party trade names as keywords with the hope of reaching highly targeted prospects. Trade name holders claim that such practices divert business from their sites, thereby damaging their brand developed in the off-line world. The author, Peter O'Connor, cites several landmark cases both in the US and Europe, and highlight the contrasting positions taken by the US and European courts in this matter.

In the next chapter titled, "E-Branding the Consumer for Cultural Presence in Virtual Communities", the author Robert Pennington explores the relationship between a company, a brand, a consumer, and the consumer's social environment (e.g., a virtual community). In the acquisition process, brands often mean the relationship between the consumer and the branded product. They can also signify the relationship between the consumer and the producer who "brands" the product. But in the consumption process, the relationship is somewhat different. Once a consumer acquires the brand, the producer is no longer part of the relationship between the brand and the consumer. Rather, a third element—the social environment (e.g., a virtual community)—replaces the producer in this triadic relationship.

The next chapter titled, "Impact of Internet Self-Efficacy on E-Service Brands", Terry Daugherty, Harsha Gangadharbatla, and Matthew S. Eastin explore the influence, if any, of consumer self-confidence in using the Internet (they call it "Internet self-efficacy) on their attitude towards e-service brands and their intention to use e-service brands. They demonstrate empirically that individuals who are experts at using the Internet are more likely to have favorable attitudes toward e-services, and hence more likely to adopt such services with ease.

Because of the global reach of e-brands, companies have to decide between globalized and localized strategies. Shintaro Okazaki and Radoslav Škapa shed light into this strategic decision in their paper titled, "Understanding Brand Website Positioning in the New EU Member States: The Case of the Czech Republic." They examine the Web site communication strategies of American MNCs in the Czech Republic and compared with those in the US, the UK, France and Germany. They found that American MNCS tend to standardize their Czech sites. They believe that the same strategy is applied to other new EU member states. They attribute this strategy to the relatively recent market entry into, and relatively small size of these markets.

In the chapter titled, "Online Consumers' Switching Behavior: A Buyer-Seller Relationship Perspective", authors Dahui Li, Glen J. Browne, and James C. Wetherbe investigate online consumers' switching behavior among different Web sites. According to them, this switching behavior depends on commitment, satisfaction, trust, comparison level of the alternatives, and the extent of non-retrievable investment.

In the chapter titled, "Understanding Consumer Reactions to Offshore Outsourcing of Customer Services", Piyush Kumar, Rajiv Mathur, and Avinabh Dhawan deal with the controversial topic of offshore outsourcing. Experts are sharply divided on the impact of offshore outsourcing of services on western economies. While industries generally favor it because of its cost advantage, labor organizations oppose it for the loss of well paying jobs in the domestic market. Despite its growing importance in the World Economy, very few studies have so far investigated how offshore outsourcing influences individual consumers, their perceptions, attitudes and behaviors. In this chapter, the authors demonstrate how offshore outsourcing of customer services can influence not only consumer perceptions about service quality and brand image, but also impact customer satisfaction, brand loyalty, complaint behavior and repurchase intentions.

In Chapter XVI titled, "An Extrinsic and Intrinsic Motivation-Based Model for Measuring Consumer Shopping Oriented Web Site Success", Edward Garrity, Joseph O'Donnell, Young Jin Kim, and G. Lawrence Sanders develop a motivation-based model to measure the success of consumer shopping web sites. In particular, they explore the influence of two factors, Decision Support Satisfaction and Interface Satisfaction, on perceived usefulness (or Task Support Satisfaction) of an online shopping site.

The next chapter comes to us from Hong Kong. In this chapter titled, "A Critical Review of Online Consumer Behavior", Christy Cheung, Gloria Chan, and Moez Limayem provide an integrative model to study online consumer behavior. Their findings indicate that the literature on online consumer behavior is rather fragmented. For example, most studies focused on the intention and adoption of online shopping while few studies investigated the repurchase behavior of online shoppers.

Because of the popularity of online shopping among various consumers segments, many traditional retailers have tapped into the new channel. These multi-channel retailers, however, must understand what factors influence consumers' decision to shop in one retail channel or another. In the chapter titled, "Multi-Channel Retailing and Customer Satisfaction: Implications for eCRM", authors Patricia Warrington, Elizabeth Gangstad, Richard Feinberg, and Ko de Ruyter investigate, based on survey data collected in the US and Europe, the influence, if any, of shopping experience on a consumer's future intention to buy. They found that shopping intentions tend to vary based on the shopping channel as well as cultural differences.

The last chapter titled, "The Effect of Information Satisfaction and Relational Benefit on Consumer's On-line Shopping Site Commitment" investigates the potential determinants of online consumers' commitment to a shopping site. Using on-line survey data collected in Korea, Chung-Hoon Park and Young-Gul Kim empirically demonstrate that two potential determinants, information satisfaction and relational benefits, are highly predictable of consumers' commitment to an online shopping site. In particular, they found that information satisfaction is influenced mostly product informational quality while relational benefit is affected mostly by service information quality.

It is my sincere hope that this collection of articles on e-branding will offer the reader a broad perspective on research and application in this emerging field.

Subir Bandyopadhyay
Indiana University Northwest, USA

Acknowledgment

I wish to thank many people who helped in preparing this book. First, I would like to thank all the researchers who contributed chapters to this book. I would like to acknowledge the help I received from IGI Global at various stages of preparation of this manuscript. Kristin Roth provided critical support as I developed the outline and unique position of the book. Meg Stocking, Jessica Thompson, and in particular, Julia Mosemann, helped me in identifying potential contributors, and providing valuable editorial feedback. Julia served as the editor during the later period of development. I especially appreciate her patience, and unhesitating support.

I am also grateful to the reviewers of this book for their many insights and helpful suggestions.

Many people encouraged me to write this book. I thank Dean Anna Rominger at the Indiana University Northwest, and my colleagues, Bala Arshanapalli and Ranjan Kini for their support and encouragement. My brothers, Sumit and Sudip, encouraged me constantly from another continent whenever we had a chance to communicate.

My wife, Soumita, and children, Aishariya and Anusuya, enthusiastically supported me throughout the process. I thank them for understanding and supporting what I was trying to do during those long hours I spent in the office.

Chapter I
Key Success Requirements for Online Brand Management

Subir Bandyopadhyay
Indiana University Northwest, USA

Rosemary Serjak
University of Ottawa, Canada

ABSTRACT

In recent years, many online brands (or e-brands) have emerged. For a brick-and-mortar brand to excel in the online environment, the brand manager must appreciate some of the key features of the Internet and make adjustments to the traditional brand management strategy. For example, the control of communication in case of online brand management lies with both the brand manager and the consumer, whereas from the traditional branding perspective, the control by and large rests with the brand manager only. We highlight the differences between traditional brand management and online brand management. We then focus on several key success factors in building a successful online brand, which we believe will help guide the brand manager through a series of steps leading to successful online branding.

INTRODUCTION

Consumer enthusiasm for online shopping is on the rise. This underlines the dichotomy of supply side and demand side of the online business. Today's online consumers demand more—they do not like limited selection, slow downloads, and inadequate navigation. The e-tailers who are unable to meet rising customer expectations are destined to fail. To operate successfully, e-tailers need a clear competitive advantage based on an attractive offering, a viable business model, and a dedicated brand management team. Success also depends on loyal customers who keep on buying products and, more importantly, bring in more loyal customers through positive word-of-mouth communication. Because the Internet is in a continuous dynamic state, firms need to follow a flexible e-brand management policy. Recent trends indicate that one viable business model could encompass both a physical brick-and-mortar presence and an Internet presence.

Marketing over the Internet implies a whole new dimension in which to engage, retain, and transact with the consumer. The future looks bright for the brand manager because the number of potential customers seems boundless. It was projected that (1) the number of computers connected to the Internet grew from 2.2 million to over 43 million worldwide between January 1994 and January 1999 and (2) the number of Internet users was over 160 million as of March 1999, with over 90% of these users having joined in the last 5 years (Hanson, 2000). A recent report showed that all of these projections have been greatly exceeded; as of December 2002, there are 580 million Internet users worldwide (Nielsen-NetRatings, 2003).

Today's most successful companies, along with companies that desire to meet with financial success, are quite aware of the power of the Internet (such as economy of scale, direct communication with the consumer across the globe, etc.). However, it is still considered a relatively new mechanism with respect to the opportunity for online brand development. Due to the relative newness of the Internet and its unknown potentials, many companies do not have a results-driven path toward developing a brand on the Internet. A preliminary step includes dissecting what brand management entails for the online marketer. Although a number of recent books (see, for example, Braunstein & Levin, 2000; Carpenter, 2000; Kania, 2000; Ries & Ries, 2000) and articles (see, for example, Aaker, 2002; McWilliam, 2000; Murphy, Raffa, & Mizerski, 2003; Sealy, 1999) have addressed the issue of e-branding, no one has articulated the critical differences between traditional and online brand management. For a brand manager, it is imperative to appreciate these differences. It is natural for a brand manager to apply his/her off-line brand experience to online branding. While this approach will work to some extent, it will fail to appreciate some of the unique features of the Internet. For example, the control of communication in case of online brand management lies with both the brand manager and the consumer, whereas from the traditional branding perspective, the control mainly rests with the brand manager only.

In the following paragraphs, we will highlight two brands—one traditional off-line brand foraying into online branding, and the other a purely online brand—to show how online branding differs from traditional branding. The first brand is Procter & Gamble's Pampers diaper. Similar to many name brands, Procter & Gamble struggles to differentiate its Pampers from its competitors'. Fortunately, its Web site (www.pampers.com) has enabled Pampers to augment its core product in a variety of ways. The notable online strategies are as follows: (1) the popular "Vantastic Sweepstakes" offered a Chrysler van full of diapers; (2) a "gift pack" provided a convenient way to send a supply of Pampers along with a Fisher-Price toy to a friend; (3) a playing center, a sharing center, and a learning center offer visitors an opportunity to explore a plethora of practical issues; and (4) the Parenting Institute offers advice from experts on a myriad of issues such as health, development, and child care (see Aaker, 2002, for more details). These unique features have made the Pampers Web site the second most popular baby-care products. It is important to note that all the strategies mentioned above are unique to the Web and are difficult to duplicate in the traditional brick-and-mortar business.

The second brand we are going to highlight is Amazon.com—a brand built primarily on the Web. Amazon.com has utilized many techniques that are unique to the Web to catch the imagination of so many people. Some of the important features of Amazon's brand management strategy are as follows (see Dayal, Landesburg, & Zeisser, 2000; and Roberts, 2003 for more details):

- *Personalization*: Amazon has developed a comprehensive database customer purchase history and buying interests. As a result, it can reach a single customer with a customized offer. Customers have the control to customize their own page and also to make recommendations directly to the company.
- *Collaboration*: Amazon collaborated with Gary Trudeau, the creator of the "Doonesbury" cartoon strip to organize a contest on the Web. First, Trudeau posted the first set of a Doonesbury strip and invited visitors to the site to complete the cartoon. Each day Trudeau would evaluate each posting and selected a winner. Trudeau finally created the last section and the 11-section cartoon was completed.
- *Self-service option*: Amazon offers a variety of self-service options in its "My Account" page. These services range from reviewing personal account transaction to changing personal information.
- *Streamlined purchase process*: Amazon offers the unique "1-Click" system that stores payment information for customers so that they do not have to fill in an order form every time they make a purchase.
- *Dynamic pricing*: Amazon offers an auction page where site visitors can observe the price variations of a product and bid for it. In the off-line world, a customer can learn about the price variations only if he/she takes the trouble to check out the prices in retail stores in the neighborhood.

It is evident that the strategies outlined above are unique to the Web. An online brand manager must appreciate the strength of these innovative tools in brand building. To that extent, a brand like Pampers, which has both an off-line and an online presence, must blend the best of off-line and online techniques to build strong brands on the Web. Online brand managers must learn to select the best technique for the branding task at hand. Unfortunately, very few studies have articulated these critical differences in off-line (or traditional) and online branding techniques.

Our paper intends to fill this important void in the online branding literature. First, we outline the importance of, and challenges to, online brand management. Next we summarize the critical differences between online and traditional brand management. Finally, we present a set of critical success factors in building a successful online brand.

THE IMPORTANCE OF ONLINE BRAND MANAGEMENT

We cannot overemphasize the importance of online brand management to an online company. According to Carpenter (2000), there are a variety of differences between online and off-line branding. Carpenter states: "In the online world, distribution has emerged as being even more important than more traditional brand-building tools. If you don't have Web allies that can get your brand in front of large numbers of people at a reasonable cost, it's unlikely that your business will thrive" (p.). One must also keep account of the market momentum, or the "Mo Factor" (Carpenter, 2000). He emphasizes the need to communicate a constant sense of momentum. Smart online marketers are aware that by having momentum behind them, the barriers to business success get dissolved. Along with the sharply focused marketer will come the strategic partner eager to develop an alliance. As a result, potential competitors will think twice about entering the category. Customers will see this particular company as a winner, which in turn, strengthens the perceived quality of the brand. Hence, momentum is a critical factor to the success of an online brand.

For an existing brand, the Internet can provide a central organizing platform for integrating marketing communication functions of a company.

Instead of looking at the Internet as another medium for information and transaction, firms must take a broader view for the brand-building process with the Internet being a critical element of the process (Aaker, 2002). The brand manager should think about joint strategy that will leverage the reach and power of the Internet to boost the sales of an online as well as an off-line brand.

Challenges to Online Brand Management

The following are challenges faced by online brand managers:

1. *Insufficient use of Internet tools*: Online marketers have yet to utilize the available online tools to an optimal level. For example, according to a business media expert, in 2003, only 5% of a company's online marketing budget is spent on permission-based e-mail, which is generally considered to be a very effective method of reaching the consumer (Ottawa Business Journal, 2003). There is also not sufficient investment in customer-friendly tools that reduce operating costs. Banks are an exception in this respect where ATMs along with online banking and telephone banking have reduced the labor cost to service customers.

2. *Price- and service-sensitive customers:* Many retailers worry that a large percentage of price-sensitive customers shop online to hunt for bargains. This can cause problems for them because they are forced to compete on the basis of price, making them vulnerable to bankruptcy. In addition, studies indicate that a common complaint related to online shopping is that the product the consumer wants is out of stock. Other complaints include the following:

- The customer did not want to pay for shipping and handling

- The site performed too slowly
- The customer was uncomfortable submitting credit card information online (security concerns)
- The customer was concerned about ability to return items

3. *Lack of understanding customer expectation:* One reason that many dot-com companies fail is due to their negligence toward recognizing their customers' expectations. A static Web site or a site that is inaccessible due to the construction of the site will at the very least annoy the potential customer, hence lowering the chances of a return visit. In addition, many users become comfortable with the layout of the Web site and drastic changes to the appearance and navigation of the Web site may make customers uncomfortable and require that users "relearn" how to use the site.

4. *Use of inaccurate performance metrics:* Another recurring problem lies in the inability for e-tailers to sustain their customers. An organization can count the number of "eyeballs" that its site receives; however, the actual number of returns is unquestionably more important and more difficult to determine. The trick is to determine if your target customers are likely to visit your site and not how many "eyeballs" your site receives.

5. *Misperception about the appropriate online branding strategy:* A final problem with online brand management is the marketer's perception that an entire shift of marketing priorities is in order. Knowledge of traditional marketing should not be shelved. As of 2004, we are still in a transition mode. It is a combination of print, television, radio, and electronic advertising that will strengthen a brand. Advertising and promotional communications should be within the context

of the investment of your customers. For example, some customers do not see the need in upgrading their Pentium III processor to a Pentium IV processor, or changing the mode of their cellphone from analogue to the improved digital mode. Instead, they want new products to be interchangeable with their existing medium of technology. What should be emphasized and promoted here is the *loyalty* and *trust* of the customer. Brand managers should adhere to keeping their online customers, along with their non-Internet customers, aware of their brand, and satisfied with the goods or services they receive. Hence, it is important that online marketers realize that the Internet is not the only medium and that some Internet users are not on the "cutting edge" of technology.

Given the problems faced by online brand managers, it is clear that most of these problems are attributable to a lack of understanding of the online brand management. Specifically, brand managers often assume erroneously that a suc-

cessful off-line or traditional branding strategy will also work for online branding.

BRAND MANAGEMENT: TRADITIONAL VS. ONLINE

What we have been implying is summed up in the following: there exists a knowledge gap between the traditional marketing approach of a brand and this new and dynamic method of e-branding on the Internet. For example, many brand managers assume erroneously that a successful off-line or traditional branding strategy will also work for online branding. Conversely, many other managers believe in a complete overhaul of the traditional brand management. It is clear from the foregoing discussion that the online brand managers are not clear about the differences, if any between traditional and online brand management. Therefore, it is important for the marketer to be aware of some of the issues regarding the differences between traditional and online brand management. Exhibit 1 outlines these key differences.

Exhibit 1.

Criterion	Traditional Brand Management	Online Brand Management
1. Focus	Predominantly on product and profit	Predominantly on customer relationship
2. Scope	Mostly a line of product	Mostly corporate branding
3. Management structure R	etail managers N	ew breed of technomanagers
4. Control of communication R	ests with the brand manager	Rests with both the brand manager and the customer
5. Targeting M	ostly one-to-many	One-to-one
6. Scope of creating brand personality	Through noninteractive television and print ads	Through interactive online chat rooms and communities

Focus

Traditional brand management primarily focuses on the product and its relationship with the consumer. Kapferer (1992) posits that the strength of a brand is reflected by the number of its customers who are brand sensitive. He characterizes brand sensitivity in terms of the relationship among brands for a given consumer for a given product category. The marketing strategy, therefore, draws more attention to the general makeup of the product. The product is marketed to better appeal to the consumer, resulting in increased sensitivity and ultimately, to better profitability.

Online brand management, on the other hand, focuses principally on better customer relations. Building a relationship with the customer through personal profiles, e-mail, video, and knowledge of their journeys on the Internet is the key to the online brand manager (Kania, 2000). Introducing a brand online requires great commitment and organization. The online brand manager is better positioned to creatively meet the needs of the customer faster and more efficiently due to the speed and the personal service option that the Internet provides. The online brand manager can also attempt to influence customers without overt marketing by utilizing customer personalization. The relationship building process allows the brand manager to get to know the likes and dislikes of his/her customer; therefore, "suggestion" advertising or guiding the customer can be possible. Amazon.com is a great example of personalized service. Once a customer has purchased a book from its Web site, Amazon.com keeps a record of the purchase. When that same customer returns to the site for another purchase, suggestions are given regarding similar literature (dependent on the previous purchase and the profile of the individual) available through its Web site. One-stop shopping is also very attractive to the average consumer who ideally wants to be able to do his/her purchasing at one time, on one site, with someone he/she knows and trusts, and save money on shipping. The brand manager has the ability to design the Web site to meet the need of the average customer. This gives the online brand manager the opportunity to retain customers and increase site visitation. Simplifying the customer's life is what the aim of a virtual store should be, and therefore one-stop shopping is a popular trend that must be addressed.

Online brand management involves branding a Web site not as an actual product, but rather as a service. Since a majority of online purchases involve the same product, online brand management needs to creatively position its Web site over its competitors' who are selling the same product. Online brand management can be more complex than traditional brand management because online purchasers are much more price sensitive. For example, Proctor & Gamble (P&G) has proven to be very effective at creating brands such as Tide and Downy. P&G is able to distinguish its brand based on physical characteristics such as how well it cleans, how nice it smells, and so forth. On the other hand, Web sites distinguish themselves by their level of service (ease of use, personalization, security) and price rather than through product characteristics.

Scope

The traditional brand manager is primarily involved in the marketing of one particular line of product that accommodates concentrated efforts at planning new product campaigns, promotional activities, and advertising. Although branding is done at different levels of brand hierarchy, such as corporate brand, family brand, and product brand, product branding is the more common approach to brand management where each product requires individual branding.

Corporate branding, as opposed to product branding, is more prevalent in online brand management, especially for the click-and-mortar companies. It is beneficial to the brand manager, not only for centering of branding efforts onto one brand but also for the clarification of the organization's position in the mind of the consumer. The Internet has produced corporate brands such as CD Now, E*trade, Yahoo!, eBay, and Autobytel. These corporate brands are challenging traditional brands for the customer's top-of-mind awareness. The classic example is the online competition between BarnesandNoble.com and Amazon.com. Studies have consistently ranked Amazon higher than BarnesandNoble.com in brand awareness. We believe this is because Amazon has successfully created an online corporate brand while Barnes and Noble has not been able to create this type of online brand recognition.

It is true that many famous brands (such as Tide, Ivory, and Vicks) have Web sites of their own. However, the link with other brands in the same corporate family remains strong in brand-specific Web sites. For example, the Web site of Tide, a P&G product, heavily cross-promotes the fabric softeners made by P&G such as Downy, Bounce, Febreze, Dreft, and Dryel.

Famous corporate brands such as GE and Kraft leverage the Web even more to augment the corporate brand. For example, GE outlines its entire product line in the Web site (ge.com) under two broad categories: home products and business products. Under the home products category, GE lists its products in such diverse product lines as appliances, lighting, consumer electronics, television programs, home comfort, and safety. GE's business products include its brands in aviation, automobiles, energy, healthcare, retail, and transportation. Similarly, Kraft lists its product line under five major food categories: beverages (e.g., Maxwell House coffee and Kool-Aid), convenient meals (Oscar Meyer bacon and Digiorno frozen pizza), cheese (e.g., Philadelphia cream cheese and Kraft grated cheese), grocery (e.g., Grey Poupon condiments and Post cereals), and snacks (Chips Ahoy! cookies).

Management

In traditional brand management, retailers work in collaboration with brand managers to make pricing and merchandising decisions. Manufacturers introduce their products to the public through stores such as Wal-Mart or Target. These retail stores sell products purchased from many manufacturers along with their store brands or private labels. Retail managers think of a marketing strategy to persuade consumers to purchase goods from their establishment. For example, Wal-Mart's marketing strategy demonstrates that it will always have lower prices than its competitors.

Online brand management demands a diverse form of management. Unlike traditional brand managers, this new breed of technomanagers must execute duties pertaining to their corporate Web site. An online brand manager's duties consist of measuring Web site traffic, purchases, and frequency of guest visits. The information gathered on visitors' preferences is utilized to develop future marketing strategies. In addition, the online brand manger is responsible for finding out why users do not complete a transaction and correct the problem if there is one. Dot-com businesses started with an intimate knowledge of Internet technology and Web audience. Online brands are marketed by people who are technically savvy, and are adept in using interactive dialogue to bring together the user and the brands.

Successful online brands are managed by individuals who consider brand management as management of values. These brand managers view their role as that of conductors, providing brand leadership but leaving the community of customers to jointly define the brand personality (de Chernatony, 2000).

Control of Communication

The brand manager controls the unidirectional communication process in the traditional brand management. This allows the manager to decide what message is more appealing to the customers. And then the message is presented to the general public through television, radio, newspapers, or magazines. If customers desire to express their thoughts and opinions about a particular product, they can call a toll-free number, or go to the retail store to fill out a comment or suggestion card.

Conversely, customers are in control of communications online. The bidirectional nature of online communication allows the customer to control communication by leaving comments at a site. This is more direct and effective than leaving comments at a retail store. This can help the brand manager create a one-to-one relationship with the customer by showing that the company cares about each and every consumer and responds to each comment. Furthermore, comments and suggestions help online managers develop Web sites that promote increased one-to-one customer communication.

Targeting

Marketers traditionally identify segments within a broader market and design brand messages to these selected segments or target markets. While there is a distinct trend toward targeting smaller segments or niches, there is a logical limit to how small a target market can become. Cost of design, manufacturing, promotion, and distribution restrict the number of product lines. Thus, targeting is done on one-to-many basis in traditional brand management. The company wants to expand its product to a large magnitude of customers. Currently, there is no way to successfully create a close relationship with customers when products are being sold in large retail stores such as Wal-Mart. These types of stores cater to large groups of people to make purchases, and hence cannot customize their offerings according to each customer's likes and preferences.

On the Web, segmentation can be even more precise because online brand managers routinely collect information on customer profiles and their online behavior patterns. For example, Amazon. com keeps preferences of previous customers. When a customer returns to the Web site, suggestions for new books are displayed on the Web page based on criteria from the past visit or purchase. This helps the customer feel like the company knows what he/she wants. All of this can be accomplished with the use of sophisticated Internet tools available to the online brand manager.

In fact, some online companies even go one step further and target individuals. This strategy of one-to-one marketing is possible when a message or product can be targeted to one individual. The Internet makes this possible by allowing the company to address each of its customers individually. Unique Web features such as e-mail, an online community, chat, Web conferencing, auctions, and cookies help in one-to-one marketing. Many sites feature elements of one-to-one marketing. For example, Dell makes custom computers as per the specification supplied by its customers. Also, CNN allows its registered users to personalize their site, MyCNN, to include news of their choice.

The ability to interact and chat with the customer one-on-one enables a brand to customize and even personalize its offerings (Travis, 2001). The online environment enables the customer to customize his/her choice of product attributes from the list of options offered by the manufacturer on its Web site. However, that is not the end—the customer may decide to become a co-creator of the product by collaborating with the brand to develop the exact product he/she needs. This is quite common for the business-to-business customers. Engineers representing suppliers and customers often collaborate intimately to produce a piece of software or hardware specially designed for the customer. The advantage of such personalization is that the customer tends to stay with the manufacturer because he/she does not want to repeat the process with another supplier.

Scope of Creating Brand Personality

Online branding offers a broader scope of creating a brand personality. Researchers found that the exposure to the brand Web site increases the brand personality (Muller & Chandon, 2003). They also found that the brand is perceived younger and more modern, as well as more sincere and trustworthy, when a visitor has a more positive attitude toward the Web site. Moreover, they found that the effect of exposure to a Web site depends on the product category: for functional/utilitarian products (such as mobile phones), the effect of exposure on youthfulness and modernity is superior than for autoexpressive products (such as luxury clothes). These results clearly indicate that the Internet offers unique opportunity to the brand manager to augment online brand personality.

Traditionally, a company tries to create a unique personality for its brand so that a customer can identify or associate with the brand. This gives a reason for the customer to return to the site over and over again. Online brands can create electronic chat rooms for discussions where actual customers represent the personalities of the brands. Interactions between customers or between customer and company produce a much more potent association than a print or television ad that uses a model to represent the target audience. In fact, there is empirical evidence to show that online communities increase repeat site visits and time spent in a given site (Kania, 2000).

But there is much more to creating a brand personality than purely offering Internet features; customers want a balance between online and off-line features. Everything that a company does and does not do contributes to its brand personality. The way it treats its employees is reflected by the way they treat the customers. Customers also see how the item the company sells is packaged, what type of delivery trucks the company uses, what events the company sponsors, and the way the company handles problems (Zyman, 2002).

KEY SUCCESS FACTORS IN BUILDING BRANDS ONLINE

The Internet offers the potential to gain new customers by generating product awareness, increasing market penetration, and gaining off-shore customers through its global reach. In order to gain these brand-building benefits offered by the Internet, a few conditions (we call them the success factors) must be satisfied. These success factors are outlined below. Note that a number of these conditions are true for traditional (or off-line) brand building as well. We emphasize, however, on their relevance for online brand building.

Create brand recognition. This is the key step to building an online brand. The first and most critical step for a pure Internet company is to develop a name that stands out in customers' minds and relates to the item that it is selling. This may sound very much like a brick-and-mortar requirement, but it is even more important for a click-and-mortar company. Since pure click-and-mortar companies do not have a physical location that customers can drive past, creating a simple but memorable name is critical. If the Web site name is too long or complicated, potential customers will become frustrated and never check out the Web site.

One of the most often cited companies for creating a short but memorable name is Amazon.com. In addition, Amazon.com created a tag line to compliment its name: "The World's Largest Bookstore." This tag line explains why Amazon.com is a fitting name for this Web site: the Amazon River is the largest in the world and Amazon.com touts its selection of books as being the largest in the world.

There are a number of ways to create brand recognition. As we mentioned above, the company needs to develop a unique name that is easy to remember and spell. Perhaps a catchy logo or phrase will make the Web site stand out in customers' minds. Some companies even create a mascot or catchy "jingle" for the company. It is also important to have promotions and to advertise the special features of the Web site, such as speedy customer service. These last two factors, promotions and special/unique features, will be addressed later.

Protect the domain name. An online brand must steadfastly protect its domain name from unrelated firms or individuals. It is quite simple to register similar domain names and variations thereof that can confuse online consumers (Murphy et al., 2003). Usually, individuals register famous brand names to attract consumers to their sites or sell them to the highest bidder. There are two types of sites that are most harmful: gripe sites and parasites (Nemes, 2000). Gripe sites include a derogatory word to the domain name such as fordsucks.com. Parasites, on the other hand, capitalize on user typing errors (such as untied. com instead of united.com for United Airlines) to score hits. A successful online company should register all possible variations to its domain name that are vulnerable to abuse. For example, Exxon registered exxonsucks.com to preempt any possible battle with a cybersquatter.

Murphy, Raffa, and Mizerski (2003) have explored the domain name registration strategies by the world's top 75 brands. The results of their study indicate that top brands of the world are aware of the importance of global and national domain name registration. However, they are not very adept in monitoring gripe sites and parasites.

Differentiate the brand. Critical success factors differ between organizations, but it is critical that online e-tailers differentiate their brand from the crowd. This can be accomplished in a variety of ways:

- Give a good first impression on the site accompanied by good navigational tools.
- Use a domain name that is easy to remember and is globally sensitive. The aim should be to attract the right customer to the site.

- Make the Web site simple yet attractive. Design the navigational tools with this in mind.
- Make the site a one-stop shop. For example, if the Web site sells coffee, offer a variety of mugs, coffee tables, picture frames, and other amenities that would complement the product and keep the consumer and his/her money at the site.
- Offer prizes. There are some consumers who are attracted by online contests and prizes. Continuing with the above example, offer a customer the chance to win a coffee table.

E-mail is at the core of a good marketing mix. Permission-based e-mail is a key element in a profitable Internet business marketing mix. Among online purchasers, 73% claim that this is their most preferred method of learning about new products, services, and promotions from online retailers (Ottawa Business Journal, 2003). This method outranks traditional distribution channels such as TV, print, direct mail, telemarketing, and direct sales. The study conducted by FloNetwork Inc. asked online buyers how they learned about Internet merchants' goods and services. Six out of 10 respondents replied that permission-based e-mail was how they usually found out about new products, services, and/or promotions. This figure is two times more than that for banner ads, and eleven times more than that of magazines and TV combined. Additionally, 7 out of 10 online buyers divulged that they click through to a company's Web site as a result of permission-based e-mail newsletters and 61% report having made an online purchase as a result of permission-based e-mail.

Get to know who is coming to the site. Investigate how and why customers visit the Web site; then create unique ways to retain the right type of customers. There are some customers who are "thrift" shoppers and are not the "ideal" customers because they only purchase items that are on sale. These customers should not constitute the target market and hence the Web site may not want to attract only these types of customers. According to Gutzman (2000), it is actually a bad thing to get the wrong people to come to a site. The problem with having the wrong people come to a site is the confusion as to who are the real customers. This will make the brand manager's task of retaining customers even harder. In short, he/she should not focus too much on statistics and should focus more on attracting the right clientele.

The long-term goal of a Web site should be to create loyal customers who are loyal to its brand. It may be necessary to attract customers through the use of price promotions in the short-run, but in the long-run these types of promotions cannot be maintained if the Web site is losing money on each and every sale, as many of the dot-com companies discovered during the recent shakeout phase.

Encourage brand loyalty. This involves satisfying the customer over and over again. Consumer satisfaction occurs when the performance of the product exceeds expectation. The online brand manager should aim for this. Do not promise service that cannot be delivered. Offer long-term warranties, if possible, because warranties add value to the product and also increase its perceived quality. The convenience of shopping on the Internet should include a convenient service or pickup for the product. Delivery should be made in a reasonable amount of time and the product should be easily returnable, if necessary.

In addition, some customers may feel more comfortable actually speaking with a "real" person. Therefore, it is important to provide customer service through other channels besides the Internet. Consider providing a toll-free phone number, fax number, online chat sessions, and other channels preferred by customers. Do not limit the brand to being a purely Internet brand; the company should strive to create a proper balance between online and off-line presence.

Finally, loyalty programs that reward the customer for repeat purchases can be advantageous

as well. For example, the brand manager could offer his/her customers a 10% discount after five purchases. By using such a program, he/she can encourage his/her customers to come back and make future purchases.

Address the privacy issue readily and openly. Given that the almost immediate concern of customers is the privacy factor involving the information they share with the company, one way to win and keep customer's loyalty is to give them more control over how their personal information is used. To ensure a better reception from customers regarding the exchange of information, Merkow (2000) recommends the adoption of the P3P in addition to posting "human-readable" privacy policies. The P3P allows customers to control how their personal identifying information is used. It is an embedded technology in the user's browser that confirms whether a site's privacy practices meets the user's predefined privacy preferences. Another popular electronic transfer system (EFT) is i-Escrow (Greenspan, 2000). The i-Escrow holds the customer's credit card funds in a trust account and the funds are not released to the seller until the customer has received the product and is satisfied with its condition. This is also an effective way to establish customer trust and provide good customer service. Another money transfer system, PayPal, has been popularized by eBay. By using PayPal, a buyer with an e-mail address can send money to a seller who has an e-mail address.

In general, the company must offer alternatives to customers in providing sensitive financial information. Some customers may prefer to give their credit card number, while others prefer to mail a check. Let the customer pay in the manner he/she feels the most comfortable with, be it by credit card, debit card, bank transfer, money order, or personal check.

Utilize cross-selling and cross-promotion to gain competitive advantage. The notion of cross-selling entails attracting customers to the site and then marketing products that are related in some way to the primary product. When the Web site is attracting the wrong customer base, cross-selling suffers. If the Web site is selling some products at a loss in hopes of cross-selling the profitable products and it hits upon price-sensitive shoppers who will buy only at the lowest price, then the company might find that all cross-selling efforts may be in vain.

In addition, a brand manager must try to develop online media relations with other Web sites. For example, hyperlinks to areas in his/her site on other Web pages can be very useful. Combine this with the use of meta-tagging. This entails including keywords in the pages describing the content of his/her site. Words used should be related to his/her business and help guide consumers to his/her Web site. Essentially, this is how a brand manager can drive traffic to his/her site. Other key elements for online promotions include submissions to online awards, online media relations, content-focused e-mail, and online contests.

In addition to these online promotions, it is important to create an off-line presence through promotions. Customers do not learn about new companies and/or products solely through the Internet. Customers live in a dynamic environment and therefore learn about new companies/Web sites through various types of media, including television, newspaper, magazines, and other media. Therefore, be sure to incorporate well-balanced promotions to attract as many new customers as possible.

Use online and traditional means to develop and manage your brand. Having an online and off-line presence can be an important factor for all brands, both established brands and start-ups. However, it is especially important that start-ups with limited resources be firm with their advertising dollars. Besides the usual online advertising opportunities such as banner ads, pop-up ads, and so forth, a company should also target off-line buyers by using advertising such as radio in a select group of cities and/or cable

television. The mix of online and off-line media is essential to established organizations. Schwab, now a successful online brokerage house, still has 250 branches in the United States, and 70% of the American population is within 10 miles of a Schwab office. However, Schwab and e-Schwab have now become one organization due to their success online (Hanson, 2000).

Measure brand performance. In all industries and in all types of markets, it has been acknowledged that from strong brand equity flows customer loyalty and profits. The world's strongest brands share similar attributes regarding their success at branding. The foremost quality an organization should truly understand and focus on is the notion that its brand excels at providing the consumer with what he/she truly desires. A product that has been construed in a manner that complements the particular attributes the brand manager wishes to convey is going to be the winner. The attributes combined with the brand's image, the service, and other tangible and intangible components will create a complete and presentable product.

Performance Metrics

The brand manager needs to determine what his/her short-term and long-term objectives are and how he/she is going to measure the success or failure of his/her initiatives. In the rush to brand online, many companies failed to measure their Web site's performance accurately. It did not seem to matter if the company was losing money. Companies were pouring money down the drain because they failed to create metrics for performance.

The number of "eyeballs" that visit a site is measured differently depending on the company objective. How it is measured is interwoven in the online branding strategy. Some companies may choose not to measure the number of visitors because that number may be meaningless. It may be more important to measure the number of repeat visitors.

Therefore, it is essential to create specific, measurable performance metrics. For example, a brand manager may want 10% of his/her current customers to reorder within 2 weeks, and 20% to reorder within 2 months, and 50% to reorder within 1 year. He/she needs to create short-run metrics to ensure that his/her company is going to reach its long-term goals during the required time frame.

Follow a consistent brand strategy. Keeping the branding strategy consistent is essential to long-term growth and perhaps survival. There is a need to find a balance between continuity in the marketing activities and the innovation that is required to keep the product "fresh" in consumers' mind. The brand manager should not confuse his/her customer by changing or modifying his/her logo or his/her marketing message in hopes of gaining new customers, since what might happen instead is that he/she loses his/her current customers without any guarantee of attracting and retaining a larger percentage of new clients. Michelob provides a good example of what can happen when a brand endures numerous repositioning. It moved from an "It's Michelob" slogan in the 1970s to "Weekends Were Made for Michelob," and from "Put a Little Weekend in Your Week" to yet another campaign in the mid-1980s with "The Night Belongs to Michelob." This resulted in an unstoppable slide in sales. In 1994, another ad campaign titled, "Some Days Are Better Than Others" was introduced. It was designed to make the point that "a special day requires a special beer." The slogan was yet again modified to "Some Days Were Made for Michelob." As a result of continuous changes in the slogan, the average consumer was left dazed and confused as to when and where Michelob should be consumed. This was reflected in the sales performance of Michelob. In 1994, sales were 2.3 million barrels, as compared to 8.1 million barrels in 1980 (Hanson, 2000).

Some Questions Still Remain Unanswered

Given the great amount of research proclaiming the power of the Internet, we can safely assume that online communication of any type is not a trend that is soon going to disappear. However, we can admit to some fault finding in the quest to brand online. As advertising via television commercials has been experiencing difficulties in retaining the attention of viewers for quite some time, advertising and promoting on the Web is now wrestling with this same problem. How does one impress a potential online customer today? How dynamic does one's Web site have to be? What type of graphics will attract one's target market? Concurrently, the issue of customer "stickiness" or loyalty to a Web site is one that is difficult to read. How does one know if online brand management is the catalyst for an increase or a decrease in online popularity and/or sales?

The following issues also deserve some attention:

- Profiles of your customers cannot all be verified for accuracy, thereby creating a problem as to how you can define your customer and then market to them accordingly.
- How can you get online shoppers to reveal their true identity in order to serve them better and to develop a relationship of trust?
- There is an unknown time investment related to spending on advertisements and promotions via the Web.
- How do you know when to stop pouring money into your online site?
- The positioning of your brand in the mind of the consumer is often unknown to the brand manager. Thus the importance of online brand management is difficult to weigh with respect to a potential repositioning of the brand—if it is in question.

CONCLUSION

Online brand management presents a twist on traditional brand management. In order to compete in today's marketplace, it asks the brand manager not to discard his/her knowledge of traditional brand management, but rather to shift his/her priorities toward the issues and contingencies regarding online brand management. Customer satisfaction must become priority. It could in fact become the company's defining competitive advantage, given that the battle for product differentiation is stronger than ever in today's marketplace. Granted that the brand manager has more opportunity than ever before to combine technology and marketing know-how to brand a product, the online world presents many challenges. As such, the brand manager must take advantage of the Internet's global reach to perpetuate his/her company's brand.

Creating an online brand can be a very difficult and time-consuming project. But remember, the most critical steps to creating an online brand are creating name recognition, providing a unique product and/or exceptional customer service, and advertising through a variety of media. It may be easy to think of these steps as a pyramid, but each of these requirements must be met to reach the ultimate goal: customer loyalty.

Online retailing has room for growth, and this gives the brand manager more reason to hone his/her brand management skills to take advantage of the increasing number of Web-savvy customers. By adhering to the issues that most affect the brand manager and ultimately the consumer, certain routes to failure can be avoided. The brand manager can use the key success factors outlined in this paper, as a strategic guide to aid in engaging, retaining, transacting, and sustaining new customers every day.

REFERENCES

Aaker, D. A. (2002). The Internet as integrator: Fast brand building in slow growth market. *Strategy+Business, 28*, 48–57.

Amazon 2002 Annual Report. www.amazon.com

Amazon.com. (1998). Gary Trudeau and Amazon.com launch "The People's Doonesbury @ Amazon.com." Press Release Archive.

Braunstein, M., & Levin, E. H. (2000). *Deep branding on the Internet: Applying heat and pressure online to ensure a lasting brand.* Roseville, CA: Prima Venture.

Carpenter, P. (2000). *E-brands: Building an Internet business at breakneck speed.* Boston: Harvard Business School Press.

Dayal, S., Landesberg, H., & Zeisser, M. (2000). Building digital brands. *McKinsey Quarterly, 2, 3.*

de Chernatory, L. (2001). Succeeding with brands on the Internet. *Brand Management, 8*(3), 186–195.

Greenspan, R. (2000). Be seen and get paid. http://Internet_com's Electronic Commerce Guide – EC Tips.

Gutzman, A. D. (2000). Unconventional wisdom: Traffic is overrated. Retrieved , from *http://ecommerce.Internet.com/solutions/tech_advisor/article/html*

Hanson, W. (2000). *Principles of Internet marketing.* Cincinnati, OH: Southwestern College Publishing.

Kapferer, J.-N. (1992). *Strategic brand management.* London: Kogan-Page.

Kania, D. (2000). *Branding.com: Online branding for marketing success.* Chicago: NTC Business Books, American Marketing Association.

Keller, K. L. (2002). *Strategic brand management: Building, measuring, and managing brand equity* (2nd ed.). Upper Saddle River, NJ: Prentice Hall.

McWilliam, G. (2000). Building strong brands through online communities. *Sloan Management Review, Spring,* 43–54.

Merkow, M. (2000). Inside the Platform for Privacy Preferences (P3P). http://Internet_com's Electronic Commerce Guide – EC Outlook.

Muller, B., & Chandon, J.-L. (2003). The impact of visiting a brand website on brand personality. *Electronic Markets, 13,* 210–221.

Murphy, J., Raffa, L., & Mizerski, R. (2003). The use of domain names in e-branding by the world's top brands. *Electronic Markets, 13*(3), 30–40.

Nemes, J. (2000). Domain names have brand impact. *B to B Chicago, 85*(12), 20–22.

Nielsen-NetRatings. (2003, February 20). Global Internet population grows an average of four percent year-over-year.

Ries, A., & Ries, L. (2000). *The 11 immutable laws of Internet branding.* New York: Harper-Collins.

Roberts, M. L. (2003). *Internet marketing: Integrating online and offline strategies.* New York: McGraw-Hill Irwin.

Sealy, P. (1999). How e-commerce will trump brand management. *Harvard Business Review, July–August,* 171–176.

Travis, D. (2001). Branding in the digital age. *Journal of Business Strategy, 22*(3), 14–18.

Wilson, P. (2000, July 4). Canadians hot for net but slow to buy online. Retrieved , from www.ottawacitizen.com

Zyman, S. (2002). The end of advertising as we know it. Hoboken, NJ: John Wiley & Sons.

This work was previously published in Contemporary Research in E-Marketing, Vol 2, edited by S. Krishnamurthy, pp. 147-167, copyright 2005 by IGI Publishing, formerly known as Idea Group Publishing (an imprint of IGI Global).

Chapter II
The Role of Blogs on a Successful Political Branding Strategy

Luis Casaló
University of Zaragoza, Spain

Miguel Guinalíu
University of Zaragoza, Spain

Carlos Flavián
University of Zaragoza, Spain

The Internet is taking on an increasingly major role in political marketing and branding strategies. This is because of the use that the public itself is making of the Internet when taking part in the decisions made by their representatives and in the events of the environment they live in. These digital citizens have found in the Internet, particularly blogs, a new way of forming relationships with politicians, by communicating with them directly, coordinating their activities with other citizens with similar political ideals or even financing electoral campaigns. This article describes the use that some political leaders have made of blogs. Therefore, we analyze the two cases that represented the beginning of the use of the Internet as a major electoral tool: Howard Dean and Wesley Clark in the Democrat primaries in the USA in the 2003-04 campaign. Thanks to the analysis of these two cases and the theories developed around the concept of social capital and virtual communities, this paper presents the main characteristics of this type of digital citizen and the possible political marketing strategies developed around them. The analysis of these cases provides various implications for better management of these political marketing tools, whose potential is yet to be discovered.

INTRODUCTION

Although the use of the Internet by public organizations is a recent phenomenon, in some countries like the USA or Singapore the Internet has become a primary way of keeping fruitful relationships with citizens. Likewise, political parties are beginning to prioritize the development of communication actions via the Internet in their political campaigns. These actions not only include promotional activities but in some cases they go beyond political messages and aim to achieve the electors' participatory attitude in the campaign and the design of the election program. This is especially remarkable in countries like the USA. As we will see throughout this work, the use of the Internet in the USA as a political marketing tool has reached relevant levels over the last few years. It has become a means to collect millions of dollars to defray campaign costs and mobilize thousands of people in support of their candidate.

The use of the Internet in electoral strategies is usually associated with virtual communities and especially the so-called blogs. According to Wikipedia.org, a blog, "*is a Web application which contains periodic, reverse chronologically ordered posts on a common webpage...The format of blogs varies, from simple bullet lists of hyperlinks, to article summaries with user-provided comments and ratings.*" The data contained in a blog did not used to be compiled and offered on the Net by an individual or an organization, but by a group of individuals acting in an altruistic but coordinated way to serve the community.

The phenomenon of blogs clearly reflects some of the changes produced by the Internet in the transmission of information. Any person may reliably express their opinion on the Internet, reaching thousands of people interested in similar issues and avoiding high costs. Moreover, blog's messages may be commented by its readers so that the errors made by the person who first published the information can be depurated. Furthermore, the quality of a news item may be assessed according to the number of readings and comments on it.

Very different issues are dealt with in blogs and at present there are between two and five million of this type of Web sites on the Internet, some of which are managed by opinion leaders, such as scientists, artists or politicians (e.g., http://weblog.siliconvalley.com/column/dangillmor/, administered by a well-known journalist specialized in the technology). Nevertheless, blogs are not only an alternative to the traditional media, such as the radio or the press. Through these Web sites, thousands of people coordinate their efforts and gather their knowledge in the interest of the community. Consequently, blogs are being used by several groups to manage their resources and coordinate their activities both in and out of the Internet. Among those groups which use blogs to improve the efficiency of their actions we can find the case of the campaign of Democratic Party presidential candidates in the USA. This is a paradigmatic example of the power of blogs, hence the remarkable interest for marketing researchers.

Considering the interest of blogs for marketing experts, the present work analyses several aspects related to the way virtual communities and blogs may affect the group's social capital and therefore the individual's democratic and civic behavior. Subsequently, we will analyze how virtual communities, as blogs, were used by Democratic candidates Howard Dean and Wesley Clark in the 2003-2004 USA presidential elections. This analysis and the literature review will allow us to delimitate digital citizen characteristics and the way he influence on his environment, to provide some recommendations for the management of electoral campaigns with the use of blogs, as well as defining the main benefits these communities may generate in the field of electoral strategies.

ANALYSIS OF THE CONCEPT OF VIRTUAL COMMUNITY

From the first studies in the 19th century to the most recent ones conducted by e- marketing researchers, communities have been given special attention due to their role in the individual's socialization and even their success in the business policy of companies. On the whole, we may define the community as a group of individuals, usually small, whose members feel committed to each other because of the common interests on a certain aspect. From a marketing perspective, Muniz and O'Guinn (2001) or Flavián and Guinalíu (2004), notice that communities (they use the term "brand community") refer to the group of consumers who voluntarily relate to each other on the basis of an interest to a brand or a product.

The influence of the Internet on the way individuals relate to their environment has been essential to exponentially increase the e-marketing researchers' interest for these social structures. Specifically, this interest mainly lies in the appearance of the so-called virtual communities (Blanchard, 2004). Virtual communities refer to groups of individuals who regularly use new technologies to establish relationships (Cothrel & Williams, 1999). In general, we may say that a virtual community is a group of people with a common interest that interact regularly in an organized way over the Internet (Ridings et al., 2002). In this respect, political blogs are a clear instance of virtual communities since they are characterized by the three fundamental markers of communities (Muniz & O'Guinn, 2001): consciousness of kind, the community's rituals and traditions, and the moral responsibility of the community's individuals.

- *Consciousness of kind*: it is the most important factor when defining a community. It refers to the feeling which makes every individual bound to the other community members and the community brand (e.g.,

admiration for a candidate, passion for belonging to a given political party). Consciousness of kind is determined by two factors: (1) legitimization, the process of establishing a difference between true and false members, that is to say, those who have opportunist behaviors and those who do not; and (2) opposition to other brands. In fact, the identification with the rest of the group is mainly based on opposition, that is, brand community is usually defined in comparison with another brand. Indeed, in the context of political blogs, which are usually developed due to the admiration for a given candidate, it is possible to find a strong feeling against candidates that belong to other political parties.

- *Rituals and traditions*: those processes carried out by community members which allow to reproduce and transmit the community meaning in and out of the community. It is usually related to the commemoration of some events (celebrate the brand history or some events, such as the satisfaction of having won the general elections). All these processes enable to reinforce brand consciousness and improve the instruction on community values. In the context of political blogs, members usually share a common ideology and values.

- *Sense of moral responsibility*: it reflects the feelings which create moral commitment among the community members, which encourages joint behaviors and allows stronger group cohesion. As a result of moral responsibility, there are two types of fundamental actions: (1) integration and retention of members, which guarantees the community survival (e.g., by spreading bad experiences suffered by those individuals who defended or chose a different ideology or political party); and (2) assistance in the correct use of the brand (e.g., by sharing information on the special interest associated to the community). For instance, in political blogs, this would take the form of the collective effort and social interactions carried out in order to develop and disseminate program ideas.

In addition, one of the main advantages of virtual communities is that, due to the Internet, these communities can overcome the space and time barriers to interaction that exist in traditional communities (Andersen, 2005). However, the characterization of virtual communities simply for replacing face-to-face communication would be too simple to comprehend a really complex concept. In this respect, it has been stated that virtual communities are able to satisfy psychological, social, and economic needs of the individual (Amstrong & Hagel, 1997). Likewise, some authors have compared virtual communities with the groups which relate through traditional means, observing that virtual communities are less robust (e.g., Romm et al., 1997). Therefore, we can refer to virtual communities as ephemeral in comparison with traditional communities in physical means. This ephemeral condition requires the following features for the virtual community to be considered an influential element on its environment (Falk, 1995): values and ideas shared by the members, and some degree of stability, growth, loyalty, and commitment among the members.

Nevertheless, it is not always possible to replace traditional tools. Thereby, we have several variables which affect the individual's decision of joining the community which may be divided into four differentiated groups (Romm et al., 1997). First, there are technological barriers. In this respect, the inherent complexity of some technologies prevents the consumer from joining virtual communities. Therefore, more simplicity in the information systems would increase the number of individuals using these virtual groups (Culnan, 1984). After overcoming technological barriers, the consumer's decision is crucially af-

fected by psychological factors (Markus, 1994). Among these factors, the individual's motivation is essential. Consequently, the fear of change or conservatism prevents joining the virtual community. A third factor, also psychological, refers to the individual's perception of the convenience of the Internet for interpersonal relationships. This factor is explained by some authors according to the *Theory of Richness*. This theory states that the richness of the media depend on their capacity to transmit complex messages (Daft, Lengel & Trevino, 1987). According to Daft and Lengel (1986), face-to-face might be the richest media, followed by the telephone and the written media. Further research considers electronic mail between the telephone and the written media (Rice, 1993), although several authors have criticized this ranking (e.g., Sproull & Kiesler, 1991). In fact, given the variants of Internet communication, it is reasonable to suppose that in some cases, it could come higher than the telephone and even come close to face-to-face communication. Finally, the most crucial factor for the development of a virtual community is the one which shows how the integration of the individual into the community depends on the adequacy of the new communication structure to the established procedures. In other words, to join a virtual community, virtual communication must be adequate for the characteristics of the group. Therefore, to develop a virtual community it will be needed:

1. To design friendly systems, easy to use, in order to avoid technological barriers.
2. To develop the virtual community around individuals highly motivated to participate in the community.
3. To design systems that facilitate the emission of complex messages (e.g., to combine images and sounds). That may increase the richness of the Internet as a communication channel and therefore, it will make the individual perceive the Internet as a product close to face-to-face communication.

4. To adapt these communication tools to the needs of the group. That is, virtual communities must replicate as far as possible the way community members interact in traditional channels.

The Influence of Virtual Communities on Social Capital and Civic Behavior

The presence of a virtual community has significant implications for the environment around it. For instance, according to Romm et al. (1997), a virtual community may influence the language used by the community members, which can develop their own language (e.g., the so-called emoticons), or the development of virtual identities, very different from real ones, due to the anonymity that Net provides to individual. In addition, virtual communities may have social and cultural effects (e.g., the transmission of cultural values).

However, one of the most important effects of virtual communities on society falls on the field of social psychology and the idea of social capital. According to Fukuyama (1999), social capital is a third type of capital, together with technical (capital goods and raw material) and human (the workers' abilities). Social capital is sustained by the trust ties existing among the society members. These ties allow the nations to develop activities of coordination and cooperation between their citizens and those from other countries. Powerful organizations able to help the development of the region are thus generated. According to Putnam (2000), the main premise of social capital is that social networks have value, so that social capital includes the collective value of all social networks (who people know?) and the inclinations that arise from these networks to do things for each other.

The lack of social capital, that is, the lack of trust between the community members, reduces

their relationships to restricted areas such as the family. This limitation also affects commercial activities and prevents the development of a competitive economic structure. Researchers have analyzed this phenomenon in regions like southern Italy, China and Latin America. All these regions have two things in common, their low per capita income and the strong influence of the family. Regions like the south and north of Italy have a very different economic development, possibly due to the fact that the northern citizens tend to relate with other people beyond restricted family environments.

Concerning virtual communities, the concept of social capital refers to the trust existing in the social nets of a community. It is the degree of trust shown by the community members which favors the development of more intense and regular relationships. Some authors have remarked that social capital may be increased as a result of the establishment of Internet-based communication tools in the community (e.g., Friedland, 1996). Due to the use of new technologies, the behavior of the community members may become more civic and democratic, increasing the ties between the individuals and their intensity. This phenomenon is the result of increasing interaction and contacts between the community members thanks to the opportunities and alternatives the Internet provides for communication and distribution of resources (Blanchard & Hom, 1998). Likewise, some authors have observed that virtual conversations may take longer than face-to-face ones, and the number of participants is higher (Rafaeli & Sudweeks, 1994). The reason is that virtuality allows disregarding the real time inherent in spoken conversations, that is, conversations may be temporally suspended and later resumed with hardly any quality loss. Furthermore, some online tools (e.g., moderated discussion forums, etc.) promote democratic participation in a virtual community since they allow the coordination of several individuals in a conversation, which is not always possible in face-to-face communication.

The Influence of Virtual Communities on Branding Strategy

In addition, one of the most important characteristics of virtual communities is that traditionally, it has been considered that participation in the activities carried out in these communities may foster consumer loyalty to the brand or interest around which the community is developed (e.g., Andersen, 2005; Algesheimer et al., 2005). For instance, we can note the work of Benyoussef et al. (2006), who found that participation in Free Software virtual communities favours consumer identification and loyalty to the Free Software. That is, once individuals participate actively in a virtual brand community, their commitment and identification with the brand or organization around which the virtual community is developed may increase (Algesheimer et al., 2005). Finally, all of these may favour higher levels of individuals' loyalty to the brand around which the virtual community is developed (Koh & Kim, 2004). Indeed, it is possible to state that a key aspect of participation in a brand community is the ongoing purchase and use of the brand products (Algesheimer et al., 2005).

This can be explained by the development of emotional ties with the brand or interest around which the community is centred that appear as a consequence of the interactions with other community members, which are usually based on topics related to the brand products (e.g., experiences with different products of the brand, support in the correct use of the brand, etc.).

Therefore, the importance of virtual brand communities is threefold. Firstly, virtual brand communities can be used by individuals to take part in discussions in order to inform and influence fellow consumers about products, brands or organizations (Kozinets, 2002). These social groups have a real existence for their participants and therefore, they can affect their members' behaviour (Muniz & O'Guinn, 2001). In fact, Almquist and Roberts (2000) point out that

consumer advocacy is one of the major factors influencing positive brand equity. Secondly, virtual communities may help to identify the needs and desires of particular individuals or groups of people (Kozinets, 2002). Therefore, it would be possible to use virtual communities to test new products or to achieve a more effective market segmentation. Lastly, active participation in virtual communities may favour higher levels of individuals' loyalty to the interest (e.g., a brand, a product, etc.) around which the community is developed (Koh & Kim, 2004).

BLOGS AND THE DIGITAL CITIZEN

Taking into account the previous considerations, blogs and virtual communities developed around a political interest (e.g., general elections, etc.) may foster the citizens' participation in political issues by expressing their opinion in the Internet in a democratic manner. It may allow reaching thousands of fellow citizens and messages may be commented by its readers. Indeed, the use of these online tools may also enhance citizens' commitment with their environment since they will take part of political decisions. Therefore, it may help to overcome some of the trends observed in recent years with regard to an individual's knowledge of political issues. According to Keeter and Delli (2002): (1) the average American is poorly informed about politics; (2) knowledge is a critical foundation for good citizenship; and (3) little change has occurred in any of these tendencies over the past years.

These individuals that have started to use online formats to participate in political issues have been traditionally called "digital citizens" (Katz, 1997). According to Katz (1997) and UCLA (2004), as the use of information technologies grows, the individuals show a more democratic profile, know the political system better and increase their voting intention. Likewise, they have a wider knowledge of their country's political life, current events, and participants. Furthermore, they read more than those consumers who make a scarce use of information technologies. Their trust in the institutions and the possibility of changing those aspects which largely affect the community's well-being is higher. They are more optimistic and their capacity to assess political decisions, far from irrational alignments with certain parties, is more significant.

However, the most relevant characteristic of the digital citizen is shown by ICPI (2004). According to this study, the digital citizen is seven times more likely to act as an opinion leader among those making up his immediate circle. This motivates him to use the Internet to influence his circle, since this medium enables him to reach more individuals rapidly and efficiently. More specifically, the digital citizen may use the following types of blogs in order to participate in political conversations and to influence fellow citizens:

- *Personal blogs*, which are developed by a given citizen who act as an opinion leader by spreading his/her own opinion,
- *Citizen communities*, which are groups of citizens that emerge in the Internet to discuss about common political issues, and
- *Political blogs*, developed by a given candidate or political party, where citizens (usually with an ideology similar to the candidate) may express their opinions regarding, for instance, the candidate's program ideas.

BLOGS AND POLITICAL BRANDING STRATEGY: THE DEMOCRATIC PRESIDENTIAL RACE IN THE USA

The influence of virtual communities on the behaviour of the individual has not gone unnoticed by the political strategists. As we have said before, digital citizens use the Internet to influence their circle and this can be especially relevant to win new voters since personal advocacy is one of the major factors influencing positive image. In addition, individuals are increasingly turning to online communication in order to obtain information on which to base their decisions (Kozinets, 2002). In this respect, individuals use virtual communities to share ideas and contact fellow consumers who are seen as more objective information sources. As a result, since 2003 one can observe how the use of virtual communities, particularly blogs, has become more common and relevant in political candidates' marketing strategies.

The Internet enables thousands of citizens to debate online on the topics they are most concerned for in their environment. The Net allows a higher participation of citizens in the political life, largely affecting the formation of public opinion (Fischer et al., 1994). Consequently, the use of information technologies as a means for the citizen to contact their political representatives directly is highly relevant (Schuler, 1996). For example, in the project Candidat 2003 (http://www.candidat2003.net), an initiative by the regional institutions of the Spanish autonomous community of Catalonia, carried out during the autonomous elections in 2003, citizens were able to ask and comment anything to candidates. The experience achieves its initial objectives, with over 3,000 consultations made to the 715 candidates standing in the elections.

However, the breakthrough in the use of Internet tools, particularly virtual communities and blogs, came with the Democrat party primary elections in the USA in 2003 and 2004. Blogs, together with other tools such as online fundraising and the coordination of citizens through Web sites like MeetUp, were widely used by the Democratic candidates Howard Dean and Wesley Clark in 2004. Nowadays, thanks to the success of these cases, most of the politicians in the world involved in any kind of elections make use of this tool to promote their campaigns and to obtain online support for their proposals. Moreover, the power of this online tool was clearly seen in the general elections in Brazil in 2006, where citizens gathered in several blogs in order to support or criticize the different candidates. For instance, concerning the president Lula da Silva, the blog "Lula Out" was formed by more than 170,000 registered users that strongly criticize his management. In turn, he found online support of more than 60,000 people in "We vote Lula for President". Therefore, due to the importance of the Dean and Clark cases, both cases will be analyzed below.

The selection of the two cases analyzed was based on the results of a first focus group made up of e-marketing and virtual community experts, which identify the most representative cases. In addition, according to Edmunds (1999), the conduction of a focus group at the beginning of the investigation may help to understand, in this case, the behaviour of the digital citizens. We then carried out an *in situ* study of the functioning of the selected blogs. To do this, following the recommendations of Kozinets (2002) regarding the conduction of ethnographic studies in the online context, the research group registered first on the blogs in order to learn as much as possible about the cultural characteristics of the group the activities carried out therein. Secondly, we took part in the debates for two weeks in order to obtain the relevant information required to evaluate the power of these blogs in the development of a successful political strategy. Finally, we also gathered information from various specialist sources.

Howard Dean Case Study

The spectacular popularity increase of Vermont Governor, Howard Dean, in his race for the USA Democratic presidential candidacy in 2003-04, was largely due to the efficient use of virtual communities by the campaign designers. A few months before the starting signal for the race, very few North American citizens knew Howard Dean and his following organization Democracy for America. However, the use of Web sites like MeetUp (http://www.meetup.com) exponentially increased his popularity.

More than 180,.000 citizens, most of them taking part in political activities for the first time, registered in MeetUp supporting Howard Dean's candidacy. They used the Internet to find other people with the same interests in order to organize and hold off-line meetings. Thus, a small group of Democrat sympathizers in a small Texas town was able to coordinate its activities with other small groups of sympathizers in other towns in the state.

Likewise, there were blogs supporting Dean, from Latinos for Dean (http://www.latinos-fordean.com/) to Mormons for Dean (http://mormonsfordean.blogspot.com/). However, the most famous blogs for Dean was Dean Nation -http://dean2004.blogspot.com/- and Blog for America - http://www.blogforamerica.com- (See Figure 1 and 2). In these Web sites, Dean followers offered their views on the candidate's program and proposed ideas to improve it. As shown by the study conducted by the Institute for Politics, Democracy & the Internet, the digital citizen is characterized to a large extent by the fact that he influences the thought and decisions of people in his immediate surroundings (IPDI, 2004). Therefore the members of this and other blogs were particularly active. They carefully analyzed the proposals of Dean and his opponents, offered their own ideas, organized rallies and even made donations to help defray the campaign on the Internet and buy merchandising products (e.g., t-shirts, mugs, bags, etc.).

Throughout 2003, Dean's online campaign raised 40 million dollars from the contributions of 280,000 people (an average of $143 per person). Dean himself expressed his gratitude for the work on behalf of his campaign, carried out mostly by supporters in small-town America: *"Thanks to all of you for your energy and your help ... I can't tell you how helpful this is. Many, many thanks..."* (See Figure 1).

Figure 1. *http://dean2004.blogspot.com/*

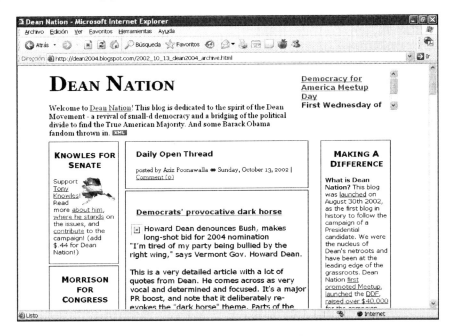

Figure 2. *http://www.blogforamerica.com*

Wesley Clark Case Study

The use of Web pages like MeetUp, fundraising for the campaign on the Internet and blogs helped not only Dean in his presidential race. Wesley Clark's candidacy was also related to the Internet. The over $2m collected through an online campaign and the fact that Clark supporters mobilized in dozens of blogs even before his candidacy was announced, were crucial for Clark's decision of leading the Democrats to the USA government

Many of the dozens of personal and group blogs which supported Clark were in the so-called Clark Community Network (http://www.forclark. com, see Figure 3). On this Web site, citizens could make contributions and organize meetings. Likewise, this Web site agglutinated blogs in the same platform so that the management and design were homogenous. Unlike the blogs in Dean's candidacy, the Clark Community Network

searched for a more participative attitude of the individuals. The Clark Community Network had a greater sense of community than Dean's Web site: the feeling of belonging to a group and the opportunity to actively participate in mapping events. In this respect, when somebody joined the Web site they were given the opportunity to create their own personal blog. Above the group of personal blogs there was a second level of group blogs where only registered users were allowed to publish after the screening of a series of moderators who voluntarily avoided inappropriate messages. All the published messages were rated by the readers between one to five, thus only those with a better rating were susceptible of being published in Clark's official campaign blog (http://campaign.forclark.com/). Consequently, the feeling of membership increased and the comments quality was motivated. This was the major difference with Dean blogs, where

Figure 3. Clark Community Network (http://www.forclark.com/)

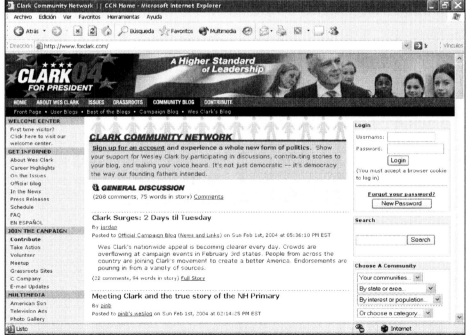

only official members of the campaign or some authorized bloggers were allowed to publish. On the other hand, Clark Community Network offered other possibilities, such as online donation or an interesting register of members who tried to recruit people for the cause, thus obtaining some kind of reward.

The analysis of the cases of Dean and Clark has enabled us to verify what a powerful support tool the Net is, with a relevant power for the citizens. Through blogs, it is possible to call thousands of voters to attend the candidate's meeting in a city; to make economic donations; to obtain up-to-date information of the events; collect opinions on ideas proposed in the campaign; recruit people who are ready to altruistically help in the campaign, among other possibilities. Consequently, a modest campaign like Governor Dean or General Clark was able to compete satisfactorily in such a complex and expensive political battle as the Democratic Party primaries.

CONCLUSION

Throughout the present research we have verified the great relevance of the Internet for the way political parties and the public in general relate with their groups of interest. Virtual communities, which first emerged as the individual's socializing elements, have become real political marketing weapons, able to reach the target segment efficiently. The opportunity for socialization offered by a virtual community increases the social capital of the group and enhances relationships with its environment. Thus we have the digital citizen, an individual who is concerned with the decisions taken by his political representatives, and who influences the people around him by means of the tools provided by the Internet.

The pronounced importance of the digital citizen has been shown by the study of the cases of the USA Democratic party primaries in the 2003-2004, which have allowed us to define

how the use of virtual communities favor the coordination of those citizens who are more aware of the progress of the society they live in, increasing their democratic attitude and a more active behavior in the interest of the community. Indeed, citizens who use the Internet to interrelate are characterized by a stronger knowledge about the world around them, as it may be observed in the big amount of Meetup's groups developed and the subjects they dealt (e.g., Blacks 4 Clark, http://www.blacks4clark.us/). Therefore, digital citizens are individuals who are socially involved in their community needs and able to consistently appreciate the initiatives promoted by political candidates.

In addition, virtual communities, and more specifically blogs, may represent an efficient weapon in electoral strategies. Blogs provide three main benefits difficult to obtain by means of traditional actions:

- Firstly, it would be possible to increase the amount of active supporters; that is, people who altruistically spread the message and recruit new voters. Indeed, blogs can be used by citizens to take part in discussions in order to inform and influence fellow individuals about different candidates. These social groups have a real existence for their participants and therefore, they can affect their members' behaviour (Muniz & O'Guinn, 2001). In fact, this citizen advocacy may be one of the major factors influencing a positive image for both candidates and political parties since fellow individuals are seen as a more objective information source (Kozinets, 2002).
- Secondly, blogs may help to identify the needs and desires of particular citizens or groups of people. In addition, thanks to these virtual communities, citizens may be able to participate in the development of the electoral program, which entails an increase of the individuals' commitment, as well as

a better adaptation of the political proposals to the society's reality.

- Lastly, active participation in these communities may favour higher levels of citizens' loyalty to the common interest (e.g., a candidate, a political party, etc.) around which the blog is developed. Thus, this result may be especially relevant for political parties due to the fact that the great efforts needed to win new voters make it increasingly necessary to reinforce the ties established with the previous ones.

In addition, blogs also allows obtaining other advantages which can be summarized in the following aspects:

- Increase of the candidate's popularity, as well as the diffusion of the program ideas.
- Fundraising to defray campaign costs.
- The online coordination of campaign meetings so that a larger number of people may be called.
- Improvement of the candidate's image, since they are perceived as a person concerned for the citizen's participation in politics.

Nevertheless, the use of blogs must be subject to following some recommendations. These aspects may be specified in the following questions:

- User-friendly systems must be designed, because technological barriers hamper the diffusion of virtual communities.
- If it is legally possible, online fundraising must be encouraged by the implementation of a payment platform.
- To motivate participation, blogs must facilitate the emission of complex messages, that is, the citizen must be given the possibility to express their opinion in a complete way, with images and sounds if necessary.
- Likewise, the citizen must be given the opportunity to contact the political lead-

ers directly. This may be achieved by the design of moderated forums which control the messages for the politician according to a series of pre-established rules.

- Although the success of blogs lies in their capacity to intensify mouth-to-mouth communication, it is also true that a promotional campaign must be designed so that the citizen has proof of the existence of these tools. Likewise, the individual must be informed about the benefits that their participation has on society, as well as being aware that their opinions will be taken into account when designing political proposals.
- In order to show a concern about citizens' needs and desires, blogs must be constantly up to date. In other words, blogs should not only be active during the election process, but every time. If they are active only in some important dates, citizens will perceive that blogs are only a tool to increase the number of voters and they may not be motivated to participate on them.
- Systems like MeetUp or similar ones must be used to coordinate the supporters' efforts and especially the calls to propaganda acts.
- Independent blogs should be firmly supported. Consequently, Web location or tools to facilitate the creation of blogs may be offered. Likewise, a network of blogs which have the reference of the campaign's Web site or official blog should be created.
- Finally, if it is technically and legally possible, it is important to reward those individuals who recruit more people or funds.

However, it is important to note that the use of virtual communities also entails some risks (Baillie, 1997). First of all, since the Internet penetration rate is still quite low in many countries, only some groups may be well represented in virtual communities; that is, those who use the Internet very often. Hence, low classes are not able to express their interests in these forums.

Secondly, it is possible that sometimes blogs, which are intended as an instrument to improve the relationships between the citizens and the administration, may become a source of arguments and confrontation where debates result in irrelevant questions. Lastly, in some cases, the management costs of these virtual communities may be quite high, since they may need hiring personnel to moderate online debates, as well as a large outlay for the design of the Web sites which support the community.

Lastly, it is necessary to decide if the events observed in the USA may be replicated in other countries. It is not easy to give an answer, since the experience out of the USA is very short. For instance, we may note the case of the autonomous elections in the Basque Country (a Spanish autonomous community) in 2005, where most of the candidates developed their own blog to interact with their online voters. However, due to the fact that the Internet penetration rate in Spain is still quite low - only 37.5% of Spaniards are frequent Internet users (INE [*National Statistics Institute*], 2005), it was not possible to assess the success of these actions. In fact, we may consider that the likelihood of a similar success for the phenomenon of blogs in other countries largely depends on the groups they are aimed at. In this respect, it is reasonable to think that the success of blogs will be higher in those groups which already form communities in traditional channels (e.g., left-wing groups, environmentalists, cultural groups), those who are more accustomed to the use of the Internet (e.g., young people), supporters with a certain party or those located in a nearby place (e.g., a city).

REFERENCES

ARMSTRONG, A. & HAGEL, J. (1997) *Net gain: Expanding markets through virtual communities.* Harvard Business School Press, MA.

ANDERSEN, P.H. (2005) Relationship marketing and brand involvement of professionals through web-enhanced brand communities: The case of Coloplast. *Industrial Marketing Management* 34, 39-51.

BAILLIE, T. (1997) A Skeptic's View of Electronic Democracy in Virtual Communities. Retrieved September 13 2005 from http://wwwucalgaryca/~dabrent/380/webproj/coms380html

BLANCHARD, A. (2004) Virtual Behavior Settings: An Application of Behavior Setting Theories to Virtual Communities. *Journal of Computer Mediated Communication* 9 (2). Retrieved September 13 2005 from http://wwwascuscorg/jcmc/vol9/issue2/blanchardhtml

BLANCHARD, A. & HORAN, T. (1998) Virtual communities and social capital. *Social Science Computer Review* 16, 293-307.

COTHREL, J. & WILLIAMS, R.L. (1999) Online Communities: Helping them Form and Grow. *Journal of Knowledge Management* 3 (I), 54-60.

CULNAN, M.J. (1984) The dimensions of accessibility to online information: implications for implementing office information systems. *ACM Transactions on Office Information Systems* 2 (2), 141-150.

DAFT, R.L. & LENGEL, R.H. (1986) Organizational information requirements media richness and structural design. *Management Science* 32 (5), 554-571.

DAFT, R.L., LENGEL, R.H., & TREVINO, L. K. (1987) Message equivocality media selection and manager performance: implications for information systems. *MIS Quarterly* 11 (3), 355-366.

FALK, J. (1995) The Meaning of the Web. Retrieved September 13 2005 from http://swissnetaimitedu/6805/articles/falk-meaning-of-the-webhtml

FINHOLT, T. & SPROULL, S. (1990) Electronic groups at work. *Organization Science* 1 (1), 41-64

FISHER, B., MARGOLIS, M. & RESNICK, D. (1994) *A New Way of Talking Politics: Democracy on the Internet.* In Annual Meeting of the American Political Science Association, New York City,

FLAVIÁN, C. & GUINALÍU, M. (2004) Virtual community: a model of successful business on the Internet. In *Advances in Electronic Marketing* (Clarke III I and Flaherty TB, Eds), pp 270-286, Idea Group Publishing Inc.

FRIEDLAND, L. (1996) Electronic democracy and the new citizenship. *Media culture and society* 18, 185-212.

FUKUYAMA, F. (1999) *The Great Disruption: Human Nature and the Reconstitution of Social Order.* Free Press, New York.

IPDI (2004) Political Influentials Online in the 2004 Presidential Campaign. Retrieved September 13 2005 from http://wwwipdiorg/Uploaded-Files/political%20influentialspdf

KATZ, J. (1997) The Digital Citizen. *Wired.* Retrieved September 13 2005 from http://www-wiredcom/wired/archive/512/netizen_prhtml

KEETER, S. & CARPINI, D.M. (2002) The Internet and an Informed Citizenry. In *The Civic Web: Online Politics and Democratic Values* (ANDERSON, DM & CORNFIELD, M. Eds). Rowman & Littlefield

MARKUS, M. L. (1995) Electronic mail as a medium of managerial choice. *Organization Science* 5 (4), 502-527.

MITCHELL, A. & KIRKUP, M. (2003) Retail development and urban regeneration: a case study of Castle Vale. *International Journal of Retail and Distribution Management* 31 (9), 451-458.

MUNIZ, A. & O'GUINN, T.C. (2001) Brand Community. *Journal of Consumer Research* 27, 412-432

PARKER, C., ANTHONY-WINTER, T. & TABERNACLE, D. (2003) Learning by stealth: introducing smaller retailers to the benefits of training and education in Barnet. *International Journal of Retail and Distribution Management* 31 (9), 470-476.

PRELL, C. (2003) Community Networking and Social Capital: Early Investigations. *Journal of Computer Mediated Communications* 8 (3). Retrieved September 13 2005 from http://wwwascuscorg/jcmc/vol8/issue3/prellhtml

PUTNAM, R.D. (2000) *Bowling Alone: The Collapse and Revival of American Community.* Simon & Schuster, New York.

RAFAELI, S. & SUDWEEKS, F. (1994) Interactivity on the nets. In *Information Systems and Human Communication Technology Divisions ICA Annual Conference*, Sydney, Australia.

RICE, R.E. (1993) Media appropriateness: using social presence theory to compare traditional and new organizational media. *Human Communication Research* 19 (4), 451-484.

RICE, R.E. & AYDIN, C. (1991) Attitudes toward new organizational technology: network proximity as a mechanism for social information processing. *Administrative Science Quarterly* 36 (June), 219-244.

RIDINGS, C.M., GEFEN, D., & ARINZE, B. (2002) Some antecedents and effects of trust in virtual communities. *Journal of Strategic Information Systems* 11, 271-295.

ROMM, CT (1999) *Virtual Politicking: Playing Politics in Electronically Linked Organizations.* Hampton Press, Cresskill NJ.

ROMM, C., PLISKIN, N., & CLARKE, R. (1997) Virtual Communities and Society: Toward an Integrative Three Phase Model. *International Journal of Information Management* 17 (4), 261-270.

SCHULER, D. (1996) *New community networks: Wired for change.* Addison-Wesley Reading, MA.

SPROULL, R. & KIESLER, S. (1991) *Connections: New Ways of Working in the Networked Organization.* MIT Press, Cambridge.

UCLA (2004) Surveying the Digital Future UCLA University. Retrieved September 13 2005 from http://wwwccpuclaedu/pdf/UCLA-Internet-Report-Year-Threepdf

Chapter III
Brand Personality of Web Search Engines:
Who is the Conqueror of the Digital Age?

Aslihan Nasir
Boğaziçi University, Istanbul, Turkey

Süphan Nasir
Istanbul University, Turkey

ABSTRACT

Today, as business becomes ever more challenging, brands become the main assets of many companies. Fierce competition forces companies to differentiate their products from those of competitors in the market. However, it is extremely difficult to create this differentiation based on the functionality attribute of the products, since advanced technology makes it possible for companies to imitate the functionality attributes. Hence, marketers begin to create personalities for their brands in order to be more appealing to the consumers. Brand personality is defined as "the set of human characteristics associated with a brand" and it is asserted that the brand personality leads to differentiation in terms of consumer perceptions and preferences. At the moment, millions of people use search engines in order to reach the most relevant information. Since search engines, as the senior actors of the online world, provide similar services, it is enormously crucial for them to create differentiation. Google is the dominant search engine brand and, in this paper, its success has been examined by utilizing the brand personality scale of Aaker (1997). This study tries to identify the brand personality dimensions that search engine companies create in the minds of Internet users by using past research on brand personality scales as a guide. Furthermore, it is also aims to determine the distinct brand personality dimensions of Google as the most preferred and used search engine. It is found that Google has been perceived as the most "competent" search engine brand. Furthermore, depending on the MANOVA results, it is shown that all three search engines have statistically significant differences only on the "competence" dimension. "Sincerity" and "excitement" are the other two dimensions which significantly differentiate Google from both MSN and Yahoo.

INTRODUCTION

Today, there has been a growing recognition about branding and brand management. There are plenty of developments such as increased globalization, fierce competition, and savvy consumers that have significantly complicated marketing practices and create challenges for the brand managers. In today's markets, it becomes difficult to develop new products with distinct features whereas it is relatively easy to copy them with advanced technological resources. Moreover, there is also a proliferation of brands as the number of brands for the same product category expands. Additionally, the Internet has completely changed the business world. Internet, as a new media channel, enables a company to efficiently target, detain and interact with its potential customers. Twenty-first century has witnessed to a rush by new and existing businesses to create their online Internet brands. But not all of them have the opportunity to show success due to fatal mistakes in brand management. In such an environment brand management, through the affective use of brand image and brand positioning, becomes extremely important. Being a major component of brand image, brand personality is the most valuable way of creating brand differentiation and hence consumer preference and loyalty.

While examining on-line branding topic, a special attention has to be given to search engines since they're continuing their activities from the very beginning of Internet age. As a result, Internet users are more familiar with the brands operating in this on-line business. Increased search engine usage among Internet users justifies the argument that a remarkable interest should be paid to the analysis of search engine branding. Search engine use is one of the top activities of the 94 million American adults who use the Internet; moreover, the search-using population totals 90 percent of all Internet users (Burns, 2005). The number of U.S. searches also grew 55 percent in December 2005 (5.1 billion searches) over December 2004 (3.3 billion searches) (Burns, 2006a). Consequently, as the search engine market continuously expands, the number of players in this market also inflates. This leads to intense competition among search engine brands. On the demand side of this market, search users prefer to use well-known search engines because they believe that well-known search engines generally provide more dependable and relevant results. On the other hand, companies that have Internet operations want to be listed in well-known and well-used search engines because these places potentially generate so much traffic (Sullivan, 2004a).

Being a preferred and well-known search engine provides crucial revenue sources to search engine brands. Revenue that comes from the paid listings is one of the most important benefits of being a leading search engine. Every major search engine with significant traffic sells paid placement listings. Anyone who runs a web site wants to be in the "top ten" results. Being listed in 11 or beyond results means that many people may miss your web site; that's why a web site with good search engine listings may see a dramatic increase in traffic (Sullivan, 2004b). Besides, revenue that comes from the advertising also plays a critical role for the survival of the search engine companies. An increasing number of advertisers allocate a portion of their budgets to the Web. In 2006, online marketing spending is expected to increase 19 percent (Burns, 2006b). Within online's increase, search engine ad spending is set to grow 26 percent this year; additionally, budget allocation for Google amounts to $3.7 million; $4.6 million for Yahoo; and $4.6 million for MSN (Burns, 2006b). As the online advertising becomes more popular, advertisers increasingly include the Internet in their marketing mix. To reach masses, advertisers prefer to give advertisements to well-known and preferable web sites. So that, being a well-known and preferable search engine brand is also very crucial to attract much more advertising, which in turn brings more revenue. However, it should also be noted that Google makes money from paid listings relevant to a searcher's query and from licensing their technology to firms such as Yahoo and the Washington Post; yet Google avoids from gaining money through ads (Keller, 2003).

In order to survive in this highly turbulent and dynamic market conditions, search engine companies have to generate a unique brand image and position their brands in a distinct place in consumers' minds and hearts. Brand personality is the major strategic tool to create the desired brand image for search engines. Thus, the purpose of this study is to examine the brand personality of the most preferable search engines, which are the gateways of Internet users to reach any information that they need. This study attempts to i) identify the brand personality dimensions that search engine companies create in the minds of Internet users by using past research on brand personality scales as a guide, and ii) determine the common and/or distinct brand personality dimensions of most preferred and used search engine.

BRAND PERSONALITY

The crucial role of brand management increases day by day as the number of brands for the same product category explodes and as the products become more similar in terms of their functionality. Furthermore, in today's marketplace, it becomes difficult to develop new products with distinct features whereas it is relatively easy to copy them with advanced technological resources. These factors force companies to create a distinct brand image and positioning in order to generate consumer preference. In his classic article, Plummer (1984) emphasized this issue and stated that brands can be explained by three types of characteristics, namely: physical attributes, functional characteristics, and brand personality. Among these three characteristics, brand personality enables marketers to give emotional values to their brands and hence by

this way they can go beyond functional utility and create brand differentiation.

In this jungle of brands, brand personality becomes one of the vital elements of brand image and brand positioning. According to American Marketing Association (AMA), brand personality is the "psychological nature of a particular brand as intended by its sellers, though persons in the marketplace may see the brand otherwise (called brand image). These two perspectives compare to the personalities of individual humans: what we intend or desire, and what others see or believe."

Even though the majority of the research on brand management concentrates on brand equity and brand image, the studies on brand personality have gained acceleration especially by the second half of 1990s. In an initial study on this topic, Plummer (1985) defined brand personality as "the characterisational aspects of the brand". Another major contribution comes from Aaker (1997) who asserted that consumers naturally attribute personality traits to brands of products. In other words, Aaker (1997) defined brand personality as the set of human characteristics associated with a brand and identified five basic brand personality traits: sincerity, excitement, competence, sophistication, and ruggedness. According to Aaker (1997), any brand can be positioned on these basic traits and the result of this multiple positioning is an assessment of the brand's personality. However, Azoulay and Kapferer (2003) criticized Aaker's brand personality scale (BPS) and her definition of brand personality as "the set of human characteristics associated with the brand" because of being too loose. Azoulay and Kapferer (2003) included aspects that explain features of the brand's identity beyond personality. Sweeney and Brandon (2006) also criticized Aaker's scale as being only comprised of positive brand attributes by excluding negative traits. In a recent study, Sweeney and Brandon (2006, p. 645) redefined brand personality "as the set of human personality traits that correspond to the interpersonal domain of human personality and are relevant to describing the brand as a relationship partner". On the other hand, Nandan (2005, p. 266) asserted that "brand personality represents the emotional characteristics of the brand". Wee Tan (2004) also investigated the brand personality topic and explored whether the human personality could be applied to the brand construct; furthermore, this paper observed whether brand personality is stable over time and in association with other brands. It was found that like human personalities, brand personalities are considered to be stable over time, that's to say brand personalities have an enduring nature (Wee Tan, 2004).

Brand personality brings several benefits to the companies operating in today's volatile and highly competitive markets. For instance, Sirgy (1982) mentioned that brand personality can increase consumer preference and usage of a brand. In her study, Fournier (1998) stated that a favorable brand personality leads to increased levels of trust and loyalty. Likewise, Kim et al. (2001) investigated the effect of brand personality on brand loyalty in cellular phone market and found that the effective use of brand personality can increase brand loyalty. Furthermore, Aaker (1996) declared that a positive brand personality provides a basis for product differentiation. Also, Keller (2003) mentioned that brand personality helps consumers differentiate among various brands in the same product category. In addition, Keller (2003) indicated that the brand should concentrate on the enhancement of brand personality in order to establish a unique positioning in the market. In their study, d'Astous and Le'vesque (2003) asserted that it is very important to understand how consumers perceive products, brands, stores and other commercial objects in terms of human attributes since it will be beneficial for the augmentation and implementation of marketing actions. The authors pointed out that being able to measure a brand's personality may help to demarcate the supreme communication strategies to set up in order to reach appropriate consumers.

Above and beyond, Biel (1992) demonstrated that a strong brand personality encourages active processing on the consumer's part. Furthermore, Aaker (1999) found that people prefer brands with which they share personality characters. It was also discovered that the congruency between brand personality and the consumer affects the relationship between the consumer and the brand (Fournier, 1998).

The studies on the topic of brand personality also give great emphasis on the application of Aaker's (1997) BPS in different sectors, across cultures and in services sector. For instance, Hosany et al. (2006) have attempted to test the relevance of BPS to tourism destinations; whereas Siguaw et al. (1999) applied Aaker's (1997) BPS to quick-service restaurants and causal dining restaurants. Aaker et al. (2001) conducted a cross-cultural research and examined to what degree basic brand personality dimensions carry universal or specific cultural meaning. On the other hand, it is also possible to see some efforts that focus on developing personality scales in distinct areas. For instance, d'Astous and his colleagues (2006) developed a personality scale for cultural festivals; whereas Venable et al. (2005) have attempted to integrate existing knowledge of brand personality in the for-profit sector with social exchange theory and trust to identify the specific dimensions of brand personality among nonprofit organizations. Similarly, Smith et al. (2006) employed Aaker's (1997) brand personality framework to assess the brand characteristics of a membership based sport organization and suggested that a modified version of framework that incorporates an additional dimension of innovation was required.

The research on brand personality by year 2000s concentrated on different aspects of the topic. For instance, Freling and Forbes (2005, p. 404) indicated that "brand personality will have a positive influence on product evaluations and that subjects exposed to a brand's personality will have a significantly greater number of brand associations; significantly greater proportion of brand associations; significantly greater unique brand associations; significantly greater proportion of congruent brand associations; and significantly greater proportion of strong brand associations". In their current study, van Rekom et al. (2006) developed and showed an approach that helps both managers and researchers establish which features form the essence of a brand.

Regardless of its importance, on-line brand personality topic received inadequate attention from the scholar world due to the recentness of the topic. One such research comes from Müller and Chandon (2003) who examined the effects of a web site on brand personality. On the other hand, in his study, Okazaki (2005) identified five underlying dimensions of on-line brand personality stimuli: excitement, sophistication, affection, popularity, and competence. Furthermore, the major contribution of Okazaki's research (2005) was its attempt to classify the brand personality stimuli in terms of cognition vs. affection framework.

RESEARCH METHODOLOGY AND RESEARCH FINDINGS

For the data collection of this study an on-line survey was prepared which was designed according to the research objectives of the paper. Since this study was concentrated on brand personality of search engine brands, on-line survey was admitted to be proper for the aforementioned purposes of this manuscript. The prepared survey was displayed for two week period on the personal web sites of the authors. The survey link was delivered to the owners of e-groups that have 500 or above members. During the two-week exhibition of the questionnaire on the Internet, a total of 238 useable questionnaires were collected and used out of 247 responses for this research.

According to a recent report by Nielsen NetRatings (2006), the market shares of the search engines that are within the scope of this study are as follows: Google (% 49.2), Yahoo (% 23.8), MSN (% 9.6), AOL (% 6.3), and finally ASK (% 2.6). However, the search engine brands that were examined in this study were limited to the brands, which comprised approximately % 82 of the market; in other words Google, Yahoo and MSN were the focus of this research. Another reason to choose only these three search engines was that they are worldwide known search engine brands. In addition, this research excluded some search engines such as AltaVista and AlltheWeb since they're Yahoo-owned sites.

Even though it was possible to see a few efforts that concentrate on generating personality scales in specific situations, it was a general trend to apply Aaker's (1997) brand personality scale in different contexts. By employing Aaker's (1997) scale, the researchers not only robust the validity of the study but also examine its applicability in online environments. Briefly, this research has attempted to analyze the brand personality of Google, Yahoo and MSN based on Aaker's (1997) five personality dimensions.

A demographic profile analysis revealed that males comprised 55.5 percent of the sample population whereas females comprised 44.5 percent of the sample population. Approximately 79 percent of the respondents were between the age range of 20-39 and of the total survey respondents, 89 percent had university or graduate study education. Almost 50 percent of the respondents indicated United States of America as their country of residence. On the other hand, 14 percent of the respondents participated to the survey from Canada and the rest of the respondents were attended from European countries such as United Kingdom, Switzerland, Sweden, Portugal, Netherlands, Turkey, Finland, Hungary, Germany, and Greece.

First of all, respondents were asked to indicate their favorite search engine. As it can be seen from the Table 1, 90 percent of the respondents indicated Google as their favorite search engine; however, 6.5 percent of the respondents chose

Table 1. Favorite search engine

	Frequency	**Percent**
AOL	2	.8
ASK	1	.4
GOOGLE	215	90.3
MSN	1	.4
YAHOO	15	6.3
Other	4	1.7
Total	238	100.0

Yahoo as their favorite search engine. MSN as a search engine was the least favorable among the respondents.

Willingness degree of the respondents to use specific on-line search engine brand were measured with five point Likert scale where 1= "not at all willing", 2= "very little willing", 3= "more or less willing", 4= "willing", and 5= "extremely willing". The results of the willingness statistics

are presented in Table 2. When the mean scores of willingness degree of respondents to use specific search engine in Table 2 are compared, it can be seen that the respondents were much more willing to use Google as a search engine (with a mean score of 4.81). On the other hand, respondents were more or less willing to use Yahoo (with a mean score of 3.39) and little willing to use MSN (with a mean score of 2.20) as a search engine. Thus, respondents are extremely willing to use Google; whereas, they are unwilling to use MSN as a search engine.

Aaker (1997) identified five underlying dimensions of brand personality and labeled these dimensions as (1) Sincerity, (2) Excitement, (3) Competence, (4) Sophistication, and (5) Ruggedness. In her study, Aaker (1997) used 42 personality traits to measure these five dimensions. "Sincerity" dimension is composed of down to earth, family oriented, small town, honest, sincere, real, wholesome, original, cheerful, sentimental, and friendly personality traits. The second dimension "excitement" includes daring, trendy, exciting, spirited, cool, young, imaginative, unique, up to date, independent, and contemporary personality traits. "Competence" dimension covers the items of reliable, hard working, secure, intelligent, technical, corporate, successful, leader and confident; whereas "sophistication" dimension embodies

Table 2. Willingness to use specific search engine

	N	**Minimum**	**Maximum**	**Mean**	**Std. Deviation**
Willingness to Use Google	238	1	5	4.81	.532
Willingness to Use Yahoo	238	1	5	3.39	1.089
Willingness to Use MSN	238	1	5	2.20	1.060

the personality traits of upper class, glamorous, good looking, charming, feminine, and smooth. Finally, "ruggedness" dimension includes the items of outdoorsy, masculine, western, tough, and rugged.

Aaker's (1997) brand personality approach was applied to this study to identify points of differentiation among brand personalities of search engines. Respondents completed this scale for each of the three-search engine. Each respondent rated three search engines on each of the 42 personality traits. Participants were asked to indicate the extent to which they thought each of the 42 personality traits described each of the search engines. Respondents indicated their responses using a five-point, Likert-type scale, where 1="not at all descriptive", 2= "very little descriptive", 3= "more or less descriptive", 4= "descriptive", and 5 = "extremely descriptive".

Mean scores of Google, MSN, and Yahoo on each of the five personality dimensions were displayed in Table 3 and in Figure 1. Perceived brand personality comparison of search engines in Figure 1 illustrated the fact that mean scores of Google with respect to five brand personality dimensions, is higher than the Yahoo and MSN, respectively. Besides, MSN gets the lowest mean scores on all of the five brand personality dimensions. Furthermore, it can be seen that Google received highest mean scores for the "competence" and "excitement" dimensions. In other words, Google as a search engine has been perceived as competent and excitement giving.

However, mean score comparison of search engines does not give an opinion whether these differences were statistically significant. In line with the purpose of this study, multivariate analysis of variance (MANAVO) was conducted in order to determine whether there are statistically significant differences among the mean scores of these three search engine brands (Google, MSN, and Yahoo) on each of the five personality dimensions (competence, sincerity, excitement, sophistication, and ruggedness).

The data must be a sample from multivariate normal populations in order to conduct MANOVA. The result of Bartlett's test of sphericity indicated that the residual covariance matrix is significantly different from an identity matrix (p=0.000). So in this study, a significance level of 0,000 satisfies the necessary level of intercorrelations between dependent variables to justify MANOVA. Moreover, to perform MANOVA the data in each cell has to come from populations with the same variance. The result of the Levene's test indicated that each of significance levels are higher than 0,05 so that Levene's test provided sufficient evidence that the error variance of the dependent variables are equal across groups.

To compare mean scores of groups, which were formed by categorical independent variable, on a set of interval dependent variables multiple analysis of variance test was applied. The research design was composed of only one independent variable (non-metric) so that no interaction is expected. The results of the multiple analysis of variance for three search engine brands (Google, MSN, and Yahoo) in respect of five brand personality dimensions were presented in the Table 4 and Table 5. Table 4 displayed the findings of the four-multivariate tests to determine whether there are statistically significant differences among the mean scores of the three search engines on each of the five personality dimensions. The multivariate tests table displays four multivariate tests of significance of search engine effect in the model. Since all of the four-multivariate tests have significance levels of 0,000, it can be asserted that mean scores of five personality dimensions vary across Google, MSN, and Yahoo. Significant differences were found on each search engine for all brand personality dimensions.

The results of multivariate tests can help us determine if there is a difference among mean scores of three search engines with respect to five brand personality dimensions. However, multivariate tests do not indicate which search engines' mean scores differ. The second step in

Table 3. Descriptive statistics of search engines on brand personality dimensions

	Search Engine	Mean	Std. Deviation
SINCERITY	Google	3.2341	.71929
	MSN	2.4453	.82059
	YAHOO	2.7503	.82508
EXCITEMENT	Google	3.7295	.83269
	MSN	2.4568	.93142
	YAHOO	2.7526	.89522
COMPETENCE	Google	3.8569	.70366
	MSN	2.6540	.87922
	YAHOO	3.0759	.96955
SOPHISTICATION	Google	2.7771	.90628
	MSN	2.2890	.94572
	YAHOO	2.4557	.94835
RUGGEDNESS	Google	2.4925	.82918
	MSN	2.0557	.90635
	YAHOO	2.2785	.83845

MANOVA is to determine which group means differ significantly from others with the help of post hoc tests. For this purpose, Scheffe post hoc test, which is a relatively strict and conservative test, has been employed so that it will be possible to depict the difference between each pair of means of search engines.

Scheffe test performs simultaneous joint pairwise comparisons for all possible pairwise combinations of means. The first column of Table 5 displays the dependent variables; whereas the next two columns illustrate the pair of means being tested. The mean difference column displays the difference between each pair of means. Confidence intervals are also displayed for the mean difference. It will be noticed that when the means differ significantly the confidence interval does not contain zero. And when the means are similar the confidence interval contains zero.

Figure 1. Brand personality comparison of search engines

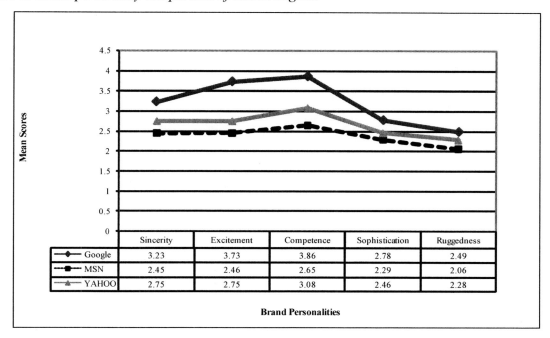

	Sincerity	Excitement	Competence	Sophistication	Ruggedness
Google	3.23	3.73	3.86	2.78	2.49
MSN	2.45	2.46	2.65	2.29	2.06
YAHOO	2.75	2.75	3.08	2.46	2.28

Brand Personalities

Table 4. Multivariate tests table[c]

Effect		Value	F	Hypothesis df	Error df	Sig.	Partial Eta Squared	Observed Power[a]
Search Engine	Pillai's Trace	1.151	28.999	15.000	699.000	.000	.384	1.000
	Wilks' Lambda	.043	90.383	15.000	638.091	.000	.650	1.000
	Hotelling's Trace	17.763	271.964	15.000	689.000	.000	.856	1.000
	Roy's Largest Root	17.510	815.972[b]	5.000	233.000	.000	.946	1.000

a *Computed using alpha = .01*

b *The statistic is an upper bound on F that yields a lower bound on the significance level.*

c *Design: Search Engine*

The question of interest at this stage is which groups significantly differ from others with respect to the mean scores of brand personality dimensions. In Table 5, asterisk (*) indicates which pair of search engines differ significantly for a specific personality dimension. The asterisks appear when the significance value is less than 0.01. Homogeneous subsets, which are displayed in Table 6 also identify homogeneous subsets of the means that are not different from each other.

Table 5. Scheffe multiple comparison test

Brand Personality Dimensions	(I) Search Engine	(J) Search Engine	Mean Difference (I-J)	Std. Error	Sig.	99% Confidence Interval	
						Lower Bound	Upper Bound
Sincerity	Google	MSN	.7888*	.12523	.000	.4049	1.1726
		YAHOO	.4838*	.12523	.001	.1000	.8676
	MSN	Google	-.7888*	.12523	.000	-1.1726	-.4049
		YAHOO	-.3049	.12563	.054	-.6900	.0801
	YAHOO	Google	-.4838*	.12523	.001	-.8676	-.1000
		MSN	.3049	.12563	.054	-.0801	.6900
Excitement	Google	MSN	1.2727*	.14072	.000	.8414	1.7040
		YAHOO	.9770*	.14072	.000	.5457	1.4082
	MSN	Google	-1.2727*	.14072	.000	-1.7040	-.8414
		YAHOO	-.2957	.14116	.114	-.7284	.1369
	YAHOO	Google	-.9770*	.14072	.000	-1.4082	-.5457
		MSN	.2957	.14116	.114	-.1369	.7284
Competence	Google	MSN	1.2029*	.13599	.000	.7862	1.6197
		YAHOO	.7810*	.13599	.000	.3642	1.1978
	MSN	Google	-1.2029*	.13599	.000	-1.6197	-.7862
		YAHOO	-.4219*	.13641	.009	-.8400	-.0039
	YAHOO	Google	-.7810*	.13599	.000	-1.1978	-.3642
		MSN	.4219*	.13641	.009	.0039	.8400
Sophistication	Google	MSN	.4881*	.14807	.005	.0342	.9419
		YAHOO	.3214	.14807	.097	-.1324	.7752
	MSN	Google	-.4881*	.14807	.005	-.9419	-.0342
		YAHOO	-.1667	.14854	.534	-.6219	.2886
	YAHOO	Google	-.3214	.14807	.097	-.7752	.1324
		MSN	.1667	.14854	.534	-.2886	.6219
Ruggedness	Google	MSN	.4368*	.13618	.007	.0194	.8542
		YAHOO	.2140	.13618	.293	-.2033	.6314
	MSN	Google	-.4368*	.13618	.007	-.8542	-.0194
		YAHOO	-.2228	.13661	.267	-.6415	.1959
	YAHOO	Google	-.2140	.13618	.293	-.6314	.2033
		MSN	.2228	.13661	.267	-.1959	.6415

Based on observed means.
* The mean difference is significant at the .01 level.

In the subset columns the subsets of means that do not differ from one another are displayed in the same column.

In sincerity homogeneous subset table, the first subset has two means ranging from 2.45 to 2.75; and the second has one mean (3.23). These

Table 6. Homogeneous subsets table

SINCERITY Scheffe		
Search Engine	**Subset**	
	1	2
MSN	2.4453	
YAHOO	2.7503	
Google		3.2341
Sig.	.054	1.000

EXCITEMENT Scheffe		
Search Engine	**Subset**	
	1	2
MSN	2.4568	
YAHOO	2.7526	
Google		3.7295
Sig.	.113	1.000

SOPHISTICATION Scheffe		
Search Engine	**Subset**	
	1	2
MSN	2.2890	
YAHOO	2.4557	2.4557
Google		2.7771
Sig.	.532	.098

RUGGEDNESS Scheffe		
Search Engine	**Subset**	
	1	2
MSN	2.0557	
YAHOO	2.2785	2.2785
Google		2.4925
Sig.	.265	.293

COMPETENCE Scheffe			
Search Engine	**Subset**		
	1	2	3
MSN	2.654		
YAHOO		3.076	
Google			3.857
Sig.	1.000	1.000	1.000

Means for groups in homogeneous subsets are displayed.
Based on Type III Sum of Squares
Alpha = .01.

results indicated that sincerity brand personality dimension for MSN and Yahoo does not differ significantly. As it can be seen from excitement, sophistication, and ruggedness homogeneous subset table, MSN-Yahoo pair does not also significantly differ from each other on excitement, sophistication, and ruggedness brand personality dimensions. However, in competence homogeneous subset table, there are three subsets and each subset has one mean (MSN=2.65, Yahoo=3,07 and

Google=3,85). This means that competence brand personality dimension is the only dimension on which Google, MSN, and Yahoo significantly and completely differ from each other.

Moreover, Google-MSN and Google-Yahoo pairs significantly differ from each other on sincerity, excitement, and competence brand personality dimension. Google completely and significantly differs from Yahoo and MSN on sincerity, excitement, and competence brand personality dimension. Google-MSN pair also significantly differs from each other on sophistication (Google=2.77 and MSN=2.28) and ruggedness (Google=2.49 and MSN=2.05) brand personality dimension. On the other hand, with respect to sophistication (Google=2.77 and Yahoo=2.45) and ruggedness (Google=2.49 and Yahoo=2.27) brand personality dimension, Google-Yahoo pair does not significantly differ from each other.

Google was perceived as being more competent (3.85), exciting (3.72) and sincere (3.23) than the other two search engines (see Table 6).

However, MSN was seen as being the least sincere, exciting and competent of the three search engine brands, but was also considered to be the least rugged and sophisticated. Yahoo was similar to Google in terms of being sophisticated and rugged. Nevertheless, Yahoo was also similar to MSN with respect to sophistication and ruggedness dimension. None of these three search engines has created a brand personality that distinguishes one search engine from the other two on the traits of sophistication and ruggedness. Google, Yahoo and MSN were viewed as being distinctive from each other only on competence personality dimension. Google (3.85) is perceived as being the most competent, followed by Yahoo (3.07), and then MSN (2.65). Furthermore, the respondents perceived Google (3.72) as being the most exciting search engine compare to Yahoo and MSN. On the other hand, Yahoo and MSN have not created a brand personality that is distinctive on the trait of excitement. Yahoo and MSN are also similar to each other on the trait of sincerity. However, Google is perceived as being the most sincere search engine and distinguishes itself from the others on the sincerity brand personality dimension as well.

CONCLUSION AND IMPLICATIONS

A comparison of brand-personality profiles reveals a differentiation among three major search engine brands. These differences might be originated from the search engines' marketing communications, the nature of the services that the search engines offer, and/or their overall performance. Brand personality can be an effective tool to differentiate one online search engine brand from another, and online brands have to use these brand personality strategies effectively as a means of brand differentiation.

Within the scope of this research, Google has been found to be the most favorite search engine brand of the respondents with a 90%. Furthermore, the search engine users indicate that they are "extremely willing" to use Google with a mean of 4.81, whereas they state that they are "more or less willing" to use Yahoo with a mean score of 3.39, and they are "very little willing" to use MSN with a mean score of 2.20. Besides, the findings of MANOVA analysis have revealed that all three search engines show statistically significant differences only on the Competence dimension, and Google has been perceived as the most competent search engine among the three.

On the Sincerity and Excitement dimensions, Google has been perceived statistically different from the other two search engines; but there is no statistically significant difference between Yahoo and MSN on these dimensions. On the other hand, the Sophistication and Ruggedness dimensions do not show considerable difference between Google and Yahoo, and MSN and Yahoo, whereas there are significant differences between Google and MSN. Briefly, Google has the highest scores for all five dimensions, and it is followed by Yahoo and MSN respectively. Additionally, except the indifference between Google and Yahoo on the Sophistication and Ruggedness dimensions, Google has been perceived as statistically different from MSN in all dimensions, and from Yahoo for Competence, Excitement and Sincerity dimensions. In the light of these statistical analyses, it appears that Google has already become the conqueror of the digital age as a search engine. That's why the following part is devoted to a comprehensive discussion about the factors that contribute to this inevitable success of Google's brand personality.

The results of this study have shown that Google's brand personality is strongly associated with Competence (e.g. intelligent, technical, reliable, successful) and Excitement (e.g. unique, up-to-date, exciting, independent, trendy). In addition, Google is moderately linked with the brand personality dimension of Sincerity (e.g. sincere, friendly, honest, cheerful, original). These findings can be largely attributed to the fact that Google as a search engine provides the most accurate and relevant information to its audience which, in turn, makes it indispensable for its users (New Atlantis, 2004). Even though Google isn't perfect, its results are still the best thing going; in fact, Google's results are so good that many users rely on it reflexively and constantly (New Atlantis, 2004). Evidence about the relevancy of Google's results comes from Search Engine Strategies Panel which revealed that people perceive Google as providing more relevant results than other search engines (Kerner, 2006). Additionally, Google performs its search engine function on a separate web page and the brand of Google only consists of search engine function. For instance, Google's email service functions on a separate web page and under the brand name of Gmail. This may be also one of the factors why Google as a search engine has been perceived as competent.

Furthermore, Hall (2007) states that in terms of technical aspects Google has the most advanced natural search algorithm and sophisticated filtering for duplicate content in order to provide relevant results. It is also found to be excellent at determining if a link is artificial or a true editorial citation (Hall, 2007). Besides, Google has a significant first-mover advantage in search engine business, which gives it an opportunity to become a generic term for search engines. In addition, the term google or the verb googling has already taken its place in today's dictionaries. According to Zumpano (2007)

Google's most noteworthy brand achievement in 2006 was the addition of the verb "to google" in two major English-language dictionaries. These may explain why Google, within the competence dimension, gets the highest scores in successful, leader, intelligent and reliable traits. Additionally, Google gets the highest scores in the traits of up-to-date, imaginative and contemporary within the excitement dimension. The results also provide a robust support to Greg Ness (2007) from Sundog who mentions that "Google imbues its operating system with usefulness, entertainment and utility for the consumer: Desktop, Docs, Spreadsheets, Search, Calendars, Picasa, Maps, Earth, YouTube, Gmail, Groups, etc." Ness (2007) also adds that "what Google provides is needed, wanted, helpful, free and almost universally available…". Moreover, for its basic search function, Google's pages are available in different languages with its simplistic web design. Additionally, despite its technical superiority everything on its page has been designed in a simple and clear way. All these factors contribute to the perception of Google as expert, authenticated, unique and exciting; in other words Google is perceived as competent and exciting. These features have positive managerial implications on Google, and they help Google strengthen its brand through appropriate marketing communications.

Google has a moderate score for Sincerity dimension which is composed of traits such as sincere, friendly, honest, cheerful, original, sentimental etc. Given that Google has themed logos to represent major holidays, and a mischievous side in the "I'm feeling lucky" option next to the search, it is not surprising that within sincerity dimension, the highest traits were cheerful, original and real. According to Rusch (2001), many things about the brand carry fun and play. Rusch (2001) describes the story of the name and logo of Google as follows: "Page came up with Google, which is a play on the word googol, meaning 10100, or 1 followed by 100 zeros…The word google is evocative of the technology involved but it is also a silly word, which makes it less apprehensive". In his article Rusch (2001) also gives place to an interview with Google's spokesperson Cindy Mc-Caffrey who mentioned that one of the founders of Google has designed the logo in a way that it reflects whimsy and fun, and with its colorful rounded edges, it's approachable and friendly but it's also serious about what it does. All these factors have an impact on Google's modest score for sincerity dimension.

However, on Sophistication dimension of brand personality scale Google has low scores. The poor performance of sophistication may also be the result of its simplicity, uncomplicated nature, and usage easiness. On the one hand, having an uncomplicated and simplistic design can attract users, but on the other hand this may lead to a perception of unsophistication and naïvety. Furthermore, by sticking only to search function and refusing to turn itself into a web portal, Google not only emphasizes its competence but also opens up new ways for parallel markets such as Google Maps, Google Earth, Google News and Blog. Hence, to some extent this lack of sophistication brings a limitation into Google's attractiveness, however, it does not lead to a damage in its image since being perceived as unsophisticated supports other brand dimensions in the case of Google.

Finally, Google (and also the other two search engine brands) receives the lowest score for the dimension of Ruggedness. This may be attributable to the nature of the service that search engine brands offer to their users. The most interesting thing is that within the ruggedness dimension, Google received the lowest trait score for the masculinity, whereas it has the highest score for the trait of Western. Furthermore, within the Sophistication dimension, the trait of feminine had been among the lowest scored traits. This finding lead us to conclude that Google as a search engine has been perceived neither with masculinity nor femininity trait, which may mean that users' perceptions about Google are free of gender.

On the other hand, the brands of Yahoo and MSN are the world's most popular web portals that cover all sort of services such as email, messenger, e-groups, news, shopping, and as well as search. And all these services are performed on the same web page and under the brand name of Yahoo and MSN. Concentration on only search engine function may be driving force for the respondents' perceptions that Google is the most competent brand of the three examined.

The users of the search engines can not position Yahoo appropriately on the five brand personality dimensions. This, in turn, leads to insufficient differentiation or improper image in the minds of the consumers. Yet, the only dimension that Yahoo gets a relatively higher mean score among the five dimensions was the competence dimension. This can be partly attributable to the fact that Yahoo was a pioneer and a major player as a web portal in online industry. Being a pioneer actor in the industry may affect the perceptions of search engine users. When compared with other search engines, it can be said that MSN does not have a clear-cut brand personality in the minds of consumers. Therefore, MSN can not create a distinct brand positioning as a search engine.

The findings of the current study have important implications for the management of all three online search engines that are investigated. It is certain that MSN and Yahoo have to position themselves in a distinctive and creative way in respondents' minds so that they may overcome the dominance of Google. Managers of MSN and Yahoo search engines have to differentiate their search engines' personalities in a favorable way from their key competitors so that the users may show high willingness to use them.

Since this study is concentrated on brand personality of search engine brands, an on-line survey is designed as a means of data collection. However, the low response rate and convenience sampling due to the nature of online surveys may be considered as the limitation of this research. Additionally, it has to be noted that the results of this study are valid when only these three brands are considered as search engines. In other words, the results can not be applicable when Yahoo or MSN are considered as web portals. Hence, there is a need for further research in order to understand brand personality of web portals such as Yahoo and MSN.

REFERENCES

Aaker, D. A. (1996). Measuring brand equity across products and markets. *California Management Review, 38,* 102-120.

Aaker, J. L. (1997). Dimensions of brand personality. *Journal of Marketing Research, 34* (3), 347-356.

Aaker, J. L. (1999). The malleable self: the role of self-expression in persuasion. *Journal of Marketing Research, 34* (3), 347-356.

Aaker, J. L., Benet-Martinez, V., & Garolera, J. (2001). Consumption symbols as carriers of culture: A study of Japanese and Spanish brand personality constructs. *Journal of Personality and Social Psychology, 81* (3), 492-508.

American Marketing Association (AMA). Definition of brand personality. *Dictionary of Marketing Terms.* Retrieved September 5, 2006, from http://www.marketingpower.com/mg-dictionary.php?SearchFor=brand+personality&Searched=1

Azoulay, A., & Kapferer, J. N. (2003). Do brand personality scales really measure brand personality? *Journal of Brand Management, 11,* 143-155.

D'Astous, A., Colbert, F., & D'Astous, E. (2006). The personality of cultural festivals: Scale development and applications. *International Journal of Arts Management, 8* (2), 14-23.

D'Astous, A., & Le'vesque, M. (2003). A scale for measuring store personality. *Psychology & Marketing, 20* (5), 455-469.

Biel, A. (1992). How brand image drives brand equity?. *Journal of Advertising Research, 32* (6), 6-12.

Burns, E. (2005). Search usage spikes as a daily online habit, *Clickz.com.* Retrieved November 20, 2005, from, http://www.clickz.com/showPage.html?page=3565561

Burns, E. (2006a). Search sees double-digit growth. *Clickz.com.* Retrieved February 9, 2006, from, http://www.clickz.com/showPage.html?page=3584126

Burns, E. (2006b). Online Seizes More of the Advertising Mix. *Clickz.com.* Retrieved February 13, 2006, from, http://www.clickz.com/showPage.html?page=3584801.

Fournier, S. (1998). Consumers and their brands: Developing relationship theory in consumer research. *Journal of Consumer Research, 24* (4), 343-373.

Freling, T. H., & Forbes, L. (2005). An empirical analysis of the brand personality effect. *Journal of Product and Brand Management, 14* (7), 404-413.

Hall, J. (2007). Google vs Yahoo vs MSN - What's the difference?. *Ecademy-Business Networking.* Retrieved February 12, 2007, from http://www.ecademy.com/node.php?id=80164&seen=1

Hosany, S., Ekinci Y., & Uysal, M. (2006). Destination image and destination personality: An application of branding theories to tourism places. *Journal of Business Research, 59,* 638-642.

Kania, D. (2001). *Branding.Com.* NTC Business Books, American Marketing Association (AMA).

Keller, K. L. (2003). *Strategic brand management: building, measuring and managing brand equity.* Upper Saddle River (NJ): Prentice Hall.

Kerner, S. M. (2006). Are Google results more relevant?. *InternetNews.com.* Retrieved April 26, 2006, from http://www.internetnews.com/dev-news/article.php/3601751

Kim, C. K., Han, D., & Park, S. B. (2001). The effect of brand personality and brand identification on brand loyalty: Applying the theory of social identification. *Japanese Psychological Research, 43* (4), 195-206.

Meyers, H., & Gerstman, R. (2001). *Branding @ the digital age.* New York: Palgrave.

Müller, B., & Chandon, J. L. (2003). The impact of visiting a brand website on brand personality. *Electronic Markets, 13* (3), 210-21.

Nandan, S. (2005). An exploration of the brand identity- brand image linkage: A communications perspective. *Journal of Brand Management, 12* (4), 264-278.

Ness, G. (2007). And some still think of Google as just a search engine company. *SUNDOG,* Retrieved April 11, 2007, from http://www.sundog.net/index.php/sunblog/comments/and-some-still-think-of-google-as-just-a-search-engine/

New Atlantis, (2004). Gaga over Google. *A Journal of Technolgy & Society. 5,* 99-101. Retrieved September 1, 2006, from http://www.thenewatlantis.com/archive/5/soa/google.htm

Okazaki, S. (2005). Excitement or sophistication? A preliminary exploration of online brand personality. *International Marketing Review, 23* (3), 279-303.

Plummer, J. T. (1984). How personality makes a difference? *Journal of Advertising Research, 24* (6), 27-31.

Rowley, J. (2004). Online branding: the case of McDonald's. *British Food Journal, 106* (2/3), 228-237.

Rusch, R. (2001). Google: The infinite quest. *Brandchannel.com.* Retrieved August 13, 2001, from http://www.brandchannel.com/features_profile.asp?pr_id=30

Siguaw, J., Mattila, A., & Austin, J. R. (1999). The brand personality scale: An application for restaurants. *Cornell Hotel and Restaurant Administration Quarterly, 40* (3), 48-55.

Sirgy, J. (1982). Self-concept in consumer behavior: A critical review. *Journal of Consumer Research, 9,* 287-301.

Smith, A. C. T., Graetz, B. R, & Westerbeek, H. M. (2006). Brand personality in a membership-based organization. *International Journal of Nonprofit and Voluntary Sector Marketing, 11* (3), 251-266.

Sullivan, D. (2004a). Major search engines and directories. *Search Engine Watch.* Retrieved March 28, 2007, from http://searchenginewatch.com/showPage.html?page=2156221.

Sullivan, D. (2004b). Buying Your Way In: Search Engine Advertising Chart. *Search Engine Watch.* Retrieved March 22, 2007, from http://searchenginewatch.com/showPage.html?page=2167941

Sweeney, J., & Brandon, C. (2006). Brand personality: Exploring the potential to move from factorial analytical to circumplex models. *Psychology & Marketing, 23* (8), 639-663.

Van Rekom, J., Jacobs, G., & Verlegh, P. W. J. (2006). Measuring and managing the essence of a brand personality. *Marketing Letters, 17,* 181-192.

Venable, B. T., Rose, G. M., Bush, V. D., & Gilbert, F. W. (2005). The role of brand personality in charitable giving: An assessment and validation.

Journal of the Academy of Marketing Science, *33* (3), 295-312.

Wee, Tan T. T. (2004). Extending human personality to brands: The stability factor. *Journal of Brand Management. 11* (4), 317-330.

Zumpano, A. (2007). Similar search results: Google wins. *Brandchannel.com.* Retrieved January 29, 2007, from http://www.brandchannel.com/features_effect.asp?pf_id=352

Chapter IV
The Naming of Corporate eBrands

Tobias Kollmann
University of Duisburg – Essen, Germany

Christina Suckow
University of Duisburg – Essen, Germany

ABSTRACT

This chapter examines whether classical brand naming concepts are sustainable for entrepreneurial firms in the Net Economy. A prior study of Kohli and LaBahn (1997) covers the formal brand naming process and gives insights into brand name objectives and criteria. To follow the research purpose, their findings have been adapted to entrepreneurial firms in the Net Economy. Three hundred nineteen e-entrepreneurs located in German business incubators were analyzed for their brand naming process. The availability of an appropriate domain name is found to be a basic driver for deciding on a brand name. The domain name influences the course of action during the naming process. Two groups were found that significantly differ in proceeding with the naming process. One group of e-entrepreneurs follows the traditional process of Kohli and LaBahn (1997), whereas the other group follows a new approach giving more emphasis on the domain name. Here, the process shows to be iterative in nature instead of a step by step procedure.

INTRODUCTION

Constant technology developments allow companies to create innovative business ideas (Kollmann, 2006), which accelerate movements especially on technology-driven electronic markets. This dynamic environment makes the development of strong (electronic) brands essential (Ibeh, Luo &

Dinnie 2005). Unstable market conditions call for stability in branding since a strong brand prospers from sustained core brand values. In this respect, e-branding encompasses all initiatives and activities of building and managing an online brand with its specific concepts, strategies and designs related to the context of the Net Economy. The rising importance of online branding or e-branding is primarily rooted in the general uncertainty and information overload online consumers attribute to online shopping. Strong e-brands create trust and give orientation during decision making at online transactions. This is the reason why more and more companies increase the efforts in online branding, especially those operating in the area of e-commerce, where trust is an essential prerequisite of customer loyalty. The increasing amount of available information on the Internet leads on the one hand to more transparency of electronic markets and empowerment of customers, which potentially results in decreasing loyalty (Ibeh, Luo, & Dinnie, 2005). Therefore, loyalty has to be regained by a strong e-brand. On the other hand, this information overload also leads to uncertainty of customers to handle vast amounts of information properly and potentially results in increased loyalty to trustful brands. Strong e-brands not only create trust, they also maintain trust.

Different from traditional brands, e-brands face the challenge of creating customer value only by means of the Internet. This comprises restrictions for e-branding in form of limited media usage (only Internet) but provides also major opportunities regarding the multiple facets of electronic networks (interactivity/individuality). Although e-branding is just about to arise from a recent practical phenomenon to a profound, theory-grounded research subject, research about e-branding is not extensive yet. In order to advance research on e-branding, traditional branding concepts need to be analysed with regard to their appropriateness in the Net Economy, before new concepts can be developed. Building a brand commences with defining and developing formal aspects of a brand, like name, logo, design and colours before the brand can be laden with meaning over time in order to develop from a simple sign to a real brand that encompasses emotional and cognitive elements. Within this process the name evolves to be the element that carries all later branding activities. Therefore, this chapter wants to advance research in e-branding by taking a closer look on the naming of e-brands. Special focus will be given to the process of how such names are created and whether this process differs from brand naming in the real economy.

BRAND NAMES

According to Anderson and Bennett (1988) *a brand* is a name, term, design, symbol, or any other feature that identifies one seller's good or service as distinct from those of other sellers. The need for differentiation becomes particularly important when considering the increasing competitiveness in consumer markets. In these markets, functional values are not sufficient anymore to distinguish a company's products from others. Rather, emotional aspects that add value to the customer's life are able to make the difference and to legitimize a price premium. Building brand equity is one form for companies to set its own brand apart from others by complementing functional values with cognitive and emotional brand traits in order to give meaning to the customer's life. Duncan states that a brand is the "perception of an integrated bundle of information and experiences that distinguishes a company and its products from competition" (Duncan, 2002, p.13). Still, a key of creating a brand is the ability to choose a name, logo, symbol, or other attributes that identify a product and already visually separate it from competitors (Keller, 2003). In developing the formal brand identity, the brand name is the first element that needs to be selected as it is the basic fundament of all branding activities. The name is the most used brand information that is communicated to customers, employees, and other stakeholders of the company, because it is the component of a brand which can be spoken or verbalized (Anderson & Bennett, 1988). The selection of a brand name therefore becomes a crucial aspect of the early branding process (Turley & Moore, 1995).

General Importance of Corporate Names

The importance of having a good corporate name lies in its significant role for corporate branding. The name must embrace all values a company wants to be known for. This name eventually becomes the umbrella for the development of the corporate brand and the driver for building brand equity in the long run. Landler, Schiller, and Therrien (1991) state that deciding on a brand name for products or services, belongs to the most important task of marketing management. Since the name of a company has even more far-reaching implications than the name for a product brand name, the selection process of corporate names should be carefully approached by top management (King 1991, Balmer 2001). In order to "differentiate a company from existing competitors and to build up entry barriers for potential competitors" (Geissler & Will, 2001, p.1) corporate branding needs to be accurately addressed already at the entrepreneurial stage. Some corporate names become major assets over time, which contribute billions of dollars to the balance sheet (Aaker, 1996). Thus, a sound corporate branding strategy is important, not only when the venture is growing, but already before the entrepreneur starts business. The creation of a catchy name must be postulated as being a fundamental stage of early brand positioning (Moore, 1995) and may not be dismissed as a creative exercise.

Corporate Brand Names in the Net Economy

Considering customers, Ward and Lee found that brand names are a source of information, which especially online shoppers use as substitutes for product information (Ward & Lee, 2000). The name is used as a mental shortcut to decrease the time of mental processing. Surfing through the Web gives customers the ability to get information very quickly, simultaneously increasing

the danger of being overloaded by information. Limited cognitive resources and time availability lead to the use of e-brands as mental shortcuts in order to decrease information overload and the time of mental processing (Einwiller, Geissler, Will, 2000). "Brand-related information customers acquire over time tend to be organized in their memories around the brand name" (Sen, 1999, p. 431). According to Baker, the brand name is the hub of a brand memory network and once a brand name is activated, a conscious retrieval of related brand information is facilitated (Baker, 2003, p. 1122). The more attributes the customer associates with the brand name, the easier it is to activate the brand memory network and the greater the scope for variation of brand messages. Thus, a strong brand name hub in the network permits customers to abbreviate cognitive processes during decision making.

To ease this mechanism, e-business companies most often have only one brand (name), which includes corporate and product brand at the same time (e.g., *google.com*; *ebay.com*; *yahoo.com*). In the corporate context, a brand has a greater impact on the whole e-branding strategy than a brand in the product context since not only customers, but also other stakeholders must be addressed with the brand. This general shift from focusing on corporate brands rather than on product brands from a company perspective goes along with a shift from reliance on product brands to reliance on corporate brands from a customer perspective (Ward & Lee, 2000). The result is a growing importance of corporate branding in the Net Economy (Leitch & Richardson, 2003; Carpenter, 2000).

The Role of Domains

Customers are not physically confronted with brands in the virtual world making brand awareness a critical factor of successful branding in the Net Economy. To reach brand awareness, the decision about the right URL is an important priority

(Keller, 2003). The domain name must be chosen with the basic brand name criteria in mind, with a great emphasis on brand recall (Keller, 2003). The actual developments in electronic markets make a strong corporate name inevitably necessary for tackling the limited cognitive capacities in processing the information overload and the resulting decline in media efficiency. That is why "corporate branding strategies outperform multibrand strategies when it comes to active brand recall" (Strebinger & Treiblmaier, 2004, p. 159) and marketing costs. Linking corporate and domain name further reduces search and advertising costs. Fiercer competition and the resulting increase of domain-name registrations make finding an available brand name a major challenge of the brand building process. This is especially true in the Net Economy, where easy access to the Web site is critical. Therefore, the match between corporate and domain name should not be the result of coincidence but of careful deliberation.

THE BRAND NAMING PROCESS

The brand naming process simply describes the formal process of how companies create brand names (Kohli & LaBahn, 1997). The goal is to have a name that is able to transfer brand values and to serve as a basis for building brand equity. Since corporate brand names function as a communication interface between the company and its stakeholders (Hatch & Schultz, 2001), its selection process is supposed to be subject to careful deliberation. Different from product brands, corporate brands not only have customers and retailers as points of contact, but also employees, shareholders, government departments, institutions, journalists, experts, and suppliers and other stakeholders (King 1991). As the focus lies on corporate brands in the Net Economy, reliable statements about the value of the name as part of the corporate brand must be achieved by a thorough analysis of the name selection process. The questions arising in this context are: how do companies select their corporate brand name to seed a strong corporate e-brand and how does this process differ from the traditional naming process?

The Traditional Naming Process

The earliest study concerning the formal brand name development process was conducted by McNeal and Zeren (1981). In their explorative study they found that the naming process tends to result in six general steps, but they did not clearly separate criteria from objectives. Shipley, Hooley and Wallace (1988) examined the naming process more extensively. They concluded that companies explicitly set branding objectives and establish branding criteria before selecting a suitable name. In their research, they identified six steps in the selection process with brand name objectives and brand name criteria being separate steps. However, the model fails to show how companies *actually* pass through the naming process; it rather shows a normative approach of the naming process. In their explorative study, Kohli and LaBahn (1997) discovered that the actual naming process results in a five step procedure, where objectives are explicitly set, but criteria are implicitly deployed during the brand name evaluation phase. The five step process of Kohli and LaBahn is presented in Figure 1.

Kohli and LaBahn's model of the naming process is the most advanced related to the naming process so far. The question is whether this model can be applied to the Net Economy. Based on Kohli and LaBahn's (1997) findings, the aim of this research paper is to investigate the corporate e-naming process in the Net Economy more thoroughly and to detect possible differences to the traditional naming process. Concerning the increasing importance of the Internet, companies nowadays are assumed to go through the naming process other than was proposed in the traditional concept. Business in the Net Economy is heavily based on operating Web sites which can only be accessed via the correct domain name. In order to ease access, minimize cost and reduce confusion, corporate and domain name are often chosen to be exactly the same. Consequently, we hypothesize that not only the search for a free domain, but also the act of registering the domain influences the naming process significantly.

Objectives of a Brand Name

For effective brand naming, the first step is setting the branding objectives, because setting explicit objectives makes the management define required achievements for future developments and give direction to the company's future way of doing business (Shipley, 1985). Shipley, Hooley, and Wallace (1988) for example, identified objectives like the *'establishment of a particular image'*, *'consumers' brand loyalty'*, *'market positioning'*, *'acceptance'*, *'product differentiation'* and *'brand reputation'*. Keller (2003) puts it more simply and says that the objective of brand name should be to

'improve brand recall' and *'brand recognition'*. In order to improve brand recall, the name should be *'simple'*, *'easy to pronounce'*, *'familiar'* and *'meaningful'* and to improve recognition, the brand name needs to be *'different'*, *'distinctive'* and *'unusual'* (Keller, 2003). Kohli and LaBahn also identified brand name objectives. Their results included for example *'to convey an intended positioning'*, *'to establish product differentiation'*, *'to establish a distinct segment'* and *'a distinctive image'*, *'to establish identification'* and *'the ease of trademark registration'*. For a possible transfer of these objectives to corporate e-brand names, product level objectives need to be transformed to company level objectives (e.g., *'product differentiation'* to *'market differentiation'*).

Selection Criteria for a Brand Name

Developing a set of brand name criteria helps to decide about an appropriate name that is able to meet defined branding goals. Entrepreneurs must follow some decision criteria in order to prioritise the brand name alternatives in favour of their goal achieving abilities. There have been numerous attempts to identify brand name selection criteria, for example by Heaton (1967), McNeal and Zeren (1981), Schloss (1981), and Berry, Lefkowith and Clark (1988). Heaton concluded that a corporate name should be *'distinctive'*, *'memorable'*, *'communicate specific favourable ideas'*, *'suggest the general types of products the company markets'*, and *'fit with specific company product lines and brand names'* (Heaton, 1967). In the study of McNeal and Zeren (1981), *'descriptiveness of product benefits'*, *'memorability'* and the *'fit with the company image'* were among the most common criteria. According to Berry, Lefkowith and Clark (1988), a name should be *'distinctive'*, *'relevant'*, *'memorable'* and *'flexible'* in order to be a potential brand name. Furthermore, possible criteria for the choice of a name might be the *'ease of recall'* and *'recognition'*, its *'distinctiveness'* or the *'transferability to other languages*

Figure 1. The brand name development process (Kohli & LaBahn, 1997)

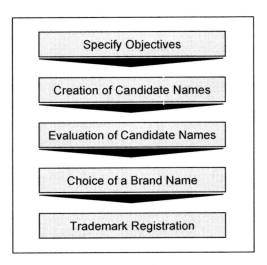

and countries' (Shipley, Hooley, & Wallace, 1988; Keller, 2003). Again, these findings are of a normative nature and fail to find out, which criteria companies really use. Additionally, the criteria found for the traditional naming process do not include any considerations of e-brands. It is suggested that, for example, *'domain name availability'* is a potentially strong criterion for the e-naming process.

THE E-BRAND NAMING PROCESS

In order to test the validity of traditional concepts of developing brand names in the context of the Net Economy, an empirical survey was conducted. The survey included not only the brand naming process itself, but also naming objectives and brand name criteria. The results are able to reflect a thorough picture of the corporate naming process on the Internet. After giving an overview of the research methodology, a discussion of the results will clarify whether the traditional concept of brand naming in the Real Economy is sustainable in the Net Economy.

Research Methodology

Rode argues "that for a corporate branding model to be relevant in the context of start-ups, the entrepreneur needs to become the centre of attention" (Rode & Vallaster, 2005, p.130). Since the naming process takes place at the very beginning of the corporate branding process, it is assumed that entrepreneurs have just completed the process and can remember details more accurately than, for example, marketing managers of established companies. We selected 319 German entrepreneurs from a list of business incubators located all over Germany. As no complete and representative list of German entrepreneurs was available for research purposes, the complete list of entrepreneurs located at business incubators enabled us to select a smaller, but representative

sample, of entrepreneurial companies. From this list we selected only those companies that were counted among the e-business sector in Germany. The entrepreneurs were personally asked about the name finding process during the start-up phase of their company via an online questionnaire. One hundred eleven entrepreneurs answered the questionnaire over three weeks in March 2006, of which 105 were completed. Companies in the sample were between one week (minimum) and 96 weeks (maximum) old with a mean of 56 weeks. Most of the respondents were the entrepreneurs themselves (52), some were the head of marketing (11), CTOs (7) and management assistants (2). The companies employed 13 people on average with one being the minimum and 46 being the maximum.

On the online questionnaire respondents had to indicate those branding objectives that their corporate name was expected to realise. Then they had to indicate the relevance of the different brand name criteria for the nomenclature of their company. In order to test whether the Internet plays a central role in the process, respondents had the possibility to additionally choose the criterion *'availability of domain name.'* To test whether the naming process itself has changed, we added two other steps that were supposed to be essential for entrepreneurial firms in the Net Economy: *'check for domain'* and *'register domain'*. The respondents were asked to set all steps into an order that best reflects their corporate naming process.

To statistically assess the naming process, we conducted a cluster analysis. With a cluster analysis, the underlying structure of a set of variables can be detected by grouping objects of similar kind into respective categories. This explorative data analysis sorts the entrepreneurs into groups in a way that their homogeneity is maximal within a group, but minimal between the groups. It simply discovers a structure in the data set without explaining their cause. With a preliminary single-linkage or "nearest-neighbour" procedure, outliers were identified and deleted. As a result, two clusters were formed that show an adequate low level of heterogeneity; one cluster comprised 51 objects (entrepreneurs) and the other 27. With the help of a discriminant function analysis, the predictive ability of the steps on one categorical dependent measure (the clusters) was explored. In fact, the discriminant function analysis is used to determine which step of the process best discriminates between the two groups of entrepreneurs.

The Ward-method allowed us to extract two clusters that show lowest heterogeneity within their groups. In addition, statistical evidence for the fact that the two clusters also significantly differ from each other (between the groups) was given by a high Eigenvalue (7.91), which is evidence for a good discriminant function. The correlation coefficient of 0.942 supports this result. Thus, 88.9% of the total variance can be explained by the difference between the groups. The classification result of 98.7 % testifies that according to the discriminant function, almost all respondents could be assigned to the cluster they originally belonged to from the cluster analysis. Thus, the division of the entrepreneurs into two groups is statistically validated.

Empirical Results

As primary objective, entrepreneurs want their corporate brand name to '*ease the identification*' with their company and the company's products (see Table 1). Identification plays an important role in the development of a corporate brand, because employees, customers, and other stakeholders must identify themselves with the corporate brand and their implicit and explicit values for a corporate brand to be successful. Especially in the fast moving e-business environment, strong identification with the brand can enhance loyalty among employees as well as customers. For creating identification, a special '*brand image*' is necessary that distinguishes corporate values from

those of competitors. Since functionality is not a point of difference in consumer markets anymore, the name is expected to '*create emotionality*'. By this, the name should be able to pursue a position in the market that clearly differentiates the company from its competitors. In some cases, the name is even expected to '*establish a new or distinct segment*' by introducing the brand/product to the market. Transparency and increasing competition in electronic markets call for stronger differentiation and emotionality, since brands cannot create value on a pure functional level anymore. An overview of the results is given in Table 1.

As can be seen from Table 2, the actual results (2nd column) differ from the traditional ones of Kohli and LaBahn (1997), which is given on the right column of the table. The direction to which a criterion moved up or down on its ranking is shown by corresponding arrows. Interesting to see is the high importance of '*recognition*' and '*recall*' of the brand name in the Net Economy. Competitors are just a mouse click away and a name that is easily memorable helps customers to find their way through the Web to the company Web site. Oftentimes, information search starts by recalling a brand name and using it for entering a domain name into the browser. If this does not lead to the requested results, the use of search engines facilitates the information search. Here, recognising a brand helps to select the right link from the list of results. Thus, not only recalling a name but also recognising a name is essential for finding information about brands on the Web. Hence, the choice of a brand name in the Net Economy should be very much influenced by memory as a selection criterion, which makes recognition a key criterion (Lerman & Garbarino, 2002).

The results also support the role of brand names as a shortcut for product information search. Additionally, difficult '*pronunciation*' or unfamiliar letter compositions prevent a correct retrieving of the brand name and a correct domain name entry in the browser. Since start-ups in the Net Economy ground their business on the domain, it would be

Table 1. Brand name objectives

	Mean[a]	Rank
Ease of Identification with company	4.14	1
Ease of Identification with company products	4.01	2
Establish a distinctive image	3.90	3
Creation of Emotionality	3.73	4
Ease of registration	3.65	5
Convey intended positioning in the market	3.64	6
Establish market differentiation	3.52	7
Establish a distinct segment	3.31	8

a: Measured on a 5-point scale: 1 = not at all important; 5 = extremely important

fatal to have such an obstacle to entering a Web site. In line with these results, the importance of *'domain availability'* becomes obvious. As 79% of the respondents indicate, their domain name is equal to their corporate name. This coherence supports our assumption that domain availability is a fundamental criterion for the corporate e-naming process.

The name is also selected according to its *'positive connotations'* and its ability to differentiate itself from others. The more evoked associations are favourable, strong and unique, the easier it is to create brand equity (Keller 2003). Although this is equally true for brands and e-brands, positive connotations are not as important as *'recall'* and *'recognition'* in the Net Economy. *'Versatility among countries'* is another criterion that drives the decision about a brand name. As a global medium, the Internet makes access to international markets very easy. This calls for brand names which are easily transferable to other countries and which are understood in different languages. As last criterion, *'ease of trademark registration'* is less decisive for e-brand names than for traditional brand names. Although failing to register a brand name may in some cases be

without consequences in the short run, increasing competition and fraud on the Web seem to make registration unavoidable for successful branding in the long run. The necessity for fast decisions especially during company foundation may lead to unreflected decisions related to brand name registrations. Eventually, the missing protection against competitors may become a danger for business continuation.

The last part of the empirical research results is looking at the formal brand name development process. As the statistical results allow a distinction between two groups of respondents, the resulting difference of proceeding in the naming process is visualised by a graphical representation in Figure 2. As the figure shows, one group follows a more traditional and classical approach, whereas the other group pursues a totally different approach. Following the traditional approach, group A develops some alternative or candidate brand names that go through an extensive evaluation phase before the entrepreneur chooses the one best suited for the realisation of the defined brand name objectives. Afterwards, a corresponding domain is checked, allowing for possible variations of the name if the domain is already

Table 3. Importance of brand name criteria

	Mean[a]	New Rank	Change	Old Rank[b]
Ease of recall	4.42	1	↑	5
Ease of recognition	4.42	1	~	3
Domain availability	4.32	2	↑	--
Positive connotations	4.19	3	~	1
Distinctiveness	4.13	4	~	4
Ease of pronunciation	3.90	5	↑	8
Overall liking	3.88	6	↓	2
Versatile among countries/languages	3.80	7	↑	10
Consistent with company image	3.73	8	~	6
Negative connotations	3.64	9	~	8
Versatile (products/markets)	3.63	10	~	9
Ease of trademark registration	3.50	11	↓	7

occupied (e.g., instead of www.xyz.com using www.xyz-software.com or www.xyz-international.com). The registration of the brand name as a trademark comes at the end. This group follows a step by step procedure that filters a name out of an accumulation of alternatives by means of specified criteria and then checks for suitable domains. This group pursues a strategy that we label "name follows domain".

Group B has no such clear procedure. This group starts with defining the naming objectives as well. They do not create alternative before they evaluate and select a name, they rather select a name that is generated by an ad hoc method like brainstorming with friends and family. They immediately check the relevant domain and if it is not available anymore they look for an alternative name and check the domain again. Once they found a name that seems suitable, they start evaluating the name according to the defined objectives and their decision criteria. If the name does not match the objectives to a certain extent, the procedure starts anew. This iterative loop continues up to the point where a name with a free domain and a good match with brand name criteria and objectives are found. Consequently, Group B develops the new corporate name by going through a cycle of picking, checking and evaluating a name until an appropriate one is found. Therefore, this strategy is labeled "name follows domain."

Following these results, the naming process of corporate brands in the Net Economy goes along two different paths. One path is similar to the traditional way of finding a brand name, whereas the other path is different and puts more emphasis on the domain. Those entrepreneurs who followed the "domain follows name" strategy, needed 14 weeks on average to find a name, the group of "name follows domain" however, only needed two and a half weeks. Overall, the shortest name finding process took one day, whereas the longest took about ten months. The Internet modifies the speed of starting a business, sometimes requiring ad hoc decisions which oftentimes include fast decisions about a corporate brand name. The difference

Figure 2. The brand name development process in the Net Economy

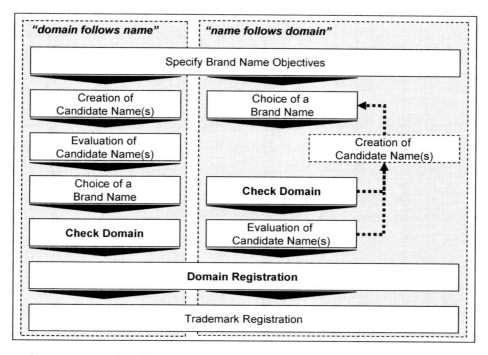

a: Cluster analysis: strategy 1 = 51 companies; strategy 2 = 27 companies

between the two groups may thus also be based upon the intensity with which the process is accomplished, which in turn depends on the speed, urgency and financial resources the entrepreneur has to deal with during the start-up phase.

Limitations

The extrapolation and generalisation of the results is restricted by some research limitations. Although the sample is representative for entrepreneurs residing at business incubators, other entrepreneurs may show different procedures when choosing a name for their e-brand. The dominance of the time consuming and intensive traditional process may be the result of this bias, since companies at business incubators tend to have higher resource endowments which, for example, decrease the necessity for fast deci-

sion-making. Expanding the sample by including entrepreneurs not residing at incubators as well will result in more confident statements about the process, and perhaps a different ration between the two groups. Additionally, the underlying reasons why the two groups differ in their naming process have not been assessed so far, which makes it difficult to derive any causal relations. This is also true for the missing assessment of performance related measures like rate of growth, turnover, or sales volume. As long as the relationship between process strategy and performance is unclear, no recommendations can be given on how to appropriately select a corporate brand name in the Net Economy. The fact the research took place via an online questionnaire is not a limitation itself, since e-entrepreneurs are assumed to be able to sophistically deal with Internet applications. Many questions required the selection of answers from a list of already given items. This potentially distorted the results in some way. Although pre-tests detected no significant problems in answering the questionnaire, clarification on word meaning or correct understanding of questions has not been possible during the research and might have lead to biased answers.

CONCLUSION

The results show supportive evidence for the necessity of extending existing research about branding in the Net Economy. The specific Internet characteristics seem to have a great impact on e-branding approaches and the way companies create and manage online brands. The importance of domain availability for example was found to heave a strong influence on the process of finding an appropriate corporate brand name in the Net Economy. The whole process of finding an adequate e-brand name is not as deliberated as traditional models suggest, the process rather takes place on an ad-hoc basis leading to a fast and unconventional manner of creating the new corporate brand. Of course, the creation of corporate brands is normally taking place during company foundation, which on itself probably makes a fast process necessary. At the early stages, entrepreneurs face resource constraints that may thus have an impact on the way e-branding activities are initiated. This is similarly true for traditional companies, but especially the search for a free domain further effects the naming process in e-business environments as our results approved. However, the majority of e-entrepreneurs follow a process that is similar to the traditional one ("domain follows name"), only varying with regard to domain search and registration, which was not tested for in prior research. This group goes along the process step by step, putting much emphasis on the brand name objectives and selection criteria. Here, the process took place during several weeks and the domain seemed to be more of a necessity than an opportunity. Compared to that group, the "name follows domain" group found their corporate e-brand name within several days and they put a lot of weight to the domain factor. Only when a good domain was available, the name was tested for pursuing branding objectives. Thus, the iterative character of the process enabled the entrepreneurs to put more emphasis on the domain when deciding on their corporate name.

Although finding a corporate brand name was proven to be a very important decision in e-branding, it is only the first of many decisions to be made in e-branding. Other aspects of the formal brand creation process as well as brand content matters need to be explored by further research in order to completely uncover the field of e-branding. Future research must also clarify how different approaches affect turnover and performance in order to deduce practical implications for e-entrepreneurs and to make suggestions for process optimizations. In this respect, the explorative nature of the present research is thought to give an impulse for future research and to serve as a basis on which to proceed with uncovering the e-branding field. Certainly, answering a lot of unsolved questions in this field bear challenges as well as opportunities for researchers to enhance e-branding research and to detect differences and similarities between e-branding and traditional branding procedures.

REFERENCES

Aaker, D. (1996) "Building Strong Brands", The Free Press, New York

Anderson, J. R. (1983) "The architecture of cognition", Harvard University Press, 1983

Anderson, P.F., Bennett P.D. (1988) "Dictionary of Marketing Terms", American Marketing Association, Chicago.

Baker, W.E. (2003) "Does Brand Name Imprinting in Memory Increase Brand Information Retention?" Psychology & Marketing, Vol.20(12), pp.1119-1136.

Balmer, J.M.T. (2001) "Corporate identity, corporate branding and corporate marketing. Seeing through the fog" European Journal of Marketing, Vol. 35, No.3/4, pp. 248-297.

Berry, L.L., Lefkowith, E.F., Clark, T. (1988) "In services: what's in a name?" Harvard Business Review Vol.66, September-October, pp.28-30.

Boyd, C.W. (1985) "Point of view: alpha-numeric brand names", Journal of Advertising Research Vol.25, no.5, pp.48-52.

Carpenter, P. (2000) "E-brands-Building on Internet Business at Breakneck Speed", Harvard Business School Press, Boston, 2000

Collins, L. (1977) "A Name to Conjure With", European Journal of Marketing, Vol. 11, No. 4/5, pp.337-364.

Duncan, T. (2002) "IMC: Using Advertising and Promotion to Build Brands", McGraw Hill, 2002

Geissler, U., Will, M. (2001) "Corporate Branding of E-Business Ventures", in: R. Sprague (ed.): Proceedings of the 34th Hawaii International Conference on System Science (HICSS), Maui, January 2001.

Hatch, M., Schultz, M. (2001) "Are the strategic stars aligned for your corporate brand?" Harvard Business Review, February, pp.128-134.

Heaton, Jr., E. E. (1967) "Testing a New Corporate Name", Journal of Marketing Research Vol. 4, No. 3, pp. 279-285.

Ibeh, K.I.N., Luo, Y., Dinnie, K. (2005) E-branding strategies of internet companies: some preliminary insights from the UK", Brand Management, Vol.12, No.5, June 2005, pp.355-373.

Javed, N. (1997) "Naming for global power", Communication World 1997, Vol.14, No. 9, pp. 32-35.

Keller, K.L., Heckler, S.E., Houston, M.J. (1998) "The effects of brand name suggestiveness on advertising recall", Journal of Marketing, 63, pp.48-57.

Keller, K.L. (2003) "Strategic Brand Management: Building, Measuring, and Managing Brand Equity", Prentice Hall 2nd edition.

King, S. (1991) "Brand-building in the 1990's", Journal of Marketing Management, 1991, 7, pp. 3-13.

Klink, R.R. (2000) "Creating Brand Names with Meaning: The Use of Sound Symbolism", Marketing Letters, 11(1), pp. 5-20.

Kohli, C., LaBahn, D.W. (1997) "Observations: Creating Effective Brand Names: A Study of the Naming Process", Journal of Advertising Research, January/February 1997, pp. 67-75.

Kollmann, T. (2006): "What is e-entrepreneurship? Fundamentals of company founding in the net economy", International Journal of Technology Management, Vol. 33, No. 4, pp. 322-340.

Landler, M., Schiller, Z., & Therrien, L. (1991) "What's in a name? less and less", Business Week, July 8, pp.66-67.

Leitch, S., Richardson, N. (2003) "Corporate branding in the Net Economy", European Journal of Marketing, Vol.37, No. 7/8 2003, pp. 1065-1079.

Lerman, D., Garbarino, E. (2002) "Recall and Recognition of Brand Names: A Comparison of Word and Nonword Name Types", Psychology & Marketing, Vol. 19 (7-8), pp.621-639.

McNeal, J.U., Zeren, L.M. (1981) "Brand Name Selection for Consumer Products", MSU Business Topics (1981), pp.35-39.

Moore, G.A. (1995) "Crossing the Chasm: Marketing and Selling High-tech Products to Mainstream Customers", New York, 1995

Murphy, J., Raffa, L., & Mizerski, R. (2003) "The Use of Domain Names in e-branding by the World's Top Brands", Electronic Markets, Vol. 13, No.3, pp.222-232

Rode, V., Vallaster, C. (2005) "Corporate Branding for Start-ups: The Crucial Role of Entrepreneurs", Corporate Reputation Review, Vol.8, No.2, pp.121-135.

Schloss, I. (1981) "Chickens and Pickles", Journal of Advertising Research, Vol. 21, No.6, pp. 47-49.

Sen, S. (1999) "The Effects of Brand Name Suggestiveness and Decision Goal on the Development of Brand Knowledge", Journal of Consumer Psychology, Vol.8, No.4, pp. 431-455.

Shipley, D. (1985) "Marketing Objectives in UK and US manufacturing companies", European Journal of Marketing, Vol.19, No.3, pp. 48-56.

Shipley, D., Hooley, G.J., Wallace, S. (1988) "The Brand Name Development Process", International Journal of Advertising, 1988, Vol.7, pp. 253-266.

Strebinger, A., Treiblmaier, H. (2004) "E-Adequate Branding: Building Offline and Online Brand Structure within a Polygon of Interdependent Forces", Electronic Markets, Vol. 14(2), pp.153-164.

Turley, L.W., Moore, P.A. (1995) "Brand name strategies in the service sector", Journal of Consumer Marketing, Vol. 12, No. 4, 1995 pp.42-50.

Ward, M.R., Lee, M.J. (2000) "Internet shopping, consumer search and product branding", Journal of Product and Brand Management, Vol.9, No.1, pp. 6-20.

Chapter V
Returns on e–Branding Investment:
Linking Pre–Acquisition Marketing Activity to Customer Profitability

Patrali Chatterjee
Montclair State University, USA

ABSTRACT

Consumer-centric organizations recognize customer relationships with brands as a source of sustainable competitive advantage that they can leverage to successfully introduce brand extensions. Marketers seeking to leverage brand equity associated with core off-line products to introduce e-brand extensions recognize that success depends on initiating brand relationships with prospective customers, as well as maintaining relationships with existing customers. This research proposes and empirically demonstrates that investment on e-branding relationships with current users generates higher returns for online extensions that have close fit with the core off-line product. In contrast, investments on nonusers have a higher return on adoption of online brand extensions that have low-fit with core products, compared to current customers and can increase overall profitability. Further, we show that Web site features like personalized e-mail and interactive aids have a significantly higher impact on customer profitability and motivate prospective consumers to move to higher levels of relationship with the firm, than financial incentives like sales promotions. Managerial implications for return on e-branding investments and future research directions are discussed.

INTRODUCTION

Firms are increasingly leveraging the equity associated with well-known and well-respected off-line brand names to develop brand extensions in the form of information or content services as documented in the business media, for example, Encyclopedia Britannica launching its online subscription service (Deleersnyder, Geyskens, Gielens & Dekimpe 2002). However, there are several examples of well-known brands that failed in their attempts to establish a stable and loyal online customer base for their e-brand extensions. Although there are several studies that have investigated how firms are using online communications and their Web sites to sustain brand relationships, and enhance brand equity for their core (and often off-line) products. There is a lack of research investigating how consumers' relationship with core brands affects their adoption and purchase of online brand extensions. Further, given the prospective that online brand extensions can cannibalize core off-line products among existing customers (Biyalogorsky & Naik 2003), it is imperative to examine how this strategy affects firm profitability.

The strategy of developing online brand extensions, primarily for service-based brands, is motivated by the desire to attract a new market composed of consumers whose category needs are either met better by competitors (competitive users) or not met by existing product offerings in the industry (nonusers in the category) (Schultz & Bailey 2000). The increasing availability of customer information and the sophistication of the technology for capturing, tracking, processing and analyzing this information now makes it possible for firms to identify, communicate and build one-to-one brand relationships with prospective and existing customers (see for example, Glazer 1991). The Internet and World Wide Web (Web, henceforth) allows firms to provide highly interactive, customized experiences, respond directly to customer's information needs and requests to

establish, nurture, and sustain long-term customer relationships at a lower cost than has been previously possible in the off-line world. More importantly, brand relationship building efforts previously directed to existing customers can be adapted to information and experience needs of prospective customers whose preferences may match benefits offered by the online extension of the brand rather than the core brand itself.

In this research we address the following questions:

1. Do existing and prospective customers differ in their response to e-branding communications by the firm?
2. Do existing and prospective customers differ in their adoption of online brand extensions and overall profitability?
3. How does the fit of online extensions compared to the core product associated with the brand affect online extension adoption behavior?
4. Does the effectiveness of financial incentives on adoption of online brand extensions differ across existing and prospective customers?

THEORETICAL BACKGROUND AND HYPOTHESES

Brand equity is defined as the differential effect brand knowledge has on consumer response to the marketing of a brand (Keller 1993). From an information economics view, Erdem and Swait (1998) argue that consumer-based brand equity is the value of a brand as a credible signal of a product's position. These definitions share the view that the value of a brand to a firm is created through the brand's effect on consumers. Most brand equity conceptualizations are further linked to consumers by emphasizing consumer-based concepts such as brand associations, brand knowledge (Keller 1993), perceived clarity and credibility of the brand information under imperfect and asymmetric information (Erdem & Swait 1998). It is clear that brand equity accrues over time via consumer learning and decision making processes.

Prior research suggests that the influence of a brand name on evaluations of a brand extension depends on the brand equity and perceptions of how well the extension "fits" the core brand category (Bottomley & Holden 2001). Brand equity can play a role in how information (e.g., attributes) is learned and encoded, and then retrieved and used in decisions and choice. These information processing effects influence part-worth evaluation and combination rules, choice set generation, and finally the decision rules used in choice. Current consumers are more likely to be familiar with the brand and its core products, and are more likely to consider attributes favorable to the brand to evaluate an online brand extension. Hence, prior research would suggest that current customers are more likely to adopt online brand extensions, compared to prospective consumers or nonconsumers.

Perceived Fit of Online Extensions with Core Products of Brand

Many researchers have considered fit to be a key factor in moderating the impact of brand equity in brand extension strategy. In general, fit is referred to as the degree to which consumers view the extension product as being similar to the existing products affiliated with the brand (Aaker & Keller, 1990; Bottomley & Holden, 2001). According to categorization theory, the degree to which brand associations are transferred from a brand portfolio to its extension brands depends on the level of perceived fit between the two (e.g., Boush & Loken, 1991). In addition, a favorable evaluation of an extension product based on family brand equity will occur only when no cues differentiate a single extension from the family brand (Fry, 1967).

There is a number of bases of fit – virtually any brand association is a potential bias – but the key bases are form similarity (physical, functional, and contextual), competence (attribute), and image (Batra et al. 1993). Online brand extensions that are similar in form to their core products (e.g., online services launched by off-line service providers etc.) are likely be to perceived as higher degree of fit compared to those that differ in form (e.g., off-line service providers selling products online and vice versa). Prior studies indicate that consumers who have high familiarity with products process product information, and evaluate these products differently from those who are less familiar. Consumers develop strong knowledge structures or schema about a product as they become more familiar with the product, and the relative degree of liking for the product becomes well-established and stable (Park & Lessig 1981). As familiarity increases, the amount of cognitive effort needed to process product-relevant information decreases (Park & Lessig 1981). According to Meyer-Levy and Tybout (1989), a positive attitude is generated in the categorization process when consumers familiar with the brand encounter brand extension with a high-fit. However, these consumers are likely to change the assessment of an extended product with low level of fit as the effort involved in categorization increases. Alternatively, preexisting attitudes may be either unformed or weak for prospective consumers, making the categorization process more difficult for both types of extensions when consumers have no or low familiarity with products (Meyer-Levy & Tybout 1989). Hence,

H1a: Current customers are more likely to adopt online brand extensions with high level of fit to core products compared to online brand extensions that have low level of fit to core products.

H1b: Prospective customers are equally likely to adopt online brand extensions that have low

level of fit to core products compared to online brand extensions that have high level of fit to core products.

Brand equity arises from two major elements, awareness and associations (Keller 1993). Awareness and associations of the brand and its communicated attributes are dynamically learned through product experience and by exposure to marketing communications for the brand. However, the strength of brand associations formed through product experience is higher than one formed through exposure to marketing communications alone (Woodside & Walser 2007). Further, the strength of brand associations grows following use of the brand over months and years (Keller 1993), and is more likely to transfer to brand extensions perceived to have high-fit with core products. Hence,

H2: The length of consumer relationship with a brand will be positively associated with the probability of adopting high-fit online extensions.

Impact of e-Branding Strategy

Prior research on interactive marketplaces suggests that product or service purchases do not merely maximize personal outcomes, but also involve exchange of relationship value between the consumer and the brand (Schultz & Bailey 2000). In addition to the core product/ service/function, prospective customers also seek brand images, and messages consistent with their attitude and emotional needs. Hence, the goal of marketing communications is not merely building awareness and preference for product and service features, but also managing customer relationship with the brand, shaping consumer preferences and behavior online and off-line.

Companies build customer relationships at many levels, depending on the nature of the target market. Borrowing from research on relationship marketing, firms use financial relationship marketing instruments (RMIs) such as rewards and pricing discounts, to start and develop the relationship (Berry 1995). Researchers suggest that sales promotions can be offered to prospective customers and are most effective in acquisition by inducing customers to enter into a relationship with the firm. However, the impact of these financial benefits on customer retention (e.g., Bolton 1998) and on customer share (or cross-selling) has been found to be small and largely ineffective with existing and loyal customers (Verhoef 2003). Hence,

H3: Prospective consumers are significantly more likely to respond to sales promotions in adopting online brand extensions compared to current customers.

At the second level, benefits with more *social* attributes may be a vital element in enhancing brand relationships. Social relationship marketing instruments (RMIs) involve personalization and customization of the relationship, communicating with customers regularly through multiple means, referring to customers by name, augmenting core service with education and entertainment. Social RMIs are better suited to longer-term brand-building efforts for customers/prospects that have a high current and/or future value to the brand but are incompatible with the current brand proposition. It is likely that some or most of them are competitors' customers. Communications and incentives that build equitable relationships, education and informational appeals, product or service experience or trials that can elicit their brand preferences, that can close the compatibility gap over time are needed. This presents opportunities for product or service innovations and variations.

E-mail newsletters are an extremely popular form of Internet-based relationship marketing instrument. Although e-mail newsletters aim to engage consumers and define their preferences, in the present environment, consumers are overwhelmed with the volume of e-mail they receive. An outbound e-mail newsletter is one-way communication, and can be largely ineffective especially if consumers do not open them (Ansari & Mela 2003). However, current consumers are more likely to notice e-mails from a company they patronize, even if they do not open them, hence the mere exposure effect on affect (Zajonc 1978) suggests,

H4: The total number of outbound e-mail newsletters sent will have a positive effect on adoption of online brand extensions for current customers but have no effect on prospective customers.

E-mail newsletters facilitate relationship building and interactive communications among nonusers of a brand, only if they open them and click on the hyperlinks. *Opt-in e-mail newsletters* require customers to opt-in or agree to receive messages from a company, and provide the opportunity to personalize the messages they receive based on their interests. However, opt-in newsletters require consumer participation in the process, and nonusers, or prospective consumers are less likely to do so compared to current customers.

Opt-in e-mail newsletters can be used to provide engaging and customized information to close the compatibility gap for new brand extensions with their existing brand schema, and move consumers from awareness to interest and liking. The easiest way to find out if e-mail newsletters are providing knowledge regarding the extended product and shaping consumer preferences is by examining the number of links clicked for a particular product. Hence,

H5a: The total number of opt-in e-mail newsletter links clicked will have a positive relationship to probability of purchasing online brand extension.

H5b: The impact of total number of opt-in e-mail newsletter links clicked on likelihood of purchasing online brand extension will be higher for high-fit extensions compared to low-fit extensions.

Level three *structural* RMIs provide structural solutions to consumers' needs and problems. *Structural* RMIs target customers with value-adding benefits for their specific needs that are difficult or expensive for competitors to provide and that are not readily available elsewhere, thereby creating a strong foundation for maintaining and enhancing relationships. Such structural RMIs create a relation-specific asset, are not portable across vendors and can create customer lock-in to the firm, and offer the highest level of sustained competitive advantage.

Zauberman (2003) showed that consumers' have a decreased propensity to search and switch after an initial investment in developing familiarity and customizing browsing experience at a site. The reluctance to switch is determined both by a preference to minimize immediate costs, and by an inability to anticipate the impact of future switching costs, not because other competitors may not offer such customization but the effort to personalize one's interface and browsing experience at a competing firm may be considerable.

Several companies have adopted the "choiceboard" (Slywotsky 2000) approach to product personalization, and have developed processes and systems for creating products according to the customers' tastes. Others, like Clairol.com allow product customization in response to changing needs of the consumer. This "choiceboard" (Slywotsky 2000) involves customers becoming coproducers (instead of simply product takers) by taking a list of product attributes and determining what they want, when and at what level. Many Web sites offer interactive tools, activities, calculators, and trackers that permit easy input and storage of personal information allowing consumers to perform what-if analyses to aid in their decision-making. Such individualized product or service tools provide value to both existing and prospective consumers.

The effect of co-creation of one's product or service is likely to lead to "learning by doing", greater involvement and lowering perceptions of risk and uncertainty regarding the extended product (Wright & Lynch 1995). Although consumers are likely to use interactive aids for all brand extensions, the returns on use of such aids are likely to be higher for nonusers and for products and services with low level of fit, because they are characterized by higher levels of risk and uncertainty, compared to extensions with high level of fit. Hence,

H6a: The impact of interactive aid usage on consumer likelihood of purchasing will be positive and higher for brand extensions with low level of fit compared to those with high level of fit.

H6b: The positive impact of interactive aid usage on the likelihood of purchasing brand extensions will be higher for prospective consumers compared to current customers.

In the next section, we present empirical data to test our hypotheses.

EMPIRICAL CONTEXT

The data for our study comes from a company (unidentified for competitive reasons) whose primary business is direct-selling of books for school-aged children, and who is the market leader in the industry. This company undertook a study to evaluate its marketing communication activities, and agreed to share their data for academic purposes. Prior to 2001, the company's customer acquisition activity involved identifying prospects through schools, after care programs, hospitals, ads in selected print magazines, mailing lists and soliciting them using direct mail. Customer demographic and preference information was collected, and a selection of books was sent every

four weeks. Customer credit cards were billed for all books sent, and credited for books returned.

The company had an informational nontransactional Web site since 1998. In fall 2000, the Web site started offering its direct mail customers the ability to go online, and choose among the books being sent to them each month. In 2001, the Web site started offering direct mail customers the ability to order books custom-published with a child's name and occasion. By fall 2002, the Web site utilized an online CRM system to communicate with its customers, and launched its e-mail newsletter program, using direct mail only to direct prospects to the Web site, or to offer promotional discounts to its current users.

In fall 2002, the company instituted free mandatory registration and started accepting orders for personalized books online, and launched a beta version of its new learning resources service, the first in the industry. Customers and nonusers of its book service were allowed to access the service free for three months after which access was restricted, unless the household paid a subscription fee. This US-based Web site provided grade-appropriate and ability-appropriate learning resources for preschool and elementary school children, with original interactive content including reference articles, encyclopedias, dictionaries, pictures, animations, video and sound clips as well as interactive applications. Webcasts with prominent authors, tutorials, online chat and community boards around topics of interest were only available to paid subscribers.

The online personalized book ordering feature allowed consumers to "create" their own storybook by inserting customers own digital photographs, choosing different story lines and geographic settings. These books can be created and edited over time. Consumers could post and share their stories on the site's community boards and purchase hard copies at their own convenience. Once ordered, these books were printed and mailed to the customers. Unlike those offered through the direct mail service, where personalization was limited to substituting a character's name with the customer name, online personalized books allowed greater level of creativity and production by the customer, and never printed unless ordered by the customer.

Clickstream Data: Usable survey, attraction and parsed clickstream data on 12,102 customers who registered at the Web site for access in Sept.-Oct. 2002, and visited the Web site at least once during the study period Jan. 1, 2003- June 1, 2003 was made available for this study. To collect valid data on exposure to marketing communication variables, this sample included current customers of the direct marketing book service and nonusers who registered for free access at the Web site with correct home addresses. Current customer's data on book purchases through both channels were also made available to us. Nonusers registered for free access at the Web site; only registration and online activity data was available. Data on profile and newsletter updates and unsubscribes, and subscription cancellations were made available in separate files. Demographic details other than the ages of children were not made available to us.

Upon registration, all customers were invited to answer a short survey in order to download age- and ability- appropriate interactive applications, games and tutorials. In addition to ages of children that would be using the service, whether home-schooled or not, grade in school, self-reported information on current and past membership with several online and off-line competing services was also collected. Consumers were offered the option to opt-in for e-mail newsletters, update their e-mail newsletter and preference profile, try the subscription service free for three months. After the free three month trial period was over, they were enrolled to the paid subscription service. If consumer opted out of the paid service, they received e-mail newsletters, personalized progress trackers, product selections and restricted access (abstracts of articles, demo versions of interactive learning activities and games).

Dependent Variables: Data on three dependent variables representing three events of interest were extracted from the clickstream of consumer activity: a binary variable indicating if the consumer ordered a personalized book or not (brand extension with high-fit); a binary variable indicating if the consumer subscribed to the trial subscription service or not (brand extension with low-fit); and a continuous variable for profit margin for each customer.

To examine if consumer perceptions of brand extension fit vary across the brand extension stimuli considered in the study, a preliminary online survey was conducted in summer 2002. Consumers at the site were asked to rate both the online personalized book ordering service and the paid online content service on similarity in form (physical, functional, and contextual), competence (attribute) and image, using the seven point scales proposed in Batra et al. (1993). Profit for each consumer was calculated using average gross margin in each of the book-selling product lines, online advertising revenues based on CPM minus costs of maintaining the consumer (using average cost of each communication unit times the number of each communication unit received by the consumer).

Marketing Communication Tools: The firm used direct mail, and e-branding communications (outbound and opt-in e-mail newsletters) to parents as their communication tools. All customers who registered online received outbound e-mail newsletters, but only those who opted in and personalized it by selecting topics of interest received personalized opt-in e-mail. These newsletters specific to either personalized book products or online service included hyperlinked article abstracts and links to daily interactive tests for each selected age group to demonstrate usefulness of the new brand extensions.

Interactive tools like event reminders, skill analyzers, online grade book, and challenge quiz contests were available to all registered online users, but usage depends on individual

Table 1. Descriptive statistics of independent variables

Variables	Operationalization	Mean	Std. Dev.	Min	Max
Customer Profit	Standardized profit for customer:gross margin on purchases and shipping minus total costs (direct mail, online costs, cost of liquidating returns)	1.4	-	-2.2	2.9
Usage of Direct Mail Book Service					
Months enrolled	Logarithm (Number of months consumer is enrolled in the direct mail book buying program)	4.21 (68.2 mths)	4.48 (88.9 mths)	0.693 (2 mths)	5.123 (172 mths)
Percent of returns	Proportion of books received from the direct mail program that were returned (personalized or customized books are non-returnable)	.24	-	0	.78
Impact of Marketing Communication Tools					
# Sales promo code	Number of times consumer received 15 percent off purchase offer	2.4	0.8	2	7
# Direct mail sent	Number of direct mail postcards with service description received	5.6	1.8	3	15
#outbound emails sent	Number of outbound emails with hyperlinked content received	18.3	4.7	15	57
# opt-in hyperlinks clicked	Number of hyperlinked articles viewed by consumer customized for their interests	9.61	2.537	0	26
# interactive aids used	Times and number of interactive aids used by the consumer	3.97	1.619	0	8
Other variables					
# children	Number of chi'dren in household	1.93	2.6	1	5
Competitor program	Whether enrolled in competing direct mail book buying program	.132	-	0	1
Website usage					
# viral emails sent	Total number of viral email referrals sent by the consumer	2.82	1.7	1	18
ln(Av. session length)	Logarithm of average session length at the website by the consumer	4.822	1.432	2.7	7.901
Other information (not used in analyses)					
Number of consumers opting in		.316	-	-	-
Number of consumers using interactive aids		.524	-	-	-
Total number of personalized books created		3	1.2	0	9
Number of customers sending viral mail		.83	-	-	-

interest. Individual reports of performance were automatically reflected in the online grade book, so parents can review their children's progress over time, across different subjects, and if desired, benchmark for that particular test across other same age kids at the site. It included online reporting of child performance with graphs and tables, which parents can use to identify specific areas of weakness.

Paying subscribers had unlimited access to all content areas and additional interactive features at the site. Each child had a personalizable portal, with MyReadingList, MyAssignments, My Favorites, MyEvents, MyFunNLearn, MyFriends pages among others. Parents could customize and monitor online grade books and MyLessonPlans for each of their children. Children and their parents had access to service branded e-mail accounts, event reminders, and could participate in online community boards, weekend chat sessions organized around learning topics, project ideas, and parenting issues.

Please note that company launched an aggressive marketing communications campaign utilizing direct mail, print ads, banner ads at prominent online properties, and search engine advertising to generate awareness, recall of their URL, and encourage consumers to register at the Web site. Since the focus of this study is on activities after online registration, the impact of these tools are not presented here. Sales promotions in the form of 15 % off any online or off-line purchase were offered throughout this period, and the number of times such offer was made to each customer was considered.

Variable Operationalization: The Web site under study uses cookies and mandatory registration, so activities of registered consumers were tracked over the study period. Current customers are those participating in the direct mail book service, and receiving book shipments by postal mail every four weeks, and they may or may not register at the Web site. Since purchase of online brand extensions (personalized books and online service) requires Web site registration, only those registered at the Web site are considered. Prospective customers have registered at the site may buy online personalized books or have paid online service membership but are not members of direct mail book service. Table 1 shows how data on the explanatory variables were collected and their descriptive statistics.

METHODOLOGY

Each member-household makes two separate decisions of interest: i.) purchase online personalized book (high-fit online brand extension) and ii.) become a paid subscriber of the online service (low-fit online brand extension) anytime after free access starts. Each of these decisions was analyzed using binary probit models. The third variable - customer profit, is an outcome variable available only to managers at the firm. Customer profit was standardized using normal distribution because profit margins across the respondent sample display large variances, and estimated using a multiple regression model. Since differences between current and prospective customers are of interest, estimations for each customer group are presented separately. We use multiple regression methods instead of ANOVAs to control for the effect of variables that may impact the dependent variables of interest, but are not considered in the conceptual framework.

RESULTS

To examine if classification of the two online brand extensions in terms of fit to the core brand is valid, a preliminary online survey was conducted for a two-week period in summer 2002. Respondents were randomly chosen, and invited to participate in the survey. There were 1,002 usable responses with a response rate of 15%. Table 2 presents mean scores for the two consumer segments and entire sample for the two online brand extensions. Overall, respondents perceived online personalized book feature to have a higher level of fit to the core brand compared to the online service (2.9 vs. 4.3, $p<0.001$), suggesting that our selection of exemplars of high and low-fit brand extensions are valid. However, there is a difference among current and prospective consumers in perceived difference of fit for the two extensions. Unlike prospective consumers, current customers perceive the difference in fit to be significantly larger (1.9 vs. 0.4, p<0.01). Thus, prospective consumers have weak schema associated with core brand, and perceive any online extension much similar to the core brand. Further, the standard deviations associated with the fit measures for prospective consumers are much higher than that of current consumers, suggesting that prospective customers have more difficulty in comparing the online brand extensions to the core brand schema.

Descriptive statistics of the variables in our model were presented in Table 1. Table 3 displays preliminary analyses of the data and provides some evidence of differences in purchases of online brand extensions among 8,018 current and prospective consumers in the sample. Overall, 2,252 consumers, or 28% of the sample have purchased online branded extensions. Current consumers made significantly more purchases of online brand extensions than prospective customers (0.33 vs. 0.17, p<0.01), however, the difference between the number of consumers purchasing online service subscriptions is marginally higher than that of personalized books (0.14 vs. 0.12, p<0.05). Purchases of both personalized books and online

services is significantly higher among current customers, compared to prospective customers (0.17 vs. 0.07, p<0.01 and 0.15 vs. 0.11, p<0.05). However, contrary to hypotheses (*H1a*) for current customers the difference in purchase probability for high-fit personalized books is not significantly higher than that for low-fit online services (0.17 vs. 0.15, p>0.05). Further, prospective consumers are more likely to purchase online service subscriptions (low-fit) compared to personalized books (high-fit), thus rejecting *H1b*.

Not surprising, the average profit for current customers is significantly higher than that for prospective consumers. This result may be because purchases of online extensions are entirely consumer-driven (pull), whereas purchases of direct mail book services for current customers is firm driven (push – promotional offers to customers). Further, given that the data applies to the introductory period of online brand extensions, when consumers perceive a high level of risk, appeals to consumers needs to established, costs of online communications and service maintenance are considerably high as the firm gains experience.

Table 4 presents estimation results for the probability of purchasing high-fit and low-fit brand extensions and customer profit for current and prospective consumers. The estimations were run with many variables, however, only those that

Table 2. Validity of online brand extension fit: Preliminary survey (standard deviations in parentheses)

Customer Segment	Online Service - Low-fit	Personalized Books – High-fit
Current n=587	2.8 (1.7) n=221	7.7 (0.8) n=366
Prospective n=415	3.1 (1.8) n=198	9.9 (2.1) n=217
Total n=1002	2.9 (1.4) n=419	2.2 (1.7) n=583

Table 3. Purchase of online brand extensions by customer segment N = 8041 users

Customer Segment	Online Service - Low-fit	Personalized Books – High-fit	Total Purchases
Current N=4023	624	687	1311
Prospective N=4018	475	296	771
Total	1099	983	2082

were significant in one or more equations were retained. Variables, as average number of unique pages browsed in a session, number of books bought through direct mail service, average dollar value of each order, age of children, education level of parents, did not achieve significance and were dropped from the final model. First, I will interpret the effects of the hypothesized variables on purchase of personalized books online (high-fit brand extension) and online service (low-fit brand extension). We are able to uncover interesting implications, because we estimate unrestricted models with separate equations for both consumer groups (unique intercepts and response coefficients), instead of confining ourselves to pooling data and estimating one set of equations.

As expected, the longer a current customer's tenure with the firm, the higher the probability that the consumer will purchase online personalized book (high-fit online brand extension), thus supporting *H2* at 0.01 level. Although there is a positive effect on purchase of online service subscription (low-fit online brand extension), it is insignificant.

The effect of sales promotions on purchase of online brand extensions varies with type of online brand extension and customer segment. The impact of sales promotion (# number of promotion codes sent) on purchase of high-fit extension (personalized book) is positive (but statistically insignificant) for both types of consumers.

However, contrary to expectations, the positive impact is marginally higher for current customers compared to prospective customers. Hence, *H3* is rejected. More important, more sales promotions have a negative impact on purchase of online service, and the effect is significant for current customers only. Sales promotions have a negative impact on profitability for current customers but a positive effect on profitability of prospective customers. This suggests that unrestricted sales promotions are a double-edged sword. They are effective in reducing uncertainty and inducing purchases, however, they subsidize purchases of current customers for products (high-fit brand extensions) they would have bought anyway, because the promotional discounts were valid for any purchase made off-line or online. Hence, firms should use restricted sales promotions designed to attract a new market of consumers for its offerings – low-fit brand extensions for current customers and high-fit brand extensions for prospective customers.

Outbound e-mail newsletters have a significant positive impact on purchase of online brand extensions for both current and prospective consumers. Current customers do not differ significantly from prospective consumers in their responsiveness to outbound e-mail newsletters in purchase of online service (low-fit brand extension). However, test of differences in response coefficients shows that greater the number of outbound e-mail newsletters

Table 4. Probability of purchasing online brand extensions and profitability

Independent Variables	Current Customer Model N=4023			Prospective Customer Model N=4018		
	Online Service	**Personalized book**	**Customer Profit**	**Online Service**	**Personalized book**	**Customer Profit**
Constant	-2.21**	-1.72***	1.39**	-1.1***	-4.13***	0.26
Usage of Direct Mail Book Service						
Months enrolled	0.21	0.47***	-0.19	--	--	--
Percent of returns	-0.07	-.46**	-.46**	--	--	--
Impact of Marketing Communication Tools						
# Sales promo code	-.27*	0.17	-0.09	-0.14	0.09	0.19
# Direct mail sent	-0.06	0.18	0.24	0.03	.22*	0.36
#outbound emails sent	.36**	.24*	.33*	.35**	.51***	0.1
# opt-in hyperlinks clicked	0.26**	0.49**	0.25	0.34**	0.12	0.79**
# interactive aids used	0.68***	0.09	0.04	.52***	.21*	.55**
Other variables						
# children	.25**	0.12	0.31	.31**	-0.19	.58**
Competitor program	0.24***	-0.07	-0.11	0.21**	-0.46***	-0.38**
Website usage						
# viral emails sent	0.12	0.34***	0.21***	-0.13	.10***	0.07*
Ln(Av. session length)	.0009***	-0.0002	0.001***	.001***	-.001***	0.0005
Personalized book purchase	-	-	0.41**	-	-	0.11
Subscribe online service	-	-	0.06	-	-	.27**
-2Log Likelihood	8000.12			6233.28		

[1] Significance levels: * P<.1, ** P<.05, *** P<.001

the more likely prospective customers will purchase personalized books online (high-fit brand extension) than current customers. Hence, *H4* is supported for high-fit online brand extension at 0.05 levels.

The total number of opt-in e-mail newsletter links clicked has a significant positive relationship to probability of purchasing online subscription service for current and prospective consumers. But the impact on purchasing personalized books online is positive for both consumer groups but insignificant for current customers only, thus supporting *H5a*. Further, the magnitude of response on purchase of personalized books online (high-fit brand extension) is higher than that for online services (low-fit brand extension) thus supporting *H5b*.

Interactive aid usage has a significantly large and positive effect on purchase of online subscription service (high-fit brand extension) compared to online services (low-fit brand extension) for both current and prospective consumers thus supporting *H6a*. However, contrary to our expectations in *H6b* the impact of interactive aid usage for prospective consumers is not significantly larger than for current customers.

Other Findings: We find that the greater the number of children in the household, the greater the likelihood that the household will subscribe to the online service, but the probability of purchasing personalized books online is insignificant. Further, consumers enrolled in a competitor's direct mail book buying program are significantly more likely to subscribe to the online service. Prospective consumers enrolled in a competitor's direct mail book buying program are significantly less likely to order personalized books online. However, analyses of clickstream data shows that prospective members create significantly more personalized books than current customers and place them in the shopping cart, but they do not buy them. These consumers are likely to be more involved in the product category, register out of curiosity to check out the competition and try out the features, but only subscribe to those

services not provided by their primary provider. It is possible that these consumers do not perceive the online personalized books to offer significantly higher value compared to customized books in the direct mail service (priced at least 25% lower than online personalized books).

The number of viral e-mails sent to refer the Web site is associated increased likelihood of purchasing online personalized books but not subscription to the online service. The number of viral e-mails sent to refer the Web site is also significantly associated with increased customer profitability. The firm can track viral behavior to identify these highly profitable e-fluentials, and target them with other benefits and experiences to reward them for their loyalty. Consumers with longer sessions (on average) at the site are significantly more likely to subscribe to the online service and current customers are associated with higher profitability than those with shorter sessions.

CONCLUSION

The burgeoning recognition that the interactive marketplace is a multi-channel environment intersects with the growing importance of managing brand- customer relationships simultaneously across multiple contact points, thus requiring the use of multiple communication tools and media. Examining relationship marketing initiatives in isolation from other communication instruments used by the firm can lead to wrong inferences.

Our empirical analyses indicate that firms with bricks-and-mortar business models, considering extending their brands to the online marketplace, have to redefine how value will be provided in the new channel. Customers of the core brand are likely to purchase online brand extensions that are perceived to have a high level of fit (online personalized books) marginally more than those with low level of fit (online services). Firms have to recognize nonusers of the core brand especially competitor's customers are attractive prospective customers of the extended online brand. They are more likely to patronize online extensions that are perceived to have a low level of fit with the core brand. As growth strategies, high and low-fit online brand extensions can be used as a product development strategy to increase current customer share of wallet. In addition, low-fit brand extensions as diversifications increase the brand franchise by attracting new customers with new products and services.

Managers can use e-branding communications to mitigate the risks associated with low-fit brand extensions for current customers. However, unrestricted sales promotions can hurt a firm's profitability, as they are ineffective in inducing current customers to purchase low-fit online brand extensions and subsidize purchases of high-fit brand extensions they would have bought anyway. Sales promotions for low-fit brand extensions will only be most effective in implementing the firm's growth strategies. Outbound e-mails are more effective than direct mail in increasing consumer acceptance of all online brand extensions.

Opt-in e-mail and interactive aids demonstrate how online brand extensions create value and product experiences that go beyond those offered by the core products of the brand. Opt-in e-mail increases current customer purchase of low and high-fit extensions. Interactive aids that require consumers to share information and invest effort in personalization are most effective, compared to other tools in demonstrating the benefits of low-fit brand extensions. Experience in learning by doing at the site had greater impact, similar to Wright and Lynch (1995)'s findings.

However, marketers cannot control or make consumers opt-in to personalize e-mail profiles or use interactive aids. The utility consumers can gain from using interactive aids are difficult or inconvenient to transfer elsewhere. Research on lock-in indicates that most consumers fail to anticipate how their prior investment will lock them in (Zauberman 2003). It is possible that consumers most likely to invest effort in the personalization process are more comfortable using Internet-based services compared to others. They (even nonusers and competitor's customers) are positively predisposed towards the firm's offerings, and may already be more engaged in brand-building communications.

The empirical context in this study has external validity, it is an actual subscription based Website. The financial dimension of the consumer relationship is of importance to the firm. The value of a brand-consumer relationship at a free or ad-supported Web site may not have a direct financial component in terms of subscription or purchase. Other behaviors, such as frequency of use, number of ads, or affiliate offers, seen and clicked, number of pages browsed, number of customer referrals may play an important role. The online brand extensions were among the first ones introduced in the industry. We had access to data for a six month period immediately following introduction, the impact of competition as other firms extended to the online marketplace could not be ascertained.

The effectiveness of online brand extensions in building revenues for core products in the brand family is an important issue, but we could not explore it here. We did not have sufficient data on cross-selling behavior at the online Web site, there were very few prospective consumers that enrolled in the direct mail book buying program, after purchasing online personalized books or subscribing to the online service in the six-month data set made available to us. Since most prospective consumers are attracted by low-fit brand extensions, preference for the core products in the brand is likely to build slowly over time, if ever. Datasets, over a longer interval of time can address these issues. This can yield interesting insights for retailers that build content and destination features at their Web sites (e.g., Amazon.com).

REFERENCES

Aaker, D.A.; Keller, K.L. (1990), "Consumer Evaluations of Brand Extensions," *Journal of Marketing*, Vol. 54, No. 1, pp. 27-41.

Ansari, A. &. Mela, C.F. (2003), "E-customization," *Journal of Marketing Research*, 40, 2 (May), 131-145.

Batra, R., Lehmann, D.R. & Singh, D. (1993), "The brand personality component of brand goodwill: some antecedents and consequences," in Aaker and Biel editor. *Brand equity and advertising*. Hillsdale, NJ: Lawrence Erlbaum Associates. pp. 83-96.

Berry, L.L. (1995), "Relationship Marketing of Services: Growing Interest, Emerging Perspectives," Journal of the Academy of Marketing Science, 23 (Fall), 236-45.

Bhattacharya, *C.B.* & Bolton, R.N. (2000), *"Relationship Marketing in Mass Markets," in Handbook of Relationship Marketing, Jagdish N. Sheth and Atul Parvatiyar, eds. Thousand Oaks, CA: Sage Publications, 327-54.*

Biyalogorsky, E. & Naik, P (2003), "Clicks and Mortar: The Effect of Online Activities on Off-line Sales," *Marketing Letters* 14 (1), pg. 21-32.

Blattberg, R.C., Getz, G. & Thomas, J.S. (2001), Customer Equity: Building and Managing Relationships as Valuable Assets. Boston: Harvard Business School Press.

Bolton, R.N. (1998), "A Dynamic Model of the Duration of the Customer's Relationship with a Continuous Service Provider: The Role of Satisfaction," Marketing Science, 17 (Winter), 45-65.

-----, *Kannan, P.K. & Bramlett, M.D. (2000), "Implications of Loyalty Program Membership and Service Experiences for Customer Retention and Value," Journal of the Academy of Marketing*

Science, 28 (Winter), 95-108.

-----, -----, *& Verhoef, P.C. (2002), "The Theoretical Underpinnings of Customer Asset Management: A Framework and Propositions for Future Research," Erasmus Research Institute in Management Working Paper No. ERS-2002-80-MKT, Erasmus University, Rotterdam.*

Bottomley, P.A. & Holden, S.J. (2001), "Do we really know how consumers evaluate brand extensions? Empirical generalizations based on secondary analysis of eight studies," *Journal of Marketing Research* 38 (2001) (4), pp. 494–500.

Boush, D.M. & Loken, B. (1991), "A Process-Tracing Study of Brand Extension Evaluation," *Journal of Marketing Research*, 28 (1), 16-28.

Christy, R., Oliver, G. & Penn, J. (1996), "Relationship Marketing in Consumer Markets," Journal of Marketing Management, 12 (1), 175-88.

Deleersnyder, B., Inge, G., Gielens, K. & Dekimpe, M.G. (2002), "How Cannibalistic is the Internet Channel? A Study of the Newspaper Industry in the United Kingdom and The Netherlands," *International Journal of Research in Marketing*, 19 (4), 337-348.

De Wulf, K., Odekerken-Schröder, G., & Iacobucci, D. (2001), "Investments in Consumer Relationships: A Cross-Country and Cross-Industry Exploration," Journal of Marketing, 65 (October), 33-50.

Erdem, T. & Swait, J. (1998), "Brand Equity as a Signaling Phenomenon," *Journal of Consumer Psychology*, 7(2), 131-157.

Dowling, G. *& Uncles, M. (1997), "Do Customer Loyalty Programs Really Work?" Sloan Management Review, 38 (Fall), 71-82.*

Garbarino, E. & Johnson, M.S. (1999), "The Different Roles of Satisfaction, Trust, and Commitment in Customer Relationships," Journal of Marketing, 63 (April), 70-87.

Georgiadis, M., Singer, M., & Harding, D. (2003), *Online Customer Practice*. McKinsey Marketing Practice white paper.

Glazer, R. (1991), "Marketing in an Information-Intensive Environment: Strategic Implications of Knowledge As An asset," *Journal of Marketing*, 55 (October), 1-19.

Keller, K.L. (1993), "Conceptualizing, measuring, and managing customer-based brand equity," *Journal of Marketing*, 57(1), pp. 1–22.

Kestnbaum, R.D., Kestnbaum, K.T., & Ames, P.W. (1998), "Building a Longitudinal Contact Strategy," *Journal of Interactive Marketing, 12* (1), 56-62.

Kozinets, R.V. (1997), "E-Tribalized Marketing?: The Strategic Implications of Virtual Communities of Consumption," *European Management Journal*, 17(3), 252-264.

Meyer-Levy, J. & Tybout, A.M. (1989), "Schema congruity as a basis for product evaluation," *Journal of Consumer Research*, 16, pp. 39–54.

Morgan, R.M. & Hunt, S.D. (1994), "The Commitment-Trust Theory of Relationship Marketing," Journal of Marketing, 58 (July), 20-38.

Park, C.W. & Lessig, P.F. (1981), "Familiarity and its impact on consumer decision biases and heuristics," *Journal of Consumer Research* 8, pp. 223–230.

Peppers, D. & Rogers, M. (1999), Enterprise One-to-One: Tools for Competing in the Interactive Age. New York: Doubleday.

Reinartz, W.J. & Kumar, V. (2002), "The Mismanagement of Customer Loyalty," Harvard Business Review, 80 (July), 86-94.

----- & ----- (2003), "The Impact of Customer Relationship Characteristics on Profitable Lifetime Duration," Journal of Marketing, 67 (January), 77-99.

Roberts, M.L. & Berger, P.D. (1999), Direct Marketing Management. Englewood Cliffs, NJ: Prentice Hall.

Rust, R.T., Zeithaml, V.A., & Lemon, K.N. (2000), Driving Customer Equity: How Customer Lifetime Value Is Reshaping Corporate Strategy. New York: The Free Press.

Schultz, D.E. & Bailey, S. (2000), "Customer/Brand Loyalty in an Interactive Marketplace," *Journal of Advertising Research*, May/Jun 2000, Vol. 40 Issue 3, 41-53.

_ & Kitchen, P.J. (2000*), Communicating Globally: An Integrated Marketing Approach*, Lincolnwood, IL: NTC Business Books.

Shapiro, C. & Varian, H. (1999), *Information Rules*. Cambridge, MA: Harvard Business School Press.

Sheth, J.N. & Parvatiyar, A. (1995), "Relationship Marketing in Consumer Markets: Antecedents and Consequences," Journal of the Academy of Marketing Science, 23 (Fall), 255-71.

Slywotsky, A.J. (2000), "The Age of the Choiceboard," *Harvard Business Review*, 78/1 (January/February), 40-41.

Verhoef, P. (2003), "*Understanding the Effect of Customer Relationship Management Efforts on Customer Retention and Customer Share Development*," *Journal of Marketing*, 0022-2429, October 1, 2003, Vol. 67, Issue 4

Winer, R.S. (2001), "A Framework for Customer Relationship Management," California Management Review, 43 (Summer), 89-108.

Woodside, A.G. & Walser, M.G. (2007), "Building strong brands in retailing," *Journal of Business Research*, Volume 60, Issue 1, January, 1-10.

Woodruff, R.B. (1997), "Customer Value: The Next Source for Competitive Advantage," Journal of the Academy of Marketing Science, 25 (Spring), *139-53.*

Wright, A. A. & Lynch, Jr., J.G (1995), "Communication Effects of Advertising vs. Direct Experience When Both Search and Experience Attributes Are Present," *Journal of Consumer Research,* 21(4), 708-718.

Zahay, D., Peltier, J.W., Schultz, D., & Griffin, A. (2004), "The Role of Transactional versus Relational Data in IMC Programs: Bringing Customer Data Together," *Journal of Advertising Research,* March, 3-16.

Zajonc, R.(1978), "Feeling and thinking: Preferences need no inferences," *American Psychologist,* 35, 151-175

Zauberman, G. (2003), "The Intertemporal Dynamics of Consumer Lock-In," *Journal of Consumer Research,* 30 (3), 405-419.

Chapter VI
Consumers' Optimal Experience on Commercial Web Sites:
A Congruency Effect of Web Atmospheric Design and Consumers' Surfing Goal

Fang Wan[1]
University of Manitoba, Canada

Ning Nan[1]
University of Oklahoma, USA

Malcolm Smith
University of Manitoba, Canada

ABSTRACT

Though marketers are aware that online marketing strategies are crucial to attract visitors to Web sites and make the Web site sticky (Hoffman et al., 1995; Morr, 1997; Schwartz, 1996; Tchong, 1998), little is known about the factors that can bring out such a compelling online experience. This chapter examines how specific Web atmospheric features such as dynamic navigation design, together with Web users' surfing goals, can lead to an optimal online experience. In addition, the chapter also examines the consequences of an optimal surfing experience on consumers' attitudes toward commercial Web sites/brands (promoted on these sites) and purchase intentions. In this chapter, we review related research on online consumer experience, identify two key antecedents of the optimal online experience, report an experiment testing the effects of these antecedents and provide insights for future research.

INTRODUCTION

Major brands in the fashion and cosmetic industry have started to have a very dynamic Web presence (e.g., www.loreal.net; www.bcbg.com). Unlike Web sites with a traditional navigation design (which is typically written in html language), these Web sites are empowered with dynamic Web atmospherics (a term adopted by Dailey 2004) such as animation, rich colors, hidden navigation bars and rich media features. On these sites, product information is neither just laid out there, nor organized by a simple navigation or site map. Instead, consumers will have to surf and "play" around in order to have a sense of site structure and to locate product information. Clearly, companies have to invest dearly to design and maintain such a dynamic Web presence. One might wonder, however, if consumers enjoy a dynamic Web interface or do they find it annoying? If a dynamic Web interface results in an enjoyable Web experience, is this positive experience transferred to an increase in brand equity and sales volume from both online and off-line channels?

Previous research (Dholakia & Bagozzi, 1999; Hoffman & Novak, 1996) suggests that a compelling online environment for Web consumers will have numerous positive consequences for commercial Web providers. On average, a good online experience can increase customer satisfaction by 40% (Bias & Mayhew, 1994) and account for 42% of most recent online purchases by US consumers (Forrester, 2001). Meanwhile, poor customer experiences can have a devastating effect on e-retailer revenues. As many as 82% of online consumers gave up their shopping attempts as a result of poor experiences in e-commerce Web sites (UsabilityNet, 2006). Moreover, online experiences have a pervasive impact on brand image and revenues of large corporations. According to Forrester research (2001), 10% of Fortune 1000 sites should be torn down because the poor online experience they provide are hurting the company's

brand. Even the technology leading firm, IBM had once been impaired by their suboptimal Web design. A massive Web redesign effort by IBM increased traffic to their online store by 120% and boosted sales by 400% (Battey, 1999). Similarly, a prominent e-commerce site, move. com experienced a 150% increase in real estate sales and significant improvement in advertising space sales after optimizing the online experience offered by their Web site (Vividence, 2001). All the real world evidence indicates that research about how to leverage the new dynamic design features to enhance consumers' online experience has important relevance to e-commerce as well as traditional companies with Web presence. Such relevance has been recognized by online executives and Internet marketing academics. As Jeff Bezos, founder and CEO of Amazon.com, pointed out, creating a compelling online experience for cyber customers is the key to a competitive advantage on the Internet (Weber, 1999).

The objective of this chapter is to examine how Web navigation design and consumers' online tasks interact to create a compelling online experience. We seek to achieve this objective by 1) reviewing related research on online consumer experience and discussing important constructs, 2) reporting an experiment on optimal consumer experience, and 3) providing insights for future research.

BACKGROUND

As companies are fighting the battle of customer acquisition via both their online and off-line channels, they have invested heavily on their Web sites to retain the attention of Web surfers who just visit their company Web site, and transform them into potential customers who would purchase either from their Web site or from their physical store (Hoffman & Novak, 2000). Though marketers are aware that online marketing strategies are crucial to attract visitors to Web sites and make the Web site sticky (Hoffman et al., 1995; Morr, 1997; Schwartz, 1996; Tchong, 1998), little is known about the factors that can bring out such a compelling online experience. This chapter examines how specific Web atmospheric features such as dynamic navigation design, together with Web users' surfing goals, can lead to an optimal online experience. In addition, the chapter also examines the consequences of an optimal surfing experience on consumers' attitudes toward commercial Web sites/brands (promoted on these sites) and purchase intentions.

Optimal Online Experience: Flow

Research has been conducted to identify efficient online marketing strategies (e.g., Morr, 1997; Schwartz, 1996; Tchong, 1998). This online marketing research has identified Web surfers' experiences to be an important factor that influences their attitudes and behaviors toward e-commerce sites. In general, a customer's on-line experience was identified as one of the most important factors that influence his/her attitude and behavior toward e-commerce sites (Dholakia & Bagozzi, 1999; Hoffman & Novak, 1996). For example, Schlosser and Kanfer (2001) reported that a positive experience with a Web site led to more frequent site visits, more focused attention to the product promoted by the site and stronger purchase intentions.

Hoffman and Novak (1996) argued that a commercially successful Web site should facilitate a state of flow for its consumers, and suggested that an important objective for online marketers is to provide for these "flow opportunities" (Hoffman & Novak, 1996). In their framework, "flow" is an optimal experience in a computer-mediated environment. It is defined as a state occurring during network navigation, characterized by a seamless sequence of responses (facilitated by machine interactivity) that the consumer finds intrinsically enjoyable, self-reinforcing, and is accompanied by a loss of self-consciousness

(Hoffman & Novak, 1996). In the context of a Web site experience, flow is the desirable consequence of the exchanges between a Web user and the Web site. Csikszentmihalyi (1982) found that a match between a task challenge and person's coping skills could facilitate the emergence of an optimal experience. However, little is known about how and why a match or the congruency between a task challenge and coping skills would yield an optimal experience.

Congruency Effect of Navigation Design and Surfing Goal on Optimal Online Experience

Navigation design is recognized as one of the most important elements that determine the success of a Web site (Whitaker, 1998). Navigation design (also referred to as navigation cues or devices (e.g., a list of links)) allows users to move to a desired section and view pages of interest (Rajani & Rosenberg, 1999). Whitaker (1998) argued that different cognitive skills are required for different navigation purposes. When these navigation devices are salient and clear enough to help users' cognitive processing of their movement in cyberspace, users are more likely to achieve an optimal experience. On the other hand, if these navigation devices are ambiguous and not user-friendly, the users are more likely to get lost in the cyberspace and, as a consequence, experience anxiety while navigating the Web.

Similarly, Steuer (1992) argued that interactions with certain Web site features can result in a more human, real-world experience, rather than just be interactions with technology. Such an online experience that mimics a real-world experience is defined as virtual reality (Steuer, 1992). He emphasized two aspects of Web features that could enhance the creation of virtual reality -- vividness and interactivity (Steuer, 1992). Vividness refers to the richness of a mediated environment as defined by its formal features (e.g., animation, color); and interactivity refers to the extent to which users can participate in modifying the form and content of a mediated environment (e.g., chat rooms and video games). Both Whitaker's (1998) and Steuer's (1992) works seem to suggest that navigation design of a Web site alone cannot bring out a positive experience for a Web site user. As noted earlier, an online optimal experience is a result of both user surfing goals and Web features.

Researchers have identified two major surfing motives for Web users--achieving an end goal (e.g., finding useful information about commercial products and services) and exploring for the sake of exploration (e.g., browsing for entertainment) (Gupta, 1995; Whitaker, 1998). Goal-oriented Web surfing has been labeled "searching" or "information seeking." When a Web user is engaged in searching, he/she looks for particular information while expending minimal time and energy. Such instrumental, goal-directed orientations have been argued to reflect purposive, task-specific behavior which leads to a directed search in order to complete such goals as prepurchase deliberation (Hoffman & Novak, 1996). Thus, searchers may surf a Web site with the deliberate goal of efficiently and effectively processing or evaluating information (Schlosser & Kanfer, 2001; Murphy, 1999).

As Whitaker (1998) pointed out, different surfing motives require different navigational and cognitive skills. For example, Wickens (1992) found that when users navigate the Web with an end goal such as information seeking, they generally use navigation devices such as frames, table of contents, navigation bars, hierarchical maps, and site maps or search engines to move toward their surfing goals (Wickens, 1992). Therefore, a static, brochure-like navigation design will serve the needs of an information seeker by presenting a clear structure of information. Achieving his/her goals should ultimately result in an optimal online experience.

On the other hand, browsing or surfing with a "fun-seeking" purpose is less task-oriented and more entertainment-oriented than information seeking. The experiential, hedonic orientations of this type of browsing reflect recreational behavior and a nonlinear search (Hoffman & Novak, 1996). Thus, whereas searchers may be motivated to find relevant information and digest it quickly without having their attention diverted, browsers may be motivated to be delighted and entertained by the Web site experience (Schlosser & Kanfer, 2001). In this case, with a purpose of enjoying the process of exploration itself, browsers are expecting sites of interests via unintended paths and unexpected hidden links. In a browsing situation, Web surfers may prefer unobtrusive and ambiguous visual cues over salient and clear ones. Therefore, a dynamic navigation design is more likely to generate an optimal experience because it serves the experiential and hedonic orientation of browsing. Therefore, dynamic Web sites with animation and hidden links are congruent with the goal of browsers.

Research across a wide variety of topics, including advertising and consumer psychology, reported congruency effects and concluded that attitudes toward advertising messages, or product evaluations are enhanced if there is a congruency between 1) advertising strategies and viewer characteristics, 2) product features and consumer characteristics, and 3) sources of the message and product features (Graeff, 1996; Kamins, 1990; Leigh, 1992; Nevite, 1999; Stafford, 1998; Solomon et al., 1992). Therefore, in our research context, we would expect that:

H1a: Web surfers with a fun seeking goal who visit a dynamic Web site (congruence) are more likely to achieve a positive Web experience and evaluate the brand positively than surfers with a fun seeking goal who visit a static Web site or surfers with an information seeking goal who visit a dynamic Web site (incongruence).

H1b: Web surfers with an information seeking goal who explore static Web site (congruence) are more likely to achieve a positive Web experience and evaluate the brand positively than surfers with an information seeking goal who visit a dynamic Web site or surfers with a fun seeking goal who visit a static web site (incongruence).

AN EMPIRICAL STUDY:

Method

A 2 (navigation design: static versus dynamic) by 2 (surfer's motive: information seeking versus browsing) online experiment was designed for this study. Two hundred and seventeen participants were recruited from a Midwestern university in the United States. Among the 217 participants, 91 were male and 126 were female. The ages ranged from 18 to 40, with both mean and median of 20.

Web sites of an existing personal care brand were selected as the commercial Web site in the study (e.g., John, Loken and Jointer (1998) adopted a real world brand in their experiments). On average, participants used this brand at least once in the past six months. The actual Web site of this brand can be characterized as a *dynamic navigation Web site*, where animation, swap images, audio clips, hidden hyperlinks are the major features of the Web site. This Web site was selected based on two criteria: (1) the site was totally made by using Macromedia Flash, which is the typical software for animated navigation design, and (2) animation, rollover images, swap menu and audio signals are the major features of its navigation design. With graphic design and Web site design software, we programmed another version of the Web site, *the static navigation Web site*, where all the animation, swap images, audio clips (music) and hidden hyperlinks were transformed into static image and text. These two Web sites have the same amount of product-related information. Detailed differences between the two Web sites can be found in Appendix 1a and 1b.

Upon arriving at the experiment site, participants were told they would take part in a Web site evaluation study. They were told that the Web site was newly designed for a personal care brand L. They were then given a short questionnaire which asked questions regarding their attitudes toward this brand and their frequency of usage of this brand. Then, they were given a URL address on paper and asked to type this URL on a Web browser. When they accessed the URL, the CGI program on the server would randomly assign them to one of the four experimental conditions and display the corresponding online experiment Web page in the Internet browser. In these experimental conditions, participants were randomly given one of the following two instructions to surf the Web site: 1) "This is a newly developed Web site. When you browse this Web site, please pay attention to product information on the Web site and you will be given a quiz on product information after you visit the Web site" (information seeking), or 2) "This is a newly developed Web site. Please try to explore this Web site and have some fun with it" (fun seeking). In addition, participants were also randomly assigned to one of the two versions of the Web site: dynamic navigation or static navigation site.

To ensure that participants spent sufficient time surfing the Web site, and to tease out amount of time spent online as a potential confounding variable, we instructed participants to spend at least five minutes on the Web site. We also implemented a built-in clock so that participants could not close the browser window until they spent five minutes on the Web site. In our pretest on 20 participants (drawn from the same student population), we asked them to browse the same Web sites at their own pace. The minimum time spent was 4.2 minutes. Therefore, we set five minutes as the minimum time limit for Web surfing in our main experiment.

Once participants were finished surfing the Web site, they closed the browsing window. A new window popped up, with an online questionnaire which was composed of questions measuring participants' attitudes toward the brand, their evaluations of their Web experience, and their behavioral intentions such as revisiting the Web site, recommending the Web site to friends, and purchasing from the Web site. When the participants completed the questionnaire, they were told to click the "submit" button located at the bottom of the screen. Then, their responses were sent back to the Web server. The CGI program on the server received the data and transformed them into a text file. Later, the data in the text file were directly imported into the Statistical Package for the Social Sciences (SPSS) for statistical analysis.

Measures

Manipulation Checks

Dynamic vs. static Web site. After surfing the Web site, participants were asked to rate the Web site with a five-point scale with 5= "Dynamic" and 1= "Static." Analysis of Variance (ANOVA) indicated a significant main effect of Web site on this scale. Participants surfing the dynamic Web site (with animation and hidden links) reported a higher mean score on the scale than those surfing the static site (4.21 versus 2.12; $F_{(1, 213)}$ = 11.86, $p < .01$).

Surfing motive. Participants were asked to indicate their agreement with the following two questions: "When I was surfing the Web site, I was paying attention to product information," "When I was surfing the Web site, I was just browsing around and having some fun." A 5-point scale was used anchored with 1 = "strongly disagree" and 5 = "strongly agree." ANOVA analysis yielded a significant main effect of surfing motive on these two items. Participants in the information seeking condition were more likely to agree with the first item (4.16 vs. 2.31, $F_{(1, 213)}$ = 9.86, $p < .01$) and less likely to agree with second item compared to participants in fun seeking conditions (2.35 vs. 4.31, $F_{(1, 213)}$ = 10.16, $p < .01$).

Dependent Measures

Attitude change. Both before and after surfing the Web site, participants were asked to indicate their attitude toward the brand by using 5-point bipolar scales anchored by 1 = "bad," "negative," "unfavorable" and 5 = "good", "positive" and "favorable." Two indices of attitude toward the brand were created by taking the average of three items for pre and posttest respectively (pretest attitude, alpha = .89; posttest attitude, alpha = .90). We created an attitude change variable by subtracting the posttest attitude scores from pretest attitude scores. The resulting variable ranged from -3, indicating a negative attitude change resulting from the exposure to the Web site, to +3, indicating a positive attitude change. This variable was used as a dependent variable in the Multivariate Analysis of Variance (MANVOA) analysis below (see Results section).

Web experience related measures. The focus of this paper is to explore the congruence effect on Web experience. To date, there has not been a measure that captures this construct. Therefore, we reviewed related measures from research on flow, Web navigation, Web personality and Web site evaluation (i.e., Chen & Wells, 1999; 2002; Chen & Rodgers, 2006; Steuer, 1992; Novak et al., 2000; Hoffman & Novak, 1996; Rodgers & Thorson, 2000) and adopted 23 items measuring attitude toward the Web site, surfing experience, emotional reactions after the surfing experience and behavioral intentions. The items consisted of a number of adjectives, or statements. Participants were asked to indicate their response to these items with a five-point scale anchored by 1 = "The adjective (or statement) does not describe my reaction toward the Web site (or my experience of surfing the site) at all" and 5 = "The adjective (or statement) very much describes my reaction toward the Web site (or my experience of surfing the site)."

A total number of 23 items were subjected to exploratory factor analysis with principal component extraction and a varimax rotation method. Factor analysis yielded three factors with factor loadings higher than .67, explaining 68.29% of the total variance. The first factor, labeled as *flow* (Novak et al., 2000) consists of items measuring participants' excitement and positive experience when surfing the Web site (refer to Appendix 2 for specific items), with an Eigen value of 10.34, explaining 44.97% of the total variance . The second factor, *Web structure*, includes items measuring how organized and easy-to-use the Web site was (Appendix 2), with an Eigen value of 3.70, explaining 16.07% of the total variance. The third factor, labeled as *Web stickiness (behavioral),* indicates participants' intentions to visit the Web site in the future and future purchase intentions after visiting the Web site (Hoffman & Novak, 2000). This factor has an Eigen value of 1.67 and explains 7.25% of the total variance (refer to Appendix 2 for factor loadings). Three variables were created by averaging their constituent items respectively (with alphas ranging from

.89 to .95) and entered as dependent variables in the MANOVA analysis.

Results

A MANOVA analysis was conducted with navigation design and surfing goal as between-subject factors and attitude change and Web experience variables as dependent variables. Means of the dependent variable by conditions are included in Appendix 3 and results of the MANOVA are described below.

Attitude change. The MANOVA analysis yielded a significant interaction effect of navigation design and surfing goal on attitude change ($F_{(1,213)} = 4.43$, $p < .05$) and non-significant main effects ($F < 1$). (See Figure 1.)

A planned contrast yielded a significant main effect of navigation design when participants were engaged in fun seeking goal ($F_{(1,213)} = 6.69$, $p < .01$), indicating that when the goal was congruent with navigation design (fun seeking goal and dynamic

Figure 1. Brand attitude change: Post-Pre

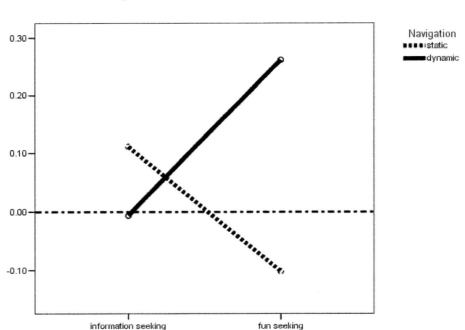

Web site), participants reported a positive brand attitude change compared to when the goal was incongruent with navigation design (fun seeking goal and static Web site) (mean = .26 vs. -.10). A planned contrast also yielded a significant main effect of surfing goal in the dynamic Web site condition ($F_{(1,213)}$ = 3.81, p < .05), providing additional evidence that congruence (dynamic Web site and fun seeking goal) led to a more positive posttest brand attitude, resulting in a positive attitude change (mean = .26 vs. -.01) compared to incongruence (dynamic Web site and information seeking goal). Therefore, these findings are more in line with predictions of H1a. However, H1b is not supported.

Flow. The MANOVA analysis yielded a significant main effect of navigation design ($F_{(1,213)}$ = 38.87, p < .001) qualified by a significant two-way interaction effect of navigation and surfing goal on flow (optimal online experience) ($F_{(1,213)}$ = 4.79, p < .05). (See Figure 2.)

A planned contrast analysis indicated a significant main effect of navigation design on flow in fun seeking conditions ($F_{(1,213)}$ = 36.69, p < .001) and a significant main effect of surfing goal in dynamic Web site conditions ($F_{(1,213)}$ = 5.8, p < .05). These findings suggest that when the surfing goal and navigation design are congruent (i.e., in the dynamic Web site and fun seeking condition), participants were more likely to experience flow (mean = 3.54) compared to when the surfing goal and navigation design are incongruent such as the fun seeking goal paired with static Web site (mean = 2.64) or information seeking goal paired with dynamic Web site (mean = 3.15). Therefore, H1a is supported. In addition, a planned contrast also revealed a significant main effect of navigation design when information seeking is the surfing goal ($F_{(1,213)}$ = 4.66, p < .05), indicating that when the goal was congruent with navigation design (information seeking and static Web site), participants were more likely to experience flow

Figure 2. Flow by navigation design and surfing goal

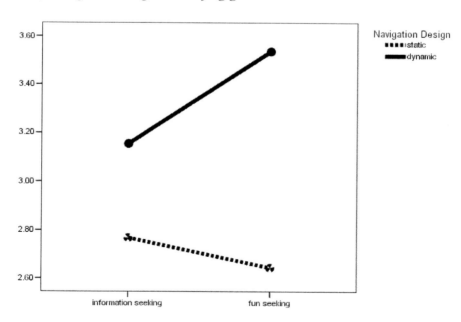

Figure 3. Web structure by navigation design and surfing goal

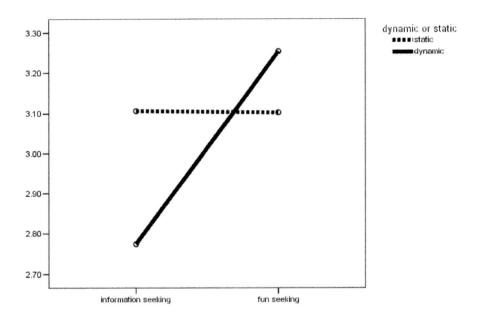

(mean = 3.15 vs. 2.77) compared to when surfing goal was incongruent with navigation design (i.e., fun- seeking goal and static Web site). Therefore, H1b is partly supported.

Web structure. The MANOVA analysis revealed a significant interaction effect of navigation and surfing goal on perceived Web structure ($F_{(1,213)}$ = 4.82, p < .05). (See Figure 3.)

A planned contrast analysis yielded a significant main effect of goal on Web structure when navigation design is dynamic ($F_{(1,213)}$ = 10.05, p < .01), suggesting that participants with fun seeking goal who surfed the dynamic Web site were more likely to provide a positive evaluation of the structure/organization of the Web site than participants with information seeking goal who surfed the dynamic Web site (mean = 3.25 vs. 2.77). However, evaluation of Web structure did not differ between participants in the fun seeking goal and dynamic Web site condition and those in fun seeking goal and static Web site condition (F < 1). Therefore, H1a is partly supported. A planned contrast also yielded another incidence of congru-

ence effect—a significant main effect of navigation design on perceived Web structure when the surfing goal is information seeking ($F_{(1,213)}$ = 4.0, p > 05). This suggests that when the surfing goal is information seeking, which is congruent with a static Web site design, participants were more likely to provide a positive evaluation of the Web structure compared to when the same surfing goal is paired with a dynamic Web site design (mean = 3.11 vs. 2.77). Similarly, a planned contrast did not yield a significant main effect of navigation design when the surfing goal is fun seeking (F > 1). Therefore, H1b is partly supported.

Web stickiness (behavioral). The MANOVA analysis yielded a significant interaction effect of navigation design and surfing goal on Web stickiness ($F_{(1, 213)}$ = 3.86, p < .05) with no significant main effect (F < 1). (See Figure 4.)

A planned contrast yielded a significant main effect of navigation design in the fun seeking condition ($F_{(1,213)}$ = 6.09, p < .05), suggesting that congruence (dynamic Web site and fun seeking goal) led to a stronger likelihood of Web sticki-

Figure 4. Web Stickiness by navigation design and surfing goal

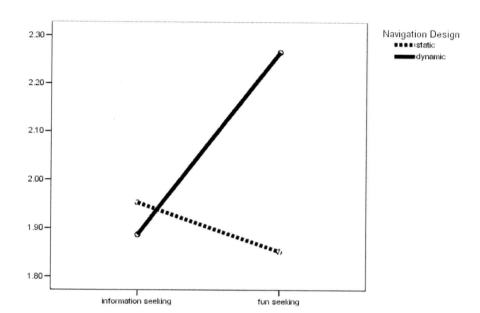

ness (i.e., revisit the site, recommend the site and purchase from the site) compared to incongruence (static Web site and fun seeking goal) (mean = 2.27 vs. 1.85). An additional planned contrast also led to a significant main effect of surfing goal in the dynamic Web site condition ($F_{(1,213)} = 4.25$, $p < .05$), revealing a positive effect of congruence (dynamic Web site and fun seeking goal) versus incongruence (dynamic Web site and information seeking goal) on Web stickiness (mean = 2.27 vs. 1.89). Again, H1a is supported. However, H1b is not supported.

CONCLUSION AND FUTURE TRENDS

The major objective of this study was to examine whether an optimal online experience can be induced by the congruence between Web design features or atmospherics (Dailey, 2006) (such as navigation design) and Web user's surfing goals.

Congruence effects have been documented in the advertising and consumer psychology literature (e.g., Nevite, 1999; Stafford, 1998; Graeff, 1996; Leigh, 1992; Solomon, Ashmore & Longo, 1992; Kamins, 1990). This past research has generally found that matching the advertising message characteristics with the audience characteristics, results in effective brand communications. However, to date, no study has been conducted to examine whether this well-documented congruence effect can be induced by matching design features of the Web site with online consumers' surfing goal. This match should facilitate an optimal online experience. The present study focused on the interaction of one specific Web feature (i.e., navigation design) with consumers' surfing goals to influence consumers' online Web experience as well as their attitude toward the brand.

We hypothesized that the pairing of an information-seeking goal and a static navigation design, or of a fun-seeking goal and a dynamic navigation design would result in an optimal online experience (i.e., positive brand attitude, more enjoyable surfing experience (flow), more positive evaluation of the Web structure and more Web stickiness by revisiting, recommending the site, and purchasing from it). Our experiment findings largely supported the congruence effect. The pairing of a dynamic navigation design with a fun-seeking goal was found to produce a more optimal online experience than the incongruent pairings such as a dynamic navigation design with an information-seeking goal, or a static navigation design with a fun-seeking goal. However, our findings indicated this congruency effect was asymmetrical. That is, the matching of a static navigation design with an information seeking goal did not result in a more optimal Web experience compared to the incongruent matching (the only exception is the evaluation of the Web structure). One plausible explanation could be that the dynamic Web site in this study, with its rolling images, hidden links, playful navigation menu, was more capable of inducing a fun and enjoyable Web experience than the static Web site regardless of the surfing motive. Therefore, our dynamic Web site may have been far more appealing to the participants. Another alternative explanation could be that participants' involvement in both the information seeking condition and fun seeking condition was low. That is, participants with an information seeking goal, who were supposed to be more involved in product information search, may have been diverted from the task by the dynamic web features. This could explain why a pairing of an information seeking goal with a dynamic Web site did not result in an inferior online experience compared to the congruent pairing of an information seeking goal with a static Web site. Future research should be conducted to explore these alternative explanations.

At the same time, our research revealed a consistent, robust, and positive effect of the dynamic navigation design and a fun-seeking surfing goal on consumers' online experience and brand attitudes. These findings send an important message to marketers: in addition to off-line brand communication channels such as traditional advertising, the Web can be a powerful and a complementary medium for consumers to experience a brand. Our research only touched the tip of the iceberg by exploring how the navigation design and consumers' surfing goal can positively affect consumers' brand experience. However, other than Web design features, marketers have explored alternative tools on the Web to energize or build a brand. For example, BMW launched an interactive Web site to promote the Z3 roaster, where consumers can customize the car, download images, and most importantly watch short films made by BMW. The Web site drew thousands of consumers to the BMW site and created an instant hype and buzz for the new product (Fournier & Dolan, 1997). Another example is the success of YouTube. This online brand is built on new, innovative content that is constantly refreshed and updated by a virtual community. Yet, given the proliferation of online brand building tools employed by marketers, little research has been carried out to systematically examine the effectiveness of these tools on brand equity. Future research needs to address these research questions so that our knowledge of the Web, as an increasingly important brand building tool, will be more sophisticated.

REFERENCES

Battey, J. (1999). IBM's redesign results in a kinder, simpler Web site. Article available at http://www.infoworld.com/cgibin/displayStat.pl?/pageone/opinions/hotsites/hotextr990419.htm

Bias, G. & Mayhew, D. (1994). *Cost-Justifying usability*. New York: Academic Press.

Csikszentmihalyi, M. (1982). Towards a psychology of optimal experience. In L. Wheeler (Ed.), *Review of Personality and Social Psychology*, 2. Beverly Hills, CA: Sage.

Chen, Q., Clifford,S., & Wells, W .D. (2002). Attitude toward the site II: New information. *Journal of Advertising Research*, 42 (2), 33-45.

Chen, Q. & Rodgers, S. (2006), Development of an instrument to measure Web site personality. *Journal of Interactive Advertising, 7(1)*. Retrieved Dec 12 2006, from http://www.jiad.org/vol7/no1/chen/index.htm

Chen, Q, & Wells, W. D. (1999). Attitude toward the site. *Journal of Advertising Research*, 39 (5), 27-38.

Dailey, L. (2004), Navigational Web atmospherics: Explaining the influence of restrictive navigation cues. *Journal of Business Research,* 57, 795-803.

Dholakia, U. R. & Bagozzi, P. (1999). Consumer behavior in digital environments. Working paper.

Forunier, S. & Dolan, R. J. (1997), "Launching the BMW Z3 roadster," Harvard Business School Case, Harvard Business Online. Retrieved Dec 30, 2006, from http://harvardbusinessonline.hbsp.harvard.edu/b01/en/common/item_detail.jhtml;jsessionid=SH2Q0JDKFMVW4AKRGWCB5VQBKE0YOISW?id=597002

Forrester Report (2001) *Get ROI from design.* Forrester Research, Inc., Cambridge, MA.

Graeff, T. R. (1996). Image congruence effects on product evaluations: The role of self-monitoring and public/private consumption. *Psychology and Marketing*, 13(5), 481-499.

Ghani, J., & Deshpande, S. P. (1994). Task characteristics and the experience of optimal flow in human-computer interaction. *Journal of Psychology*, 128(4), 381-392.

Gupta, M., & Gramopadhye, A. (1995). An evaluation of different navigational tools in using hypertext. *Computers & Industrial Engineering*, 29, 437-442.

Hoffman, D. L., & Novak, T. P. (1996). Marketing in Hypermedia computer-mediated environments: Conceptual foundations. *Journal of Marketing*, 603, 50-69.

Hoffman, D. L., & Novak, T. P. (2000). Measuring the customer experience in online environments: A structural modeling approach. *Marketing Science*, 19(1), 22-24.

Hoffman, D. L., Novak, T. P., & Chatterjee, P. (1995). Commercial scenarios for the Web: Opportunities and challenges. *Journal of Computer Mediated Communication*, 1(3). Retrieved Dec 12, 1995, from shum.huji.ac.il/j cmc/vol1/issue3/hoffman.html.

John, D. R., Loken, B., & Jointer, C. (1998), The negative impact of extensions: Can flagship products be diluted? *Journal of Marketing*, 62 (1), 19-33.

Kamins, M. A. (1990). An investigation into the 'match-up' hypothesis in celebrity advertising: When beauty may be only skin deep. *Journal of Advertising*, 19 (1), 4-13.

Lieigh, J. H. (1992). Modality congruence, multiple resource theory and intermedia broadcast comparisons: An elaboration. *Journal of Advertising*, 21(2), 55-63.

Morr, T. (1997). You can build it, but will they come back On The Highway. *SEMA News*, June. Specialty Equipment Market Association.

Murphy, J. (1999). Surfers and searchers: An examination of Web-site visitors' clicking behavior. *Cornell Hotel & Restaurant Administration Quarterly*. 40(2), 84.

Neviite, N. & Kanji, M. (1999). Orientations towards authority and congruency theory. *International Journal of Comparative Sociology*, 40(1), 160.

Novak, T. P., Hoffman, D. L., & Yung, Y. (2000). Measuring the customer experience in online environments: A structural modeling approach. *Marketing Science*, 19(1), 22-42.

Rajani R. & Rosenberg D. (1999) "Usable?...or not?...factors affecting the usability of web sites. *CMC Magazine*, 1-5 (January).

Rodgers, S. & Thorson, E. (2000). The interactive advertising model: How users perceive and process online ads. *Journal of Interactive advertising*, 1(1). Retrieved Dec 12 2006, from http://www.jiad.org

Schwartz, E. I. (1996). Advertising webonimics 101. *Wired*, 4.02 Electrosphere section, February.

Schlosser, A. E. & Kanfer, A. (2001, May). *Impact of product interactivity on searchers' and browsers' judgments: Implications for commercial Web site effectiveness.* Paper presented at the Advertising and Consumer Psychology Conference on "Online Consumer Psychology: Understanding How to Interact with Consumers in the Virtual World," Seattle, WA.

Solomon, M. R., Ashmore, R. D., & Longo, L. C. (1992). The beauty match-up hypothesis: Congruence between types of beauty and product images in advertising. *Journal of Advertising*, 21, 23-34.

Stafford, M. R. (1998). Advertising sex-typed services: The effects of sex, service type, and employee type on consumer attitude. *Journal of Advertising*, 27(2), 65-82.

Steuer, J. (1992). Defining virtual reality: Dimensions determining tele-presence. Journal of Communication, 42(2), 73-93.

Tchong, M. (1998). ICONOCAST. *Imagine Media, Inc.* Retrieved on Dec 12 2006 from http://www.iconocast.com/

UsabilityNet (2006). The business case for usability. Article available at http://www.usabilitynet.org/management/c_business.htm

Vividence, Corp. (2001) Moving on up: Move.com improves customer experience. Article available at: http://www.vividence.com/public/solutions/our+clients/success+stories/movecom.htm.

Weber, J. (1999). The bottom line. *The Industry Standard*, 5, 2-9.

Whitaker, L. A. (1998). Human navigation. In Forsythe, C., Grose, E. & Ratner, J. (Eds.) *Human Factors and Web Development*. Lawrence Erlbaum Associations.

Wickens, C. D. (1992*). Engineering psychology and human performance*. New York: Harper Collins.

ENDNOTE

[1]   The first two authors contributed to this manuscript equally.

APPENDIX 1A

Dynamic Navigation Design: Snapshot of First Page

APPENDIX 1B

Static Navigation Design: Snapshot of the First Page

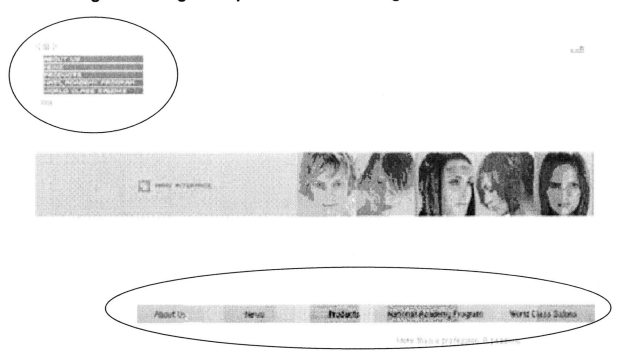

Note: There are three major differences between the two versions. First, on the dynamic Web site, a drop-down navigation menu is hidden in the upper-left hand corner. Only when users move around the mouse cursor and finally put it on the small gray square icon in the upper-left hand corner, the drop-down menu will be displayed. In contrast, in the experimental Web page, the menu is exposed in the same position and in static form. The other difference is the navigation bar at the bottom of the two pages. Second, on the dynamic Web site, the navigation bar only displays part of the optional links and it keeps rolling constantly. Once users put their mouse cursor on it, the navigation bar stops rolling and allows users to click on a link. On the static Web site, all the links in the navigation bar are exposed and stay static. Third, the female images on the dynamic Web site keep rolling, following the rhythm of the music. However, on the static Web site, these images stay static.

APPENDIX 2

Scale Items

Scale	Item	Factor loadings	Alpha
Flow	Cool	.845	.95
	Entertaining	.787	
	Exciting	.820	
	Flashy	.793	
	Lively	.774	
	Unique	.806	
	Attractive	.781	
	This site is appealing	.778	
	Time flew by while on this site.	.677	
	I experienced enjoyment during the Web navigation.	.678	
	I found this site is interesting.	.782	
Web structure	I got lost while navigating this site.	.759	.90
	This site is well-organized.	.723	
	The navigation of this site is easy to use.	.827	
	This site has clear layout.	.836	
	I experienced the feeling of being in control during Web navigation.	.724	
	It's easy to get around in this site.	.836	
	This site provides clear directions on where to go.	.678	
	I feel confused by this site.	.717	
Web stickiness (behavioral)	I would like to visit this Website again.	.773	.89
	I will recommend this Website to my friend.	.802	
	If possible, I will purchase products from this Website.	.870	

APPENDIX 3

Means of flow, Web structure, Web stickiness and attitude change by navigation design and search motive

	Dynamic web site		Static web site	
	Fun-seeking	Information-seeking	Fun-seeking	Information-seeking
Flow	3.54 (.76)	3.15 (.90)	2.64 (.87)	2.77 (.71)
Web structure	3.25 (.82)	2.77 (.94)	3.10 (.66)	3.11 (.75)
Web Stickiness (behavioral)	2.27 (1.15)	1.89 (.89)	1.85 (.89)	1.95 (.79)
Brand Attitude Change	.26 (.76)	-.01 (.91)	-.10 (.79)	.11 (.62)

Note: Numbers in parentheses represents standard deviations.

Chapter VII
Nonlinear Pricing in E–Commerce

José J. Canals-Cerdá
Federal Reserve Bank of Philadelphia, USA

ABSTRACT

Internet markets are usually under the command of a market intermediary that charges fees for its services. Differences in quality across items being sold allow the market intermediary to employ lucrative nonlinear pricing strategies and to offer different levels of service. For several years now, eBay has been using a nonlinear pricing policy that offers sellers the opportunity of having their items listed first when buyers search for specific products in return for an additional fee. A similar pricing strategy is also used in other online markets like Overstock.com and ArtByUs.com, and is also employed by search engines when sponsored links are displayed first. In this paper we analyze this topic from a theoretical and empirical perspective. Intuitively, potential buyers are more likely to examine items listed first and sellers of high quality items are more likely to pay an extra fee in order to have preferential access to buyers. In the theoretical section of the paper we analyze the optimal pricing policy of the market intermediary in a market with heterogeneous goods. In the empirical sections of the paper we analyze a unique panel of approximately 2,200 art auctions from artists who sell their own work through eBay. We use our data to quantify the overall impact of this pricing policy on the revenues of the sellers and the market intermediary. As expected, this pricing policy creates a selection effect by which sellers of the most valuable paintings are willing to pay an extra fee in order to gain access to a large pool of potential buyers. Our results also indicate that the pricing policy implemented by eBay increases revenues significantly for sellers and for the market intermediary when compared with a single-price policy and acts as a coordination mechanism that facilitates the match between buyers and sellers.

INTRODUCTION

Online markets are usually under the control of a market intermediary. The intermediary, by matching buyers with sellers, acts as a necessary catalyst for trade and can charge fees for its services. Faced with heterogeneous customers, the intermediary has an incentive to offer different levels of service to different customers subject to different fees. Intuitively, sellers of high quality items may be willing to pay an extra fee in order to gain access to a large pool of potential buyers because they benefit the most from having many buyers competing for their product in an auctions market.

In this paper, we analyze theoretically and empirically a specific pricing strategy employed by eBay. For several years now, eBay has been using a simple nonlinear pricing strategy, or as they call it "Featured Plus!" (FP). This pricing strategy works by giving sellers the option of having their item listed first when buyers look for a specific item, artwork in our data, at an extra fee. Items that are not featured will be listed after the featured items along with thousands of other pieces of artwork that are posted on eBay daily. The basic idea behind "Featured Plus!" is that items that are listed first will attract a larger number of potential buyers because buyers incur a lower search cost when looking at these items. The same kind of strategy is also used in other online markets, like overstock.com or artbyus. com. Search engines also employ a similar pricing strategy when sponsored links are displayed at the top of the results page.

Theoretically, we build a simple model of a two-side market controlled by a market intermediary and develop some insights on the optimum pricing policy of the market intermediary. We also present some comparative statics results. Empirically, we analyze a unique panel data of approximately 2,200 art auctions from artists who sell their own work through eBay without the help of an agent or a gallery, also known as "self-representing"

artists. We use our data to quantify the effect of this pricing policy on the revenues of the sellers and the market intermediary. As expected, this pricing policy creates a selection effect by which sellers of the most valuable paintings are willing to pay an extra fee in order to gain access to a large pool of potential buyers. This kind of auction commands a higher price than standard auctions and a higher probability of sale. Our results also indicate that the pricing policy implemented by eBay increases revenues significantly for sellers and for the market intermediary when compared with a single-price policy and acts as a coordination mechanism that facilitates the match between buyers and sellers.

The paper proceeds as follows. In the theoretical background section, we develop a theoretical model that illustrates the properties of alternative price policies available to the market intermediary in a two-sided market. In the section on empirical application, we present a brief description of the eBay marketplace and the data to be used in the empirical analysis along with some descriptive statistics. In the section on empirical methodology, we develop the econometric methodology to be used in our analysis of the data. In the empirical results section, we present estimation results and analyze the outcome from a policy experiment.

THEORETICAL BACKGROUND

Consider a market controlled by an intermediary. The market intermediary matches sellers with potential buyers and in return charges a fee for this service. The market serves a large number of sellers and potential buyers. Without loss of generality, assume that the number of sellers in the market correspond to the unit interval and that there are K potential buyers per seller. For simplicity, we will treat K as if it was a positive real number, when in fact it has a more intuitive interpretation as a positive integer. As a result of the match between a seller and K potential buyers the object may be sold to a single buyer, the highest bidder in the case of eBay, or alternatively the object may remain unsold. For simplicity, we abstract from the mechanism of exchange and assume that an increase in the number of potential buyers increases the seller's willingness to pay (WTP) for the match, denoted as $W(\bullet)$. In the case of eBay this is clearly the case. An increase in the number of auction participants is likely to increase the expected sale price for two reasons, first because it increases the probability of a "good match," or a sale, and second because an increase in the number of bidders increases the level of competition for the item being sold, and the sale price. Consistent with our data, we also assume that the market intermediary serves a group of heterogeneous sellers with different willingness to pay functions. For simplicity, we assume that there are only two different types of sellers, the type 1 or "high-value" sellers and the type 0 or "low-value" sellers, with willingness to pay functions $W_j(k)=\theta_j W(k)$, $j=0,1$, and with $\theta_1>\theta_0$. Denote the proportion of type 1 sellers as λ and the proportion of type 0 sellers as $(1-\lambda)$. Assuming that the "willingness to pay function" is sufficiently smooth, we have that $W'(k)>0$. It is also reasonable in this framework to assume that $W''(k)<0$.[b]

Optimal Nonlinear Pricing Policy

Differences in willingness to pay across sellers allow the market intermediary to employ profitable nonlinear pricing strategies and to offer different levels of service to different types of customers. [c] Formally, the optimal pricing policy from the perspective of the market intermediary can be represented by a vector $((p_1,k_1),(p_0,k_0))$, $j=0,1$, with p_j representing the fee associated with a guaranteed match with k_j potential buyers, which is aimed at type j sellers. In this context, the viable optimum should satisfy a number of constraints: (1) It should be a feasible allocation, that is the number of buyers matched with sellers should

equal the total number of buyers in the market; (2) sellers must be willing to pay for the services offered by the intermediary; (3) Since the market intermediary cannot force any seller into buying a particular type of service, a type j seller should prefer option (p_j,k_j) over the alternative, for $j=0,1$. The second and third kind of constraints are usually referred to in the theory of incentives literature (Laffont & Martimort, 2002) as the "individual rationality constraints" and the "incentive-compatibility constraints." We will refer to the first constraint as the market intermediary's "resource budget constraint." As it is usually the case in this type of setting, we only need to verify the individual rationality constraint for the low value seller and the incentive-compatibility constraint for the high value seller. It can be easily verified that the other constraints are also satisfied at the optimum. Intuitively, the optimal price policy will be such that the high value seller will prefer option 1 only marginally, thus necessarily making this option less attractive to the low value seller. Formally, the problem of the market intermediary can be represented as the solution to the following maximization problem

$$\text{Max } \lambda p_1+(1-\lambda)p_0$$
$$\text{St: (a) } \lambda k_1+(1-\lambda)k_0 = K$$
$$\text{(b) } \theta_0 W(k_0) \geq p_0$$
$$\text{(c) } \theta_1 W(k_1) - p_1 \geq \theta_0 W(k_0) - p_0$$

Because the market intermediary benefits from high prices, restrictions (b) and (c) will be satisfied as equalities at the optimum. Thus, from (b) we have that (1) $p_0=\theta_0 W(k_0)$ and from (c) we have that (2) $p_1=p_0+\theta_1(W(k_1)-W(k_0))>p_0$, or equivalently $p_1=\theta_1 W(k_1)-(\theta_1-\theta_0)W(k_0)$. These equations have an interesting economic interpretation. The first equation indicates that the fee to be paid by the low value seller equals her maximum WTP. The second equation indicates that the fee to be paid by the high value seller is higher than p_0 but lower than her maximum WTP, $\theta_1 W(k_1)$, with the difference being just high enough to make option

1 marginally more attractive to a type 1 seller than the alternative. Thus, because of (a), (1) and (2) the maximization problem can be reduced to a simple one-variable optimization of the function $\lambda[\theta_0 W(k_0)+\theta_1(W(k_1)-W(k_0))]+(1-\lambda)\theta_0 W(k_0)$, for $k_0=(1-\lambda)^{-1}(K-\lambda k_1)$ and $0 \leq k_1 \leq \lambda^{-1}K$, and the first order condition (FOC) for optimality can be derived easily. In particular, the following representation of the FOC for an interior solution accepts a simple economic interpretation

(3) $\lambda[\theta_1 W'(k_1)+\lambda(1-\lambda)^{-1}(\theta_1-\theta_0)W'(k_0)]=\lambda\theta_0 W'(k_0)$

Observe that the intermediary's gain from matching an additional potential buyer to group 1 is $\lambda\Delta p_1/\Delta k_1 \approx \lambda[\theta_1 W'(k_1)+\lambda(1-\lambda)^{-1}(\theta_1-\theta_0)W'(k_0)]$ while the intermediary's gain from taking one buyer from group 1 and adding it to group 0 is $(1-\lambda)\Delta p_0/\Delta(-k_1)) \approx \lambda\theta_0 W'(k_0)$. The optimal value, denoted k_1^*, is such that these two quantities are the same. The optimal price policy satisfies $p_1^* > p_0^*$ and in order to make alternative 1 more attractive to the high-value seller it should also be the case that $k_1^* > K > k_0^*$. A corner solution is also possible. If the difference in types $(\theta_1-\theta_0)$ is large enough and/or λ is large enough it could be optimal for the market intermediary to serve only high value sellers, in which case the optimal policy will be one of the form $(p_1=\theta_1 W(k_1),k_1=\lambda^{-1}K)$. That is, potential buyers would be matched evenly among type 1 sellers and the fee would be equal to a type 1 agent's maximum willingness to pay.[d] A corner solution in which only the low-value buyers are served does not exist. As long as there are high value sellers, it is in the best interest of the market intermediary to serve them. The revenues of the market intermediary can be implicitly defined as $\theta_0 W(k_0^*)+\lambda\theta_1(W(k_1^*)-W(k_0^*))$.

Some Simple Analytics

Based on the above model we can derive some simple results. First, an increase in K, λ, θ_0 or θ_1 increases profits for the market intermediary.

Intuitively, the market intermediary will benefit from an increase in the number of potential buyers, the number of high value sellers or the willingness to pay of any seller's type. While we have set the size of the seller's pool equal to one for simplicity, it is intuitively clear that a proportional increase in the pool of sellers would also result in an increase in profits for the market intermediary. What about the optimal price policy $((p_1^*,k_1^*),(p_0^*,k_0^*))$? An increase in the proportion of high value sellers, λ, will induce the market intermediary to extract higher rents from the high value seller. The market intermediary can achieve this goal with an increase in k_1^* and the optimal price p_1^*, as well as a decrease in k_0^* and p_0^* as a result. Similarly, an increase in the WTP of high-value sellers represented by an increase in θ_1 will result in an increase in the optimal k_1^* and p_1^* and a decrease in k_0^* and p_0^*. An increase in the WTP of low-value sellers represented by an increase in θ_0 will result in an increase in k_0^* and p_0^* and a decrease in k_1^* and p_1^*. For illustrative purposes we will demonstrate the last statement analytically taking as given an increase in k_0^* and, consequently, a decrease in k_1^*. Observe that, the optimal price strategy is implicitly defined by equations (1), (2) and (3), taking partial derivatives of equations (1) and (2) with respect to θ_0 we get that

(1') $\partial p_0^*/\partial\theta_0 = W(k_0^*) + \theta_0 W'(k_0^*) \cdot \partial k_0^*/\partial\theta_0$, with $\partial k_0^*/\partial\theta_0 = -\lambda(1-\lambda)^{-1} \cdot \partial k_1^*/\partial\theta_0 > 0$

(2') $\partial p_1^*/\partial\theta_0 = \theta_1 W'(k_1) \cdot \partial k_1^*/\partial\theta_0 - (\theta_1-\theta_0)W'(k_0) \cdot \partial k_0^*/\partial\theta_0 < 0$

Thus, we confirm that $\partial p_0^*/\partial\theta_0 > 0$ since all the elements in the right side of equation (1') have a positive sign. We also confirm that $\partial p_1^*/\partial\theta_0 < 0$ since $\partial k_1^*/\partial\theta_0 < 0$ and all other components in this equation are positive. Finally, as the difference $(\theta_1-\theta_0)$ converges to zero, or $\theta_1=\theta_0=\theta$, the nonlinear pricing policy converges to the optimal single price policy for an homogeneous population of sellers, with $k=K$ and $p=\theta W(K)$.

Alternative Pricing Policies

We now compare the outcomes from three alternative pricing policies. Efficient distribution of buyers across sellers can be achieved by means of a *perfect price discrimination* policy (PPD). In this case, the market intermediary's optimal policy can be represented by a price vector $(p_j^P, k_j^P)_{j=0,1}$, with $p_j^P = \theta_j W(_j^P)$, with FOC for optimality $\theta_0 W'(k_0^P) = \theta_1 W'(k_1^P)$ and with $k_0^P = (1-\lambda)^{-1}(K - \lambda k_1^P)$. In this setting, the market intermediary captures the entire consumer surplus from sellers. This is the optimal policy from the perspective of the market intermediary. This policy results in an efficient allocation of buyers across sellers, in the sense that the marginal value of an additional potential buyer to each group of sellers is the same. In most cases, the market intermediary cannot distinguish between a high-type and a low-type seller. Thus, the PPD is not a viable pricing policy in general.

A viable, second-best, price policy from the perspective of the market intermediary is the *nonlinear pricing* strategy described in the section on theoretical background. We can show that $\theta_1 W'(k_1^*) > \theta_0 W'(k_0^*)$, which implies that the marginal value of an additional potential buyer is higher for high-value sellers' group. Thus, this policy results in an inefficient allocation of buyers across sellers. Also, unlike with PPD, in this case the price paid by the high-value seller is less than her WTP for the reasons already explained, and the difference is equal to $(\theta_1 - \theta_0)W(k_0)$.

Finally, we can also consider a standard *single-price* policy, (p^s, k^s). The optimal single-pricing policy can take two forms depending on whether the market intermediary caters to high-value sellers only or to the whole population of sellers. Clearly, if the market intermediary caters to the high-value seller only we have that $k^s = \lambda^{-1}K$, and the optimal price has to satisfy the condition $\theta_1 W(\lambda^{-1}K) \geq p^s$. That is, the price cannot be higher than the maximum WTP of the high-value seller. Clearly, in this case the optimal price will be equal to $\theta_1 W(\lambda^{-1}K)$ and the market intermediary' revenues will be equal to $\lambda\theta_1 W(\lambda^{-1}K)$. On the other hand, if the market intermediary caters to both types of sellers the optimal pricing policy will be of the form (p^s, k^s) with $k^s = K$ and $\theta_0 W(K) \geq p$. Clearly at the optimum this last inequality will be binding and the market intermediary' revenues will be equal to $\theta_0 W(K)$. It will be optimal for the market intermediary to serve all sellers' types for values of λ relatively close to zero or when the difference $(\theta_1 - \theta_0)$ is small.[e] In this case the price paid by the high-value seller is less than her WTP and equal to $(\theta_1 - \theta_0)W(K)$. This single-price policy also results in an inefficient allocation of buyers across sellers. More precisely, we have that $K = k_1^s < k_1^* < k_1^P$, with k_1^P representing the efficient allocation of potential buyers to high-value sellers.

Until now we have focused our attention on the relationship between the seller and the market intermediary. An additional source of market value that is not explicitly addressed in our model is the consumer welfare extracted from a buyer/seller's match. In particular, if a match with a high-value seller produces a larger welfare for the buyer then it may be the case that even k_1^P is too small from the perspective of maximizing social welfare. We have also ignored other issues of potential important in two-sided markets like competition between market intermediaries, network effects, and the price elasticity of each side of the market (Bolton & Tieman, 2005; Eisenmann, Parker & Van Alstyne 2006). Thus, it is conceivable that other types of price policies not considered in this section may be preferred in certain kinds of two-side markets (Rochet & Tirole, 2005).[f]

EMPIRICAL APPLICATION: THE MARKET AND THE DATA

Sellers on eBay offer objects for auction by posting a description of the item being auctioned, including pictures. Buyers browse through thousands of auctions organized by category and subcategory; buyers can also use a powerful search engine. Additional information about eBay can be found in Bajari and Hortacsu (2004).

Between August and December 2004, we collected eBay data on art auctions from a group of "self-representing artists," that is, artists who sell their own artwork on eBay without representation. The data were collected without any specific criteria in mind other than the artists included in our dataset were selected from a group of artists who posted items on auction regularly, as reflected by their completed listings. All the auctions in our dataset follow the English Auction format.[g] The key feature of this type of auction is that the highest bidder at the end of the auction wins the item at a price equal to the second highest bid. Also, because of the design of the English auction it can be shown that the final auction price should coincide with the maximum willingness to pay of the second highest bidder, at least in theory.

For each auction, we collected four different types of information: item characteristics, auction characteristics, bidding history, and artist reputation. Characteristics specific to the object being auctioned include information on the height, width, medium (acrylic, oil, etc.), and ground (stretch canvas, paper, wood, etc.). Auction characteristics include the opening bid, the shipping and handling fees and the "style" or eBay category in which the object is being listed (abstract, pop, whimsical, etc.). At the end of the auction the final auction price is collected if the auction was successful. Because auctions on eBay follow the second price English auction format, the final auction price represent the maximum willingness to pay by the second highest bidder, if there are two or more bidders, or the reservation

price in the case of a single bidder. We also collect information on the type of feedback received by the seller in previous transactions (positive, neutral, negative). We use these data to define two variables: the first one represents the number of unique buyers prior to the current auction, which could be interpreted as a measure of the artist's customer base on eBay, and the second one represents the feedback rating as reported on eBay defined as the percentage of positive feedbacks. Descriptive statistics for a set of characteristics for the artworks auctioned and other relevant variables of the auctions in our sample are reported in Tables 1 and 2. We observe that all of the artists in our sample have excellent feedback ratings, with most of them having perfect feedback ratings. In addition, most of the artists in our sample have ample experience selling on eBay. FP paintings are more than twice the size of non-FP paintings in average. There are also significant differences in the distribution of FP/non-FP paintings according to style, medium and ground, as illustrated in Table 2. In particular, FP auctions seem to be highly concentrated among these characteristics that command the highest prices: for style, these are abstract, modern, and pop; for medium, these are acrylic, oil, and collage; and for ground it is primarily one, stretch canvas. According to the auctions' FP/not-FP status, in our data, FP items sell with 88% probability while non-FP items sell with 49% probability. For the subgroup of successful auctions FP-auctions attract more than five bidders while non-FP auctions attract less than two bidders in average. Also, the average market value of FP paintings is $223, or more than four times higher than that of non-FP paintings, which is $49. Thus, the data indicates that FP paintings are significantly different from non-FP paintings. Overall, these results suggest, with caveats, that the benefits derived by the artist from the FP status is an increase in the probability of sale and an increase in the final selling price.

Before we proceed with a thorough econometric analysis of the data we use simple reduced form regression methods in order to understand to what extent the information contained in our dataset contributes to explaining the observed variation in auction prices. Table 3 presents results from logarithmic regressions of sale price as a function of painting and artist's characteristics. It also presents results from linear probability models for the FP choice. Model 1 describes a log-linear regression of final auction price as a function of painting size measured in square feet. We find that size is an important determinant of price. A one square feet increase in size in a two square feet painting is predicted to increase price by approximately 45%. This simple model explains 64% of the variation in sale price as measured by the R-square. Model 2 including controls for artist feedback, size, style, medium, and ground, explains approximately 77% of the variation in prices.

In Models 3 and 4 we report estimation results from discrete choice models of the artist's FP choice. A simple linear probability model including controls for painting size only explains approximately 31% of the variation in FP choice. A linear probability model including controls for artist's feedback, size, style, medium, and ground, explains approximately 47% of the variation in FP choice. The size of paintings appears to be an important determinant of FP status. The coefficients associated to size are highly significant in both models estimated. A one-unit increase in size, measured in square-feet, increases the FP probability by 8% in the more general model. Overall, the information available in the data does a remarkable job at explaining sale prices and FP choices.

THE EMPIRICAL METHODOLOGY

For each art-auction in our data we observe a vector of characteristics described in the previous section, the FP status of the auction and the bid history including all bids, except for the highest

one, if the auction is successful or the opening bid if the auction ends with zero bids. In our empirical specification we model the FP choice on the part of the artist as well as the final selling price of the artwork both for FP auctions and for standard auctions. Thus, the econometric model consists of three equations, one for each of the processes under study: (1) the FP choice; (2) the sale price for FP auctions; (3) the sale price for standard auctions. Next we describe each one of these equations separately. After that, we present the econometric methodology for joint estimation of our model equations.

Equation 1: The "Featured Plus!" Choice. Featuring an auction increases the number of potential buyers and thus, increases expected revenues. There are also nonpecuniary returns from featuring a painting, which may influence an artist's FP choice. For instance, artists may also extract utility from the fact that their painting is being viewed, and appreciated, by many potential buyers.[h] For this reason, we choose not to model the FP choice as a profit maximizing decision on the part of the artist. Instead, we propose a flexible discrete-choice framework. Formally, denote by F_{ij}^* the unobservable net utility of artist j from featuring artwork i. In this framework, $F_{ij} = I(F_{ij}^* > 0)$ represents the FP choice, with $I(F_{ij}^* > 0)$ an index function equal to one if $\{F_{ij}^* > 0\}$ and equal to zero otherwise. We assume that $F_{ij}^* = F^*(Z_{ij}) + \varepsilon_{ij}$, with Z_{ij} representing a vector of characteristics, and ε_{ij} representing other idiosyncratic factors affecting this choice. In this framework, the probability of the FP choice is denoted as $P_{ij}^1 = P(F_{ij}^* > 0)$ while the alternative is denoted as $P_{ij}^0 = 1 - P_{ij}^1$. For simplicity we will assume a probit specification.

Equations 2 & 3: The Transaction Price. The final transaction price is specific to the artist's FP choice. Thus, we model the final price for auctioned item i using a standard log-normal regression equation with a different specification for FP and non-FP auctions. Formally, assume $ln\ p_{ij}^F = \varphi^F(Z_{ij}) + u_{ij}^F$, with F=1,0 representing the FP and non-FP states, Z_{ij} representing a vector of characteristics for item i from artist j and u_{ij} representing the price's random component measuring other auction-specific determinants of prices not included in the vector of explanatory variables.

The Likelihood: The opening bid of an auction, denoted by b_{ij}, is set by the seller and represents the minimum value that the seller is willing to accept. As a result, only these items that are valued by the potential buyers at a price above b_{ij} will be sold, and we observe the transaction price only for those items that sell. For those items that do not sell we only know that the market valuation of the item is less than b_{ij}. Denote the density and distribution of u_{ij}^F as $g_u^F(\cdot)$ and $G_u^F(\cdot)$, respectively. When the item is sold, the probability of a transaction price p_{ij} is equal to $g_{ij}^F = g^F(ln\,p_{ij}^F - \varphi^F(Z_{ij}))$. Similarly, when the item is not sold, and the transaction price is not observed, we can only infer that { $ln\,p_{ij}^F = \varphi^F(Z_{ij}) + u_{ij}^F < ln\,b_{ij}$ }, with associated probability $G_{ij}^F = G_u^F(ln\,b_{ij} - \varphi^F(Z_{ij}))$. With this information at hand, we can determine the contribution to the likelihood of auction ij,

$$LF(Z_{ij}, b_{ij}, p_{ij}; \ s = s_{ij}, F=F_{ij}) = P_{ij}^F \cdot (s_{ij} \cdot g_{ij}^F + (1 - s_{ij})G_{ij}^F),$$

with F=0,1 denoting the FP choice, and s_{ij} equal to one if the item is sold, and zero otherwise. While we have imposed a parametric assumption of normality for the residuals ε_{ij}, u_{ij}^0 and u_{ij}^1 this assumption should have little impact on the results given the superior explanatory power of the observed vector of painting/auction/artist characteristics.

Finally, to ascertain the validity of our econometric specification we augment our model by allowing for the presence of unobserved heterogeneity. More precisely, if there are relevant

elements in the vector of explanatory variables Z_{ij} that are unobservable to the econometrician this could introduce an omitted variable bias in our analysis. We can incorporate this concept into our econometric model by assuming that $Z_{ij} = (X_{ij}, \delta_{ij})$ with X_{ij} representing the observed vector of characteristics and δ_{ij} representing an unobserved component of Z_{ij}, or unobserved heterogeneity. Empirically, we address this issue using the popular semiparametric approach described in Heckman and Singer (1984). Subject to the standard assumptions of a random effects model, this approach hypothesizes a discrete distribution with finite support as a good approximation to the true distribution of the unobserved heterogeneity component. In this framework, the contribution to the likelihood of an observation can be computed as

$$LF(X_{ij}, b_{ij}, p_{ij}; s = s_{ij}, F=F_{ij}) = \sum_{h=1,\ldots H} q_h \cdot LF(X_{ij}, b_{ij}, p_{ij}; s = s_{ij}, F=F_{ij}, \delta_{ij} = \delta_h),$$

with H representing the number of points of support of the discrete distribution of δ_{ij}, $q_h \geq 0$ the probability associated to a realization δ_h, with $\sum_{h=1,\ldots H} q_h = 1$, and $\sum_{h=1,\ldots H} q_h \cdot \eta_h = 0$ a mean restriction required for identification.[i]

EMPIRICAL RESULTS

Model specification: We estimate several versions of the empirical model described in the previous section. In the first model estimated, a vector of instruments captures differences across auctions. These instruments include two measures of the artist's reputation; characteristics of the object being auctioned describing dimensions, styles, medium, and ground; and characteristics of the artist auctioning the painting. If there are differences in quality across artists, in addition to those captured by the vector of instruments, the model parameters could potentially be biased. For this reason, in the second model estimated we also include artists' specific fixed effects. In addition, if there are differences in the quality of paintings that are not captured by the vector of observable characteristics and artists' specific fixed effects, the estimation results will be biased due to selection of paintings into FP/non-FP auctions according to the unobserved quality component. Thus, the third model estimated builds on the previous models by allowing for the possible existence of unobserved differences across auctions in addition to these measured by the vector of instruments and the artists' specific fixed effects. Therefore, this model controls for two sources of unobserved heterogeneity: artist's specific unobserved heterogeneity, that is constant across auctions from a specific artist, and object specific unobserved heterogeneity that varies across auctions. The implementation of this model is described at the end of the previous section. To preserve the simplicity and parsimony of the models, we exclude from the final model specification variables that are highly insignificant (t-values close to zero), and small in magnitude, in those instances in which this does not affect the overall interpretation of results.

Interpretation of Results: Qualitatively the results are similar to the single-linear-equation results of Table 3. However, the advantages of model presented in the section on imperial methodology cannot be overlooked. Our model controls for censoring and the differences in sale price between FP and non-FP auctions as well as explicitly takes into account the potential endogeneity of the FP choice. Furthermore, the maximum likelihood joint estimation of the model equations improves estimation efficiency. The results for models with and without artist specific fixed effects are similar. For this reason, we present estimation results for the models with fixed effects only (Tables 4 and 5).

Interestingly, we observe that the contribution of the unobserved heterogeneity component to each model equation in Table 5 is small in mag-

nitude and insignificant. This is consistent with findings from our reduced form analysis indicating that the vector of observable characteristics does a very good job at explaining most of the observed variation in the endogenous variables. Thus, the evidence strongly suggests that the vector of observable characteristics accurately captures differences in characteristics across paintings. A likelihood-ration hypothesis test shows that unobserved heterogeneity has no statistically significant impact on the results. Thus, we will concentrate our attention in the fixed effects model of Table 4 without unobserved heterogeneity. As observed in reduced form models, size is an important positive determinant of FP status and price. A one feet increase in size increases price by about 15% for FP paintings and by about 30% for non-FP paintings. Taking into account that FP paintings are more than twice than non-FP paintings in size, the effect of size on FP/non-FP paintings are similar. Another important determinant of price is the artist's feedback rate. A 1% increase in the good feedback rating increases average sale price by 38% for non-FP paintings and by 30% for FP paintings, but only the first effect is significant probably due to the limited variation in this variable across FP paintings. In addition, an increase in 100 unique buyers increases average prices by about 7%. Finally, some other variables that we do not discuss here associated to style, medium and ground also have a significant impact in sale price, but these effects are in general not consistent across the FP/non-FP groups.

Policy simulation. Here we attempt to understand the effect of the "FP" non-linear pricing strategy on the revenues of eBay as well as the revenues of the artists and the probability of sale. To accomplish that goal, we use our estimated model of Table 4 to simulate the effects of the FP non-linear pricing strategy on this market. The results from this simulation exercise are presented in Table 6. The upper section of this table includes real revenues calculated directly from the data while the lower section includes values from our policy simulation exercise. Looking at these values we observe that average seller revenues are also significantly higher for FP Paintings, $168, than for paintings from standard auctions $37. Overall, the 508 FP auctions in our sample generate $79,065, while the 1,729 standard auctions generate $31,181, in artists' revenues. Also, FP paintings generate most of eBay's revenues in our sample. Of the close to $16,000 in revenues about $13,500 are generated by FP auctions and only $2,500 are generated by standard auctions. While FP auctions only account for about 20% of the auctions, their sale price and their probability of sale are much higher than that of standard auctions, and this contributes to their much higher fees paid to eBay. But more important is the $20 FP fee which by itself represents about seven times the average eBay's revenues from non-FP auctions.

The lower section of Table 6 includes results from our policy simulation exercise. Our theoretical model suggests that standard fees would be higher under a single-pricing policy, that is, one that does not allow for the FP option. However, without knowledge of eBay's profit function we cannot determine quantitatively the magnitude of this effect. Thus, we pursue a second best alternative that consists of asking how market revenues for eBay and for the artists would change if all the FP auctions in our data were posted as standard auctions instead. To answer this question we perform policy simulations using the estimated model of Table 4. For a given vector o parameters and for any given FP auction in our data we generate 100 realizations of the model residuals and generate the corresponding market outcomes. Also, we generate the standard errors for our simulated values by repeating the simulation exercise for 100 draws of the vector of parameters generated from the empirical parameters' distribution. Only these values in Table 6 that are generated by simulation are presented in bold along with the associated

standard errors. The simulated/predicted probability of sale is 66%, which is significantly less that the 87% observed for FP auctions but still much higher than the 49% probability of sale for standard auctions. Thus, our results suggest that the observed differences in the probability of sale between standard and FP auctions are in part the result of a selection effect by which the best paintings are usually posted as FP auctions. The simulated/predicted average revenues for eBay are $7 which is significantly less than the $28 observed in our data. In particular, the observed eBay's revenues from FP auctions are 13,425 but when the FP option is not allowed in our simulations revenues from this group of auctions are reduced to 2,874. This provides additional evidence of the importance of the FP fees for eBay. The average simulated/predicted revenues for artists are $152, a 10% decrease over the real revenues in FP auctions. However, selection also plays a role in our simulations. Since the probability of sale is lower in our simulations than in the real data, the average quality of paintings sold in our simulation exercise is higher than the average quality of paintings sold in a real FP auction. If we account for this selection effect, the reduction in price is about 20%, or $32 which is higher than the $20 FP fee collected by eBay. Thus, our simulations suggest that FP pricing is a worthwhile option for sellers of good quality paintings. Furthermore, combining revenues of artists on eBay we observe that FP auctions generate $92,493 in market revenues while the simulated alternative would generate only $51,097, or a 45% reduction in market revenues.

CONCLUSION

This paper investigates the effect of a specific type of nonlinear price policy in the market for art by self representing artists on eBay. For several years now, eBay has been using a simple nonlinear pricing strategy, or as they call it "Featured

Plus!" (FP). This type of pricing policy works by giving sellers the option to incur an extra fee at the time of posting their items for sale and in return having these items listed first when buyers search for specific categories.

As suggested by the theory and illustrated by our empirical analysis, auctions for high value items are for the most part concentrated in the group of FP auctions. FP auctions attract a much larger number of potential buyers than standard auctions. Also, this kind of auction commands a higher price than standard auctions and a higher probability of sale. The size of the artwork seems to be an important determinant of price and FP status even after controlling for artists' fixed effects. Also, artists' that have been in the market for a long period of time, and that have a large customer base, benefit from the existence of repeated buyers. EBay allows buyers to rate their shopping experience, this rating is used to create a reputation index and we use this index as a measure of artists' reputation. Interestingly, this measure of reputation has a significant positive effect on the selling price.

We use the results from our empirical methodology to conduct simulations based on the estimated model with artists' fixed effects. The results indicate that the FP policy has an important positive effect on revenues for eBay and for the sellers in this market. Auctions for high-value items benefit from the existence of the FP option even though the associated fee to eBay is high. Non-FP auctions are more common than FP auctions but contribute significantly lower fees to eBay than FP auctions and account for a small proportion of the overall revenues. Our theoretical and empirical results also suggest that the FP option acts as a coordination mechanism that facilitates the match of the best artists and the best artwork with buyers looking for the best art. These results underscore the relevance of pricing policies and other kinds of market mechanisms that promote the best match between buyers and sellers.

REFERENCES

Bajari, P., & Hortacsu, A. (2004): "Economic Insights from Internet Auctions," Journal of Economic Literature, Vol. XLII, 457-486.

Baker, M., & Melino, A. (2000), "Duration Dependence and Nonparametric Heterogeneity: A Monte Carlo Study," Journal of Econometrics 96, 357-393.

Bolton W., & Tieman, A.F. (2005) "Skewed Pricing in Two-Sided Markets: An IO Approach," Available at SSRN: http://ssrn.com/abstract=665103.

Canals-Cerda, J.J., & Gurmu, S. (2007), *"Semiparametric Competing Risk Analysis," Econometrics Journal, Vol. 10, No. 10, pp.* 193-215.

Cowen, T., & Tabarrok, A. (2000). "An Economic Theory of Avant-Garde and Popular Art, or High and Low Culture," Southern Economic Journal, Vol. 67, No. 2, pp. 232-253.

Eisenmann, T.E., G.G. Parker, M. Van Alstyne (2006). "Strategies for Two-Sided Markets." Harvard Business Review, October, 1-12 .

Heckman J., & Singer, B. (1984) "A Method for Minimizing the Impact of Distributional Assumptions in Econometric Models for Duration Data." Econometrica, Vol. 52, No. 2., pp. 271-320.

Klemperer, P. (2004). "Auctions: Theory and Practice." Princeton University Press. Also available online at http://www.paulklemperer.org/index.htm.

Laffont, J.J., & Martimort, D. "The Theory of Incentives: The Principal-Agent Model," Princeton University Press, 2002.

Maskin, E. & Riley, J.G. (1984) "Monopoly With Incomplete Information." Rand Journal of Economics, 15, Summer.

Mussa, M., & Rosen, S. (1978) "Monopoly and product quality." Journal of Economic Theory 18, 301-317.

Rochet, J.J., & Tirole, J. (2005) "Two-Sided Markets: A Progress Report." The Rand Journal of Economics, forthcoming.

Tirole, J. (1988) "The Theory of Industrial Organization." The MIT press.

ENDNOTES

a   Katrina Beck provided excellent editorial assistance. Excellent research assistance was provided by David Donofrio, Tyson Gatto, Woong Tae Chung, Kelvin Tang and Jason Pearcy. We are grateful to Kristen Stein, artist and eBay power-seller, for answering many questions on the functioning of eBay and on bidders and artist behavior. These are the views of the author, and should not be attributed to any other person or organization, including the Federal Reserve Bank of Philadelphia.

b   That is, a seller's willingness to pay for a match with an additional potential buyer is decreasing with k.

c   Seminal contributions to the nonlinear pricing literature include Mussa and Rosen (1978) and Maskin and Riley (1984). The model developed in this section is closely related to the exposition in Tirole (1988).

d   In a more complex model in which two types of sellers serve two different types of buyers it may always be optimal for the market intermediary to serve both types of sellers.

e   In particular, under the reasonable assumption that the market intermediary's marginal cost of service is zero, it will be profitable to serve only high-value sellers if their proportion λ satisfies $\lambda\theta_1 W(\lambda^{-1}K) \geq \theta_0 W(K)$.

f   "For two-sided networks, pricing is a complicated affair. Platform providers have to choose a price for each side, factoring in the impact on the other side's growth and willingness to pay" (Eisenmann, Parker & Van Alstyne 2006).

g   Definition of English auction from wikipedia.org: "In an English auction (also called an Open-outcry auction), the auctioneer begins the auction with the reserve price (lowest acceptable price) and then takes larger and larger bids from the customers until no one will increase the bid. The item is then sold to the highest bidder." Also, see Klemperer(2004) for a comprehensive survey of the literature on Auctions.

h   See Cowen and Tabarrok (2000) for an economic model of the artist's decision making.

i   In our empirical work H is set to 2. A similar assumption is made in many other papers using the Heckman-Singer approach. Montecarlo studies by Baker and Melino (2000) and Canals-Cerda and Gurmu (2007) show that this assumption usually performs very well.

APPENDIX

Table 1. Descriptive statistics for relevant variables

	Feature Plus! Posting				Regular Posting			
	Average	**Std**	**Min**	**Max**	**Average**	**Std**	**Min**	**Max**
Square Feet	5.40	3.10	0.44	24.00	1.92	2.40	0.02	24.00
eBay Feedback	99.92	0.15	99.24	100.00	99.73	0.31	98.99	100.00
# of feedbacks	4.80	2.69	0.70	16.22	5.25	2.55	0.75	16.50
Sale Price	223.25	132.00	21.10	1441.41	49.37	55.99	3.01	595.55
# of bidders*	5.26	2.71	1	17	2.35	1.61	1	10
# of bids*	13.47	9.09	1	49	4.04	4.37	1	29
% Sold	87.60%				48.93%			
N. Obs.	508				1729			

Note: the '# of unique feedbacks' variable is measured in hundreds of feedbacks by unique buyers. Sale price includes shipping costs. (*) Indicates average values computed with respect to sold items.

Table 2. Frequency distributions and average selling price by subgroups

	Feature Plus! Auction			Regular Auction		
STYLE	**Av. Price**	**Freq.**	**% Freq.**	**Av. Price**	**Freq.**	**% Freq.**
Abstract	247.43	341	67.13	84.09	547	31.64
Contemporary	187.32	83	16.34	111.16	443	25.62
Cubist	194.64	68	13.39	71.95	230	13.30
Folk	101.79	44	8.66	38.57	401	23.19
Modern	254.19	324	63.78	79.93	232	13.42
Urban	118.14	6	1.18	30.64	514	29.73
Pop	176.58	160	31.50	36.52	1106	63.97
Other	106.01	122	24.01	37.09	977	56.51
MEDIUM						
Acrylic	231.22	300	59.06	55.35	913	52.81
Pen and Ink	0	0	0.00	32.49	33	1.91
Collage	236.90	66	12.99	34.91	468	27.07
Oil	206.74	138	27.17	85.10	187	10.82
Other	40.15	4	0.33	28.29	128	7.41

continued on following page

Table 2. continued

GROUND

Stretch Canvas	228.60	485	95.47	83.74	624	36.09
Canvas Panel	103.82	4	0.79	33.76	183	10.58
Cardboard	142.84	3	0.59	23.05	177	10.24
Paper	65.84	7	1.38	25.31	514	29.73
Other	159.64	9	1.77	65.45	231	13.36

Table 3. Results from log-linear regressions and linear probability models

Dependent	Log-Linear Regressions				Linear Probability Model			
	Model 1		Model 2		Model 3		Model 4	
Variable	Log(sale price)				"Feature Plus!" indicator			
	Coef.	**t-val.**	**Coef.**	**t-val.**	**Coef.**	**t-val.**	**Coef.**	**t-val.**
FEEDBACK								
# feedbacks			0.029	3.56			0.007	2.11
eBay Feedback			0.336	3.96			0.237	8.05
DIMENSION								
Square-Feet	0.546	38.04	0.307	18.1	0.144	26.91	0.086	13.26
Square-Feet^2	-0.025	21.91	-0.011	10.2	-0.006	-15.62	-0.003	-7.48
STYLE								
Abstract			-0.229	3.08			-0.035	-1.06
Contemporary			-0.078	1.51			-0.066	-3.23
Cubist			-0.081	1.23			-0.031	-1.19
Folk			0.009	0.20			-0.062	-3.30
Modern			0.581	12.5			0.226	11.18
Urban			0.151	2.61			-0.059	-2.60
Pop			-0.222	3.10			0.064	1.92
MEDIUM								
Acrylic			-0.302	2.97			-0.042	-1.23
Pen and Ink			-0.273	1.80			-0.044	-0.71
Collage			-0.146	1.43			0.083	2.36
Oil			0.063	0.58			0.144	3.76

continued on following page

Table 3. continued

GROUND

Stretch Canvas		0.544	7.30	0.218	8.66
Canvas Panel		-0.081	0.90	-0.026	-0.80
Cardboard		-0.302	3.29	0.088	2.62
Paper		-0.310	3.67	0.068	2.31
R-square	0.6368	0.7685		0.3170	0.4785

T-values are in absolute value. Log-linear regression models are estimated using the sub-sample of sold paintings. For the linear probability model, the results are qualitatively very similar to those obtained using probit and logit models.

Table 4. Estimation results for the model with fixed effects

	Item Valuation					
	Featured Choice		Featured Item		Non-Featured Item	
	Coef.	t-val.	Coef.	t-val.	Coef.	t-val.
FEEDBACK						
# feedbacks	0.0540	0.92	0.0783	3.89	0.0642	6.61
eBay Feedback	5.4315	6.97	0.3069	0.81	0.3850	3.41
DIMENSION						
Square-Feet	0.7899	9.58	0.1496	5.85	0.3007	16.26
Square-Feet²	-0.0248	5.81	-0.0043	2.87	-0.0112	10.43
STYLE						
Abstract	0.1255	0.34	-0.2785	1.76	-0.0406	0.41
Contemporary	-0.2426	0.84	0.2007	2.38	-0.1305	2.23
Cubist	-0.5625	1.39	-0.3158	2.21	0.3867	4.67
Folk	-0.5756	1.96	-0.4005	3.72	0.1903	3.48
Modern	1.7585	6.61	0.3124	4.38	0.2635	3.71
Urban	-1.5717	2.85	0.2172	0.95	0.3820	6.26
Pop	0.7460	2.12	-0.2632	1.81	0.1153	1.26
MEDIUM						
Acrylic	-1.6979	5.18	0.0752	0.92	-0.0188	0.20
Pen and Ink					0.0223	0.16
Collage					0.1184	1.14
Oil	-0.9539	2.09	0.1581	1.18	-0.0821	0.76
GROUND						
Stretch Canvas	2.9457	8.62	0.3536	2.77	0.6318	8.75
Canvas Panel					0.2108	2.45

continued on following page

Table 4. continued

					-0.1265	1.52
Cardboard					-0.1265	1.52
Paper					-0.1488	1.69
Sigma			0.4478	24.77	0.5675	22.63
Artist FE.	Yes		Yes		Yes	
	N. Obs.	2237		**LLF**	-7224.60	

T-values are in absolute value. For featured items we include a single "stretch canvas" dummy

Table 5. Estimation results for the model with unobserved heterogeneity & fixed effects

	Item Valuation					
	Featured Choice		**Featured Item**		**Non-Featured Item**	
	Coef.	**t-val.**	**Coef.**	**t-val.**	**Coef.**	**t-val.**
FEEDBACK						
# feedbacks	0.0308	0.49	0.0739	3.52	0.0641	6.61
eBay Feedback	5.3624	6.52	0.3070	0.80	0.3865	3.43
DIMENSION						
Square-Feet	0.7910	8.84	0.1481	5.75	0.2992	16.16
Square-Feet^2	-0.0244	5.23	-0.0042	2.73	-0.0111	10.30
STYLE						
Abstract	0.1091	0.29	-0.2940	1.87	-0.0453	0.46
Contemporary	-0.2905	0.96	0.2052	2.43	-0.1318	2.25
Cubist	-0.4748	1.13	-0.2911	2.01	0.3890	4.69
Folk	-0.8590	2.76	-0.4273	3.93	0.1925	3.52
Modern	1.7963	6.46	0.3189	4.50	0.2633	3.70
Urban	-2.2960	2.41	0.0766	0.18	0.3819	6.25
Pop	0.7408	2.06	-0.2753	1.92	0.1087	1.19
MEDIUM						
Acrylic	-1.6625	4.81	0.0900	1.09	-0.0163	0.17
Pen and Ink					0.0228	0.16
Collage					0.1239	1.20
Oil	-1.2806	2.52	0.1690	1.28	-0.0760	0.70
GROUND						
Stretch Canvas	3.3071	8.19	0.3827	2.73	0.6275	8.67
Canvas Panel					0.2054	2.38

continued on following page

Table 5. continued

Cardboard				-0.1294	1.55
Paper				-0.1544	1.76
Sigma		0.4459	24.13	0.5675	22.58
Unobs. Het. Coef.		-0.0015	0.37	0.0126	0.00
Artist FE.	Yes		Yes		Yes
N. Obs.	2237		**LLF**	-7220.17	

T-values are in absolute value. For featured items we include a single "stretch canvas" dummy.

Table 6. Simulation of eBay Revenues and Artists' Revenues Based on the Model of Table 4

	Market Revenues						
	Average Revenues				**Total Revenues**		
	Sold Paintings		**Unsold Paintings**				
	Non-FP	FP	Non-FP	FP	Non-FP	FP	Overall
EBay Revenues	2.94	28.45	1.50	23.01	2502	13428	15930
Seller Revenues	36.64	167.51			31181	79065	110245
					TOTAL:	92493	126176

	Not "FP" Option Allowed: Simulated Revenues for Paintings in FP Group				
	Average Revenues			**Total Revenues**	
	Sold Paintings		**Unsold Paintings**		
	FP		FP		FP
EBay Revenues	7.17 (0.98)		2.72 (0.32)		2874
Seller Revenues	152.4 (39)				51097
				TOTAL:	53970
% Sold	0.66 (0.12)				

Seller revenues are net of shipping costs and eBay revenues. Simulated values represented in bold

Chapter VIII
The E–Mode of Brand Positioning:
The Need for an Online Positioning Interface

S. Ramesh Kumar
IIM, Bangalore

ABSTRACT

Brand positioning is a crucial strategy to any brand's strategy. Given the rapid development of technology and it impact on online strategies, changing lifestyles of consumers and the consumer interaction required as a part of contemporary brand strategy, there may be need for brands to synergize their positioning strategies with online positioning strategies. This would enable brands to adapt to an environment which is increasingly becoming digital. The paper after taking into consideration the published literature on brand positioning, attempts to formulate online positioning strategies using different aspects of brand positioning, price, customer interactivity and consumer community orientation. Implications for marketing managers are provided.

INTRODUCTION

Brand positioning has been the cornerstone of marketing strategy in the recent times in fast moving consumer product categories, durable categories and services. It would be difficult to think of a strategy for any brand without a well thought-out strategy for entering the consumer's psyche (Ries and Trout,1987).

Thus, Nike's success could be attributed to the positioning that it is worn by the world's best athletes as reflected by the Michael Jordan campaign (Trout and Rivkin,1999). While the challenges concerned with positioning strategies still remain with the marketers, the environment has been changing with the influence of web-based marketing. In the year which closed in Sept.1999, there was an increase of 221.5% of the goods which were traded over the Internet. Consumer goods registered an increase of 665% increase over the same period (Wind and Mahajan,2001).

The consumer is becoming more evolved in terms of information control. The consumer is no longer likely to receive information without the interactive component being present when he/she gets involved in consumer decision making. Hence, the traditional positioning strategies may not succeed as segments are becoming smaller and less homogenous (Solomon,2003). A number of established brands have also started using the Internet and the Web to adapt to the changing environment. Some of the global brands to make this transition include Levi's, Dockers and Barbie (Ries and Ries, 2000).

Even in a developing country like India where less than 5% of the total retail sales come from organized supermarkets/malls and the penetration of the Internet is miniscule, supermarkets like Subiksha and FabMall(www.fabmall.com) have started online marketing of groceries and consumer goods. Fabmall started as an online store at Bangalore with books and misic and over a period of time has added several categories like groceries jewelry and gifts. It has since added physical retail stores around the city of Bangalore. Today, its model attempts to synergize the advantages of retail outlets and online dimensions. The physical retailing model of the company has grown from revenues of Rupees(Rs) 4 million to Rs 15 million per month from April 2003 to November 2003 (Kumar and Mahadevan,2003).

The trend of having multiple channels to reach the consumers could result in building a good brand besides the profitability aspects. Subiksha is a discount grocery store at Chennai(previously known as Madras) which deals with low priced groceries. The store has a network of stores around the city and has started online operations by which customers could order groceries. The unique aspect of this store is that the residential neighborhoods are located close to the network of stores and hence the delivery charges which are normally significant get saved.

This integration of physical and online presence is commonly observed in global brands. Charles Schwab transacts 80% of its business over the Internet but increased its offline presence as both channels would be required to service its customers (Lindstorm, Peppers and Rogers,2001). Tesco, the UK based retail chain with 600 stores, 60,000 product-lines and 10 million customers who are members of a loyalty program has illustrated how the combination of online and offline retailing could develop a successful retail brand. Amazon.com with a customer base of 8.4 million and 66% of sales being contributed by repeat purchasers is a brand which has an association of customizing products (books, music etc) to the needs of consumers by suggesting a number of options which they may not have otherwise considered (Rust, Zeithamal and Lemon ,2000).

Given the rapid challenges in the marketing environment and consumer lifestyles and the growing influence of technology with regard to consumer retailing and marketing communications (e.g. advergaming and SMS messages), there is a distinctive need to explore new conceptual frameworks for the concept of positioning. There are two stages which would lead to the development of such frameworks which could assist practitioners in a marketing environment. The first stage is concerned with analyzing the existing dimensions of brand positioning with a view to examine how they could be used for a brand which will have both online and offline retail channels. The next stage is to develop a framework for categories of consumer products from the insights gained from the first stage.

Different Dimensions of Brand Positioning

The challenge for marketers in India is not just to create an online experience: there is a need to "move" the consumer from the traditional ways of buying to the digital ways of buying after understanding certain shopping aspects which are unique to the Indian context. While some of these aspects may invole providing a kiosk in a traditional store for customers to browse though several dimensions of brand comparison, the most critical factor is the manner in which such prospective buying experiences are communicated. Given the Indian diversity with regard to demographics and psychographics, positioning challenges need to be market-specific and product-specific. The second challenge is to ensure that positioning propositions of brands are fullfilled and this involves infrastructure demanded by positioning startegies in a manner which would bring in price differentiation.

There are various dimensions which could be used for positioning a brand. Brand equity is a set of assets and liabilities linked to a brand, its name or symbol. Brand loyalty, brand name awareness, perceived quality, brand associations and other brand assets like patents and trademarks are some of the components of brand equity (Aaker,1991). Brand positioning involves developing, nurturing and sustaining brand associations and brand imagery in such a way that it offers a long-term competitive edge through the consistency of such associations which could be called as sustainable competitive proposition or SCP (Kumar,2003). Hence, most components of brand equity could be used to develop positioning strategies.

Loyalty as a Positioning Dimension

Amazon.com uses loyalty as a strong positioning strategy. It provides a customer not just value in terms of the price of the merchandise. Rather, its unique value comes from specific strategies like recommendation of book and music titles after capturing the customer's preferences on its database. It found that customers who bought books also bought CDs and expanded its product-line base to satisfy the base of loyal customers. It could be noted that the interactive nature of online marketing was effectively made use of by Amazon.com and this enabled the company to sustain a dialog with its customers.

Peapod, an online grocery shopping store in the U.S. has sustained the loyalty of its customers based on its "virtual supermarket" strategy. Customers could access a list of categories, brands in the categories,(continue)brands by package size, by unit price or in some cases even by nutritional value. Customers could have standardized and special shopping lists which could be used by them any time. The customer retention rate for Peopod is 80%.the retail outlet also uses the Internet to develop "learning relationships" by which it could adapt itself to the needs of consumers (Gilmore and Pine,2000).

In both the Amazon.com and Peapod cases, the organization uses customization and interaction with customers to gain loyalty and the outlets are positioned on "value-based customization". In contrast, in a typical brick-and-mortar outlet the loyalty is built up in a different manner. Tesco has collected massive data on its customers and divided them into 5000 needs segments. It sends coupon assortments to various customers depending on their needs and the redemption rate of these coupons is 90%(Kotler,2003). From 1980 to 1993,the number of sales promotion coupons distributed tripled from 100 billion to 300 billion in the U.S and the number of coupons redeemed has only grown over only by about a third since 1981 (Hallberg,1995).

Shoppers Stop in India which has a considerable degree of loyalty also attempts to research the needs of consumers in terms to formulate its loyalty programs. Large offline retail outlets could develop loyalty-related positioning by analyzing the purchase data of consumers belonging to different segments. As the number of consumers in these offline retail formats are likely to be large in numbers, "value based loyalty" arises from the purchase patterns. FabMall uses recency of purchase, frequency of purchase and monetary value(RFM) to formulate its loyalty programs. RFM could be useful both in offline and online retailing environment. It is possible for a multiple channel retailer (with both online and offline channels) to follow strategies which would enhance loyalty. In a country like India where shopping for both fast moving consumer goods and durable categories like TV, music system and kitchen appliances could be a ritual of entertainment, it is possible for a retailer to provide information on the web and attract retail traffic base on the information being given on the web for a specific segment (Kumar,2002).

By this approach while the information provided enables a consumer to be appraised of the offerings of the company, the "touch and feel" factor- a major prerequisite in the Indian shopping context- is also retained. This would be possible only for a specific segment of a market (niche) as the penetration of computers is low in India. The positioning of the brand is based on information support as well as the retail service when the customer visits the retail outlet. There has been a proliferation of brands in most categories and the traditional positioning methods may not result in customer retention. In a low involvement category like soap, consumers will have a tendency to try out many brands even if they express a dominant loyalty to one brand. In other low involvement categories like anti septic lotion or floor cleaning solution, penetration levels have to be enhanced especially in developing markets. In both these kinds of categories, there is a need to combine offline and online positioning strategies and hence mass based advertising approach which has been followed for decades may not produce sustainable outcome in terms of brand loyalty.

In the case of soaps, India brands continue to position themselves on fragrance, skin care and prevention of bad odor while expanding on herbal offerings. One Indian herbal soap brand Ayush claims that it would kill 99% of seven types of bacteria in its advertisement. Pears, a well known glycerine soap has launched the germ shield variant. Another brand Lifebuoy with variants is positioned as a family soap on the health platform and the brand has been in the Indian context for more than four decades. Lyril which was positioned on product freshness with its lime ingredient and "waterfall" freshness has not been doing well in recent times because of highly competitive positioning strategies. All four brands mentioned are from the same company and except for the herbal brand the other brands have a distinctive identity of their own and they have been nurtured for several decades by the company.

Given such a competitive situation, positioning has to go beyond the traditional imagery created by advertisements and the blitz of mass media. It may be worthwhile to follow the principle of combining the product benefit with the life benefit (Buchhold and Wondemann, 2000) while the positioning strategy is being formulated by brands in the competitive context. Incidentally, Lifebuoy was also positioned for several decades as a soap with a germ killing action to the rural target segment characterized by a lower income and a different type of lifestyle. In fact, using a Lifebuoy a few decades back in the rural areas meant that the consumer has graduated to a branded offering from several low-end regional substitutes. Pears is a high priced soap which has a small niche market and it has been positioned on long term skin care. At the outset there is a need to provide differentiation in terms of how the product benefit of brands is relevant to the respective segment and even to segment the market combining life benefit with the product benefit would be useful. The product benefit of a herbal brand like Ayush (killing of bacteria) may be relevant for a target segment which is exposed to the dust and pollution of the environment in a developing country like India.

Children and several thousands of middle class consumers of soaps travelling by crowded buses can be the target segment. The life benefit for this target segment is to stay fresh in the context to which they are exposed to. Lifebuoy which is currently positioned to the urban target segment as a "family soap" on the health platform (rather than on its original germ killing proposition)could have the same demographic segment but address the same life benefit of staying fresh with regard to consumers who are exposed less of the dusty environment-probably self employed business people who do not travel to work as the target segment for Ayush.

The Internet enters into the mix as an information channel. It could provide information on the various brands, the various life benefits,the context (user situation) in which the core benefit of the brand could offer the maximum benefit and the ingredients used by each brand which is appropriate to the context (user situation). From this approach, it is clear that there is a very clear differentiation not only in terms of benefits offered by the brands but also in terms of usage situation which is very strong criteria to segment consumers. Consumers would be able appreciate how they are made to select the offering closest to their needs (not just in terms of fragrance or odor prevention which is very generic). This would make them buy the brand more frequently as there is a strong rationale to buy the specific brand (than just trying a few brands as more a variety seeking behavior). The problem of low penetration of the Internet in India (and hence the information) could be addressed at the important retail outlet and consumers could be educated by the company at these outlets with digital kiosks.

Sheseido a cosmetic brand in Japan has outlets where consumers could simulate several color combinations to sit their skin/ desired aesthetic appeal and if they wish they could leave their details on the database (Johansson and Nonka,1996). For the category of soaps, for instance consumers could take a look at the kinds of ingredients and their benefits based on life benefit for an appropriate segment. With the database the company could obtain feedback on the effectiveness of the claims of the brand used by the consumers. This method of contemporary positioning even for a low involvement product category could enable a brand to build up a relationship with the consumer base than just satisfying the positioning function of differentiating the offering from the competitors. Customer lifetime value has to consider the duration of loyalty and the profitability of customers during the duration of loyalty (Reinartz, Thomas and Kumar, 2003). In a specific category the duration of loyalty is critical and the contemporary positioning suggested is likely to result in a longer duration of loyalty. Besides the company which has several brands across a price spectrum, the duration of loyalty could also enable the consumer to graduate to updated offerings. One of the reasons for customer migration is because the consumer does not find the company offering a broad spectrum of offerings which the consumer could adapt to based on his changing lifestyles (Coyles and Gokey, 2002).

Positioning Framework-I

My framework (Figure 1) uses two dimensions-price and interactivity with consumers to provide guidelines for marketers to position their products on the dimension on loyalty:

The framework has four dimensions from which a brand can choose to employ its online and offline positioning strategies depending on the selection of target segment for the brand. This framework would also be useful to develop specific "loyalty associations" through appropriate reward systems as applicable for the respective segment. Needs to be integrated with the framework more systematically. For example, low price-low interactivity(LEAD consumers as a target segment) would clearly understand that

Figure 1.

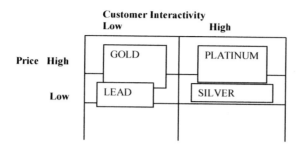

they would not be in a position to get rewards on loyalty as they are a part of the bargaining segment which is only price conscious. The understanding comes from the positioning signal provided by the company's reward system for retaining customers.(continue) reak down into smaller paragraphs. Such type of positioning is not possible through traditional ways.

For a brand which wants to consider high price, high customer interactivity (PLATINUM consumers as a target segment), the company should customize its product (even a tea brand could do this) to the consumer based on the finer needs of the consumer and the Internet based interactivity could be used for changes in customization whenever it is required by the customer when it is bought frequently. For example, a brand of glycerine soap may customize such an offering based on the constant feedback received on usage, changing climatic conditions and the customer's skin specific reaction to the brand. The high-end customer getting involved in this interaction with the brand also perceives a value for the price he is paying and is aware that the price conscious consumer is clearly differentiated by the brand. The Internet could throw up several customization options and give the customer specific guidelines on product usage after ascertaining the feedback on brand performance with the inclusion of a dermatologist. A new variant of the soap could be initially introduced exclusively through a loyal base of consumers belonging to this segment and this adds exclusivity to the value positioning.

High price and low customer interactivity(GOLD segment of consumers) could find application in hedonic products like coffee, tea and perfumes. While the interactivity may not be much on product performance it may associated with trends or recipes and the interaction may low but customer information on new offerings may be required. This is the type of interaction would be helpful to build a relationship with customers by emphasizing the superiority of the offering taking into consideration the category and competition together. An interesting example could be provided from the readymade apparel industry which ahs a number of brands generally positioned on lifestyle aspects. The brand Van Heusan has brought in a fabric which reduces the temperature of the wearer. Another brand Louis Phillippe has introduced a shirt which is called "Permpress" (it offers a fabric which remains permanently pressed because of a specific technology). Even diapers which has a very low penetration in the Indian market could be a category which involves high price and low customer interactivity. These categories could reach out to the consumer on the net with information on the state of the art work in the category and how such critical applications are treated with technology to deliver the relevant benefits to consumer. This approach would also add credibility to the brand. Product development efforts could also be highlighted and if the brand is able to get a testimonial from the scientific community on the credibility of claims ,they could be discussed on the web. Providing consumption related services could be another dimension which may be appropriate to this segment. For example, a new user of baby foods may be interested in clarifying a few doubts about the usage and web is a very effective strategy for providing a service of this kind.

Low price, high customer interactivity(SILVER segment of consumers) may not be a very feasible option for the company as costs of maintaining a system of this kind may offset the profits but there are a few aspects which could be considered for this segment. While individual consumer-specific information may not be a distinctive possibility, there could be a web page which addresses the common concerns of consumers regarding the product. The brand offering this service would have to be priced slightly higher than the one in low price, low customer interactivity. If a company offering several shampoo brands the mid-priced brand could have some customer interactivity if not a high interactivity. The brand could answer a few questions on hair care in the web site and the buyer of the brand could be given a pass word with which she could get three specific question of her choice answered. SILVER target segment of consumers offer the possibility of a future potential in terms of interactivity as well as prices and hence could be moved to other segments. The four aspects of loyalty positioning could be useful in a variety of product/market situations and each aspect conveys a distinctive positioning which is likely to enhance customer loyalty in the appropriate segment.

Positioning Framework-II

There are two dimensions of positioning strategies, namely perceived quality and associations which have been successful in the marketing history in both developed and developing markets. It would be useful for marketers to consider them while attempting the positiong synergy suggested in this article. These dimensions are portrayed in the backdrop of specific situations/contexts which reflect the realities of Indian markets. The contextual aspects are given in such a way that the positioning strtegies suggested with these vital dimensions would be one of the primary components of a brand's startegy.

Perceived Qality as a Positioning Dimension

Perceived quality has three aspects-objective quality based on the performance of the brand on the intended direction, manufacturing quality in terms of how defect free the brand is and product based quality which is associated with features, parts/ingredients and services offered by the brand (Aaker,1991).Perceived quality is the psychological because it involves consumers' perception of how the brand addresses their needs. The expectations of the target segment is crucial in assessing perceived quality. There may be two kinds of televisions one an up market plasma version and the other an entry level model. Both of these versions are targeted towards different segments. the higher end consumer would expect specific features, the state of the art features which would also add some symbolic appeal to the television (which is normally kept in the visitors' hall in the typical Indian household) and effective after sale service when there is a need for it. The expectations of the lower-end customer would be very different and hence perceived quality would be different for these two segments.

Perceived quality is used by the consumer in his decision making. A customer who is convinced of the perceived quality of a car would select the brand from among several alternatives. This aspect is especially applicable for a premium priced brand. There are several car brands competing in the higher-end of the market. While offline strategies would be associated with conventional advertising support, online promotion could be done at through the Internet highlighting certain aspects which could not be done in an advertisement. For example the engineering excellence in terms of safety or comfort could be conveyed through a special effect film the features and benefits which could be shown to the prospective customer after assessing his needs .The preferences of several individuals could vary and several dimensions associated with the brand could be shown in accordance with the preferences of each individual prospective consumer. Perceived quality of an offering could also be enhanced by the services offered. OnStar is a service offered by General Motors and several millions of consumers have availed this service. The service ranges from remotely opening the door of a car (when the consumer loses the key), to tracking the car when it is stolen (Prahalad and   ,2004). The very positioning of such a service triggers a superior quality of service beyond the mundane after sale service offered by car makers. Retail outlets of such brands could demonstrate such instances through simulations when consumers visit the outlets to learn more about the brand. Internet could also be used to carry the experience of consumers who have used the features of a brand (as testimonials) prospective consumers are thus encouraged to have a dialog with consumers who have experienced the brand .Such word of mouth references on reliability (which could be quick from a variety of consumers on the web/e mail) could enhance the perceived quality of the brand as reliability is one of the factors affecting product quality. Other aspects of product quality like serviceability, finish (look and feel of the product), features and durability (Garvin,1984) could also be dealt with in the web. Besides customers experts from specific fields of engineering well known in the respective fields like designers and engineers could offer an impartial assessment of the brand and its competitors. If the brand offers a product which is superior to that of competitors ,this approach of using experts to compare brands would be more effective than the company sponsored comparison based advertisements in which several competing brands are compared on a number of factors. The brand could also showcase the internal systems in the organization which

assure quality on several aspects of the brand. There are also extrinsic cues that could influence perceived quality of the brand (Schiffman and Kanuk,2002). The brand and its advertising are extrinsic cues that could influence perceived quality. A brand like Sony can mention the various high tech experiments it had carried out to enhance its entertainment products in its web site .Consumers may not understand the technology involved but are likely to perceive the products of the brand as high in quality. The digital media in combination with such information creates a quality perception among consumers because elements of advertising enter the consumers' awareness as technology portrayed through digital media is used as a metaphor for quality of the product (Zaltman,2003).

Associations as Positioning Dimensions

A number of dimensions of brand associations could be nurtured for positioning purposes. Prominent among them are product attributes ,customer benefits, lifestyle associations, celebrity associations and user imagery. Product attribute association is concerned with the association of a specific characteristic of the brand with its positioning. For example, Volvo is associated with safety and Mercedez is associated with its engineering excellence. In the digital context

digitizability would be the extent to which the existing functional attribute could be converted into information based functionality (Wind and Mahajan,2001).This offers interesting possibilities for e positioning of brands. National Semiconductor offers a simulation program on its web site which would enable engineers to plug in their own parameters to experiment with their designs. Over 5,00000 engineers keep coming back to Cisco's web site (Seybold and Marshak,2000).

In consumer product categories too such aspects of positioning (digitizable positioning) is possible. Tide the brand of detergent has a web site in which consumers could find information on removal of various kinds of stains. Amazon. com offers consumers several kinds of information which would enable them to consider several alternatives revolving around their preferences.

E positioning of brands extend the conventional positioning to offer whole customer experience which spans the entire decision making stages of consumer's selection process from pre purchase to post purchase(Bloch,1995). The lifestyle positioning associated with a number of consumer categories too could effectively use e positioning to be in line with the changing environment.

Consumer community is a concept which is evolving rapidly with the online marketing context cyberspace offers several innovative types of positioning.(continue)

Forrester Research estimates that there were 4,00000 communities in the year 2000 existed on the Internet (Solomon,2002). Gartner G2 opines that by 2005,fifty percent of all Fortune 1000 companies will launch virtual communities linked their web site.(Zetlin and Pfleging,2001). Sony's www.station.com has millions of users who participate in computer gaming online. Toyota has a digital racing game called Tundra and as gaming's popularity has been increasing marketers are merging advertisements which are interactive and they are placed with online games and this kind of technique is known as advergaming(Solomon,2003). Ninety four percent of British youth have mobile phones (Dana,2001) and Neslte held an innovative context for its brand Kitkat which involved mobile phones. Offline lifestyle positioning, high tech gadgets as status symbols and cyberspace meeting spaces with an evolving youth population offers several online positioning strategies which could be sued in synchronization with lifestyle brand associations. The concept of consumer mindset (Gollwitzer,1986) distinctively divides the consumer mindset into two categories -goal oriented mindset and experiential mindset. The goal oriented mindset may be focused on feature based information where as the experiential mind set may be directed towards hedonic

or sensual pleasure and this aspect could be used in online positioning of brands with contests and games being a trigger to make the hedonic mindset more involved for sensual pleasure. Over a period of time a brand could build a community of users who would be able to display brand passion as in the case of Harley Davidson. Celebrity associations have been increasingly used in the recent times both globally and In India. Pepsi. Coke, Nerolac Paints, Cadbury's, Perk (chocolates) and Dabur's over the counter medicinal offerings in consumables and Palio and Santro in passenger cars, Victor two wheelers (motorcycles) Samsung (washing machines) and Sahara (airlines) are some of the categories in which celebrities have been used in the Indian context.

Santro was a car introduced by Hyundai a few years back and the brand has crossed 1,00000 cars in terms of sales in 2003-2004 in a total passenger car market of one million. Santro was literally an unknown brand and also had a "tall boy" design unknown to Indian consumers. The brand initially used a topical male celebrity to create awareness about the brand and later after the brand picked up in terms of sales, it introduced a topical female celebrity and positioned the brand as "sunshine " brand with the imagery of the advertisement indicating a clear lifestyle positioning. The buyers of the brand are urban young adults who are upwardly mobile I terms of aspirations, income and status. The celebrity positioning was strengthened (by the inclusion of the second celebrity) after the product was accepted for its functional features like design and performance and comfort. It is surprising even such a celebrity oriented advertising , very rarely brands use online positioning to "connect" with these target segment especially in durable categories. An online consumer chat session with the celebrities starring in the brand's advertisement (for example in Santro's) on the functional features of the car and the celebrities' experience with the car brand would have added fun and charismatic credibility to the campaign. Fanta the orange flavored soft drink from Coca Cola company uses celebrities in its TV commercials and the script and the visual revolves around humor. An online session with consumers with the humor theme and the brand would have added excitement to the brand and in soft drink category excitement is a useful positioning .In durable categories ,an expert could also be roped in with the celebrity to provide a commentary on brand benefits and an online program could be made available on the brand's web site for consumers to access any time.

A chat among the registered consumers as a rub-off strategy could also open up the possibilities of a community of brand users being formed. User imagery is another positioning dimension which is very useful in a competitive environment full of communication clutter. User imagery is very useful because the viewers of the advertisement using the imagery would be able to readily figure out the typical user depicted by the brand and this is very important especially because there are several brands vying for the attention of the consumer. Fast track is a brand of watch targeting youngsters in urban markets and the advertising imagery shows the watch alongside a can of soft drink /beer (as perceived by the consumer with the can's image in India)indicating that it is clearly positioned towards youth who belong to the "cola/beer" culture and the imagery speaks volumes about the lifestyle association of the brand. Johnson &Johnson clearly carries the images of children when its products are advertised.

Imagery for an edible oil brand could be different because the product is more under the focus of the consumer than the typical user imagery. Online positioning could carry complementary imagery (complementing the print/TV advertisement imagery) to create an "experience ".A chocolate drink aimed at youth could carry several innovative imagery visuals linking the typical drinker of the brand and the pleasure of the drinker in having consumed the brand. Experiential marketing which involves several sense organs (Schmitt,1999) could be used by brand with their graphics on the web. A high end shaving razor which claims several technological points towards providing consumer benefits could create a product imagery on the web (supplementing the user imagery in offline advertising) which could vividly portray the finer aspects of the razor with the linked up benefits. Online advertising imagery as an extrinsic cue concerned with the brand could provide a significant enhancement of the intention to try the product in the case of consumables and could offer an enhanced image for durable categories. Such imagery could also provide information on product usage whether it is a recipe for a new fast food or for the first time user of a fully automatic washing machine. A consumer may buy a vacuum cleaner but may not know how to use it and company based offline assistance is "time bound" and an online format would be available to the consumer any time she wants it. .Timestyles of consumers differ depending on their personality (Cotte, Ratneshwar and Glen Mick,2003) and hence online communication would take in to consideration several types of consumers' personality.   Given the variety of associations and the contexts in which they could be put to use   the following frame work (Fig.2) with two dimensions namely attribute orientation and Online customer community orientation would enable marketers to choose a strategy best suited to their product/market situation:

Positioning Framework-III

Given the fact that almost half the population in the Indian subcontinent is below the age of 25 years,the youth segment is an attractive one for several fast moving consumer good categories. Changing lifestyles and the diffusion of digital products and the emrgence of neo-youth segements like software professionals offer tremendous scope for synergising offline and online positioning strategies with a focus on "community orientation". Consider a 2x2 matrix formed by Functional attributes(high, low) and Consumer Community(high, low). This provides us with an interesting way to explore positioning brands.

A brand could have a high attribute orientation and a high community orientation. Brands which have been launched on lifestyle to build itself over the years but which are required to enhance their attributes due to intense competition could follow this approach. Close up is a brand of toothpaste which was launched in the mid-seventies in India with the lifestyle appeal of "Close up smile" which featured a boy and girl with romantic overtones. Over the years the brand has followed the same positioning slant and has been targeting the youth. With competitive brands following the same approach and brands from several other categories following similar positioning the brand seems to have lost its positioning luster. The brand could be revitalized by an online contest that emphasizes the functional attributes of the product.

A brand having a low attribute orientation could have a high community orientation. Brands faced with low levels of product differentiation could develop a community of brand users in a sustained manner. Mountain Dew's positioning which involves a group of youth is in tune with the online community orientation.

Low online community orientation with high attribute orientation could be applied to brands in any category which is highly innovative and sustains a product-line which addresses the changing customer needs. While community orientation could help any brand to build itself, in a country like India where mass markets rule volumes, a durable category brand like Haier (the Chinese brand which has already entered India) may like to address the mid-market and develop a strong product attribute association with thousands of consumers who may not have personal access to computers.

Low attribute orientation and low online consumer community orientation would be suitable to a number of "no-frill" brands at the lower end of the market which compete with unorganized offerings (offerings which are marketed at the local market and the ones which may not may not be marketed in a systematic manner or the offerings which may not have completed the legalities required for marketing them) required for marketing the offerings in the category in a market like India (electrical appliances, watches and foot-wear in the Indian market are examples of such product categories).

Other Topical Dimensions/Issues in Positioning

Points of difference associations (PODs) are strong, favorable and unique brand associations for a brand and they may involve performance attributes or imagery which is unique to the brand (Keller,2003). The various combinations of offline and online positioning strategies could establish an appropriate POD for a brand in a given competitive context. The other aspect which was advocated by Keller was the points of parity association (POPs) which deals with category parity associations and competitive parity associations. category parity associations refer to the extent to which a brand matches what consumers expect in a specific category.

Competitive parity associations refer to the extent to which a brand's associations matches with that of its competitive brand's association with regard to its strengths. For example if a new brand of car is launched in the market, competitive POP refers for instance to the state of the art features of the brand which matches with that of an existing competitive brand. It advantage of combining offline positioning and online positioning is that in offline positioning involving TV or print advertisements (for example performance attributes of a detergent brand) could be highlighted and POP could be established. Online positioning of the brand (like that of Tide's) could establish the POD with suggestions on how the detergent brand could be used for various types of clothes or on how stains could be removed. Positioning could also involve linking attributes and benefits of the brand with the values which may be relevant to the target segment to which the brand is positioned. This concept is known as laddering (Renolds and Gutman,1988)

MARKETING IMPLICATIONS- CREATING A SYNERGY BETWEEN OFFLINE AND ONLINE POSITIONING

Brands could be categorized as functional brands, symbolic brands and hedonic brands from the view point of brand positioning and this categorization is aimed at managing brand meaning over the period of a brand's lifecycle (Park, Jaworski and MacInnis,1996).This is very useful concept for brand positioning as it builds up a brand with a clear focus even when the brand attempts to enter a related diversification. When a brand has a strong functional appeal in terms of attributes an benefits and if the company is able to sustain a product-line with several offerings of the brand (over a period of time) having a focus on functional attribute or benefits, it could choose online and offline positioning which has a focus on such dimensions.

Hero Honda is a two wheeler bike company which entered the Indian context during the mid-eighties and for almost two decades it has focused on functional attributes/benefits with regard to all its offerings namely Hero Honda CD100, Hero Honda SS, Hero Honda Splendor and Hero Honda Passion. The last two offerings have had a symbolic positioning in terms but even such symbolism has been highlighted with additional features of the bike. While the brand has a clear focus on attributes, symbolism has been added

based on innovative features. Hero Honda could have an online positioning which illustrates the processes within the factory on quality control, the rigor with which material is sourced from suppliers and quality control with regard to suppliers to emphasize the efforts the company is taking with regard to the attributes which consumers receive. the brand. The brand could also convey the developmental efforts being taken by the company to enhance customer-friendly features. This kind of *"secondary online positioning"* could build up credibility for the brand as consumers would also spread this information through word-of-mouth.

CONCLUSION

In sum, I am arguing that even in a developing market with low Internet penetration levels, the Web could be used as a channel to position a product effectively. Web sites could be designed to distribute product information that would enhance the differentiation of the brand in the marketplace.

REFERENCES

Aaker, David A. (1991), "Managing Brand Equity - Capitalizing on the Value of a Brand Name", The Free Press, pp.16-85.

Aaker, David A.and Joachimsthaler(2000), "Brand Leadership", The Free Press, pp. 243.

Bloch, Peter (1995), "Seeking the Ideal Forces; Product Design and Consumer Response", Journal of Marketing, 59, pp.16-29.

Buchhold, Andreas and Wordemann Wolfram(2000), "What makes Winning Brands Different", pp.21-26.

Cotte, June, Ratneswar R and Glen Mick David(2003), "The Times of their lives; Phenomenological and Metaphorical Characteristics of Consumer Timestyles", forthcoming article in Journal of Consumer Research, pp.2-4.

Coyles, Stephanie and Gokey C Timothy(2002), "Customer Retention is not enough", The McKinsey Quarterly, No.2, pp.1-6, www.mckinseyquarterly.com

Dana, Mike(2001), " M Commerce will Outperform E Commerce", RCR Wireless News 20, No.2, 4

Gilmore H. James and Pine B. Joseph II, (2000), "Markets of One, Creating Customer - Unique Value through Customer", HBS, pp.62-65.

Gollwitzer M. Peter (1996), "The Volitional Benefits of Planning". Gollwitzer P. Peter and John A. Bargh (Eds.), "The Psychology of Actions, Living Cognition and Motivation or Behavior", Guilford Press, pp.287-312.

Hallberg Garth, (1995), "All Consumers are Not Created Equal" John Wiley and Sons, 19.

Johansson K. Johny and Nonaka Ikujiro, (1996), "Relentless, The Japanese Way of Marketing", Harper Business, pp.143-148.

Keller Lane Kevin, (2003), "Strategic Brand Management, Building, Measuring and Managing Brand Equity", Prentice Hall of India, pp.132-149.

Keller Lane Kevin, Sternthal Brian and Tybout Alice, (2002), "Three Questions You Need to Ask About Your Brand", Business Review, pp.3-8.

Kotler Philip, "Marketing Management", 11ed. (2003), Pearson Education, 623.

Kumar S. Ramesh, (2002, Conceptual Issues in Consumer Behaviour – Indian Context", Pearson Education, pp.82-89.

Kumar S. Ramesh, (2002), "Managing Indian Brands", Vikas, pp.299-300.

Kumar K and Mahadevan B, (2003), "Evolution of Business Models in B2C E Commerce; The Case of Fabmall", Management Review, Vol.15, No.4, pp.23-30.

Linstrom Martin, Peppers Don and Rogers Martha, (2001), "Clicks, Bricks and Brands", Kogan, pp.24.

Park C. Whan, Jaworski J. Bernard and MacInnis J. Deborah, (1996), "Strategic Brand Concept – Image Management", Journal of Marketing, pp.135-145.

Prahalad and C K Ramaswamy Venkat, (2004), "Future of Competition - Co-Creating Unique Value with Customers", HBS, pp.83-85.

Reinatz W, Thomas J and Kumar V, (2003), "Linking Acquisition and Retention to Maximize Profitability", Working paper, University of Connecticut.

Reynolds J. Thomas and Gutman Jonathan, (Feb/Mar 1988), "Laddering Theory; Method, Analysis and Interpretation", Journal of Advertising Research, pp.11-23.

Ries Al and Trout Jack, (1987), "Brand Positioning; The battle in the Mind", Tata McGraw Hill, pp.1-5.

Ries Al and Laura Ries, (2000), "Immutable Laws of Internet Branding", Harper Collins.

Rust Roland J, Zeithmal Valarie A and Lemon N. Katherine, (2000), "Driving Customer Equity, How Customer Lifetime Value is Reshaping Corporate Strategy", The Free Press, pp.223-241.

Schiffman G. Leon and Kanuk, Lazer Leslie(2002), "Consumer Behavior", Pearson Education, pp.141-153.

Schmitt H. Bernd(1999), "Entrepreneurial Marketing", The Free Press, pp.71.

Seybold Patricia and Marshak T. Ronni(2000), "Customers.com", Times Business, pp.99-102.

Solomon Michael(2003), "Conquering the Consumer Mindspace", Amcom 10, pp.151-153.

Trout Jack and Rivkin Steve(1999), "The Power of Simplicity", Tata McGraw Hill, 55.

Wind Yoram and Mahajan Vijay(2001), "Digital Marketing", John Wiley and Sons, pp.210-320.

Zaltman Gerald(2003), "How Consumers Think Insights into the Mind of the Market", HBS, pp.80-90.

Zetlin M and Pfleging, (Oct 2001), "Creators of Online Community", Computer World 29, 34.

This work was previously published in Contemporary Research in E-Marketing, Vol 2, edited by S. Krishnamurthy, pp. 304-321, copyright 2005 by IGI Publishing, formerly known as Idea Group Publishing (an imprint of IGI Global).

Chapter IX
Job Search at Naukri.com:
Case Study of a Successful Dot–Com Venture in India

Sanjeev Swami
Indian Institute of Technology Kanpur, India

INTRODUCTION

Until 1997, job seekers in India would wait the whole week for the weekly supplements of various newspapers, or sundry employment journals and gazettes to learn about the vacancies and job openings in the industry. Then came the Internet and threatened to push the days of white envelopes to oblivion. In India, a forerunner in ushering in the change in the way one looks at job-hunting today is a relatively small, but rapidly growing company, Naukri.com. Today, it is regarded as one of the most resourceful destinations for job seekers, ranging from a seasoned professional to a recent graduate. According to the CEO of Naukri. com, the major challenge that the organization currently faces is the management of growth. The company had steadily grown from Rs. 40 lacs to Rs. 1 crore to a Rs. 20 crore company in

the year 2004. The next year's target is Rs. 45 crores.[b] Management of such rapid growth in such a short period of time requires effective strategies not only to attract talent, but also to retain it. Therefore, in the middle of 2004, the challenges facing Naukri.com involved the issues related to organizing its e-business and the proper management of its growth.

JOB SEARCH METHODS AND THE ADVENT OF E-RECRUITMENT

Job Search Methods: General Approaches

Several methods have been recognized as the standard methods of job search in the U.S. and other parts of the world (http://www.bls.gov/oco/

oco20042.htm). A representative list of these methods, along with their comparative description, is provided below.

(i) *Personal contacts / Networking* – In this method, the family, friends, and acquaintances of the job seeker offer one of the most effective ways to find a job. They may help the candidate directly or put him/her in touch with someone else who can. Such *networking* can lead to information about specific job openings, many of which may not be publicly posted. Networking, or referrals, has emerged as one of the most productive ways to find a job in recent years, and has been loosely defined as follows -- *When you let others know that you are looking for a job, and they let someone else know, and so on*

(ii) *Executive Search Firms* – The job seeker may contact firms which specialize in searching executives for their clients with a certain background and qualification. However, an executive search firm's primary function is usually to find "stars" for their clients, and they place less emphasis on placing outplaced or unemployed candidates.

(iii) *Business Directories / Company Sites* – A relatively recent approach towards job search is to visit various companies' sites on the Internet which are in the area of expertise of the candidate. A list of major companies in a specific field may be available at sites such as Hoovers.com. At a company's site, links, such as, *Employment Opportunities, Careers, Join Us*, and so on, are provided. E-mail addresses are usually provided so that the interested candidates could mail their resumes electronically. Alternatively, the candidate may directly contact the company by getting its contact information from business directories.

(iv) *Employment Agencies and Career Consultants* – Most of the employment agencies operate on a commission basis, with the fee dependent upon a percentage of the salary paid to a successful applicant, paid either by the candidate or the hiring company. Although employment agencies can help save time and contact employers, the commission costs may sometimes outweigh the benefits. There are other agencies which usually specialize in jobs for secretaries, administrative assistants, clerks, and other clerical workers. They may sometimes test the prospective candidates in typing, Word, Excel, Access, PowerPoint or other skills, and may even provide training for the same.

(v) *Job Fairs* – Many companies send their representatives to job fairs for the purpose of recruiting new candidates. These fairs are generally held at large convention or outplacement career centers, and promoted in local newspapers or on the Internet. These events provide great networking opportunities with prospective employers.

(vi) *School Career Planning and Placement Offices* – College/university placement offices help their students and alumni find jobs. They set up appointments and allow recruiters to use their facilities for interviews. Placement offices may also have lists of jobs for on-campus, regional, nonprofit, and government organizations. Students can receive career counseling and testing and job search advice. At career resource centers, the students may attend workshops on such topics as job search strategy, resume writing, letter writing, and effective interviewing; critique drafts of resumes and watch videotapes of mock interviews; explore files of resumes and references; and attend job fairs conducted by the placement office. These remain one of the easiest and most attractive methods of finding a job.

(vii) *Classified Ads* – The "Wanted" ads in the newspapers is one of the most traditional methods of recruitment. However, one must realize that not all of the job openings are listed in these ads. Also, the classified ads sometimes do not give all of the important information. They may offer little or no description of the job, working conditions, or pay. Some ads do not identify the employer, and only provide a post office box number to which the candidate can mail the resume, thus making follow-up inquiries very difficult. Some ads offer out-of-town jobs; others advertise employment agencies rather than actual employment opportunities. Usually the Sunday or Weekend editions of the newspapers carry the most listings. Other outlets for these ads are in the form of business magazine ads and Employment News Bulletins.

(viii) *Internet Networks and Resources* – The Internet provides a variety of information, including job listings and job search resources and techniques. Several sites have emerged in this category; the examples include Naukri.com in India, and monster.com in the U.S. The job listings are generally posted by the field or discipline, and a search using keywords is recommended for such sites. Some Web sites provide national or local classified listings and allow jobseekers to post their resumes online. Others offer advice on how to search for a job, prepare for an interview, or write resumes. These sites allow candidates to send their resume to an employer by e-mail or to post it online.

(ix) *Government / State Employment Service Offices* – The State employment service, sometimes called Job Service, operates in countries like USA in coordination with the U.S. Department of Labor's Employment and Training Administration. Local offices, found nationwide, help jobseekers find jobs and help employers find qualified workers at almost no cost to either. These also sponsor database services, such as, *America's Job Bank* (http://www.ajb.org, sponsored by the U.S. Department of Labor), which is an Internet site that provides a database of over one million jobs Nationwide, creates and posts resumes online, and sets up an automated job search. The state employment offices also provide *services for special groups, such as,* veterans, dislocated workers, military personnel and youths. Information on obtaining a position with the Federal Government is also through telephone-based systems.

(x) *Professional Associations* – Many professions have associations that offer employment information, including career planning, educational programs, job listings, and job placement. The associations' services are generally available to only the members of the association.

(xi) *Labor Unions* – Labor unions provide various employment services to members, including apprenticeship programs that teach a specific trade or skill.

(xii) *Community Agencies* – Many nonprofit organizations, including religious institutions and vocational rehabilitation agencies, offer counseling, career development, and job placement services, generally targeted to a particular group, such as women, youths, minorities, ex-offenders, or older workers.

Job Search Methods: Indian Scenario

In the Indian context, the job search methods have not been as elaborate as listed above. The methods also varied according to the graduation degree of the candidate. While private companies were quite willing to visit the campuses of engineering and business schools throughout the country, they were not so eager to recruit from the colleges of non-professional degree courses such as arts, education, humanities, and so on. Consequently, school placement offices (Method (vi) above) were the most popular option for business and engineering graduates. For other types of candidates, the classified ads option (vii) was one of the predominant one. Another attractive option was to prepare for the competitive examinations for clerical or executive positions in public sector banks, government jobs, administrative services, and so on. Although not widely documented, it was widely believed that the networking or referral option (i) also worked reasonably well in the Indian environment. Some employment agencies and career consultants (iv) were also present in India, but there role was restricted to only a very small percentage of the job-seeking population. Lately, however, the role of placement consultants and some newer methods in job search had increased with the advent of Internet, outsourcing, proliferation of software firms, and entry of multinational and global corporations in India. The newer methods included executive search (ii), Internet resources (viii), and professional associations (x). Other options, such as job fairs (v), state employment offices (ix), labor unions (xi), and community agencies (xii), were either dysfunctional or virtually non-existent in India.

The communication methods of prospective employers with job-seekers had also adapted to the advancement of technology. Initial communication methods predominantly involved print media ads such as those in newspapers and magazines. In addition, a local gazette "Employment Bulletin" carried the major advertisements on a periodic basis. As radio was one of the most affordable means of entertainment and information gathering, a radio program "Employment News" also gave the relevant information about jobs. Subsequently, with the diffusion of televisions in the market, some job-related information also started appearing on national and regional networks. The latest occurrence in this trend has been that of e-recruitment job search option. The promise of instant delivery, paperless transaction, lower cost, and access to a large amount of information made this a really attractive option.

E-Recruitment Market in India

Similar to the software industry, the e-recruitment industry also performed reasonably well in the years 2002 onwards. The market witnessed a healthy growth rate of 80% to 100%. Growing at approximately 100 percent, the players, which have emerged as the clear winners are — Naukri.com, JobsAhead.com, Jobstreet.com and Monster.com. (Source: Internet). The online job market is expected to grow faster than the conventional recruitment market, and is likely to capture sizeable share of traditional channels like newspaper recruitment advertising. From an estimated Rs 25 crore in 2002, the online job market was expected to reach Rs 45 crore in the year 2004. This promised to be a phenomenal progress, which would defy the trends of the dotcom washout. Arun Tadanki, president of Monster Asia, agrees, "The economy is very strong and the recruitment market is booming. The jobs market is one of the best in recent years." Tadanki estimates India's online recruitment sector will clock revenues of between Rs. 750-800 million during 2004, which is about 12 per cent of the total recruitment market. "In two years time it could shoot up to 25 per cent," Tadanki says. Stuart McKelvey, Monster's Group President for the Asia-Pacific, was also quite optimistic about e-recruitment market and estimated that the online opportunity for hiring in India is growing at 80-90 per cent each year.

BACKGROUND OF NAUKRI.COM

Historical Perspective

The vision of Naukri.com is: *To create a platform where, in 20 years time, every Indian who is looking for a job can find one.* In March 1997, as the influence of the Internet was beginning to grow in India, Naukri.com was launched as a floorless employment exchange. It was conceived as a platform for employers and job seekers to meet and exchange information. The site was launched with databases of jobs, resumes and placement consultants. In October 1997, the service went commercial. By then, more than 50 companies had tried out the services offered by Naukri.com and were satisfied with the response received. Since then, the client list has increased to over 7500 companies.

Info Edge, the holding company of Naukri. com, started in 1989 and became Info Edge (India) Private Limited on May 1, 1995. It was in the business of selling reports and project marketing related consulting services to its clients. Info Edge also provided management consulting services to a number of clients in India and abroad. In 1991, the Department of Telecommunications (DoT) of Government of India began to experiment with Videotex services. Info Edge put in its application as information providers – people who would run a database. The mechanism proposed involved a central server in one place. Several databases would reside on the server. Each database would be accessed by public through terminals in different telephone exchanges on payment of a fee. Consequently, Info Edge advertised for information providers. The complete project concept was called "Jobnet." The Videotex pilot project of DoT, however, did not take off and Info Edge was eventually forced to abandon its plans for this service. Over the next few years, Info Edge evaluated the idea of providing job information to the public independently, but was unable to identify a financially viable technology backbone till the Internet entered India.

Today, Naukri.com aims to provide Indians with Indian qualifications the maximum opportunity for their career growth. It has also been promoted in all parts of the globe, where Indian qualifications are acceptable, and clients have been enlisted. Over 10% of its current corporate client list consists of companies located in USA, Africa, Middle East and Far East. Similarly, about 5% of the job-seekers approaching Naukri.com are non–resident Indians wanting to return to India. The financial performance of Naukri.com from 1999 to 2003 is given in Table 1.

Naukri.com planned to rake in Rs.450 million in sales in the fiscal year ending March 31, 2005 on increasing online traffic.[d] Despite the recent merger of its two major competitors, JobsAhead. com and Monsterindia.com, Naukri.com said it was well poised to achieve 100 percent sales growth in the current fiscal over the previous year's

Rs.220 million. Naukri.com claimed it had emerged as the fastest growing recruitment site in the Indian market with 10,500 clients, offices in 18 locations across the country, over 64,000 live job listings and a rapidly expanding resume database.

B2B or B2C Site?

Since Naukri.com has both job seekers and corporates as their customers, there is some confusion as to whether it is a B2B or B2C site. According to Sanjeev Bikhchandani, it is both B2B and B2C. It is essentially a medium where Naukri. com enables handshakes between corporate and prospective employees. They are able to meet on the Naukri.com web site.

Business Model of Naukri.com

Naukri.com has had a clear revenue model from the beginning. As with any other business, there has to be a direct inflow of revenue for services rendered. While it has a select few services that are free to both job seekers and job-providers, the majority of its services are paid for by one of the two segments. 90% of Naukri.com's revenues come from the corporate clients, and the remaining 10% of the revenue comes from job-seekers. Naukri.com is open to the idea of secondary revenue sources like advertisements on its site. However, as Naukri.com's entire focus was on

Table 1. Financial performance of Naukri.com (1999-2003)

	1999	2000	2001	2002	2003
Revenue	21.14	37.64	96.44	379.00	907.00
Costs Incurred	1.90	4.12	20.69	28.98	130.96
Gross Profit	**19.24**	**33.52**	**75.75**	**350.02**	**776.04**
Selling/General/ Administrative Exp	15.40	29.93	265.85	402.15	620.32
Depreciation/ Amortization	0.80	1.90	18.13	46.00	55.00
Other Expenses	0.37	0.50	3.52	16.35	20.70
Total Operating Expense	**16.57**	**32.33**	**287.50**	**464.50**	**696.02**
Operating Income	2.67	1.19	(211.75)	(114.48)	80.02
Income Before Tax	**2.67**	**1.19**	**(211.75)**	**(114.48)**	**80.02**
Income After Tax	2.67	1.19	(211.75)	(114.48)	80.02

providing recruitment solutions, such a mode of revenue generation was not vigorously pursued. Says Sanjeev Bikhchandani (CEO, Naukri.com), on secondary sources of revenue, "If somebody pops in with an advertisement, we don't refuse him." A brief description of the services provided by Naukri.com, both paid and free, is provided in a later section. As Naukri.com has grown, it has been conscious of controlling expenses, especially advertising, which has been one of the pitfalls of many a dotcom businesses. A diagrammatic representation of the business model of Naukri.com is presented in Figure 1.

Tracing the Growth of Naukri.com

One of the most important factors that made Naukri.com profitable was the founder's tight leash on the expenses. Started with self-funding in 1997, Naukri.com did not have deep pockets to begin with. Naukri.com did not face many problems procuring finances, human resources and the entire infrastructure. This was primarily because the parent company, Info Edge, was already in the business of preparing reports and databases. It employed three data entry operators and asked them to put some jobs into the database

Figure 1. Business model of Naukri.com

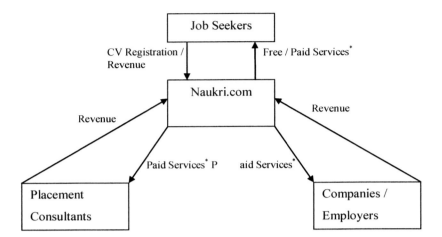

* Description of services referred here is provided in Section 4

structure. The technology person, who was a part-time employee, was then asked to convert this into a website. The name "Naukri.com" was thought of and registered. To begin with, finances were not a problem because the staff consisted of three data entry operators and a part time technology person. The web site was served out of a hired server in the United States. The hiring cost of the server was US $25 per month. Slowly, as business began to pick up, Info Edge closed down all other business and put all the staff to work on the Naukri.com business. Says Sanjeev Bikhchandani, "And before we knew it, the thing just kept growing and growing and expanding. And we had to slowly close the other businesses and put all the staff here and this thing began to make money."

The investment in the first three years was to the tune of Rs. 25 lacs. The company kept its overheads low, refused to splurge on advertising and promotions, and sailed through the dotcom bust with little problem. According to Bikhchandani, "We had a small team and a lot of our marketing was done via word of mouth and some ads in print." It was only after Bikhchandani was cer-

tain in his mind that there was a huge market for e-recruitment in India that he decided to invest more in expansion. In mid-2000, the company approached ICICI Bank, which picked up a stake in the venture, providing it with the capital needed to spread its wings.

From just one office in Delhi in the year 2000, the company then crossed state borders to have 15 offices in 13 cities nationwide. Naukri.com now covers cities like Noida, Gurgaon, Chandigarh, Mumbai, Pune, Ahmedabad, Baroda, Indore, Chennai, Hyderabad, Bangalore, Cochin, Coimbatore and Kolkata. There is one office in California, U.S.A., which looks after overseas operations.

The Brain Wave

Sanjeev Bikhchandani, CEO, is not just another netpreneur. He is an IIM Ahmedabad graduate who left his cushy job at SmithKline Beecham to try his luck in the topsy-turvy world of Internet marketing. Bikhchandani, during his IIM Ahmedabad days, got placed in SmithKline Beecham before the regular placements season began at

IIM Ahmedabad. Therefore, he was drafted in a voluntary position into the placement office to help out the companies visiting the campus. It was here that he noticed that two blue chip companies, Citibank and Hindustan Lever Limited, literally coming to blows over talent. He realized then that companies would go to any length for talent and expressed in his own words, "When I saw this, I realized that, listen, there is literally a war for talent, I saw it first hand."

This war for talent registered in Bikhchandani's mind but took a back seat and in 1989, he joined SmithKline Beecham as a brand manager for the brand for kids' health drink "Horlicks". He and all his colleagues used to sit in an open hall. When the latest issue of the business magazine *Business India* would come in the office, all his colleagues would start reading it from the back because the appointment advertisements were at the back. The interesting thing that he observed here was that all the people who were flipping through appointment advertisements were not hunting for a job. This led Bikhchandani to realize that probably jobs were a very high interest category and even if one is not searching for a job, he/she looks at the list of opportunities. Finally, one more thing that Bikhchandani noticed was that almost every day, his colleagues used to receive calls from placement consultants. Even though his colleagues were not interested in taking up a new job, they would take the calls and talk to those placement consultants.

These observations helped Bikhchandani figure out that there is a huge fragmented database of jobs with different placement consultants and jobs are a high interest category. If somebody could consolidate the database of live jobs and put it at one place and continuously update it that would be a very powerful product and money could be made out of this. Bikhchandani realized this by the end of 1989 and early 1990. He quit his job in October 1990 and along with a partner started the company Info Edge (India) Private Limited. This company was initially into databases, trade-mark-searching services, report writing, and so on. But the jobs database idea remained dormant in his mind.

Why the Name Naukri.com?

While there are many factors that contributed to making Naukri.com a success story, part of the credit goes to its unique nomenclature. The Naukri.com team had intentions of giving the web site an English name. A number of names were thought of, such as, jobsindia, indiajobs, employindia, indiaemploy, careerindia, careersindia, indiacareers, employmentIndia, recruitmentindia. To their disappointment, however, all these names were already registered. Therefore, a compromise had to be made and a decision was made to name the web site Naukri. Opponents of this name said that this name was down market and had the connotation of "servitude" (*naukar*) attached to it. But the name was retained because of its memorability and uniqueness. Interestingly, Sanjeev Bikhchandani considers the brand name to be an asset for his company. Bikhchandani says "It's turned out to be a great asset for us. At that time, I thought it would be a handicap." Moreover, he did not believe that the Hindi name would be a handicap in the southern part of India for the simple reason that Hindi movies are released in south India and they are avidly watched there.

Why Naukri.com Was Not Affected by the Dotcom Meltdown?

The parent company of Naukri.com is 14 years old. It launched Naukri.com in March 1997 and operated for three years without venture capital. Since venture capital funding was not taken upfront, the company had to make money in order to survive. Dotcoms itself are just about 7 years old and were not fashionable at a time when Naukri.com was launched. Therefore, by the time dotcoms became popular, Naukri.com was already profitable and that too without venture capital funding. Venture capital funding was taken merely to scale up an existing profitable model.

Bikhchandani claims the dotcom bust in fact helped Naukri.com. When the competitors came into India, they had a high cost model and did not know how to make money because of their unfamiliarity with the market. Naukri.com, on the other hand, was already making money. Naukri.com did not spend their money on advertising. They just put it in a bank, put feet on the street, hired sales people, built client relationships and opened new offices. When the meltdown actually happened, the competitors could not get a second round of funding whereas Naukri.com did not need a second round of funding. This helped Naukri.com in beating competition.

During the meltdown, foreign competitors like monster, jobstreet, jobsdb came to India with the promise of sending Indian technical man power abroad. The meltdown resulted in a reduced demand for Indian technical manpower. The foreign portals then lost interest in the Indian

market. There was additional pressure on them in the United States also. Bikhchandani says, "We used the last four years of meltdown very, very profitably in consolidating our business, building our brand, moving in a planned manner, not spending our money foolishly and really strengthening our position. So the meltdown actually helped us because it really killed our competition."

Organizational Structure

The organization chart of Naukri.com is presented in Figure 2.

Human Resource Management at Naukri.com

The profiles of various management personnel at Naukri.com is presented in Appendix I. It is clear from the management profiles that Naukri.com has a fairly sophisticated pool of talent in its management. The work environment at Naukri.com is

Figure 2. Organization Chart of Naukri.com

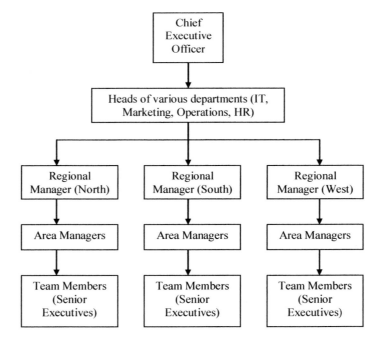

also very open and friendly. According to the HR manager, problems are resolved by discussions. Even if it is an inter-departmental issue, appointments are not required for discussions with the personnel of the other department. For instance, if the marketing team were working on product development, they would need to work in close coordination with technology because technology is ultimately going to deploy the product over the net. If the marketing people have any queries, then they can straight away walkup to the technology people and get the issue resolved.

People at Naukri.com are given opportunities to learn even at the cost of making mistakes. In the words of the HR manager, "People here get a lot of opportunity to learn by making mistakes, I would say. Because a lot of responsibility is given and space is given, that you try out things and try to learn on your own." The management at Naukri.com also encourages idea generation. When a new member joins a team, he/she is only assigned a task. How to accomplish the task is his/her prerogative. This prompts the new team member to formulate new ideas to do the assigned task in the best possible way. Since organizational issues are recognized as one of the major challenge areas that Naukri.com is facing, during recruitment, attention is paid to ensure that the selected candidate has the right kind of attitude that would help him/her to fit into the system. Says the HR manager "If the attitude is right, people will always learn the skills of doing the task." The regional offices themselves hire employees from the campus recruitment for the regional offices, while the head office helps the regional offices when lateral recruitment is to be done. This assistance is provided to them in terms of short-listing the candidates and conducting telephonic interviews. The regional offices themselves proceed with the final interview and selection process.

PRODUCT/SERVICE OFFERINGS OF NAUKRI.COM

The products offered by Naukri.com are aimed at two broad groups of customers – 1) recruiters and 2) job-seekers. The products for each group are explained below.

Products for Recruiters

Naukri.com offers a range of services to the recruiters. A brief description of each product/service follows:

a. **Best Places to Work:** An exclusive section for top companies, this is the first section that appears on the Naukri.com home page. Naukri.com develops a career micro-site for the customer company with a link from the home page. This ensures maximum branding and visibility to a company's recruitment requirements. This package provides the web-enabled Response Management Software, and e-Apps, free of cost.

b. **Job Gallery:** A listing in this section makes the client company directly accessible from the Naukri.com home page. Vacancy listings may be customized like the vacancies in a newspaper. Client company is seen with other quality organizations and vacancies are highlighted.

c. **Hot Vacancies:** This is the premium job listing service provided by Naukri.com to its clients. This gives the client company's vacancies greater visibility in a less cluttered space and they get listed with other quality jobs. Their listing gets covered in the Classifieds section, where free Job Alerts are done for the client company's vacancies and a logo is included on listings.

d. **Classifieds:** Designed to be brief and to the point, the format ensures easy access of information. Vacancies are listed in specific and relevant categories, thereby ensuring a higher degree of relevant response.

e. **Resume Database Access:** RESDEX for short, this product makes the client company's recruitment exercise simple, targeted, and focused as an "in your hands" solution. The client may search profiles that are specific to the clients' requirements and access fresh and active job seekers anytime from anywhere. RESDEX contains the highest quality resumes available in India today.

f. **Electronic Application:** This product is also referred to as e-Apps. The e-Apps Response Management System reduces times spent on managing applications by 80%. CV's are collected in a database format, which can be used to filter out relevant candidates from a large pool in a matter of minutes.

The first four services are job-posting services. The point to note here is that all of the above services/products offered by Naukri.com to employers are paid products/services.

Products for Job-Seekers

Naukri.com offers a range of services to the job seekers. A brief description of each product/service follows:

a. **Resume Flash:** Naukri.com has a database of 1000 leading placement consultants in India. For the requisite fee, Naukri.com sends the job seeker's resume to 800 or 1000 placement consultants. The choice of the number of consultants to whom the job seeker wants to have his/her resume sent is entirely his/hers.

b. **Resume Development:** Naukri.com's experts help the job seeker to develop a powerful and effective resume. This service is also rendered for a fee.

c. **Job Mail:** All the jobs posted on the site are first matched with a job seeker's profile and if there is a fit, the job listing is e-mailed to the prospective employee. This service may be subscribed to for a 3 or a 6-month period.

d. **Job Alert:** All the vacancies that Naukri.com gets are mailed to the job seeker. This is a free service.

e. **Resume Display:** In the Paid Resume Display option, the job seeker's CV is visible to all recruiters / HR Managers / Placement Consultants who visit Naukri.com looking for candidates free of charge to them. This service may be subscribed to for a period from 6 months to 1 year.

f. **Resume Manager:** This is a free service in which the job seeker's CV is visible only to Naukri.com's clients who have purchased the RESDEX product from Naukri.com.

In addition to the above products/services, Naukri.com also offers certain services such as short-listing candidates and organizing walk-in interviews which no other medium does. This makes Naukri.com an end-to-end recruitment solutions provider.

Technology Involved

Because the services offered by Naukri.com are deployed over the Internet, it requires a very sound technological backup. The organization has a 20 strong team of technology persons, out of which, 16 are on the software development side. This team is entrusted with the responsibility of continuously improving and upgrading existing products and adding new products.

Naukri.com has 10 servers in a server farm in the United States. The technology team in India manages those servers. The web site is served from the servers in the United States. The head office has about 250-300 personal computers, which are used for the daily operations. The operating system used is Linux, the web servers used are Apache, the RDBMS software used is MySQL and the programming language employed is PHP. According to Sanjeev Bikhchandani, not a lot of data mining is done at Naukri.com.

Product and Service Pricing Strategy

The basic strategy of Naukri.com is to be present at every price point in the market – right from Rs. 500 to Rs. 9 lacs. Presence at all the price points enables Naukri.com to service low budget customers, and, at the same time, have high end customers. A price list of Naukri.com's products/ services is appended at the end. The low priced services are there to basically enable penetration. To quote Sanjeev Bikhchandani, "Essentially our old strategy is penetration – to make the medium popular." There is grading in the price charged within a product also. For example, for one of the products RESDEX, the price can range anywhere between Rs. 15,000 to Rs. 1.5 lacs, depending on how many login's the customer wants, and whether the customer wants it for one month, three months or a year. Similarly, there are a number of other pricing options available.

CONSUMER SEGMENTS

The key segments in a B2B sense that Naukri. com serves are recruitment consultants and corporates. Within the placement consultant segment, it was found that consultants catering to different industries are different from each other in terms of their recruitment solution requirements. For instance, placement consultants serving the IT sector would be quite different from the other placement consultants. Within the corporate segment, the segmentation is by the verticals, that is, by the industry type. Segmentation is also done according to the size of companies. In some cases, segmentation is also done geographically.

Naukri.com serves all these segments and is a leader in all the segments. Naukri.com has been able to achieve a position of leadership in all these segments primarily because of the fact that it was the first mover in the online recruitment market. "I think one of the best-kept secrets of most market leaders is being the first mover. The fact that we moved three years before anybody else really helped us because we understood the customer, we understood the recruiter, we understood the medium, we understood the technology that has to work in order to make money", informs Sanjeev Bikhchandani. Also, because Naukri.com's knowledge of the Indian customer went a long way in contributing to the overwhelming success of Naukri.com. Bikhchandani believes that the foreign companies had to adapt their pricing strategy and their business model and there they floundered.

COMPETITION

Naukri.com's two closest competitors are Jobstreet.com and JobsAhead.com in the Indian market. However, some big multinational competitors, such as Monster.com, have also set up their Indian operations, namely, Monsterindia. com. The screens-shots of the websites of various competitors are provided in Appendix II. The details of these websites are presented below.

Jobstreet.com

Launched in 1995, JobStreet.com has also grown rapidly to become one of the leading Internet Recruitment websites in the Asia-Pacific. JobStreet. com offers a comprehensive suite of interactive recruitment services. International and local Asian corporations recruit from JobStreet.com's pool of talent and manage their recruitment process through uniquely developed software applications via the Internet. The web site has 2.5 million users and has country specific web sites for Singapore, Malaysia, India and Philippines. It has the following products and services on offer:

a)   Online Job Posting

- Employers can post jobs at their India site
- Email notification to suitable candidates through automated job alerts
- Browsing candidates are able to apply online immediately to posted job advertisements
- SiVA (JobStreet's online recruitment management system) Resume Management Application to zero-in on the right candidate

b)   JobStreet SELECT

- Screen applications and conduct first round interviews

c)   JobStreet IMPACT

- Employer career website management
- Access to candidate database
- Integrate all candidate data in SiVA (JobStreet's online recruitment management system) to the company's HR system.

d)   Other Services

- Online Testing – Employers can evaluate applicants with customizable online tests
- Targeted Banners
- Newsprint Ads - Candidates apply online to employers newsprint ads and process them with SiVA (JobStreet's online recruitment management system)

In addition to the above-mentioned products, JobStreet also has secondary sources of revenue, such as the facility given to clients to advertise on their web site.

JobsAhead.com

JobsAhead has a team of over 125 personnel spread across 8 metropolitan cities in India. It has the unique distinction of powering the job section of India's largest horizontal portals like Yahoo. Recently, in May 2004, US-based global leader in online jobs, Monster Worldwide Inc., announced that it has acquired JobsAhead.com for consideration of Rs 40 crores. [e] The website gets around 5.5 million unique visitors every month and has 2.7 million resumes posted on it. It has close to 5,000 corporates as its clients.

The deal involved acquisition of a company named Webneuron Services, which runs JobsAhead.com. JobsAhead.com was among early entrants in India's e-recruitment space, where it competes primarily with naukri.com. "India is an important and strategic market with vast pool of skilled manpower. We set eyes on India as it has one of fastest growing recruitment markets," says Stuart McKelvey, Monster Worldwide Group President (Asia Pacific). The original promoters of JobsAhead.com, which include Mr. Dalmia and Vice Chairman Mr. Alok Mittal, will continue to play their respective roles in new entity. They will benefit monetarily from acquisition besides venture capitalist ChrysCapital, which invested around Rs 25 crore in the company.

Prior to the merger with Monster, JobsAhead.com offered the following products/services to job-seekers.

a)   **Right Resume:** Resume writing service
b)   **Resume Blaster:** Sends resumes of job seekers to placement consultants all over the country and to the middle-east (for an extra fee).
c)   **Resume Highlighter:** Highlights the posted resume of jobseeker so that it may easily catch the attention of the recruiter/placement consultant.

d)   **Placement Directory:** Complete directory of top placement consultants across India and abroad.

e)   **Career Booster:** A package providing all the services listed above.

For employers, JobsAhead offers the following products/services:

a)   **Database Access:** Paid access to the database of job seekers.

b)   **Job Listings:** Employers can advertise their jobs on JobsAhead and let their jobs viewed by over 1 million job-seekers.

c)   **Stingers:** Employers' jobs can be directly delivered into job-seekers' mail boxes or the job seeker can be called for a walk-in interview.

This online job company has also been the only player globally to develop role-based matching techniques (MarksMan), which in conjunction with text-based resume search (TextStar), has significantly improved customer experience. MarksMan allows corporates to search for candidates by their current job role or designation. It defines the job requirement in a single phrase thereby reducing the cumbersome filling of search forms. A single click search, MarksMan classifies the recruitment market into 23 categories and 600 roles that users can easily understand. Users can further refine their search based on industry, experience, location and key skills.

TextStar works for the employers' company by allowing the user to perform a search on all the contents of a candidate's resume. This tool is similar to Google in its functionality. JobsAhead claims that the use of this tool makes any recruitment effort "100% more accurate."

Monsterindia.com

Monsterindia.com is a flagship brand of Monster Worldwide (NASDAQ Symbol: MNST), which is a leading online global careers network and hiring management resource. It was founded in 1994 by Chief Monster, Jeff Taylor, and at present, has sites in 20 countries around the world.

As part of its India strategy, Monster Worldwide Inc, the parent of job site Monster.com, has bought Indian Web site JobsAhead.com as a part of a global acquisition drive to boost revenues.[f] The deal, worth about Rs. 400 million ($9.6 million), is Monster's fourth acquisition in less than three months and is the first buyout in India, which is Asia's third largest economy and home to booming software and telecoms industries. JobsAhead. com, which focuses on IT and BPO recruitment will now be fully owned by Monster India. Monster Asia President and Managing Director Arun Tadanki said that the combined entity will have close to 3500 clients from across the industry and companies of various sizes. "The new entity will also have data base of 25 lacs job applications and unduplicated traffic of 55 lacs job seekers, which is twice as large as our nearest competitor," with an obvious reference to Naukri.com.

It offers products / services to three consumer segments – 1) job-seekers, 2) employers, and 3) movers. The *job-seekers* could search for jobs, build and post their resumes and access a number of pages of career information and advice. It also offered the regular e-recruitment facilities, such as resume registration and e-mail alerts. The job-seekers could also use the Monster site as a networking platform. The products for *employers* included searching the candidates in Monster's Resume Database tool, building the company's own private candidate database with the tool Career Site Hosting, leveraging the company's brand by letting candidates learn more about the company with the tool Employer Profiles, and streamlining the hiring process with the Hiring Tools, Applicant Tracking and Candidate Screening products. In addition, Monster also provided unique solutions to the large workforce moving from one location to another. To this segment, it offered services like finding a local real estate agent, getting instant mortgage rates, and planning the move within a short period of time. These services were provided on Monstermoving.com, positioned as "Your One-Stop Moving Resource."

Comparison of Competitors

The business models of the competitors are largely similar to each others. Except for the moving services offered by Monster.com, all of the models involved a mixture of services for both employers and job seekers. Job seekers are usually allowed free posting of resumes and the employers are charged to access the database.

There was considerable confusion as to which company was the market leader in online jobs market-space in India. According to some estimates, JobsAhead.com has a 40 per cent share of the online jobs market, while monster.com has another 25 per cent. "Together, we will be almost twice as large as the next player (naukri.com)," Mr. Dalmia of JobsAhead.com added. [g] According to comScore MediaMetrix, which is an international company that independently tracks traffic on the Internet, Monster and JobsAhead together got 55 lacs unduplicated (i.e., unique) visitors in April 2004 compared with 26 lacs for the nearest competitor. Despite the recent merger of its two competitors, JobsAhead.com and Monster, Naukri.com said it was well poised to achieve 100 percent sales growth in the current fiscal over the previous year's Rs.220 million. On the merger of JobsAhead.com with Monster, Sanjeev Bikhchandani, CEO of Naukri.com, claimed: "We are ahead of both JobsAhead.com and Monster combined in terms of traffic, daily additions, resume database and client base...Post merger, even clients are realizing the power of Naukri.com as a unified force credibly offering services and targeting sales of between Rs.400 million and Rs.450 million over sales of Rs.220 million in 2003-04." [h]

MARKETING STRATEGY OF NAUKRI.COM

Initial Marketing Strategy (1997-2000)

The initial marketing strategy was geared towards fulfilling two objectives. The first objective was to get the companies and placement consultants to list their jobs on the web site and the second one was to get job seekers to visit the site. Towards achieving the first objective, an intensive search exercise was carried out. The team went through the previous issues of several newspapers and magazines, went to libraries, scanned Yellow Pages and built a mailing list that contained names and addresses of approximately twenty four thousand companies and placement consultants who had placed an advertisement for jobs in the last five years. Letters were mailed out to them with information about the service. At the same time, another list of newspapers and magazines was compiled. Letters were also sent to these newspapers and magazines informing them of the introduction of this unique service. Advertising was also done but on a very small scale. It was restricted to small-classified displays in newspapers. In effect, initially, the marketing strategy of Naukri.com was based on direct mailing and it was actually a very low cost one.

Current Marketing Strategy (2001-2004)

The marketing strategy currently being followed by Naukri.com is "two pronged" one, in the words of their marketing manager Ayesha Kapur. Naukri.com reaches out to two segments primarily – the job seekers and the employers. To reach out to recruiters, Naukri.com has a 130–140 strong sales force across the country that go around and meet the clients face to face, introduce them to the products and explain them. The mechanism adopted to reach out to the other segment, that is, the job seekers, is aggressive advertising. The aggressive advertising has kept momentum only during the last year (2003-2004). Naukri.com has been advertising on television and the print media and is now exploring radio as a medium for advertising its services and products. Advertisement on television has included promotion during the India–Australia cricket game series telecast on the national T.V. network, *Doordarshan,* in the year 2001.

Such aggressive advertising is a new feature of Naukri.com. Earlier, when the company was a start up and the revenue was not as much as it is today, advertising was done on a much smaller scale. Says Ayesha Kapur, "So two years ago, when our revenues were about Rs. 4 crores, accordingly the ad budget was something smaller than what it was last year. This year we are targeting Rs. 20 crores. Accordingly our ad budgets have also grown."

For the year 2004, the marketing budget of Naukri.com is close to Rs. 4-5 crores. The figure of how much to spend on advertising is arrived at by taking into consideration a number of factors like what needs to be done in the north, south, east or west India, which media to use for advertising, and so on. Also, the company is now looking at advertising as more of an investment rather than an expense.

Sanjeev Bikhchandani is of the opinion that a service should be advertised only if advertising is producing results. According to him, Naukri.com did not advertise aggressively earlier because they "did not have the wherewithal to take advantage of advertising". Now that the market is booming, management at Naukri.com believes that this is the right time to advertise. Therefore, when Naukri.com was a start up, focus was on development of business, growing products, and increasing product offerings. Once venture capital funding was taken, a conscious decision was taken to shift focus to grow business, invest in infrastructure, develop offices all over the country and advertise.

Alliances with Other Organizations

Media alliances with various media houses like Hindustan Times, New Indian Express, and The Telegraph also form a part of the marketing strategy of Naukri.com. The management says that they also consider themselves as a media company. They have a certain reach and the newspapers have their own reach. Therefore, there are always some people that Naukri.com manages to reach and some people that the newspaper houses manage to reach. The deals thus sealed require the newspapers to provide some advertising space to Naukri.com. Naukri.com, on its part, promotes these newspapers on its web site, in a bartering kind of arrangement. These alliances, thus, give the company frequent advertising and also save the company a lot of money.

Advertising over the Internet is primarily accomplished by means of alliances with established sites like MSN and Yahoo. In these deals, MSN or Yahoo places a banner or a text link on their site. Depending on the number of click-throughs, number of CV registrations and number of banner impressions, payment is made to MSN and Yahoo. There is no revenue sharing arrangement between Naukri and MSN or Yahoo. The objectives of online advertising are similar to that of television and print advertising – drive CV registration. But promotion over television and print has the additional objective of branding, which is not there in Internet advertising.

Positioning of Naukri.com

The services of Naukri.com are positioned in a different fashion for job seekers and employers. The positioning for employers is end-to-end recruitment solutions. For some key clients, Naukri.com has done first round of short listing, and organized walk in interviews, but those types of services are rendered to only key accounts.

For job seekers, the positioning is essentially in terms of the largest database of jobs that Naukri.

com claims to have in its possession. It also claims to have jobs in its database that are of a much superior quality as compared to the jobs in the database of the competitors. Value proposition is also a part of the positioning. Naukri.com promises the following advantages to its customers, both the job seekers and employers:

- National and global reach
- Recruitment costs reduced by 80%
- Hiring cycle time reduced by over 60%
- Reduced junk and irrelevant responses
- Confidentiality
- Several options to suit varying recruitment needs
- Management of responses through Naukri.com's e-recruitment software application

Product/Service Development at Naukri.com

The sales force of Naukri.com is in constant touch with the clients. The sales team brings back feedback on a daily basis. This forms the major source of intelligence and is one of the main inputs that go into new product development. The needs of the HR managers in various sectors are studied thoroughly to determine the features that may be incorporated into the new product. Other modes of intelligence gathering include looking at competitor's web sites and products, and analyzing what the market is demanding. This is then followed by the discussion with technology team. They determine the best way in which the new product may be deployed over the Internet. Other departments like finance and operations play their respective roles in new product development.

Interestingly, no formal marketing research is done for intelligence gathering purpose. Most of the information is what the clients give to the sales people of Naukri.com. Marketing team at Naukri believes that the clients would be honest while revealing information because business here is primarily based on relationships that develop

over a period of time. Says Ayesha Kapur, "It is not a question of making a sale once and not seeing them again. It is not like, say for instance, advertising in print, where there is not that hand holding, being in touch with clients." The product development team adds two to three features to their products on a daily basis based on the feedback they receive through the sales team. The marketing team dispatches a lot of corporate communication to their clients to make the clients aware of the small improvements that have been made to the existing products. But most of the talking is still done by the sales team.

Co-Branding

Naukri.com is very clear in this regard. It will not indulge in any sort of promotion that dilutes its brand. As mentioned earlier, several alliances have been forged with media houses like Hindustan Times, etc., but none of them can be strictly called a co-branding exercise. Naukri.com did a co-branded section with Business Today called "Jobs Today". But in that venture too, according to the marketing manager of Naukri.com, Business Today stood on its own strength and Naukri.com stood on its own strength. The section "Jobs Today" no longer appears in Business Today as it has been discontinued.

Innovative Mailing

Instead of sending out plain brochures to corporate clients, marketing team at Naukri.com has an innovative theme-based direct mailing. For instance, they created a "Stress Ball" campaign, the theme of which was "Squeeze the Stress Out of Recruiting". Then, for the response management team, a puzzle was created with the theme "Take the Puzzle Out of Recruiting". This, according to Ayesha Kapur, is helping because "….everyone gets a brochure every now and then through a courier but if you get something that's interesting, you look at it, it's got a theme around it, you can squeeze it, play around with it. It's a little bit more interesting".

Offline Presence

Naukri.com brought out a magazine that had all the jobs listed and was sold on the news stands. But that has taken a back seat lately. This magazine was brought out with the intention of catering to those people who did not have access to the Internet or those who did not have the time to navigate through the site and find relevant jobs. The magazine was intended to be a ready reckoner with the Top 1500 jobs listed. The jobs were classified in terms of different functional areas, different levels in terms of seniority – senior level, middle level, junior level, freshers, and so on. However, at the moment, it appears that the reason why it has taken a back seat is because the online business is doing very well. Therefore, the management is just focusing on the online business in terms of all their resources of management, technology, operations, and humans.

THE FUTURE OF NAUKRI.COM

Naukri.com has got elaborate market expansion plans for the future. It plans to take its existing products to new markets outside India. The markets that are being eyed include the United States of America and the Middle East. If there is a requirement for Indian talent in those markets, then Naukri.com wants to be in a position to satisfy those demands by allowing the recruiters there to come in contact with the talent in India. The ultimate goal of Naukri.com is to be a global hub for Indian talent.

As far as mergers and acquisitions are concerned, Sanjeev Bikhchandani does not see a need for it in the foreseeable future. He says "We do not need mergers. We are doing well in the current state. And, at least in the foreseeable future, we know we don't need to merge. As far as acquisitions are concerned, we are growing so fast without acquisition, we feel we don't need an acquisition." Also, Naukri.com is not contemplating an Initial Public Offer in the near future because, according to Sanjeev Bikhchandani, companies go for IPO's in order to raise money and since Naukri.com is internally generating all the money it needs, he does not feel that there is a need for an IPO.

Are those viewpoints likely to change with the merger of Monster.com and JobsAhead.com?

ENDNOTES

[1] Corresponding Author: Assistant Professor, Department of Industrial and Management Engineering, Indian Institute of Technology Kanpur, India, Email: sswami@iitk.ac.in. The author thanks these MBA students for their work on this case- Neelabhro Deb, Sudhir Nagle, Sreejith Ummathiriyan, and Bindumadhavi P.

[2] U.S. $ = Rs. 45.00 (approx.), Units conversions: 1 lacs = 0.1 million, 1 crore = 0.1 billion

[3] "Monster Worldwide buys India's JobsAhead.com for $9.6 mn," [http://www.expressindia.com/fullstory.php?newsid=31796#compstory, May 25, 2004]

[4] "Naukri.com to generate Rs.450 mn in sales in 2004-05," [http://www.keralanext.com/news/index.asp?id=38521, June 8, 2004]

[5] "Monster India buys JobsAhead.com," [http://www.deccanherald.com/deccanherald/may262004/b1.asp, May 26, 2004]

[6] Monster Worldwide buys India's JobsAhead.com for $9.6 mn, [http://www.expressindia.com/fullstory.php?newsid=31796, May 26, 2004]

[7] "Monster acquires JobsAhead," http://autofeed.msn.co.in/pandoraV2/output/30C606E3-C4D6-4B25-BDD3-

143

8A0CBCD359EB.asp, [May 26, 2004]

8   IndiaNews:Naukri.comtogenerateRs.450mn
in sales in 2004-05, http://www.keralanext.
com/news/index.asp?id=38521 [June8,2004]

APPENDIX I

Profiles of Management Personnel of the Company

Sanjeev Bikhchandani (CEO): He is 38 years old. He did his graduation from St. Stephen's College Delhi in B.A. (Economics). Subsequently, he completed MBA from Indian Institute of Management, Ahmedabad. He has been associated with MNC's like SmithKline Beecham and Lintas. IIM Ahmedabad, IMT Ghaziabad, Times School of Marketing and Delhi School of Communication have invited him as a guest lecturer in the functional area of marketing. He has been the former editor of "Careers" – the career supplement of Pioneer and has co-authored two books on job hunting and careers. He is also the member, Editorial Advisory Board, Encyclopedia Britannica India, student's edition.

V. N. Saroja (COO): She is 33 years old. She did her graduation in mathematics from Hindu College in 1988 and followed it up with a MBA from Indian Institute of Ahmedabad in 1990. After a five-month stint at IFCI, she began freelance consulting and preparation of multi-client reports. Clients included NASSCOM, Vedika Software, HTA, Trikaya Grey, Garware, Wallropes, Salora and some NRI's amongst others. She has been a visiting faculty at IMT Ghaziabad and National Institute of Advertising and has been associated with Info Edge since 1991. She has been with Naukri.com ever since its inception.

Ambrish Raghuvanshi (CFO & Head – HR): He is 40 years old. He holds a Bachelors degree in Commerce, is a Chartered Accountant and an MBA from XLRI, Jamshedpur. He has worked with MNC banks like HSBC, Standard Chartered and Bank of America where he was VP of the Corporate and Investment Banking.

Simeryn Jeyadev (Head, Operations): She is 38 years old. She started her career in 1985 with ABC Placement Consultants and moved to NIIT Ltd. in 1988 where she held various responsibilities including sales, center administration, training, co-ordination and corporate communications.

Hitesh Oberoi (Head - Sales and Marketing): He is 30 years old. He is a Computer Science engineer from IIT Delhi and an MBA from IIM Bangalore. He was formerly with Hindustan Lever Limited.

Anil Lall (Head of Technology): He is 37 years old and has 14 years experience in software development. He graduated in commerce from Bhagat Singh College in the year 1986.

Vivek Khare (General Manager – Technology): He is 30 years old. He did his M.Sc. (Physics) from IIT Kanpur and MBA from Birla Institute of Management Technology, New Delhi. Previously, he was employed with FIITJEE.

Sharad Malik (Advisor): He is 38 years old and is an electrical engineer from IIT Delhi. He did M.S. and Ph.D. in Computer Science from University of California, Berkeley in 1987 and 1990 respectively. Currently he is a Professor in the Department of Electrical Engineering, Princeton University and also serves as a consultant to a number of companies in the Silicon Valley technology companies.

Sushil Bikhchandani (Head – US Operations): He is 45 years old. He did his B.Tech (Computer Science – 1978) from IIT Delhi. He did his MBA from IIM Ahmedabad. In 1986, he completed his Ph.D. in Economics from Stanford University. Currently, he is a professor at the Anderson Graduate School of Business at the University of California, Los Angeles.

Surabhi Motihar (Head – Product Development): She is 36 years old and did her graduation in Economics from St. Stephen's College, Delhi in the year 1986. In 1989, she finished her MBA from Indian Institute of Management Ahmedabad. She worked as a marketing executive in Nestle India Limited where she was responsible for product management (Maggi noodles).

APPENDIX II

Screen shots of Different Websites Referred in the Case

This work was previously published in Contemporary Research in E-Marketing, Vol 2, edited by S. Krishnamurthy, pp. 58-87, copyright 2005 by IGI Publishing, formerly known as Idea Group Publishing (an imprint of IGI Global).

Chapter X
Trademark Infringement in Pay-Per-Click Advertising

Peter O'Connor
IMHI, Essec Business School, France

INTRODUCTION

Since its launch in 1994, the Web has continued to grow at a phenomenal rate, from an estimated one billion Web documents in 2001 to over eleven billion in January 2005 (Gulli & Signorini, 2005). For most users, navigating this ever expanding sea of data has become a significant challenge. Search engines – sites that maintain indexes of Web content – allow users to specify words / phrases and return a list of sites that potentially match these criteria – have become a key way of finding information on the Web. Google, the world's largest search engine is estimated to have indexed over 8 billion pages (Sullivan, 2004c) and to be used in nearly 50% of consumer searches (Nielsen NetRatings, 2006). Over 6.4 billion individual searches took place during May 2006 within the USA alone (Comscore, 2006). Clearly being favourably positioned in such search results

is very important for site owners wishing to get visibility to the online consumer.

In the beginning, search engines were unbiased, striving to display the results that provided the most relevant answers to user queries (Sullivan, 2002). While many were supported by advertising, in general this took the form of banner advertisements – graphical adverts displayed across the top of the page and clearly differentiated from the engine's search result listings. Today, however, search engines need more workable business models to meet the substantial costs of maintaining their databases and improving their technology (Princeton Research Associates, 2002). For that reason, many now market their ability to route consumers towards specific Web sites - blurring the line between their 'results' and their 'advertisements'. Like tour guides supplementing their income by bringing potential customers to restaurants or gift shops, many search engines now actively direct users to sites which have paid for positioning on their results pages (Lastowka, 2002).

In most cases, these paid placements are based on advertisers bidding for the specific keywords under which they wish to be displayed. For example, an online sports retailer might wish to appear whenever users enter "running shoes" as a search criterion. Bidding on these keywords would insure that the sports retailer's site is displayed prominently in the resulting search listing. Controversy has arisen, however, over the use of trademarked terms as keyword triggers. For example, can the same online retailer bid on the keyword "Nike" and / or use the trademark "Nike" in the copy of the advert subsequently displayed, thus potentially diverting shoppers who might otherwise have bought directly from Nike.com - the Web site of the trademark owner? Clearly doing so compromises Nike's brand equity – its monopolistic right to be able to profit from its investment in building up the Nike brand (Arvidsson 2006). As George (2006, p 215) puts it "brands are the placards by which modern consumers choose their products". Corporations rely on brands to stimulate consumer awareness and foster an affinity for their products (Spinello 2006). Legal protection against brand infringement comes from trademark law – a subsection of intellectual property law that prevents third parties from benefiting from the value and goodwill built up in a brand (Gallafent 2006). However, such legislation has developed in the off-line world. How do its principles and practices transfer to e-commerce? While still a developing subject, this paper examines the ethical and legal position surrounding trademark infringement in a specific area of the electronic arena – within paid search advertising. The paper explains the rational behind the problem, outlines the current legal situation and offers advice as to how trade name owners can better protect their e-brand.

BACKGROUND

Search engines have become an essential tool, with search volumes increasing at over 20% per year as users struggle to find relevant information on the ever expanding World Wide Web (Sen, 2005). Research has shown that users – in addition to using search engines to perform searches - now also often type site URLs directly into search boxes, suggesting that they use search engines not just as data harvesting tools but for navigation (Smith, 2005). Given such dependence, gaining a favourable position in search results listings is important for anyone wishing to gain exposure to online consumers and maximise traffic. Research by Jupiter Media shows that 93% of users do not look past the first two pages of search results (Thompson, 2004), while Sen (2005) claims that users hardly ever go beyond the first three pages – approximately the top 30 listings - making inclusion in this subset of results essential for consideration by the customer. Search engine marketers use two primary techniques to try to increase their positioning in search result listings. *Search engine optimisation* focuses on manipulating Web page structure and content in order to be naturally ranked highly under particular search terms, while *paid placement* instead pays for position, usually on a competitive cost-per-click basis.

Organic Search Engine Optimisation

Search engines use specialized software, known as 'spiders', to crawl the Web, classifying each page they encounter and adding it to their database so that it will subsequently appear in search result listings. Marketers try to manipulate these spiders to give their pages favourable positions by modifying their pages' HTML (for example the title tag, meta-tags, headings or links) and / or page content to convince the spider's ranking algorithm that the page is highly relevant to the search terms desired, and that thus it should give that page a higher purported relevancy than competing pages in the search-results listing for the specified terms (Sen, 2005).

Organic search engine optimisation, as this is known, suffers from several limitations. Firstly, the search engine's proprietary classification algorithms are both secret and complex, making it difficult to identify what modifications might be needed to get better positioning. Classification algorithms change frequently and thus any gain achieved by modifications may subsequently be lost. Each search engine stresses different issues, and thus optimising for one may negatively affect positioning on others. Lastly, the modified pages must be reevaluated by the classification algorithm for any changes to be taken into account. Although spiders revisit periodically, it can take up to 120 days for the results of modifications to take effect (Sen, 2005). Site owners can speed up this process by paying search engines to carry out the review within a fixed time frame and to check back for updates more regularly, a process known as *paid inclusion*. However, this does not guarantee that the site will be listed under a particular set of search terms or have a favourable position, merely that it will be reindexed in a timely fashion. Thus, search engine optimisation is time consuming and costly, and offers little guarantee of success in terms of consistently high rankings. Marketers have to adapt to ever changing classification strategies to both maintain position and improve rankings (Pasternack, 2006). Such limitations and uncertainty are driving many marketers towards using paid placement to help insure that their sites are favourably positioned.

Paid Placement

Instead of spending time manipulating sites with little guarantee of success, paid placement allows advertisers to pay for positioning in search results listings (Sen, 2005). Such sponsored links are acquired by competitively bidding on specific keywords, usually on a Pay-per-Click (PPC) ba-

sis, with the advertiser making the highest bid generally appears first when a user searches for that keyword (Sullivan, 2004b). For example, if an advertiser wished to appear in top position for "running shoes", he might agree to pay 25 cents per click. If no one else offered to pay more, then he would appear in the number one spot. If someone else later decided to pay 26 cents, then he would fall to number two position unless he increased his bid to regain the top listing (Sullivan, 2004d).

A number of different paid search networks exist, with the biggest being Google AdWords and Yahoo! Search Marketing (formerly known as Overture) (Krol, 2006). These are networks in the sense that in addition to displaying adverts within their own results listings, both also syndicate sponsored listings to a large number of third party sites (Sullivan, 2004b). For example, Google places sponsored listings on other search engines (such as Ask.com and AOLSearch), on content sites (such as the NewYorkTimes.com, HowStuffWorks and MySpace), as well as a large number of smaller sites that allow Google to crawl their content and integrate relevant adverts in return for a revenue share as part of its Adsense program (Sen, 2005). Some of the sites powered by Yahoo! Search Marketing include Altavista, CitySearch, CNN and NationalGeographic.com.

Sponsored listings are usually (but not always) segregated from organic search results and labelled as adverts. Their position on the results page can vary. For example, on its own search results pages, Google normally displays its sponsored listings (known as AdWords) down the right-hand side of the screen, separated from organic results by a vertical bar (Burden, 2005). Yahoo!, in contrast, displays its sponsored listings above and in the same format as its organic results, with the term ("sponsored") appearing beside each link. Google also sometimes positions sponsored matches above its organic listing, but shaded in a different colour to clearly distinguish such listings from normal results. However, particularly on syndicated sites, the line between 'results' and 'advertisements' has become blurred (Lastowka, 2002). According to Sullivan (2004a), with traditional media like print or television, consumers can identify adverts as they look different from normal content. Over time they have established criteria to help them determine which is which. However, on search engines, sponsored listings have only become commonplace relatively recently, which is not much time for consumers to develop clues as to what is an advert (Sullivan, 2002). Thus, combined with the lack of obvious differentiation on many sites, it is questionable as to whether the consumer actively distinguishes between paid and natural search results listings. This issue has prompted the U.S. Federal Trade Commission to issue guidelines about how search engines should disclose paid content to avoid such confusion.

Using paid placement overcomes many of the limitations of search engine optimisation, as it effectively guarantees visibility under the desired set of keywords (Haig, 2001). Adverts appear instantly, can be changed at will, and the advertiser has total control over position, title, content, and even where the user is taken if they click on the link. Changes in the search engine's ranking algorithm have no effect and adverts can be precisely targeted thus increasing the likelihood of delivering highly qualified traffic (Hansell, 2006). Payment is performance based (usually cost per click basis) and, with a set budget per advert per day, costs are known in advance and entirely performance based. Because of these advantages, paid placement has become the search engine marketing strategy of choice for most online sellers (Sen, 2005). It accounted for approximately 83% of the estimated $5.75 billion spent on search engine marketing in 2005, compared to just 11% for organic search optimisation (Krol, 2006).

TRADEMARKS AND PAID PLACEMENT

A trademark is anything that, when used in connection with the sale of goods or services identifies the source, sponsorship or affiliation of the goods or services (Heilbronner, 2006). Trademark law is a subsection of intellectual property law, which also contains patent and copyright law (Skibell & Kazemi, 2005). However, unlike other areas of intellectual capital law, with trademark law the focus is on the protection of the consumers rather than the property owner. Both patents and copyright provide exclusivity to the property owner, allowing them alone to reap the economic benefits associated with that property for a limited period of time. Trademarks, on the other hand, protect consumer by allowing them to associate a particular trademark with a particular company, assuring them that the origin of the product bearing that trademark is in fact genuine (Popov, 2005). As Skibell and Kazemi (2005) point out, whether the consumer has a preference for, or a dislike of a particular product, trademarks allow them to make decisions based on their previous experiences with that product. In the absence of such protection, unscrupulous producers could use the goodwill established by another company to confuse the consumer.

Trademarks do not have to be registered with any government office in order to be established, although registration with the United States Patents and Trademark Office (USPTO) results in greater legal protection (Tysver, 2005). Unregistered trademarks are called "common law" trademarks, and rights under these trademarks arise by virtue of the use of the mark in question by a business for some purpose including, for example, the marketing of a product or service (Heilbronner, 2006). The most important attribute of a common law trademark is that it is limited in scope. Generally, and because common law rights only exist as a result of use in a particular area, the territorial scope of common law trademark rights is the geographic area of use, business presence and reputation (Heilbronner, 2006).

An estimated 20% of online searches are for trademark terms (Elixir Systems, 2006). Trademark owners argue that in such cases consumers are searching for information about, or to purchase, the mark holder's products. When trademarks are used by third parties as keywords in paid search engine marketing, the resulting bias in the search result listings may mean that the customer is diverted to the third party site, and the products sold indirectly (thus necessitating the payment of an unnecessary mark-up or commission) or even diverted to competitors and the sale lost entirely.

There is considerable evidence that bidding on trademarks is highly effective. DoubleClick claim that most buyers start their searches with generic terms, but rely on branded searches to find sites in the period immediately leading up to purchase. Searches for brand names become more prominent as the purchase date approaches, peaking in the session in which the sale actually occurs (DoubleClick, 2005). There is also evidence that branded searches may be more effective, with 16% of searchers who made a supplier related search making an instant purchase compared to only 5% of those who searched on more generic terms (DoubleClick, 2005). Hitwise also maintain that traffic from branded search terms has the highest conversion ratio, so brand hijacking can have a real impact on a company's bottom line (Hitwise, 2006). Despite the effectiveness of branded search, studies estimate that trademark owners are responsible for only 7% of all brand bidding on search engines (Plave, 2005). It's clear that customers are being diverted by third parties and that businesses around the world are losing millions of dollars in revenue as a result of trademark infringements in paid search.

To combat such abuse, trademark owners are often obliged to themselves participate in paid placement, engaging in costly bidding wars with competitors to protect trademarks that they have already established in the off-line world. However, legal remedies are also available to protect trade names in such situations. The legal position is outlined in the following section, and practical advice as to how to more thoroughly protect a brand in the online search environment is then presented.

THE LEGAL PERSPECTIVE

Initial legal precedent on trademarks in paid placement comes from cases involving pop-up advertising on the Internet. While one of the initial cases (Washington Post Newsweek Interactive Company *v.* Gator) found that the triggering of pop-up adverts based on a trademark was deceptive, several subsequent cases ruled that such practices were allowable. For example, in both U-Haul *v.* WhenU and Wells Fargo *v.* WhenU, the courts found in favour of the defendant as it ruled that WhenU merely used the marks for a "pure machine linking function" and in no way advertised or promoted the trademark holders' Web address or any other trademark. The court held that there was no trademark infringement as WhenU only used the trademarks in its directory to determine which adverts to display to customers and, since adverts appeared in a separate window, did not hinder access to the trademark holder's Web sites.

However, a subsequent ruling (1-800 Contacts *v.* WhenU) introduced an argument that is often still used today in trademark cases in the online environment – *likelihood of customer confusion*. During this case, the plaintiff presented strong expert and survey based evidence that demonstrated how users presented with pop-up adverts on the 1-800 Contacts' Web site perceived them to be generated by and approved by the Web site owner, leading the judge to conclude that there was a strong likelihood that customers would be confused as a result of the appearance of the pop-ups (Ripin, 2003). As such confusion would allow third party sites to benefit from the trademark, such usage was deemed to be unfair, the pop-up advertising network was deemed to have infringed 1-800 Contacts' trademark and such usage prohibited.

Trademark use in meta-tags provides further legal precedent (Lastowka, 2002). Meta-tags are hidden lines of code on every HTML page that are used to describe a page's contents to visiting spiders. While search engine operators maintain that they no longer give much emphasis to meta-tags in their ranking algorithms, most Web marketers still consider it important to include appropriate phrases (including trademarks) as meta-tags on pages to help with organic ranking (Oliva, 2004). Competitors could also include these same trademarks in their meta-tags in order to try to appear alongside or above the company's site in search results listings (Howell, 2006). However, such usage has in general been found to be unlawful.

While early rulings focused on trademark infringement under a likelihood-of-confusion analysis (as with pop-up adverts discussed above), Brookfield Communications Inc *v.* West Coast Entertainment Corp. introduced a more useful *initial-interest-confusion* argument (Lastowka, 2002). Even though "moviebuff" was a registered trademark of Brookfield Communications, West Coast Entertainment intended to set up a site at Moviebuff.com and use moviebuff in the meta-tags of its pages. Prohibiting the use of the domain name, the court introduced a landmark judgment on meta-tag use. While consumers viewing search results influenced by such meta-tags would be unlikely to be confused as to which was the real Brookfield site (thus negating the likelihood-of-confusion argument previously used), the court ruled that there existed the real possibility of initial-interest-confusion – "the diversion of potential customers from the Web site they were seeking to another site, based on the belief that the second site is associated with the original one sought". The crux of this concept is that the

users will be satisfied with the second site or be sufficiently distracted so that they will never arrive at or return to the site they initially wanted. If meta-tags placed West Coast's site among "moviebuff" results, this might divert consumers searching for Brookfield to alternative sites. The court compared this to a misleading billboard that directed consumers to exit a highway at the wrong place or to posting a sign with another's trademark in front of one's store, and ruled that such practices were not acceptable (Ripin, 2003). However, the court did note that West Coast would be permitted to use the more generic term "movie buff", which it described as a "descriptive term … routinely used in the English language to describe a movie devotee."

The UK Courts delivered a similar judgement in Road Tech Computer Systems Limited *v.* Mandata (CMS Cameron McKenna LLP, 2000). Mandata used Road Tech's registered trademarks in its meta-tags and also elsewhere in hidden text in its Web site. When Road Tech complained, Mandata removed some, but not all, of the offending meta-tags and refused to provide an undertaking not to use such trademarks in the future. Road Tech successfully sought judgment on admissions in relation to trademark infringement and summary judgment in respect of passing off (CMS Cameron McKenna LLP, 2000). Thus it is clear that the unauthorized use of trademarks (registered or not) in meta-tags is actionable in circumstances where they are being used to lure searchers away from the trademark owner's Web site.

However, it's also worth noting that the search engines themselves have never been held liable in such cases (CMS Cameron McKenna LLP, 2000). While they of course facilitate the practice, in most court cases they have been characterized as passive conduits duped and outwitted by the infringing meta-tags (Lastowka, 2002). While ruling have been issued against the third party sites using the trademarked keywords, search engines have to date escaped prosecution. No recorded decision has to date held a search engine liable, even thought all meta-tag cases involved search engines and even when the search engine has been put on notice as to trademark abuse (CMS Cameron McKenna LLP, 2000).

Given such clear precedents, trademarks use in paid placement should follow similar logic. When third parties bid on trademarks or use trademarks in the titles or copy of their adverts, they are intentionally trying to appear in the results for search terms of the trademark owner. As the test for infringement looks to initial interest confusion, it is difficult to see why the legal position should be different, and the courts have largely supported this argument. For example, in Nissan Motor Co. Ltd *v.* Nissan Computer Corp., the court ruled that there was no good cause for not extending the protection offered in meta-tag cases to infringements in paid search placement (Lastowka, 2002). The message is clear – when a trademark is being abused, the owner can take legal action against the advertiser to both prevent further infringement and recover damages for lost business (Thompson, 2004). While each case is very fact specific, with the court needing to assess whether the activities are likely to cause consumer confusion, likelihood of success is high, particularly when infringing sites represent the trademark owner's competitors and are using the trademark to generate business for themselves (Thompson, 2004).

However, the success of any legal action depends on being able to prove the likelihood of customer confusion. For example, in GEICO *v.* Google Inc & Overture Services, GEICO claimed that the search networks infringed upon its trademarks when it sold them as keywords to competitors, causing sponsored links to appear next to the GEICO site in search results. GEICO claimed this was likely to confuse consumers, and that that the sponsored links were misleading as they implied an association between GEICO and the companies displayed (Mirchin, 2005). According to the U.S. Trademark Act, to be liable for trademark infringement, a defendant must use

the trademark "in commerce" and "in conjunction with the sale, offering for sale, distribution, or advertising of goods and services." Google had previously argued in this same case that it only used GEICO's trademark in its computer coding and that such an invisible process could not constitute infringement. The court overruled this argument, and thus the question became one of whether the use of a trademarked word as a keyword trigger was likely to confuse consumers as to the source of the sponsored links (Mirchin, 2005). To prove infringement, GEICO needed to show that use of its trademark was "likely to confuse an ordinary consumer as to the source or sponsorship of the goods" – that is, it did not need to prove actual confusion, merely likelihood of confusion (Mirchin, 2005). However, the survey data presented by GEICO failed to achieve this, with the court concluding that "initial interest confusion" is more difficult to prove in the electronic environment than in the real world. While it might be time-consuming or expensive to retrace your steps if confused by a highway billboard using another company's trademark, in the online world all you need to do is click the "Back" button (Mirchin, 2005).

However, the court did rule that consumers were indeed confused when trademarks were included in the heading or text of adverts. However, this has less relevance as the search networks claim that they remove adverts which use trademarked terms in advertising titles or copy without the owners' permission (Mirchin, 2005). The case was settled under terms of confidentiality, but is important for Google as it gives the company a meaningful legal argument to support their continued use of trademark terms as keyword triggers. Similar rulings have been delivered outside the US. For example, in Germany Nemetschek *v.* Google ruled that it is advertisers, not the search networks, who are responsible for the keywords chosen. However, it also ruled that the search networks need to be able to disqualify trademark terms as soon as they have been informed of violations. Similarly, in Metaspinner media GmbH *v.* Google, the court ruled that there is neither trademark infringement nor unfair competition as long as the trademark does not appear in the advert text, implying that use as a keyword trigger is permissible (Anon, 2005b).

The positioning of sponsored links on a search results page may help to determine the likelihood of customer confusion. As discussed above, positioning varies among search engines. Google's approach appears least likely to create consumer confusion that could give rise to a charge of infringement. On Google, the sponsored links appear to the right side of the page rather than within the search results themselves (Thompson, 2004). On others search engines, including Altavista and Yahoo, the sponsored links appear above the actual search results – meaning that they often appear above the listing for the actual trademark owner's site. These sponsored links are often only distinguished by having the terms ("sponsored") appear beside the link, making them harder to distinguish from organic listings. Still other search engines (such as Dogpile) and sites to which the search networks syndicate their listings have the highest likelihood of confusion because they make no differentiation between sponsored links and actual search results (Thompson, 2005).

Thus, in the US at least, the search networks are legally justified in allowing advertisers to bid on trademarked terms as keywords for paid search engine marketing. Despite this, most search networks claim to be committed to helping trademark owners to protect their brands by formally prohibiting the use of trademarks as keywords or in advertising copy. However, such claims are not in fact completely accurate. While (outside the US) Google will prevent advertisers from bidding solely on trademarks themselves, it will not disable keyword phrases composed of trademarks used in combination with more generic terms – for example "Ford trucks" - the generic term "trucks" combined with the trademark "Ford" (Thompson, 2004). Similarly, Yahoo!

Search Marketing requires the trademark owner to provide evidence of confusion before disabling keywords (Thompson, 2004), and specifically allows such bidding where the linked page primarily provides comparison data (Seda, 2004). The search networks are protected in such behaviour under arguments of comparative advertising and fair use. For example, in Smith *v.* Channel the Ninth Circuit held that informational use of a rival's trademark in advertising is acceptable as long as the use is not false or misleading (Thompson, 2004). Similarly, in Playboy Enterprises Inc. *v.* Netscape Communications Corp., the court ruled that the search engines could never be sure that a searcher was not looking for information on the generic word "playboy" rather than the trademark "Playboy". In the court's opinion, generic terms, even when sold to competitors for their trademark value, are incapable of possessing a trademark meaning (Lastowka, 2002).

COMBATTING TRADE NAME ABUSE

Given the importance of search in gaining exposure with consumers, protection of a company's brand in the online environment has become an essential task. The best defence is a good offence, and thus trademark owners need to be proactive about finding and stopping those who seek to profit from their brand (Wehr, 2005). Search audits need to be conducted on a regular basis, examining both paid and organic search results for evidence of trademark infringement (Pattison, 2006). Where abuse is discovered, procedures by which both the search network in question and the advertiser are contacted to demand discontinuation should be established. While expensive, time consuming and sometimes frustrating, not doing so will undoubtedly result in business being diverted to competing sites.

The search networks have in general taken a hands-off approach to dealing with this issue.

Most placed the burden of responsible use on advertisers themselves, arguing that it is the latter who are abusing the system, and that trademark owners must resolve any infringement directly with each offender (Wehr, 2005). Google in particular actively promotes the use of trademarks as potential keyword triggers in the U.S. market, and, as discussed above, refuses to disqualify trademarks used in conjunction with generic terms worldwide. Trademark owners thus have to pursue the advertiser directly. However, actually doing so can be problematic. Finding the offender can be difficult as domain name registrations can now legitimately hide the owner's contact details, and sites may be deliberately registered in foreign countries where enforcement is more difficult.

Where the contact details of the offending site can be established, a cease and desist letter from the company's lawyer can be highly effective, with Seda (2004) estimating that 90% of infringements can be stopped in this way. Smaller sites in particular will usually discontinue their use of trademarks to avoid a legal battle, although in some cases legal action may be necessary. For this, evidence of abuse needs to be collected as by the time such an action gets to court, the illegal adverts in question will have disappeared. Thus it's important to capture a history of the activity (using screen captures) with as much detail as possible (Wehr, 2005). Specialised companies now exist to perform such audits, gather appropriate evidence and legally challenge persistent offenders.

Trademark owners also need to actively participate in the major paid search networks. Not only will this give them insider access to information on who is bidding or their trade names as keywords, but it will also help overcome the uncertainty of search engine optimisation and insure that their site is always listed prominently in relevant consumer searches. When combined with effective monitoring and management of trademark use on such networks, such actions should also be extremely cost effective as only the minimum bid should ever need to be paid since third parties should not be able to bid on trademarked terms without permission, and any clicks (and therefore any costs) should deliver highly qualified prospects.

CONCLUSION AND FUTURE PERSPECTIVES

Search has become an incredibly important part of the online promotion and selling process. Favourable positioning in relevant search results has become a key to success in the e-commerce environment. As the above discussion has demonstrated, paid placement has become the online marketing strategy of choice for many companies. On the paid search networks, bidding on third party trade names as keywords is effective in that it delivers highly targeted prospects, but it is also clearly controversial. Trade name holders claim that such practices divert business away from their sites, thus damaging the brand that they have already developed in the off-line world. In general the courts support this argument, but fail to attribute blame to the search networks that facilitate this process, forcing mark holders into the frustrating and difficult process of having to pursue legal action against multiple individual advertisers.

While in the US, search networks are legally justified in allowing advertisers to bid on trademarked terms, in the international arena, courts are increasingly placing at least some liability on the search networks for such infringements (Anon, 2005a). For example, a number of high profile cases in France - including Viaticum / Luteiciel *v.* Google, Louis Vuitton *v.* Google, Le Meridien *v.* Google and Accor *v.* Overture - have all ruled that search networks are guilty of trademark infringement when they allow advertisers to bid on trademarked terms or suggest such terms as potential triggers in their keyword suggestion tools. In all cases, the networks have been ordered to discontinue displaying the infringing adverts, delete the trademarks in question from their keyword generator and pay substantial damages to the trade name holders (Speer 2005). In each of these cases, the courts focused not on the likelihood of customer confusion but on the rights of the trademark holders and dilution of the brand, moving the legal argument from one of protecting customers to treating trademarks as a property of value for the mark holder (Anon 2005c). In fact in the Le Meridien case, the plaintiff did not even provide any evidence that any of its competitors had ever selected its trade names as keywords, merely demonstrating that Google might suggest the word "Meridien" as a keyword and that a search for that word might trigger adverts posted by its competitors (Hugot & Hugot, 2005). As Skibell and Kazemi (2005) point out, without any evidence of infringing adverts existing, it is impossible to prove customer confusion, and thus the French courts have in fact preemptively acted to protect the trademark, reflecting its value as a property asset of the mark holder.

A similar philosophy is emerging in the US with the introduction of the Trademark Dilution Revision Act of 2005 (Manning-Magid, Cox & Cox 2006). Although intended for use with trademarks in general, this Act may have unintended consequences for trademark use in paid placement by granting higher levels of protection to trademark owners in the online environment. As in the European situation, rather than basing infringements solely on the likelihood of customer confusion, this Act regards trademarks as the property of the mark holder (Skibell & Kazemi, 2005). Attempts by others to benefit from or falsely associate themselves with such marks are thus prohibited. While in the past legal remedies under dilution arguments only provided recourse to holders of famous trademarks and in very limited circumstances (Tysver, 2005), the 2005 Act greatly expands the definition of dilution and the range of marks to which it can be applied. While as yet largely untested in law, actions regarding

infringements in paid search engine marketing using this justification have a high likelihood of success and thus severely threaten the methods of operations and business models of the paid search networks.

These developments are driving a change in attitude in the major search networks. For example, in 2006 Yahoo! announced that they would no longer allow PPC advertisers to advertise or bid on trademarked terms (Pattison 2006). "On March 1, 2006, Yahoo! Search Marketing will modify its editorial guidelines regarding the use of keywords containing trademarks. Previously, we allowed competitive advertising by allowing advertisers to bid on third-party trademarks if those advertisers offered detailed comparative information about the trademark owner's products or services in comparison to the competitive products and services that were offered or promoted on the advertiser's site. In order to more easily deliver quality user experiences when users search on terms that are trademarks, Yahoo! Search Marketing has determined that we will no longer allow bidding on keywords containing competitor trademarks."

This leaves Google as the only major search network that currently allows advertisers to bid on trademarks as keywords. However, even this approach is softening, perhaps in response to the European rulings. Currently, if a trademark owner objects to the use of its trademark, Google has one commercial policy for the US/Canada and another for the rest of the world. If a trademark owner outside the US or Canada objects to a company using its trademarked terms in the actual content of the advert or in trigger keywords, Google will investigate and require the advertiser to remove the term from the content and/or keyword list. For example, suppose British Airways (BA) complains that Japan Airlines (JAL) purchased the use of the 'British Airways' keyword to trigger JAL ads. Upon BA's presentation of certain proof as set forth in Google's trademark policy, Google will prevent Japan Airlines from continuing to use the trademarked terms to trigger JAL-sponsored links (Mirchin, 2005). However, within the US Google is still maintaining a strong stance in allowing (and even actively encouraging) advertisers to bid on trademarked search terms (Olsen 2004). Thus, if Microsoft complains that Apple is using the word 'Microsoft' in the heading or text of its sponsored link advertising, Google will require Apple to remove the word. However, if Microsoft objects to Apple's purchase of the word 'Microsoft' as a keyword trigger in the US market, Google will not take any action. Given the importance of advertising revenues to the company, this is not surprising, but it is questionable as whether it is sustainable in the long term.

It's clear that the legal position with regard to trademark use in search engine paid placement is still developing and that few clear answers or precedents are available. However, given the growth in the importance of paid search on the Web, these issues need to be clarified in the short run to provide guidance for both advertiser and trademark holder as to what is acceptable and what is not. As the saying goes – watch this space!

REFERENCES

Anon (2005a) Google's AdWords under attack – Overview over the pending lawsuits, www.linksandlaw.com/adwords-pendinglawsuits.htm, Retrieved 29 December, 2006

Anon (2005b) AdWords lawsuits in Germany – Preispiraten decision, www.linksandlaw.com/adwords-google-germany-preispiraten.htm Retrieved 29 December, 2006

Anon (2005c) AdWords lawsuits in France – Trademarks as keywords illegal? www.linksandlaw.com/adwords-google-keyword-lawsuit-France.htm , Retrieved 29 December, 2006

Arvidsson, A. (2006) Brand Value. *Journal of Brand Management*, 13 (3), pp 188-192.

Burden, D. (2005). Marketing's haiku challenge. *Marketing (UK), 24 August 05,* 26.

Comscore (2006) Google sees its US search market share jump a full point in May, marking tenth consecutive monthly gain, Press Release, June 21.

CMS Cameron McKenna LLP. (2000). *Meta-tagging on search engines.* London.

DoubleClick, (2005) Search Marketing: It's Not About Your Brand, It's About the Customer, Smart Marketing Report, Jan / Feb (Online), Retrieved 29 December, 2006

Elixir Systems. (2006). *Online Reputation Management: Protect your brand.* Scottsdale, AZ.

Gallafent, R. (2006) Branding: The demands of the client, the needs of society and the effect of the law. *Journal of Brand Management*, 13 (3), pp 201-205.

George, A. (2006) Brand rules: When branding lore meets trade mark law. *Journal of Brand Management*, 13 (3), pp 215-232.

Gulli, A., & Signorini, A. (2005). *The indexable Web is more than 11.5 billion pages.* Poster proceedings of the 14th international conference on World Wide Web, Chiba, Japan.

Haig, M. (2001) The great search debate, e-volve, November 29, pp 47-51

Hansell, S. (2006, 16/8/06). Seek (on the Web) and the advertisers shall find you. *International Herald Tribune,* p. 13.

Heilbronner, M., Heilbronner, S. & Estis Green, C. (2006) *Profits and Pitfalls of Online Marketing: A Legal Desk Reference for Travel Executives,* TIG Global LLC, New York.

Hitwise. (2006) *Best Practice for Search Engine Brand Management.* London.

Hugot, O. & Hugot, J. (2005) Preliminary Relief Granted Against Google France in Adwords

Case", Juriscom.net, Feb 2, Retrieved 12 September, 2006

Krol, C. (2006, 16/1/06). Search engine marketing up 44% in 2005. *B to B, 91,* 3.

Lastowka, F. G. (2002). Search Engines Under Siege: Do Paid Placement Listings Infringe Trademarks. *Intellectual Property & Technology Law Journal, 14*(7), 1-7.

Manning Magid, J., Cox, A. & Cox, D. (2006) Quantifying Brand Image: Empirical Evidence of Trademark Dilution. *American Business Law Journal,* 43 (1) pp 1-42.

Mirchin, D. (2005). Google wins U.S. keyword case. *Information Today,* 22(9), 1-5.

Nielsen NetRatings. (2006). *MegaView Search Engine Ratings.* NewYork: Nielsen NetRatings.

Oliva, R. (2004). Playing the Search: So little time, so many sites. *Marketing Management* (April), 48-51.

Olsen, S. (2004) *Google plans trademark gambit.* CNET News April 13th

Pasternack, D. (2006). Good Organic Rankings Aren't Enough. In M. Alam Khan (Ed.), *Essential Guide to Search Engine Marketing.* New York, NY: Courtenay Communications Corporation.

Plave, L. (2005) *E-Business Legal Survival Kit,* DLA Piper Rudnick Gray Cary, Washington DC

Pattison, W. (2006, 9 March 2006). *Trademark Infringement Issues for Pay-per-Click (PPC) Advertisers.* Retrieved 25 August, 2006.

Popov, A. (2005) The extraterritorial reach of the Lanham Act over trademarks on the Internet: Adapting the Lanham Act to global e-commerce or an unjustified extension of US laws? Journal of Internet Law, May, pp 19-28

Princeton Research Associates. (2002). *A Matter of Trust: What Users Want From Web Sites - A Report on Consumer Concerns About Credibility of Web Sites.* Yonkers, New York: Consumer Reports WebWatch.

Ripin, P. (2003) Hotel Internet Marketers Beware: Pop-up and Keyword Advertising Threaten Your On-Line Brand. American Hotel & Lodging Association Knowledge Base. Retrieved 12 September, 2006

Seda, C. (2004). *Search Engine Advertising.* Indianopolis, IN: New Riders.

Sen, R. (2005). Optimal Search Engine Marketing Strategy. *International Journal of Electronic Commerce, 10*(1), 9-25.

Skibell, R. & Kazemi, N. (2005) The Unanticipated Consequences of the Trademark Dilution Revision Act for Search engine Advertising. *Journal of Internet* Law, 9 (5), pp 1, 6-16.

Smith, S. (2005). The Emerging Search Economy. *e-content* (Jan / Feb), 31.

Speer, L. (2005) (French Translation) French Trademark Ruling Against Google Keyword Advertising Upheld on Appeal (French Translation), Commerce & Law Report, pp 296-297.

Spinello, R. (2006) Online brands and trademark conflicts: A Hegelian perspective. *Business Ethics Quarterly,* 16 (3), pp 343-367.

Sullivan, D. (2002, 2 July). *FTC Recommends Disclosure to Search Engines.* Retrieved 3 September, 2006

Sullivan, D. (2004a, 22 November). *Buying your way in: Search Engine Advertising Chart.* Retrieved 2 September, 2006

Sullivan, D. (2004b, 13 Aug). *Pay Per Click Search Engine.* Retrieved 2 September 2006

Sullivan, D. (2004c). *Search Engine Wars V Erupts.* Retrieved 27 August, 2005

Sullivan, D. (2004d, 5 July). *Submitting via Paid Listings: Overture & Google Adwords.* Retrieved 2 September 2006

Thompson, C. (2004). Search Engines Invite New Problems. *Marketing Management* (April), 52-53.

Tysver, D. (2005) Trademark Dilution, www. bitlaw.com/trademark/dilution.html. Retrieved 3 September 2006

Wehr, L. (2005, 10 May). *Thieves, Scallywags and Scoundrels: Combating Trademark Infringement in Search.* Retrieved 28 August, 2006

Chapter XI
E–Branding the Consumer for Cultural Presence in Virtual Communities

Robert Pennington
Fo Guang University, Taiwan

ABSTRACT

Brands have evolved from signs of property rights to signs of product attributes to signs of consumer attributes. Brands have become an important mode of consumer communication, identifying and distinguishing consumers as social objects within consumer market culture. Virtual communities have evolved from telephonic verbal communication to highly interactive electronic media that provide rich audio-visual sensory detail that gives consumers a sense of being in an environment. As a fundamentally cultural phenomenon, marketing communication reflects shared patterns of consumer thoughts, feelings, emotions and behaviors. Virtual communities are particularly suited for communication in consumer culture because they afford consumers authentic cultural presence. Culture depends on communication. Communication depends on symbols. Symbols constitute electronic environments. E-branding affords consumers the necessary tools to communicate their roles and relationships in virtual consumer culture environments for transfer to actual consumer culture environments. Consumption in actual environments results in brand viability and marketing success.

INTRODUCTION

This chapter discusses brands as critical design elements in virtual communities. All human behavior communicates, including brand consumption, which is so important to consumer culture that any electronic environment without brands will seem unrelated to any actual environment. The increasing use of electronic technology in marketing communication requires that marketers understand the culture of consumption and function of brands as consumer communication. This understanding will enable marketers to create effective electronic environment designs for product and brand trial and to integrate electronic environments with other marketing communication.

This chapter is about the evolution of brands and virtual communities, projecting that evolution into future trends. The chapter begins by discussing the evolution of brands from signs of property rights to signs of consumer properties. The next section discusses the evolution of virtual communities. The following sections discuss culture generally, the system of meanings in consumer culture, culture in virtual communities, communicating culture through products and brands, and branding consumption. The final section discusses future trends, a continuing evolution, in which marketers design virtual communities that include brands to give consumers a sense of being in those communities.

EVOLUTION OF BRANDS

Brands are signs. Originally, brands were statements of property, that is, the right to possess, use, enjoy, and dispose of an object. Brands were necessary to distinguish objects that were difficult to distinguish by their own inherent properties, that is, attributes or characteristics. Brands further developed into statements of the outcome of product use when the attributes that cause the outcome were difficult to distinguish. That is, brand evolved to signify the expected outcome of human interaction with products.

Originally, brands most often occurred in the context of the products to which they were attached. By association, products first signified objects and second, the outcome on the environment of interacting with the product. Contemporary brands, however, most often occur within the context of marketing communication. That is, brands most often occur within the context of other signs. Therefore, consumers interpret brands based upon the context of communication more than upon product use or relationship with the producer.

Brands are not always depicted attached to products in marketing communication. Even when marketing communication does depict a product with which a brand is associated, the depiction is not the product itself (Mick, 1986). The depiction itself is a cultural representation with its own cultural meaning derived from cultural context. Within marketing communication, brands acquire meaning by association with other meaningful symbolic cultural elements. Indeed, marketing communication is critical to managing brand meaning. To the extent that brand meaning is connected to the product at all, brand meaning derives from the cultural meaning of the product or its symbolic representation.

McCracken (1990) has explained how marketing communication transfers cultural meaning to products, which then transfer meaning to consumers who use them. In fact, the product is a peripheral element in meaning transfer, important chiefly because consumers generally cannot acquire the brand without acquiring the product. The success of counterfeits demonstrates the greater importance of brands in relation to products.

Because brands derive significance from a context detached from any product, consumers can consume a brand without consuming the product that increasingly serves merely as a vehicle for the brand. Contemporary marketing communication identifies the target segment using symbolic elements that signify the target's attributes. By association in the context of marketing communication, brands signify the attributes of their target consumers. In brand consumption, the expected outcome of interacting with the brand is the acquisition of the target attributes.

Brands are not about products; they are about consumers. This chapter discusses brands as signifying consumers in the context of online interaction. This perspective does not apply to all brands in all situations. In some cases, brands signify products or objects to which they are attached. Indeed, this use of brands is important to e-commerce. In other cases, brands signify relationships that exist between consumers and products, consumers and producers, and consumers and resellers. This chapter, however, examines brands as signifying consumers' cultural, social, psychological, and philosophical relationships. In other words, the focus is on brands as they signify consumers' relationships with other consumers, with themselves and with the rest of the world.

All brands signify a relationship between consumers and an environment. However, brands differ on which environment, which aspect of that environment and which consumers they relate. In online environments consumers cannot physically inspect and evaluate the products or services offered. Branded products and services afford consumers assurance of certain specific attributes and standards of quality. This is a return to the early period of branding in the actual marketplace in which consumers looked for brands for assurance (Editors 1988). With the possibility of counterfeit products and services, however, a branded Web site affords further assurance. The policies of Amazon.com and eBay have made them into recognized brands that signify a secure relationship.

Such brands assure that physical interaction with a product or service will result in a desired modification of the physical environment. However, these brands do not signify the modification of the physical environment. Rather, they signify assurance. To succeed in a competitive environment, any competitor must meet consumers' non-compensatory decision-making criteria. Assurance becomes a standard that all brands must meet. When all brands signify the same level of assurance, a parity situation exists in which consumers assume assurance.

Ironically then, when all competing brands signify assurance, none of them especially signifies assurance within the framework of consumers' decision-making criteria. Each brand carries equal significance of assurance in relation to competing brands. Effectively, each brand signifies every other competing brand. Further, competing brands will likely match any successful product or performance change in another brand. Therefore, brands lose their capacity to signify distinctions in product features or performance.

Consumers, however, will still use brands to signify distinction. The new distinctions will be consumer-created. Although consumers may report product or performance distinctions where none exist, the actual distinctions are among consumers themselves. Consumers distinguish, compare and identify themselves, projecting those distinctions, comparisons and identities onto the brands they choose. Consumers brand themselves and each other in creating virtual communities (McWilliam 2000). The challenge for brand managers in the parity environment, then, is to signify distinctions among consumers. Those distinctions are based not only on cultural categories (Pennington 2006), but also upon cultural accepted methods for dealing with experience and modifying environments.

The following sections discuss relationships among consumers and how brands signify those relationships in virtual communities. The discussion treats online behavior as occurring in a cultural environment, with recognizable and detectable patterns of behavior. It builds upon previous work on marketing in virtual reality, presence in virtual environments and methodology for distinguishing idiosyncratic behavior from shared patterns. Further, it builds upon previous work on brands as a nonverbal language in consumer culture and the semiotics of brands in consumer discourse. This chapter explains how brands provide the forms, patterns, and symbols with which consumers deal with the electronic environment. The result is an e-culture in which brands signify consumers and their interrelationships.

VIRTUAL COMMUNITIES

Although Lynd's (1939) definition of culture referred to inhabitants of a geographical area, communication theorists of the early twentieth century had already argued that electronic communication could create communities independent of geographic contiguity (Susman, 1984). Electronic media began the progression toward virtual communities by breaking the geographic boundaries altogether. Although people could still share characteristics with others in their geographic communities, electronic media illustrated shared characteristics with others in distant communities. Culture was no longer bound by geography. The pseudoenvironment was one of cultural and social location. Behavior in response to the pseudoenvironment of social and cultural location, however, continued to occur in the actual world of the geographic environment.

Further development of technology created more sophisticated pseudo-environments, virtual environments. In virtual communities, people can group themselves by choice more easily than they can in geographic environments. Presence, the sense of being in an environment (Gibson, 1977) depends up the range and detail of sensory inputs the environment provides and on the ability to effect change in the environment in real time. Vividness, the range and detail of sensory inputs, and interactivity, the ability to effect change, not only provide a greater sense of presence in the cultural and social environments. They also

allow human behavior in the actual world to have consequences in the pseudoenvironment. The result is that consumers in the actual world respond to a pseudoenvironment with behavior in the actual world that has consequences in the pseudoenvironment.

Virtual communities comprise the inhabitants of e-locations created through technology. Consumers' sense of presence in e-communities depends, in part, on the vividness of the online experience. The concept of vividness refers to the range and detail of sensory inputs that technology provides. But vividness also refers to the sense of social location, which depends upon the range and detail of social inputs.

In virtual communities, just as in actual communities, consumers organize and deal with their experience by creating and choosing sets of forms, patterns and symbols. They create a culture that makes experience meaningful. As social concepts within the online culture, consumers choose forms, patterns, and symbols to place themselves in relation to other concepts of the online culture.

Therefore, the vividness of the virtual community depends not only on the technology but on the cultural significance of the content as well. Technology must provide range and detail of a meaningful cultural environment to evoke a sense of cultural presence. In actual communities, material goods constitute a code through which members define themselves (Baudrillard, 1988). The online environment is composed only of signs, not actual goods. For the online environment to be culturally meaningful, the signs must conform to the material cultural code of the target.

Studies of virtual communities (VCs) treat VCs as almost purely abstract. Although VCs form through the mediation of electronic devices, the VCs themselves are available for sensation only as verbal text (Bagozzi & Dhloakia, 2006). The significance of meaning of verbal text may be shared through social or cultural convention. But, except in the reader's imagination, verbal text lacks both the range and depth of sensory inputs and the interactivity necessary for a sense of presence. Indeed, as discussed in the literature, VCs call attention to the mediating role of technology that users must fail to acknowledge for a sense of presence. Except for the visual evidence of verbal text, then, VCs are not only impersonal but also intangible in the human sense. From this perspective, the only tangible attribute of VCs is the technology that mediates them. Or as Marx (1967) observed, relationships increasingly occur between objects rather than between people.

Memmi (2006) discusses virtual communities as a progression of the movement away from *Gemeinschaft*, the tradition community based on location, and toward *Gesellschaft*, modern communities based on association (Tönnies, 1963). However, the association-based character of virtual communities reflects technological limits that are disappearing rapidly. Increasingly, technology affords development of communities based on virtual locations, which implies a potential for a movement toward *e-Gemeinschaft*.

People join VCs to fulfill communication needs (c.f. Gupta & Kim, 2007; Memmi, 2006). Bagozzi and Dholakia (2006) define VCs as mediated social spaces in the digital environment that allow groups to form and be sustained primarily through ongoing communication processes.

All human behavior communicates (Watzlawick, Bavelas & Jackson, 1967). Further, all products of human behavior communicate. Verbal text is only one category of artifact. Any evidence of human interaction with the environment is an artifact that communicates. A sense of presence in a VC depends upon the interactivity and vividness of the VC. Vividness demands a richness of detail in communication. The greater the range of communication forms, the greater the likelihood of a sense of presence in the VC.

Yet Memmi (2006) suggests that vividness be a criterion for excluding telephony from consideration as a VC. He also suggests that telephony be excluded from consideration as a VC because

the technology is long established. If the purpose in studying VCs is to study recent technology only, then telephony can be excluded. However, newer technology and techniques integrate actual voice communication, such as voice-over-Internet protocol (VIOP), with other forms of audio-visual communication. Projecting new design considerations for VC development must include telephony. Most important, voice communication, whether actual or synthetic, contributes to a sense of presence by making more inputs available for sensation.

According to Preece (2000), a VC is a community of people with common interest of shared purpose, whose interactions are governed by policies in the form of tacit assumptions, rituals, protocols, rules and laws and who use computer systems to support and mediate social interaction and to facilitate a sense of togetherness. In essence, Preece has defined a culture sustained through the use of computer systems. This is an e-consumer e-culture in which both products and brands communicate cultural information. That is, products and brands are the social hieroglyphics that Marx (1967) described.

VC studies have derived categories based on analysis of participants needs: shared interest, relationship building, transaction and fantasy (Hagel & Armstrong, 1997; Talukder & Yeow, 2007). But these categories are not mutually exclusive. This chapter concerns marketing communication within VCs. Therefore, the principle category of concern would seem to be transaction. However, relationship is, in fact, the dominant concern.

For example, Daugherty, Li & Biocca (2001) and Li, Daugherty & Biocca (2002) conducted product-trial studies in which consumer experience in virtual reality applied to product use in actual reality. But as Ritson & Elliot (1999) pointed out, marketing study methodology often excludes by design the context within which a product is used and which gives the product its meaning. In the studies cited above, the product was a camcorder, which is most often used within a social context. Therefore, a study of product use in virtual reality that excludes any social context ignores product meaning. In other words, a valid virtual product trial must occur within the context of a VC.

A complete sense of virtual community depends upon the completeness of features and attributes available for sensation. A sense of presence depends upon vividness, which comprises not only the range of senses the environment stimulates, but also the amount of detail available for sensation (Pennington 2006). An environment that conspicuously lacks expected detail fails to elicit an empirical sensation of reality (Pennington 2001). An environment that fails to offer visual and auditory sensation of social objects is unlikely to elicit a sustainable sense of community.

CULTURAL ENVIRONMENT

Culture is a unifying theory of interrelated concepts. This definition derives from social science literature that considers culture to be "all the things that a group of people inhabiting a geographical area do, the ways they do things and the ways they think and feel about things, their material tools and their values and symbols" (Lynd 1939).

We can identify culture operationally by observing patterns that not only account for, but also shape individual behavior. Culture is the shared, learned patterns of thoughts, feelings, appetites, and behaviors, based upon a climate of values, for organizing or adapting to the natural and social environments (Pennington 2001a). We can recognize culture through the artifacts of those patterns.

Perhaps without realizing that they were doing so, marketers have studied culture for many years. The study of consumer behavior is a study of culture, as is the study of values and lifestyles, psychographics and other common research areas. These areas are not outside of culture, but rather integral components of culture. Although we can

inquire legitimately into the effects of culture on behavior, we can inquire just as legitimately into the effects of behavior on culture. The patterns we observe in the artifacts of human behavior or that we elicit through research are evidence of cultures and subcultures. The greater the commonality of occurrence, the more confident we are that we have found evidence of a culture. Distinguishing commonalities within larger patterns are evidence of subcultures.

In marketing, when we observe commonalities in behavior we call the groupings segments rather than cultures. But even common demographic groupings reflect cultural concepts and definitions. We study categories of age, sex, income, education, taste and so forth, because they are culturally significant. Each category attribute stands in a distinct cultural relation to other attributes of the same category. Each attribute has some distinguishing pattern of thought, emotion or behavior made tangible through an associated, culturally designated and recognizable object, symbol or object as symbol. These objects and symbols allow community members to identify, compare and distinguish their roles in relation to others. In consumer culture, the objects and symbols are products and brands.

CONSUMER MEANING

"Consumer" is a paradigmatic class of all those whose marketplace activities go beyond the satisfaction of material needs and wants. Consumers communicate through marketplace activity and marketplace signs. To be human is to communicate (Watzlavick, Bavels & Jackson, 1967). Those who are not consumers also communicate through marketplace activity. But for consumers, communication plays a major role in that activity. As a paradigmatic class, consumers are distinct from those who are not consumers. As a paradigm example, each consumer is identical to each other. But within the class, further classifications permit consumers to compare and distinguish themselves.

All consumers are not alike, as any beginning marketing student knows intuitively. Some distinctions have tangible foundations. To say that a consumer is female is one such distinction that implies not all consumers are female. Physical attributes determine whether a consumer is female, but those attributes may often elude observation. Consumption allows identity with or distinction from that attribute, which is discrete and has a binary opposite, male.

Some distinctions have less tangible foundations. To say that a consumer is feminine is such a distinction within the paradigmatic class that implies not all consumers are feminine and has a binary opposite, masculine. But feminine is not a discrete attribute; one consumer can be more or less feminine than another. And a consumer can be male and feminine or female and masculine. Although tangible and observable, the distinctions between feminine and masculine, and the degrees of those qualities, are not physical characteristics. Behavior patterns prescribed by a cultural code define femininity and masculinity.

Within consumer culture, categories of consumers actualize their attributes through a specified code. Consumption objects are components of that code (Douglas & Isherwood, 1996). Without the objects that the code specifies, a consumer is a cultural commodity with no identity. In fact, without the specified objects, the consumer is not even a consumer, but merely an indistinguishable human being. Outside the code, people are no more distinguishable than kernels of corn.

Within the code as well, consumers face a continuing process of identifying, comparing, and distinguishing themselves. As the market becomes saturated with a paradigm class of consumption objects, the object class itself loses the capacity to distinguish among consumers. In the use of such objects, consumers once again become cultural commodities. When all consumers have automobiles, for example, they cease to be consumers be-

cause consumption specifies a relationship, which supposes the possibility of distinction. When an object class loses the capacity to distinguish, the code then requires an additional object class to communicate distinction. However, because object acquisition and storage has a practical limit, the code of consumer culture has created a symbolic distinction within paradigm classes, that is, brands.

COMMUNICATING E-CULTURE

The core of culture is communication (Hall, 1969). Culture provides consumers with an inventory of meaningful objects and signs with which to communicate and recognize concepts and relationships. Because culture is learned and shared, dissemination depends upon access to communication. To disseminate culture, formal institutions and organizations tend to utilize formal mechanisms such as schools, churches, and other formal meetings. Products and signs acquire and retain meaning through explicit definitions and expressions.

Although consumption is not a formal institution, it is a significant form of cultural communication. Within consumer culture, consumption is an act of encoding, decoding, and deciphering that requires mastery of the consumption code (Bourdieu, 1984). This cultural code specifies the use and display of artifacts (Douglas & Isherwoood, 1996). Through shared experience, consumers learn to use products for artifactual communication (Mick, 1986). Consumption is the process of consumers communicating their cultural identities (Levy, 1986). The communication takes place not only between consumers and producers but also between consumers and others, even reflexively between consumer and self (Nöth, 1988; Williamson, 1978).

Because consumer culture is informal, its communication mechanisms are also informal. Artifacts acquire meaning through implicit definition and expression. Consumers acquire competence in cultural meanings through repetition of informal contact similar to language acquisition outside of formal education.

Before the advent of mass communication, the dissemination of culture tended to be limited to those within a geographic area in which people had regular interpersonal contact. Oral tradition tended to insure cultural stability. Early recorded communication tended to be time-based; the same message was available to many generations of receivers with little change in content.

Mass communication laid the foundation for virtual communities by expanding the boundaries of communities and decreasing the importance of oral communication in disseminating culture. Culture defined media and their relationships to other cultural concepts. Media disseminated the culture that gave rise to them and within which they operated (Pennington, 2000b).

In the early 1920s, Lippman (1965) noted the insertion of a pseudoenvironment between man and his environment. Human behavior became a response to the pseudo-environment, but with consequences in the actual environment. Media then disseminated those consequences within the context of the pseudoenvironment to which humans responded with actual-world consequences. The situation was ideal for the emergence of consumer culture and marketing. Mass media disseminated pseudoenvironment culture in which consumption of specific products, and increasingly brands, were the appropriate behaviors for dealing with pseudoenvironment experiences.

BRANDING CONSUMPTION

Most human behavior involves interaction with either a physical or social object. Every interaction modifies the physical or social environment in some way. Gibson (1977) used the term "affordance" to mean the result of interaction with an object, that is, the modification of the environ-

ment. Every affordance is a potential brand. A company Web site is a cultural tool that affords consumers the ability to acquire other cultural tools. The result of interacting with the Web site includes information, in the sense of uncertainty reduction, and acquisition. The company name brands the specific triadic relationship that binds the consumer, the object (the Web site) and the interaction result.

As morphemes in consumer culture, brands convey meaning. And as in other forms of communication, brands as morphemes can convey more than one meaning depending on the context. In the acquisition process, brands often mean the relationship between the consumer and the branded product. They can also signify the relationship between the consumer and the producer. The fundamental qualities of such relationships are trust and assurance that interaction between the consumer and the branded object will afford the desired modification of the actual physical environment.

However, a general assertion that all brands signify a relationship between a consumer and a company may overstate the importance of that relationship. In the consumption process, a brand signifies another relationship. Once a consumer has acquired the brand, it belongs to the consumer, not to the marketer (Schultz & Barnes, 1995). The consumer owns the right to possess, use, and enjoy the brand. It is the consumer's property. From that point at least, the brand stands for a triadic relationship that does not include the marketer. Often, the triadic relationship includes a resulting modification of a social environment.

Holt (2004) asserts that consumers participate in cultural myths through brand consumption. In fact, however, brands signify metaphors for qualities that consumer culture values. The culture treats the attributes attached to consumers as if they were independent of consumers. Through brand consumption, consumers attach qualities to themselves, signifying their roles in relation to other roles. Consumers do not so much form an emotional bond with the brand as with the role that the brand signifies. The consumer no more forms an emotional bond with the brand than a plumber forms an emotional bond with the word "plumber," no matter how much they may enjoy that occupation.

What brands signify is intangible, abstract. Therefore, physical resemblance is not possible. A sign that becomes the concrete form of an abstract concept becomes the icon of that concept. For example, good aesthetic taste has no tangible form. But Starkist, through the persona of Charlie the Tuna, utilized icons of good taste to make a point about tunas that taste good as opposed to tuna with good taste. In the process, they imbued the brand with both meanings of good taste.

The word "plumber" has an intensive meaning, which is the qualities or characteristics that an object, in this case a social object, must have for the word to apply accurately. The word applies to a social and cultural role. The word also has an extensive meaning, which is all of the objects to which the word accurately applies within a culture, that is, all those who play the specific role. Similarly, a brand has an intensive meaning, which, is the qualities or characteristics of the cultural role it signifies. A brand also has an extensive definition, which is the set of all consumers who play the cultural role that the brand signifies.

Even in modern economic systems with great division of labor, culture expects multiple roles. A plumber may also be a parent, baseball player, golfer, photographer, conservationist, and more. Each word signifies a different cultural category with various attributes, qualities, characteristics or specific roles. A single individual may fit into all of those categories, each with its own attribute of role, such as centerfielder or duffer. Consumer culture expects individual consumers to communicate their multiple categories with specific respective attributes through multiple brand consumption.

Marketing communication serves as a lexicon of brand meaning (McCracken, 1986). However,

for the consumer code to have any meaning outside of the purely lexical, it must have some relation to actual experience (Pennington 2002). This is fundamentally important to marketers because to continue providing consumers with cultural meanings, marketers require revenue generated by consumer spending. Although consumption as culture is merely symbolic, the viability of the culture requires the actual-world consequence of purchase.

Marketing communication composes a pseudoenvironment. Attitude change based upon marketing communication is a response to the pseudoenvironment. The results of that attitude change can have consequences in the actual environment. Brands consumed in the actual environment effect attitude change by communicating about the actual consumer rather than an endorser selected by a marketer. The relationship between brand and actual consumer can ratify or modify attitude toward the brand that is a response to the pseudoenvironment.

Meaning established in the pseudoenvironment enables consumers to recognize relationships in the actual environment. Consumers refer to marketing communication for trust and assurance that a brand signifies actual social and cultural qualities. Integrity is an antecedent of trust, which is a precursor to transactions (Mayer, Davis & Schoorman, 1995; McKnight, Choudhury & Kacmar, 2002). Brands that establish integrity of meaning are likely to realize transactions in the actual world. Therefore, integrated communication is essential to the management of brand meaning.

Products can convey virtually any cultural meaning (McCracken, 1986). But brands have even greater capacity to convey meaning because, as symbols, that is their only capacity. Consistency of use establishes meaning (Pinker, 1994). Holt (2004) asserts that myth brands must violate that principle periodically. But he has actually misinterpreted the market change. Brands signify cultural roles rather than entire myths.

Consistency of signification requires periodic adjustments in the cultural symbols associated with that role. Just as the Morton Salt girl, Betty Crocker and Aunt Jemima have undergone periodic symbolic upgrades to maintain cultural significance; consumers undergo periodic symbolic upgrades to maintain cultural significance. To maintain consistency of use within a cultural role, a brand must match the symbolic changes culture associates with that role.

FUTURE TRENDS

Lippman (1965) referred to all mediated environments as pseudoenvironments. This included all marketing communication. But he could not foresee how technology would advance in the ninety years after he wrote. Technology affords consumers the opportunity to expand their environments into virtual environments and virtual communities. Further, Lippman's was an outsider's perspective. From the outsider's view, no actual environment exists in media. Although that is technically correct, when technology provides sufficient vividness and interactivity, consumers on some level do not acknowledge the mediation of technology. They experience presence, the sense of being in the environment. From the insider's view then, the environment does exist. And from Kant's (1977) perspective, people only observe appearances anyway.

Lippman (1965) also observed people's tendency to interpret others according to stereotypes. But people interpret all experiences according to cultural stereotypes. And just as people tend to interpret others based upon a small number of observable attributes, they tend to interpret all experiences based upon a similarly small number of attributes. In the online environment, this means that many sensory inputs may be absent, yet consumers will still interpret the experience as actual. The stereotypical attributes of sight, sound and interactivity in virtual communities evoke interpretations assigned by culture in actual environments.

Culture provides the shared framework or schema for interpreting experience. Any experience comprises current sensory inputs perceived and interpreted according to previous experiences and interpretations, which are not components of the actual environment. Consumers respond to their interpretations of an actual environment, not to the actual environment itself. In a virtual community environment, consumers similarly respond to their interpretations of the environment, not to the signs or other stimuli that compose the environment. Therefore, whether the environment is actual or pseudo is irrelevant because to the consumer, the interpretation is always actual; it can never be pseudo.

As discussed previously, technology affords consumers a sense of presence, the failure on some level to acknowledge technological mediation. With a sense of presence, the consumer is in the environment. The range and depth of sensory inputs combined with real time responses to physical inputs elicit interpretations similar to those associated with previous actual experiences having similar inputs. Eventually, the signs that stand for actual experiences not only displace but also become actual experiences.

Consumers can have a sense of being in virtual community through their ability to interact with the online physical environment. However, presence is incomplete without interaction with the social and cultural environment. As in the actual world, consumers must communicate about themselves in the online world. They must be able to interpret others through the observable meaningful attributes that culture defines. They must have the capacity to communicate their cultural identities.

Just as actual environments do, virtual communities afford consumers the capacity to use consumption objects to communicate. Consumer interaction with virtual consumption objects can have virtual consequences. For the purpose of actual-world marketing, those consequences must be parallel to the consequences of inter-action with actual objects in the actual world. Driving an online automobile, for example, must have similar consequences online as driving an actual automobile. However, the social and cultural consequences must be similar as well, if not identical.

Identical social and cultural consequences are possible, although identical physical consequences are not, because the virtual community is only a physical approximation created by technology. A consumer may have a strong sense of presence in driving an automobile online, but physically, that consumer remains in the same location. However, social and cultural consequences are the conse-quence of communication, which depends on signs. Technology utilizes culturally meaningful signs to compose the online environment. The response to the online environment is by nature a cultural response.

The virtual community can be a practice environment through which consumers can ob-serve symbolic behaviors for social and cultural consequences. Further, consumers can test their own symbolic behaviors in order to observe social and cultural consequences. Current technology affords consumers the opportunity to engage in symbolic behaviors that approximate actual behaviors. Technology affords consumers the capacity to select culturally meaningful physical attributes of a desired online appearance. More important, however, technology affords consum-ers the opportunity to associate themselves with culturally meaningful signs and observe responses in a risk-free environment.

Virtual communities offer marketers a richer opportunity to collect data on consumer choices and respond rapidly in modifying the environ-ment. As I have discussed previously (Pennington, 2001a), marketers can collect data on consumer choices and probabilities of occurrence based upon previous consumer choices and consumer attri-butes. An important consequence is that online

environments afford marketers the possibility of more timely upgrades to the symbolism surround-ing the cultural roles that brands signify.

As opposed to traditional media, interactive electronic media afford marketers greater con-trol over brand meaning with greater input from consumers. Brands acquire meaning from the contexts within which they occur (Pennington, 2004a). With traditional media, marketers can control the cultural signs in message presented, but they have limited control over the context within which the message occurrs. Marketers can select media, vehicles and even time, but they cannot select the surrounding content. Rather, they select based upon previous or proposed content. But content rarely matches perfectly the message of marketing communication. Interactive electronic media afford marketers complete control over content with the opportunity to create a sense of presence.

A list of universal cultural concepts available for branding has already been compiled. Osgood, May & Miron (1975) have listed concepts common to dozens of cultures. They have also provided a list of modifiers to distinguish further the rela-tionships among concepts across cultures. Within any culture, all concepts have distinguishing properties or attributes that allow identification and distinction according to the cultural code. Within consumer culture, brands are cultural markers critical to identifying and distinguishing cultural concepts in both actual environments and virtual communities.

Pennington (2001) discussed an approach to computer-assisted design (CAD) for consumer generated virtual communities. The vividness and interactivity available in those virtual re-alities evoke the sense of presence (Pennington, 2004). Both articles discuss giving tangible form to virtual communities, that is, taking virtual communities out of the realm of imagination and making them available for sensation. Previously, making social objects available for sensation has been a challenge. Increasingly, electronic games offer a solution to that challenge by using avatars to represent players. The technique extends easily to consumer avatars.

Avatars are the tangible features users give themselves, to make themselves available for sensation by others in time and space of online environments. Observers do not sense the actual person as object. But according to (Kant 1977), observers in the actual world do not sense actual objects but only the appearances in the time and space. Just as consumers in actual environments, avatars convey information to identify and distinguish themselves through conspicuous consumption of brands.

Without any observation distinction, each avatar would be just a commodity. But without observable distinctions, consumers are just commodities. Within consumer culture, behaviors and products associated with those behaviors can distinguish. But within a pattern of behaviors and products, brands are the cultural tool for further distinction. This is true not only for actual consumers but also for their avatars in virtual communities.

Consumers do not always compete with each other in the process of distinction, comparison and identity. To say that a consumer is masculine makes no sense unless culture recognizes the possibility of being not masculine. But consumers do not have to compete to determine who is masculine. All consumers who exhibit behaviors culturally associated with masculinity can be masculine. Of course, consumers can and do compete to determine who is more or less masculine, feminine, youthful, honest, attractive, intelligent or any other quality that culture designates as variable and valuable. In part, the competition determines not only which consumers possess more or less of a quality, but also the observable behaviors and artifacts that signify the varying degrees of a quality.

Brands are a key component of the cultural signification process. As such, brands do not always compete with each other. To say that one brand of deodorant is masculine makes no sense unless another brand can be not masculine, that is, feminine or neutral. However, to the extent that culture recognizes degrees of masculinity, one brand can signify a greater or lesser degree of masculinity than other brands. For example, one brand can be "the best a man can get." In order to establish such significance, marketing communication must associate a brand with observable behaviors and artifacts culturally designated as corresponding to the degree of a quality.

Often, other brands are among the culturally designated artifacts. Indeed, one can expect to find other brands among the artifacts because consumers rarely use a single brand in a vacuum. The virtual community that includes only a single brand lacks the cultural vividness necessary for a sense of presence. Multiple brands are part of the consumer code.

Just as no two consumers are identical, no two brands are identical. Each brand modifies consumer identity. In combination, brands interact to refine consumer identity. Therefore, e-branding consumers requires carefully analyzed cultural meanings of brand combinations rather than single brand placement in virtual communities.

REFERENCES

Attneave, F. (1959). *Applications of information theory to psychology: A summary of basic concepts, methods, and results.* New York: Henry Holt and Company, Inc.

Bagozzi, R. P. & Dholakia, U. M. (2006). Intentional social action in virtual communities. *Journal of Interactive Marketing,* 16(2), 2-21.

Baudrillard, J. (1988). *Selected writings.* Translated by Mark Poster. Stanford, CA: Stanford University Press.

Bourdieu, P. (1984). *Distinction: A social critique of the judgement of taste.* Translated by Richard

Nice. Cambridge, MA: Harvard University Press.

Daugherty, T. M., Li, H. & Biocca, F. (2001). Consumer learning and 3D e-commerce: The effects of sequential exposure of a virtual experience relative to indirect and direct product experience on product knowledge, brand attitude and purchase intention. In Frank Biocca, (Ed.), *Proceedings of the experiential e-commerce conference* (CD-ROM). East Lansing, Michigan: Michigan State University.

Douglas, M. & Isherwood, B. (1996). *The world of goods: Toward an anthropology of consumption.* New York: Routledge.

Editors of Advertising Age. (1988). *Proctor & Gamble: The house that Ivory built.* Lincolnwood, IL: NTC Business Books.

Fournier, S. (1998). Consumers and their brands: Developing relationship theory in consumer research. *Journal of Consumer Research,* 24 (March), 343-373.

Gibson, J. J. (1977). The theory of affordances. In R. Shaw & J. Bransford, (Eds.) *Perceiving, acting and knowing: toward an ecological psychology* (pp. 67-82). Hillsdale, New Jersey: Lawrence Erlbaum Associates.

Gupta, S. & Kim, H.W. (2007). Developing the commitment to virtual community: The balanced effects of cognition and affect. *Information Resources Management Journal,* 20(1), 28-45.

Hall, E. T. (1969). *The hidden dimension.* Garden City, NY: Anchor Books.

Hirschman, E. C. & Thompson, C. J. (1997). Why media matter: Toward a richer understanding of consumers' relationships with advertising and mass media. *Journal of Advertising,* 26 (1), 43-60.

Holt, D. B. (2004). *How brands become icons.* Boston: Harvard Business School Press.

Huang, W.-Y., Schrank, H., & Dubinsky, A. J. (2004). Effect of brand name on consumers' risk perceptions of online shopping. *Journal of Consumer Behavior,* 4(1), 40-50.

Kant, I. (1977). *Prolegomena to any future metaphysics.* (P. Carus, Trans., J. W. Ellington, Rev.). Indianapolis, Indiana: Hackett Publishing Company, Inc.

Levy, S. J. (1986). Meanings in advertising stimuli. In J. Olson & K. Sentis (Eds.), *Advertising and consumer psychology* (Vol. 3) (pp. 214-226). New York: Praeger Publishers.

Li, H., Daugherty, T., & Biocca, F. (2002). Impact of 3-D advertising on product knowledge, brand attitude, and purchase intention: The mediating role of presence. *Journal of Advertising,* 31(3), 43-57.

Lippman, W. (1965). *Public opinion.* New York: The Free Press.

Lynd, R. S. (1939). *Knowledge for what? The place of the social sciences in American culture.* Princeton: Princeton University Press.

Marx, K. (1967). Commodities. In *Capital: A critique of political economy.: Vol 1. The process of capitalist production.* (S. Moore & E. Aveling, Trans.). New York: The International Publishers Co.

Mayer, R. C., Davis, J. H., & Schoorman, F. D. (1995). An integrative model of organizational trust. *The Academy of Management Review,* 20(3), 709-734.

McCracken, G. (1990). Culture and consumer behavior: An anthropological perspective. *Journal of the Market Research Society,* 32(1), 3-11.

McCracken, G. (1986). Culture and consumption: A theoretical account of the structure and movement of the cultural meaning of consumer goods. *Journal of Consumer Research,* 13 (June), 71-84.

McKnight, D. H., Choudhury, V., & Kacmar, C. (2002). Developing and validating trust measures for e-commerce: An integrative typology. *Information Systems Research*, 13(3), 334-359.

McWilliam, G. (2000). Building strong brands through online communities. *Sloan Management Review*, 41(3), 43-54.

Memmi, D. (2006). The nature of virtual communities. *AI & Society*, 20(3), 288-300.

Mick, D. G. (1986). Consumer research and semiotics: Exploring the morphology of signs, symbols and significance. *Journal of Consumer Research* 13 (September), 196-213.

Nöth, W. (1988). The language of commodities: Groundwork for a semiotics of consumer goods. *International Journal of Research in Marketing*, 4(3), 173-186.

Osgood, C. E., May, W. H. & Miron, M. S. (1975) *Cross-cultural universals of affective meaning.* Urbana, IL: University of Illinois Press.

Osgood, C., Suci, G., & Tannenbaum, P. (1957). *The measurement of meaning.* Urbana, IL: University of Illinois Press.

Pennington, R. (2000a). Brands as the language of consumer culture. *Journal of Global Competitiveness*, 8(1), 318-329.

Pennington, R. (2000b). The theory is the press: A view of the press as developer of informal theory. Phoenix: Association for Education in Journalism and Mass Communication Annual Convention (Communication Theory and Methodology Division).

Pennington, R. (2001a). Signs of marketing in virtual reality. *Journal of Interactive Advertising*, 2(1), <http://jiad.org/vol2/no1/pennington>.

Pennington, R. (2001b). The conceptual definition of culture in advertising, marketing and consumer research literature. In M. Roberts & R. L. King (Eds.), *Proceedings of the 2001 Special Asia-Pacific Conference of the American Academy of Advertising* (pp. 34-40). Gainesville, FL: The University of Florida.

Pennington, R. (2004a). Brands, culture and semiotics (revisited) in creative strategy development. In P. Ribeiro Cardoso & S. Nora Gaio (Eds.), *Publicidade e Comunicação Empresarial: Perspectivas e Contributos* (pp. 29043). Porto, Portugal: Edições Universidade Fernando Pessoa.

Pennington, R. (2004b). Revising a psycho-linguistic application of information theory for the consumer psychology of brands. In J. D. Williams, W.-N. Lee & C. P. Haugtvedt (Eds.), *Diversity in Advertising* (pp. 201-214). Hilldale, NJ: Lawrence Erlbaum Associates, Inc.

Pennington, R. (2005). Affording cultural and social presence in e-marketing. In Y. Gao (Ed.), *Web Systems Design and Online Consumer Behavior* (pp. 305-318). Hershey, PA: The Idea Group Inc..

Pennington, R. (2006). A cultural framework for studying youth, brands, and lifestyles. In P. Ribeiro Cardoso, S. Nora Gaio & J. Pérez Seoane (Eds.), *Jovens, Marcas e Estilos de Vida* (pp. 15-24). Porto, Portugal: Edições Universidade Fernando Pessoa.

Pinker, S. (1994). *The language instinct.* New York: William Morrow and Company, Inc.

Porra, J & Parks, M. S. (2006). Sustainable virtual communities: Suggestions from the colonial model. *Information Systems and eBusiness Management*, 4(4), 309-341.

Preece, J. (2000). *Online communities: Designing usability, supporting sociability.* New York: John Wiley & Sons.

Ritson, M. & Elliott, R. (1999). The social uses of advertising: An ethnographic study of adolescent advertising audiences. *Journal of Consumer Research*, 26(December), 260-277.

Schultz, D. E. & Barnes, B. E. (1995). *Strategic advertising campaigns* (4th ed.). Lincolnwood, IL: NTC Business Books.

Susman, W. I. (1985). *Culture as history: The transformation of American society in the twentieth century.* New York: Pantheon Books.

Talukder, M. & Yeow, P. H. P. (2007). A comparative study of virtual communities in Bangladesh and the USA. *The Journal of Computer Information Systems,* 47(4), 82-90.

Tönnies, F. (1957). *Gemeinschaft and Gesellschaft.* (C. P. Loomis, Ed. And Trans.). East Lansing, MI: Michigan State University Press.

Watzlawick, P., Bavelas, J. B. & Jackson, D. D. (1967). *Pragmatics of Human Communication.* New York: W. W. Norton & Company.

Williamson, J. (1978). *Decoding advertisements: Ideology and meaning in advertising.* London: Marion Boyars.

Chapter XII
Impact of Internet Self–Efficacy on E–Service Brands

Terry Daugherty
The University of Texas at Austin, USA

Harsha Gangadharbatla
Texas Tech University, USA

Matthew S. Eastin
The University of Texas at Austin, USA

ABSTRACT

As the Internet expands to include individual applications such as banking, shopping, information gathering, and so on, brand managers and marketers have turned to the Internet to utilize it as an effective branding vehicle. Consequently, understanding how the Internet could be used effectively in e-branding becomes imperative. One barrier to a successful utilization of the Internet as a branding tool is the rate at which individuals adopt and use the various e-services made available to them. As will be discussed, adoption depends, in part, on the users' level of Internet self-efficacy. This chapter illustrates a conceptual framework for understanding Internet self-efficacy and presents findings from an exploratory experiment designed to investigate the link between self-efficacy, attitudes toward e-services and individuals' likelihood of using such e-services. Results are presented and managerial implications for e-service providers are drawn.

INTRODUCTION

The Internet has radically impacted the field of marketing as many companies recognize the potential of this unique medium for efficiently delivering targeted messages, generating sales, and facilitating two-way communication with consumers (Hoffman &Novak, 1996). Marketers have been taking advantage of this new medium in their marketing communications efforts since branding a product online can be relatively quick and easy (Kania, 2000). One of the areas significantly impacted by the advent of the Internet is the service sector (Krishnan & Hartline, 2001). Popularly referred to as e-services, the 2007 spending in this area is expected to reach $565 million in North America according to the Service & Support Professionals Association (SSPA) (BusinessWire, 2006). Therefore, both e-services and the use of the Internet in branding such services have begun to play a pivotal role in today's e-commerce driven society.

Many firms such as , www.ebay.com, www. ancestry.com, and www.fedex.com have been able to create strong online brands by taking advantage of this new and powerful medium (Fisk, Grove, & John, 2004) by providing traditional services online. The success of eBay is a good example of how the service industry has greatly benefited from taking its services online. From a small company to a large marketplace with over 125 million users worldwide, eBay's success story is phenomenal (CBS 60 Minutes, 2005). So, how does eBay do it without any sort of inventory or products to sell or ship? By providing the service of an online marketplace for individuals to transact and auction items so much so that thousands have quit their day jobs to become full-time merchants on eBay making its market value worth more than Bloomingdale's, Macy's, Sears, and Toys 'R Us all put together (CBS 60 Minutes, 2005).

Despite the growing financial worth of the e-service industry and the increasing number of players in the sector, very little research has been done to understand consumer usage and adoption of such services online. One of the factors influencing adoption of e-services that is frequently mentioned in literature is the role of consumer perceptions of technology and their ability to use it, which is often referred to as Internet self-efficacy. Internet self-efficacy or consumer confidence in using the Internet plays a significant role in influencing the perception and adoption of service brands online (Daugherty, Eastin & Gangadharbatla, 2005).

The current chapter begins with a brief description of e-service industry and details the use of the Internet as a branding tool for service-oriented businesses. We then review literature in the area of e-service adoption and Internet self-efficacy and develop a theoretical framework that postulates a link between Internet self-efficacy, attitudes toward e-services and the likelihood of using such services. In order to test the relationship between the proposed constructs, we run a simple laboratory experiment. Results are presented, and both theoretical and practical implications are drawn.

LITERATURE REVIEW

Understanding the E-Service Industry

A service is defined as "a deed, performance, and/or effort" offered in exchange by a company to a consumer (Hoffman & Bateson, 1997, p. 5; Rathmell, 1966 p. 33) and includes four distinguishable characteristics such as intangibility, simultaneity, heterogeneity, and perishability (Fisk, Grove & John, 2004). Intangibility refers to a company's ownership of an offering because customers are unable to claim physical ownership of an "experience," "time," or the "process." For example, when a customer pays for or uses the services of a Web site like www.mapquest.com (e.g., popular consumer site that provides directions and map services, among other offerings, for both commercial and consumer locations), they cannot claim ownership of that service. The process or the experience is not the customer's property to keep forever. Once the service is performed the user has to live with the memory or effect of that service as opposed with taking it home as one would in the case of a tangible good, such as a chair purchased at a retail store or automobile from a dealership. Similarly, if sophisticated processes are involved in providing a particular service—say, finding an airline ticket using search aggregators—the purchase or ownership is limited only to the service and not to the process itself. Simultaneity on the other hand, refers to the fact that for most services both the production and consumption occurs simultaneously. For instance, in the case of an online brokerage firm offering stock trading services, both the product and consumption of the service provided happen at the same time. Production of the service begins as the user starts a trade and ends the moment the trade is complete. A tangible good like a chair or a car is produced at a factory for later consumption whereas in the case of a customer using an online trading site, both production and consumption are happening simultaneously. This is the case with most services, the production and consumption happen simultaneously. Third, heterogeneity refers to the difficulty involved in standardizing the quality of service. It is easier to standardize the quality of a mass produced tangible product rather than a service that relies heavily on user perception. For example, a slow Internet connection may hinder consumer perception of an online retailer because pages take longer to load, or a poor graphics card may limit the visual quality of a site designed to provide health care information relying on interactive tutorials. Regardless of the issue, perception of a service not only depends on internal quality from the company but also external consumer characteristics. Finally, perishability refers to the fact that most services

cannot be stored before consumption. Airlines flying with empty seats cannot store those seats for a later flight. Similarly, empty theater seats cannot be stored for a later show.

Having examined the definition and the distinguishing characteristics of a service, let us now turn to e-services. E-service as a concept goes beyond being "a deed, effort, or performance" (Hoffman & Bateson, 1997, p. 5). E-service relates to the "deed, effort, or performance" as delivered with the mediation of information technology. Rowley (2006) defines e-service as "deeds, efforts or performances whose delivery is mediated by information technology (including the Web, information kiosks and mobile devices p.340)." Featherman and Pavlou (2003) use the following definition: assets—information, business processes, computing resources, applications—made available via the Internet as a means of driving new revenue streams and creating efficiencies (p. 451-452). Examples include the service element of e-tailing, customer support and service, and service delivery (Rowley, 2006). Most organizations today realize the important role the Internet plays in providing services online in terms of convenience, speed, communication and utility while providing great incentives for customers to engage in these services over off-line usage. For instance, www.Blockbuster.com and www.usps.com are traditional off-line service businesses migrating online. The convenience of ordering a movie without leaving your home is certainly something many cable and satellite companies (e.g., video-on-demand) have recognized as well as the video rental industry (e.g., Netflix). Whether it is because of increased competition, an evolving media consumption experience, or advancements in technology, Blockbuster is now offering many of their services online while providing free shipping and the unique flexibility of allowing its customers to exchange movies rented online in-store. The United States Postal Service (USPS) on the other hand has reduced its store traffic considerably by going online with their "Let the Post Office Come to You" free package and pickup option. To this end, the Internet is changing the service industry through online versions of existing services and the introduction of new and unique services. To cite another example, www.myheritage.com provides comprehensive tools for genealogy research. Also included on their Web site is a free service that applies advanced face recognition technology for personal photos and family history.

There are many reasons why companies are taking their services online. First, recent advances in technology have created a plethora of "technology-based self services" (Dabholkar et al., 2003). Technology-based self services make businesses cost-effective and efficient by taking advantage of decreased costs as a result of customers moving online and servicing themselves (Schultze, 2003). Thus, customer acquisition costs and service costs are considerably reduced due to reduced human intervention (Iqbal et al., 2003). Second, these benefits translate into reduced transaction costs for the end-customer along with the advantage of reduced product search associated with e-service (Steinfield & Whitten, 2000). Further, e-services are also capable of delivering consumers high quality in-depth product information at anytime of the day (Rowley, 2006). Lastly, e-services and recent developments in technology empower the customer with new service tools like *intelligent agents* (Glynn, 1997) and *service robots* (Fisk, Grove, & John, 2004). For instance, priceline.com uses similar tools to perform tasks previously performed by travel agents. Customers cannot only search for available flights at cheap fares but also name their own price and buy tickets online. Most PC-based banking services utilize agent-based software to allow individuals to bank, transfer funds from one account to another, pay bills, check account balances, and perform almost all transactions online at the convenience of their homes at any given time of the day. Even when a company's core product is not a service, firms have ventured to implement and include some

kind of service element in their product bundle. For instance, Amazon.com started by selling books (a tangible item) and now offers such e-services as wish lists and recommendations to complement their core product, thereby creating a unique interactive experience for their customers. Therefore, in addition to the growth of service companies, e-service is becoming important for manufacturers of goods as well (Rust, 1997).

Branding E-Services

The Internet plays an important role in the branding of services online. With the advent of the Internet companies can create and launch a campaign within hours or days as opposed to several weeks and months with TV, magazines, and other traditional media (Kania, 2000). For example, Amazon.com has been consistently identified as one of The Top 100 Global Brands according to Business Week (August, 2005) and recently placed as high as 68th one spot ahead of Kraft and higher than such brands as Adidas, Rolex, Porsche, and Tiffany & Co., which have all been around much longer than Amazon.com. Amazon.com was able to achieve this feat by taking advantage of the Internet's capacity to reach a large audience quicker than other traditional media. The rapid pace with which Internet users are growing makes a strong case of taking branding strategies online.

Implementing traditional branding strategies online is often referred to as e-branding or cyberbranding and is defined as "the hands-on experience and immediate involvement with a brand online prior to the purchase of a product or service" (Breakenridge, 2001). In other words, e-branding refers to the changes in the traditional branding process to include a "virtual brand experience" and "interactivity" with a product as a result of using the Internet strategically (Kania, 2000). Virtual product experiences are psychological and emotional states that consumers undergo while interacting with products in a virtual environment (Li, Daugherty, & Biocca, 2001), such as the Internet. Shopping online provides consumers with an opportunity to experience products and brands virtually, and this experience is similar to a direct experience with a product or brand as both are interactive in nature (Daugherty, Li & Biocca, 2005). Interactivity refers to some "real-time dialogue in which the involved entities (human or otherwise) play both the role of the sender and receiver of information at some point in the dialogue" (Roehm & Haugtvedt, 1999. p. 32). Interactivity has also been defined as the "extent to which users can participate in modifying the form and content of a mediated environment in real time" (Steuer, 1992. p84). Certainly, within the context of the Internet, interactivity is a multidimensional construct and has been described as both the ability to communicate with people (person interactivity) and access information (machine interactivity) (Hoffman & Novak 1996). As a form of communication, interactivity is measured in terms of the level of responsiveness between users along a continuum ranging from one-way discourse to the reactive interaction of two-way communication (Rafaeli & Sudweeks, 1997). This perspective acknowledges that interactivity can occur either through a medium or without and is differentiated by the extent to which the communicator and audience facilitate each other's communication needs (Ha & James, 1998). However, Hoffman and Novak (1996) emphasize that the Internet's potential as an efficient marketing channel not only stems from what they refer to as a many-to-many communication medium but also from the ability of consumers to interact with as well as create content. Marketers today are relying on the Internet and technological advantages to reach consumers while positioning brands in competitive environments by offering consumers varying degrees of experiences and interactivity (Li, Daugherty & Biocca, 2001; 2003; Nash 2000). For example, Marketwatch.com offers numerous tools such as Interactive Charting

and Virtual Stock Exchange information on its Web site, which allows users to conduct effective research, create and maintain portfolios online, and take part in interactive online discussions. Past brand managers would create messages for mass audiences that established a brand image which was essentially the same for everyone, however, e-branding allows managers to target individuals with highly personalized messages based on the interaction between the marketer and the customer causing brands to mean different things to different people (Kania, 2000). The new media consumer desires and actively seeks "interactivity" and "virtual brand experiences" that go beyond what traditional media have to offer (Kania, 2000), and thus, companies are developing brand images specifically for new media consumers. For instance, Dove (www. dove.com) offers interactive quizzes, real beauty e-cards, share your view discussion forums, and contests to create multimedia content among other things. A print ad for Dove does not allow for such personalized interaction with the brand. This, in essence, is how the Internet is changing the branding process.

The influence of the Internet on the branding process is particularly important for the service sector (Krishnan & Hartline, 2001). The reason e-branding is crucial for service industries online is because tangible goods are easier to evaluate than intangible services. Meaning, it is easier for consumers to touch, examine, and compare different tangible goods before the actual purchase, yet the intangible nature of the service industry makes it difficult for consumers to evaluate the quality of one service in comparison to another without actually experiencing both, which makes branding of services critical and more important (Onkvisit & Shaw, 1989). The second reason why e-branding is more important for services than for tangible goods is because consumers undergo a more complex decision process while purchasing services than when choosing physical goods (Darby & Karni, 1973), and have a more difficult time evaluating the quality and content of a service before, during, or post purchase (Bharadwaj et al., 1993). This complexity and difficulty involved in selecting services strengthens the case for greater importance of e-branding since the Internet is capable of two-way communication, interactivity, and high consumer control. Despite the realization of the importance of e-branding of services, there has been comparatively little research done in this area to understand the factors that influence the effectiveness of branding strategies—in terms of attitudes and behavior intentions—and the ultimate adoption of e-services. In the following section, we review studies that examine consumer usage of e-service and identify factors that influence the ultimate adoption of such services with particular emphasis on one important factor called Internet self-efficacy.

Research on Consumer use of E-Services

To date, e-service research has examined various topics such as e-service quality, its dimensions, and measurement; elements of Web experience; relationship of this experience with consumer satisfaction, behavior, and loyalty (Rowley, 2006). However, an area that is being increasingly identified as crucial is consumer usage (or behavior) of e-services, and the cognitive, affective, and conative indicators of this usage behavior (Rowley, 2006) or in other words, understanding the factors that influence usage/adoption of e-services. There has not been any research that explains how consumers evaluate e-services for adoption (Featherman & Pavlou, 2003). Measurement of consumer responses to e-service strategies in terms of their satisfaction ratings, attitudes, and behavior intentions is a relatively under researched area (Rust & Lemon, 2001). As a result, not much is known about what consumers want from e-service technologies (Meuter et al., 2000) and how this growing phenomenon of the service industry online is affecting consumer behavior.

Understanding how consumers respond to e-services is important because many experts point to inadequate service and negative consumer experiences as potential hindrances to the growth of e-services in general (Bettua, 1999). E-service goes beyond Web sites with discussion forums, online chat helplines, e-mail reminders, and status updates. The real opportunity for providing services online though lies in the Internet's potential to communicate with consumers in an interactive two-way form, achieve a high degree of personalization and provide real-time adjustments to a firm's offerings (Rust & Lemon, 2001). In other words, effective e-service branding strategies go beyond good Web site design with simply an easy means to contact and communicate with the company. The next generation of consumers expects a lot more from e-service providers in terms of an enhanced buying experience (Pine & Gilmore, 1999), increased control (Bolton & Lemon, 1999; Hui & Bateson, 1991), and a high degree of personalization with needs that change depending on the situation (Belk, 1975; Rust & Lemon, 2001). The new and all-powerful consumer has come to expect these things as part of the service to be provided at no extra cost. Given this rapidly changing environment, the number of choices today's consumers have, and the ease with which they can switch brands, it is becoming increasingly difficult to gain and retain customers (Murphy, 2000).

Unlike basic e-commerce transactions, adoption of e-services is more complex as consumers enter a more long-term relationship with "faceless e-service providers" (Featherman & Pavlou, 2003 p. 452). Technology adoption certainly plays an important role in the effectiveness of e-services (Rowley, 2006) and the branding of such services online. In the case of e-services, technology constitutes the mediated environment through which the service is provided and thus an integral part of the process that cannot be ignored. The mediated environment of the Internet affects consumers in a number of ways including their learning process, how they perceive the quality of e-services, and ultimately, their adoption of e-services. Among the factors that influence the process of adoption of technology systems, the ones frequently mentioned are (1) perceived risk (Bauer, 1967; Featherman & Pavlou, 2003; Pavlou, 2001), (2) perceived usefulness and (3) perceived ease of use of the system (Davis et al., 1989). Perceived usefulness and perceived ease of use are similar to Bandura's (1997) concept of self-efficacy. Both perceived usefulness and perceived ease of use have been shown to predict adoption of technology systems (Featherman & Pavlou, 2003; Moon & Kim, 2001; Pavlou, 2001; Teo et al., 1999; Venkatesh & Davis, 2000).

As the Internet continues to evolve, the ability to brand effectively is linked to the innovation and adoption of technology (Breakenridge, 2001), especially for companies providing e-services. Technological services represent investments in establishing a relationship of equity that manifests itself in terms of both attitude and behavior (Kannan, Wagner & Velarde, 2002). With corporate implementation and consumer adoption of e-services ongoing, understanding how and why people are deciding to use such services becomes increasingly important to brand providers and managers. Several factors have been identified within the literature for consumer adoption of e-services with researchers suggesting that adoption of e-services, such as online shopping, investing and banking, is best predicted by individual's reported level of self-efficacy (Eastin, 2002; Hsu & Chiu, 2004; LaRose & Eastin, 2002). Thus, the following section examines the role of Internet self-efficacy in conjunction with the adoption of e-services.

Role of Internet Self-Efficacy in the Adoption of E-Services

Two factors that influence consumer satisfaction with e-services are "control" and "perception of control" (Hui & Bateson, 1991). Increasing control

or the perception of control can lead to increased levels of satisfaction. One way to increase control and/or the perception of control is to provide customers more choices. For instance, Hui and Bateson (1991) in a laboratory experiment varied the level of consumer control by giving subjects more choices and observed that increased levels of control led to more pleasant service experience. Another way to increase the sense of perceived control is to provide customers with the option of self-service (Rowley, 2006), which is precisely how many companies use the Internet. However, this perception of control is dependent of individual level factors such as locus of control (Bradley & Sparks, 2002) and self-efficacy (Eastin, 2002; Hsu & Chiu, 2004).

Locus of control deals with attributing outcomes to either self or an external entity (Lefcourt, 1981). Depending on individuals' life experiences, they tend to attribute the results or outcomes to either themselves or their environment. If an individual consistently experiences success as a result of their actions, they are more likely to develop a belief in self-control. On the other hand, if one perceives the results or outcomes to be random and unreliable, one is more likely to believe in external control (Bradley & Sparks, 2002). Self-efficacy is the belief "in one's capabilities to organize and execute the courses of action required to produce given attainments" (Bandura, 1997 p. 3). Although both these concepts are similar in that they refer to "future-oriented beliefs," the concept of self-efficacy "relates to expectations of control over behaviors rather than control over outcomes" (Bradley & Sparks, 2002, p. 313). Therefore, when concerned with behavior and behavioral intentions such as likelihood of adopting e-services, the impact or role of self-efficacy is more prominent than that of locus of control.

This impact of self-efficacy on e-service adoption becomes particularly important when e-service is conceptualized as self-service. Self-service, as noted earlier, is one way to increase the perceived sense of control. Some researchers describe e-service as essentially a self-service experience (Meuter et al., 2000) and Rowley (2006) claims that "all e-service is predominantly self-service, whether it is delivered through a Web page on a PC, a mobile device, or a kiosk" (p. 343). Self-service demands that customers learn how to navigate and service themselves in the absence of a service agent to assist them (Solomon et al., 1985). Customer experiences depend vastly on their performance in the new environment, and this could influence their perception and evaluation of service quality (Rowley, 2006), significantly impacting the behavior of individuals and their responses to e-branding efforts.

One approach to understanding the use of information technology is through Bandura's (1986, 2001) Social Cognitive Theory (Compeau & Higgins, 1995; Eastin & LaRose, 2000; LaRose & Eastin, 2002). Social Cognitive Theory includes a complex triadic causal structure that establishes the development of competency and regulation of action (Bandura, 1986, 2001). Through the development of knowledge structures, cognitive models of action are created that serve to guide behavior. Consequently, this cognitive guidance is a crucial component to the developmental stages of a behavior. In particular, one cognitive factor that has been explained as an influential variable is perceived confidence, more commonly referred to as self-efficacy (Bandura, 1997). As a primary self-regulatory mechanism, self-efficacy simply refers to the level of confidence an individual has toward a given behavior. This confidence represents the internal belief "in one's capability to organize and execute the courses of action required to produce given attainments" (Bandura, 1997, p. 3).

Numerous studies have also investigated the impact of self-efficacy on consumer decision-making and behavior (Bearden, Hardesty, & Rose, 2001; Bettman, Johnson, & Payne, 1991; Fleming & Courtney, 1984); however, none have

directly examined the role of Internet self-efficacy on attitudes and behavior intentions. Literature on self-efficacy suggests that the construct has different meanings depending on the context. For instance, it may refer to a person's trust in another, another person's ability to perform a task, a person's judgment about a future event, or even one's belief in their own ability (i.e., self-confidence) (Barbalet, 1998). The feeling of confidence in one's ability has been characterized as essential for any behavior to take place because this belief serves as a form of self-assurance (Dequech, 2000). With regard to using the Internet, personal confidence in one's ability to successfully understand, navigate, and evaluate content should alleviate doubts and suspicions when dealing with e-services. In other words, individuals' level of Internet self-efficacy should relate to their heightened beliefs about products or services encountered online. These beliefs formed reflect a consumer's perceived capability in using the Internet to accomplish tasks (Eastin & LaRose, 2000). Subsequently, "as Internet self-efficacy (i.e., beliefs) increases, then attitudes toward the object of those beliefs, will also increase" (Ajzen & Sexton, 1999, p. 118).

Research to understand adoption of technologies and user behavior has applied Fishbein and Ajzen's (1975) theory of reasoned action (TRA) as an explanatory model. This framework considers the beliefs that an individual has about a behavior and the actions taken from those beliefs. This approach has had some success predicting the uses of technologies such as personal computers (Davis, Bagozzi, & Warsaw, 1989) but modifications to this theory by Ajzen (1991) suggests that an individual's perceived ability, or confidence, to perform a behavior could also play an important role in the adoption process. This modification is popularly known as the Theory of Planned Behavior (TPB). For instance, applying TPB to e-services, the perceived complexity of service experience could influence the formation of attitudes and internal perceptions but depends on an individual's level of self-efficacy or confidence in using the new technology.

Researchers have positively linked Internet self-efficacy to online performance, prior experience, and Internet use (Eastin & LaRose, 2000; Compeau & Higgins, 1995). There is evidence pointing to a positive causal relationship between previous experiences (both actual and vicarious) and individuals' levels of self-efficacy (Staples, Hulland, & Higgins, 1998). For instance, a positive interaction reinforces and increases self-efficacy while negative interactions weaken it (Eastin, 2005). More precisely, Eastin and LaRose (2000) showed that previous Internet usage in terms of the number of months spent using the Internet positively affected individuals' levels of self-efficacy. In turn, Internet self-efficacy has been found to positively impact some e-commerce activities, such as online banking (Eastin, 2002). In a laboratory experiment Eastin (2002) identified subjects with high levels of self-efficacy and assigned them a technology oriented task, such as the electronic transfer of money, to identify whether or not they were likely to adopt such an online service. The results indicated that those participants with higher levels of self-efficacy were more likely to adopt and perform such an action. Meaning, it is reasonable to assume that confidence in one's ability to use the Internet can positively influence one's willingness to adopt and use e-services because internal beliefs are associated with actual behavior.

With an increase in the extent to which individuals feel capable and secure with their decisions and behavior, a person is better equipped at making decisions and feels confident about their behavior (Bearden et al., 2001). However, behavior is more strongly associated with one's attitude toward that action when deliberate cognitive processing is involved (Fazio & Towles-Schwen, 1999, p. 99). Because Internet self-efficacy does not represent a form of deliberate cognitive processing directly associated with the behavior in question (i.e., willingness to use e-services), attitude toward an e-service brand should exude a stronger direct influence on behavior. Certainly with the corporate implementation and consumer adoption of e-services ongoing, understanding what factors influence the acceptance and use of services online becomes increasingly important to brand managers engaged in e-commerce today. To examine how Internet self-efficacy and brand attitude influence the decision to adopt and/or use e-services online, a theoretical model (Figure 1) is proposed. In order to test these theoretical relationships, select variables from the model were examined using an online banking simulation (Figure 2). While distinct hypotheses were posited from the literature, the principal research

Figure 1. Proposed model examining the relationship between self-efficacy, attitude and behavior

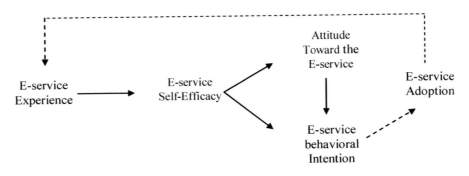

proposition was that a positive relationship exits between self-efficacy and attitude toward the brand thus increasing the likelihood of adoption of an e-service.

Examining the Relationship of Internet Self-Efficacy

Data were collected from a purposive sample of 64 professionals from two nonprofit groups in Central Ohio. The average age of participants was around 42 years old. Thirty-five percent of respondents were male, and 65% of the respondents were female. Fifty-one percent of the sample was African-American, 47% were Caucasian and 1.5% of respondents indicated as being other. Reported income among respondents ranged from $15,000 to more than $105,000 per year. Twenty-four percent of the sample earned between $15,000 and $30,000; 24% earned between $30,001 and $45,000; 27% of the sample earned between $45,001 and $75,000; and finally, about 23% of the sample earned more than $75,000. Education levels varied from some high school to graduate school grads. Sixteen percent of the sample graduated from high school, with another 21% of the respondents attending some college. The majority of the samples, 43%, were college grads with another 12% attending or graduating from graduate school. Prior to exposure to the banking simulation, around 62% of respondents reported that they had never banked online. The other 38% reported using online banking minimally for checking account balances, transferring funds and occasionally paying bills online.

Participants were initially contacted for this study through their nonprofit organizations, and a cash donation was made to each of the participating organizations in the name of the participant. Understanding that participation was voluntary, participants were randomly assigned to one of two conditions: pretest/posttest or posttest only. In the posttest only condition, respondents

viewed a computer screen and were given some basic instructions about the functionality of the simulation software and then asked to spend time exploring each of the options available (i.e., transfer funds, online bill pay, set up new accounts). After viewing the simulation, the posttest only group completed a paper questionnaire that asked about their experience using the simulation. In the pretest/posttest condition, respondents were asked to complete a paper questionnaire assessing their attitudes towards and understanding of online banking. After the pretest, respondents in this group viewed the same simulation software as the posttest only group, followed by additional questions on the second part of the paper survey.

Established seven-point semantic differential scales were used to test the proposed variables with reliability assessment conducted on Internet self-efficacy, attitude and behavior intention using Cronbach's Alpha (Internet self-efficacy M=5.50, SD=1.36, α = .92; attitude toward the e-service M=3.83, SD=1.21, α = .94; behavior intent M=4.25, SD=1.22, α = .88), with all exceeding the generally accepted guideline of .70 (Hair, Anderson, Tatham, & Black, 1998, p.118). Composite measures for each of the scales were then constructed to represent the multiple items and used in the subsequent analysis to reduce measurement error.

Overall, the data fit the model shown in Figure 2, $\chi^2(2) = 4.51$, $p < .05$; CFI = .98; RMSEA = .10. From this model, experience with the online banking (as e-service) stimulus produced a significant relationship with online banking self-efficacy (β = .41), which subsequently significantly influenced attitude toward online banking (β = .53) and the intention to adopt (β = .51). Although not significant, attitude toward online banking also positively predicted the intention to adopt (β = .07). From these relationships, 17% of the variance in self-efficacy, 28% of the variance in attitude, and 31% of the variance in behavioral intention was predicted.

Figure 2. Model examining the relationship between self-efficacy, attitude and behavioral intention

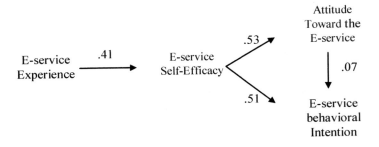

CONCLUSION AND IMPLICATIONS

E-services and branding of such services online is an area that is becoming increasingly important. With millions of dollars spent every year on e-services (BusinessWire, 2006), it becomes imperative that we better understand the factors that influence the outcome (and success) of e-branding strategies when it comes to services online or e-services. The current chapter presents a framework of understanding the effect on one such individual level factor, Internet self-efficacy, on individuals' attitude toward e-services and their likelihood of adopting such services. While the successful adoption of any new consumer technology used for business purposes requires a certain level of user knowledge, overcoming deficient self-efficacy and attitudes are prerequisites to effectively move customers toward e-services (Eastin 2002; LaRose & Eastin 2002). Findings presented from the exploratory small-scale study provide evidence to support the relationship between Internet self-efficacy and attitudes, which in turn predict customer likelihood of adoption. In other words, individuals who are experts at using the Internet are more likely to have favorable attitudes toward e-services or services online. Being experts, they can be expected to adopt such services with ease as well.

While there are many potential factors that could influence an individual's ultimate adoption of an e-service, this particular chapter focused on only one factor, self-efficacy. Although self-efficacy can be thought of as something outside the control of brand managers, we strongly believe that it is still an important variable and its effect on adoption has indirect implications for managers. For instance, furthering our understanding of the effect of self-efficacy on e-service adoption may help managers devise effective e-service Web sites that take into the account the influence of individual consumer level experience factors. Hence, the establishment of a relationship between Internet self-efficacy, brand attitude and behavior (adoption) for e-services is of importance to both academic scholars interested in theoretical research as well as professionals focused on branding online. E-service managers may not be able to directly change individual level self-efficacy but there are a number of implications for strategies that take "individual level differences in self-efficacy" into account while formulating effective means to increase adoption rates.

Implications for Managers

The e-service sector is highly competitive considering that it costs about 20-30% higher to acquire a customer for an online business than for traditional businesses (Reichheld & Schefter, 2000). Furthermore, Reichheld and Schefter (2000) also suggest that retaining customers and building loyalty is a crucial prerequisite to surviving in a highly competitive online business environment as start-up companies can boost their profits by 25 to 95% just by retaining 5% more customers. By recognizing the importance of Internet self-efficacy and its contribution to e-service adoption, brand managers will be able to acquire new customers, retain old ones by building brand loyalty, and improve their overall strategic decision-making. A direct implication is that by influencing individuals' "perceived" levels of self-efficacy, marketers could potentially impact their attitudes towards e-services and their likelihood of adoption. Internet self-efficacy is dependent on a number of factors such as prior experience, time spent online and physical limitations that may not be under the direct control of marketers and e-service providers but by designing sites that are easier to navigate they can surely influence the confidence level. Web sites that increase visitor's perceived sense of control, interactivity, and virtual brand experiences are more likely to elicit favorable attitudes, which in turn translate to behavioral intentions and actual adoption of services offered on those sites. E-service providers are able to increase the customer's sense of perceived control through a number of strategies, such as providing them with opt-in and name-removal mechanisms and giving customers the option of choosing the means of communication—e-mail, chat or phone. Increased sense of control contributes to an increase in self-efficacy levels leading to a favorable attitude and ultimate adoption of e-services.

Another strategy for brand managers is to use different strategies that address differing levels of self-efficacy. For instance, e-service sites designed to store individuals' information so as to make later purchases easy with "one-click purchase" options might fare well with individuals low on

self-efficacy rating. For example, Amazon.com has an easy "one-click ordering" that uses all stored information to allow for purchases with just one click. Such services address the technological and navigational burden expected of novice users. Similarly, for experienced users high on self-efficacy rating, other features that allow for customization, in-depth navigation, or personalization might help bring an increased sense of confidence. Google.com, for example, offers customization and multiuser document facilities among a number of other advanced services on its homepage that are rather simple to implement but nonetheless help in enhancing confidence.

Self-efficacy levels can also be influenced in other ways such as by educating the customer. E-service providers that include easy to follow tutorials on their Web sites and demo versions of their software showing the Web site's useful and important features and functions will help build and instill confidence in their customers. Also recommended are brief surveys that could help understand how e-service customers differ or are similar in levels of self-efficacy reported. It is e-service providers that attempt to increase a user's level of confidence be it while navigating their Web site or while filling the initial online registration form that will succeed in the long run. This success would be in not only acquiring new customers but also in retaining them in this highly competitive environment.

Finally, because customer expectations are shaped by technology in this information economy, the effective use of e-services to improve business efficiency will enable companies to develop new markets and improve their competitive positions (Rust & Kannan, 2002). E-services that combine different technologies such as ATMs, telephones, cell phones, PC, and Web TV have a greater chance of tapping into consumer segments high in technology self-efficacy, thereby taking e-service to the next level.

The model proposed and tested in this chapter is simplistic in that only one factor is illustrated as linked to attitudes. Of course, Internet self-efficacy is only one of many factors that can potentially impact e-branding, as illustrated throughout this book. Consumer attitudes and the likelihood of adopting e-services may also be dependent on such other factors as perceived risk in terms of privacy and security. Even Internet self-efficacy itself could be an outcome of many factors although only one factor—prior e-service experience—was considered in this chapter. Socioeconomic factors, such as income levels, parental success, social group or peer group influence, and demographic factors, like age and gender, can also influence an individual's self-efficacy level. Further modifications to the model in terms of these additional constructs should be considered as future research directions. Despite these limitations, the authors feel that the current chapter presents a right step in the direction of advancing our initial understanding of e-service adoption and the various factors that influence e-branding of such businesses online.

REFERENCES

Ajzen, I., & Sexton, J. (1999). Depth of Processing, Belief congruence, and Attitude-Behavior Correspondence. In Chaiken, S. & Trope, Y. (Eds.), *Dual-Process Theories in Social Psychology* (pp. 117-138). New York, NY: The Guilford Press.

Bandura, A. (1997). *Self-Efficacy: The Exercise of Control*. Freeman, New York, NY.

Barbalet, J. M. (1998). *Emotions, Social Theory, and Social Structure: A Macrosociological Approach*. Cambridge: Cambridge University Press.

Bauer, R. (1967). Consumer behavior as risk taking. In: Cox, D. (Ed.), *Risk Taking and Information Handling in Consumer Behavior*. Harvard University Press, Cambridge, MA.

Bearden, W. O., Hardesty, D. M., & Rose, R. L. (2001). Consumer Self-Confidence: Refinements in Conceptualization and Measurement. *Journal of Consumer Research, 28*(June), 121-134.

Belk, R. W. (1975). Situational variables and consumer behavior. *Journal of Consumer Research, 2* (December), 157-164.

Bettman, J. R., Johnson, E., & Payne, J. W. (1991). Consumer Decision-Making. In Robertson Thomas S., and Kassarjian Harold H. (Ed.), *Handbook of Consumer Behavior* (pp. 54-80). Englewood Cliffs, NJ: Prentice Hall.

Bettua, M. (1999). Rethinking e-commerce service. *Call Center Solutions, 18* (July), 148-150.

Bharadwaj, S, G., Varadarajan, P.R., & Fahy, J. (1993). Sustainable competitive advantage in service industries: a conceptual model and research propositions. *Journal of Marketing, 57* (Oct.), 83-99.

Bolton, R. N., & Lemon, K. N. (1999). A dynamic model of customers' usage of services: Usage as an antecedent and consequence of satisfaction. *Journal of Marketing Research, 36* (May), 171-186.

Bradley, G. L., & Sparks, B. A. (2002). Service locus of control: its conceptualization and measurement. *Journal of Service Research, 4* (4), 312-24.

Breakenridge, D. (2001). *Cyberbranding: Brand Building in the Digital Economy*. Upper Saddle River, NJ: Prentice Hall.

BusinessWeek (2005). *The Top 100 Brands: Here's How We Calculate the Power in a Name*. August, 2005 [Online Available at http://www.businessweek.com/pdfs/2005/0531_globalbrand.pdf]

BusinessWire (2006). *North American Technology Service and Support Spending Expected to Top $1.4 Billion for 2007*, According to the SSPA. Online available at http://www.findarticles.

com/p/articles/mi_m0EIN/is_2006_Dec_18/ai_n16912392

CBS 60 Minutes (2005). *eBay's bid for success: Internet auction site racking up big gains*, transcript available online at http://www.cbsnews.com/stories/2002/10/30/60II/main527542.shtml

Compeau, D., & Higgins, C. (1995). Computer self-efficacy: Development of a measure and initial test. *MIS Quarterly, 19*, 189-211.

Darby, M. R. & Karni, E. (1973). Free competition and the optimal amount of fraud. Journal of Law and Economics 16 (April), 67-86.

Daugherty, T., Li, H., & Biocca, F. (2005). Experiential E-commerce: A Summary of Research Investigating the Impact of Virtual Experience on Consumer Learning. In Curt Haugtvedt, Karen Machleit & Richard Yalch (Eds.), *Online Consumer Psychology: Understanding and Influencing Consumer Behavior in the Virtual World* (pp. 457-490). Lawrence Erlbaum Associates.

Daugherty, T., Matt, E., & Gangadharbatla, H. (2005). eCRM: Understanding Internet Confidence and the Implications on Customer Relationship Management. *Advances in Electronic Marketing.* Irvine Clarke & Theresa B. Flaherty (eds.), Idea Group Publishing, 67 – 82.

Davis, F. D., Bagozzi, R. P., & Warsaw, P. R. (1989). User Acceptance of Computer Technology: A Comparison of Two Theoretical Models. *Management Science, 35*(8), 983-1003.

Dequech, D. (2000). Confidence and Action: A Comment on Barbalet. *Journal of Socio-Economics, 29*(6), 503-516.

Dabholkar, P.A., Bobbitt, L.M., & Lee, E.J. (2003). Understanding consumer motivation and behavior related to self-scanning in retailing: implications for strategy and research on technology-based self-service. *International Journal of Service Industry Management, 14*(1), 59-95.

Dowling, G., & Staelin, R. (1994). A model of perceived risk and intended risk-handling activity. *Journal of Consumer Research, 21*, 119-134.

Eastin, M. S. (2002). Diffusion of E-commerce: An Analysis of the Adoption of Four e-commerce Activities. *Telematics and Informatics, 19*(3), 251-67.

Eastin, M. S. (2005). Teen Internet Use: Relating Social Perceptions and Cognitive Models to Behavior. *CyberPsychology & Behavior, 8*(1), 62-75.

Eastin, M. S., & LaRose, R. L. (2000). Internet Self-Efficacy and the Psychology of the Digital Divide. *Journal of Computer-Mediated Communication. 6.* Available [Online]: http://www.ascusc.org/jcmc/vol6/

Fazio, R. H., & Towles-Schwenn, T. (1999). The MODE model of attitude-behavior processes. In S. Chaiken & Y. Trope (Eds.), *Dual process theories in social psychology* (pp. 97–116). New York: Guilford Press.

Featherman, M. S. & Pavlou, P. A. (2003). Predicting e-services adoption: a perceived risk facets perspective. *International Journal of Human-Computer Studies, 59*, 451-474.

Fishbein, M., & Ajzen, I. (1975). Belief, Attitude, Intention, and Behavior: An Introduction to Theory and Research. Reading, MA: Addison-Wesley.

Fisk, R. P., Grove, S. J., & John, J. (2004). *Interactive Service Marketing* (2nd ed.). Boston: Houghton Mifflin Co.

Fleming, J., & Courtney, B. E. (1984). The Dimensionality of Self-Esteem II: Hierarchical Facet Model for Revised Measurement Scales. *Journal of Personality and Social Psychology, 46*(February), 404-421.

Fournier, S. (1998). Consumers and Their Brands: Developing Relationship Theory in Consumer

Research. *Journal of Consumer Research, 24*(4), 343-373.

Gefen, D., & Straub, D. (2000). The relative importance of perceived ease-of-use in IS adoption: a study of e-commerce adoption. *Journal of Association for Information Systems, 1*(8), 1-20.

Glynn, W. J. (1997). Building Future Relationships. Marketing Management, Chicago: *American Marketing Association, 6* (Fall), 34-36.

Ha, L., & James, E. L. (1998). Interactivity Reexamined: A Baseline Analysis of Early Business Web Sites. *Journal of Broadcasting & Electronic Media, 42*(4), 457-474.

Hair, J. F., Anderson, R. E., Tatham, R. L., & Black, W. C. (1998). *Multivariate Data Analysis* (5th ed.). Upper Saddle River, NJ: Prentice Hall.

Hoch, S. J., & Deighton, J. (1989). Managing What Consumers Learn from Experience. *Journal of Marketing, 53* (April), 1-20.

Hoffman, D. L., & Thomas P. N. (1996). Marketing in Hypermedia Computer-Based Environments: Conceptual Foundations. *Journal of Marketing, 60* (July), 50-68.

Hoffman, K. D., & Bateson, J. E. G. (1997). *Essentials of Service Marketing.* The Dryden Press, Fort Worth, TX.

Hsu, M. H., & Chiu, C. M. (2004). Internet Self-efficacy and Electronic Service Acceptance. *Decision Support Systems, 38* (3), 369-381.

Hui, M. K., & Bateson, J. E. G. (1991). Perceived control and the effects of crowding and consumer choice on the service experience. *Journal of Consumer Research, 18* (September), 174-184.

Iqbal, A., Verma, R., & Baran, R. (2003). Understanding consumer choices and preferences in transaction-based e-services. *Journal of Service Research, 6*(1), 51-65.

Kania, D. (2000). Branding.com: Online branding for marketing success. Chicago: NTC Business Books, American Marketing Association.

Kannan, P.K.,Wagner, J., & Velarde, C. (2002). Initiatives for Building e-Loyalty: A Framework and Research Issues. In Michael Shaw (ed.) *E-Business Management: State-of-the-Art Research, Management Strategy, and Best Business Practices.* New York: Kluwer.

Kotler, P. (2000). *Marketing Management: The Millennium Edition,* New Jersey: Prentice-Hall Inc.

Krishnan, B. C., & Hartline, M. D. (2001). Brand Equity: Is It More Important in Services? *Journal of Services Marketing, 15*(2), 328-342.

LaRose, R., & Eastin, M. S. (2002). Is Online Buying Out of Control? Electronic Commerce and Consumer self-regulation. *Journal of Broadcasting and Electronic Media, 46*(4), 549-564.

Lefcourt, H. M. (1981). *Research with the Locus of Control Construct. Volume 1: Assessment Methods.* New York: Academic Press.

Li, H., Daugherty, T., & Biocca, F. (2001). Characteristics of Virtual Experience in Electronic Commerce: A Protocol Analysis. *Journal of Interactive Marketing, 15*(3), 13-30.

Li, H., Daugherty, T., & Biocca, F. (2003). The Role of Virtual Experience in Consumer Learning. *Journal of Consumer Psychology, 13*(4), 395 – 405.

Meeker, M. (1997). *The Internet Advertising Report.* New York, NY: Harper Business.

Meuter, M. L., Ostrom, A. L., Roundtree, R. J., & Bitner, M. J. (2000). Self-Service Technologies: Understanding Consumer Satisfaction with Technology-Based Service Encounters. *Journal of Marketing, 64*(3), 50-64.

Moon, J., & Kim, Y. (2001). Extending the TAM for world-wide-web context. *Information and Management, 28,* 217-230.

Murphy, T. (2000). *Web Rules: How the Internet is Changing the Way Consumers Make Choices,* Chicago, IL: Dearborn Financial Publishing, Inc.

Nash, S. (2000). Online Catalogs Will Come to Life and You'll View Merchandise From Every Side. PC Magazine, January 2000. [Online available at] http://www.zdnet.com/pcmag/stories/trends/0,7607,2418240,00.html

Onkvisit, S., & Shaw, J.J., (1989), "Service marketing: image, branding and competition", Business Horizons, 32 (1), 13-18

Parasuraman, A. (2000). Technology Readiness Index (TRI): A Multiple-Item Scale to Measure Readiness to Embrace New Technologies. *Journal of Service Research, 2*(4), 307-320.

Pavlou, P. (2001). *Integrating trust in electronic commerce with the technology acceptance model: model development and validation.* AMCIS Proceedings, Boston, MA.

Pine, B. J., & Gilmore, J. H. (1999). *The Experience Economy.* Boston: Harvard Business School Press.

Rafaeli, S., & Sudweeks, F. (1997). Networked Interactivity. *Journal of Computer-Mediated Communication, 2*(4), [On-line] Retrieved June 10, 2002, from http://www. http://www.ascusc.org/jcmc/vol2/issue4/rafaeli.sudweeks.html.

Rathmell, J. M. (1966).What Is Meant by Services? *Journal of Marketing,* 30 (4), 32-36.

Reichheld, F., & Schefter, P. (2000). E-loyalty your secret weapon. *Harvard Business Review,* July-August, 105-13.

Roehm, H. A., & Curtis P. H. (1999). Understanding Interactivity of Cyberspace Advertising. In

David W. Schumann & Esther Thorson (Eds.) *Advertising and the World Wide Web,* 27-39.

Rowley, J. (2004). Online Branding. *Online Information Review, 28* (2), 131-138.

Rowley, J. (2006). An analysis of the e-service literature: towards a research agenda. *Internet Research, 16*(3), 339-359.

Rust, R. T. (1997). The dawn of computer behavior: Interactive service marketers will find their customer is not human. *Marketing Management, 6* (fall), 31-34.

Rust, R.T,, & Kannan, P. K. (2002). Preface. *E-service: New Directions in Theory and Prac*tice. Roland Rust & P. K. Kannan (eds.), New York, NY: M.E. Sharpe.

Rust, R. T., & Lemon, K. N. (2001). E-service and the Consumer. *International Journal of Electronic Commerce, 5*(3), 85-101.

Schultze, U. (2003). Complementing self-serve technology with service relationships: the customer perspective. *E-service Journal, 3*(1), 7-31.

Solomon, M. R., Suprenant, C., Czepiel, J. A, & Gutman, E. G. (1985). A role theory perspective on dyadic interactions: the service encounter. *Journal of Marketing, 48,* 99-111.

Staples, D. S., Hulland, J. S., & Higgins, C. A. (1998). A self-efficacy theory explanation for the management of remote workers in virtual organizations. *Journal of Computer Mediated Communication, 3,* 1-38. Available online at www.ascusc.org/jcmc/vo3/

Steinfield, C., & Whitten, P. (2000). Community level socioeconomic impacts of electronic commerce, Journal of Computer Mediated Communication, 5(2). Available online at http://www.ascusc.org/jcmc/vol5/issue2/steinfield.html

Steuer, J. (1992). Defining Virtual Reality Dimensions Determining Telepresence, *Journal of Communication,* 42 (4), 73-93.

Teo, S., Lim, V., & Lai, R. (1999). Intrinsic and extrinsic motivation in Internet usage. *Omega International Journal of Management Studies, 27*, 25-37.

Venkatesh, V. & Davis, F. D. (2000). Theoretical extension of the technology acceptance model:

Four longitudinal field studies. *Management Science*, 46 (2), 186-204.

Zhang, X., & Prybutok, V. R. (2005). A consumer perspective of e-service quality. *IEEE Transactions on Engineering Management, 52*(4), 461-77.

Chapter XIII
Understanding Brand Website Positioning in the New EU Member States:
The Case of the Czech Republic

Shintaro Okazaki
Universidad Autónoma de Madrid, Spain

Radoslav Škapa
Masaryk University Brno, Czech Republic

ABSTRACT

This study examines Websites created by American multinational corporations (MNCs) in the Czech Republic. Utilizing a content analysis technique, we scrutinized (1) the type of brand Website functions, and (2) the similarity ratings between the home (US) sites and Czech sites. Implications are discussed from the Website standardization versus localization perspective.

INTRODUCTION

Both academics and practitioners have long debated whether advertising messages should be standardized. The proponents of standardization argue that the use of uniform advertising would provide significant cost benefits, thus improving company performance in the short run, while creating a consistent brand image in multiple markets. In contrast, the proponents of localization contend that ignoring the cultural, social, and economic characteristics of particular markets would cause psychological rejection by local consumers, thus decreasing profits in the long run. The debate has also produced a compromised or hybrid approach, which suggests that whether to standardize or localize advertising in a given market is a question of degree, and it is necessary to analyze many factors on a case-by-case basis (Mueller, 1991).

This debate is not limited to traditional media. As multinational corporations (MNCs) integrate their marketing communication with an emergent interactive medium, websites are becoming increasingly important for brand marketing and customer relationship management in multiple markets. This is because the Internet is, by definition, a *glocal* medium, which allows companies to create localized content with global access. In fact, many MNCs have established so-called "global gateway" sites with several language options. Consumers can first choose the language, then seek the information they desire. In this regard, the content of the local sites may need to be adapted to local consumers' tastes and preferences, in terms of design, layout, copy, message, and so forth. (Okazaki and Alonso, 2002).

Okazaki (2005) examined websites created by American MNCs' in four EU member states (i.e., the UK, France, Germany, and Spain), and found a high level of localization in website communication strategy. This research extends Okazaki's exploration into the new EU member states, by conducting a content analysis of the MNCs' websites created in the Czech Republic. Specifically, we address the following questions: (1) What types of brand website functions are used? (2) To what extent are the Czech sites standardized?

SIGNIFICANCE OF THE STUDY

This study will be an interesting addition to the literature of global information technology for two reasons. First, prior research provides little information on how the content created by the most globally diffused information technology, the Internet, has been standardized in foreign markets. Information managers in global markets should be aware of a question of transmitting culturally bound meanings into local sites. Secondly, this study addresses how design features and website functions can be used as a tool to create a universal imagery in global websites. Specifically, this study explores one of the most understudied countries in Europe: the Czech Republic. After joining the European Union, studies on information technology in this new member state is almost non-existent, thus, this research makes a unique contribution to the literature.

ENLARGEMENT OF THE EUROPEAN UNION

In 2004, the enlargement of the European Union increased its member states from 15 to 25, by adding 10 countries: Cyprus, the Czech Republic, Estonia, Hungary, Latvia, Lithuania, Malta, Poland, Slovakia, and Slovenia. In 2007, two more countries, Romania and Bulgaria became the member states, making the Union of 27 countries. This drastic expansion changed the way multinational corporations (MNCs) operate their businesses in Europe. Because of these countries' low labour costs and investment incentives (e.g., tax reduction, construction aid, etc.), many firms moved their production facilities from other regions to these new member states. For example, Sheram and Soubbotina (2000) report that "Countries seen as more advanced in market reforms—the Czech and Slovak Republics, Hungary, and Poland—attracted almost three-quarters of foreign investment" in transition economies. In fact, Poland received approximately $6.4 billion in foreign direct investment in 2003, an increase of $360 million over the previous year (MacKay 2004).

As these new EU Member States experience rapid economic expansion, global marketing influences consumers in them more and more. Their product experiences increasingly resemble those of their "Western" neighbours. In this light, it is reasonable to argue that the role of advertising in everyday consumption has also undergone a drastic transition, in both content and executions. For example, in the Czech Republic, advertising spending reached 563 million euros in 2004, while the average annual growth rate over the last 5 years has been 5%. Multinational corporations (MNCs) are the largest advertisers in these countries.

MEDIA USAGE IN EASTERN AND CENTRAL EUROPE

The Czech Republic

In the Czech Republic, television has traditionally been the primary vehicle for advertising, accounting for 46% of the MNCs' marketing budgets. Print media is the second medium with 34%, while outdoor advertising (i.e., billboard) is third, with 8% of total advertising expenditure (OMD Czech, 2005). However, the rapid growth of the Internet has significantly affected this media distribution. According to the Czech Publishers Association, the share of Internet advertising has been estimated at approximately 4%, or 25 million Euro (760 millions CZK), with a growth rate of almost 80% in 2004 (Unie vydavatelů, 2005). The telecommunications, financial, and automobile companies are the heaviest users of the Internet as an advertising medium (Unie vydavatelů, 2005).

In 2005, nearly 30% of Czech households had a personal computer (Czech Statistical Office, 2005). Internet penetration is increasing steadily in the Czech Republic. Nowadays, 35% of the adult population in the Czech Republic uses the Internet, almost twice the number of Internet users in 2000. The Czech Republic has thus clearly outmatched other Central European countries: for example, Bulgaria (16%), Hungary (22%), and Poland (31%). However, it has not yet achieved the levels of Internet penetration in Estonia (51%) or Slovenia (56%). The most dynamic increase is found in older people (GfK, 2006), even though the Internet use remains the domain of younger

people. A quarter of Czech citizens have an Internet connection at home.

Searching for information is one of the most frequent activities on the Internet, according to a survey by the Czech Statistical Office (2005). In the most recent quarter to be surveyed, 62% of the Internet users used the Internet to find information about goods and services, 54% used it to find and download professional texts, 38% looked for services related to travel and accommodation, 36% to read and download on-line newspapers and magazines, and 28% to play or download games or music. However, the number of individuals with e-shopping experience increased rapidly between 2005 and 2006 (the survey was carried out in the first quarters of 2005 and 2006): it amounted to 14% in 2006, while a year before it had been only 6% (Czech Statistical Office, 2006). The most popular items in the Internet shopping are electronics, books, journals, textbooks, tickets and travel services, and accommodation. Online shopping is typically used more by men than women, and by the younger generation groups, between 25 and 45 years.

Approximately 12,500 Czech enterprises purchased goods or services via the Internet in 2003, almost 30% of the total number. The value of Internet purchases reached 2.8% of total purchases, and the value of Internet sales reached nearly 2.1% of total sales in these enterprises.

Poland and Hungary

Along with the Czech Republic, Poland and Hungary make up the fastest-growing economic region within the new EU member states. For example, the rapid transformation of the Polish economy is reflected in the accelerated growth of its advertising market. Between 1996 and 1999, average annual growth in advertising expenditure was more than 40%, which can be attributed to the drastic structural changes, and the subsequent economic boom, in this period. With regard to media share, television was the most popular

(48%), with print media second (35%). On-line advertising, including websites, remains far behind traditional media, representing approximately 1% of total media spending (Zenith Optimedia, 2004). The telecommunications, financial, and automobile industries are the heaviest users of the Internet for advertising, promotion, and transactions (Agora, 2005).

In 2005, 30% of households in Poland had the technical possibility of the Internet access. In term of quality of connections, the survey found that only 16% of Polish households used a broadband connection. The significant disparity in the Internet infrastructure is between urban areas and the countryside, where the penetration of broadband connections is four times lower than in urban areas (Eurostat, 2005).

The Internet usage by Polish enterprises is below the EU average: in 2005, 87% of enterprises used the Internet connection. The share of broadband the Internet connections was 43%. More than 67% of companies have their own website homepage (Eurostat, 2006). Online purchases have not yet become popular. Only 5% of Polish consumers ordered goods or services via the Internet in 2005 (Eurostat, 2006). According to the survey by GfK (2006), only 4% of the Internet users make a purchase on the Internet once a month or more. A further 6% buy online once every two to three months, while 18% go online sporadically with the intention of buying something. The most frequently purchased items include books, CDs, clothes, and shoes. Less frequently, people buy DVDs and air tickets (GfK, 2006).

In B2B the situation is similar. In 2005, only 9% of the enterprises surveyed ordered products or services via the Internet. Sales via the Internet were lower, with only 4% of enterprises selling via the Internet. In 2005, turnover from e-commerce via the Internet amounted to 1.6% of total turnover (Eurostat, 2005).

Similarly, the Hungarian market has shown a drastic growth in market size and advertising spending. According to the Budapest Business Journal (BBJ, 2004), advertising expenditure in television media reached 213 million euros by 2003. The print media also showed a drastic growth, to spending of 212 million euros. In 2003, the online advertising market expanded by approximately 30%, achieving a 2% share of the total media market. The principal reasons for this growth were an increased number of the Internet users in younger generations, and the rapid proliferation of broadband high-speed connection. The largest online advertisers include car dealers, telecommunication companies, beer makers, and cosmetics firms (BBJ, 2003).

Other EU Member States

In 2005, Slovenia had the highest rate of the Internet usage in the new member states, both for households (48%), and for enterprises (96%) (Eurostat, 2006). The lowest rates of access were in Lithuania, for households (16%), and in Latvia, for enterprises (75%). The largest disparities in the Internet access between households and enterprises were recorded in the Czech Republic, Lithuania, and Slovakia. The number of individuals who have never used the Internet outweighs the number of regular users in the new member states. That differs from the situation in the old member states.

There is also disparity in the presence of companies' websites on the Internet. In January 2005, 62% of enterprises in the EU were equipped with a website, but only 49% in the new member states. The lowest percentages of companies with websites were found in Latvia, Hungary, and Lithuania. Most enterprises use the content of their web presentations mainly to market their products. Less than half use it to display catalogues of their products, services, and prices. One quarter use websites to offer after-sales service to their customers. Apart from the Czech Republic, enterprises in the new member

Table 1. Descriptive statistics

	Population[1]	GDP per capita[2]	Advertising spending[3]	Advertising spending as % of GDP[4]	Internet penetration[5]	Internet household penetration[6]	No of local domains[7]	Online spending[8]	Internet Advertising spending[9]
Czech Rep.	10,288.9	73.6	769,186	0.65	50	29	1,502,537	7	22,734
Cyprus	776.0	88.9	89,073	0.54	33.6	37	75846	2	n.a.
Estonia	1,339.9	59.8	107,744	0.79	51.8	46	449,036	n.a.	3,607
Hungary	10,057.9	62.5	1,029,874	0.91	30.4	32	1,176,592	7	21,302
Latvia	3,385.7	48.6	129,961	0.81	45.2	42	132,204	1	7,277
Lithuania	2,280.5	52.1	150,07	0.50	35.9	35	240,592	2	3,086
Malta	407.7	71.7	n.a.	n.a.	33	53	20,673	n.a.	n.a.
Poland	3,8101.8	49.7	1,862,672	0.55	29.9	36	5,001,786	6	32,885
Slovakia	5,391.6	57.1	n.a.	n.a.	46.5	27	486,020	0	n.a.
Slovenia	2,010.3	81.9	242,656	0.64	55.5	54	64,284	9	5,484
EU 10	74,040.3	64.6			44	39	9,149,570		

Note: 1. Data in thousands for the 1st of January 2007. Source: Eurostat (2007)

2. GDP (in PPS per capita) in 2005. EU25= 100%. Source: Eurostat (2007).

3. Global advertising expenditure 2006. In $US Thousands. Initiative Innovation (2007).

4. Initiative Innovation (2007) and The World Factbook, Central Intelligence Agency (2007)

5. Internet Usage in the European Union. Penetration (% Population) in 2007. Source: Internet World Stats (2007).

6. Percentage of households who have Internet access at home in 2006. Source: Eurostat (2007).

7. Number of local domains based on number of top-level domain in January 2007. Source: ISC Internet Domain Survey (2007).

8. The Internet turnover as percentage of the total turnover of enterprises with 10 or more employees in 2006. Source: Eurostat (2007).

9. Global advertising expenditure 2006. In thousands of $. Initiative Innovation (2007).

states registered lower rates than the EU average for purchases, sales, and for total sales on the Internet, as a percentage of their overall turnover (Eurostat, 2006).

The e-readiness rankings of the Economist Intelligence Unit can be seen as a complex indicator of the level of ICT of a country's infrastructure. The index is a weighted collection of nearly 100 quantitative and qualitative criteria, which assesses the "state of play" of a country's information and communications technology (ICT) infrastructure, and the ability of its consumers, businesses, and governments to use ICT to their benefit. In the 2006 e-readiness rankings, Estonia achieved the best position of all the new EU member states (27th), whereas Latvia (39th) was lowest. By comparison, ten of the fifteen old EU members were in the top 20.

The Networked Readiness Index, published annually in the Global Information Technology Report, is a similar index. This index captures such aspects as available ICT infrastructure, and actual levels of ICT usage, and its purpose is to understand more thoroughly the impact of ICT on the competitiveness of nations. In this index, Estonia again scored best amongst the new members. Latvia and Poland had the lowest ratings.

STANDARDIZATION VS. LOCALIZATION

The issue of standardization arises from the desirability and feasibility of using a uniform marketing mix (4Ps) across national markets (Szymanski et al., 1993). Advertising has been examined more often than the other elements of this mix (Agrawal, 1995; Zandpour et al., 1994). A *standardized* approach is the use of uniform messages with no modification of headings, illustrations, or copy, except for translation in international markets (Onkvisit and Shaw, 1987). The standardized school of thought argues that consumers anywhere in the world are likely to

share the same wants and needs (Elinder, 1961; Levitt, 1983). On the other hand, the *localized* approach asserts that consumers differ across countries, and therefore advertising should be tailored according to culture, media availability, product life cycle stages, and industry structure (Synodinos et al., 1989; Wind, 1986). Combining these two extremes, the third school of thought states that the appropriateness of standardization depends on economic similarity, market position, the nature of the product, the environment, and organizational factors (Jain, 1989).

In the 1970s, empirical evidence showed a high degree of localization, due to both increasing nationalistic forces, and various well-publicized advertising blunders in the 1960s (Agrawal, 1995). This trend reversed, to favour standardization, in the 1980s, and went along with a drastic rise in the number of multinational advertising agencies (Yin, 1999). During this period, a series of content analysis studies attempted to identify cross-cultural differences between Japanese and U.S. advertising (Hong et al., 1987; Madden et al., 1986; Mueller, 1987).

In the 1990s, localization seemed to remain popular among MNCs operating in various regions of world markets. Harris (1994) found that 69% of 38 MNCs (19 American and 19 European) standardized their advertising campaigns to some extent throughout the EC markets, whilst the rest of the sample localized. Interestingly, only 8% of the sample used totally standardized advertising, providing "little evidence of any widespread practice of standardized pan-European advertising campaigns" (Harris, 1994). Kanso and Nelson (2002) found that 62% of 193 firms (both American and non-American subsidiaries) in Finland and Sweden use localization, and place a strong emphasis on local cultures. Similarly, Samiee et al. (2003) found that MNCs operating in Southeast Asia tend to localize advertising. They examined 113 firms in Hong Kong, PRC, Taiwan, and Singapore, and found that both environmental

Table 2. Network and e-readiness statistics

	Networked Readiness Index [1]	Networked Readiness Index (Rank) [1]	e-readiness rankings [2]	e-readiness rankings, general index [2]	e-readiness rankings, Connectivity index [2]	e-readiness rankings, Business Environment index [2]	Enterprises selling via Internet 2005 in % [3]	Enterprises availability of the Internet 2005 in % [3]
Czech Republic	0.36	32	32	6.14	4.90	7.39	13	92
Cyprus	0.36	33	n.a.	n.a.	n.a.	n.a.	4	85
Estonia	0.96	23	27	6.71	6.60	7.81	8	90
Hungary	0.27	37	32	6.14	4.80	7.34	4	78
Latvia	-0.03	52	39	5.30	3.95	7.21	1	75
Lithuania	0.08	44	38	5.45	4.65	7.28	6	86
Malta	0.51	30	n.a.	n.a.	n.a.	n.a.	16	90
Poland	-0.09	53	32	5.76	4.30	7.28	5	87
Slovakia	0.19	41	36	5.65	4.05	7.35	7	92
Slovenia	0.34	35	28	6.34	5.90	7.45	12	96

Note: n.a. = not available.
1. Global Information Technology Report 2005-2006
2. Economist Intelligence Unit (2006).
3. Eurostat (2005).

and economic factors were the primary drivers of this tendency.

WEBSITE POSITIONING AS GLOBAL INFORMATION MANAGEMENT

Although these issues have been debated for decades in traditional media, a new stream of research has emerged recently, on the standardization versus localization of global websites in multiple markets. With the rapid expansion of the Internet, and the resulting connections between local, regional, and international markets, an increasing number of MNCs are shifting from off-line to on-line marketing. This frequently entails creating a diverse range of websites in multiple markets (Donthu and Garcia, 1999). By 2001, more than 36 million domains for commercial websites had already been established: these "dot coms" are projected to attract an astonishing $6.8 trillion in business by 2004 (Forrester, 2002; Internet Software Consortium, 2001).

Such numbers incline observers to see the Internet as a door to the "global village wonderland", as advocated by Levitt (1983): that is, an entity that creates an environment for more standardized marketing communication in world markets. Product-based websites are replacing such shopping venues as mail-order catalogues and television-based home shopping, and also offer a new format for global advertising among culturally and linguistically diverse groups (Pastor, 2001). An increase in the quantity and quality of product/ brand information on the Internet is generating extraordinary consumer interest, which extends beyond physical and political boundaries (Donthu and Garcia, 1999). Accordingly, Roberts and Ko (2001) asserted that websites, with their ability to uniformly blend textual and visual content, constitute the best communication medium in which to develop brand images.

One roadblock that MNCs face involves localized websites: primarily, the need to satisfy the linguistic requirements of a diverse population of potential customers (Warden et al., 2002). According to Quelch and Klein (1996), establishing localized relationships with international consumers is best achieved by creating regional Web content. However, creating regional commercial websites may not be cost-effective if, to elicit return visits, a company is obliged to update information continuously. Such intense website maintenance on a regional level can jeopardize consistent brand strategies, by eliminating the "advantage of centralized management of a firm's Websites" (Warden et al., 2002).

In a pioneering study, Okazaki and Alonso (2002) examined Japanese websites in Japan, Spain, and the U.S.A., and found that cultural dimensions (power distance, uncertainty avoidance, masculinity – femininity, individualism-collectivism, and long-term orientation) and communication style (high context versus low context) were the primary drivers of cross-cultural differences in MNCs' website communication strategies. Focusing on more operational aspects, Okazaki (2005) examined American brands' website standardization in France, Germany, Spain, and the UK. He argued that the progress of the EU enlargement and economic integration via the euro provided firms with an incentive to use a uniform website communication across the EU member states. However, the findings were mixed, in that the level of standardization of American brands' websites in the European countries was low, compared to their respective home-country (American) websites. On the other hand, differences within the EU were minimal: the websites created within the European markets were somewhat "regionalized", especially for durable and industrial goods.

A summary of prior research on website content analysis is shown in Table 3.

Table 3. Prior research on website content analysis

Year	Authors	Countries examined	Unit of analysis	Analyzed content	Sample size	Statistical design
1999	Ju-Pak	US, UK & S.Korea	Product-based websites	Information content, creative strategies, design	110 (EE.UU.) 100 (UK) 100 (S.Korea)	Chi-square, ANOVA
1999	Oh, Cho & Leckenby	US & S.Korea	Target ads	Information content, creative strategies	50 for each country	Chi-square
1999	Yoon & Cropp	US & S.Korea	Brand websites	Information content, emotional appeals, cultural aspects	20 for each country	Chi-square
2000	Lee & Sego	US & S.Korea	Banners	Information content, emotional appeals, colours, etc.	252 in total	Chi-square
2000	Chung & Ahn	US & S.Korea	Banners	Information content, "call-to-action" messages, demographics, etc.	251 (EE.UU.) 221 (S.Korea)	Chi-square
2000	Yoon	US	Product-based websites	Information content, celebrity endorsement, etc.	200 in total	Chi-square, ANOVA
2002	Okazaki & Alonso	Japan, Spain & EE.UU.	Product-based websites	Information content, cultural values, creative strategies	20 for each country	Chi-square, ANOVA
2002	Dou, Nielsen & Tan	Canada, Denmark & Malaysia	Commercial websites	Communication systems, transactional functions, etc.	150 for each country	ANOVA
2002	Zahir, Dobing & Hunter	26 countries	National portals	Linguistic aspects, design, colours, Hofstede's cultural dimensions, etc.	26 portals	Descriptive stat
2003	Robbins & Stylianou	16 countries	Corporate websites	Design, presentation, links, security, information content, financial content, corporate information, etc.	90 in total	ANOVA
2005	Okazaki	US, UK, France, Germany & Spain	Brand websites	Brand website functions, similarity ratings	244	ANOVA, discriminant analysis, multiple regression

COMMUNICATION IN THE GLOBAL WEBSITE ENVIRONMENT

What is the primary factor influencing MNCs that operate in European markets? They now face more and more pressure to generate more comprehensive marketing strategies on the web. Among the various forms of the online environment, websites have been one of the most popular platforms, allowing consumers to see, consult, and obtain product-related information at any time, anywhere. Such websites can be seen as a new form of global marketing communications, offering opportunities to strengthen effective relational marketing in international markets (Robert and Ko, 2002). The creation of a localized URL in Europe, therefore, may be a necessary strategic move, because cultural and linguistic barriers are perhaps the most difficult obstacles to overcome in marketing communications across European nations (Kahle, Beatty, and Mager, 1994). Such localization, however, could cost a great deal. Hence, MNCs may intuitively favour standardization, given the benefits associated with offline marketing standardization, such as consistent brand image and corporate identity, cost savings, and organizational control. Furthermore, websites seem to be an effective medium for establishing a global brand image, by offering consistent textual and visual information to international consumers. Unfortunately, there seems to be a lack of empirical research regarding the standardization versus localization issue in the online environment, leaving important questions unanswered.

What are the determining factors in international marketing communications on the web? In a recent criticism of the slow progress of international advertising research, Taylor and Johnson (2001) argue that the standardization debate should "focus on what executions can be standardized and when they can be standardized". Following this suggestion, this study intends to fill this gap, by identifying to what extent MNCs have adopted a standardized approach for their websites created in European markets. In order to ensure cross-national data equivalency, we examined only the websites created by America's top brands for the UK, France, Germany, and Spain. These countries differ importantly in terms of cultural and linguistic characteristics, but are relatively homogeneous in socioeconomic conditions and technological infrastructure, and have online markets of a reasonable size.

Furthermore, 3.3%, 6.5%, and 8.1% of the world's online population consist of French, German, and Spanish speaking consumers, respectively, compared to 35.2% of English speakers (Global Reach, 2003). Therefore, these four countries represent an important segment of world online consumers. On the other hand, the languages spoken in the new EU member states, such as Polish or Czech, account for a very small portion of the online population. In fact, the impact of these countries, on both the world economy and the world online population, is negligible (Table 4). Thus, an important question arises: is it worthwhile for MNCs to consider local adaptation in such new markets? Or is it better to use a standardization approach in these markets, to take advantage of cost savings and efficient website maintenance? To address these questions, this study will examine websites created by MNCs for the Czech Republic.

CONCEPTUAL FRAMEWORK

Figure 1 shows the conceptual framework for this study. These concepts are essentially based on the matrix proposed by Quelch and Klein (1996), who suggested two primary models of website: the communication model and the transaction model. Originally, their matrix was not intended to be a theoretical model for formal testing, but since then it has been used as a conceptual base (e.g., see Dou, Nielsen, and Tan, 2002). In our modified matrix, communication and transaction feature form two ends of one axis, which should be balanced with the other axis, consisting of fact and image. The resulting four quadrants need to be effectively combined to achieve the desired level of website standardization. The components in each quadrant can be considered the most relevant programmes for website brand communications.

The extent of website standardization should be determined on the basis of the two major roles of global online programmes: (1) to enhance worldwide transactions by establishing a localized relationship, and (2) to develop a standardized brand image, using the appropriate combination of content, graphics, backgrounds, and multimedia effects in all the MNC's websites in different languages (Roberts and Ko, 2003). In the following

Table 4. World online population and language use

Language type	Internet access [1]	% of world online pop.	Total pop. [1]	GDP [2]	% of world economy	GDP per capita [3]
English	238.5	35.2	508	n.a.	n.a.	n.a.
Non-English	439.8	64.8	5,822	n.a.	n.a.	n.a.
European Languages (non-English)	238.1	35.1	1,218	12,968	30.3	n.a.
Czech	4.0	n.a.	12	121	n.a.	10.0
Dutch	13.2	2.0	20	575	n.a.	28.5
Finnish	2.8	n.a.	6	142	n.a.	23.6
French	22.7	3.3	77	1517	4.2	19.7
German	44.4	6.5	100	2,679	5.8	26.8
Greek	2.0	n.a.	12	189	n.a.	15.8
Hungarian	1.6	n.a.	10	96	n.a.	9.6
Italian	24.1	3.6	62	1,251	3.6	20.1
Polish	6.9	n.a.	44	359	n.a.	8.1
Portuguese	19.3	2.8	176	1,487	3.6	8.4
Romanian	2.4	n.a.	26	108	n.a.	4.2
Russian	18.4	2.7	167	822	1.8	4.9
Scandinavian languages (total)	13.5	2.0	20	550	1.3	27.9
Serbo-Croatian	1.0	n.a.	20	n.a.	n.a.	n.a.
Slovak	1.0	n.a.	6	47	n.a.	8.7
Slovenian	0.7	n.a.	2	22.9	n.a.	10.9
Spanish	54.8	8.1	350	2500	8.9	7.1
Turkish	4.6	n.a.	67	431	n.a.	6.4
Ukrainian	0.9	n.a.	47	115	n.a.	2.3
TOTAL EUROPEAN LANGUAGES (non-English)	238.1	35.1	1,218	12,968	33.9	n.a.
TOTAL ASIAN LANGUAGES	201.7	29.7	n.a.	n.a.	n.a.	n.a.
TOTAL WORLD	648.7		6,330	41,400	n.a.	n.a.

Note: 1 US$ in million; 2 US$ in billion, 3 US$ in Thousand.
Source: Global Reach (2003)

section, each principal featu·e of our proposed model is therefore analyzed in the light of these perspectives.

METHODOLOGY

This study adopts content analysis as a research methodology. This method has been widely used in cross-cultural research (Brislin, 1980), as well as in the Internet research (McMillan, 2000; Okazaki and Alonso, 2002).

Company selection. A website content analysis was performed, to examine the degree of website standardization of American brands' websites created for the Czech market. Methodological recommendations from prior research were adopted, to establish a high reliability (Dou et al., 2002; Okazaki and Alonso, 2002; Philport and Arbittier, 1997). To create a dataset, a ranking of "The 100 Top Global Brands" from *BusinessWeek (2002)* was used. Only brands with America as country of origin (by the classification of *BusinessWeek*) were chosen to match home versus host country website pairs. In total, 66 brands were found, of which 34 brands had websites in the Czech

Republic. Here, it is important to note that these firms are considered as representative of American firms doing business in the Czech Republic, because their Internet presence can be considered as the initial step of market entry mode.

Coding categories. Next, a detailed coding sheet was first developed, with detailed operational definitions. The variables include (1) brand website functions, and (2) similarity ratings (Table 5). With regard to the former, the coding categories were adopted from Okazaki (2005), who suggested 23 website communication functions. Similar categories have been suggested in the past (e.g., Ghose and Dou, 1998; Leogn, Huang, and Stanners, 1998). Each variable was measured on a categorical dichotomy as to the existence of each function on a website. Values of "1" and "0" were assigned for answers of "Yes" and "No", respectively. For example, websites that had appropriate information associated with "job/career development" were assigned "1" for this attribute. Those that did not were assigned "0". These values were considered dependent variables in the analysis. The similarity rating refers to the degree of similarity between home-country and host-country websites. This "similarity rating"

Figure 1. Conceptualization of website program standardization

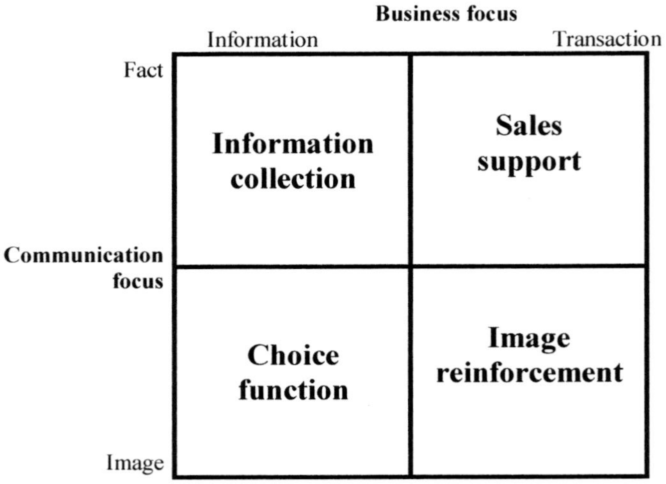

measure was also adopted from Okazaki (2005), and was originally inspired by Mueller (1991). The textual and visual components of websites created for local markets were assessed for the extent to which they were similar or dissimilar to those created at home. The similarity rating was coded for each pair of websites (i.e., U.S.A.-Czech sites) on a five-point semantic scale, ranging from "very different" (coded as 1) to "very similar" (coded as 5), with an intermediate scale point "not determinable" (coded as 3). The components included copy, headlines, text, layout, colour, photographs associated with the product, with human models, and with background scenes, illustrations, charts, graphs, and interactive images.

Coding instrument. All coding instruments were originally prepared in English, and then translated into Czech, using the "back translation" technique. Each typology was supplemented with additional examples, to give a better illustration. The unit of analysis was determined as the homepage, which has been considered a central gate to Web-based communication. This is appropriate, given the primary objective of the study: to identify major differences in the main text, pictures, and graphics. We examined the first and second levels of websites, because it is practically impossible to scrutinize every detail of an entire site. The existence of online brand communications was primarily determined by the main menu or index provided on the homepage. For instance, if the menu included a link labelled "corporate information", the site was coded as having this variable. The only exception occurred when analyzing direct or indirect online transactions, because in some cases these functions may not be listed on the main index. In this case, the coders were asked to examine the submenu of the websites.

Coder training and reliability. Following the recommendations by Kolbe and Burnett (1991), two bilingual Czech judges, both of whom were unaware of the purpose of the study, were hired and first trained to grasp the operational definitions of all the variables. During the training period, the coders practised independently, by examining 20 randomly chosen websites from non-American firms. Then, the coded results were compared, and differences were reconciled through discussion. An inter-judge reliability was calculated using the reliability index suggested by Perreault and Leigh's reliability index (I_r) (1989). Various researchers consider this estimation method to be the best among available alternatives (e.g., Kolbe and Burnett, 1991).

As Table 6 shows, the majority of the resulting indexes far exceeded a widely accepted minimum .80???, and was thus deemed satisfactory. It was recognized that there would be a potential loss of information in similarity evaluation between American and Czech sites, because non-native English speakers had analyzed American websites. However, it was accepted that such potential bias was minimized by the coders' extensive preparation: the subjective interpretation of textual information was minimal, since the coders were responsible for examining only *major* copy, headlines, and text on the websites. Otherwise, they were instructed to objectively measure the similarity of non-textual information.

RESULTS

Table 7 summarizes the frequency distribution of brand website functions. For the sake of comparison, the information provided in Okazaki's (2005) previous exploration was used as a reference with regard to the U.S., UK, French, and German markets. This comparison should help our understanding of MNCs' website standardization in existing versus new EU member states.

The Chi-square analysis detected significant differences in 8 categories: global/local site options, general product information, investor relations, online purchase, email contact, promotion/prizes/sweepstakes, culture/entertainment, and guest book/customer feedback. It appears

Table 5. Measurement schemes

Measure	Coding categories	Scale type
Brand website functions	Global/Local site options, Corporate information, Corporate news release, Product/ Brand news release, General product information, Brand specific information, Investor relationships, Direct online transaction, Indirect online transaction, Office/Store locator, Country/Language option, Search engine, Jobs/Career development, Promotion/Prizes/ Sweepstakes, Education/Training, Culture/Entertainment, Client registration/Log-in, Guest book/Customer feedback, E-mail alert, FAQs, Free download, Sitemap, Links	Nominal scale (Yes=1, No=0)
Similarity ratings	Company logo, Company logo placement, Major copy, Major copy placement, Major headline, Major headline placement, Major text, Layout in top half / right half, Layout in bottom half / left half, Colour in top half / right half, Colour in bottom half / left half, Major photograph 1 (product), Major photograph 2 (human model), Major photograph 3 (background scene), Major illustrations, Major chart or graph, Interactive image 1 (flash as opening), Interactive image 2 (pop-ups), Interactive image 3 (animated banners), Interactive image 4 (layers, pop-unders, etc.)	Interval scale (1=very different, 5=very similar)

Table 6. Intercoder reliability

Measure	Coding categories	Perreault & Leigh's *Ir*
	Brand specific information	0.82
Brand website functions	Client registration/Log-in	0.91
	Corporate information	1.00
	Corporate news release	0.97
	Country/Language option	1.00
	Culture/Entertainment	0.97
	Direct online transaction	1.00
	Education/Training	0.94
	E-mail alert	1.00
	FAQs	1.00
	Free download	0.94
	General product information	0.97
	Global/Local site options	0.94
	Guest book/Customer feedback	1.00
	Indirect online transaction	1.00
	Investor relations	0.97
	Jobs/Career development	0.97
	Links	0.91
	Office/Store locator	1.00
	Product/Brand news release	1.00
	Promotion/Prizes/Sweepstakes	0.97
	Search engine	1.00

continued on following page

Table 6. continued

	Sitemap	1.00
Similarity ratings	Text	0.91
	Major photograph: product	0.75
	Major photograph: model	0.56
	Major photograph: background scene	0.92
	Major illustrations	0.82
	Major chart or graph	
	Layout in top half / right half	0.93
	Layout in bottom half / left half	0.98
	Headline placement	0.74
	Headline	0.69
	Copy placement	0.73
	Copy	0.91
	Company logo placement	0.95
	Company logo	0.96
	Colour in top half / right half	0.93
	Colour in bottom half / left half	0.91

that American MNCs tend to apply a different website communication strategy in the Czech market because, in prior research, Okazaki (2005) found significant differences in only 3 of 23 variables, suggesting that the frequency of the usage of brand website functions in the UK, France, Germany, and Spain was relatively uniform. In observing the frequencies of brand website functions in the Czech sites, email contact was used more frequently, but the other tools were used much less than in the other markets.

Next, in order to capture the relationships between the brand website functions and country domain, we performed a multiple correspondence analysis via optimal scaling technique. This method is appropriate for nominal variables, from which a multidimensional map can be created. We used the existence of the brand website functions (yes or no) as descriptive variables, and the type of country domain (U.S.A. or Czech Republic) as classification variables. Figure 2 shows the resulting biplot component loadings. As clearly seen, the majority of brand website functions are more closely associated with U.S. sites (represented by "1"), while only a limited number of brand website functions are associated with Czech sites (represented by "2"). Specifically, global/local site options, links, and indirect online transactions are concentrated in the lower left quadrant (which U.S. sites appear to dominate), but the rest of the brand website functions are concentrated in the upper right quadrant (where Czech sites appear to dominate).

Lastly, Table 8 summarizes the results of the similarity ratings. A higher similarity rating indicates a higher degree of standardization. As the results clearly show, the similarity between the American and Czech sites was notably higher, especially in logo, copy, and colour. In comparison with the other sites, headlines and major pho-

Table 7. Results of brand website functions

1. Brand website features	US (n=66)	UK (n=57)	France (n=49)	Germany (n=57)	**Czech (n=34)**	*p*
Global/Local site options	37.9	84.2	65.3	75.4	**64.4**	.000
Corporate information	89.4	86.0	87.8	84.2	**86.1**	.956
Corporate news release	53.0	54.4	55.1	59.6	**55.6**	.983
Product/Brand news release	51.5	49.1	53.1	52.6	**55.6**	.990
General product information	80.3	84.2	83.7	78.9	**47.2**	.000
Brand specific information	75.8	68.4	73.5	68.4	**69.4**	.858
Investor relationships	45.5	26.3	16.3	22.8	**11.1**	.001
Online purchase	71.2	42.1	42.6	43.9	**25.0**	.000
Email contact	22.7	31.6	28.6	24.6	**77.8**	.000
Office/Store locator	33.3	33.3	32.7	26.3	**13.9**	.346
Country/Language option	62.1	57.9	71.4	61.4	**52.8**	.536
Search engine	68.2	57.9	55.1	50.9	**52.8**	.442
Jobs/Career development	62.1	47.4	46.9	54.4	**61.1**	.374
Promotion/Prizes/Sweepstakes	56.1	63.2	44.9	47.4	**11.1**	.000
Education/Training	39.4	33.3	26.5	24.6	**25.0**	.331
Culture/Entertainment	47.0	57.9	53.1	42.1	**13.9**	.001
Client registration/Log-in	51.5	36.8	38.8	36.8	**41.7**	.398
Guest book/Customer feedback	78.8	82.5	75.5	77.2	**22.2**	.000
E-mail alert	25.8	15.8	20.4	19.3	**25.0**	.483
FAQs	18.2	22.8	16.3	19.3	**8.3**	.647
Free download	19.7	26.3	26.5	28.1	**36.1**	.643
Sitemap	45.5	42.1	44.9	36.8	**38.9**	.905
Links	4.5	12.3	8.2	3.5	**19.4**	.053

Note: The data of the US, UK, France and Germany are based on Okazaki (2005)

tographs also exhibit higher similarity. On this basis, it appears clear that the American MNCs tend to create highly standard\]zed websites in the Czech Republic.

DISCUSSION

This study attempts to examine the website communication strategy used by American MNCs in a new EU member state, the Czech Republic. We performed a content analysis of 34 Czech sites created by America's top brands in terms of brand website functions, and similarity between the home and host sites. The findings indicate that American MNCs appear to standardize their Czech sites. Given that the Czech Republic is a growing market that attracts more and more foreign direct investment, this case could be

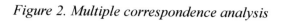

Figure 2. Multiple correspondence analysis

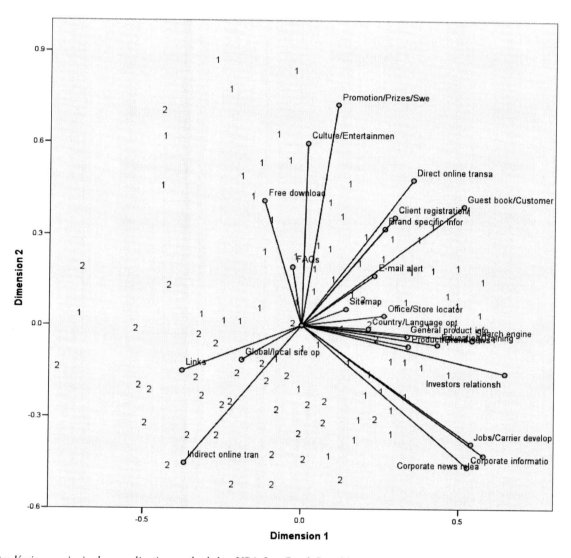

Note: Varimax principal normalization method. 1 = USA, 2 = Czech Republic

Table 8. Results of similarity ratings

Components	UK (n=57)	France (n=49)	Germany (n=57)	**Czech (n=34)**
Company logo	4.51	4.61	4.39	**4.58**
Major copy	1.43	1.36	1.14	**4.00**
Major headline	1.23	1.17	1.02	**3.47**
Major text	2.84	2.53	2.68	**2.32**
Layout	3.35	3.32	3.29	**3.88**

considered indicative of the general tendency in the other new EU member states.

First, American MNCs tend to use general product information less frequently in the Czech market than in the other EU markets, which suggests two possible scenarios. First, they have not yet commercialized their products in this market, and therefore dispose of little information. In this case, the primary objective of their websites would be to provide a preliminary information platform in a new market. Second, they might have needed to localize product information to a great extent, especially in the local language, with more adapted product usage. However, it appears that the most logical conclusion would be that the lack of online product information is because American firms are still in the very early mode of market entry in the Czech Republic.

The second scenario seems very unlikely when we address the following question: Why would large multinational firms devote resources to extensive adaptations of Czech websites? The country's population is only 10 million and, according to the most recent Eurostat (2006), only 19% of Czech homes had the Internet access in 2005, including 5% with broadband connections. As much as 63% of the population has never used the Internet. Only one in six people who used the Internet (5.5%) bought anything online in 2005, and these purchases were limited largely to electronic goods (2.1%), books (1.6%), and clothing (1.1%). Therefore, if the total market

in a given product category is currently only 100,000 or so, and if adapting the website is only going to improve website effectiveness by 5% to 10%, is there any incentive to adapt and then to continue managing that adaptation? Consistent with this argument, our findings indicate that online purchase functions are rarely used in the Czech sites. This suggests that American MNCs may have neither distribution channels nor local investors in the Czech market. Similarly, the much less frequent use of guest book/customer feedback indicates that American brands are less willing to offer personalized contact to the local Czech consumers, probably because of the unavailability of local outlets, representatives, or staff. In contrast, in the Czech Republic, they offer general email addresses more frequently than in the other countries, as an alternative contact mode for general inquiries.

Third, by the same token, culture/entertainment and promotion/prices/sweepstakes are used much less in the Czech market than in the others, because these elements need to be matched to local consumer tastes, and require more personalized content. It would make little sense to offer presents or incentives when the companies actually have no local sales activities.

Finally, a surprisingly high level of similarity ratings for both textual and visual components indicates a lack of any cultural adaptation of websites to the Czech market. This contrasts with Okazaki's (2005) findings regarding American MNCs' website strategy in the UK, France, Germany, and

Spain, where clearly localized websites have been created in the existing EU member states. This finding is consistent with the frequency of brand website functions: the Czech sites use far fewer brand website functions with highly standardized textual and visual components.

It is clear that American MNCs consider the EU a single market, and one that is strategically dissimilar to their home market. If we observe only the websites created in the "older" member states, there seems to exist a "regionalization" strategy across Europe, in that the level of similarity ratings among the European samples was relatively uniform. This may be due to the close geographical proximity of the three countries, which would, logically, provide more opportunities for personal interaction and the accumulation of greater knowledge. However, in the case of the Czech Republic, website adaptation has not yet advanced, probably due to many unknown factors: in particular, specific information regarding local consumers' tastes and preferences.

To make our findings more objective, we should recognize a few limitations. First, the current study examined only one country that has recently joined the European Union. Future research should expand this study into other new EU member states, especially Poland and Hungary, because these two countries, along with the Czech Republic, are the most economically developed regions. Because of the extreme scarcity of research related to these countries, any such extension will contribute significantly to the literature. Second, while content analysis could provide useful information regarding the manifest content, the findings should be treated with caution. The findings by no means explain practitioners' "true" intentions in website communication strategy. In this regard, it will be interesting to extend this study in the future, by conducting a questionnaire survey of advertisers and marketers who are actually responsible for the new EU member states.

LIMITATIONS

While this study makes significant contributions to the global information management literature, some important limitations must also be recognized. First, content analysis is, by definition, an observational method that examines only manifest content. Our findings have little or nothing to do with marketers' "true" intentions on global website positioning. Second, our unit of analysis was limited to the menu and submenu of the homepages. However, it is possible that a more localized strategy might have been observed in further links. Finally, we examined only one of the new EU member states, thus, any generalization of our findings should be treated with caution.

FUTURE RESEARCH DIRECTIONS

First, future extensions should examine websites created for the other new EU member states, such as Poland, Hungary, Latvia, Lithuania, and Malta. Information technology management for website positioning in these countries is virtually unknown, and analyzing brands' websites positioning in these countries should help us to draw more generalisable implications. In particular, researchers are planning to examine Polish and Hungarian websites in the next stage because, in these countries, the total online as well as offline advertising spending is substantial, in comparison with the other new EU member sates.

Second, in furthering our explorations, content analysis methodology should be improved. Specifically, we need to examine the level of standardization or localization at deeper levels of websites. While this study scrutinized the first level of websites or homepages, some may claim that much information was lost by ignoring the second and third levels of websites. For example, the lack of direct online transactions need not necessarily mean that the website does not have a link to the online shopping sites of different companies. This was the case for consumer electronics, in that computer or office machine products are sold on "general" e-commerce (or even auction) sites. More specific coding instructions should be established, to enable the coders to improve their analysis with a higher level of inter-coder reliability.

Third, we also should conduct a survey that targets foreign subsidiaries' managers. It will be interesting to compare the findings of this paper with the managers' perceptions. In particular, several questions appear of special interest. For example, are their websites created or controlled locally or globally? What level of control do senior executives of foreign subsidiaries actually have of their electronic commerce planning and executions?

Finally, in an attempt to capture a clearer picture of global website positioning in multiple markets, more collaboration will be needed by researchers in information systems management and other disciplines: in particular, marketing management. Needless to say, a higher level of international cooperation is necessary to conduct more objective and reliable data collection in multiple markets.

REFERENCES

Agora (2005). Advertising market. Available: http://www.agora.pl/agora_eng/1,60209,2385752.html?menu=7.

Agrawal, M. (1995). Review of a 40-year debate in international advertising. *International Marketing Review*, 12 (1), 26-48.

ARBOmedia (2005). Standardní reklamní rok přinese médiím 17,8 miliard. Available: http://www.arbomedia.cz/strany/ipwc/w2a.asp?id=133

ARBOmedia (2005). Standardní reklamní rok přinese médiím 17,8 miliard". Available: http://www.arbomedia.cz/strany/ipwc/w2a.asp?id=133.

Brislin, R.W. (1980). Translation and Content Analysis of Oral and Written Material. In H. C. Triandis and Berry, J. W. (eds.), *Handbook of Cross-cultural Psychology* (Vol. 2, pp. 389-444), Boston: Allyn and Bacon.

Budapest business journal (2003). Web-based advertising making ground. September 16, 2003, Available: http://www.bbj.hu.

Budapest business journal (2004). Online advertising boom. August 18, 2004, Available: http://www.bbj.hu.

BusinessWeek (2002). The 100 Top Brands. August 5, 95-99.

Czech Publishers Association (2006). Internetová reklama v roce 2005 přesáhla 1 miliardu Kč. Press release, Available: http://www.unievyda-vatelu.cz.

Czech Statistical Office (2006), *The survey on ICT usage in households and by individuals in the Czech Republic in 2006* (in Czech).

Donthu, N. and A. Garcia (1999). The Internet Shopper. *Journal of Advertising Research* 39 (5), 52-58.

Dou, W., U.O. Nielsen, and C.M. Tan (2002). Using corporate websites for exporting marketing. *Journal of Advertising Research*, 42 (5), 105-115.

Economist Intelligence Unit (2006), *The 2006 e-readiness rankings*.

Elinder, E. (1961). How International Can Advertising Be?" in S. W. Dunn (ed.), *International Handbook of Advertising*, NY: McGraw-Hill, 59-71.

Eurostat (2005), *Europe in figures: Eurostat yearbook 2005*.

Eurostat (2006), *Community survey on ICT usage in households and by individuals.*

Forrester (2002), *Forrester's Global eCommerce Predictions For 2004.* Available: http://www.forrester.com/home/0,6092,1-0,FF.html

GfK (2006). Increasingly more kids use the Internet. One in three Polish Internet users willing to buy music on the Internet. Press release, Available: http://www.gfk.pl/podstrona.php?page=/page.php?id=630&ltr=.

Ghose, S. and Dou, W. (1998). Interactive Functions and Their Impacts on the Appeal of Internet Presence Sites. *Journal of Advertising Research,* 38 (2), 29-43.

Harris, G. (1994). International Advertising Standardization: What Do the Multinationals Actually Standardize?" *Journal of International Marketing,* 2 (4), 13-30.

Hong, J.W., Muderrisoglu, A. and Zinkhan, G.M. (1987). Cultural differences and advertising expression: a comparative content analysis of Japanese and U.S. magazine advertising. *Journal of Advertising,* 16 (1), 55-62, 68.

Internet Software Consortium (2001), *Distribution of Top-Level Domain Names by Host Count, Jul 2002.* Online: http://www.isc.org/ds/WWW-200207/dist-bynum.html.

Jain, S.C. (1989). Standardization of International Marketing Strategy: Some Research Hypotheses. *Journal of Marketing,* 53 (January), 70-79.

Ju-Pak, K.H. (1999). Content dimensions of Web advertising: a cross-national comparison. *International Journal of Advertising,* 18 (2), 207-231.

Kanso, A. and Nelson, R.A. (2002). Advertising Localization Overshadows Standardization. *Journal of Advertising Research,* 42 (1), 79-89.

Kolbe, R. H. and M. S. Burnett. 1991. "Content-Analysis Research: An Examination of Applica-

tions with Directives for Improving Research Reliability and Objectivity". *Journal of Consumer Research,* 18 (September), 243-250.

Koudelova, R. and J. Whitelock (2001). A cross-cultural analysis of television advertising in the UK and the Czech Republic. *International Marketing Review,* 18 (3), 286-300.

Leong, E.K.F., Huang, X. and Stanners, P.J. (1998). Comparing the Effectiveness of the Web site with Traditional Media. *Journal of Advertising Research,* 38 (5), 44-51.

Levitt, T. (1983). The Globalization of Market. *Harvard Business Review,* 61(May/June), 92-102.

Mackay, S. (2004). Parliament Approves New Government. *Executive Perspectives: Poland, Price Waterhouse Coopers.* Available: http://www.pwcglobal.com/.

Madden, C.S., Caballero, M.J. and Matsukubo, S. (1986). Analysis of information content in U.S. and Japanese magazine advertising. *Journal of Advertising,* 15 (3), 38-45.

McMillan, S.J. (2000). The Microscope and The Moving Target: The Challenge of Applying Content Analysis to The World Wide Web. *Journalism and Mass Communication Quarterly,* 77 (1), 80-98.

Mueller, B. (1991). An analysis of information content in standardized vs. specialized multinational advertisements. *Journal of International Business Studies,* First Quarter, 23-39.

OBP (2001). Advertising in Poland. Available: http://www.obp.pl/03-raport/2001/advertising_in_poland.htm

Oh, K.W., Cho, C.H. and Leckenby, J.D. (1999). A Comparative Analysis of Korean and U.S. Web Advertising. *Proceedings of the 1999 Conference of the American Academy of Advertising,* Gainesville: University of Florida, 73-77.

Okazaki, S. (2005). Searching the Web for global brands: How American brands standardise their websites in Europe. *European Journal of Marketing*, 39 (1/2), 87-109.

Okazaki, S. and Alonso, J. (2002). A content analysis of Web communication strategies: Cross-cultural research framework and pre-testing. *Internet Research: Electronic Networking, Applications and Policy*, 12 (5), 380-390.

OMD Czech (2005). Odhady reklamních výdajů. Available: http://www2.omd.com/OMDOffice/section/subsection.asp?CompanyID=9&SubSectionID=105.

Onkvisit, S. and Shaw, J.J. (1987). Standardized International Advertising: A Review and Critical Evaluation of the Theoretical and Empirical Evidence. *The Columbia Journal of World Business*, 22 (Fall), 43-55.

Perreault, W.D. and L.E. Leigh (1989). Reliability of nominal data based on qualitative judgments. *Journal of Marketing Research*, 26 (May), 135-148.

Philport, J.C. and J. Arbittier (1997). Advertising: Brand communications styles in established media and the Internet. *Journal of Advertising Research*, 37 (2), 68-76.

Quelch, J.A. and Klein, L.R. (1996). The Internet and International Marketing. *Sloan Management Review*, 38 (Spring), 60-75.

Roberts, M.S. and Ko, H. (2001). Global Interactive Advertising: Defining What We Mean and Using What We Have Learned. *Journal of Interactive Advertising*, 1 (2), Online: http://www.jiad.org/vol1/no2/roberts/index.html.

Root, F.R. (1994), *Entry Strategies for International Markets*. Heath, Washington DC: Lexington.

Sheram, Katherine, and Tatyana P. Soubbotina (2000), *Beyond Economic Growth: Meeting the Challenges of Global Development*, Washington D.C.: World Bank.

Taylor, Charles R., P. Greg Bonner and Michael Dolezal (2002). Advertising in the Czech Republic: Czech perceptions of effective advertising and advertising clutter. In Charles R. Taylor (ed.), *New direction in International Advertising Research* (Vol 12, pp. 137-149), San Diego, CA: Elsevier.

Taylor, C.R. and Johnson, C.M. (2002). Standardized vs. specialized international advertising campaigns: What we have learned from academic research in the 1990s. *New Directions in International Advertising Research*, 12, 45-66.

Synodinos, N., Keown, C. and Jacobs, L. (1989) Transitional Advertising Practices: A Survey of Leading Brand Advertisers. *Journal of Advertising Research*, 29 (2), 43-50.

Szymanski, D.M, Bharadwaj, S.G. and Varadarajan, P.R. (1993). Standardization versus Adaptation of International Marketing Strategy: An Empirical Investigation. *Journal of Marketing*, 57 (October), 1-17.

TNS Factum (2004). Firemní weby a marketing. Available: http://www.factum.cz/tz93.html.

TNS Factum (2005). Češi a reklama v roce 2004. Available: http:// www.factum.cz/tz124.html.

Unie vydavatelů (2005). Internetová reklama v roce 2004 dosáhla 760 milionů Kč. Available: http://www.uvdt.cz/download.aspx?id_file=209.

van REPEN, Erica, Rik Pieters, Jana Fidrmucova and Peter Roosenboom (2000). The Information Content of Magazine Advertising in Market and Transition Economies. *Journal of Consumer Policy*, 23, 257–283.

West, Douglas C. and Stanley J. Paliwoda (1996). Advertising adoption in a developing market economy: The case of Poland. *International Marketing Review*, 13 (4), 82-101.

World Advertising Resource Center (WARC) (2004). *European Marketing Pocket Book*.

Zandpour, F., Campos, V., Catalano, J., Chang, C., Cho, Y.D., Hoobyar, R., Jiang, H.F., Lin, M.C., Madrid, S., Scheideler, P. and Osborn, S.T. (1994). Global Reach and Local Touch: Achieving Cultural Fitness in TV Advertising. *Journal of Advertising Research*, 34 (5), 35-63.

Zenith Optimedia (2004). Poland's advertising market in 2004. Available: http://www.eniro.com/AR/EN/2004/filter.asp?filename=eniro04_016.html

ADDITIONAL READING

Batra, R., Myers, J.G. and Aaker, D.A. (1996). *Advertising Management,* Prentice Hall, Englewood Cliffs, NJ.

De Mooij, M. (1998). *Global marketing and advertising: Understanding cultural paradox*. Sage Publications, Thousand Oaks, CA.

Duncan, T. and Ramaprasad, J. (1995). Standardized multinational advertising: The influencing factors. *Journal of Advertising*, 24(3), 55-67.

Ghose, S. and Dou, W. (1998). Interactive functions and their impacts on the appeal of Internet presence sites. *Journal of Advertising Research*, 38(3), 29–43.

Ha, L. and James, E.L. (1998). Interactivity reexamined: A baseline analysis of early business Web sites. *Journal of Broadcasting and Electronic Media*, 42(4), 457-469.

Hwang, J.S., McMillan, S.J. and Lee, G. (2003). Corporate Web sites as advertising: An analysis of function, audience, and message strategy. *Journal of Interactive Advertising*, 3(2), Available: http://jiad.org/vol3/no2/mcmillan/index.htm

Jain, S. (1989). Standardization of international marketing strategy: Some research hypotheses. *Journal of Marketing*, 53(1), 70-79.

Krippendorff, K. (1980). *Content analysis: An introduction to its methodology*. Sage Publications, Newbury Park, CA.

Laroche, M., Kirpalani, V.H., Pens, F. and Zhou, L. (2001). A model of advertising standardization in multinational corporations. *Journal of International Business Studies*, 32(2), 250-65.

Lynch, P.D., Kent, R.J. and Srinivasan, S.S. (2001). The global Internet shopper: Evidence from shopping tasks in twelve countries. *Journal of Advertising Research*, 41(3), 15-22.

Okazaki, S. and Alonso, J. (2003). Right messages at the right site: on-line creative strategies by Japanese multinational corporations. *Journal of Marketing Communications*, 9(4), 221-239.

Okazaki, S. and Alonso, J. (2003). Beyond the Net: Cultural Values Reflected in Japanese Multinationals' Web Communication Strategies. *Journal of International Consumer Marketing*, 16(1), 47-70.

Okazaki, S. (2004). Do multinationals standardise or localise? The cross-cultural dimensionality of product-based Web sites. *Internet Research: Electronic Networking, Applications and Policy*, 14(1), 81-94.

Tharp, M. and Jeong, J. (2001). Executive insights: The global network communications agency. *Journal of International Marketing*, 9(4), 111-131.

Warden, C.A., Lai, M. and Wu, W.Y. (2003). How world-wide is marketing communication on the World Wide Web? *Journal of Advertising Research*, 43(5), 72-84.

This work was previously published in Handbook of Research on Global Information Technology Management in the Digital Economy, edited by M. Raisinghani, pp. 99-117, copyright 2008 by Information Science Reference, formerly known as Idea Group Reference (an imprint of IGI Global).

Chapter XIV
Online Consumers' Switching Behavior:
A Buyer–Seller Relationship Perspective

Dahui Li
University of Minnesota Duluth, USA

Glenn J. Browne
Texas Tech University, USA

James C. Wetherbe
Texas Tech University, USA

ABSTRACT

Limited studies have investigated online consumer loyalty and retention from a relationship orientation in electronic commerce research. It is important to understand the differences in relationship orientations between people who have the propensity to stick to particular web sites ("stayers") and people who have the propensity to switch to alternative web sites ("switchers"). This study proposes a relationship-based classification schema consisting of five dimensions, i.e., commitment, trust, satisfaction, comparison level of the alternatives, and non-retrievable investment. Data were collected from 299 college students who had experience with e-commerce websites. Using discriminant analysis, we found that stayers and switchers were significantly different along the five research dimensions. Satisfaction with the current website was the most important discriminant factor, followed by trust, commitment, comparison level of alternative websites, and non-retrievable investment in the current website. Implications of the findings for researchers and practitioners are discussed.

INTRODUCTION

With the development of electronic commerce, more and more companies have conducted online business transactions with their customers. Why consumers consistently stick to a website ("stayers") or switch to an alternative website ("switchers") has drawn considerable attention from the research community (e.g., Chen & Hitt, 2002; *Park & Kim, 2006;* Pavlou & Gefen, 2004) due to the ease of jumping from one website to many alternative websites that offer similar products or services with the mere click of a mouse.

This paper conducts a study to compare stayers and switchers in online consumer markets based on relationship marketing theories. We define stayers as those consumers who have the propensity to stay with a particular website in the future. Switchers, on the other hand, are those consumers who have no propensity to use the website in the future. The abundant literature in relationship marketing has provided sufficient theoretical foundations for the present study. Guided by an integrated model of buyer-seller relationships in the conventional marketplace (Wilson, 1995), this study investigates how online consumers' switching behavior varies along five salient relationship factors drawn from the model (commitment, trust, satisfaction, comparison level of the alternatives, and non-retrievable investment). We believe that these factors will influence the quality of buyer-seller relationships in the *online* environment.

An investigation of switching behavior will contribute to our understanding of the differences between technology adoption/acceptance and continuous use of the technology. Information systems researchers have found that users' beliefs and attitudes in pre-adoption and post-adoption are different (e.g., Parthasarathy & Bhattacherjee, 1998). The present study will extend these previous findings by providing understanding as to why some adopters stay with a website (post-adoption retention) and others switch (post-adoption attrition) in the online environment.

Studying online consumers' switching behavior is also important for marketing research and practice. From the business side, acquiring a customer is much more difficult and more inefficient than keeping a customer. Costs associated with acquiring new customers are five times the costs of retaining customers (Keaveney, 1995). In the context of e-commerce, a high quality buyer-seller relationship is important because keeping existing customers and attracting new customers are so expensive and it is so easy to switch online (Reichheld & Schefter, 2000).

With these motivations in mind, this paper reports the results of an empirical study. In the next section, we discuss the conceptual background and develop the research hypotheses. The research method for the empirical study is then explained, followed by a discussion of the data analysis and results. Finally, we discuss the findings and draw implications for researchers and practitioners.

THEORETICAL BACKGROUND

Several studies have investigated online switching behaviors. Keaveney and Parthasarathy (2001) found that online consumers' previous behavioral patterns (e.g., service usage), attitudes (e.g., risk-taking, satisfaction, and involvement), and demographic characteristics (e.g., income and education) were significant discriminating factors between stayers and switchers. In an investigation of the online brokerage industry, Chen and Hitt (2002) found that online consumers' system usage and the breadth and quality of alternative online service providers were significant in predicting switching behavior. Gupta et al. (2004) found that consumers switching from off-line to online transactions paid attention to channel risk, search effort, and learning effort.

In addition to these exploratory empirical studies, other researchers have started to apply well-established models and theories to examine online consumer behaviors and customer loyalty (e.g., Gefen, Karahanna, & Straub, 2003; Pavlou, 2003; *Park & Kim, 2006*). The first stream of such literature is based on conventional consumer behavior theories, which suggest that satisfaction and switching barriers are significant antecedents of customer loyalty and retention (e.g., Bhattacherjee, *2001; Flavian, Guinaliu, & Gurrea., 2006; Park & Kim, 2006*). This stream is also called the "transactional" view of online buyer-seller relationships (Benbasat & DeSanctis, 2001), and emphasizes the importance of providing economic benefit, profit, efficiency, and effectiveness to attract and satisfy consumers.

The second stream of research examines relationship marketing theories, which predict that a customer's commitment to and trust in a business relationship are the main reasons for him or her to stay with a business (Morgan & Hunt, 1994). This relational view considers online buyer-seller relationships as personalized, interpersonal social and psychological exchanges and emphasizes the effects of social and psychological factors (such as commitment and trust) on customer retention (Benbasat & DeSanctis, 2001). Most previous e-commerce literature has investigated the significant role of trust (e.g., Pavlou, 2003; Pavlou & Gefen, 2004). Recently, some studies have started to examine commitment (e.g., *Park & Kim, 2006*).

The current study continues to investigate the differences between switchers and stayers from this relational view of online buyer-seller relationships. The theoretical framework of this study is Wilson's integrated model of buyer-seller relationships for conventional marketing research (Wilson, 1995). The model consists of 13 important factors that are believed to predict the development and success of marketing relationships. We posit that Wilson's model provides an important framework for examining online buyer-seller relationships. Following Wilson's suggestion, we limit our focus to how consumers view buyer-seller relationships in the consumer

market. We emphasize five factors from Wilson's model, which are commitment, trust, satisfaction, comparison level of the alternatives, and non-retrievable investment. In the following sections, we review the literature concerning these five variables and develop research hypotheses. A summary of the research variables and our review of supporting literature are shown in Table 1.

RESEARCH HYPOTHESES

Commitment. Commitment is the most important relationship factor and is central to the success of many buyer-seller relationships (Ganesh, Arnold, & Reynolds, 2000; Morgan & Hunt, 1994). People usually realize the importance of keeping a relationship because the benefits for them are inseparable from the benefits for their partners. Highly committed individuals generally believe that the relationship will continue in the future, so they try to maximize their efforts to stay in the relationship (Garbarino & Johnson, 1999; Morgan & Hunt, 1994).

Studying the effect of commitment in online buyer-seller relationships is important because commitment may be difficult to develop. However, we posit that it is possible for an individual to develop commitment to a particular website. A consumer's consistent interactions with the website may be attributed to his or her commitment level toward the business. If a consumer stays with a website, this may result from the commitment level toward maintaining his relationship with the website (*Park & Kim, 2006*). Thus, we hypothesize

H1: Stayers have higher levels of commitment to current websites than switchers.

Trust. Trust is the basic mechanism used to build and maintain a relationship and fosters a long-term orientation in marketing relationships (Morgan & Hunt, 1994). In business-to-consumer

Table 1. Research variables and supporting literature

Variables in Wilson's Model	Definition and Similar Terms Used in Other Studies	Selected Supporting Literature
Commitment	Stayers have higher levels of commitment to current websites than consumers who switch websites. Similar terms: bonding mechanism	Garbarino & Johnson, 1999; Ganesh, Arnold, & Reynolds, 2000; Morgan & Hunt, 1994; Park & Kim, 2006
Trust	Stayers trust current websites more than switchers trust current websites.	Gefen, Karahanna, & Straub, 2003; Morgan & Hunt, 1994; Pavlou, 2003; Pavlou & Gefen, 2004;
Satisfaction	Long-term judgment based on past interactions with an online website over time, rather than single transaction-based satisfaction that is usually an immediate post-buying judgment	Bhattacherjee, 2001; Flavian, Guinaliu, & Gurrea., 2006; Ganesh, Arnold, & Reynolds, 2000; Keaveney & Parthasarathy, 2001
Comparison Level of the Alternatives	Perceived desirability of alternative website to the present relationship with the current website Similar terms: quality of alternatives; relational benefit; use of multiple suppliers, pool size of suppliers	Anderson & Narus, 1990; Chen & Hitt, 2002; Hart & Saunders, 1997; Park & Kim, 2006; Rusbult, Martz, & Agnew, 1998
Non-Retrievable Investment	The extent and importance of resources attached to the relationship with the current website. Similar terms: sunk cost, switching cost, investment size, asset specific investment	Anderson & Narus, 1990; Chen & Hitt, 2002; Hart & Saunders, 1997; Rusbult, Martz, & Agnew, 1998

relationships, trust is a predictor of Internet buyers' positive attitudes toward online shopping (Gefen, Karahanna, & Straub, 2003). Many different positive outcomes may be generated from trusting the vendor's website (Pavlou, 2003; Pavlou & Gefen, 2004). If a consumer does not receive positive results, his trust belief toward the website will be reduced or destroyed, and the consumer may terminate further interactions and switch to other vendors. Thus we hypothesize

H2: Stayers trust current websites more than switchers trust current websites.

Satisfaction. We define satisfaction as a long-term judgment based on past interactions with an online website over time, rather than single transaction-based satisfaction that is usually an immediate post-buying judgment. Satisfaction is an important predictor of the intention to use an information system continuously (Bhattacherjee, 2001). Consumers' future buying intentions and behavior can be predicted by their satisfaction with a product or service (e.g., Burnham, Frels, & Mahajan, 2003; Ganesh, Arnold, & Reynolds, 2000). Using data collected from the customers of a national online service provider, Keaveney and Parthasarathy (2001) found that people who continued to use the online service could be significantly discriminated from switchers in terms of their level of satisfaction with the service. The significant effect of satisfaction on online customer loyalty has also been reported in several studies of online buyer-seller relationships (e.g., Bhattacherjee, *2001; Park & Kim, 2006*). Thus, we hypothesize

H3: Stayers are more satisfied with their current websites than are switchers.

Comparison Level of the Alternatives. Comparison level of the alternatives refers to the perceived desirability of alternative websites to the present relationship with the current website

(Anderson & Narus, 1990). It measures how much an individual's needs could be fulfilled by other relationships. In the IS literature, Hart and Saunders (1977) have suggested that the smaller the "supplier pool size," the greater the buyer's dependence on the supplier in an EDI relationship. Marketing research has also shown that dependence on a current supplier will be low if there are many good alternative suppliers available in the marketplace (e.g., Anderson & Narus, 1990). In online consumer markets, comparison level of the best alternative website also influences the dependence of online consumers on the present website (Chen & Hitt, 2002). If there is a group of high quality websites available, dependence on the present website will be affected and online consumers are more likely to switch to an alternative website. Thus, we hypothesize

H4: Switchers are more aware of the comparison level of alternative websites than are stayers.

Non-Retrievable Investment. Non-retrievable investment refers to the extent and importance of resources attached to the relationship with the current website (Anderson & Narus, 1990; Burnham, Frels, & Mahajan, 2003; Chen & Hitt, 2002). The value of such resources will be lowered or lost if the relationship is ended. Thus, non-retrievable investment acts as a powerful psychological incentive to persist in a relationship. According to Burnham, Frels, and Mahajan (2003), switching costs can be classified further as extra expenditure of time and effort (procedural cost), loss of financial resources (financial cost), and psychological discomfort (relational cost). In the online environment, a consumer could feel tied to the present website whenever he recalls the time, money, and effort invested. Further, the anticipation of switching costs such as searching for alternative sites and then learning how to use one may discourage consumers from abandoning the current website for another. Thus, we hypothesize

H5: Stayers value non-retrievable investment more than do switchers.

RESEARCH METHOD

All the scales were adapted from Morgan and Hunt (1994) and Rusbult, Martz, and Agnew (1998) (we have omitted the scales for space purposes). Seven-point Likert scales were utilized. Preliminary investigations were conducted to test the validity of these scales.

The survey method was used to collect data. Student subjects at a large public university were the respondents of the survey. To ensure appropriate motivation, students were given course credit for completing the questionnaire. One of the major advantages of collecting data from university students is that they typically have considerable experience with different types of e-commerce websites. Students are very active users of Internet applications and participants in e-commerce activities. In fact, 18-34 year-olds are the heaviest users of the Internet (comScore, 2004; Forrester Research, 2005) compared with other groups in the population. Further, consumers around age 20 have been found to be savvy about online shopping (Forrester Research, 2005). Therefore, student samples have been found feasible for research concerning online behavior and have been used in several recent studies (e.g., Agarwal & Karahanna, 2000; Gefen, Karahanna, & Straub, 2003; Meinert, Peterson, Criswell, & Crossland, 2006). In our study, the sample statistics indicate that our college student sample is representative of 18-34 year-old users.

The questionnaires were formatted into two versions. One version asked the student to name an e-commerce website (defined as a website that conducts business transactions) that the student would continue using in the near future, while the other version asked the student to name an e-commerce website with which the student did not intend to continue. We asked students to subjectively select one website from a variety of websites. Asking respondents to subjectively report switching behaviors among a group of service providers has been utilized in previous literature (e.g., Chakravarty, Feinberg, & Rhee, 2004; Ganesh, Arnold, & Reynolds, 2000; Keaveney & Parthasarathy, 2001). In our study, each student randomly received one version of the questionnaire. Two screening questions were asked to check whether the respondent had enough experience with the e-commerce website to be evaluated. The first question was: How long have you used this website? The second was: During the time period you checked in question (1), how often did you visit this website? Following the screening questions, the respondents were asked to respond to survey questions. Finally, demographic information was collected.

We adopted a two-step approach to classify a respondent as a stayer or a switcher. The first step was based on the version of the questionnaire. If a questionnaire asked a respondent to report a web site that the individual did not plan to use in the future, the respondent was classified as a "switcher"; otherwise, the respondent was classified as a "stayer." In the second step, we examined the respondent's answers to three survey questions about his intention to stay with the website. Using intention to measure actual behavior is consistent with the Theory of Reasoned Action (Fishbein & Ajzen, 1975). The scale used was from Agarwal and Karahanna (2000). If a respondent was classified as a "switcher" in the first step, but the intention to stay was high (above the median score), the response was removed. If a respondent was classified as a "stayer," but the intention was below the median score, the response was also removed.

Three hundred sixty-five questionnaires were distributed in eight business courses. Juniors, seniors, and graduate students were surveyed, representing all majors in the college. Fifty-four respondents who had used the reported website for less than three months and no more than ten times were excluded from the study. In the classification step, noted above, 12 responses were excluded. In the end, 299 responses were kept in the sample, of which 158 were staying responses and 141 were switching responses.

DATA ANALYSIS AND RESULTS

We examined the reliability and validity of the scales using LISREL 8.3 (Table 2 and Table 3). While the overall chi-square for the measurement model was significant ($P^2(142)=223.02$, $p<0.001$), other fit indices showed that the model had a good fit with the data (RMSEA=0.046, SRMR=0.042, GFI=0.92, AGFI=0.90, NFI=0.96, NNFI=0.98, CFI=0.98). To evaluate scale reliability and convergent and discriminant validity, we followed the guidelines from Fornell and Larcker (1981). All item loadings were significant and exceeded 0.7. Composite reliabilities of research constructs ranged from 0.88 to 0.95. Average variance extracted (AVE) ranged from 0.64 to 0.78 and all the square roots of AVEs exceeded their respective inter-construct correlations. Thus, the validity and reliability of the scales were acceptable.

Table 2. Measurement model

Item	Mean	Standard Deviation	Standard Loading
COMMT1	3.41	1.94	0.86
COMMT2	2.90	1.67	0.82
COMMT3	3.42	1.85	0.83
TRUST1	4.77	1.63	0.82
TRUST2	4.65	1.73	0.95
TRUST3	4.79	1.64	0.88
SATIS1	4.42	2.09	0.96
SATIS2	4.33	2.08	0.97
SATIS3	4.27	2.03	0.81
SATIS4	3.95	1.74	0.84
SATIS5	4.56	1.82	0.83
COMPA1	4.33	1.84	0.85
COMPA2	4.01	1.87	0.84
COMPA3	4.21	1.83	0.93
COMPA4	4.48	1.86	0.84
INVES1	2.78	1.68	0.75
INVES2	2.96	1.68	0.81
INVES3	3.47	1.79	0.84
INVES4	3.38	1.81	0.80

Fit Indices: $\square 2(142)=223.02$ (p<0.001), RMSEA=0.046, SRMR=0.042, GFI=0.92, AGFI=0.90, NFI=0.96, NNFI=0.98, CFI=0.98

Table 3. Reliability and inter construct correlations

CONSTRUCT	AVE	RELI	COMMT	TRUST	SATIS	COMPA	INVES
COMMT	0.70	0.88	0.84				
TRUST	0.78	0.92	0.66	0.88			
SATIS	0.78	0.95	0.77	0.84	0.88		
COMPA	0.75	0.92	-0.59	-0.54	-0.65	0.87	
INVES	0.64	0.88	0.61	0.28	0.35	-0.32	0.80

AVE   is Average Variance Extracted, computed as $[(\Gamma(8^2)]/[(\Gamma(8^2) + \Gamma(\gamma))]$
  RELI   is Composite Reliability, computed as $[(\Gamma(8))^2]/[(\Gamma(8))^2 + \Gamma(\gamma))]$
  Square roots of AVE are shown on the diagonals of the correlation matrix

Table 4. Overall discriminant analysis

	Research Variable	Group Means			Wilks' Lambda	F
		Switchers (n=141)	Stayers (n=158)	Difference		
H1	COMMITMENT	2.20	4.20	2.00	0.62	178.83*
H2	TRUST	3.64	5.73	2.09	0.54	250.31*
H3	SATISFACTION	2.73	5.72	2.99	0.29	740.13*
H4	COM. LEVEL	5.25	3.18	-2.07	0.63	174.82*
H5	NON-RETR. INVES.	2.87	3.68	0.81	0.92	24.37*

* p<0.001; Canonical Discriminant Function: Eigenvalue=2.6, Canonical correlation=0.85, Wilks' Lambda=0.278, □2(5)= 377.44 (p<0.001);

Classification Results: Percentage correctly classified (hit ratio): Analysis Sample: 93.3%; Holdout Sample: 93%; Proportional chance criterion=50%; Maximum chance criterion=53%.

After the scales were validated, we tested the research hypotheses using multiple discriminant analysis (Hair, Anderson, Tatham, & Black, 1995). The independent variables were commitment, trust, satisfaction, comparison level of the alternatives, and non-retrievable investment.

Results of the analyses are shown in Table 4. The overall canonical discriminant function was significant, with Wilks' Lambda = 0.278 and $P^2_{(5)}$ = 377.44 (p<0.001). This indicated that stayers can be discriminated from switchers. As for the predictability of the discriminant function,

the percentages correctly classified (or hit ratios) for the analysis sample (93.3%) and the holdout sample (93%) were above the proportional chance criterion (50%) and the maximum chance criterion (53%). This indicates that the classification was highly accurate.

As shown in Table 4, all tests of the group-mean differences were significant at the " = 0.001 level. The directions of the mean differences between switchers and stayers show that all the hypotheses were supported. Compared with switchers, stayers were more committed to maintaining the relationship with the current website (H1) (mean difference = 2.00, $F_{(1,297)}$ = 178.83, p<0.001), consistent with studies in conventional buyer-seller relationships (e.g., Garbarino & Johnson, 1999). Stayers showed a higher level of trust in the current website than did switchers (H2) (mean difference = 2.09, $F_{(1,297)}$ = 250.31, p<0.001). Stayers were more satisfied with the interactive experience with the current website (H3) (mean difference = 2.99, $F_{(1,297)}$ = 740.13, p<0.001), and less aware of the comparison level of the alternative websites (H4) (mean difference = 2.07, $F_{(1,297)}$ = 174.82, p<0.001), consistent with previous studies (e.g., Anderson & Narus, 1990; Keaveney & Parthasarathy, 2001). Finally, stayers were more aware of the size of the non-retrievable investment (H5) (mean difference = 0.81, $F_{(1,297)}$ = 24.37, p<0.001).

DISCUSSION

This study has investigated the differences between switchers and stayers in the context of online buyer-seller relationships, based on an integrated buyer-seller relationship model (Wilson, 1995). Our empirical study has shown that stayers are more committed to online businesses than switchers. However, the mean value of commitment for stayers (4.20) in this study is relatively low compared with the commitment levels reported in other types of relationships (e.g., Morgan & Hunt, 1994; Garbarino & Johnson, 1999). This suggests that due to the limited capacity of Internet as a transmission medium between consumers and websites, commitment is not easily developed in the online consumer market.

Stayers were also found to trust online businesses more than switchers, consistent with other studies (e.g., Gefen, Karahanna, & Straub, 2003). Unlike commitment, trust was quite high on a relative basis for consumers in the present study (mean values: 5.73 for stayers, 3.64 for switchers). It is reasonable to speculate that consumers are

well aware of the potential risk inherent in online transactions. If a consumer decides to participate in a transaction, he or she must have a strong perception of the trustworthiness of the online business to minimize the perception of the risk.

This study has also found that stayers are more satisfied with the current online business and less aware of the comparison level of alternative online businesses, consistent with previous research (e.g., Anderson & Narus, 1990; Ganesh, Arnold, & Reynolds, 2000; Keaveney & Parthasarathy, 2001). If a consumer is more satisfied with the current business, he or she may be reluctant to look for alternative websites. On the other hand, switchers usually are not satisfied with the current online business and thus look for alternative websites (and are also therefore able to evaluate the quality of alternatives). Based on the coefficient of satisfaction (Wilks' Lambda=0.29) in the discriminant function, we conclude that satisfaction is the most important factor in discriminating switchers from stayers in online consumer markets.

Although stayers put more weight on the size of the non-retrievable investments than do switchers, the mean values of investment size (stayers = 3.68; switchers = 2.87) on a 7-point Likert scale are relatively low, suggesting that neither switchers nor stayers put a great deal of weight on their investments in websites. It is possible that the effect of investment size varies for different types of B2C websites. For example, the effect might be very high for banking or other financial sites. The fact that we pooled different types of websites in our empirical study may have led to a low effect for investment. However, Chen and Hitt (2002) found that when multiple factors (such as customer characteristics and firm characteristics) were modeled together with switching costs, the effect of switching costs was not significant in explaining customer switching. Thus, questions concerning the issue of investment size by online users remain.

CONCLUSION

Limitations

There are several limitations in the present study. First, this study may have omitted some important factors, such as product price, incentives, rebates, business reputation, and customer referrals, in the online business environment because the research variables were selected from an established model (Wilson, 1995). Second, we did not investigate whether there is an interaction effect between the business-to-consumer relationship and the website-to-consumer relationship. It is not clear whether these two types of relationships are separate or intertwined. Third, because of the specially defined sample in the current study, the generalizability of the findings may be limited. Although college students are in many ways prototypical Internet users, their behavior may be different from that of other consumers among the Internet population (e.g., Agarwal & Karahanna, 2000; Forrester Research, 2005; Gefen, Karahanna, & Straub, 2003). Finally, this research utilized only respondents' subjective data rather than objective measures.

Implications for Research

The first contribution of the present study is applying the integrated buyer-seller relationship model (Wilson, 1995) to online consumer markets. The empirical results provide support for the external validity of the model in online business-to-consumer relationships. Second, the five relationship factors we investigated may be used as a classification schema of online consumers, providing a useful starting point for additional research.

An online consumer's continuous patronage of a particular web site is arguably analogous to an IS user's continuous use of an IS. We speculate that relationship variables such as commitment and trust might be applied to IS implementation research. After adopting, adapting, accepting, and using an IS, a user may have developed a relationship orientation toward using the IS in the latter stages of IS implementation. Future studies could conduct empirical tests of the relational variables in the context of conventional IS. Future studies may also investigate whether and how an IS user develops a relationship with an IS during the IS-user interaction process.

Implications for Practice

For online companies such as Dell Computers, eBay.com, and Amazon.com, consumer retention is especially vital to their success. The results of this study, as well as some previous research, show that there is reason for considerable optimism in making websites sticky. Online consumers have a clear inclination toward loyalty and their behaviors are not very different from people in conventional markets. The five factor classification schema can serve as an alternative for businesses to capture the profiles of online consumers. Adopting such an approach will improve the effectiveness of businesses in retaining customers.

Consumers' commitment to online businesses is difficult to develop and is not as strong as commitment in other contexts. This suggests that it is not practical for online businesses to expect persistent and long-term relationship orientations from online consumers. However, various incentive mechanisms other than those focused on relationship building and maintenance may need to be initiated. An online business may adopt different methods to enhance its customer satisfaction level. For example, a company may use its web site to retain, or "lock," a consumer, by keeping personal data. When people enter a significant amount of personal data at a website, they are typically reluctant to change vendors and enter the data again (White, 2004).

In summary, the present research has examined online consumers' switching behavior among different websites. Whether a consumer intends to stay with a website or switch to another was shown to depend on commitment, trust, satisfaction, comparison level of the alternatives, and non-retrievable investment. Future research can add additional insights into this important area of electronic commerce research.

REFERENCES

Agarwal, R., & Karahanna, E. (2000). Time flies when you're having fun: Cognitive absorption and beliefs about information technology usage. *MIS Quarterly, 24,* 4, 665-694.

Anderson, J.C., & Narus, J.A. (1990). A model of distributor firm and manufacturer firm working partnerships. *Journal of Marketing, 54,* 1, 42-58.

Benbasat, I., & DeSanctis, G. (2001). Communication challenges: A value network perspective. In G.W. Dickson and G. DeSanctis (Eds.), *Information technology and the future enterprise: New models for managers* (pp. 144-162). New Jersey: Prentice-Hall.

Bhattacherjee, A. (2001). Understanding information systems continuance: An expectation confirmation model. *MIS Quarterly, 25,* 3, 351-370.

Burnham, T.A., Frels, J.K., & Mahajan, V. (2003). Consumer switching costs: A topology, antecedents, and consequences. *Journal of the Academy of Marketing Science, 31,* 2, 109-126.

Chakravarty, S., Feinberg, R., & Rhee, E. (2004). Relationships and individuals' bank switching behavior. *Journal of Economic Psychology, 25,* 4, 507-527.

Chen, P.Y., & Hitt, L.M. (2002). Measuring switching costs and the determinants of customer retention in Internet-enabled businesses: A study of the online brokerage industry. *Information Systems Research, 13,* 3, 255-274.

comScore. (2004). Marketers take note: The elusive 18-34 year-old is habitually online. Retrieved April 18, 2006, from http://www.comscore.com/press/release.asp?press=445.

Fishbein, M., & Ajzen, I. (1975). *Belief, attitude, intention, and behavior: An introduction to theory and research.* MA: Addison-Wesley.

Flavian, C., Guinaliu, M., & Gurrea, R. (2006). The role played by perceived usability, satisfaction and consumer trust on website loyalty. *Information & Management, 43,* 1, 1-14.

Fornell, C., & Larcker, D.F. (1981). Evaluating structural equations with unobservable variables and measurement error. *Journal of Marketing Research, 18,* 1, 39-50.

Forrester Research (2005). Young consumers are the first "technology everywhere" generation. Retrieved April 18, 2006, from http://www.forrester.com/ER/Press/Release/0,1769,1051,00.html

Ganesh, J., Arnold, M.J., & Reynolds, K.E. (2000). Understanding the customer base of service providers: An examination of the differences between switchers and stayers. *Journal of Marketing, 64,* 3, 65-87.

Garbarino, E., & Johnson, M.S. (1999). The different roles of satisfaction, trust, and commitment in customer relationships. *Journal of Marketing, 63,* 2, 70-87.

Gefen, D., Karahanna, E., & Straub, D. (2003). Trust and TAM in online shopping: An integrated model. *MIS Quarterly, 27,* 1, 51-90.

Gupta, A., Su, B., & Walter, Z. (2004). An empirical study of consumer switching from traditional to electronic channels: A purchase-decision process perspective. *International Journal of Electronic Commerce, 8,* 3, 131-161.

Hair, J.F. Jr, Anderson, R.E., Tatham, R.L., & Black, W.C. (1995). *Multivariate data analysis* (4th ed.). New Jersey: Prentice-Hall.

Hart, P., & Carol, S. (1997). Power and trust: Critical factors in the adoption and use of electronic data interchange. *Organization Science*, 8, 1, 23-42.

Keaveney, S.M. (1995). Customer switching behavior in service industries: An exploratory study. *Journal of Marketing*, 59, April, 71-82.

Keaveney, S.M., & Parthasarathy, M. (2001). Customer switching behavior in online services: An exploratory study of the role of selected attitudinal, behavioral, and demographic factors. *Journal of the Academy of Marketing Science*, 29, 4, 374-390.

Meinert, D.B., Peterson, D.K., Criswell, J.R., & Crossland, M.D. (2006). Privacy policy statements and consumer willingness to provide personal information. *Journal of Electronic Commerce in Organizations*, 4, 1, 1-17.

Morgan, R.M., & Hunt, S.D. (1994). The commitment-trust theory of relationship marketing. *Journal of Marketing*, 58, 3, 20-38.

Park, C., & Kim, Y. (2006). The effect of information satisfaction and relational benefit on consumers' online shopping site commitments. *Journal of Electronic Commerce in Organizations*, 4, 1, 70-90.

Parthasarathy, M., & Bhattacherjee, A. (1998). Understanding post-adoption behavior in the context of online services. *Information Systems Research*, 9, 4, 362-379.

Pavlou, P.A. (2003). Consumer acceptance of electronic commerce: Integrating trust and risk with the technology acceptance model. *International Journal of Electronic Commerce*, 7, 3, 101-134.

Pavlou, P.A., & Gefen, D. (2004). Building effective online marketplaces with institution-based trust. *Information Systems Research*, 15, 1, 37-59.

Reichheld, F.F., & Schefter, P. (2000). E-loyalty: Your secret weapon on the web. *Harvard Business Review*, 78, 4, 105-113.

Rusbult, C.E., Martz, J.M., & Agnew, C.R. (1998). The investment model scale: Measuring commitment level, satisfaction level, quality of alternatives, and investment size. *Personal Relationships*, 5, 4, 357-391.

White, T.B. (2004). Consumer disclosure and disclosure avoidance: A motivational framework. *Journal of Consumer Psychology*, 14, 1&2, 41-52.

Wilson, D.T. (1995). An integrated model of buyer-seller relationships. *Journal of the Academy of Marketing Science*, 23, 4, 335-345.

This work was previously published in Journal of Electronic Commerce in Organizations, Vol 5, Issue 1, edited by M. Khosrow-Pour, pp. 30-42, copyright 2007 by IGI Publishing, formerly known as Idea Group Publishing (an imprint of IGI Global).

Chapter XV
Understanding Consumer Reactions to Offshore Outsourcing of Customer Services

Piyush Sharma
Nanyang Business School, Singapore

Rajiv Mathur
Percom Limited, New Delhi, India

Abhinav Dhawan
team4U Outsourced Staffing Services, New Delhi, India

ABSTRACT

Offshore outsourcing is a fast-growing aspect of the world economy today and it has drawn attention from policy makers as well as public at large in many developed countries. However, there is hardly any research on how outsourcing of customer services may influence individual consumers, their perceptions, attitudes and behaviors. In this chapter, the authors first review the extant literature in the country-of-origin and services marketing areas to highlight key concepts and theories relevant to this area. Next, they show how offshore outsourcing of customer services may influence consumer perceptions about service quality, brand image and brand loyalty on one hand and impact customer satisfaction, complaint behavior and repurchase intentions on the other. The role of several relevant demographic and psychographic variables is also discussed. Finally, the findings from a survey-based study among customers in three developed countries (US, UK and Australia) are reported along with a discussion of managerial implications and future research directions in this area.

INTRODUCTION

Background

Outsourcing is a fast-growing aspect of the world economy with worldwide spending on outsourcing estimated to cross $6 trillion by the end of 2005 (Corbett, 2002). Forrester Research estimates that by 2015, 3.3 million jobs accounting for $136 billion in wages will move offshore to countries such as India, China and Russia (McCartney, 2003). According to latest estimates by Gartner, IT outsourcing global revenue alone was predicted to grow from $184 billion in 2003 to over $256 billion in 2008 (Blackmore et al., 2005) and IDC estimates business process outsourcing (BPO) in Europe to grow from $43 to $72 billion Euros between 2002 and 2005. Clearly these are very large numbers and companies around the world seem to be relentlessly pursuing outsourcing to benefit the end customers by reducing cost and improving productivity.

However, existing research on offshore outsourcing is primarily focused on the labor and ethical issues of outsourcing and effects of strategic outsourcing decisions on organizations with hardly any attention on how it may influence individual customers (Clott, 2004). Similarly, critics of outsourcing have so far focused on the changing employment patterns, globalization of the labor force, and its effects on individual employees and organizations with little consideration to the end-customers. On the other hand, based on their experience in recent years organizations have already become more cautious about outsourcing and conscious of the need to protect their reputation, brand image, core skills and property rights (Reilly, 1997). Some of the emerging potential downsides of outsourcing include dilution of company's image, lower customer satisfaction, reduced brand loyalty and an increase in customer complaints due to real or perceived concerns about cultural differences, lower service standards and loss of privacy (Cor-

nell, 2004; Data-Monitor, 2004; Economist, 2001; Kennedy, 2002; Roy, 2003).

Consumers and Offshore Outsourcing

In a recent customer survey by American Banker/Gallup (2004) it was found that two-thirds (71%) of the respondents were aware of offshore outsourcing to lower-cost countries. Among those aware, a whopping 78% held an unfavorable opinion about it and more than 80% said they would feel better if outsourcing did not take away American jobs and only less than half would feel better if it made American companies more competitive in the global marketplace (51%) or if it improved American companies' profits (46%). However, besides these general surveys, there is very little research that could specifically help organizations understand the effects of offshore outsourcing of customer service on individual customers, their perceptions, attitudes and behavior.

On the other hand, there is a large body of knowledge in the area of country-of-origin (COO) phenomenon which demonstrates that customers have distinctly different perceptions and attitudes about foreign products and services (Gronroos, 1999; Javalgi et al., 2001; Javalgi et al., 2003; Kotabe et al., 1998; Lovelock, 1999; Nicoulaud, 1989; Ruyter et al., 1998). Specifically, it is shown that products and services from less developed countries are evaluated unfavorably by customers in developed countries due to negative perceptions about their quality. In the context of offshore outsourcing of customer services, it is shown that some customers may not want to speak to a customer care representative from a particular country (Briggs, 2005) and some of them believe that continuing outsourcing of call centres abroad will diminish customer satisfaction (Hayward, 2004). However, there is little research in consumer behavior or marketing literature about the socio-psychological process underlying these customer perceptions.

In this chapter we address this important gap in existing research by combining learning from existing literature in the COO and services marketing areas to this emerging field. Specifically, we address the following questions in this chapter:

1. Are customers aware of offshore outsourcing of customer services in general?

2. Are they aware of offshore outsourcing of customer services in their own day-to-day lives?

3. How do they perceive offshore outsourcing of services in general?

4. How do they evaluate their own experiences with offshore outsourcing of customer services?

5. How does offshore outsourcing of customer services influence brand image, brand loyalty, customer satisfaction, customer complaint behavior and repeat purchase intentions?

BACKGROUND

What is Offshore Outsourcing?

Outsourcing is a contractual agreement between the customer and one or more suppliers to provide services or processes that the customer is currently providing internally (Fan, 2000). In other words, outsourcing occurs when an organization transfers some of its tasks to an outside supplier (Siems & Ratner, 2003). The benefits of outsourcing are well-known: (1) reduce cost, (2) improve quality, service and delivery, (3) improve organizational focus, (4) increase flexibility and (5) facilitate change. Numerous studies portray the strategic benefits of offshore outsourcing for firms as a means to reduce costs, improve asset efficiency, and increase profits (Quinn, 1997).

However, in recent years organizations have become more cautious about moving towards outsourcing and conscious of the need to protect their reputation, brand image, core skills and property rights (Reilly, 1997). According to Kennedy companies risk *losing potential customers* for the parent brand due to poor customer relationship management by outsourced sub-contractors. Similarly, companies in UK have been warned of a possible customer backlash if they continue to offshore jobs to lower-cost economies, as further domestic job cuts will undoubtedly harm their *corporate image* (Data-Monitor, 2004). Suppliers of outsourced services also play a key role in influencing outsiders' opinions of the organization (Trapp, 1999).

Dell Computers returned its business help desk from India to North America last year because of an *increase in complaints* from its customers about the Indian employees' perceived heavy reliance on scripted answers and lack of expertise required for solving complex computer problems (Cornell, 2004). Moreover, due to concerns that Indian call centers may have distinctly *lower service standards* than the British ones, many 'exported' jobs deal with simple customer account queries and the more complex enquires are serviced in UK (Data-Monitor, 2004). Some American medical-transcription firms even refuse to outsource work to India due to *concerns about privacy of information*, despite potential savings of up to 50% (Economist, 2001). There are also concerns about how many American medical and financial services firms are shifting information-processing work to low-wage countries that lack tough privacy laws, leaving the most sensitive details of the lives of millions of their customers *vulnerable to lax security and in the hands of malicious identity thieves* (Swartz, 2004a, 2004b).

COO, Customer Ethnocentrism and Offshore Outsourcing

Customer ethnocentrism represents a preference for domestic products on the basis of nationalistic feelings and ethnocentric customers are shown to be reluctant to buy foreign products, because of a sense of loyalty towards their home country (Shimp, 1984; Shimp & Sharma, 1987). Customer ethnocentric tendencies can also lead to negative attitudes towards foreign products in general and researchers have identified several antecedents and moderating factors of customer ethnocentricity in the product-sector (Sharma et al., 1995). These include four social–psychological antecedents: 'openness to foreign cultures', 'patriotism', 'conservatism', and 'collectivism/individualism' together with four demographic factors: 'age', 'gender', 'education' and 'income' along with two moderating factors: 'perceived necessity of the product' and 'perceived economic threat of foreign competition'.

Ruyter et al. (1998) extended this theory to the services sector and using an empirical study with Dutch customers, they confirmed the generalizability of the ethnocentric model and provided evidence of the fact that COO effects do play a role in customers choice behaviour towards international services. They were also able to replicate Sharma et al.'s (1995) findings with respect to all social–psychological antecedents. Other researchers have explored the influence of customer patriotism, conservatism and ethnocentrism (Ali-Sulaiti & Baker, 1998; Gronroos, 1999; Kaynak et al., 1994). On the other hand, offshore outsourcing in the manufacturing industry has been acknowledged by COO researchers in the form of hybrid products i.e. products which may be designed in one country, whose components may be produced in another country and which may be assembled in yet another country (Chao, 1993b, 2001; Han & Terpstra, 1988; Tse & Lee, 1993). Using Osgood and Tannenbaum's (1955) congruency principle these researchers argue that there is a congruency among the different COO elements which influences customer attitudes towards a hybrid product. This has led COO researchers to conceptualize it as a multidimensional construct and incorporate its various dimensions in their research e.g. uni-national versus bi-national products (Han & Terpstra, 1988), country

of components versus assembly (Tse & Lee, 1993), country of design versus assembly (Sauer et al., 1991) country of assembly versus parts versus design (Chao, 1993a, 2001) and multiple COO facets as a result of global outsourcing (Li et al., 2000).

Using a similar approach, we argue that offshore outsourcing of customer services has converted many conventional services into hybrid forms wherein various components of many services are now performed in different countries. For example, in healthcare services doctors in the US examine their patients physically and record their observations into their dictaphones. Next, these recordings are digitized and uploaded into the servers of medical transcription companies based in Indian cities like Bangalore and Gurgaon where skilled operators decipher these and complete the documentation such as patient records and billing. Similarly, call center operators based in another country like Philippines or Singapore may handle queries from these patients. Researchers have also shown that customers are increasingly becoming aware of such practices followed by more and more businesses that they deal with every day and hence, it is important to study how this awareness would influence their perceptions, attitudes and behavior towards these businesses (Brown & Chin, 2004).

CONCEPTUAL FRAMEWORK

Prior research in COO area has linked it with several psychographic variables including consumer ethnocentrism, patriotism, conservatism and openness to foreign cultures on one hand and demographic variables such as age, gender, education, occupation, country of birth, residence and citizenship (Ali-Sulaiti & Baker, 1998; Sharma et al., 1995). Specifically, it is shown that highly ethnocentric, patriotic, conservative and less open to foreign cultures consumers are more likely to have negative perceptions about imported products and services. Similarly, older, female, less educated, blue-collar workers and consumers who are born and brought up in developed countries are shown to be more ethnocentric.

Based on these findings in prior literature, we argue that all these demographic variables would also act as antecedents of consumer perceptions about businesses and brands that use offshore outsourcing of customer services. Moreover, we suggest that all the above psychographic variables may not have a direct effect but a moderating influence on consumer perceptions about service quality, customer satisfaction, brand image, brand loyalty, repeat purchase intentions and complaint behavior. Next we discuss how two of these variables (i.e., home country and consumer ethnocentrism) influence different aspects of consumer perceptions, attitudes and behavior.

Service Quality Perceptions

Many services which used to be performed within one country or indeed just one city are now per-

formed in two or more countries around the world. This has resulted in an interaction between the customers and service providers from two different cultural and socio-economic backgrounds especially in contact-based services (Clark et al., 1996). Managing these interactions has never been an easy task because close cultural relationships within a society and the way various services are offered in that society make it extremely difficult to market services internationally (Dahringer, 1991). In fact, even within one's own country perceived nationality of a service provider may be more important to the customers than the supplementary or extra services offered by the provider as seen in the study of national stereotype effects on the selection of professional healthcare service providers (Harrison-Walker, 1995). To summarize these findings, customer ethnocentric tendencies do affect customer evaluation of services that are perceived to be foreign or provided by foreigners and generally this effect is negative if the COO of these service providers is less developed compared to the home country.

Figure 1. Conceptual framework

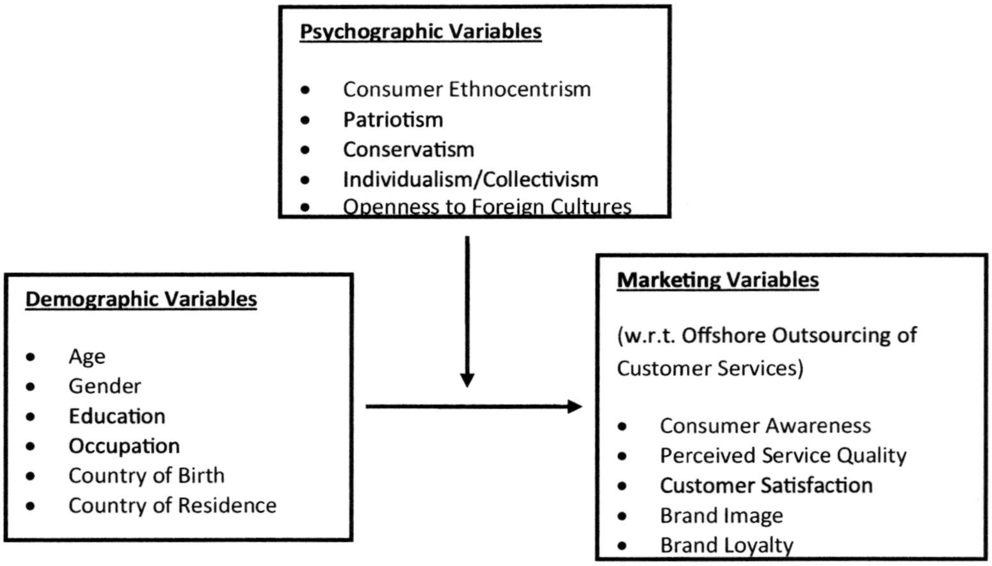

Psychographic Variables

- Consumer Ethnocentrism
- Patriotism
- Conservatism
- Individualism/Collectivism
- Openness to Foreign Cultures

Demographic Variables

- Age
- Gender
- Education
- Occupation
- Country of Birth
- Country of Residence

Marketing Variables

(w.r.t. Offshore Outsourcing of Customer Services)

- Consumer Awareness
- Perceived Service Quality
- Customer Satisfaction
- Brand Image
- Brand Loyalty

Customer Satisfaction

Service Quality consists of customer perceptions of the goodness-of-service provided to them (Cronin Jr. & Taylor, 1992; Parasuraman et al., 1988) and customer satisfaction is conceptualized as an affect-laden fulfillment response to service received (Oliver, 1997). As such, the cognitive perception of service quality logically precedes the affective judgment of satisfaction and therefore, perceptions of service quality are shown to be an antecedent of customer satisfaction (Brown & Chin, 2004). Hayward (2004) suggests that continuing outsourcing of call centres abroad will diminish customer satisfaction, because it is associated with relatively lower levels of service quality. Hence, offshore outsourcing of customer services may lead to lower customer satisfaction for some consumers because they may perceive a decline in the quality of service they received from overseas service representatives.

Repurchase Intentions

Customer satisfaction is directly and positively related to repurchase intentions because satisfied customers are more likely to want to experience the same satisfactory experience again and again (Anderson & Sullivan, 1993; Brown & Chin, 2004; Butcher et al., 2001; Cronin Jr. & Taylor, 1992; Hellier et al., 2003). Therefore, it is likely that customers who have negative perceptions about firms that use offshore outsourcing of customer services, may not like to continue purchasing that firm's products or services. In other words, offshore outsourcing may lead to a decline in repeat purchase intentions for some consumers because they may not like to deal with offshore service representatives or perceive the quality of their service to be distinctly lower compared to local staff of the same company in their home country.

Brand Image

Researchers have shown customers' perceptions about product quality to be positively associated with their perceptions of brand image (Steenkamp, 1990). Similarly, service quality is shown to be closely related to brand image across a wide range of industries such as hospitality (Francese & Renaghan, 1990), auto insurance and copy service (Arora & Stoner, 1996), life insurance (Hill, 1996), travel and tourism (Gilbert & Hewlett, 2003) and cruise lines (Ahmed et al., 2002). Similarly, customer satisfaction has been positively associated with brand image (Mayer et al., 2003; Palacio et al., 2002; Selnes, 1993). Therefore, the customer perceptions about service quality and their level of satisfaction with offshore outsourced customer services would influence their perceptions about brand image. In other words, offshore outsourcing of customer services by companies may lead to erosion in their brand image in the minds of those consumers who have negative perceptions about the quality of service offered by the overseas service representatives.

Brand Loyalty

Service quality is positively associated with customer loyalty although this relationship appears to be stronger at the company level rather than at the interpersonal level (Wong & Sohal, 2003). Similarly, it is found that service quality is positively associated with emotional satisfaction, which is positively associated with both customer loyalty and relationship quality (Wong, 2004). Several studies have found a strong positive association between customer satisfaction and brand loyalty across several service categories such as telecommunications (Kim et al., 2004), financial services (Chernatony et al., 2004) and travel (McCaskey & Symes, 2004). Hence, offshore outsourcing of customer services would influence customers' brand loyalty through its association with their perceptions about service quality and their level of customer satisfaction.

Complaint Behavior

It is fairly well-established in extant literature that customer lack of satisfaction often triggers the process of complaining and this effect is stronger in case of services compared to products (Bearden & Teel, 1983; Crié, 2003; Gronhaug & Gilly, 1991; Singh & Pandya, 1991; Singh & Wilkes, 1996). Based on this, it is argued that offshore outsourcing of customer services would influence customers' complaint behavior because of its strong association with their level of satisfaction and perceived quality of service. In other words, some customers when faced with a dissatisfactory service experience, are more likely to complain if this service encounter involved an offshore service representative rather than a local one in their home country.

EMPIRICAL FINDINGS

To test the impact of offshore outsourcing on customer perceptions, a survey was conducted in three developed countries namely, United States (US), United Kingdom (UK) and Australia with 100 customers each, resulting in a total sample size of 300. Graduate students were used to approach shoppers at local malls in these countries and recruited to participate in the survey. The survey questionnaire consisted of the following well-established scales with a Likert-type seven-point response format, to measure all the constructs used in this study: Customer Ethnocentrism (Sharma et al., 1995), Brand Image (Aaker, 1996), Brand Loyalty (Quester & Lim, 2003), Service Quality (Parasuraman et al., 1988), Customer Satisfaction (Oliver, 1997), Repurchase Intentions (Hellier et al., 2003), Customer Complaint Behavior Scale (Singh, 1988). The questionnaire

had three parts. First, the customers were asked to rate one of their existing service providers (e.g. Bank, Insurance company, Healthcare provider, Mobile phone service provider etc.) using these scales. Next, they were asked if they were aware of offshore outsourcing of customer services and asked to complete the same scales again assuming if the same provider were to outsource its customer services to some offshore locations in a less developed Asian country (e.g. India, Philippines or Thailand). Finally, they were asked to complete the customer ethnocentrism scale and their demographics such as gender and age were also recorded.

We conducted exploratory factor analysis and reliability tests on all the scales used and found high factor loadings on the expected factors (> 0.60) and high Cronbach's alpha values for all the scales (> 0.70). Next we used ANOVA to compare the average scores for all these scales across the two conditions i.e. offshore outsourcing (yes or no). Thereafter, each participant was classified as low (N=196, M=3.7) and high (N=104, M=4.9) on their customer ethnocentrism scores using a median split. There was no significant difference in average consumer ethnocentrism scores across the three countries. Finally, the average scores for each scale were compared across low and high ethnocentric groups for each country. All the results are summarized in Table 1 and 2.

As seen from Table 1, customers in all the three developed countries have distinctly less favorable perceptions about service quality, lower customer satisfaction and greater complaint behavior towards firms which use offshore outsourcing of customer services. However, the findings on brand image, brand loyalty and repurchase intentions were mixed, with customers in US and Australia showing lower brand image, those in Australia showing lower repurchase intentions and those in UK showing a less favorable brand image for companies using offshore outsourcing.

On the other hand, as seen in Table 2 we found high ethnocentric customers were found to

Table 1. Mean Comparison – Offshore Outsourcing (ANOVA)

	United States		United Kingdom		Australia		Overall	
	No	Yes	No	Yes	No	Yes	No	Yes
Service Quality	5.6	4.5 [a]	4.8	4.2 [b]	6.0	4.9 [a]	5.5	4.5 [a]
Customer Satisfaction	5.4	4.7 [b]	4.5	4.0 [c]	5.8	5.0 [b]	5.2	4.6 [b]
Repurchase Intention	4.9	4.8	5.1	4.8	5.9	5.2 [b]	5.3	4.9 [c]
Brand Image	4.5	4.2 [c]	5.5	5.2	5.5	4.5 [a]	5.2	4.6 [c]
Brand Loyalty	4.3	4.1	5.7	5.1 [b]	6.3	5.9	5.4	5.0 [c]
Complaint Behavior	4.9	5.7 [b]	5.7	6.2 [c]	4.0	4.7 [b]	4.9	5.5 [b]

[a] $p < 0.001$, [b] $p < 0.01$, [c] $p < 0.05$

Table 2. Mean Comparison – Customer Ethnocentrism (ANOVA)

	United States		United Kingdom		Australia		Overall	
	Low (69)	High (31)	Low (62)	High (38)	Low (65)	High (35)	Low (104)	High (196)
Service Quality	4.9	3.7 [a]	3.5	4.6 [a]	4.0	5.4 [a]	4.1	4.6 [b]
Customer Satisfaction	5.2	3.6 [a]	3.2	4.5 [a]	4.4	5.3 [a]	4.3	4.5
Repurchase Intention	4.9	4.6 [c]	4.3	5.1 [b]	4.8	5.4 [a]	4.7	5.0 [c]
Brand Image	4.3	3.9 [c]	4.5	5.6 [a]	4.1	4.7 [a]	4.3	4.7 [c]
Brand Loyalty	4.1	4.0	4.6	5.4 [b]	5.2	6.3 [a]	4.6	5.2 [b]
Complaint Behavior	5.4	6.3 [a]	6.6	6.0 [b]	5.1	4.2 [a]	5.7	5.5

[a] $p < 0.001$, [b] $p < 0.01$, [c] $p < 0.05$

have distinctly lower perceptions about service quality, customer satisfaction, repurchase intentions, brand image and brand loyalty along with greater complaint behavior, towards companies using offshore outsourcing of customer services (with the sole exception of brand loyalty among American consumers). We also compared the various scores across gender and different age-groups. As in prior literature, females and younger customers were found to be less ethnocentric and less influenced by offshore outsourcing, compared to older males.

Overall, with this study we were able to demonstrate that consumer awareness of offshore outsourcing to less developed countries by companies does have a negative influence on the perceptions, attitudes and behaviors of customers in developed countries. These influences are strongest on service quality, customer satisfaction and complaint behavior, probably because these are a direct consequence of inter-personal interaction with service providers in offshore locations. On the other hand, these influences are less strong on brand image, brand loyalty and repurchase intentions, probably because there are other factors that have a greater influence on these e.g. involvement, perceived need and high exit barriers.

CONCLUSION

In this chapter, we discuss the implications of offshore outsourcing for consumer behavior in general and its influence on consumer perceptions, attitudes and behaviors in particular. We first reviewed extant literature in the international and services marketing areas and then combined learnings from these two, to first conceptualize offshore outsourcing of customer services as a "hybrid service" and then develop a new conceptual framework. We also described a survey-based study undertaken in three developed countries (US, UK and Australia), which was used to test our hypotheses based on this new conceptual framework.

It is expected that this line of research would make managers more sensitive to the need to understand the challenges in managing the relationships between customers and their offshore service providers, and also draw more academic researchers to this emerging research area. The findings of similar studies may also suggest possible areas for improvement in a wide range of operational and strategic areas in the management of international services organizations e.g. human resources management, operations management, joint-venture and partner alliances management. Organizations with a high reliance on offshore outsourcing of customer services would be well-advised to draw up specific action plans to incorporate these learnings into their recruitment, training and retention programs, operations manuals, telesales scripts and other related materials for their offshore service representatives. Moreover, they may also need to develop customer education programs targeting those customers who are likely to have negative perceptions about the quality of service delivered by offshore service representatives. Such programs may be delivered through mass-media campaigns as well as specifically targeted direct marketing efforts and should attempt to convince the customers about the benefits of offshore outsourcing to them in terms of lower prices for services offered to them. Services organizations may even need to adjust their loyalty management or rewards programs for their regular customers to make sure that they are able to retain them.

Moreover, it would also be very useful to extend this line of research to the Business-to-business (B2B) context because that area contributes to a significant proportion of the overall offshore outsourcing business. On one hand, the service standards expected by buyers of professional services could be much more stringent compared to individual consumers whereas on the other hand the exit-barriers in the buyer-seller relationship in this context could also be much stronger because of the money involved and other contractual obligations. Moreover, the awareness of the COO of offshore service providers and perceptions about their service quality could also be much stronger in the B2B context. Therefore, future researchers in this area could try to explore these relationships in the B2B context as well, besides validating and replicating these findings in Business-to-consumer (B2C) context.

Finally, future researchers may expand upon our study in many ways. We measured the customer behaviors such as repeat purchase and complaint behavior only indirectly i.e. in terms of behavioral intentions. Future researchers may attempt a more direct measure for more robust results by looking at consumer panel data to track repeat purchase and complaint patterns. Similarly, due to operational limitations we did not measure customer reactions to offshore outsourcing to specific target countries but future research into this may provide some useful insights into this phenomenon.

REFERENCES

Aaker, D. A. (1996). Measuring Brand Equity across Products and Markets. *California Management Review, 31*(May), 191-201.

Ahmed, Z. U., Johnson, J. P., Ling, C. P., Fong, T. W., & Hui, A. K. (2002). Country-of-origin and brand effects on consumers' evaluations of cruise lines. *International Marketing Review, 19*(2/3), 279-302.

Ali-Sulaiti, K. I., & Baker, M. J. (1998). Country of origin effects: a literature review. *Marketing Intelligence & Planning, 16*(3), 150-199.

American Banker, & Gallup. (2004). *What Americans Think About Overseas Outsourcing*: American Banker/Gallup.

Anderson, E. W., & Sullivan, M. W. (1993). The antecedents and consequences of customer satisfaction for firms. *Marketing Science, 12*(2), 125-143.

Arora, R., & Stoner, C. (1996). The effect of perceived service quality and name familiarity on the service selection decision. *The Journal of Services Marketing, 10*(1), 22.

Bearden, W. O., & Teel, J. E. (1983). Selected determinants of consumer satisfaction and complaint reports. *Journal of Consumer Research, 20*(1), 21-28.

Blackmore, D., DeSouza, R., Young, A., Goodness, E., & Silliman, R. (2005). *Forecast: IT Outsourcing, Worldwide, 2002-2008 (Update)*: Gartner.

Briggs, B. (2005). Offshore Outsourcing Poses Risks. *Health Data Management, 13*(2), 68-78.

Brown, S. P., & Chin, W. W. (2004). Satisfying and Retaining Customers through Independent Service Representatives. *Decision Sciences, 35*(3), 527-550.

Butcher, K., Sparks, B., & O'Callaghan, F. (2001). Evaluative and relational influences on service loyalty. *International Journal of Service Industry Management, 12*(4), 310-327.

Chao, P. (1993a). Partitioning Country of Origin Effects. *Journal of International Business Stud-ies, 24*(2), 291-306.

Chao, P. (1993b). Partitioning Country-of-Origin Effects: Consumer Evaluations of a Hybrid Product. *Journal of International Business Studies, 24*(2), 291-306.

Chao, P. (2001). The Moderating Effects of Country of Assembly, Country of Parts, and Country of Design on Hybrid Product Evaluations. *Journal of Advertising, 30*(4), 67-81.

Chernatony, L. d., Harris, F. J., & Christodoulides, G. (2004). Developing a Brand Performance Measure for Financial Services Brands. *The Service Industries Journal, 24*(2), 15.

Clark, T., Rajaratnam, D., & Smith, T. (1996). Toward a theory of international services: marketing insights in a world of nations. *Journal of International Marketing, 4*(2), 9-28.

Clott, C. B. (2004). Perspectives on Global Outsourcing and the Changing Nature of Work. *Business and Society Review, 109*(2), 153-170.

Corbett, M. F. (2002). Outsourcing's next wave. *Fortune*(July 15).

Cornell, C. (2004). Offshore Options: Outsourcing operations to overseas providers can save you money or cause you pain. The choice is yours. *Profit, 23*(4), 87-88.

Crié, D. (2003). Consumers' complaint behaviour. Taxonomy, typology and determinants: Towards a unified ontology. *Database Marketing & Customer Strategy Management, 11*(1), 60-79.

Cronin Jr., J. J., & Taylor, S. A. (1992). Measuring service quality: A reexamination and extension. *Journal of Marketing, 56*(55-68).

Dahringer, L. D. (1991). Marketing services internationally: barriers and management strategies. *Journal of Services Marketing, 5*(3), 5-17.

Data-Monitor. (2004). Axa/Abbey: a passage to India. *3*(3), 16-17.

Economist. (2001). Back office to the world. *359*(8220), 59-61.

Fan, Y. (2000). Strategic outsourcing: evidence from British companies. *Marketing Intelligence & Planning, 18*(4), 213.

Francese, P. A., & Renaghan, L. M. (1990). Data-Base Marketing: Building Customer Profiles. *Cornell Hotel and Restaurant Administration Quarterly, 31*(1), 60-63.

Gilbert, D., & Hewlett, J. (2003). A method for the assessment of relative brand strength: A UK tour operator example. *The Service Industries Journal, 23*(2), 166.

Gronhaug, K., & Gilly, M. C. (1991). A transaction cost approach to consumer dissatisfaction and complaint actions. *Journal of Economic Psychology, 12*(1), 156-183.

Gronroos, C. (1999). Internationalization strategies for services. *Journal of Services Marketing, 13*(4/5), 290-297.

Han, C. M., & Terpstra, V. (1988). Country-of-origin effects for uni-national and bi-national products. *Journal of International Business Studies, 19*(Summer), 235-255.

Harrison-Walker, L. J. (1995). The relative effects of national stereotype and advertising information on the selection of a service provider. *Journal of Services Marketing, 9*(1), 47-59.

Hayward, M. (2004). I showed them the future and they ignored it. *Management Today*(Sep), 68-69.

Hellier, P. K., Geursen, G. M., Carr, R. A., & Rickard, J. A. (2003). Customer repurchase intention: A general structural equation model. *European Journal of Marketing, 37*(11/12), 1762-1800.

Hill, J. (1996). Keeping customers loyal at Liverpool Victoria Friendly Society. *Managing Service Quality, 6*(4), 27-31.

Javalgi, R. G., Cutler, B., & Winans, W. A. (2001). At your service! Does country of origin research apply? *Journal of Services Marketing, 15*(6/7), 565-582.

Javalgi, R. G., Griffith, D. A., & White, D. S. (2003). An empirical examination of factors influencing the internationalization of service firms. *Journal of Services Marketing, 17*(2/3), 185-201.

Kaynak, E., Kucukemiroglu, O., & Kara, A. (1994). Consumer perceptions of airlines: a correspondence analysis approach in an airline industry. *Management International Review, 34*(3), 235-254.

Kennedy, C. (2002). Name and shame: If you outsource, beware. Your brand may be in tatters through appalling customer service - and you may never know it. *Director, 56*(5), 23.

Kim, M.-K., Park, M.-C., & Jeong, D.-H. (2004). The effects of customer satisfaction and switching barrier on customer loyalty in Korean mobile telecommunication services. *Telecommunications Policy, 28*(2), 145.

Kotabe, M., Murray, J. Y., & Javalgi, R. G. (1998). Global sourcing of services and market performance: an empirical evaluation. *Journal of International Marketing, 6*(4), 10-31.

Li, Z. G., Murray, L. W., & Scott, D. (2000). Global Sourcing, Multiple Country-of-Origin Facets, and Consumer Reactions. *Journal of Business Research, 47*, 121-133.

Lovelock, C. H. (1999). Developing marketing strategies for transactional service operations. *Journal of Services Marketing, 13*(4/5), 278-289.

Mayer, K. J., Bowen, J. T., & Moulton, M. R. (2003). A proposed model of the descriptors of service process. *The Journal of Services Marketing, 17*(6/7), 621.

McCartney, L. (2003). A shore thing. *CFO-IT Magazine*(Spring), 60–63.

McCaskey, D., & Symes, S. (2004). Travel Inn: everything you want for a good night's sleep - 100 per cent satisfaction guarantee or your money back. *International Journal of Contemporary Hospitality Management, 16*(3), 167.

Nicoulaud, B. (1989). Problems and strategies in the international marketing of services. *European Journal of Marketing, 23*(6), 55-66.

Oliver, R. L. (1997). *Satisfaction: A behavioral perspective on the consumer.* New York, NY: McGraw-Hill.

Osgood, C. E., & Tannenbaum, P. H. (1955). The Principle of Congruity in the Prediction of Attitude Change. *Psychological Review, 62*(1), 42-55.

Palacio, A. B., Meneses, G. D., & Perez, P. J. (2002). The configuration of the university image and its relationship with the satisfaction of students. *Journal of Educational Administration, 40*(4/5), 486-505.

Parasuraman, A., Zeithaml, V. A., & Berry, L. L. (1988). SERVQUAL: A multiple-item scale for measuring consumer perceptions of service quality. *Journal of Retailing, 64,* 12-37.

Quester, P., & Lim, A. L. (2003). Product involvement/brand loyalty: is there a link? *Journal of Product & Brand Management, 12*(1), 22-38.

Quinn, J. B. (1997). *Innovation Explosion: Using Intellect and Software to Revolutionize Growth Strategies.* New York: Free Press.

Reilly, P. (1997). Outsourcing: employers becoming cautious. *Management Services, 41*(6), 9-11.

Roy, M. (2003). Outsourced call centres damage long-term effort. *Precision Marketing*(Nov 7), 14.

Ruyter, K. d., Birgelen, M. v., & Wetzels, M. (1998). Consumer ethnocentrism in international services marketing. *International Business Review, 7,* 185-202.

Sauer, P. L., Young, M. A., & Unnava, H. R. (1991). An Experimental Investigation of the Processes Behind the Country-of-Origin Effects. *Journal of International Consumer Marketing, 3*(2), 29-59.

Selnes, F. (1993). An examination of the effect of product performance on brand reputation, satisfaction and loyalty. *European Journal of Marketing, 27*(9), 19-35.

Sharma, S., Shimp, T. A., & Shin, J. (1995). Consumer ethnocentrism: A test of antecedents and moderators. *Journal of the Academy of Marketing Science, 23*(1), 26-37.

Shimp, T. A. (1984). Consumer ethnocentrism: The concept and a preliminary empirical test. *Advances in Consumer Research, 11,* 285-290.

Shimp, T. A., & Sharma, S. (1987). Consumer ethnocentrism: Construction and validation of the CETSCALE. *Journal of Consumer Research, 24*(August), 280-289.

Siems, T. F., & Ratner, A. S. (2003). Do What You Do Best, Outsource the Rest. *Southwest Economy*(Nov/Dec).

Singh, J. (1988). Consumer Complaint Intentions and Behavior: Definitional and Taxonomical Issues. *Journal of Marketing, 52*(January 1988), 93-107.

Singh, J., & Pandya, S. (1991). Exploring the Effects of Consumers' Dissatisfaction Level on Complaint Behaviours. *European Journal of Marketing, 25*(9), 7-21.

Singh, J., & Wilkes, R. E. (1996). When consumers complain: a path analysis of the key antecedents of consumer complaint response estimates. *Journal of the Academy of Marketing Science, 24*(4), 350-365.

Steenkamp, J.-B. E. M. (1990). Conceptual Model of the Quality Perception Process. *Journal of Business Research, 21*(4), 309-333.

Swartz, N. (2004a). Much More Than Jobs Being Outsourced. *Information Management Journal, 38*(3), 3.

Swartz, N. (2004b). Offshoring Privacy. *Information Management Journal, 38*(5), 24-26.

Trapp, R. (1999). Blunder Boss. *The British Journal of Administrative Management*(Jul/Aug), 12-16.

Tse, D. K., & Lee, W.-N. (1993). Removing Negative Country Images: Effects of Decomposition, Branding and Product Experience. *Journal of International Marketing, 1*(1), 57-75.

Wong, A. (2004). The role of emotional satisfaction in service encounters. *Managing Service Quality, 14*(5), 365.

Wong, A., & Sohal, A. (2003). Service quality and customer loyalty perspectives on two levels of retail relationships. *The Journal of Services Marketing, 17*(4/5), 495-511.

Chapter XVI
An Extrinsic and Intrinsic Motivation–Based Model for Measuring Consumer Shopping Oriented Web Site Success

Edward J. Garrity
Canisius College, USA

Joseph B. O'Donnell
Canisius College, USA

Yong Jin Kim
Sogang University, Korea & State University of New York at Binghamton, USA

G. Lawrence Sanders
State University of New York at Buffalo, USA

ABSTRACT

This paper develops a new model of web information systems success that takes into account both intrinsic and extrinsic motivating factors. The proposed model begins with the Garrity and Sanders model of technologic acceptance and develops an extended nomological network of success factors that draws on motivation and flow theory.

INTRODUCTION

The Technology Acceptance Model (TAM) has been the dominant framework for explaining the acceptance and use of information technology for nearly twenty years (Keil, Beranek, & Konsynski, 1995). In particular, research has found that Perceived Usefulness and Perceived Ease of Use are important predictors of the acceptance of information systems technologies (Adam, Nelson, & Todd, 1992; Davis, 1989; Doll, Hendrickson, & Deng, 1998).

The difficulty comes in applying the TAM model to the Web shopping experience. Unlike traditional organizational information systems, web systems are used for a variety of activities including both work and pleasure. This leads to a disconnect in terms of applying the Perceived Usefulness and Perceived Ease of Use constructs to the shopping experience because they are typically not the only driving forces behind web use (Moon & Kim, 2001).

Recent research has extended the TAM model to the Web environment by including intrinsic motivating factors to take into account a wider and more realistic assessment of users' goals (Hackbarth, Grover, & Yi, 2003; Koufaris, 2002; Moon & Kim, 2001; Venkatesh, 2000).

For example, Koufaris (2002) examined the dual role of the consumer in using a web-based system environment, where an individual can be viewed as both a computer user and a consumer. When viewed as a consumer, Koufaris argues that Perceived Shopping Enjoyment (an intrinsic motivator) is important for on-line shopping since it can have an impact on attitudes and usage intentions. His rationale was based on the findings of Jarvenpaa & Todd (1997a; 1997b). The Koufaris study found that enjoyment was critically important for on-line shopping.

However, their model did not adequately explain Perceived Usefulness and Ease of Use and their nomological net did not integrate TAM with their intrinsic motivation factor, Perceived Shopping Enjoyment.

This paper uses the Garrity and Sanders (1998) model as a vehicle to integrate the individual as a consumer perspective, wherein Shopping Enjoyment is used as an intrinsic motivator, and the individual is also viewed as a computer user, wherein Perceived Usefulness is used as an extrinsic motivator and is implemented using Task Support Satisfaction. Our approach treats Shopping Enjoyment as a state variable that emerges from the interaction between the user and the information system. This perspective is consistent with flow theory (Ghani & Deshpande, 1994; Trevino & Webster, 1992), motivation theory (Deci, 1971; Scott et al., 1988) as well as environmental psychology (Mehrabian & Russel, 1974).

This paper contributes to the literature in three ways. Firstly, the proposed model provides a nomological network of success factors that provides a better understanding of how intrinsic and extrinsic motivation factors impact the use of systems in general and websites in particular. Secondly, this paper incorporates two dimensions, Decision Support Satisfaction and Interface Satisfaction, as antecedent variables to expand our understanding of Perceived Usefulness (implemented as Task Support Satisfaction). Thirdly, Decision Support Satisfaction not only provides for enhanced explanatory power in the model, but it can also offer important insights into the decision support provided by consumer shopping-oriented web information systems (Garrity et al., 2005). This is especially important because consumer shopping-oriented web information systems differ from conventional DSS in a number of ways, including and most notably that consumers have an extensive and different decision making process from managers (O'Keefe & McEachern, 1988).

LITERATURE REVIEW

Garrity and Sanders Model of IS Success and the GSISS Model

Garrity and Sanders (1998) adapted the DeLone & McLean (1992) model and proposed an alternative model in the context of organizational systems and socio-technical systems. They developed a user satisfaction inventory comprised of questions from six well-developed instruments. Garrity and Sanders expand on the DeLone and McLean model by identifying four major factors they assert are the basic underlying constructs that make up existing success measures in the IS field (Figure 1). They validate these constructs using a modified Delphi technique whereby IS research experts mapped existing measurement items into one of four factors.

The four factors they identify are *Task Support Satisfaction, Decision Support Satisfaction, Interface Satisfaction,* and *Quality of Work Life Satisfaction.*

In order to better understand the underlying dimensions, Kim et al. (2004) developed and tested a revised model, which arranges the IS success dimensions into a nomological net in order to further understand IS success and to test the construct validity of their dimensions. The revised or detailed model, called Goal Satisfaction-based IS Success Model (GSISS Model) is presented in Figure 2.

Although the origins of the GSISS model are derived from general systems theory and TAM is derived from the Theory of Reasoned Action (Ajzen & Fishbein, 1980; Fishbein & Ajzen, 1975), the GSISS model is related to TAM. Essentially, Interface Satisfaction is equivalent to Perceived Ease of Use; and Task Support Satisfaction is equivalent to Perceived Usefulness. In essence, Usefulness is expanded in the GSISS model into two components: usefulness toward task accomplishment or overall job support (Task Support Satisfaction) and usefulness toward decision making (Decision Support Satisfaction). Since most jobs are composed of both decision making and clerical or processing tasks, the GSISS model provides additional precision and usefulness above and beyond TAM.

Extrinsic and Intrinsic Motivation: Flow Theory and Shopping Enjoyment

Extrinsic motivation is defined as the motivation to perform an activity because it is perceived to produce valued outcomes that are distinct from the

Figure 1. Garrity and Sanders (1998) model of IS success

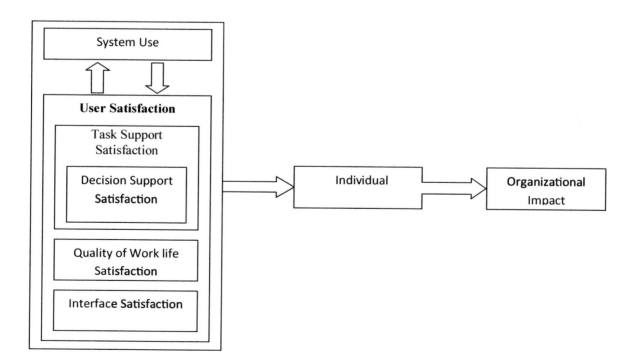

Figure 2. GSISS model: Goal satisfaction-based IS success model

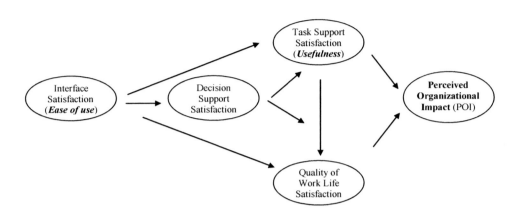

activity itself (Webster & Martocchio, 1992). For example, one may be motivated to use information technology because it helps one to achieve better job performance. Thus, Perceived Usefulness or Task Support Satisfaction would be regarded as extrinsic motivators. In contrast to this, intrinsic motivation is the motivation to perform the activity due to the direct reinforcement of performing the activity per se´. An example of this is Enjoyment towards the system (Davis, Bagozzi, & Warshaw, 1992).

The TAM model was first modified and extended to include intrinsic motivation using the variable Enjoyment (Davis, Bagozzi, & Warshaw, 1992). An intrinsic motivating variable or construct that has recently received a great deal of attention in web-based technology utilization studies is "Computer Playfulness" or "Playfulness" (Hoffman & Novak 1996; Novak, Hoffman, & Yung, 2000; Moon & Kim, 2001; Novak, Hoffman, & Duhachek, 2003; Pace, 2004). Playfulness has been operationalized in a number of ways however, most researchers start with the definition based on the pioneering work on Flow theory by Csikszentimihalyi (1975). Csikszentimihalyi's work on flow theory emphasizes the role of a *specific context* rather than *individual differences* in explaining human motivated behaviors. Csikszentimihalyi defines the "flow" as "the holistic sensation that people feel when they act with total involvement."

Flow theory focuses on the *state of Playfulness* which emphasizes the interaction of the individual in a *specific context*, whereas a strict interpretation of the original TAM model, which is based on the theory of reasoned action (TRA), requires that individual beliefs impact attitudes through Perceived Usefulness and Perceived Ease of Use (Davis, et al., 1989). Thus, TAM forces researchers to treat all variables as antecedents to Ease of Use and Perceived Usefulness. Therefore, intrinsic motivation factors such as Playfulness or Enjoyment cannot be easily incorporated into TAM unless these variables are treated as traits of individuals (as done by Moon & Kim, 2001), but this is in direct contradiction to flow theory.

RESEARCH MODEL AND HYPOTHESES

Integrating intrinsic motivation into a model of IS Success requires decisions on two major issues: (1) the selection of a variable or construct to operationalized intrinsic motivation, and (2) the decision to model intrinsic motivation as either a state variable or as a trait variable.

First, we prefer the use of Shopping Enjoyment as a measure of intrinsic motivation since intrinsic motivation is concerned with, and defined as the performance of an activity for the inherent reward of doing the activity itself; Enjoyment has the advantage of simplicity and also has a great deal of face validity. Finally, Shopping Enjoyment is a more specific measure that is applicable in the consumer-oriented, web-based application domain.

Second, we view intrinsic motivation and specifically, Shopping Enjoyment, as a function of the interaction of the individual within a *specific context* (with the computer-based artifact or interface). Such an interpretation is consistent with flow theory and the perspective of environmental psychology. According to Mehrabian and Russel (1974), emotional responses to the environment mediate the relationship between the environment and one's behavior. Figure 3 displays the research model and hypotheses, now termed the Integrated Web Information System Success Model (IWISSM).

Consumer Trust in the Web Retail Environment

Consumer trust in the web retail environment is critical for B2C ecommerce where the possibility exists that a web retailer can take advantage of online consumers. Trust in the web retail environment is the "willingness of the consumer to rely on the [web retailer] when there is vulnerability for the consumer" (Jarvenpaa et al., 1999, p. 2). Consumer vulnerability relates to the risk that customers encounter when visiting a problematic site during a purchase. In this context, web retailers may use personal information to the detriment of the consumer, purchased products may not meet consumer specifications, and or the delivery of purchased products may be late or may not occur at all (O'Donnell, Ferrin, Glassberg, & Sanders, 2004).

Consumers' Trust in the web retailer has been empirically shown to influence their Intention to Use the merchant site for Ecommerce purposes (Gefen, Karahanna, Straub, 2003; Jarvenpaa, Tractinsky, Saarinen, & Vitale, 1999; Jarvenpaa, Tractinsky & Vitale, 2000). Gefen, Karahanna & Straub (2003) suggest that Trust increases the Perceived Usefulness of the site by improving

Figure 3. An integrated model of Web information system success (IWISSM)

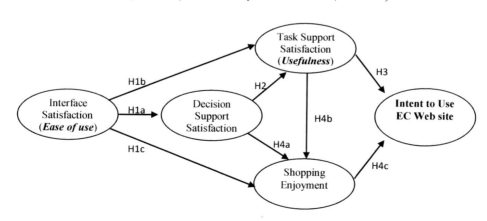

the perceived likelihood that consumers will gain expected benefits of product purchases from the site.

Individual Characteristics

One can expect certain individual characteristics (or traits) to be related to Computer Shopping Enjoyment. Webster and Martocchio (1992) and Hackbarth et al. (2003) found strong associations between Computer Experience and Playfulness (which has a component of Shopping Enjoyment). Koufaris (2002) also found strong correlations between a consumer/computer user's Product Involvement and Shopping Enjoyment. Product Involvement is defined as the degree to which a consumer is involved with or finds a particular product to be interesting, fascinating, or enjoyable to use. Since a user of a web-based consumer pur-

chasing website is both a consumer and a computer user, one's experience level (or Self-Efficacy) and one's degree of Product Involvement should influence one's degree of Shopping Enjoyment in a particular web information system context. Table 1 summarizes the study hypotheses.

METHODOLOGY

Data Collection and Experimental Procedure

In order to examine the proposed model in this study, we identified three diverse, commercial web sites for selecting a digital camera: myCamera. com, Active Buyers Guide, and Amazon.com. "myCamera.com" is a digital camera comparison

Table 1. Hypotheses

	Hypothesis
H1a	Interface Satisfaction positively influences Decision Support Satisfaction.
H1b	Interface Satisfaction positively influences Task Support Satisfaction.
H1c	Interface Satisfaction positively influences Shopping Enjoyment.
H2	Decision Support Satisfaction is positively associated with Task Support Satisfaction.
H3	Task Support Satisfaction positively affects Intention to Use EC Website.
H4a	Decision Support Satisfaction positively affects Shopping Enjoyment.
H4b	Task Support Satisfaction positively affects Shopping Enjoyment.
H4c	Shopping Enjoyment positively affects Intention to Use EC Website.
H5a	Product Involvement positively affects Shopping Enjoyment.
H5b	Web Skills positively affects Shopping Enjoyment.
H5c	Trust positively affects Intention to Use EC Website.

guide that lists products and their corresponding critical attributes in a table or list format. "Active Buyers Guide," is a sophisticated decision guide for the purchase of digital cameras. This website provides a number of features and functions to guide a user to "narrow down" the large potential list of products. "Amazon.com" was selected because it represents a very successful commercial website that includes a feature not present in the other two experimental sites – "the average customer rating." The average customer rating features gives users the opportunity to see how other consumers rate the various products.

The data collection was conducted in two steps. First, a pilot test was performed involving 52 subjects and 104 observations. It was used to test the experimental procedure and to refine the items and constructs used in the study. It also enabled the researchers to clarify the wording, content and general layout of the survey instrument.

Next, the actual experiment was conducted. Students in an introductory computer course at a large research university were given a questionnaire set consisting of two identical sets of survey items for each of the two websites assigned. Student subjects were assigned at random to one of 6 possible website combinations. Subjects were given an overview of the task and told that they had a budget of $200 and were asked to select the best camera from the website. This budget restriction was used to ensure a moderately involved cognitive task. Specifically, subjects were instructed to visit the website listed on their questionnaire packet, select a digital camera from the website, and then to fill-out the questionnaire. Each questionnaire included a section requiring subjects to list the price, make and model of the camera selected from the website. Subjects were then told to repeat this procedure for the second website listed on their packet. Subjects were given one week to complete the experiment and were given extra credit in the course for their participation. In addition, as extra incentive subjects were informed that completed questionnaires would be placed in a raffle drawing for gift certificates to Circuit City. A total of 300 sets of questionnaires were distributed. One-hundred and ninety (190) questionnaire sets were returned for a response rate of 63% (190/300).

Demographics

Tables 2 and 3 show the demographic and web access information and the web use and web skills for the subjects of this study. Microsoft Internet Explorer was the major Web browser used and over 90% of the subjects had some prior experience with Internet shopping. Interestingly, the majority (over 60%) of the subjects accessed the Internet through their home office to perform the assignment given for this study.

Operationalization of Research Variables

Measures for Product Involvement and Web Skills were adapted from Koufaris (2002). Product Involvement was described on the questionnaire as – "We would like to know how interested you are in digital cameras. Please use the series of descriptive words listed below to indicate your level of interest." The instrument then listed two 7-point semantic differential scales ranging from Un-Exciting to Exciting and from Boring to Interesting. Web Skills was implemented using a 7-point Likert scale, anchored by Strongly Disagree to Strongly Agree:

1. I am very skilled at using the Web,
2. I know how to find what I want on the Web, and
3. I know more about using the Web than most users (See items G6-G8 in Table 3).

The other major questionnaire items are shown in Appendices 1-3. The variables in the study were operationalized based on a variety of sources and existing instruments.

Table 2. Descriptive statistics on demographics and Web access

Demographic Information	N	Minimum	Maximum	Mean	Std. Deviation
Age (in years)	189	18	48	**22.21**	4.308
Gender	188	Male 79 (42%), **Female 109 (58%)**			
Browser used for this survey	187	**Microsoft Internet Explorer 169 (90.4%)** AOL Browser 10 (5.3%) Netscape Navigator 7 (3.7%)			
Location where the Internet was accessed	151	**Home using network 74 (49.0%)** School 48 (31.8%) Home using modem 20 (13.2%) Work place using network 5 (3.3%) Work place using modem 4 (2.6%)			

Table 3. Descriptive statistics on Web use and Web skills

Web Use/Skills Information	N	Minimum	Maximum	Mean	Std. Deviation
G6. I am very skilled at using the Web	188	1	7	**5.74**	1.333
G7. I know how to find what I want on the web	188	1	7	**5.88**	1.309
G8. I know more about using the web than most users	188	1	7	**5.26**	1.336
How would you rate your experience with Web technology?	188	1	7	**5.28**	1.089
How many **hours** per week do you use the Internet?	187	0	100	**16.21**	13.584
How many **hours** per week do you spend overall on a computer?	188	0	100	**25.59**	20.039
How long have you been using the Internet?	175	**Between 1 and 1.5 years 170 (97.1%)** More than 3 years 2 (1.1%) Less than 6 months 2 (1.1%) Between 6 months and 1 years 1 (0.6%)			
Number of purchases you have made through the Internet in the last year	189	**1-5 times 91 (48.1%)** 11 or more 53 (28.0%) 6-10 times 32 (16.9%) Never 13 (6.9%)			

Order Effects and Treatment Effects

The survey questionnaires were designed in six different formats with identical measures (Each set of the questionnaires includes two web sites for assessment out of three with the order of web sites reversed for each of the website pairs). Order effects during the experiments were investigated. The results of two-way ANOVA (Table 4) showed that there was no statistically significant difference in Behavioral Intention to Use (the website) caused by the order of the presentation of the Web sites on the questionnaire.

The order of site presentation (or evaluation) did not appear to affect respondents' decisions about which site they preferred to buy a digital camera. As shown in Table 5, there was no significant interaction effect between the selected site to buy from and the order of evaluation of e-commerce sites.

ANALYSIS AND RESULTS

We employed the Partial Least Squares (PLS) approach to analyze the data. The emphasis of

Table 4. Tests of between-subjects effects

Source	Sum of Squares	Df	Mean Square	F	Sig.
SITE	12.432	2	6.216	2.945	.054
SITE * SORD	.987	2	.493	.234	.792
Error	785.264	372	2.111		
Total	7206.778	378			
Corrected Total	798.912	377			

Note: Dependent Variable: Behavioral Intention to Use an EC Web site
 SITE: Target e-commerce sites (Amazon, Decision Guide, and MyCamera.com)
 SORD: Site evaluation Order by respondents

*Table 5. Selected site to buy from * Site Evaluation Order Cross-tabulation*

	Site Evaluation Order		Total
	1	2	
Buy from Amazon	63	65	128
Buy from Decision Guide	68	60	128
Buy from MyCamera.com	58	64	122
Total	189	189	378

Note: Pearson Chi Square value =.826 and p=.662.

PLS is on predicting the responses as well as in understanding the underlying relationship between the variables (Tobias, 1999). PLS is a powerful approach for analyzing models and theory building because of the minimal demands on measurement scales, sample size, and residual distributions (Fornell, 1982). In addition, the component-based PLS avoids two serious problems, inadmissible solutions, and factor indeterminancy (Fornell & Bookstein, 1982). SEM approaches, such as LISREL and AMOS, are not able to deal with non-standardized distributions (Fornell, 1982), and they can yield non-unique or otherwise improper solutions in some cases (Fornell & Bookstein, 1982). PLS is not as susceptible to these limitations (Wold, 1974; Wold, 1985).

Assessment of the Measurement Model

PLS analysis involves two stages: (1) the assessment of the measurement model, including the reliability and discriminant validity of the measures, and (2) the assessment of the structural model. For the assessment of the measurement model, individual item loadings and internal consistency were examined as a test of reliability (See Table 6). Individual item loadings, and internal consistencies greater than 0.7 are considered adequate (Fornell & Larker, 1981).

As shown in Table 6, loadings for all measurement items are above 0.8 (except for I1 in Interface Satisfaction), which indicates there is sound internal reliability. The almost uniformly

Table 6. Measures, loadings, and weights

Decision Support Satisfaction			Task Support Satisfaction			Interface Satisfaction			BI to use EC Web site		
Item	Loadings	Weight	Item	Loadings	Weight	Item	Loadings	Weight	Item	Loadings	Weight
D7	0.8984	0.2818	T7	0.8510	0.3550	I1	0.7904	0.1749	U2	0.8953	0.3563
D8	0.9246	0.2819	T9	0.9020	0.3674	I5	0.8392	0.1784	U5	0.9432	0.3724
D9	0.9096	0.2965	T10	0.9228	0.3973	I8	0.8622	0.2174	U6	0.9254	0.3568
D10	0.8686	0.2534				I92	0.8965	0.2050			
						I13	0.8774	0.1997			
						I16	0.8645	0.1936			
Shopping Enjoyment			Web Skills			Product Involvement			Trust		
P4	0.8828	0.2778	G6	0.9568	0.3736	PI3	0.8920	0.4707	TR1	0.8709	0.1717
P5	0.9274	0.2800	G7	0.9382	0.3929	PI4	0.9389	0.6179	TR2	0.8584	0.1929
P6	0.9214	0.2637	G8	0.8753	0.3130				TR3	0.9230	0.1859
P7	0.9294	0.2722							TR4	0.8772	0.1526
									TR5	0.9134	0.2104
									TR6	0.9161	0.2054

Note: Items were not included if either: (1) loadings are less than 0.7 and (2) bivariate correlations are higher than .60.

Table 7. Composite reliability (CR) and average variance extracted (AVE)

Constructs	CR	AVE	Formula
Decision Support Satisfaction	0.9449	0.8109	$CR = (\sum \lambda_i)^2 / [(\sum \lambda_i)^2 + \sum_i var(\epsilon_i)]$
Task Support Satisfaction	0.9214	0.7965	$AVE = \sum \lambda_i^2 / [\sum \lambda_i^2 + \sum_i var(\epsilon_i)]$
Interface Satisfaction	0.9425	0.7322	
Shopping Enjoyment	0.9539	0.8377	
Web Skills	0.9460	0.8539	
Product Involvement	0.9121	0.8384	
Trust	0.9596	0.7984	
Behavioral Intention to Use EC Web site	0.9441	0.8492	

Note: λ_i is the component loading to an indicator and $var(\epsilon_i) = 1 - \lambda_i^2$

distributed weights show each item contributes to each construct equivalently. We used PLS-Graph Version 2.91.03.04 to perform the analysis.

Reliability and Validity Tests

In assessing the internal consistency for a given block of indicators, the composite reliability (CR), also referred to as convergent validity (see Werts, Linn, & Joreskog, 1974), was calculated. All the CR values are over 0.9, which suggests that the parameter estimates are sound (Table 7).

The Average Variance Extracted (AVE) was also calculated. AVE measures the amount of variance that a construct captures from its indicators relative to the variance contained in measurement error. This statistic can be interpreted as a measure of reliability for the construct and as a means of evaluating discriminant validity (Fornell & Larker, 1981). AVE values should be greater than 0.50. All AVEs for the constructs used in this study are greater than 0.70. This indicates that more than 70% of the variance of the indicators can be accounted for by the latent variables.

Table 8. Correlations of latent variables

	DSS	IFS	TSS	SE	WSKL	PI	TR	BI
Decision Support Satisfaction	(0.901)							
Interface Satisfaction	0.628	(0.856)						
Task Support Satisfaction	0.699	0.604	(0.892)					
Shopping Enjoyment	0.522	0.458	0.613	(0.915)				
Web Skills	0.107	0.226	0.057	0.119	(0.924)			
Product Involvement	-0.039	-0.075	-0.029	-0.074	-0.123	(0.915)		
Trust	0.421	0.459	0.400	0.429	0.217	-0.129	(0.894)	
Behavioral Intention to use	0.532	0.422	0.680	0.668	0.007	-0.031	0.402	(0.922)

Note: the number in parenthesis is the square root of AVE.

The AVE can also be used to assess discriminant validity. The AVEs should be greater than the square of the correlations among the constructs. That is, the amount of variance shared between a latent variable and its block of indicators should be greater than shared variance between the latent variables. In this study, the square-roots of each AVE value are greater than the off-diagonal elements (Table 8). This indicates that there exists reasonable discriminant validity among all of the constructs. The correlation between Decision Support Satisfaction and Task Support Satisfaction appears to be a little high although valid in terms of discriminant validity criteria. Such a close but distinctive relationship between Decision Support Satisfaction and Task Support Satisfaction was expected (see Garrity & Sanders, 1998)). Hence, Decision Support Satisfaction together with Task Support Satisfaction can be used to provide more insight into the features of the Web site.

Assessment of the Structural Model

The path coefficients in the PLS model represent standardized regression coefficients. The suggested lower limit of substantive significance for regression coefficients is 0.05 (Pedhazur, 1997). In a more conservative position, path coefficients of 0.10 and above are preferable. As shown in Figure 4, all path coefficients except Product Involvement to Shopping Enjoyment, Web skills to Shopping Enjoyment, and Trust to Behavioral Intention are over 0.10 thus satisfying both conservative criteria and the suggested lower limit. They are also statistically significant at $p = 0.001$. Overall, the IWISSM model explains a significant amount of variation in the dependent variable, Intention to Use the EC Website ($R^2 = 0.57$). Both Task Support Satisfaction as a measure of extrinsic motivation and Shopping Enjoyment as a measure of intrinsic motivation are significant predictors of Intention to Use the EC Website.

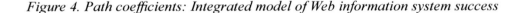

Figure 4. Path coefficients: Integrated model of Web information system success

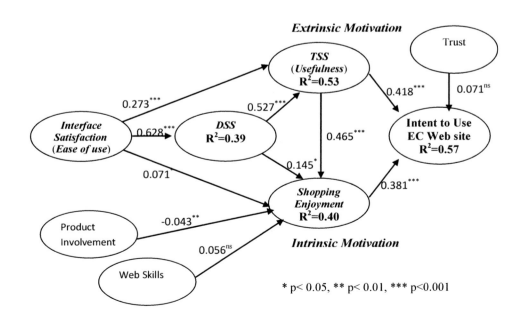

Table 9. Summary of hypothesis testing

	Hypothesis	Support	Significance Level
H1a	Interface Satisfaction positively influences Decision Support Satisfaction.	Yes	$p < 0.001$
H1b	Interface Satisfaction positively influences Task Support Satisfaction.	Yes	$p < 0.001$
H1c	Interface Satisfaction positively influences Shopping Enjoyment.	Yes	$p < 0.001$
H2	Decision Support Satisfaction is positively associated with Task Support Satisfaction.	Yes	$p < 0.001$
H3	Task Support Satisfaction positively affects Intention to Use EC Website.	Yes	$p < 0.001$
H4a	Decision Support Satisfaction positively affects Shopping Enjoyment.	Yes	$p < 0.001$
H4b	Task Support Satisfaction positively affects Shopping Enjoyment.	Yes	$p < 0.001$
H4c	Shopping Enjoyment positively affects Intention to Use EC Website.	Yes	$p < 0.001$
H5a	Product Involvement positively affects Shopping Enjoyment.	No	
H5b	Web Skills positively affects Shopping Enjoyment.	No	
H5c	Trust positively affects Intention to Use EC Website.	No	

The IWISSM model is also a nomological network and can be used to test the construct validity of the success dimensions. Constructs in a nomological network are considered valid if they predict or are predicted by the other constructs consistent with theoretical models and past research (Bagozzi, 1980; Straub, Limayem, & Karahanna-Evaristo, 1995). As shown in Figure 4, a high R^2 for each endogenous variable in the structural model demonstrates that this model can be used to predict each of the success dimensions within the nomological net.

Specifically, over 50% of the variance in Task Support Satisfaction is explained via Interface Satisfaction and Decision Support Satisfaction, and by the indirect effects of Interface Satisfaction through Decision Support Satisfaction. In addition, close to 40% of the variation in Decision Support Satisfaction is explained by Interface Sat-

isfaction. Over 40% of the variance in Shopping Enjoyment is explained by Interface Satisfaction, Decision Support Satisfaction, and Task Support Satisfaction and the indirect effects of Interface Satisfaction through Decision Support and Task Support Satisfaction. However, Product Involvement, Web Skills and Trust do not provide for significant paths in the model. Table 9 summarizes the results of the hypothesis testing.

DISCUSSION

Interestingly, the major information systems success dimensions from the Garrity and Sanders model all yielded significant path coefficients in the structural model test of the IWISS model (Figure 4). Both the extrinsic motivating factor, Task Support Satisfaction, and the intrinsic motivating factor, Shopping Enjoyment, yielded significant paths to the dependent variable, Intention to Use the EC Web site and helped to explain over 56% of the variance ($R^2 = 0.57$). The model lends support to the IWISS model.

In the web-based, consumer shopping environment, the primary intrinsic motivating factor is Shopping Enjoyment. That is, users are motivated by the holistic experience of interacting with computer technology in a manner that promotes enjoyment, (and perhaps also captivates their attention, and maintains their curiosity).

Interface Satisfaction is shown as a significant factor in determining Decision Support, Task Support Satisfaction and indirectly through those dimensions to Shopping Enjoyment (Intrinsic Motivation). This is consistent with the proposed model, since computer tools that are easy to use with well-designed interfaces should be enjoyable and captivating (Shopping Enjoyment), aid in the support of decision making (Decision Support Satisfaction), and support the entire task process (Task Support Satisfaction).

It is interesting to note that the additional variables from previous web use studies were not statistically significant. That is, hypotheses H5a, H5b, and H5c are not supported. Although Trust has a 0.40 correlation with Intent to Use the EC Website, its path is not significant in the model. In other words, the IWISS model accounts for most of the variation in Intent to Use the EC Website ($R^2 = 0.57$) but Trust does not add significant explanation of Intent to Use the EC Website above and beyond what is already explained by the main IS Success factors. The high correlations between Trust and the main dimensions of the IWISS model can also be observed in Table 8 and indicate the likelihood of shared variance within the model.

Study results suggest that Trust does not directly influence Intention to Use the web site *which appears contradictory to prior studies* involving TAM constructs (Gefen, Karahanna, & Straub,

2003; O'Donnell, Ferrin, Glassberg, & Sanders, 2004). However, in the development of the IWISS model we were not specifically interested in modeling Trust as an additional, endogenous variable or dimension of IS success. In our view, the level of Trust of a website by a user is best modeled as an independent variable or predictor but not as a component of IS success.

Upon closer examination, *Trust is significantly related to the major dimensions of the model, including Task Support (Perceived Usefulness) and Intention to Use, which is consistent with prior studies of Trust* (Table 8). The major difference in this study is that the IWISS model already accounts for significant variation in Intention to Use and Trust (modeled only as a direct effect on Intention to Use) does not explain significant variation above what is already predicted[3].

A further explanation of Trust in this study relates to study participants' perceived level of vulnerability (Risk) in using the sites. In the absence of Risk, Trust is not important in choosing one's actions (Lewis & Weigert, 1985; Rousseau et al., 1998). It may be inferred that the level of Perceived Risk could have lessened the importance of Trust in our study.

In order to test for moderating influences of Perceived Risk on Trust's direct impact on Intention to Use, we divided the study sample into a High Risk group and a Low Risk Group based on respondents' answers to the following questionnaire item: "I would use my credit card to purchase from this Web site." Subjects that felt their use of the website was a High Risk undertaking would be reluctant to use their credit card for purchases, whereas subjects in the Low Risk group are those that are willing to use their credit card.

The correlation between Trust and Intention to Use was 0.13 for the Low Risk group. This was not statistically significant at the 0.05 level. However, the correlation between Trust and Intention to Use for the High Risk group was 0.33, which was significant at the 0.01 level. In addition, the difference in the correlations between the two samples is significant[2] (p<0.01, t-statistic = 3.5). The results lend support to the notion that Trust directly impacts Behavioral Intention to Use, but only when the level of Perceived Risk is relatively high. Further research should investigate the influence of varying levels of Perceived Risk on the relative importance of Trust on Intention to Use a web site.

Finally, the Shopping Enjoyment factor (Intrinsic Motivation) was modeled as a function of Interface, Decision Support, and Task Support Satisfaction, as well as Product Involvement, and Web Skills. Although this model explained over 40% of the variation in Shopping Enjoyment ($R^2 = 0.40$) both Product Involvement and Web Skills did not have significant path coefficients to Shopping Enjoyment. This suggests that Shopping Enjoyment, as implemented in our study, is correctly modeled as a "state variable," meaning that it is a situational characteristic of the interaction between an individual and the situation. Since Interface Satisfaction, Decision Support and Task Support Satisfaction were the primary determinants of Shopping Enjoyment, this implies that the human computer interaction environment exerts a stronger influence on Shopping Enjoyment than these individual trait variables.

The nomological network presented in this paper along with the results regarding Shopping Enjoyment differ from other researchers findings on intrinsic motivation, such as Venkatesh (2000). Venkatesh (2000) and Moon & Kim (2001) view intrinsic motivation via Playfulness as an individual difference variable (trait) that is system-independent. Our results offer an alternative explanation of how intrinsic motivation (viewed as Shopping Enjoyment) fits within the realm of web-based information systems success and Use. Future research will have to explore Playfulness or Enjoyment as a component of the IS success model, especially in web-based environments.

CONCLUSION

The IWISS model extends the work of Koufaris (2000) and others by providing and validating a nomological network of factors based on motivation and flow theory and the Garrity and Sanders (1998) model. One of the objectives of this research project was to compare the IWISS model to TAM. In the IWISS model, Perceived Usefulness is expanded into two closely related but separate dimensions – Task Support Satisfaction and Decision Support Satisfaction. The two dimensions provide additional precision and explanatory power that is helpful to both system designers, who want to design specific support features, and for researchers, who wish to evaluate the system's impact on Task Support or Decision Support Satisfaction (Figure 5).

An important goal of our research was to understand why users find web systems acceptable and useful, and indeed this is important for both researchers and practitioners involved in web-based

Figure 5. Path coefficients: A comparison of TAM and IWISSM TAM model

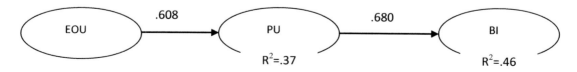

BI = Behavioral Intention to Use the website, EOU = Ease of Use (Interface Satisfaction), PU = Perceived Usefulness (Task Support Satisfaction).

Table 10. Summary of Selected Studies of Website Usage and Explained Variance

Literature	Dependent	Independent	Explained Variance (R^2)
This Paper, IWISSM Model	Intention to Use EC Website	Task Support, Decision Support, Interface Satisfaction, Shopping Enjoyment, (Trust, Product Involvement, Web Skills)	0.57
Koufaris (2002)	Intention to Return	Perceived Usefulness, Shopping Enjoyment, (Perceived Control, Concentration, Perceived Ease of Use)	0.55
Moon and Kim (2001)	Behavioral Intent to Use Web	Perceived Usefulness, Ease of Use, Attitude toward using	0.38
Venkatesh (2000)	Behavioral Intention to Use	Perceived Usefulness, Computer Self-Efficacy, Perceptions of External Control, Computer Anxiety, Objective Usability (Playfulness, Perceived Enjoyment, Ease of Use)	0.35
Lederer et al., (2000)	Web site Usage	Ease of Use, Usefulness	0.15

(Variables in parentheses are insignificant within the model tested).

systems development. From a practical standpoint, systems that are judged successful become a part of the organizational decision making framework and or part of the organization's system structure and processes. Additionally, IS success models are used by researchers who wish to build models and enhance our understanding of the factors that generate successful systems. A by-product of this empirical research is the development of normative guidelines that will then be used by practitioners. It is thus imperative for IS success models to be both valid and precise enough to be useful for developing practical guidelines.

The IWISS model provides for additional explanatory power and provides for a greater understanding of the complex factors that may be used to predict web site use. As Table 10 il-lustrates, this has received significant research attention over the past decade.

From a researchers perspective, the IWISS model is both a nomological network that can be used to test the construct validity of the variables involved in technology acceptance and IS Success measurement as well as a path for conducting future research. Future research can apply an empirical test of the model for the further enhance-ment and understanding of information systems success measurement and prediction.

REFERENCES

Adams, D.A.; Nelson, R.R.; & Todd, P.A. (1992). Perceived usefulness, ease of use, and usage of information technology: A replication. *MIS Quarterly*, 16(2), 227-247.

Agarwal, R. & Prasad, J. (1999). Are individual differences germane to the acceptance of new information technologies? *Decision Sciences*, 30(2), 361-391.

Ajzen, I. & Fishbein, M. (1980). *Understanding attitudes and predicting social behavior*. Englewood Cliffs: Prentice Hall.

Bagozzi, R.P. (1980). *Causal methods in marketing*. New York: John Wiley and Sons.

Csikszentimihalyi, M. (1975). *Beyond boredom and anxiety*. San Francisco: Jossey-Bass.

Davis, F.D. Bagozzi, R.P., & Warshaw, P.R. (1992). Extrinsic and intrinsic motivation to use computers in the workplace. *Journal of Applied Social Psychology*, 22(14), 1111-1132.

Davis, F.D. (1989). Perceived usefulness, perceived ease of use, and user acceptance of information technology. *MIS Quarterly*, 13(3), 319-340.

Davis, F.D.; Bagozzi, R.P.; & Warshaw, P.R. (1989). User acceptance of computer technology: a comparison of two theoretical models. *Management Science*, 35(8), 982-1003.

Deci, E.L. (1971). Effects of externally mediated rewards on intrinsic motivation. *Journal of Personality and Social Psychology*, 18, 105-115.

DeLone W.H. & McLean, E.R. (1992). Information systems success: The quest for the dependent variable. *Information Systems Research*, 3(1), 61-95.

Doll, W.J.; Hendrickson, A.; & Deng, X. (1998). Using Davis's perceived usefulness and ease of use instruments for decision making: A confirmatory and multi-group invariance analysis. *Decision Sciences*, 29(4), 839-869.

Doll, W.J. & Torkzadeh, G. (1988). The measurement of end-user computing satisfaction. *MIS Quarterly*, 12(2), 259-274.

Fishbein, M. & Ajzen, I. (1975).*Belief, attitude, intentions and behavior: An introduction to theory and research*. Boston: Addison-Wesley.

Fornell, C., & Larcker, D. (1981). Evaluating structural equation models with unobservable variables and measurement error. *Journal of Marketing Research*, 18, 39-50.

Fornell, C. (1982). *A second generation of multivariate analysis*. New York, NY: Praeger.

Fornell, C. & Bookstein, F.L. (1982). Two structural equation models: LISREL and PLS applied to consumer exit-voice theory, *Journal of Marketing Research*, 19(4), 440-452.

Franz, C.R. & Robey, D. (1986). Organizational context, user involvement and the usefulness of information systems. *Decision Sciences*, 17(3), 329-356.

Garrity, E.J.; Glassberg, B.; Kim, Y.J.; Sanders, G.L.; & Shin, S.K. (2005). An experimental investigation of web-based information systems success in the context of electronic commerce. *Decision Support Systems*, 39(3), 485-503.

Garrity, E.J. & Sanders, G.L. (1998). Dimensions of information systems success measurement, in *Information Systems Success Measurement*. Garrity, E.J. & Sanders G.L (eds.), Hershey: Idea Group Publishing, 13-45.

Gefen, D.; Karahanna, E.; & Straub, D. (2003). Trust and TAM in online shopping: An integrated model. *MIS Quarterly* 27(1), 51-90.

Ghani, J.A. & Deshpande, S.P. (1994). Task characteristics and the experience of optimal flow in human-computer interaction. *The Journal of Psychology*. 128(4), 381-391.

Ghani, J.A., Supnick, R., & Rooney, P. (1991). The experience of flow in computer-mediated and in face-to-face groups. J.I. DeGross, I. Benbasat, G. DeSanctis, & C.M. Beath, (eds.) *Proceedings of the 12th International Conference on Information Systems*, New York, 229-237.

Goodhue, D.L. (1990). Developing a theory-based measure of user satisfaction: The task systems fit questionnaire. *Working Paper, Information and Decision Sciences, University of Minnesota.*

Hackbarth, G.; Grover, V.; & Yi, M.Y. (2003). Computer playfulness and anxiety: positive and negative mediators of the system experience effect on perceived ease of use. *Information and Management*, 40, 221-232.

Hoffman, D.L. & Novak, T.P. (1996). Marketing in hypermedia computer-mediated environments: Conceptual foundations. *Journal of Marketing*, 60, 50-68.

Jarvenpaa, S.L.; Tractinsky, N.; Saarinen, L.; & Vitale, M. (1999). Consumer trust in an Internet store: A cross-cultural validation. *Journal of Computer Mediated Communications.* 5(2) 1-35.

Jarvenpaa, S.L.; Tractinsky, N.; & Vitale, M. (2000). Consumer trust in an Internet store. *Information and Technology Management*, 1(1), 45-71.

Jarvenpaa, S.L.; & Todd, P.A. (1997a). Is there a future for retailing on the Internet? R.A. Peterson, (ed.) *Electronic Marketing and the Consumer.* Thousand Oaks, CA: Sage.

Jarvenpaa, S.L.; & Todd, P.A. (1997b). Consumer reactions to electronic shopping on the World Wide Web. *International Journal of Electronic Commerce*, 1(2), 59-88.

Keil, M.; Beranek, P.M.; & Konsynski, B.R. (1995). Usefulness and ease of use: Field study evidence regarding task considerations. *Decision Support Systems*, 13(1), 75-91.

Kim, Y.J., E.J. Garrity, G.L. Sanders, and B.A. Sherman. (2004). A means-end model of IS success: Toward understanding the cognitive structure of IS users. *Working Paper State University of New York at Buffalo.*

Koufaris, M. (2002). Applying the technology acceptance model and flow theory to online consumer behavior. *Information Systems Research*, 13(2), 205-223.

Lederer, A.L., Maupin, D.J., Sena, M.P., & Zhuang, Y. (2000). The technology acceptance model and the World Wide Web. *Decision Support Systems*, 29(3), 269-282.

Lewis, D., & Weigert, A. (1985). Trust as a social reality. *Social Forces*, 63, 967-985.

Mathieson, K. (1991). Predicting use intentions: Comparing the technology acceptance model with the theory of planned behavior. *Information Systems Research*, 2(3), 173-191.

Mayer, R.C. & Davis, J.H. (1999). The effect of the performance appraisal system on trust for management: A field quasi-experiment. *Journal of Applied Psychology*, 84(1), 123-136.

Mehrabian, A. & Russel. (1974). *An approach to environmental psychology.* Cambridge, MA.: MIT Press.

Moon, J. & Kim, Y. (2001). Extending the TAM for a world wide web context. *Information and Management*, 38, 217-230.

Novak, T.P., Hoffman, D.L., & Yung, Y.F. (2000). Measuring the customer experience in online environments: A structural modeling approach. *Marketing Science*, 19(1), 19-42.

Novak, T.P., Hoffman, D.L., & Duhachek, A. (2003). The influence of goal-directed and experiential activities on online flow experiences. *Journal of Consumer Psychology*, 13(1-2), 3-16.

O'Donnell, J.B.; Ferrin, D.L.; Glassberg, B.; & Sanders, G.L. (2004). The influence of web site characteristics on consumer trust and the purchase decision. *Working Paper, Canisius College.*

O'Keefe, R.M. & McEachern, T. (1998). Web-based customer decision support systems. *Communications of the ACM*, 41(3), 71-78.

Pace, S. A grounded theory of the flow experiences of web users. (2004). *International Journal of Human-Computer Studies*, 60(3), 327-363.

Pedhazur, E.J. (1997). *Multiple regression in behavioral research: Explanation and prediction.* Fort Worth: Harcourt Brace College Publishers.

Rousseau, D.M.; Sitkin, S.B.; Burt, R.S.; & Camerer, C. (1998), Not so different after all: A cross-disciplined view of trust. *Academy of Management Review*, 23(3), 393-404.

Sanders, G.L. (1984). MIS/DSS success measure. *Systems, Objectives, Solutions*, 4, 29-34.

Scott, W.E., Farh, J., & Podaskoff, P.M. (1988). The effects of intrinsic and extrinsic reinforcement contingencies on task behavior. *Organizational Behavior and Human Decision Processes*, 41, 405-425.

Straub, D.; Limayem, M.; & Karahanna-Evaristo, E. (1995). Measuring system usage: Implications for IS theory and testing. *Management Science.* 41(8), 1328-1342.

Tobias, R.D. (1999). *An introduction to partial least squares regression.* SAS Institute, Inc., 1-8.

Trevino, L.K. & Webster, J. (1992). Flow in computer-mediated communication: Electronic mail and voice mail evaluation and impacts. *Communication Research*, 19(5), 539-573.

Venkatesh, V. (2000). Determinants of perceived ease of use: Integrating control, intrinsic motivation, and emotion into the technology acceptance model. *Information Systems Research*, 11(4), 342-365.

Webster, J., & Martocchio, J.J. (1992). Microcomputer playfulness: Development of a measure with workplace implications. *MIS Quarterly*, 16(2), 201-226.

Werts, C.E.; Linn, R.L.; & Joreskog, K.G. (1974). Interclass reliability estimates: Testing structural assumptions. *Educational and Psychological Measurement*, 34(1), 25-33.

Wold, H. (1974). Causal flows with latent variables, *European Economic Review*, 5, 67-86.

Wold, H. (1985). Partial least squares, in *Encyclopedia of Statistical Sciences*, Kotz, S. & Johnson, N.L. (eds.), 6, New York: Wiley, 581-591.

ENDNOTES

[1]   Some items from frequently used instruments were classified by the expert panel as "out of place," and were later identified as independent variables.

[2]   The correlations were first converted to z-scores and a two-tailed test of significance was performed to determine if the correlations were drawn from the same population.

[3]   Our main concern was to test the validity of the Integrated Web Information System Success Model. Alternatively, Trust could also be modeled as an antecedent to Task Support Satisfaction.

APPENDIX 1

Operationalization of Latent Variables: Decision Support, Task Support, Interface Satisfaction

	Decision Support Satisfaction	
D7	This Web site improves the quality of my purchasing decision. making.	Sanders (1984)
D8	Use of this Web site enables me to make better purchasing decisions.	Sanders (1984)
D9	This Web site assists me in making a decision more effectively.	Davis (1989)
D10	Use of this Web site enables me to set my priorities in making the purchase decision.	Sanders (1984)
	Task Support Satisfaction	
T7	I could come to rely on this Web site in performing my task.	Sanders (1984)
T9	Using this Web site enables me to accomplish tasks more quickly.	Davis (1989)
T10	This Web site makes it easier to do my task.	Davis (1989)
	Interface Satisfaction	
I1	This Web site contains understandable graphics.	Adapted from Lederer et al (2000)
I5	Learning to use this Web site was easy for me.	Davis (1989)
I8	This Web site is user-friendly.	Davis (1989), Doll & Torkzadeh (1988), Goodhue (1990)
I9	This Web site is easy to use.	Davis (1989), Doll & Torkzadeh (1988), Goodhue (1990)
I13	It would be easy for me to become skillful at using this Web site.	Davis (1989)
I16	This Web site is easy to navigate.	Lederer et al (2000)

APPENDIX 2

Operationalization of Latent Variables:
Behavioral Intention to Use, Shopping Enjoyment

	Behavioral Intent to Use	
U2	The use of this Web site would be critical in my future decisions.	Adapted from Franz & Robey (1986)
U5	I intend to increase my use of this Web site in the future.	Agarwal & Prasad (1999)
U6	In the future, I plan to use this Web site often.	Adapted from Moon & Kim (2001)
	Shopping Enjoyment	
P4	I found this Web site interesting.	Ghani, et al. (1991)
P5	I found my Web site visit enjoyable.	Ghani, et al. (1991)
P6	I found my Web site visit exciting.	Ghani, et al. (1991)
P7	I found my Web site visit fun.	Ghani, et al. (1991)

APPENDIX 3

Operationalization of Latent Variable: Trust

	Trust	
TR1	I would be comfortable dealing with this retailer having responsibility for the delivery of the product.	Adapted from Mayer & Davis (1999)
TR2	I would be comfortable dealing with this retailer, even if I could not monitor its actions.	Adapted from Mayer & Davis (1999)
TR3	This retailer is trustworthy.	Jarvenpaa et al. (2000)
TR4	This retailer wants to be known as one who keeps promises and commitments.	Jarvenpaa et al. (2000)
TR5	I trust that this retailer keeps my interests in mind.	Jarvenpaa et al. (2000)
TR6	This retailer's behavior meets my expectations.	Jarvenpaa et al. (2000)

* *Note: All questionnaire items in Appendices use a 7-point Likert scale, varying from Strongly disagree to Strongly agree.*

This work was previously published in Journal of Electronic Commerce in Organizations, Vol 5, Issue 4, edited by M. Khosrow-Pour, pp. 18-38, copyright 2007 by IGI Publishing, formerly known as Idea Group Publishing (an imprint of IGI Global).

Chapter XVII
A Critical Review of Online Consumer Behavior

Christy MK Cheung
City University of Hong Kong, Hong Kong

Gloria WW Chan
City University of Hong Kong, Hong Kong

Moez Limayem
City University of Hong Kong, Hong Kong

ABSTRACT

The topic of online consumer behavior has been examined under various contexts over the years. Although researchers from a variety of business disciplines have made significant progress over the past few years, the scope of these studies is rather broad, the studies appear relatively fragmented and no unifying theoretical model is found in this research area. In view of this, we provide an exhaustive review of the literature and propose an integrative model of online consumer behavior so as to analyze the online consumer behavior in a systematic way. This proposed framework not only provides us with a cohesive view of online consumer behavior, but also serves as a salient guideline for researchers in this area. We conclude our paper with a research agenda for the study of online consumer behavior.

INTRODUCTION

Online consumer behavior has become an emerging research area with an increasing number of publications per year. The research articles appear in a variety of journals and conference proceedings in the fields of information systems, market-ing, management, and psychology. A review of these articles indicates that researchers mostly draw theories from classical consumer behavior research, such as behavioral learning (Skinner, 1938), personality research (Folkes, 1988), information processing (Bettman, 1979), and attitude models (Fishbein, 1975).

A close examination of the literature in this area reveals that most of the components of consumer behavior theory have been applied to the study of online consumer behavior. However, the application is not as straightforward as simply borrowing the components and applying them. There are still significant differences between offline and online consumer behavior that warrant a distinguishing conceptualization. For example, Vijayasarathy (2001) integrated the web specific factors (online shopping aid) into the theory of reasoned action (TRA) to better explain consumer online shopping behavior. Song and Zahedi (2001) built on the model of the theory of planned behavior (TPB) and examined the effects of website design on the adoption of Internet shopping.

A review of online consumer research reveals that the scope of published studies is rather broad, the studies appear relatively fragmented with contradictory results, and only very few prior studies (e.g., Jarvenpaa and Todd, 1996; Koufaris et al., 2001) have attempted to systematically review and develop a framework for the study of this important research area. In this vein, the objectives of this study are: (1) to provide a systematic and exhaustive review of online consumer behavior research, (2) to identify important constructs that are specific to the context of online purchasing, (3) to propose an integrated framework that enhances our understanding of the underlying driving factors of online consumer behavior, and (4) to provide directions for future research in this area.

The paper is organized as follows. Section II outlines the research approach and Section III describes the results and the literature analysis. Section IV presents an integrated framework for the study of online consumer behavior. Finally, Section V addresses the discussion, and Section VI concludes the paper by considering the future research agenda in this area.

A STRUCTURED RESEARCH APPROACH

Prior literature provides us with a rich foundation on which to build a research framework for the study of online consumer behavior. As suggested in Douglas et al. (1994), strong theoretical and conceptual frameworks can be developed through an integration of constructs from different research traditions and disciplines. In the current study, we review the prior literature of online consumer behavior and analyze the theories and the underpinning factors.

A systematic and structured approach in search and review is strongly recommended in writing sound IS literature reviews (Webster and Watson, 2002). In this study, we conducted an exhaustive and systematic electronic search using ProQuest, Social Science Citation Index, and IEEE Xplore. Moreover, we conducted a literature search in the EC-specific journals including *International Journal of Electronic Commerce* and *Internet Research: Electronic Networking Applications and Policy*. In addition to the search for referred journal articles, we included three IS-related conference proceedings (AMCIS, HICSS, ICIS) in our literature search and analysis.

The literature search was based on keywords such as "online shopping", "Internet shopping" and "online consumer purchasing behavior". Each article was reviewed and screened in order to eliminate the articles that were not pertinent to the current focus. A total of 355 articles in the area of online consumer behavior were identified from 1994 to June 2002. For any study to be included in our analysis, it has to focus primarily on consumer purchasing behavior on the Web. Electronic copies of most articles were obtained from digital libraries and online databases.

LITERATURE ANALYSIS RESULTS

The 355 articles were analyzed and classified in terms of publication year, title, and the underlying theory/framework. We believe that this clarification provides fruitful insights about online consumer scholars. In particular, this analysis helps researchers discover deficiencies and identify potential unexplored research opportunities in this area.

Historical Overview

The importance of an emerging research area is reflected in the increasing number of publications per year. The number of articles in the online consumer behavior literature has risen dramatically in the past four years, with over 120 articles being published in 2001 (see Figure 1).

Publications

Research on online consumer behavior appears in a variety of journals and conference proceedings in the fields of Information Systems, Marketing, Management and Psychology. In Information Systems it appears that online consumer behavior research is not yet part of the mainstream. As is typical for an emerging research area, most articles appear in new, innovative journals such as the *International Review of Retail, Distribution and Consumer Research, International Journal of Electronic Commerce* and *Internet Research: Electronic Networking Applications and Policy.* We expect that as this research area matures, articles will begin to find their way into more established journals such as *MIS Quarterly* and *Information Systems Research.* Moreover, it is interesting to find that many non-IS journals such as the *International Review of Retail* and *Distribution and Consumer Research,* rank the highest in terms of number of articles published in this area. This illustrates the importance of this research area to MIS and related disciplines. Table 1 shows the ranking of the journals that have published articles in online consumer behavior.

Figure 1. Number of publications by year

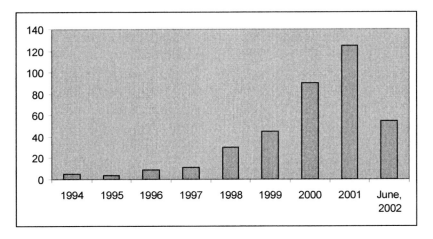

Table 1. Number of online consumer behavior research studies in journals

Journals	Count
The International Review of Retail, Distribution and Consumer Research	24
International Journal of Electronic Commerce	18
Internet Research: Electronic Networking Applications and Policy	11
Communications of the ACM	8
Information & Management	7
Journal of Marketing Communications	7
Electronic Markets	6
Journal of Marketing Practice: Applied Marketing Science	6
Quarterly Journal of Electronic Commerce	6
Electronic Commerce Research	5
Business Strategy Review	7
Decision Support Systems	7
Journal of Business Research	7
Journal of Computer Information Systems	7
Journal of Retailing	7
Marketing Management	7
IEEE Transactions on Systems, Man and Cybernetics, Part A	7
International Journal of Human-Computer Studies	3
Management of Engineering and Technology	3
MIT Sloan Management Review	3
Journal of Consumer Marketing	3
California Management Review	2
e-Service Journal	2
International Journal of Retail & Distribution Management	2
Journal of Advertising Research	2
Journal of Industrial Economics	2
Management Decision	2
Marketing Science	2
Psychology & Marketing	2
International Journal of Information Management	2
International Journal of Service Industry Management	2
Journal of Computer-Mediated Communication	2

Underlying Theory and Framework

As part of our analysis, we identified the theories that are used by the authors of the 355 papers surveyed. Findings show that the Theory of Reasoned Action (TRA) and its family theories including the Technology Acceptance Model (TAM) and the Theory of Planned Behavior (TPB) are the dominant theories in this area. Expectation-Confirmation Theory (ECT) and Innovation Diffusion Theory (IDT) have also been repeatedly tested in the study of online consumer behavior. Table 2 lists the five most frequently used theories and their corresponding references.

The findings show that most authors depend heavily on theories from the TRA family (TPB, TAM, and TRA), while other useful theories such as the flow theory are ignored. Researchers, therefore, should try to explore new theories and frameworks and investigate online consumer behavior from different perspectives and angles.

AN INTEGRATED FRAMEWORK FOR THE STUDY OF ONLINE CONSUMER BEHAVIOR

The prevalence of the Internet has aroused enormous interest in the study of consumer-based

Table 2. References of online consumer behavior research

Theory	References
Expectation – Confirmation Theory	[7] [8] [57]
Innovation Diffusion Theory	[7] [8] [36] [88] [99] [101]
Technology Acceptance Model	[6] [7] [8] [13] [18] [43] [56] [66] [75] [77] [88] [89]
Theory of Planned Behavior	[6] [7] [8] [20] [51] [56] [75] [76] [89] [100] [104]
Theory of Reasoned Action	[43] [51] [52][53] [56] [60][76] [100] [110] [111]

electronic commerce in recent years. In particular, the focus of prior studies was on investigating factors affecting the intention and adoption of consumer online purchase.

Early studies in online consumer behavior largely sought to explore how consumers adopt and use online purchase. Specifically, the emphasis was on the antecedents of consumer online purchasing intention and adoption. Companies, however, have started to realize that in the digital economy, competitors are just a click away. Initial adoption by consumers is only the first step towards overall success, and companies that succeed in their e-business initiatives are adept at creating and maintaining a long-term sustainable relationship with loyal customers. Thus, research in the consumer continuance behavior (repurchase) becomes increasingly salient.

Online Consumer Behavior: Intention, Adoption, and Continuance

Our literature review revealed that no prior study has attempted to link the three key concepts of intention, adoption, and continuance and investigate the process of online consumer purchase as a whole.

Fishbein's Attitudinal Model

Fishbein's attitudinal model has been widely used in the marketing context (Lilien et al., 1992) and this paradigm provides researchers with a useful lens for examining the factors explaining consumer purchasing intention and adoption. According to this model, behavior is predominantly determined by intention. Other factors like attitudes, subjective norms, and perceived behavioral control are also shown to be related to an appropriate set of salient behavioral, normative, and control beliefs about the behavior. However, Fishbein's model stops at the adoption level and does not capture other important factors that explain and predict consumer continuance behavior (repurchase).

Expectation-Confirmation Model

The expectation-confirmation model (Oliver, 1980), on the other hand, focuses on the post-purchase behavior. It is a widely used model in the consumer behavior literature, particularly in explaining consumer satisfaction and repeat purchase. Satisfaction is the central notion of this model and it is formed by the gap between expectation and perceived performance. The expectation-confirmation theory suggests that if the perceived performance meets one's expectation, confirmation is formed and consumers are satisfied. Bhattacherjee (2001b) stated that satisfied users are more likely to continue the IS use.

Determinants of Online Consumer Behavior

Existing studies on the determinants of online consumer behavior can be separated into five major domain areas including individual/consumer characteristics, environmental influences, product/service characteristics, medium characteristics, and online merchant and intermediary characteristics. Table 3 summarizes the five domain areas and highlights the key constructs used in explaining online consumer behavior.

The impact of Individual/Consumer characteristics on the intention and adoption of IS/IT is a dominant research perspective in the IS literature (Zmud, 1979). In the context of online consumer behavior, Goldsmith (2000) and Limayem et al. (2000) found that personal innovativeness is a personality trait explains consumer online buying intention. Bellman et al. (1999) and Kim and Lim (2001) focused on the demographic variables to explain online consumer purchasing. Gefen (2002) and Lee (1999) focused on online repurchase and contended that consumer trust and consumer satisfaction were the key antecedents of continued purchase.

Table 3. Determinants of online consumer behavior

Domain Area	Description	Key Constructs I	llustrative Research
Individual/ Consumer Characteristics	Referring to internal individual factors and behavioral characteristics	Attitude Demographics Flow Motivation Perceived Risk Personal Innovativeness Satisfaction Trust	[6][13][51][52][75][76] [3][12][59][92][114][118] [63][85][119][120] [18][83][98][104][110] [9][43][51][52][67][81] [36][38][75][76][93] [7][8][44][65][66] [43][51][52][65][89][97]
Environmental Influences	Referring to the structural influences, including market-related issues (uncertainty, competition, and concentration), national and international issues (legal structure, trade restrictions, and culture).	Exposure Perceived Behavioral Control Subjective Norm	[59][60][88][103] [6][9][63][75][76][103] [6][56][75][76][88][100]
Product/Service Characteristics	Referring to knowledge about the product, product type, frequency of purchase, tangibility, and product quality.	Price Product Knowledge Product Type	[50][73][87][98][104] [9][40][67][69][94] [9][44][73][92][118]
Medium Characteristics	Referring to both traditional IS attributes (ease of use, quality, security, and reliability) and web specific factors (navigation, interface, and network speed).	Convenience Ease of Use Information Quality Navigation Security Shopping Aids Usefulness	[18][59][67][69][93] [13][18][43][72][87][88] [44]59][65][87][119][120] [13][18][67][72][87] [65][72][73][87][98] [42][72][111][112] [6][13][18][43][88]
Merchants and Intermediate Characteristics	Referring to the key attributes/features of the online stores.	Brand Privacy and Security Control Service Quality	[43][51][52][97][115] [59][67][69][87][95] [33][78][97][104][109]

Environmental factors refer to the structural influences from the electronic commerce (EC) environment, including market-related issues (uncertainty, competition, and concentration), national and international issues (legal structure, trade restrictions, and culture). According to Markus and Soh (2002), structural influences are "physical, social, and economic arrangements that shape EC business models and influence individual and organizational use of the Internet". In the context of online consumer behavior, several researchers (e.g., Limayem and Khalifa, 2000; Limayem et al., 2000) provided evidence for the significant influence of subjective norm and perceived behavioral control on online consumer purchasing intention and adoption.

Jarvenpaa and Todd (1996) argue that price, quality, and product type are the three key elements in shaping consumers' perception. In suggested fragmentation, product/service characteristics mainly refer to knowledge about the product, product type, frequency of purchase, tangibility, differentiation and price. Bobbitt and Dabholkar (2001) examined the impact of product knowledge and product type on online purchasing intention and adoption. Liao and Cheung (2001) and Jarvenpaa and Todd (1996) postulated that price has a significant impact on online purchasing intention and online purchasing adoption respectively.

Figure 2. Framework of online consumer behavior

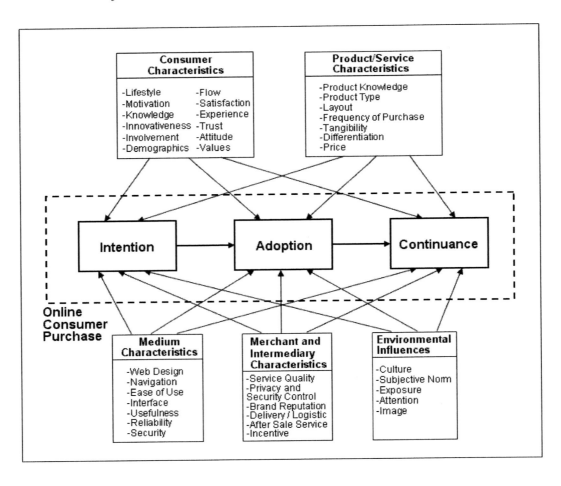

Characteristics of systems have been extensively studied in the IS literature. Traditional IS attributes such as ease of use, quality, security and reliability are included in the study of electronic commerce systems. Additionally, web specific factors such as ease of navigation, interface and network speed are also considered in the current study. Chau et al. (2000) examined the effects of presentation mode, search engines, and navigation structure of product items on the adoption of Internet shopping.

Spiller and Lohse (1998) have suggested a broad classification of Internet retail stores as well as the key attributes and features of online stores. These studies provided us with a better insight into the study of online merchant and intermediary characteristics. In the current study, we included factors like service quality (e.g., Liu and Arnett, 1999; Ruyter et al., 2001), privacy and security control (e.g., Lee and Park, 2001; Lee, 2002), brand/reputation (e.g., Heijden e al., 2001; Jarvenpaa, 1999; Jarvenpaa et al., 2000), delivery/logistic (e.g., Goldsmith and Bridges, 2000; Liang and Huang, 1998), after sales services (e.g., Lee, 2002) and incentive (e.g., Bhattacherjee, 2001a) in our framework of online consumer behavior.

An Integrative Model of Online Consumer Behavior

Intention, adoption, and continuance are the key building blocks of our proposed framework of online consumer behavior. The five domain areas were integrated into the key constructs (intention, adoption, and continuance) and to form a framework (as shown in Figure 2) for the study of online consumer behavior. This proposed framework not only provides us with a cohesive view of online consumer behavior, but also serves as a salient guidance for researchers in this research area.

In the following section, we implicitly investigated the three key elements by mapping prior literature into the five domains. For example, the impact of age on intention was investigated by one study and the impact of age on adoption was investigated by seven studies. However, no study explored the link between age and continuance.

Consumer Online Purchase Intention

Based on the theory of reasoned action and other related theories in this research area, the key factors of attitude, subjective norm, and perceived behavior control are largely postulated as the determinants of consumer online purchase intention (e.g. Bhattacherjee, 2000; Keen et al., 2000; Limayem et al., 2000). Similarly, perceived ease of use and perceived usefulness stemming from technology acceptance model (TAM), have also received enormous attention (e.g. Chau et al., 2000; Lin and Lu, 2000).

Trust and perceived risk (e.g. Jarvenpaa et al., 2000; Pavlou, 2001; Ruyter e al., 2001) have been widely investigated in the study of consumer online purchase intention. Some recent studies (e.g. Cheung and Lee, 2001 & 2001a; Lee and Turban, 2001) focused primarily on the trust formation process in the context of Internet shopping. Product/service characteristics, are the key research topics are product type (e.g. Bobbitt and Dabholkar, 2001; Sohn, 1999) and price (e.g. Degeratu et al., 2000; Liang and Lai, 2001). For instance, Sohn (1999) argued that products like CDs, books or canned food which do not require a physical examination before being purchased are easier to sell on the Internet. Brand/reputation (e.g. Jarvenpaa et al. 2000; Ruyter et al., 2001) and service quality (e.g. Ruyter et al., 2001, Song and Zahedi, 2001) are also important in affecting online purchase intentions.

Consumer Online Purchase (Adoption)

As is the case for consumer online purchase intention, researchers (e.g. Bobbitt and Dabholkar, 2001; Chau et al., 2000; Goldsmith and Bridges, 2000; Koufaris et al., 2001; Limayem et al., 2000; Raijas and Tuunainen, 2001; Vellido et al., 2000) extensively employed attitudinal theoretical models in the study of consumer online purchase and thoroughly investigated the antecedent factors like intention, attitude, subjective norm, perceived behavior control, ease of use, and perceived usefulness.

Moreover, we observed a significant number of empirical studies that proposed and tested factors affecting consumer online purchase. Compared to the study of intention, the studies of consumer online purchase are quite fragmented and widely dispersed in the five main categories. For examples, demographics (e.g. Bellman et al., 1999; Bhatnagar et al., 2000; Li et al., 1999; Phau and Poon, 2000; Ramaswami et al., 2000) have been widely considered in the study of online consumer behavior. Researchers primarily investigated factors such as age, gender, income, education, and the like in determining consumer online purchase. In terms of medium characteristics, a number of web specific factors including navigation (e.g. Chau et al., 2000; Liang and Lai, 2002), interface (e.g. Schoenbachler and Gordon, 2002), security (e.g. Goldsmith, 2001; Kim and Lim, 2001), accessibility (e.g. Chen and Sukpanich, 1998; Lee, 2002), social presence (e.g. Kumar and Benbasat, 2001) and online shopping aid (e.g. Vijayasarathy, 2001) have been widely investigated in these prior studies. In terms of merchant and intermediary characteristics, factors like privacy and security protection (e.g. Kim and Lim, 2001; Lee, 2002) and brand/reputation (e.g. Ruyter et al., 2001; Ward and Lee, 2000) are frequently studied in consumer online purchase adoption.

Consumer Online Repurchase (Continuance)

Research on continuance is in its infancy. Bhattacherjee (2001a) is one of the very first attempts to explain consumer online repurchasing behavior. His proposed model was formulated on the basis of expectation and confirmation theory (ECT), and postulated satisfaction, confirmation, and loyalty incentives as salient factors affecting consumer online repurchasing.

Our literature review and analysis revealed that prior research on consumer online repurchase placed more emphasis on the impact of psychological factors. For instance, considerable attention has been given to the study of trust (Fung and Lee, 1999; Lee et al., 2000) and satisfaction formation (Khalifa and Liu, 2001) in the context of consumer-based electronic commerce. Very few studies, however, have attempted to investigate the impact of product/service characteristics, medium characteristics, and merchant and intermediary characteristics on consumer online repurchasing. Liang and Lai's (2002) was one recent study that explored the impact of web page design such as navigation, security, search attribute, and shopping aids. Similarly, Gefen and Devine (2001) focused on merchant characteristics and investigated the effect of service quality on consumer online purchase continuance using SERVQUAL.

DISCUSSIONS

Electronic commerce is rapidly changing the way people do business all over the world. In the business-to-consumer segment, sales through the web have been increasing dramatically over the last few years. Customers, not only those from well-developed countries but also those from developing countries, are getting used to the new shopping channel. Understanding the factors that affect intention, adoption and repurchase are important for researchers and practitioners alike.

Our analysis of over 300 research articles on online consumer behavior has showed that this research area has received tremendous attention over the past few years. Most of the studies have borrowed theories from consumer behavior research and over emphasized the factors affecting a consumer's intention and adoption of online shopping while ignoring the factors leading to repurchase. Our review illustrates the need for a unifying framework that can guide research in this important area. Consequently, the proposed model shows how five important factors (consumer characteristics, environment influences, product/service characteristics, medium characteristics, merchant and intermediary characteristics) are related to three key elements (intention, adoption, repurchase).

Antecedents of Intention, Adoption and Continuance

Our findings confirm that online consumer behavior is still immature and exhibits an important research potential. The impact of several constructs of TPB, TRA and TAM such as attitude, subjective norms, and perceived behavioral control has been widely studied while other important factors have been ignored. As illustrated in Figure 2, factors related to consumer characteristics like demographics, personality, value, lifestyle, consumer resources, and knowledge were not explored. In addition, factors related to the medium characteristics (network availability, reliability, stability, speed, externalities, information quality, shopping aids medium richness and convenience), and environmental influences (culture and reference groups) have not been fully investigated in prior studies.

In terms of adoption, we found that consumer characteristics and medium characteristics are the key categories that most prior research explored. For example, characteristics such as demographics, lifestyle, motivation, behavioral characteristics, knowledge, attitude, intention, personal innovativeness, experience, trust, perceived risk, satisfaction, involvement and flow are well-tested and extensively studied. In addition, factors related to merchant and intermediary characteristics including website design, network reliability, search, network speed, usefulness, information quality, search attribute, shopping aids, channel, convenience and enjoyable are frequently explored.

Compared to intention and adoption, continuance is an under-researched area. The impact of factors like trust and satisfaction in the domain of consumer characteristics, ease of use, usefulness and search attribute in the domain of medium characteristics, and delivery in the domain of merchant and intermediary characteristics on continuance are yet to be investigated.

CONCLUSION AND AGENDA FOR FUTURE RESEARCH

The purpose of this study was to conduct a thorough analysis of the literature in the area of online consumer behavior. A research framework was suggested to better understand existing studies and to highlight under-researched areas. Our findings show that the literature on online consumer behavior is rather fragmented. Most studies investigated intention and adoption of online shopping while continuance behavior (repurchase) is seriously under-researched. Moreover, our analysis helped us to identify several fruitful directions for future research.

1. Future research could use our suggested framework as a basis to empirically explore the factors affecting the online consumer purchasing process.

2. Our findings show that existing studies focus on the factors affecting intention of buying from the web. They do that by using TRA and its related theories. We therefore encourage researchers to explore theories from different disciplines and use them to study consumers' adoption and continuance of online shopping. For example, Csikszentmihalyi (1975) introduced the concept of flow, which he defined as "the holistic experience that people feel when they act with total involvement". Some researchers (Csikszentmihalyi, 1990; Ghani and Desh-

pande, 1994; Trevino and Webster, 1992) advocated the use of the concept of flow to better understand purchase and repurchase from the web (Chen et al., 1998; Rettie, 2001). We, therefore, believe flow theory is useful in explaining consumers' continuance behavior.

3. We invite researchers to pay more attention to the under-researched areas highlighted by our analysis. For instance, researchers can explore new variables in the five categories (consumer characteristics, environmental influences, product characteristics, medium characteristics, and merchant and intermediary characteristics) and empirically test how these factors affect intention, adoption and continuance.

4. Moe and Fader (2000) suggest that both planned and unplanned visit/purchase will affect future purchase decisions. However, our analysis of over 300 research articles showed that there are only very few studies examining unplanned purchase. Koufaris (2002) is the first to explore the relationship between unplanned and online consumer behavior. Unplanned behavior (for example, browsing visit without specific intention to buy) in fact is stimuli-driven and occasionally results in unplanned purchase (Janiszewski, 1998; Jarboe and McDaniel, 1987). We believe that the web provides several types of stimuli and we urge researchers to examine the process of online unplanned purchase.

5. Classical consumer behavioral theories provide researchers with a good starting point in understanding online consumer behavior. However, we should take the IT component into serious consideration when doing research in online consumer behavior. Instead of blindly borrowing theories and models from other disciplines, we as IS researchers should work out our own behavioral models declaring what is unique and

specific to the context of consumer-based electronic commerce.

Finally, it is important to note that classical theories such as TRA and related theories constitute only a starting point in understanding online consumer behavior. Researchers should carefully consider the artifact and its impact on online consumer behavior. Therefore, we believe that the time has come for IS researchers to start building their own theories instead of applying theories from other disciplines.

REFERENCES

Ambrose, P.J. and Johnson, G.J. (1998). A Trust Based Model of Buying Behavior in Electronic Retailing. In *Proceedings of the Fourth Americas Conference on Information Systems (AMCIS 1998)*. Baltimore, 263-265.

Andrade, E.B. (2000). Identifying Discriminating Variables of Online and Offline Buyers: A Perceived-Risk Approach. In *Proceedings of the Sixth Americas Conference on Information Systems (AMCIS 2000)*. Long Beach, 1386-1392.

Bellman, S.; Lohse, G.L. and Johnson, E.J. (1999). Predictors of Online Buying Behavior. *Communications of the ACM*, 42(12), 32-38.

Bettman, J.R. (1979). *An Information Processing Theory of Consumer Choice*, Reading, Mass.: Addison-Wesley.

Bhatnagar, A.; Misra, S. and Rao, H.R. (2000). On Risk, Convenience, and Internet Shopping Behavior - Why Some Consumers are Online Shoppers while Others are Not, *Communications of the ACM*, 43(11), 98-105.

Bhattacherjee, A. (2000). Acceptance of E-Commerce Services: The Case of Electronic Brokerages, *IEEE Transactions on Systems, Man and Cybernetics, Part A*, 30(4), 411-420.

Bhattacherjee, A. (2001a). An Empirical Analysis of the Antecedents of Electronic Commerce Service Continuance, *Decision support systems*, 32(2), 201-214.

Bhattacherjee, A. (2001b). Understanding Information Systems Continuance: An Expectation Confirmation Model, *MIS Quarterly*, 25(3), 351-370.

Bobbitt, L.M. and Dabholkar, P.A. (2001). Integrating Attitudinal Theories to Understand and Predict Use of Technology-Based Self-Service: The Internet as an Illustration, *International Journal of Service Industry Management*, 12(5), 423-450.

Borchers, A. (2001). Trust in Internet Shopping: A Test of a Measurement Instrument. In *Proceedings of the Seventh Americas Conference on Information Systems (AMCIS 2001)*. Boston, 799-803.

Boyer, K.K.; Hallowell, R. and Roth, A.V. (2002). E-Services: Operating Strategy. A Case Study and a Method for Analyzing Operational Benefits. *Journal of Operations Management*, 20(2), 175-188.

Case, T.; Burns, O.M. and Dick, G.N. (2001). Drivers of On-Line Purchasing among U.S. University Students. In *Proceedings of the Seventh Americas Conference on Information Systems (AMCIS 2001)*. Boston, pp. 873-878.

Chau, P.Y.K.; Au, G. and Tam, K.Y. (2000). Impact of Information Presentation Modes on Online Shopping: An Empirical Evaluation of a Broadband Interactive Shopping Service. *Journal of Organizational Computing and Electronic Commerce*, 10(1), 1-22.

Chen, H.; Wignad, R.T. and Nilan, M. (1998). Optimal Flow Experience in Web Navigation, Effective Utilization and Management of Emerging Information Technologies. In *Proceedings of the Ninth Information Resources Management Association International Conference*, Idea Group Publishing, Boston, MA.

Chen, L.D. and Sukpanich, N. (1998). Assessing Consumers' Involvement in Internet Purchasing. In *Proceedings of the Fourth Americas Conference on Information Systems (AMCIS 1998)*. Baltimore, 281-283.

Cheung, C.M.K. and Lee, M.K.O. (2001). Trust in Internet Shopping: Instrument Development and Validation Through Classical and Modern Approaches. *Journal of Global Information Management*, 9(3), 23-32.

Cheung, C.M.K. and Lee, M.K.O. (2001a). Trust in Internet Shopping: A Proposed Model and Measurement Instrument. In *Proceedings of the Seventh Americas Conference on Information Systems (AMCIS 2001)*. Boston, 681-689.

Childers, T.L.; Carr, C.L.; Peck, J. and Carson, S. (2001). Hedonic and Utilitarian Motivations for Online Retail Shopping Behavior. *Journal of Retailing*, 77(4), 511-535.

Citrin, A.V.; Sprott, D.E.; Silverman, S.N. and Stem, D.E. (2000). Adoption of Internet Shopping: The Role of Consumer Innovativeness. *Industrial Management & Data Systems*, 100(7), 294-300.

Csikszentmihalyi, M. (1975). *Beyond Boredom and Anxiety*, Jossey-Bass, San Francisco, CA.

Csikszentmihalyi, M. (1990). *Flow: The Psychology of Optimal Experience*, Harper & Row, New York, NY.

Degeratu, A.M.; Rangaswamy, A. and Wub, J. (2000). Consumer Choice Behavior in Online and Traditional Supermarkets: The Effects of Brand Name, Price, and other Search Attributes. *International Journal of Research in Marketing*, 17(1), 55-78.

Dobie, K.; Grant, J. and Ready, K. (2001). Product Motivation and Purchasing Activity: An Exploratory Study of Consumers' Intention Purchasing Activity. *Journal of Promotion Management*, 6(1/2), 31-43.

Douglas, S.P.; Morrin, M.A. and Craig, C.S. (1994). Cross-National Consumer Research Traditions. In G. Laurent, G. Lilien, and B. Bras, ed., *Research Traditions in Marketing*, Kluwer, Boston, MA.

Engel, J.F.; Blackwell, R.D. and Miniard, P.W. (2001). *Consumer Behavior*, The Dryden Press Series in Marketing.

Eroglu, S.A.; Machleit, K.A. and Davis, L.M. (2001). Atmospheric Qualities of Online Retailing - A Conceptual Model and Implications. *Journal of Business Research*, 54(2), 177-184.

Fishbein, M. (1967). Attitude and Prediction of Behavior. In M. Fishbein, ed., *Readings in Attitude Theory and Measurement*, New York: John Wiley, 477-492.

Fishbein, M.; and Ajzen, I. (1975). *Belief, Attitude, Intention and Behavior: An Introduction to Theory and Research*, Reading, MA: Addison-Wesley Publishing Company.

Folkes, V.S. (1988). Recent Attribution Research in Consumer Behavior: A Review and New Directions. *Journal of Consumer Research*, 14, 548-565.

Friedman, B.; Kahn, Jr P.H. and Howe, D.C. (2000). Trust Online. *Communication of the ACM*, 43(12), 34-40.

Fung, R.K.K. and Lee, M.K.O. (1999). EC-Trust (Trust in Electronic Commerce): Exploring the Antecedent Factors. In *Proceedings of the Fifth Americas Conference on Information Systems (AMCIS 1999)*. Milwaukee, 517-519.

Gefen, D. (2000). E-Commerce: The Role of Familiarity and Trust. *Omega*, 28(6), 725-737.

Gefen, D. and Devine, P. (2001). Customer Loyalty to an Online Store: The Meaning of Online Service Quality. In *Proceedings of the Twenty-Second International Conference of Information Systems (ICIS 2001)*. New Orleans, 613-618.

34.Gefen, D. (2002). Customer Loyalty in E-Commerce. *Journal of the Association for Information Systems*, 3, 27-51.

Ghani, J.A. and Deshpande, S.P. (1994). Task Characteristics and the Experience of Optimal Flow in Human-Computer Interaction. *Journal of Psychology*, 128(4), 381-91.

Goldsmith, R.E. (2000). How Innovativeness Differentiates Online Buyers. *Quarterly Journal of Electronic Commerce*, 1(4), 323-333.

Goldsmith, R.E. and Bridges, E. (2000). E-Tailing VS Retailing: Using Attitudes to Predict Online Buying Behavior. *Quarterly Journal of Electronic Commerce*, 1(3), 245-253.

Goldsmith, R.E. (2001). Using the Domain Specific Innovativeness Scale to Identify Innovative Internet Consumers. *Internet Research: Electronic Networking Applications and Policy*, 11(2), 149-158.

Grandon, E.E. and Ranganathan, C. (2001). The Impact of Content and Design of Web Sites on Online Sales. In *Proceedings of the Seventh Americas Conference on Information Systems (AMCIS 2001)*. Boston, 920-926.

Griffith, D.A.; Krampf, R.F. and Palmer, J.W. (2001). The Role of Interface in Electronic Commerce: Consumer Involvement with Print Versus On-Line Catalogs. *International Journal of Electronic Commerce*, 5(4), 134-153.

Han, H.J.; Ocker, R. and Fjermestad, J. (2001). An Investigation of University Students' On-Line Shopping Behavior. In *Proceedings of the Seventh Americas Conference on Information Systems (AMCIS 2001)*, Boston, 930-933.

Haubl, G. and Trifts, V. (2000). Consumer Decision Making in Online Shopping Environments: The Effects of Interactive Decision Aids. *Marketing Science*, 19(1), 4-21.

Heijden, H.v.d.; Verhagen, T. and Creemers, M. (2001). Predicting Online Purchase Behavior: Replications and Tests of Competing Models. In *Proceedings of the Thirty-Fourth Annual Hawaii International Conference on System Sciences*, Maui, HI, USA, IEEE Computer Society, Los Alamitos, CA.

Ho, C.-F. and Wu, W.-H. (1999). Antecedents of Customer Satisfaction on the Internet: An Empirical Study of Online Shopping. In *Proceedings of the Thirty-Second Annual Hawaii International Conference on Systems Sciences*, Maui, HI, USA, IEEE Computer Society, Los Alamitos, CA.

Hoffman, D.L. and Novak, T.P. (1996). Marketing in Hypermedia Computer-mediated Environments: Conceptual Foundations. *Journal of Marketing*, 60, 50-68.

Hoffman, D.L.; Novak, T.P. and Peralta, M. (1999). Building Consumer Trust Online. *Communications of the ACM*, 42(4). 80-85.

Huang, M.-H. (2000). Information Load: Its Relationship to Online Exploratory and Shopping Behavior. *International Journal of Information Management*, 20(5), 337-347.

Janiszewski, C. (1998). The Influence of Display Characteristics on Visual Exploratory Search Behavior. *Journal of Consumer Research*, 25(3), 290-301.

Jarboe, G. R. and McDaniel, C. D.(1987). A Profile of Browsers in Regional Shopping Malls. *Journal of the Academy of Marketing Science*, 15(1), 46-53.

Jarvenpaa, S.L. and Todd, P.A. (1996). Consumer Reactions to Electronic Shopping on the World Wide Web. *International Journal of Electronic Commerce*, 1(2), 59-88.

Jarvenpaa, S.L. (1999). Consumer Trust in an Internet Store: A Cross-Cultural Validation.*Journal of Computer-Mediated Communication*, 5(2).

Jarvenpaa, S.L.; Tractinsky, N. and Vitale, M. (2000). Consumer Trust in an Internet Store. *Information Technology & Management*, 1(1-2), 45-71.

Jones, J.M. and Vijayasarathy, L.R. (1998). Internet Consumer Catalog Shopping: Findings from an Exploratory Study and Directions for Future Research.*Internet Research: Electronic Networking Applications and Policy*, 8(4), 322-330.

Jungwon, L.; Jinwoo, K. and Jae, M.Y. (2000). What Makes Internet Users visit Cyber Stores Again? Key Design Factors for Customer Loyalty. In *Proceedings of the Conference on Human Factors in Computing Systems,* The Hague, Netherlands.

Kannan, P.K. and Kopalle, P.K. (2001). Dynamic Pricing on the Internet: Importance and Implications for Consumer Behavior. *International Journal of Electronic Commerce*, 5(3), 63-83.

Keen, C.; Ruyter, K.D.; Wetzels, M. and Feinberg, R. (2000). An Empirical Analysis of Consumer Preferences Regarding Alternative Service Delivery Modes in Emerging Electronic Service Markets. *Quarterly Journal of Electronic Commerce*, 1(1), 31-47.

Khalifa, M. and Liu, V. (2001). Satisfaction with Internet-Based Services: A Longitudinal Study. In *Proceedings of the Twenty-Second International Conference of Information Systems (ICIS 2001)*, New Orleans, 601-606.

Kim, D.J.; Cho, B. and Rao, H.R. (2000). Effects of Consumer Lifestyles on Purchasing Behavior on the Internet: A Conceptual Framework and Empirical Validation. In *Proceedings of the Sixth Americas Conference on Information Systems (AMCIS 2000)*, Long Beach, 688-695.

Kim, S.Y. and Lim, Y.J. (2001). Consumers' Perceived Importance of and Satisfaction with Internet Shopping. *Electronic Markets*, 11(3), 148-154.

Kimelfeld, Y.M. and Watt, J.H. (2001). The Pragmatic Value of On-Line Transactional Advertising: A Predictor of Purchase Intention. *Journal of Marketing Communications*, 7(3), 137-157.

Koivumaki, T. (2001). Customer Satisfaction and Purchasing Behavior in a Web-based Shopping Environment. *Electronic Markets*, 11(3), 186-192.

Koufaris, M.; Kambil, A. and Labarbera, P.A. (2001). Consumer Behavior in Web-Based Commerce: An Empirical Study. *International Journal of Electronic Commerce*, 6(2), 115-138.

Koufaris, M. (2002). Applying the Technology Acceptance Model and Flow Theory to Online Consumer Behavior. *Information System Research*, 13(2), 205-223.

Kumar, N. and Benbasat, I. (2001). Shopping as Experience and Web Site as a Social Actor: Web Interface Design and Para-Social Presence. In *Proceedings of the Twenty-Second International Conference on Information Systems (ICIS 2001)*, New Orleans, 449-454.

Lee, M.K.O. (1999). Comprehensive Model of Internet Consumer Satisfaction, *Unpublished Working Paper, City University of Hong Kong*.

Lee, J.; Kim, J. and Moon, J.Y. (2000). What Makes Internet Users Visit Cyber Stores Again? Key Design Factors for Customer Loyalty. In *Proceedings of the Conference on Human Factors in Computing Systems*, The Hague, Netherlands, 305-312.

Lee, D. and Park, J. (2001). On the Explanation of Factors Affecting E-Commerce Adoption. In *Proceedings of the Twenty-Second International Conference of Information Systems (ICIS 2001)*, New Orleans, pp. 109-120.

Lee, M.K.O. and Turban, E. (2001). A Trust Model for Consumer Internet Shopping. *International Journal of Electronic Commerce*, 6(1), 75-91.

Lee, P.M. (2002). Behavioral Model of Online Purchasers in E-Commerce Environment. *Electronic Commerce Research*, 2(1-2), 75-85.

Li, H.; Kuo, C. and Russell, M.G. (1999). The Impact of Perceived Channel Utilities, Shopping Orientations, and Demographics on the Consumer's Online Buying Behavior. *Journal of Computer-Mediated Communication*, 5(2).

72. Liang, T.P. and Huang, J.S. (1998). An Empirical Study on Consumer Acceptance of Products in Electronic Markets: A Transaction Cost Model. *Decision Support Systems*, 24(1), 29-43.

72. Liang, T.P. and Lai, H.J. (2002). Effect of Store Design on Consumer Purchases: An Empirical Study of On-Line Bookstores. *Information & Management*, 39(6), 431-444.

73. Liao, Z. and Cheung, M. (2001). Internet-Based E-Shopping and Consumer Attitudes: An Empirical Study. *Information & Management*, 38(5), 299-306.

74. Lilien, G.L.; Philip, K. and Sridhar, M.K. (1992). *Marketing Models*, New Jersey: Prentice Hall.

75. Limayem, M. and Khalifa, M. (2000). Business-to-Consumer Electronic Commerce: A Longitudinal Study. In *Proceedings of the Fifth IEEE Symposium on Computers and Communications*, 286-290.

76. Limayem, M.; Khalifa, M. and Frini, A. (2000). What Makes Consumers Buy from Internet? A Longitudinal Study of Online Shopping. *IEEE Transactions on Systems, Man & Cybernetics, Part A (Systems & Humans)*, 30(4), 421-432.

77. Lin, J.C.-C. and Lu, H. (2000). Towards an Understanding of the Behavioral Intention to Use a Web Site. *International Journal of Information Management*, 20(3), 197-208.

78. Liu, C. and Arnett, K. (1999). Assessing the Customer Behavioral Intentions on the Web: A

Research Model. In *Proceedings of the Fifth Americas Conference on Information Systems (AMCIS 1999)*, Milwaukee, WI, 307-309.

79. Luna, D. and Gupta, S.F. (2001). An Integrative Framework for Cross-Cultural Consumer Behavior. *International Marketing Review*, 18(1), 45-69.

80. Markus, L. and Soh, C. (2002). Structural Influences on Global E-Commerce Activity. *Journal of Global Information Management*, 10(1), 5-12.

81. Miyazaki, A.D. and Fernandez, A. (2001). Consumer Perceptions of Privacy and Security Risks for Online Shopping. *The Journal of Consumer Affairs*, 35(1), 27-44.

82. Moe, W.W. and Fader, P.S. (2001). Uncovering Patterns in Cybershopping. *California Management Review*, 43(4), 106-117.

83. Moe, W. W. and Fader, P. S. (2000). *Which Visits Lead to Purchase? Dynamic Conversion Behavior at E-Commerce Sites*. University of Texas.

84. Muthitacharoen, A. (2000). Consumer's Preference Between the Internet and Conventional Stores (An Exploratory Study). In *Proceedings of the Sixth Americas Conference on Information Systems (AMCIS 2000)*, Long Beach, 1373-1379.

85. Nel, D.; Niekerk, R.v.; Berthon, J.-P. and Davies, T. (1999). Going with the Flow: Web Sites and Customer Involvement. *Internet Research: Electronic Networking Applications and Policy*, 9(2), 109-116.

86. Oliver, R.L. (1980). A Cognitive Model for the Antecedents and Consequences of Satisfaction. *Journal of Marketing Research*, 17, 460-469.

87. Page, C. and Lepkowska-White, E. (2002). Web Equity: A Framework for Building Consumer Value in Online Companies. *Journal of Consumer Marketing*, 19(3), 231-248.

88. Parthasarathy, M. and Bhattacherjee, A. (1998). Understanding Post-Adoption Behavior in the Behavior in the Context of Online Services. *Information Systems Research*, 9(4), 362-379.

89. Pavlou, P.A. (2001). Integrating Trust in Electronic Commerce With The Technology Acceptance Model: Model Development And Validation. In *Proceedings of the Seventh Americas Conference on Information Systems (AMCIS 2001)*, Boston, 816-822.

90. Pereira, R.E. (1998). Factors Influencing Consumer Purchasing Behavior in Electronic Commerce. In *Proceedings of the Fourth Americas Conference on Information Systems (AMCIS 1998)*, Baltimore, 450-452.

91. Phau, I. and Poon, S.M. (2000). Factors Influencing the Types of Products and Services Purchased over the Internet. *Internet Research: Electronic Networking Applications And Policy*, 10(2), 102-113.

92. Phau, I. and Poon, S.M. (2000). An Exploratory Study of Cybershopping in Singapore. *Quarterly Journal of Electronic Commerce*, 1(1), 61-75.

93. Raijas, A. and Tuunainen, V.K. (2001). Critical Factors in Electronic Grocery Shopping. *International Review of Retail, Distribution and Consumer Research*, 11(3), 255-265.

94. Ramaswami, S.N.; Strader, T.J. and Brett, K. (2000). Determinants of On-Line Channel Use for Purchasing Financial Products. *International Journal of Electronic Commerce*, 5(2), 95-118.

95. Ranganathan, C. and Ganapathy, S. (2002). Key Dimensions of Business-to-Consumer Web Sites. *Information & Management*, 39(6), 457-465.

96. Rettie, R. (2001). An Exploration of Flow During Internet Use. *Internet Research: Electronic Networking Applications and Policy*. 11(2), 103-113.

97. Ruyter, K.d.; Wetzels, M. and Kleijnen, M. (2001). Customer Adoption of E-Service: An Experimental Study. *International Journal of Service Industry Management*, 12(2), 184-207.

98. Schoenbachler, D.D. and Gordon, G.L. Multi-Channel Shopping: Understanding What Drives Channel Choice. *Journal of Consumer Marketing*, 19(1), 42-53.

99. Senecal, S. (2000). Stopping Variables in Online Buying Processes: An Innovation Diffusion Approach. In *Proceedings of the Sixth Americas Conference on Information Systems (AMCIS 2000)*, Long Beach, 1380-1385.

100. Shim, S.; Eastlick, M.A.; Lotz, S.L. and Warrington, P. (2001). An Online Prepurchase Intentions Model: The Role of Intention to Search. *Journal of retailing*, 77(3), 397-416.

101. Siu, N.Y.M. and Cheng, M.M.-S. (2001). A Study of the Expected Adoption of Online Shopping – The Case of Hong Kong. *Journal of International Consumer Marketing*, 13(3), 87-106.

102. Skinner, B.F. (1938). *The Behavior of Organisms: An Experimental Analysis*, New York: Appleton Century Crofts.

103. Sohn, C. (1999). The Properties of Internet-based Markets and Customers' Behavior. In *Proceedings of the Fifth Americas Conference on Information Systems (AMCIS 1999)*, Milwaukee.

104. Song, J. and Zahedi, F.M. (2001). Web Design in E-Commerce: A Theory And Empirical Analysis. In *Proceedings of the Twenty-Second International Conference of Information Systems (ICIS 2001)*, New Orleans, 205-220.

105. Spiller, P. and Lohse, G. L. (1998). A Classification of Internet Retail Stores. *International Journal of Electronic Commerce*, 2(2), 29-56.

106. Spiteri, L.F. (2001). Information Architecture of Business-to-Consumer E-Commerce Websites.

Part I: The Online Catalogue of Selected Video Retailers. *Journal of Information Science*, 27(4), 239-248.

107. Sukpanich, N. and Chen, L. (1999). Antecedents of Desirable Consumer Behaviors in Electronic Commerce. In *Proceedings of the Fifth Americas Conference on Information Systems (AMCIS 1999)*, Milwaukee, 550-552.

108. Trevino, L.K. and Webster, J. (1992). Flow in Computer-Mediated Communication. *Communication Research*, 19(5), 539-73.

109. Vellido, A.; Lisboa, P.J.G. and Meehan, K. (2000). Quantitative Characterization and Prediction of On-Line Purchasing Behavior: A Latent Variable Approach. *International Journal of Electronic Commerce*, 4(4), 83-104.

110. Vijayasarathy, L.R. and Jones, J.M. (2000a). Intentions to Shop Using Internet Catalogues: Exploring the Effects of Product Types, Shopping Orientations, and Attitudes towards Computers. *Electronic Markets*, 10(1), 29-38.

111. Vijayasarathy, L.R. and Jones, J.M. (2000b). Print and Internet Catalog Shopping: Assessing Attitudes and Intentions. *Internet Research: Electronic Networking Applications and Policy*, 10(3), 191-202.

112. Vijayasarathy, L.R. (2001). The Impact of Shopping Orientations, Product Types, and Shopping Aids on Attitude and Intention to Use Online Shopping. *Quarterly Journal of Electronic Commerce*, 2(2), 99-113.

113. Vijayasarathy, L.R. and Jones, J.M. (2001). Do Internet shopping Aids Make a Difference? An Empirical Investigation. *Electronic Markets*, 11(1), 75-83.

114. Vrechopoulos, A.P.; Siomkos, G.J. and Doukidis, G.I. (2001). Internet Shopping Adoption by Greek Consumers. *European Journal of Innovation Management*, 4(3), 142-153.

115. Ward, M.R. and Lee, M.J. (2000). Internet Shopping, Consumer Search and Product Branding. *Journal of Product & Brand Management*, 9(1), 6-20.

116. Warrington, T.B.; Abgrab, N.J. and Caldwell, H.M. (2000). Building Trust to Develop Competitive Advantage in E-Business Relationships. *Competitiveness Review*, 10(2), 160-168.

117. Webster, J. and Watson, R.T. (2002). Analyzing the Past to Prepare for the Future: Writing a Literature Review. *MIS Quarterly*, 26(2), xiii-xxiii (13-23).

118. White, G.K. and Manning, B.J. (1998). Commercial WWW Site Appeal: How Does it Affect Online Food and Drink Consumers' Purchasing Behavior? *Internet Research: Electronic Networking Applications and Policy*, 8(1), 32-38.

119. Wolfinbarger, M. and Gilly, M. (2000). Consumer Motivations for Online Shopping. In *Proceedings of the Sixth Americas Conference on Information Systems (AMCIS 2000)*, Long Beach, 1362-1366.

120. Wolfinbarger, M. and Gilly, M.C. (2001). Shopping Online for Freedom, Control, And Fun. *California Management Review*, 43(2), 34-55.

121. Zmud, R.W. (1979). Individual Differences and MIS Success: A Review of the Empirical Literature. *Management Science*, 25(10), 966-979.

This work was previously published in Journal of Electronic Commerce in Organizations, Vol 3, No 4, edited by M. Khosrow-Pour, pp. 1-19, copyright 2005 by IGI Publishing, formerly known as Idea Group Publishing (an imprint of IGI Global).

Chapter XVIII
Multi–Channel Retailing and Customer Satisfaction:
Implications for eCRM

Patricia T. Warrington
Texas Christian University, USA

Elizabeth Gangstad
Purdue University, USA

Richard Feinberg
Purdue University, USA

Ko de Ruyter
University of Maastricht, The Netherlands

ABSTRACT

Multi-channel retailers that utilize an eCRM approach stand to benefit in multiple arenas - by providing targeted customer service as well as gaining operational and competitive advantages. To that end, it is inherent that multi-channel retailers better understand how satisfaction – a necessary condition for building customer loyalty – influences consumers' decisions to shop in one retail channel or another. The purpose of this study was to examine the influence of shopping experience on customers' future purchase intentions, both for the retailer and for the channel. Using a controlled experimental design, U.S. and European subjects responded to a series of questions regarding the likelihood making a future purchase following either a positive or negative shopping encounter. Results suggest that shopping intentions vary based on the shopping channel as well as cultural differences.

INTRODUCTION

Retailers are being advised that the future of retail will belong to those who execute seamless multi-channel access (Chu & Pike, 2002; Close, 2002; Johnson, 2004; Pastore, 2000; Thompson, 2003). The reason is quite simple—retailers must be where shoppers want them, when they want them…anytime, anywhere, and in multiple formats (Feinberg, Trotter, & Anton, 2000). If customers want to shop from a store, retailers must have a physical location; if customers want to shop over the telephone, retailers must be available by phone; if customers want to shop over the Internet, retailers must be accessible online. And, in the future, if customers want to shop via a wireless device, retailers must be available by wireless. Multi-channel access is considered one of the top 10 trends for all businesses in the next decade (Ernst & Young, 2003; Feinberg & Trotter, 2003; Levy & Weitz, 2003). Indeed, surveys show that consumers not only want multi-channel access, they expect it (Burke, 2000; Johnson, 2004).

Electronic customer relationship management (e-CRM) has the potential to enable retailers to better meet the needs of their customers across retail formats and, at the same time, maximize the strategic benefits of a multi-channel strategy. By effectively using modern information technology, retailers are able to offer shoppers the advantages of a one-to-one relationship, yet reap the profit savings that accrue from mass-market operating efficiencies (Chen & Chen, 2004). Customer retention lies at the heart of e-CRM. As such, e-CRM is increasingly viewed as vital to building and maintaining customer loyalty.

The research on e-CRM has been very conceptual in nature outlining research agendas and possible strategic models of the nature and scope of e-CRM (e.g., Parasuraman & Zinkham, 2002; Varadarajan & Yadav, 2002). The most recent review of the e-CRM literature suggests that we really know three things about e-CRM (Zeithaml, Parasuraman, & Malhotra, 2002).

1. E-CRM is multidimensional and each study examines a "favorite" attribute it finds to be important. But, as yet, we do not know if ease of use, privacy, site design, or any of a variety of attributes is determinant of some e-CRM outcome.

2. Consumers really care about e-CRM after negative online shopping or service experiences. Consumers seem less concerned with e-CRM issues following routine Web interactions.

3. While there is anecdotal evidence to suggest e-satisfaction to be important for purchase, repurchase, and loyalty, the evidence is simply not empirical and/or strong.

In reading Zeithaml et al.'s (2002) review of the e-CRM literature, it appears that e-CRM is seen as an independent issue from other points (channels) of satisfaction. The conceptual point of this study is that e-CRM is part of a broader issue of customer satisfaction. What happens in the "e" channel, what happens in the store channel, and what happens in any other channel has an effect within the channel it occurs and in the retailer's other channels.

Satisfaction is a key determinant of retail customer loyalty (Cronin, Brady, & Hult, 2000). To date, the extant research is relatively silent regarding the effect of shopping satisfaction (or dissatisfaction) on consumers' channel choices. The goal of this study was to assess the effect of a satisfactory/dissatisfactory shopping experience on customers' future shopping intentions for the retailer, the shopping channel, and alternative shopping channels. What is the likelihood of purchase from a retailer in the same or different channel following a positive or negative shopping experience? There is some evidence to suggest that multi-channel shoppers are actually not very loyal to any particular retailer (Reda, 2002). As such, this study employs an experimental design to determine what effect experience (satisfying, dissatisfying) in a particular channel (store, catalog, or Internet) will have on a customer's decision to shop with the same retailer in the same channel, a different retailer in the same channel, and the same retailer in a different channel.

CUSTOMER SATISFACTION AND MULTI-CHANNEL RETAILING

Multi-channel access allows retailers to reach a greater market and to leverage their skills and assets to increase sales and profits. It allows a single organization to overcome the limitations of any single channel. The goal of retailing is to attract consumers, keep consumers, and increase "wallet share," and a multi-channel presence increases the probability of all three (Chu & Pike, 2002).

One can construct an argument for the importance of multi-channel retailing for retail success by noticing that most of retail sales on the Internet are done by multi-channel retailers (Johnson, 2004). Research on multi-channel retailing has focused on the factors that drive channel choice (e.g., Burke, 2000; Chu & Pike, 2002; Inman, Shankar, & Ferraro, 2004; Wu, Mahajan, & Balasubramanian, 2003) and the nature of the multi-channel shopping experience generally (Burke, 2000). As reported by Chu and Pike (2002), the National Retail Federation's Shop.org found that 78% of online shoppers also made a purchase at the retailer's physical store and 45% bought merchandise from the retailer's catalog. The same study reported that 23% of catalog shoppers also shopped at the retailer's Internet site (e.g., an Eddie Bauer catalog shopper also purchased at eddiebauer.com). Only 6% of store shoppers purchased from the retailer's online site. However, slightly more than half of catalog shoppers and 75% of store shoppers search for pre-purchase information online.

Unfortunately, research has neglected the complex relationship between shopping experiences and future shopping behavior in a multi-channel environment. The complexity of the relationship between store-based, catalog, and online shopping extends beyond the mere description of what people are doing inter- and intra-channel. It encompasses the relationship between encounters in one channel and subsequent decisions to shop in the same or another channel. Is a good experience in one channel equivalent to a good experience in another channel as it relates to future channel choice? Indeed a recent study showed very clearly that there are tradeoffs that consumers make between channels and these tradeoffs are not equal; a positive/negative experience differs in value depending on the channel and the resulting choices differ as well (Keen, Wetzels, de Ruyter, & Feinberg, 2004).

Substantial research supports the premise that satisfaction/dissatisfaction of customer experience in a store has a direct impact on the probability of revisit to the store (e.g., Feinberg, 2001; Fornell, Johnson, Anderson, Cha, & Bryant, 1996; Loveman, 1998; Rust & Zahorik, 1993; Rust, Zeithaml, & Lemon, 2000). Satisfaction is generally viewed as the foundation for any marketing relationship (e.g., Morgan & Hunt, 1994; Selnes, 1998). Research on e-retailing has been founded on the same premise with the same general finding: customer satisfaction is related to return visits to a Web site (Balasubramanian, Konana, & Menon, 2003; Freed, 2003; Reibstein, 2002; Zeithaml et al., 2002). The belief in customer satisfaction as the "prime directive" of the retail-consumer relationships is further supported by the extensive range of popular books on the subject (e.g., Blanchard & Bowles, 1993; Sewell & Brown, 2002). If customer satisfaction is important for decisions in one channel alone, there is likely to be some relationship between the satisfaction in one channel and future channel decisions. Multi-channel retailers will benefit from understanding the nuances of these effects and be better able to successfully implement and fine tune e-CRM strategies.

HYPOTHESIS DEVELOPMENT

Even if a one-to-one relationship between experience and choice is subject to some variation, it is clear that there should be a relationship. Positive retail encounters influence the likelihood that consumers will revisit and possibly buy again from a retailer on future shopping trips (Cronin et al., 2000). Thus, satisfied shoppers are likely to shop again from a given retailer in the same channel (i.e., store, catalog, or Internet). In other words, a positive experience with Retailer A in a particular channel (e.g., store) will have an impact on a subsequent decision to patronize Retailer A in that same channel.

H1: *There is a direct positive relationship between a satisfying shopping experience with a retailer in a given channel and a consumer's willingness to patronize the retailer in the same channel in the future.*

A favorable shopping experience with a retailer in a particular channel is likely to increase the possibility of shopping with the retailer across all channels. Brand recognition and the value associated with the retailer in one channel is transferred to the retailer in all channels in the same manner that positive beliefs about a core brand favorably influence consumers' evaluations of the brand's extensions (e.g., Randall, Ulrich, & Reibstein, 1998). This effect occurs as a result of a categorization process whereby feelings and beliefs are transferred by association to other stimuli that are similar. For example, a consumer's positive experience with a multi-channel retailer in the store channel leads to the belief that the consumer will have a positive shopping experience at the retailer's Web site or from the retailer's catalog. Negative experiences should lead to lower probability in the same way; that is, a negative shopping experience at the retailer's store lowers the probability of shopping at the retailer's Internet site or from their catalog.

H2: *There is a direct positive relationship between a satisfying shopping experience with a retailer in a given channel and a consumer's willingness to patronize the retailer in a different channel in the future.*

Finally, it is likely that consumers show a preference for shopping in a particular channel. Whereas some consumers prefer store-based shopping, non-store retail, particularly the Internet, is increasing in popularity. Despite a lack of empirical evidence, it is logical to assume a satisfying shopping experience in a given channel will influence preference for that channel in the future. Thus, it is expected that a positive shopping experience online is likely to build a consumer's confidence in shopping online, which, in turn, enhances the likelihood of shopping online in the future. Similarly, a positive catalog shopping experience is likely to reinforce a consumer's decision to shop and purchase from catalogs in the future. Alternatively, a negative shopping experience in a given channel is likely to have an unfavorable impact on the probability of shopping in the channel in the future.

H3: *There is a direct positive relationship between a satisfying shopping experience in a given channel and a consumer's willingness to shop in the same channel in the future.*

METHODOLOGY

A 3 (shopping channel) by 2 (shopping experience) factorial design was employed to test the hypotheses. An experimental design was chosen as a first attempt at looking at this issue because of the high degree of control and ability to achieve cause and effect understanding of this issue. To add to the conceptual validity, the study was replicated with a European sample. As a result, the experimental design was a 2 (U.S., Dutch) x 3 x 2.

Stimulus Material

A scenario approach was employed to manipulate shopping channel and shopping experience. A shopper was described as having either a satisfactory or dissatisfactory shopping experience in one of three different shopping channel contexts (store, Internet, or catalog). Subjects in each sample (U.S., Dutch) were randomly assigned to read one of the six scenarios (see Appendix A for the scenarios).

A pretest with a U.S. sample was conducted to confirm that the positive retail shopping experience generated greater positive effect than the negative shopping experience. The stimulus material used for the study in Holland was identical to that of the U.S. study since all student subjects in Holland take their classes in English. Pretests indicated that the manipulations were effective in the Dutch sample and that there were no sources of misunderstanding.

Dependent Measures

A series of six questions were developed to assess future shopping intentions. Subjects were asked to indicate the likelihood the shopper described in the scenario would make a future purchase from the same retailer in the same channel, from the same retailer in a different channel, from a different retailer in the same channel, or from a different retailer in a different channel. Responses were recorded using 5-point scales ranging from not likely at all (1) to extremely likely (5) (see Appendix A for item descriptions).

Procedure

A convenience sample of undergraduate students was drawn from two universities; 148 of the 353 subjects were enrolled at a major Midwestern university in the U.S. The remaining 205 subjects attended a well-known university in Holland. Subjects were instructed to read the short narra-

tive appropriate for their experimental condition. Subjects then completed a manipulation check question followed by the set of six dependent measures for assessing future shopping intentions.

RESULTS

Preliminary Analysis

A check for the shopping experience manipulation yielded a significant main effect (p<.05) with the negative experience leading to a less satisfactory response than the positive experience. There were no interactions. Thus, the manipulation of shopping experience was successful.

Hypothesis Testing

ANOVA was used to determine whether shoppers would be willing to return to the same retailer in the same channel following a satisfactory shopping experience. The analysis revealed a main effect for shopping with the retailer again in the same channel. As hypothesized, when subjects were asked the likelihood of repurchase from the same retailer in the same channel, a negative shopping experience led to a lower probability of repurchase (M = 1.60) than a positive shopping experience (M = 4.30). Thus, H1 was supported.

The analysis also showed that the probability of purchasing again in the same channel from the same retailer is not equal for all channels $(F(2, 341) = 6.67, p <.05)$. Subjects in the store treatment group were significantly more likely to repeat purchase from the same retailer in the same channel than those in either the catalog or Internet treatment groups. This was primarily due to the variation between the channel treatment groups in the U.S. sample. In other words, a significant interaction was found between country (i.e., U.S., Dutch) and shopping channel $(F(1, 341)=4.2, p<.05)$. Subjects in the U.S. store treatment group were significantly more

Table 1. ANOVA findings

	^FG	^FC	^FE	$^FG*C$	$^FC*E$	$^FG*E$	$^FG*E*C$	R^2	Overall^F
Same Retailer Same Channel	3.24	6.67*	1022.07*	4.21*	.34	.31	.92	.76	98.62*
Same Retailer Different Channel	15.82*	5.69*	294.15*	5.34*	3.43*	1.50	2.30	.51	32.61*
Different Retailer Same Channel	3.36	23.59*	19.57*	2.53	33.30*	1.58	.33	.30	13.56*

*Note: G = U.S./Dutch, C = Channel (Internet/Store/Catalog), E = Shopping Experience(Satisfactory/Dissatisfactory) * p < .05*

likely to return to the same retailer/same channel (M=3.33) than store subjects in the Dutch sample (M=2.95). Essentially, there was no significant difference in the likelihood of purchasing again from the same retailer/same channel among the three channel treatment groups in the European sample (Table 2). In contrast, in the U.S. sample, the likelihood of purchasing again from the same retailer/same channel was significantly greater for the store treatment group than for the catalog and the Internet treatment groups (p>.05).

H2 predicted that a satisfying shopping experience with a particular retailer would increase the likelihood of shopping again with the retailer in other channels. ANOVA indicated that shopping channel interacted with shopping experience (F(1,341)= 3.43, p<.05). More specifically, the likelihood of purchasing from a retailer in a different channel was significant for all three channel treatment groups; however, shopping experience affected channel treatment groups differently. Subjects in the store treatment group (M=3.49) were less willing than Internet (M= 3.63) or catalog subjects (M=3.85) to consider shopping from the retailer in a different channel following a satisfactory experience. Similarly, subjects in the store treatment group were the least likely to consider a future purchase from the retailer in a different channel following a negative shopping experience (Table 3). These findings lend support for H2.

Additionally, a significant interaction was found between shopping channel and country (F (1,341)=5.34, p<.05). Subjects in the U.S. store treatment group were significantly more likely (M=3.10) than store subjects in the Dutch sample (M=2.43) to make a future purchase from the retailer in a different channel (Table 2). Whereas, very little difference occurred between shopping channel treatment groups in the U.S. sample, the likelihood of shopping again from the same retailer in a different channel varied significantly across treatment groups in the Dutch sample with means of 2.43, 2.89, and 3.06 for store, catalog, and Internet, respectively.

According to H3, the greater the shopping satisfaction, the more likely shoppers will be to return and shop again from the same channel. The findings from H1 provide some support for this hypothesis as consumers were indeed willing to revisit the retailer in the same channel following a satisfactory shopping encounter. To test H3, the subjects were asked the likelihood of shopping in the same channel from a *different* retailer. The data analysis revealed a significant main effect for shopping experience (F(1, 341)=19.57, p<.05), a significant main effect for shopping channel (F (2, 341)= 23.59, p<.05), and a significant shopping channel by shopping experience interaction (F(2,341)=33.3, p<.05). When asked the likelihood of making a future purchase from a different Internet retailer, subjects in the satisfied Inter-

Table 2. Means: U.S. and Dutch subjects by channel

Same Retailer Same Channel

Channel	U.S.	Dutch
Internet	2.76	2.95
Store	3.33	2.95
Catalog	2.92	2.67

Same Retailer Different Channel

Channel	U.S.	Dutch
Internet	3.08	3.06
Store	3.10	2.43
Catalog	3.18	2.89

Different Retailer Same Channel

Channel	U.S.	Dutch
Internet	2.90	3.05
Store	3.25	3.70
Catalog	2.72	2.65

net treatment group were more likely (M=3.15) than subjects in the dissatisfied treatment group (M=2.80) to do so. Conversely, subjects in the satisfied store treatment group were less likely (M=2.73) than subjects in the dissatisfied store treatment group (4.22) to make a future purchase from a different store retailer. There was not a significant difference among the two shopping experience treatments for the catalog subjects. The implications of this finding will be discussed in the following section. The findings provide only partial support for H3.

DISCUSSION AND IMPLICATIONS

The primary objective of this study was to examine the effect of retail channel (i.e., store, catalog, and Internet) and shopping experience on future shopping intentions. To provide further support

for the findings, samples were drawn from both the U.S. and the Netherlands.

As predicted, the findings for H1 show that a satisfying shopping experience will increase the likelihood of returning to shop with the retailer again in the same channel. While this finding is not surprising, the analysis suggests that there is significantly greater variation in this effect across retail channels among U.S. shoppers than among Dutch shoppers. Thus, cultural differences may affect how consumers respond to satisfying (or dissatisfying) experiences in different retail channels.

The findings for H2 suggest that satisfactory shopping experiences will encourage customers to patronize a retailer in more than a single channel. On the other hand, negative shopping experiences will decrease the likelihood customers will shop with the retailer in alternative channels. Whereas, subjects' responses across channels were similar for positive experiences, future purchase intentions for negative shopping experiences varied. This finding supports the notion that channels are not neutral vessels of experience but differ in important ways. In this study, Internet shoppers were significantly more likely to patronize another channel (with the same retailer) than were store shoppers or catalog shoppers following a dissatisfactory experience. Intuitively, this seems reasonable as Internet shoppers are usually store shoppers as well, but store shoppers are not always Internet shoppers. In other words, when a consumer's Internet shopping encounter is less than satisfactory, the person is likely to attribute some of the negative experience to the channel. For a store shopper, the negative encounter will weaken the likelihood the person will consider shopping with the retailer online or through a catalog. Thus, channel characteristics play a role in how a negative encounter influences a shopper's future shopping intentions.

Finally, the findings from H3 further demonstrate the impact that retail channels may have on influencing consumers' future shopping

Table 3. Means: Positive/negative shopping experience by channel

Same Retailer Same Channel

Channel	Experience	
	Positive	Negative
Internet	4.20	1.51
Store	4.41	1.87
Catalog	4.14	1.45

Same Retailer Different Channel

Channel	Experience	
	Positive	Negative
Internet	3.63	2.52
Store	3.49	2.05
Catalog	3.85	2.22

Different Retailer Same Channel

Channel	Experience	
	Positive	Negative
Internet	3.15	2.80
Store	2.73	4.22
Catalog	2.62	2.74

intentions. The response to shopping experience was similar for subjects in the catalog treatment groups. Based on this result, dissatisfied catalog shoppers were equally as likely as satisfied catalog shoppers to consider making a future purchase from a catalog retailer in the future. The effect of a negative catalog shopping encounter seems to have very little effect on the decision to shop in the future from catalog retailers. A negative shopping encounter significantly increased the likelihood that a store shopper would purchase from a competing store retailer. Interestingly, the effect was reversed for the Internet shoppers. A negative shopping encounter significantly de-

creased the likelihood that an Internet shopper would purchase from a competing Internet retailer. In other words, satisfied Internet shoppers were more likely than dissatisfied Internet shoppers to express a willingness to purchase from a competing Internet retailer. Thus, satisfied Internet shoppers will return to the channel again but not the retailer. In essence, all Internet retailers benefit from positive Internet experiences. On the other hand, dissatisfied Internet shoppers will not only choose another retailer, but they will also choose another channel. This could mean that repeat purchase behavior, and even customer loyalty, is more difficult to sustain in the Internet channel as compared to other retail channels. Further research is needed to more thoroughly investigate these interpretations.

CONCLUSION

If retailers are offering shoppers multiple channel options now, it is expected that pressure will increase for all retailers to do so in the future. The findings of this study suggest that above all else channel satisfaction/dissatisfaction is a significant issue—but not in an equal way. For some channels, satisfaction/dissatisfaction has a greater or lesser impact. In addition, channels are not all equal. Independent of satisfaction and dissatisfaction the likelihood of switching channels and switching retailers differs across the three channels studied.

Here are the major lessons learned from this study:

1. A positive experience is the prime directive for any retailer hoping to keep a consumer loyal to any particular channel.

2. A positive experience in the Internet channel may actually increase the likelihood of trying the Internet channel of another retailer. This may have significant implications for e-retailing. Clearly the goal of e-retailing is

to move store and catalog customers to "e." Yet in doing so a retailer may dig their own grave by also making it likely the consumer will try another Internet retailer also. If their experience at that site is more positive than the original retail site the unintended side effect of moving a consumer to "your" site is destroyed.

3. The European/American differences are important. The differences by sample group suggest that there are differing retail experiences across cultures, and these differences affect consumer behavior. The lack of consistency in the findings here suggests that cross-cultural studies need to be very careful in explaining and generalizing their findings. European studies need to be sensitive to the fact that their results might differ from U.S. results and vice versa. Internet/store/catalog shopping in the U.S. differs from Europe, and these differences may result in consumer behavior that differs for the same stimulus environment.

There are a number of multi-channel opportunities for retailers. Retailers can leverage strong brand value by adding channels. For example, Internet-only retailers can establish brand equity by opening physical stores or merging with an existing store-based retailer (e.g., Sears's acquisition of Lands' End). Multi-channel retailing leverages advertising and marketing expenses as well as distribution and supplier networks. Benefits of a multi-channel strategy to store-based retailers include access to expanded demographic and psychographic segments, opportunity to drive cross-channel traffic, and the ability to use existing stores for distribution and return of merchandise purchased off-line. And, as this study shows, multi-channel retailing leverages customer satisfaction. Customer satisfaction in one channel transfers to other channels. Successful multi-channel retailing is contingent on understanding the variation in consumer responses that positive/negative shopping experiences produce in different channels and different cultures. Channel-specific e-CRM strategies that take into account these variations should contribute positively to improved customer service and operational efficiencies.

Multi-channel retailing will clearly be a growth industry for retailing (Wagner, 2002) if for no other reason than multi-channel consumers spend more (Jupiter Communications, 2000; Stringer, 2004). Promotions and incentives will need to be multi-channel. Customer service as well as operational systems and processes will need be integrated and customized for each channel. The customer's interaction with a retailer's brand should be seamless across all channels. More research is clearly needed to better understand how the customer's experience in one channel affects the behavioral responses toward other channels.

As an experimental study using scenario-based research, emphatic statements like "x or y increase or decrease purchase" (or probabilities of purchase) are tenuous at best. The study involves a sample of consumers who tell us what they think is likely to happen: imagined positive/negative experiences and real positive/negative experiences may affect "real" purchase behavior and intentions in different ways. Yet, the clear cause and effect relationships uncovered may illuminate what does happen, and so there is value in encouraging experimental work in this particular area.

This research shows that the assumption that e-CRM is equivalent to CRM in non-Internet channels is not complete. Too many studies appear to be focused on the examination of the antecedents and composition of e-CRM and not its consequences both within and across retail channels. In effect, e-CRM has the potential to create positive benefits for the multi-channel retailer in the form of positive effect (i.e., customer satisfaction) across all the retailer's channels as well as positive effect for the channel in general.

REFERENCES

Balasubramanian, S., Konana, P., & Menon, N. (2003). Customer satisfaction in virtual environments: A study of online trading. *Management Science, 49*, 871-889.

Blanchard, K., & Bowles, S. (1993). *Raving fans: A revolutionary approach to customer service.* New York: William Morrow.

Burke, R. (2000). *Creating the ideal shopping experience: What consumers want in the physical and virtual store.* Retrieved from www.kelley. iu.edu/retail/research/iukpmg00b.pdf

Chen, Q., & Chen, H. (2004). Exploring the success factors of eCRM strategies in practice. *Database Marketing & Customer Service Strategy Management, 11*, 333-343.

Chu, J., & Pike, T. (2002). *Integrated multichannel retailing (IMCR): A roadmap to the future.* IBM Institute for Business Value. Retrieved August 5, 2004, from http://www-1.ibm.com/services/strategy/e_strategy/integrated_multi_channel.html

Close, W. (2002). CRM at work: Eight characteristics of CRM winners. *Defying the Limits, 3*, 66-68.

Cronin, J., Jr., Brady, M., & Hult, G. (2000). Assessing the effects of quality, value, and customer satisfaction on consumer behavioral intentions in service environments. *Journal of Retailing, 76*, 93-218.

Ernst & Young. (2003). *Global online retailing.* Retrieved from http://www.ey.com/GLOBAL

Feinberg, R. (2001). Customer service and service quality. In G. Salvendy (Ed.), *Handbook of industrial engineering* (pp. 651-664). New York: John Wiley and Sons.

Feinberg, R., & Trotter, M. (2003). The customer access evolution: Leveraging touch points for customer acquisition, retention, and wallet share. *Defying the Limits, 2*, 30-35.

Feinberg, R., Trotter, M., & Anton, J. (2000). At any time- from anywhere- in any form. *Defying the Limits, 1*, 296-304.

Fornell, C., Johnson, M. D., Anderson, E. W., Cha, J., & Bryant, B. E. (1996). The American customer satisfaction index: Nature, purpose, and findings. *Journal of Marketing, 60*, 7-18.

Freed, L. (2003). *The insiders view of e-retailing 2003.* Retrieved August 5, 2004, from,www. foreseereults.com

Inman, J., Shankar, V., & Ferraro, R. (2004). The roles of channel-category associations and geodemographics in channel patronage. *Journal of Marketing, 68*, 51-71.

Johnson, C. (2004). *The growth of multichannel retailing.* A Forrester document prepared for the National Governor's Association and the National Conference of State Legislatures. Retrieved from www.nga.org/cda/files/0407MULTICHANNEL. PDF

Jupiter Communications. (2000, August 29). *Multichannel shoppers buy more, but 76 percent of retailers unable to track then across channels.* Retrieved from http://retailindustry.about. com/library/bl/bl_jup0829.htm

Keen, C., Wetzels, M., de Ruyter, K., & Feinberg, R. (2004). E-tailers versus retailers: Which factors determine consumer preferences. *Journal of Business Research, 57*, 685-695.

Levy, M., & Weitz, B. (2003). *Retail management* (5th ed.). New York: McGraw-Hill.

Loveman, G. (1998). Employee satisfaction, customer loyalty, and financial performance: An empirical examination of the service project chain in retail banking. *Journal of Service Research, 1*, 18-31.

Morgan, R., & Hunt, S. (1994). The commitment-trust theory of relationship marketing. *Journal of Marketing, 58,* 20-38.

Parasuraman, A., & Zinkham, G. (2002). Marketing and serving customers through the Internet: An overview and research agenda. *Journal of the Academy of Marketing Science, 30,* 286-295.

Pastore, M. (2000). *Future of e-tail lies with multichannel retailers.* Retrieved August 5, 2004, from http://cyberatlas.internet.com/markets/retailing/article/0,1323,6061_417411,00.html

Randall, T., Ulrich, K., & Reibstein, D. (1998). Brand equity and vertical product line extension. *Marketing Science, 12,* 356-379.

Reda, S. (2002). Active multi-channel shoppers may be a liability, less loyal than other on-line shoppers. *Stores Magazine, 84*(9), 78-82.

Reibstein, D. (2002). What attracts customers to online stores and what keeps them coming back. *Journal of the Academy of Marketing Science, 30,* 465-473.

Rust, R., & Zahorik, A. (1993). Customer satisfaction, customer retention, and market share. *Journal of Retailing, 69,* 193-215.

Rust, R., Zeithaml, V., & Lemon, K. (2000). *Driving customer equity: How customer lifetime value is reshaping corporate strategy.* New York: The Free Press.

Selnes, F. (1998). Antecedents and consequences of trust and satisfaction on buyer-seller relationships. *European Journal of Marketing, 3,* 305-322.

Sewell, C., & Brown, P. (2002). *Customers for life: How to turn that one buyer into a customer for life.* New York: Doubleday.

Stringer, K. (2004, September 3). Shoppers who blend store, catalog, Web spend more. *The Wall Street Journal,* p. A7.

Thompson, B. (2003). *Multi-channel service: Boosting customer value and loyalty.* RightNow Technologies. Retrieved from http://www.rightnow.com/resource/crm-whitepapers.html

Varadarajan, R., & Yadav, M. (2002). Marketing strategy and the Internet: An organizing framework. *Journal of the Academy of Marketing Science, 30,* 296-312.

Wagner, T. (2002). Multichannel customer interaction. *Defying the Limits, 1,* 277-280.

Wu, F., Mahajan, V., & Balasubramanian, S. (2003). An analysis of e-business adoption and its impact on business performance. *Journal of the Academy of Marketing Science, 31,* 425-447.

Zeithaml, V., Parasuraman, A., & Malholtra, A. (2002). Service quality delivery through Web sites: A critical review of extant knowledge. *Journal of the Academy of Marketing Sciences, 30,* 362-375.

APPENDIX A

Store Scenario/ Satisfying Shopping Experience

Betsy is very interested in purchasing a camera, and she estimates that the cost will be in the $200 to $500 range. After doing research she has determined that one brand and model is perfect for what she needs and it is in her price range. She decides to make the purchase at a store. After making the purchase, she is happy with her shopping experience. Betsy thinks she has made a great purchase for the money. Betsy is now interested in purchasing a DVD player. After research, she knows what brand she wants and what it will cost.

Store Scenario/Dissatisfying Shopping Experience

Betsy is very interested in purchasing a camera, and she estimates that the cost will be in the $200 to $500 range. After doing research she has determined that one brand and model is perfect for what she needs and it is in her price range. She decides to make the purchase at a store. After making the purchase she is unhappy with her shopping experience. Betsy thinks she has wasted her money. Betsy is now interested in purchasing a DVD player. After research, she knows what brand she wants and what it will cost.

Four additional scenarios were created: Internet, satisfying shopping experience; Internet, dissatisfying shopping experience; catalog, satisfying shopping experience; catalog, dissatisfying shopping experience.

How likely is it that Betsy will buy from:	Not at all likely	Unlikely	Neither likely nor unlikely	Likely	Extremely likely
1. The same store[a]	1	2	3	4	5
2. A different store	1	2	3	4	5
3. A catalog from that same retailer[b]	1	2	3	4	5
4. The Internet Web site of the same retailer[b]	1	2	3	4	5

a. The dependent measures were adapted to match each scenario (e.g., item 1 for the Internet scenario read: The same Internet site.

b.Items 3 and 4 were summated and a mean was generated to represent the likelihood of shopping in a different channel.

Chapter XIX
The Effect of Information Satisfaction and Relational Benefit on Consumer's On-Line Shopping Site Commitment

Chung-Hoon Park
Samsung SDS, Korea

Young-Gul Kim
Graduate School of Management, KAIST, Korea

ABSTRACT

Among the potential determinants of consumers' commitment to on-line shopping site are information features of the web site because on-line shopping consumers have to base their judgment solely on the product or service information presented on the site. When consumers are satisfied with such information features and perceive clear benefits from their relationships with the site, we can expect them to be more committed to the site. In this study, we investigate the relationship between such determinants and consumers' commitment to an on-line shopping site. Results of the on-line survey with 1,278 Korean customers of on-line bookstores and ticketing services indicate that information satisfaction and relational benefit are highly predictable of consumers' commitment to an on-line shopping site. In addition, we found that information satisfaction is affected most by product information quality while relational benefit is strongly related to service information quality. These results seem to reflect the consumers' different perceptual weights to different information contents of the web sites in forming their web site perceptions.

INTRODUCTION

Shopping at an on-line site is like shopping through a paper catalog because both involve mail delivery of the purchases and in both cases customers cannot touch or smell the items (Lighter and Eastman, 2002). So the promise of e-commerce and on-line shopping depends, to a great extent, on user interfaces and how people interact with computers (Griffith, et al., 2001). Moreover, the characteristics of information presentation, navigation, order fulfillment in an interactive shopping medium is considered a more important factor in building e-commerce trust than in the traditional retailing (Alba, et al., 1997; Reynolds, 2000).

However, while information contents of a web site might be an important determinant of consumers' on-line shopping behavior, there has been little empirical research on how such information features affect consumers' commitment to a shopping site on the web (Hong, et. al., 2005). This study examines how information features and other related technical and social aspects of an on-line shopping site affect consumers' commitment to such sites. The study was conducted in Korea that is leading the world in the deployment and usage of high speed internet infrastructure (IMD, 2005). Korean consumers' extensive use of online shopping would provide an appropriate context for studying online consumer behaviors.

The paper is organized as follows. First, we review information aspects of an on-line shopping site. Second, based on the literature, we develop a research model and a set of hypotheses to be tested, Third, in the research methodology section, the procedures for hypothesis testing and the testing results are described. Finally, we discuss the key findings and implications of this study and propose future research issues.

LITERATURE REVIEW

Prior studies on on-line shopping (Lohse and Spiller, 1998; Szmanski and Hise, 2000; Liu and Arnett, 2000) classify the attributes of an on-line store into four categories: merchandise, customer service and promotions, navigation and convenience, and security. These studies, however, did not recognize the fact that information aspects of these service attributes may affect the consumers' satisfaction and perceived benefits with the shopping site, eventually determining their commitment to the site. In this section, for each category of the service attributes, the importance of information for achieving consumer website commitment is confirmed from the literature.

Merchandising includes product related characteristics such as assortment, variety, and product information. According to Lohse and Spiller's study (1998), big on-line stores are less effective than the small ones at converting site traffic into sales because consumers have difficulty in finding the products they seek. It is argued that since a primary role of an on-line store is to provide price-related information and product information to help reduce consumers' search cost (Bakos, 1997), more extensive and higher quality information available on-line leads to better buying decisions and higher levels of consumer satisfaction. (Peterson, 1997; Lightner and Estman, 2002). For instance, on-line shopping stores can offer hyperlinks to more extensive product information such as price comparison, product testimonials (e.g. book reviews at an on-line book store), and product demonstrations (e.g. software downloads).

The second attribute category for an on-line store is customer service and promotion. Customers want careful, continuous, useful communication, across geographic barriers (Lose and Spiller, 1998). These attributes are frequently identified as a salient dimension to determine the store choice behavior in both on-line and off-line stores (Jarvenpaa and Todd, 1997; Kolesar and Galbraith, 2000). The third attribute category is navigation and convenience. This is related to the user interface of an on-line store (Szymanski and Hise, 2000). Store layout, organization features, as well as ease of use are considered in this category. Since user interface of an on-line store influences the experience of the consumers interacting with the retailer's product or service offerings (Griffith, 2001), a well-designed user interface system may reduce consumers' cost of searching and information processing time, minimizing the effort needed to perform choice and purchasing tasks (Hoque and Lose, 1999). Finally, security of on-line transactions continues to dominate the discussions on e-commerce (Elliot and Fowell, 2000; Szymanski and Hise, 2000; Liao and Cheung, 2001). Consumers are concerned about disclosing their private and financial information (Malhotra, et al., 2004). While most on-line shopping sites provide personal information a privacy protection policy and guarantee for transaction security, they do not offer detailed information on how transaction and personal data are secured (Gauzente, 2004).

Eventually, it can be seen that these four attributes of on-line shopping sites are about how to provide relevant information to meet consumers' needs for decision making in purchasing. Thus, the discussion about the critical factors in consumers' commitment to on-line shopping store needs to be focused on the availability of information (Wolfinbarger and Gilly, 2001). The availability of information considers not only product or service information but also convenience and personalization for retaining customers. It depends on the degree to which information can be employed by consumers to predict their probable satisfaction with subsequent purchases. By cultivating their customer database and proactively offering

desired information, an on-line store is actively inviting its customer to revisit its site (Srinivasan, and et al., 2002). Consequently, the success of an on-line store will be determined by the ability to tailor their information to meet the consumers' needs (DeLone and McLean, 2004).

RESEARCH MODEL AND HYPOTHESES

We have developed a research model of explaining the relationship between information features of the service attributes and consumer's commitment to an on-line shopping site. As independent variables, information quality dimensions was chosen, that correspond with the four online store attributes - product information quality for merchandising , service information quality for customer service and promotion, user interface quality for navigation and convenience, and security. Site awareness, which is not part of the online store attributes, has been added since it is an important aspect of the relational benefit based on the marketing literature.

As dependent variables, site commitment was chosen from the relationship marketing literature. As mediating variables to affect consumer's relational attitude, we introduce consumer information satisfaction and relational benefits. We describe the research model in Figure 1. Conceptualization of variables and its hypothesis are explained below.

Information Satisfaction

Information satisfaction refers to consumers' dis/satisfaction with an overall information service encounter (Crosby and Stephens, 1987) - which means navigating through web pages and contents in an on-line service context. This is different from the overall satisfaction that refers to the consumers' overall evaluation of an organization based on all encounters and experiences with that particular

Figure 1. Research model

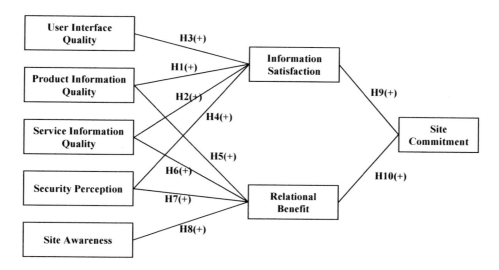

organization (Jones and Suh, 2000). In this study, we conceptualize information satisfaction as "an emotional reaction to the experience provided by the overall information service."(adapted from Westbrook, 1983).

According to the IS literature, information quality and user interface quality are believed to affect user information satisfaction (Wang and Strong, 1996; DeLone and McLean, 2004). Information provided by the on-line store is divided into product information and service information. Product information includes product attribute information, consumer recommendations, evaluation reports, etc. Service information that most on-line stores provide includes membership information, FAQ's, ordering and delivery information, and promotion, etc.

To evaluate product and service information, we adopted six components of information quality from user information satisfaction research. They are relevancy, recency, sufficiency, playfulness, consistency, and understandability (Wang and Strong, 1996; Moon and Kim, 2001, DeLone and McLean, 2004). Information presented by on-line stores should support customer service and product search. Such information should be

helpful and relevant in predicting the quality and utility of a product or service (Wolfinbarger and Gilly, 2001). To satisfy consumers' information needs, such information should be up-to-date in presenting products and services, sufficient to help consumers make a choice, consistent in representing and formatting the content, and easy to understand (Wang and Strong, 1996; Zhang, et al., 2000; McKinney, et al., 2002). Enjoyment, entertainment, and humor are important factors to form consumer's revisiting intention to web sites (Childers, and et al., 2001; Moon and Kim, 2001; Koufaris, 2002; O'Cass and Fenech, 2003). Therefore, playfulness is a salient factor in the web-based presentation information.

H1: There is a positive relationship between information satisfaction and product information quality.

H2: There is a positive relationship between information satisfaction and service information quality.

User interface quality is related to system layout, navigation sequence, and convenience to search for a product or information, or simply to browse (Szymanski and Hise, 2000; Molla and Licker, 2001; McKinney, et al., 2002; Hong, et al., 2004). Since a purchasing transaction can be adversely influenced by the poor on-line store design, it is essential to understand the effects of different layouts, and organizational, browsing, and navigation features on consumers' behavioral intention (Lose and Spiller, 1998; Hong, et al., 2004). On-line stores facilitate consumers' navigation by providing features such as search functions, guided navigation, and site maps. So in this research, we developed items corresponding to ease of navigation, convenience of searching for and ordering products as user interface quality measures.

H3: There is a positive relationship between information satisfaction and user interface quality.

Another important factor affecting information satisfaction in the web environment is security. Consumers are concerned about on-line payment security, reliability, and privacy policy of the on-line store (Gefen, 2000). So, security is a critical factor in acquiring and retaining consumers as on-line shopping service users. Basically, security concerns in e-commerce can be divided into concerns about user authentication and concerns about data and transaction security (Elliot and Fowell, 2000; Szymanski and Hise, 2000; Liu, et al., 2004; Gauzente, 2004). According to the prior research, as perception of security risk decreases, satisfaction with the information service of on-line stores is expected to increase.

H4: There is a positive relationship between information satisfaction and security perception.

Relational Benefit

In a traditional commercial service relationship, prior research has shown that relational benefit

is an antecedent to building a long-term relationship (Ravald and Gronroos, 1996; Gwinner, et al., 1998; Patterson and Smith, 2001). According to Gwinner, et al., (1998), relational benefit is defined as "the benefit customers receive from long-term relationships above and beyond the core service performance." The literature suggests that an important part of relational benefit is the sense of reduced anxiety, trust, and confidence that customers experience. Trust is a key-mediating variable in relational exchanges (Morgan and Hunt, 1994; Garbarino and Johnson, 1999) and risk reduction is a key outcome of the service relationships (Berry, 1995). Although this sense of confidence and trust may be inextricably tied to the quality of the core service, it is perceived as the independent benefit of a long-term relationship (Ravald and Grönroos, 1996).

Based on the previous discussion of relational benefit, we focused on the role of risk reduction, minimization of information search and transaction cost, and cognitive consistency as part of the relational benefit in an on-line shopping context. Since consumer decision-making efficiency improves when the information processing task is simplified and bounded (Sheth and Parvaytiyar, 1995), one would expect that consumers intend to maintain a relationship with the marketer to improve his/her future decision-making. Consumers may be able to reduce information search and transaction cost by maintaining a relationship with a credible on-line store that satisfies their information needs.

H5: There is a positive relationship between the product information quality and relational benefit.

H6: There is a positive relationship between the service information quality and relational benefit.

Besides affecting consumers' evaluation of overall information service, as discussed earlier, assurance of security also plays an important role in trust forming by reducing the consumers' concerns about personal data abuse and vulnerability of transaction data (Liu, et al., 2004). Consumers want detailed information on how their private and transaction data are secured (Elliot and Fowell, 2000). So, if the perceived level of security assurance meets consumer's expectations, a consumer may be willing to disclose his/her personal information and try to purchase with comfort.

H7: There is a positive relationship between security perception and relational benefit

In the service marketing literature, an external source of information about a company, corporate image, reputation, and awareness were identified as important factors in the overall evaluation of the firm and its service (Zeithaml and Bitner, 1997). Apart from corporate image as a function of accumulated purchasing/consumption experience over time, most companies also provide external informational events (e.g. advertising or public relations) to attract new customers and keep existing customers (Andreassen and Lindestad, 1998).

We introduce site awareness as perception by consumers about an on-line shopping store that is based on external information events like advertising and word-of-mouth communication. It is defined as the "ability of a buyer to recognize or recall that a site is a member of a certain service category." (adapted from Aaker, 1991). This construct indicates consumers' perception of extrinsic information cues about an on-line store and is assumed to have an impact on customers' choice of a company when service attributes are difficult to evaluate.

H8: There is a positive relationship between site awareness and relational benefit.

As summarized, we expect consumers to perceive the relational benefits of an on-line store

(i.e., on risk reduction, information searching, and transaction cost minimization), as a result of their evaluation of the information features of that on-line store.

Site Commitment

Commitment is an essential ingredient for a successful long-term relationship (Dwyer, et al., 1987; Morgan and Hunt, 1994). Commitment has been defined as "an enduring desire to maintain a valued relationship" (Moorman, et al., 1992) or "a tendency to resist change" (Pritchard, et al., 1999). It plays a key-mediating role in formation of consumers' loyalty and future behavioral intention (Garbarino and Johnson, 1999; Morgan and Hunt, 1994; Pritchard, et al., 1999).

In the service marketing literature, service quality, perceived value, and satisfaction are considered as antecedents of commitment (Grönroos, 1990; Hocutt, 1998; Shemwell, et al., 1998). That is, consumer's emotional and judgmental reaction to products or services is a key influential factor for consumers' commitment. The psychological benefit and trust are also essential ingredients for enhancing commitment (Grönroos, 1990). They are validated to be more important than special treatment or social benefits in consumer relationships with service firms (Gwinner, et al., 1998).

Based on the prior research, we expect information satisfaction and relational benefit to play a key role in forming consumers' site commitment to an on-line store. Information satisfaction indicates the consumer's overall evaluation of the on-line store's information service and relational benefit represents a cumulative psychological perception about the store.

H9: There is a positive relationship between relational benefit and site commitment.

H10: There is a positive relationship between information satisfaction and site commitment

RESEARCH METHODOLOGY

For greater generalizability, the proposed research model was validated through a large-scale field survey based on the multiple-item method where each item was measured based on a 5 point Likert scale from 'strongly disagree' to 'strongly agree'. All operational definitions of the study constructs are summarized in Appendix I. If possible, constructs that have already been used and validated by other researchers were adopted. Constructs that have not been used or developed previously are evaluated and adapted from the relevant literature as to how they might be operationalized, and then were validated by pilot testing. The measurement items are shown in Appendix II.

Sampling and Data Collection

The unit of analysis in this study is the individual consumer who has experience with purchasing products at on-line stores. In deciding on the target on-line stores, we applied control to the several factors. While price advantage and product quality are important factors affecting consumer purchasing behavior in any on-line shopping, since the interest of this study is focused on investigating the relationship between information characteristics and consumer commitment, we decided to select the on-line bookstores and movie ticketing services that have a fixed price policy. It was documented that consumers do interact more on-line than off-line with these product categories in Korea (KNSO, 2003). For the study, we selected three on-line bookstores and two ticketing services in Korea with the highest sales volume. At these stores, price policy (e.g. no discount policy), delivery service, and payment process were almost identical.

To collect the consumer perception data, we built an on-line survey web site that was hyper-linked to each target on-line bookstore – Kyobo, Jongro, and Youngpung – and ticketing service – Tiketlink and Maxmovie and the survey period was from three to four weeks for each bookstore and ticketing service(during from October to November at 2003). The target subjects were Korean consumers who had memberships at the on-line bookstores and ticketing services. We provided coupons or cyber money as a reward for the survey participation in the form of gift vouchers for books and free ticket or bonus points at the on-line store. Total number of participants was 1577. From the sample, we excluded the 161 cases of missing data and 139 cases of no membership ID number and finally used 1278 respondents for our analysis. For each site, the number of valid samples was 274 for Kyobo, 171 for Jongro, and 157 for Youngpung, 436 for Maxmovie, and 240 for Ticketlink.

As shown in Table 1, the distribution of respondents' gender, age, and occupation is somewhat skewed. But a national survey on the computer and internet usage which was conducted at National Internet Development Agency of Korea in 2004 (NIDA, 2004), reveals the similar demographic patterns among the Korean on-line shoppers - female consumers outnumber male consumers almost two to one, and young people in the twenties account for more than 60% of the people purchasing tickets and books on-line. So it can be said that respondent profile in Table 1 presents a realistic picture of the Korean consumers' on-line shopping service usage patterns.

Reliability and Validity of Instrument

Content validity defines how representative and comprehensive the items were in presenting the hypothesis. It is assessed by examining the process that was used in generating scale items (Straub, 1989). In this research, definitions of user interface quality, information quality, and security perception were developed based on the review of theory and research in information systems and other disciplines. Six items were selected for information quality, four items for user interface quality, and four items for security perception.

Table 1. Descriptive statistics of the respondent profile

Measure	Items	Frequency	Percent
Gender	Female	889	69.6
	Male	378	29.6
	Missing	11	0.8
Age	≤ 19	63	4.9
	20-29	891	69.7
	30-39	275	21.5
	≥ 40	35	2.7
	Missing	15	1.2
Occupation of Respondents	White collar employee	383	30.0
	Student	478	37.4
	Professional	181	14.2
	Self-employed	41	3.2
	Housewife	34	2.7
	Teacher	45	3.5
	Technical person	40	3.1
	Retired	18	1.4
	Missing	58	4.5
Time to use Internet (total access time)	≤ 1 hour per a day	176	13.8
	2-5	837	65.5
	6-9	163	12.7
	≥ 10	75	5.9
	Missing	27	2.1
Purchase frequency (during the last year)	≤ 2	456	35.7
	3 ~ 4	267	20.9
	5 ~ 6	187	14.6
	7 ~ 8	146	11.4
	≥ 9	216	16.9
	Missing	6	0.5

For developing the scales for site awareness, information satisfaction, relational benefit, and site commitment, we looked to the current marketing and service marketing literature. Four items were selected for site awareness, three items for information satisfaction, four items for relational benefit, and four items for commitment.

In this study, we follow the Straub's (1989) process of validating instruments to test construct validity in terms of convergent and discriminant validity. Convergent validity is the degree to which multiple attempts to measure the same concept are in agreement. For testing convergent validity, we evaluated the item-to-total correlation that is the correlation of each item to the sum of the remaining items. Items whose item-to-total correlation score was lower than 0.4 were dropped from further analysis.

Discriminant validity is the degree to which measures of different concepts are distinct. The discriminant validity of each construct was assessed by principal component factor analysis with VARIMAX rotation. As shown in Appendix III., the confirmatory factor analysis for independent variables yielded five distinct factors: user interface quality, product information quality, service information quality, security perception, and site awareness. Factor loadings for all variables were greater than 0.54 with no cross-construct loadings, indicating good discriminant validity. Together, the five observed factors accounted for 61% of the total variance.

To validate the appropriateness of the factor analysis, we applied several measures to the entire correlation matrix. Here, Bartlett's test of sphericity (p=0.000) indicates the statistical probability that the correlation matrix has significant correlations among at least some of the variables, and the Kaiser-Meyer-Olkin measure of sampling adequacy (0.908) showed acceptable sampling adequacy (Hair et al., p 99, 1998).

Next, we conducted the second factor analysis to investigate the distinctions among the dependent variables: information satisfaction, relational benefit, and site commitment. As shown in the table, factor loadings for the three variables were greater than 0.60 with no cross-construct loadings,

and the three observed factors accounted for 64% of the total variance.

Internal consistency reliability is a statement about the stability of individual measurement items across replications from the same source of information The Cronbach Alpha coefficient was used to assess reliability of the measures (Straub, 1989). As shown in Appendix III, reliability coefficients were acceptable for all constructs, ranging from 0.8687 for service information quality to 0.6712 for relational benefit. While all the reliability figures were higher than 0.6, the lowest acceptable limit for Cronbach's alpha suggested by Hair, et al (1998), variables with reliabilities lower than 0.8 deserve further refinement in the future research.

Table 2. Result of hypotheses tests

Model [a]	R^2	Adj. R^2	Std. β	t-value	VIF	Hypothesis result
(1) *Information Satisfaction* (INFSAT)						
INFSAT =UIQ + PIQ + SIQ + SEC + e	0.357	0.355				
UIQ			0.301	10.453[b]	1.641	H1 was supported
PIQ			0.258	9.050[b]	1.609	H2 was supported
SIQ			0.122	4.222[b]	1.644	H3 was supported
SEC			0.053	2.059[c]	1.295	H4 was supported
(2) *Relational benefit* (BENEF)						
BENEF = PIQ + SIQ + SEC + SA + e	0.306	0.304				
PIQ			0.175	6.264[b]	1.436	H5 was supported
SIQ			0.282	9.890[b]	1.489	H6 was supported
SEC			0.204	7.619[b]	1.306	H7 was supported
SA			0.064	2.576[c]	1.138	H8 was supported
(3) *Site Commitment* (COMMIT)						
COMMIT = INFSAT + BENEF + e	0.360	0.359				
INFSAT			0.452	18.686[b]	1.164	H9 was supported
BENEF			0.261	10.780[b]	1.164	H10 was supported

[a] *INFSAT, Information Satisfaction; BENEF, Relational benefit; COMMIT, Site Commitment; UIQ, User Interface Quality; PIQ, Product Information Quality; SIQ, Service Information Quality; SEC, Security Perception; SA, Site Awareness* [b] $p<0.001$; [c] $p<0.05$

Testing the Hypothesis

Hypotheses 1, 2, 3, and 4 examine the factors affecting information satisfaction. They are user interface quality, product information quality, service information quality, and security perception. Entering the variables in a single block, as shown in table 2, we found that 39% of the variance in information satisfaction is explained by user interface quality, product information quality, service information quality, and security perception ($R^2 = 35.5\%$, F-value=176.513, $p<0.001$). At the 0.001 significance level, user interface quality and product information quality were significantly related to information satisfaction, while service information quality and security perception were found to affect information satisfaction at the 0.05 significance level.

Hypotheses 5, 6, 7, and 8 examine the factors affecting relational benefit. They are product information quality, service information quality, security perception, and site awareness. To investigate the hypotheses, entering the variables in a single block, we found that 31% of the variance for relational benefit is explained by product information quality, service information quality, security perception, and site awareness ($R^2 = 30.4\%$, F-value=139.912, $p<0.001$). At the 0.001 significance level, product information quality, service information quality, and security perception were significantly related to relational benefit. Site awareness was also found to affect relational benefit at the 0.05 significance level.

Hypotheses 9 and 10 examine the links between both information satisfaction and relational benefit and consumer's site commitment. The result in

Table 3. Testing the mediation effect of information satisfaction and relational benefit

	(1)		(2)		(3)		(4)	
	IV → INFSAT		IV → BENEF		IV → COMMIT		IV → COMMIT *(Mediator included)*	
	Std. β	t-value	Std. β	t-value	Std. β	t-value	Std. β	t-value
Independent variables [a] (IV):								
UIQ	0.301	10.453[b]	N/A	N/A	0.163	5.336[b]	0.027	0.908
PIQ	0.258	9.050[b]	0.175	6.264[b]	0.105	3.483[b]	-0.001	-0.043
SIQ	0.122	4.222[b]	0.282	9.890[b]	0.201	6.607[b]	0.124	4.315[b]
SEC	0.053	2.059[c]	0.204	7.619[b]	0.137	5.047[b]	0.090	3.533[b]
SA	N/A	N/A	0.064	2.576[c]	0.137	5.356[b]	0.089	3.741[b]
Mediators [a]:								
INFSAT							0.363	13.153[b]
BENEF							0.165	6.180[b]

[a] *INFSAT, Information Satisfaction; BENEF, Relational benefit; COMMIT, Site Commitment; UIQ, User Interface Quality; PIQ, Product Information Quality; SIQ, Service Information Quality; SEC, Security Perception; SA, Site Awareness;* [b] *p<0.001;* [c] *p<0.05*

Table 3 shows that information satisfaction and relational benefit explain 35% of the variance in site commitment ($R^2 = 35.9\%$, F-value=359.024, p<0.001). At the 0.001 significance level, information satisfaction and relational benefit were significantly related to site commitment.

Tests on Mediating Effects

According to Kenny (2001), the following three conditions must hold to support the mediating effect of a construct (see also Baron and Kenny, 1986):

1. The independent variable must have a significant association with the dependent variable;
2. The independent variable must have a significant association with the mediator; and
3. When both the independent variable and the mediator variable are included as predictors, the mediator must have a significant effect on the dependent variable.

Complete mediation is supported when the beta coefficient for the independent variable in Condition 1 is significant, and the same coefficient in Condition 3 is not. Otherwise (still assuming all three conditions hold), partial mediation is supported (Baron and Kenny, 1986; Kenny, 1998). In Table 3, we report the results of the tests for mediation. The columns labeled (1), (2), (3), and (4) correspond to conditions 1-3. Mediation is indicated when all the beta coefficients, in column (1), (2), and (3) are significant and the beta coefficients of mediators in column (4) are also significant. To assess the strength of the mediation, column (4) reports the beta coefficients for the independent variables when both they and the mediators are included.

The results Table 3 clearly support the notion that information satisfaction and relational benefit variables mediate the effect of user interface quality, product and service information quality, site awareness, and security perception on site commitment.

Table 4. Results of stepwise regression analysis: Moderating effect of on-line service type

Model [a]	Std. β	t-value	R^2	Adj. R^2	ΔR^2	df.	F-value	F Change
Full Model[#]			0.431	0.429	0.070	3/1271	192.510 [b]	52.483 [b]
Mediator Variables								
INFSAT	0.285	7.886[b]						
BENEF	0.409	11.330[b]						
Moderator Variables								
ST	0.300	2.616[c]						
Interaction Effects								
ST x BENEF (Residuals)	- 0.390	- 3.571[b]						
ST x INFSAT (Residuals)	0.377	3.378[b]						

[a] *INFSAT, Information Satisfaction; BENEF, Relational benefit; COMMIT, Site Commitment; ST, Service Type*
[b] *p<0.001;* [c] *p<0.05;* [#]*Model: COMMIT = INFSAT + BENEF + ST + ST x BENEF + ST x INFSAT +* e

Consumer Commitment in Different Types of On-Line Shopping Service

To examine whether the basic relationship between information satisfaction and relational benefit and site commitment is moderated by the different types of on-line shopping (book purchase vs. movie ticketing), we have conducted the stepwise regression analyses (Atuahene-Gima and Li 2000). The procedure is as follows: First, the overall significance of a model comprising all antecedents and moderators is evaluated. Then, we add the interaction terms to the regression model and examine the increase in R^2. If the increase in R^2 is significant, it indicates the presence of the moderating effect. When this is the case, the individual interaction terms are then examined.

An equation for the moderated regression analyses and the results are presented in Table 4. Here, we note that, since cross-product terms generally correlate strongly with their constituent variables, we used the residual centering method which uses residuals from regressing the cross-product term on its constituent variables to extract pure non-linear terms. When the modera-

tor is service type and the dependent variable is site commitment, we found that addition of the interaction terms with the antecedents to the regression equation yields a significant increase in R^2 (F change = 52.483, $p < 0.001$). In particular, it is noteworthy that information satisfaction appears to be more effective in case of the on-line bookstore than for the on-line ticketing service ($\beta = 0.377$, $p < 0.001$). As the regression results show, the intervention of relational benefit is more visible in increasing site commitment at the on-line ticketing service than at the on-line bookstore ($\beta = -0.390$, $p < 0.01$).

For more in-depth understanding of the moderating effects, we conducted two more regression analyses with the data set split into two; one was for the on-line bookstore and the other was only for the on-line ticketing service. The results of the separated regression analyses are also shown graphically in Figure 2. There are two lines in each graph, representing on-line bookstore and ticketing service. Also, each line has two values; one is the beta coefficient and the other is the intercept value from each regression analysis.

Figure 2. Graphical representation of on-line service type's moderating effect

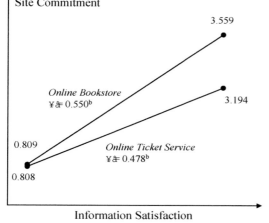

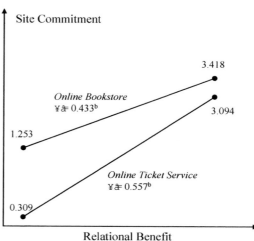

[b] $p < 0.001$

In the graph on the relationship between information satisfaction and site commitment, as information satisfaction increases, site commitment value for on-line bookstore increases steeply ($\beta = 0.550$). On the other hand, the line for on-line ticketing service is relatively flat ($\beta = 0.478$). Thus, we can confirm that the effect of information satisfaction on site commitment is affected by the type of on-line shopping. On the other hand, in the second graph on the relationship between relational benefit and site commitment, as relational benefit increases, site commitment value for on-line ticket service increases steeply ($\beta = 0.557$) and the line for on-line bookstore is relatively flat ($\beta = 0.433$).

Based on this analysis, we expect that the product information and user interface, which are strongly related to information satisfaction, might be more important in consumers' decision making for repeat patronage at the on-line bookstore than at the on-line ticketing service. For the same rationale, consumers who visit and purchase tickets at the on-line ticketing service site are expected to consider security and service information, which are strongly linked to relational benefit, as more important factors for their repeat patronage than customer of the on-line bookstore.

FINDINGS AND DISCUSSION

We found that consumers' commitment to an on-line store is highly related to information satisfaction and relational benefit. At the same time, information satisfaction and relational benefit were found to be significantly affected by product and service information quality, user interface quality, and security perception. These results imply that information richness of an on-line store, for the fixed price, standardized product such as book or movie, is an important factor that affects each consumer's commitment to the site. However, among the information feature variables, consumers' security percep-

tion was found to be of less important than other information quality dimensions contrary to the argument in the previous literature that security is a critical factor in acquiring and retaining consumers as on-line shopping service users. This may have been due to the fact that all three bookstores and two ticketing services were the top players in their market in Korea, providing a very high level of security infrastructure and management. However, whether there exists a cultural difference between Korean and western consumers toward their security perception needs to be further verified in the future research.

Another interesting finding of this study is the differential effect of product information and service information on different mediating variables - information satisfaction and relational benefit. Information satisfaction is affected more strongly by product information quality than by service information quality. Conversely, relational benefit is more strongly related to service information quality than to product information quality. These results may suggest that consumers have different perceptual weights toward the on-line store's information features. That is, in searching and purchasing, product information quality is a critical feature that affects the consumer. It is consistent with the prior discussion that the key benefit of e-commerce is the availability of organized and classified information, which enables consumers to reduce their information search and processing costs (Bakos, 1991; Alba, et al., 1997). On the other hand, consumers seem to consider service information quality as a more important factor in assessing the relational benefit of e-commerce in terms of reducing the transaction cost and risk.

In addition, a comparative analysis with two different on-line shopping domains – bookstore and movie ticketing service – shows that on-line service type has a significant effect on the relationship between information satisfaction and relational benefit and site commitment. In the on-line ticketing service context, relational benefit is more important in site commitment formation but, in the on-line bookstore, information satisfaction has stronger effect on site commitment formation. This finding leads us to believe that on-line shopping site operators need to find out what particular set of information features or service options might be effective in securing consumers' commitment to their site.

CONCLUSION AND FUTURE RESEARCH

Although our findings provide meaningful implications for on-line stores, our study has several limitations. First, although our model considers on-line store attributes as factors affecting consumer purchase behavior, since other factors such as price and promotion (e.g. loyalty program, price discount rate) were not included, our model does not explain the effect of price sensitivity and loyalty program on consumer purchase behavior with our model. Second, although this study has been conducted at the individual level of analysis, our sample data was collected from the customer-base of only three companies for on-line bookstore and two for on-line ticketing service. So, lack of organizational variance may have affected our result. Third, the literature review has been limited to the available e-commerce literature that predominantly comes from non-Korean social contexts. In the future, the literature related to Korea' business and cultural context needs to be used. Finally, due to the nature of web-survey, we were not able to provide the response rate or conduct the non-respondent bias analysis.

Main contribution in this study is the empirical validation of consumer behavior in the on-line shopping context. We investigated the perceptual difference of consumer's emotional and cognitive response to on-line shopping store attribute by comparative analysis between two different service types. Although much research on on-line store classification and its attribute

has been conducted, little is known about the empirical evidence of consumer response to service attributes in a specific service type. So, academically, this study provides a seminal work for future research on various service categories in on-line context and, for the practice in the on-line shopping industry, the results of this study present the general guidance to develop the strategy of on-line shopping site design and operation for promoting consumers' revisiting and repeat patronage to each service category.

For future research, it seems worthwhile to focus on the differences in consumer behavior according to product diversification and breadth of service domain. Moreover it is also worthwhile to conduct a comparative research on the differences of consumer behavior between off-line stores and on-line stores. Further study should also be conducted on consumers' relational behavior, and the differential effect of trust, commitment, and information satisfaction on purchasing behavior between relationship-oriented customers and transaction-oriented customers in an on-line shopping context (Garbarino and Johnson, 1999). To explain the effect of price sensitivity and loyalty program on consumer purchase behavior, future studies may test these constructs along with our research model. Moreover, many attempts to develop e-satisfaction, e-SERVUQAL, or e-Commerce metrics have been conducted (Szymanski and Hise, 2000; Devaraj, et al., 2002; McKinney, et al., 2002; DeLone and McLean, 2004). Our study may be applied to developing and validating e-commerce metrics that measure overall performance of an on-line store.

REFERENCES

Aaker, David A. (1991), *Managing brand equity*, New York: The Free Press.

Alba, Joseph, John Lynch, Barton Weitz, Chris Janiszewski, Richard Lutz, Alan Sawyer, & Stacy

Wood (1997), "Interactive home shopping: Consumer, retailer, and manufacturer incentives to participate in electronic marketplaces," *Journal of Marketing*, Vol. 61, pp. 38-53

Andreassen, Tor Wallin and Bodil Lindestad (1998), "Customer loyalty and complex services," *International Journal of Service Industry Management*, Vol. 9, No.1, pp.7-23

Atuahene-Gima, K., and Li, H. (2000), "Marketing's Influence Tactics in New Product Development: A Study of High Technology Firms in China", Journal of Product Innovation Management, Vol. 17, pp. 451-470.

Bailey, James E. and Sammy W. Pearson (1983), "Development of a tool for measuring and analyzing computer user satisfaction," *Management Science*, Vol. 29, No.5, pp.530-545

Bakos, J. Yannis (1991), "A strategic analysis of electronic marketplaces," *MIS Quarterly*, September, pp. 295-310

Bakos, J. Yannis (1997), "Reducing Buyer Search Costs: Implications for electronic marketplaces," *Management Science*, Vol. 43, No. 12, pp. 1676-1692

Baron, Reuben M. and David A. Kenny (1986), "The moderator-mediator variable distinction in social psychological research: Conceptual, strategic, and statistical considerations," *Journal of Personality and Social Psychology*, Vol. 51, No. 6, pp. 1173-1182

Berry, Leonard L. (1995), "Relationship marketing of services-growing interest, emerging perspectives," *Journal of the Academy of Marketing Science*, Vol. 23, No. 4, pp.236-245

Childers, Terry L., Christopher L. Carr, Joann Peck, and Stephen Carson (2001), "Hedonic and utilitarian motivations for online retail shopping behavior," *Journal of Retailing*, Vol. 77, pp. 511-535

Crosby, Lawrence A. and Nancy Stephens (1987), "Effects of relationship marketing on satisfaction, retention, and prices in the life insurance industry," *Journal of Marketing Research*, Vol. 24, pp. 404-411

DeLone, William and Ephraim R. McLean (2004), "Measuring e-commerce success: applying the DeLone & McLean information systems success model," *International Journal of Electronic Commerce*, Vol. 9, No. 1, pp. 31-47

Devaraj, Sarv, Fan, Ming, and Kohli, Rajive (2002), "Antecedents of B2C channel satisfaction and preference: validating e-commerce metrics," *Information Systems Research*, Vol. 13, No.3, pp. 316-333

Dwyer, F. Robert, Paul H. Schurr, and Sejo Oh (1987), "Developing buyer-seller relationships," *Journal of Marketing*, Vol. 51, 11-27

Elliot, Steve and Sue Fowell (2000), "Expectations versus reality: a snapshot of consumer experiences with internet retailing," *International Journal of Information Management*, Vol. 20, pp. 323-336

Garbarino, Ellen and Mark S. Johnson (1999), "The different roles of satisfaction, trust, and commitment in customer relationships," *Journal of Marketing*, Vol. 63, 70-87

Gauzente, Claire (2004), "Web merchants' privacy and security statement: How reassuring are they for customers? Two sided approach," *Journal of Electronic Commerce Research*, No. 5, No.3, pp.181-198

Gefen, D. (2000), "E-commerce: The role of familiarity and trust,"*Omega*, Vol. 28, No.6, pp. 725-737.

Griffith, David A. and Robert F. Krampf, and Jonathan W. Palmer (2001), "The role of interface in electronic commerce: consumer involvement with print versus online catalogs," *International Journal of Electronic Commerce*, Vol. 5, No. 4, pp. 135-153

Gronroos, Christian (1990), "Relationship Approach to Marketing in Service Contexts: The Marketing and Organizational Behavior Interface," *Journal Business Research*, Vol.20, pp.3-11

Gwinner, Kevin P., Dwayne D. Gremmler, and Mary Jo Bitner (1998), "Relational benefits in services industries: The customer's perspective," *Journal of the Academy of Marketing Science*, Vol. 26, No.2, pp.101-114

Hair, J.F., Jr., R.E. Anderson, R.L. Tatham,and W.C. Black (1998), Multivariate Data Analysis, Fifth Edition, Upper Saddle River: Prentice-Hall, Inc.

Hocutt, Mary Ann (1998), "Relationship dissolution model: antecedents of relationship commitment and the likelihood of dissolving a relationship," *International Journal of Service Industry Managment*, Vol. 9, No. 2, pp.189-200

Hong, Weiyin, James Y. L. Thong, and Kar Yan Tam (2005), "The effects of information format and shopping task on consumers' online shopping behavior: a cognitive fit perspective," *Journal of Management Information Systems*, Vol. 21, No.3, pp. 149-184

Hoque, Abeer Y. and Gerald L. Lohse (1999), "An information search cost perspective for designing interfaces for electronic commerce," *Journal of Marketing Research*, Vol. 36, No.3, pp.387-394

IMD World Competitiveness Center Yearbook (2005), IMD Business School, Geneva, Switzerland.

Jarvenpaa, Sirrka L. and Peter A. Todd (1997), "Consumer reactions to electronic shopping on the World Wide Web," *International Journal of Electronic Commerce*, Vol.1, No.2, pp.59-88

Jones, Michael A. and Jaebeom Suh (2000), "Transaction-specific satisfaction and overall satisfaction: an empirical analysis," *Journal of*
Services Marketing, Vol. 14, No. 2, pp. 147-159

Kenny, David A., "Mediation," 2001, (Accessed January 2002), [http://nw3.nai.net/~dakenny/mediate.htm]

KNSO (Korea National Survey Office), (2003), "The Annual Results of e-Commerce Transaction Survey in 2002," (Accessed July 2003) [http://www.nso.go.kr/eng/releases/e_suec0144.htm]

Kolesar, Mark B. and R. Wayne Galbraith (2000), "A services-marketing perspective on e-retailing: implications for e-retailers and directions for further research," *Internet Research*, Vol. 10, No.5, pp.424-438

Koufaris, Marios (2002), "Applying the technology acceptance model and flow theory to online consumer behavior," Information Systems Review, Vol. 13, No. 2, pp.205-223

Liao, Ziqi and Michael Tow Cheung (2001), "Internet-based e-shopping and consumer attitudes: an empirical study," *Information and Management*, Vol. 38, pp. 299-306

Lightner, Nancy J. and Caroline Eastman (2002), "User preference for product information in remote purchase environment," Journal *of Electronic Commerce Research*, Vol.3, No.3, pp.174-186

Liu, Chang and Kirk P. Arnett (2000), "Exploring the factors associated with web site success in the context of electronic commerce," *Information and Management*, Vol. 38, pp. 23-33

Liu, Chang, Jack T. Marchewka, Jun Lu, and Chun-Sheng Yu (2004), "Beyond concern: a privacy – trust- behavioral intention model of electronic commerce," *Information & Management*, Vol., 42, pp. 127-142

Lohse, Gerald L. and Peter Spiller (1998), "Electronic shopping," *Communications of ACM*, Vol. 41, No. 7, pp 81-89

Malhotra, Naresh K., Sung S. Kim, and James Agarwal (2004), "Internet users' information privacy concerns(IUIPC): The construct, the scale, and a causal model," *Information Systems Research,* Vol. 15, No. 4, pp. 336-355

McKinney, Vicki, Yoon, Kanghyun, and Zahedi, Fatemeh "Mariam" (2002), "The measurement of web-customer satisfaction: an expectation and disconfirmation approach," Information Systems Review, Vol. 13, No.3, pp. 296-315

Molla, Alemayehu and Paul S. Licker (2001), "E-commerce systems success: an attempt to extend and respecify the DeLone and McLean model of IS success," *Journal of Electronic Commerce Research,* Vol.2, No.4, pp.131-139

Moon, Ji-Woon and Young-Gul Kim (2001), "Extending the TAM for a World-Wide-Web context," *Information and Management,* Vol.38, pp. 217-230

Moorman, Christine, Gerald Zaltman, and Rohit Deshpande (1992), "Relationships between providers and users of market research: the dynamics of trust within and between organizations," *Journal of Marketing Research,* Vol. 29, pp. 314-328

Morgan, Robert M. and Shelby D. Hunt (1994), "The Commitment-Trust theory of Relationship marketing," *Journal of Marketing,* Vol.58, pp.20-38

NIDA (National Internet Development Agency of Korea) report (2004), "Survey on the computer and internet usage," www.nida.or.kr

O'Cass, Aron and Tino Fenech (2003), "Web retailing adoption: exploring the nature of internet users," *Journal of Retailing and Consumer Services,* Vol.10, pp. 81-94

Patterson, Paul G. and Tasman Smith (2001), "Relationship benefits in service industries: a replication in a southeast asian context," *Journal of services marketing,* Vol. 15, No.6, pp. 425-443

Peterson, Robert A., Sridhar Balasubramanian, and Bart J. Bronnenberg (1997), "Exploring the implications of the internet for consumer marketing," *Journal of the Academy of Management Science,* Vol. 25, No.4, pp.329-346

Pritchard, Mark P., Mark E. Havitz, and Dennis R. Howard (1999), "Analyzing the commitment-loyalty link in service contexts," *Journal of the Academy of Management Science,* Vol. 27, No. 3, pp. 333-348

Ravald, Annika and Christian Gronroos (1996), "The value concept and relationship marketing," *European Journal of Marketing,* Vol. 30, No. 2, pp. 19-30

Reynolds, Jonathan (2000), "eCommerce: a critical review," *International Journal of Retail & Distribution Management,* Vol. 28, No.10, pp. 417-444

Shemwell, Donald J., Ugur Yavas, and Zeynep Bilgin (1998), "Customer-service provider relationships: an empirical test of a model of service quality, satisfaction, and relationship-oriented outcomes," *International Journal of Service Industry Management,* Vol. 9, No.2, pp. 155-168

Sheth, Jagdish N. and Atul Parvatiyar (1995), " Relationship marketing in Consumer Markets: Antecedents and Consequences," *Journal of the Academy of Marketing Science,* Vol. 23, No. 4, pp. 255-271

Srinivasan, Srini S., Rolph Anderson, and Kishore Ponnavolu (2002), "Customer loyalty in e-commerce: an exploration of its antecedents and consequences," *Journal of Retailing,* Vol. 78, pp.41-50

Straub, D.W. (1989), "Validating instruments in MIS research" *MIS Quarterly,* Vol. 13, No. 2, pp. 147-169.

Szymanski, David M. and Richard T. Hise (2000),

"e-satisfaction: an initial examination," *Journal of Retailing*, Vol. 76, No. 3, pp.309-322

Wang, Richard Y. and Diane M. Strong (1996), "Beyond accuracy: What data quality means to data consumers." *Journal of Management Information Systems*, Vol. 12, No.4, pp.5-34

Westbrook, Robert A. et al. (1983), "Value-percept disparity: An alternative to the disconfirmation of expectations theory of consumer satisfaction," *Advances in consumer research*, Vol. 10, pp. 256-261

Wolfingbarger, Mary and Mary C. Gilly (2001), "Shopping Online for freedom, control, and fun," *California Management Review*, Vol. 43, No.2, pp. 34-55

Zeithaml, Valarie A. and Mary Jo Bitner (1997), *Services Marketing,* Singapore, p.114, McGraw-Hill.

Zhang, Xiaoni, Kellie B. Keeling, and Robert J. Pavur (2000), "Information quality of commercial web site home pages: an explorative analysis," *in Proceedings of the Twenty First International Conference on Information Systems*, Brisbane, Australia, pp.164-175

APPENDIX 1

Definitions and References of Key Constructs

Constructs	Definition	References
User Interface Quality	Customer perception of degree to convenience and user friendliness in using a web site system	Szymanski and Hise, 2000 Griffith, et al., 2001
Product Information Quality	Customer perception of the quality of information about product that is provided by a Web site (Relevancy, Recency, Sufficiency, Understandability, Consistency, Playfulness)	Wang, et al., 1996 DeLone and McLean, 2004 Bailey and Pearson, 1983
Service Information Quality	Customer perception of the quality of information about service that is provided by the Web Site. (Relevancy, Recency, Sufficiency, Understandability, Consistency, Playfulness)	Wang, et al., 1996 DeLone and McLean, 2004 Bailey and Pearson, 1983
Security Perception	Customer perceptions about the ability of an on-line store's controlling and safeguarding of transaction data from misappropriation or unauthorized alteration	Bailey and Pearson, 1983;
Site Awareness	The customer's ability to recognize or recall that a site is a member of a certain service category	Aaker, 1991
Information Satisfaction	Emotional response to the experience provided by the overall information service	Westbrook, 1983
Relational Benefit	Benefit customers receive from long-term relationships above and beyond core service performance	Gwwinner, et al. 1998
Site Commitment	An enduring desire to maintain a valued relationship with the site	Moorman, et al., 1992

APPENDIX 2

Measurements of Instrument of Key Constructs

Construct	Items (anchors: strongly disagree/ strongly agree)	Cronbach Alpha
Independent Variables		
User Interface Quality	1. This site is convenient to search for a book (ticket) 2. This site is convenient to order a book (ticket) 3. This site is easy to navigate wanted pages 4. This site is user friendly	0.7143
Product Information Quality	1. This site provides up-to-date book (ticket) information 2. This site provides sufficient book (ticket) information 3. This site presents book (ticket) information easy to understand 4. The book (ticket) information is consistent 5. The book (ticket) information is playful 6. The book (ticket) information is relevant	0.8216
Service Information Quality	1. This site provides up-to-date service information 2. This site provides sufficient service information 3. This site present service information easy to understand 4. The service information is consistent 5. The service information is playful 6. The service information is relevant	0.8680
Site Awareness	1. Neighbors know this site very well 2. This site is very famous as an Internet bookstore (ticketing service) 3. This site is known through the advertising media (TV, newspaper, Internet, etc.)	0.6787
Security Perception	1. My private information is managed securely on this site 2. I am sure that payment information will be protected in this site 3. This site provides detailed information about security 4. *I am afraid that my private information will be used in an unwanted manner (R)*	0.7630
Mediators and Dependent Variable		
Information Satisfaction	1. I am satisfied with the information service of this site compared to other shopping sites 2. Information service of this site satisfies my expectations 3. I am satisfied with the overall information service of this site	0.7690
Relational benefit	1. At this site, I am able to reduce the time to purchase wanted books (ticket) 2. At this site, I am able to reduce efforts to purchase wanted books (ticket) 3. At this site, I am able to purchase wanted books (ticket) that are hard to purchase at other stores 4. I will receive credible customer service from this site	0.6667
Site Commitment	1. I will not change my book (ticket) shopping site in the future 2. I will continuously purchase books (tickets) at this site in the future 3. I will recommend this site to other people 4. I will visit this site first when I want to buy books (tickets)	0.8765

Web site provides various types of information that evokes consumers' interest like humor, links to other sites of interest, and appetizer information, on-line games, gossips, and video clips. So this types of information, that we mean, is playful

APPENDIX 3

Construct Validity and Reliability of Measures

Construct	Item label	Eigen value	Factor loading	Item to total correlation	Cronbach alpha	Variance explained	Cumulative percentage
Independent Variables							
User Interface Quality	UIQ1	2.084	0.521	0.467	0.7143	9.5%	9.5%
	UIQ2		0.566	0.486			
	UIQ3		0.726	0.522			
	UIQ4		0.750	0.531			
Product Information Quality	PIQ1	3.348	0.570	0.480	0.8216	15.2%	24.7%
	PIQ2		0.783	0.672			
	PIQ3		0.714	0.647			
	PIQ4		0.622	0.586			
	PIQ5		0.644	0.536			
	PIQ6		0.696	0.608			
Service Information Quality	SIQ1	3.686	0.735	0.652	0.8680	16.8%	41.5%
	SIQ2		0.788	0.690			
	SIQ3		0.772	0.686			
	SIQ4		0.735	0.702			
	SIQ5		0.609	0.587			
	SIQ6		0.688	0.682			
Security Perception	SEC1	2.103	0.777	0.596	0.7630	9.5%	51%
	SEC2		0.795	0.636			
	SEC3		0.743	0.562			
Site Awareness	SP1	1.916	0.772	0.509	0.6787	8.7%	59.7%
	SP2		0.811	0.538			
	SP3		0.673	0.432			
Mediators and Dependent Variable							
Information Satisfaction	INFSAT1	2.115	0.801	0.605	0.7690	19.2%	19.8%
	INFSAT2		0.732	0.605			
	INFSAT3		0.796	0.610			
Relational benefit	BENEF1	2.078	0.653	0.444	0.6667	18.9%	38.1%
	BENEF2		0.656	0.472			
	BENEF3		0.749	0.416			
	BENEF4		0.666	0.471			
Site Commitment	COMMIT1	2.931	0.854	0.772	0.8765	26.6%	64.7%
	COMMIT2		0.823	0.774			
	COMMIT3		0.733	0.687			
	COMMIT4		0.748	0.714			

This work was previously published in Journal of Electronic Commerce in Organizations, Vol 4, Issue 1, edited by M. Khosrow-Pour, pp. 70-90, copyright 2006 by IGI Publishing, formerly known as Idea Group Publishing (an imprint of IGI Global).

Compilation of References

----- & ----- (2003), "The Impact of Customer Relationship Characteristics on Profitable Lifetime Duration," *Journal of Marketing, 67 (January), 77-99.*

-----, -----, & Verhoef, P.C. (2002), "The Theoretical Underpinnings of Customer Asset Management: A Framework and Propositions for Future Research," *Erasmus Research Institute in Management Working Paper No. ERS-2002-80-MKT, Erasmus University, Rotterdam.*

-----, Kannan, P.K. & Bramlett, M.D. (2000), "Implications of Loyalty Program Membership and Service Experiences for Customer Retention and Value," *Journal of the Academy of Marketing Science, 28 (Winter), 95-108.*

_ & Kitchen, P.J. (2000), Communicating Globally: An *Integrated Marketing Approach,* Lincolnwood, IL: NTC Business Books.

Aaker, David A.and Joachimsthaler(2000), "Brand Leadership", The Free Press, pp. 243.

Aaker, D. (1996) "Building Strong Brands", The Free Press, New York

Aaker, D. A. (1996). Measuring Brand Equity across Products and Markets. *California Management Review, 31*(May), 191-201.

Aaker, D. A. (2002). The Internet as integrator: Fast brand building in slow growth market. *Strategy+Business, 28,* 48–57.

Aaker, D.A.; Keller, K.L. (1990), "Consumer Evaluations of Brand Extensions," *Journal of Marketing,* Vol. 54, No. 1, pp. 27-41.

Aaker, David A. (1991), "Managing Brand Equity - Capitalizing on the Value of a Brand Name", The Free Press, pp.16-85.

Aaker, David A. (1991), *Managing brand equity,* New York: The Free Press.

Aaker, J. L. (1997). "Dimensions of Brand Personality". Journal of Marketing Research. 34 (3), pp. 347-356.

Aaker, J. L. (1999). "The Malleable Self: The Role of Self-Expression in Persuasion". Journal of Marketing Research. 34 (3), pp. 347-356.

Aaker, J. L., Benet-Martinez, V. and Garolera, J. (2001). "Consumption Symbols as Carriers of Culture: A Study of Japanese and Spanish Brand Personality Constructs". Journal of Personality and Social Psychology. 81 (3), pp. 492-508.

Adams, D.A.; Nelson, R.R.; & Todd, P.A. (1992). Perceived usefulness, ease of use, and usage of information technology: A replication. *MIS Quarterly,* 16(2), 227-247.

Agarwal, R. & Prasad, J. (1999). Are individual differences germane to the acceptance of new information technologies? *Decision Sciences,* 30(2), 361-391.

Agarwal, R., & Karahanna, E. (2000). Time flies when you're having fun: Cognitive absorption and beliefs about information technology usage. *MIS Quarterly,* 24, 4, 665-694.

Agora (2005). Advertising market. Available: http://www. agora.pl/agora_eng/1,60209,2385752.html?menu=7.

Agrawal, M. (1995). Review of a 40-year debate in international advertising. *International Marketing Review*, 12 (1), 26-48.

Ahmed, Z. U., Johnson, J. P., Ling, C. P., Fong, T. W., & Hui, A. K. (2002). Country-of-origin and brand effects on consumers' evaluations of cruise lines. *International Marketing Review, 19*(2/3), 279-302.

Ajzen, I. & Fishbein, M. (1980). *Understanding attitudes and predicting social behavior.* Englewood Cliffs: Prentice Hall.

Ajzen, I., & Sexton, J. (1999). Depth of Processing, Belief congruence, and Attitude-Behavior Correspondence. In Chaiken, S. & Trope, Y. (Eds.), *Dual-Process Theories in Social Psychology* (pp. 117-138). New York, NY: The Guilford Press.

Alba, Joseph, John Lynch, Barton Weitz, Chris Janiszewski, Richard Lutz, Alan Sawyer, & Stacy Wood (1997), "Interactive home shopping: Consumer, retailer, and manufacturer incentives to participate in electronic marketplaces," *Journal of Marketing*, Vol. 61, pp. 38-53

Ali-Sulaiti, K. I., & Baker, M. J. (1998). Country of origin effects: a literature review. *Marketing Intelligence & Planning, 16*(3), 150-199.

Amazon 2002 Annual Report. www.amazon.com

Amazon.com. (1998). Gary Trudeau and Amazon.com launch "The People's Doonesbury @ Amazon.com." Press Release Archive.

Ambrose, P.J. and Johnson, G.J. (1998). A Trust Based Model of Buying Behavior in Electronic Retailing. In *Proceedings of the Fourth Americas Conference on Information Systems (AMCIS 1998).* Baltimore, 263-265.

American Banker, & Gallup. (2004). *What Americans Think About Overseas Outsourcing*: American Banker/ Gallup.

American Marketing Association (AMA). Dictionary of Marketing Terms. http://www.marketingpower.com/mg-dictionary.php?SearchFor=brand+personality&Searched=1

ANDERSEN, P.H. (2005) Relationship marketing and brand involvement of professionals through web-enhanced brand communities: The case of Coloplast. *Industrial Marketing Management* 34, 39-51.

Anderson, E. W., & Sullivan, M. W. (1993). The antecedents and consequences of customer satisfaction for firms. *Marketing Science, 12*(2), 125-143.

Anderson, J. R. (1983) "The architecture of cognition", Harvard University Press, 1983

Anderson, J.C., & Narus, J.A. (1990). A model of distributor firm and manufacturer firm working partnerships. *Journal of Marketing, 54*, 1, 42-58.

Anderson, P.F., Bennett P.D. (1988) "Dictionary of Marketing Terms", American Marketing Association, Chicago.

Andrade, E.B. (2000). Identifying Discriminating Variables of Online and Offline Buyers: A Perceived-Risk Approach. In *Proceedings of the Sixth Americas Conference on Information Systems (AMCIS 2000).* Long Beach, 1386-1392.

Andreassen, Tor Wallin and Bodil Lindestad (1998), "Customer loyalty and complex services," *International Journal of Service Industry Management*, Vol. 9, No.1, pp.7-23

Anon (2005) AdWords lawsuits in France – Trademarks as keywords illegal? www.linksandlaw.com/adwords-google-keyword-lawsuit-France.htm , Retrieved 29 December, 2006

Anon (2005) AdWords lawsuits in Germany – Preispiraten decision, www.linksandlaw.com/adwords-google-germany-preispiraten.htm Retrieved 29 December, 2006

Anon (2005) Google's AdWords under attack – Overview over the pending lawsuits, www.linksandlaw.com/adwords-pendinglawsuits.htm, Retrieved 29 December, 2006

Ansari, A. &. Mela, C.F. (2003), "E-customization," *Journal of Marketing Research*, 40, 2 (May), 131-145.

ARBOmedia (2005). Standardní reklamní rok přinese

médiím 17,8 miliard. Available: http://www.arbomedia. cz/strany/ipwc/w2a.asp?id=133

ARBOmedia (2005). Standardní reklamní rok přinese médiím 17,8 miliard". Available: http://www.arbomedia. cz/strany/ipwc/w2a.asp?id=133.

ARMSTRONG, A. & HAGEL, J. (1997) *Net gain: Expanding markets through virtual communities.* Harvard Business School Press, MA.

Arora, R., & Stoner, C. (1996). The effect of perceived service quality and name familiarity on the service selection decision. *The Journal of Services Marketing, 10*(1), 22.

Arvidsson, A. (2006) Brand Value. *Journal of Brand Management*, 13 (3), pp 188-192.

Attneave, F. (1959). *Applications of information theory to psychology: A summary of basic concepts, methods, and results.* New York: Henry Holt and Company, Inc.

Atuahene-Gima, K., and Li, H. (2000), "Marketing's Influence Tactics in New Product Development: A Study of High Technology Firms in China", Journal of Product Innovation Management, Vol. 17, pp. 451-470.

Azoulay, A. and Kapferer, J.N. (2003). "Do Brand Personality Scales Really Measure Brand Personality?". Journal of Brand Management. 11, pp. 143-155.

Bagozzi, R. P. & Dholakia, U. M. (2006). Intentional social action in virtual communities. *Journal of Interactive Marketing*, 16(2), 2-21.

Bagozzi, R.P. (1980). *Causal methods in marketing.* New York: John Wiley and Sons.

Bailey, James E. and Sammy W. Pearson (1983), "Development of a tool for measuring and analyzing computer user satisfaction," *Management Science*, Vol. 29, No.5, pp.530-545

BAILLIE, T. (1997) A Skeptic's View of Electronic Democracy in Virtual Communities. Retrieved September 13 2005 from http://wwwucalgaryca/~dabrent/380/web-proj/coms380html

Bajari, P., & Hortacsu, A. (2004): "Economic Insights from Internet Auctions," Journal of Economic Literature, Vol. XLII, 457-486.

Baker, M., & Melino, A. (2000), "Duration Dependence and Nonparametric Heterogeneity: A Monte Carlo Study," Journal of Econometrics 96, 357-393.

Baker, W.E. (2003) "Does Brand Name Imprinting in Memory Increase Brand Information Retention?" Psychology & Marketing, Vol.20(12), pp.1119-1136.

Bakos, J. Yannis (1991), "A strategic analysis of electronic marketplaces," *MIS Quarterly*, September, pp. 295-310

Bakos, J. Yannis (1997), "Reducing Buyer Search Costs: Implications for electronic marketplaces," *Management Science*, Vol. 43, No. 12, pp. 1676-1692

Balasubramanian, S., Konana, P., & Menon, N. (2003). Customer satisfaction in virtual environments: A study of online trading. *Management Science, 49*, 871-889.

Balmer, J.M.T. (2001) "Corporate identity, corporate branding and corporate marketing. Seeing through the fog" European Journal of Marketing, Vol. 35, No.3/4, pp. 248-297.

Bandura, A. (1997). *Self-Efficacy: The Exercise of Control.* Freeman, New York, NY.

Barbalet, J. M. (1998). *Emotions, Social Theory, and Social Structure: A Macrosociological Approach.* Cambridge: Cambridge University Press.

Baron, Reuben M. and David A. Kenny (1986), "The moderator-mediator variable distinction in social psychological research: Conceptual, strategic, and statistical considerations," *Journal of Personality and Social Psychology*, Vol. 51, No. 6, pp. 1173-1182

Batra, R., Lehmann, D.R. & Singh, D. (1993), "The brand personality component of brand goodwill: some antecedents and consequences," in Aaker and Biel editor. *Brand equity and advertising.* Hillsdale, NJ: Lawrence Erlbaum Associates. pp. 83-96.

Batra, R., Myers, J.G. and Aaker, D.A. (1996). *Advertising Management,* Prentice Hall, Englewood Cliffs, NJ.

Battey, J. (1999). IBM's redesign results in a kinder, simpler Web site. Article available at http://www.infoworld. com/cgibin/displayStat.pl?/pageone/opinions/hotsites/ hotextr990419.htm

Baudrillard, J. (1988). *Selected writings*. Translated by Mark Poster. Stanford, CA: Stanford University Press.

Bauer, R. (1967). Consumer behavior as risk taking. In: Cox, D. (Ed.), *Risk Taking and Information Handling in Consumer Behavior*. Harvard University Press, Cambridge, MA.

Bearden, W. O., & Teel, J. E. (1983). Selected determinants of consumer satisfaction and complaint reports. *Journal of Consumer Research, 20*(1), 21-28.

Bearden, W. O., Hardesty, D. M., & Rose, R. L. (2001). Consumer Self-Confidence: Refinements in Conceptualization and Measurement. *Journal of Consumer Research, 28*(June), 121-134.

Belk, R. W. (1975). Situational variables and consumer behavior. *Journal of Consumer Research, 2* (December), 157-164.

Bellman, S.; Lohse, G.L. and Johnson, E.J. (1999). Predictors of Online Buying Behavior. *Communications of the ACM*, 42(12), 32-38.

Benbasat, I., & DeSanctis, G. (2001). Communication challenges: A value network perspective. In G.W. Dickson and G. DeSanctis (Eds.), *Information technology and the future enterprise: New models for managers* (pp. 144-162). New Jersey: Prentice-Hall.

Berry, L.L. (1995), "Relationship Marketing of Services: Growing Interest, Emerging Perspectives," Journal of the Academy of Marketing Science, 23 (Fall), 236-45.

Berry, L.L., Lefkowith, E.F., Clark, T. (1988) "In services: what's in a name?" Harvard Business Review Vol.66, September-October, pp.28-30.

Berry, Leonard L. (1995), "Relationship marketing of services-growing interest, emerging perspectives," *Journal of the Academy of Marketing Science*, Vol. 23, No. 4, pp.236-245

Bettman, J. R., Johnson, E., & Payne, J. W. (1991).

Consumer Decision-Making. In Robertson Thomas S., and Kassarjian Harold H. (Ed.), *Handbook of Consumer Behavior* (pp. 54-80). Englewood Cliffs, NJ: Prentice Hall.

Bettman, J.R. (1979). *An Information Processing Theory of Consumer Choice*, Reading, Mass.: Addison-Wesley.

Bettua, M. (1999). Rethinking e-commerce service. *Call Center Solutions, 18* (July), 148-150.

Bharadwaj, S, G., Varadarajan, P.R., & Fahy, J. (1993). Sustainable competitive advantage in service industries: a conceptual model and research propositions. *Journal of Marketing*, 57 (Oct.), 83-99.

Bhatnagar, A.; Misra, S. and Rao, H.R. (2000). On Risk, Convenience, and Internet Shopping Behavior - Why Some Consumers are Online Shoppers while Others are Not, *Communications of the ACM*, 43(11), 98-105.

Bhattacharya, *C.B.* & Bolton, R.N. (2000), *"Relationship Marketing in Mass Markets," in Handbook of Relationship Marketing, Jagdish N. Sheth and Atul Parvatiyar, eds. Thousand Oaks, CA: Sage Publications, 327-54.*

Bhattacherjee, A. (2000). Acceptance of E-Commerce Services: The Case of Electronic Brokerages, *IEEE Transactions on Systems, Man and Cybernetics, Part A*, 30(4), 411-420.

Bhattacherjee, A. (2001). An Empirical Analysis of the Antecedents of Electronic Commerce Service Continuance, *Decision support systems*, 32(2), 201-214.

Bhattacherjee, A. (2001). Understanding information systems continuance: An expectation confirmation model. *MIS Quarterly,* 25, 3, 351-370.

Bhattacherjee, A. (2001). Understanding Information Systems Continuance: An Expectation Confirmation Model, *MIS Quarterly*, 25(3), 351-370.

Bias, G. & Mayhew, D. (1994). *Cost-Justifying usability.* New York: Academic Press.

Biel, A.(1992). "How Brand Image Drives Brand Equity?". Journal of Advertising Research. 32 (6), pp. 6-12.

Biyalogorsky, E. & Naik, P (2003), "Clicks and Mortar: The Effect of Online Activities on Off-line Sales," *Marketing Letters* 14 (1), pg. 21-32.

Blackmore, D., DeSouza, R., Young, A., Goodness, E., & Silliman, R. (2005). *Forecast: IT Outsourcing, Worldwide, 2002-2008 (Update)*: Gartner.

BLANCHARD, A. & HORAN, T. (1998) Virtual communities and social capital. *Social Science Computer Review* 16, 293-307.

BLANCHARD, A. (2004) Virtual Behavior Settings: An Application of Behavior Setting Theories to Virtual Communities. *Journal of Computer Mediated Communication* 9 (2). Retrieved September 13 2005 from http://wwwascuscorg/jcmc/vol9/issue2/blanchardhtml

Blanchard, K., & Bowles, S. (1993). *Raving fans: A revolutionary approach to customer service*. New York: William Morrow.

Blattberg, R.C., Getz, G. & Thomas, J.S. (2001), Customer Equity: Building and Managing Relationships as Valuable Assets. Boston: Harvard Business School Press.

Bloch, Peter (1995), "Seeking the Ideal Forces; Product Design and Consumer Response", Journal of Marketing, 59, pp.16-29.

Bobbitt, L.M. and Dabholkar, P.A. (2001). Integrating Attitudinal Theories to Understand and Predict Use of Technology-Based Self-Service: The Internet as an Illustration, *International Journal of Service Industry Management*, 12(5), 423-450.

Bolton W., & Tieman, A.F. (2005) "Skewed Pricing in Two-Sided Markets: An IO Approach," Available at SSRN: http://ssrn.com/abstract=665103.

Bolton, R. N., & Lemon, K. N. (1999). A dynamic model of customers' usage of services: Usage as an antecedent and consequence of satisfaction. *Journal of Marketing Research, 36* (May), 171-186.

Bolton, R.N. (1998), "A Dynamic Model of the Duration of the Customer's Relationship with a Continuous Service Provider: The Role of Satisfaction," Marketing Science, 17 (Winter), 45-65.

Borchers, A. (2001). Trust in Internet Shopping: A Test of a Measurement Instrument. In *Proceedings of the Seventh Americas Conference on Information Systems (AMCIS 2001)*. Boston, 799-803.

Bottomley, P.A. & Holden, S.J. (2001), "Do we really know how consumers evaluate brand extensions? Empirical generalizations based on secondary analysis of eight studies," *Journal of Marketing Research* 38 (2001) (4), pp. 494–500.

Bourdieu, P. (1984). *Distinction: A social critique of the judgement of taste*. Translated by Richard Nice. Cambridge, MA: Harvard University Press.

Boush, D.M. & Loken, B. (1991), "A Process-Tracing Study of Brand Extension Evaluation," *Journal of Marketing Research*, 28 (1), 16-28.

Boyd, C.W. (1985) "Point of view: alpha-numeric brand names", Journal of Advertising Research Vol.25, no.5, pp.48-52.

Boyer, K.K.; Hallowell, R. and Roth, A.V. (2002). E-Services: Operating Strategy. A Case Study and a Method for Analyzing Operational Benefits. *Journal of Operations Management*, 20(2), 175-188.

Bradley, G. L., & Sparks, B. A. (2002). Service locus of control: its conceptualization and measurement. *Journal of Service Research, 4* (4), 312-24.

Braunstein, M., & Levin, E. H. (2000). *Deep branding on the Internet: Applying heat and pressure online to ensure a lasting brand*. Roseville, CA: Prima Venture.

Breakenridge, D. (2001). *Cyberbranding: Brand Building in the Digital Economy*. Upper Saddle River, NJ: Prentice Hall.

Briggs, B. (2005). Offshore Outsourcing Poses Risks. *Health Data Management, 13*(2), 68-78.

Brislin, R.W. (1980). Translation and Content Analysis of Oral and Written Material. In H. C. Triandis and Berry, J. W. (eds.), *Handbook of Cross-cultural Psychology* (Vol. 2, pp. 389-444), Boston: Allyn and Bacon.

Brown, S. P., & Chin, W. W. (2004). Satisfying and

Retaining Customers through Independent Service Representatives. *Decision Sciences, 35*(3), 527-550.

Buchhold, Andreas and Wordemann Wolfram(2000), "What makes Winning Brands Different", pp.21-26.

Budapest business journal (2003). Web-based advertising making ground. September 16, 2003, Available: http://www.bbj.hu.

Budapest business journal (2004). Online advertising boom. August 18, 2004, Available: http://www.bbj.hu.

Burden, D. (2005). Marketing's haiku challenge. *Marketing (UK), 24 August 05*, 26.

Burke, R. (2000). *Creating the ideal shopping experience: What consumers want in the physical and virtual store*. Retrieved from www.kelley.iu.edu/retail/research/iukpmg00b.pdf

Burnham, T.A., Frels, J.K., & Mahajan, V. (2003). Consumer switching costs: A topology, antecedents, and consequences. *Journal of the Academy of Marketing Science*, 31, 2, 109-126.

Burns, E. (2005). Search Usage Spikes as A Daily Online Habit. Available at: http://www.clickz.com/showPage.html?page=3565561

Burns, E. (2006). Online Seizes More of the Advertising Mix. Available at: http://www.clickz.com/showPage.html?page=3584801.

Burns, E. (2006). Search Sees Double-Digit Growth. Available at:. http://www.clickz.com/showPage.html?page=3584126

BusinessWeek (2002). The 100 Top Brands. August 5, 95-99.

BusinessWeek (2005). *The Top 100 Brands: Here's How We Calculate the Power in a Name*. August, 2005 [Online Available at http://www.businessweek.com/pdfs/2005/0531_globalbrand.pdf]

BusinessWire (2006). *North American Technology Service and Support Spending Expected to Top $1.4 Billion for 2007*, According to the SSPA. Online available at http://www.findarticles.com/p/articles/mi_m0EIN/

is_2006_Dec_18/ai_n16912392

Butcher, K., Sparks, B., & O'Callaghan, F. (2001). Evaluative and relational influences on service loyalty. *International Journal of Service Industry Management, 12*(4), 310-327.

Canals-Cerda, J.J., & Gurmu, S. (2006), "*Semiparametric Competing Risk Analysis,*" *Econometrics Journal (*Forthcoming).

Carpenter, P. (2000) "E-brands-Building on Internet Business at Breakneck Speed", Harvard Business School Press, Boston, 2000

Carpenter, P. (2000). *E-brands: Building an Internet business at breakneck speed*. Boston: Harvard Business School Press.

Case, T.; Burns, O.M. and Dick, G.N. (2001). Drivers of On-Line Purchasing among U.S. University Students. In *Proceedings of the Seventh Americas Conference on Information Systems (AMCIS 2001)*. Boston, pp. 873-878.

CBS 60 Minutes (2005). *eBay's bid for success: Internet auction site racking up big gains*, transcript available online at http://www.cbsnews.com/stories/2002/10/30/60II/main527542.shtml

Chakravarty, S., Feinberg, R., & Rhee, E. (2004). Relationships and individuals' bank switching behavior. *Journal of Economic Psychology*, 25, 4, 507-527.

Chao, P. (1993a). Partitioning Country of Origin Effects. *Journal of International Business Studies, 24*(2), 291-306.

Chao, P. (1993b). Partitioning Country-of-Origin Effects: Consumer Evaluations of a Hybrid Product. *Journal of International Business Studies, 24*(2), 291-306.

Chao, P. (2001). The Moderating Effects of Country of Assembly, Country of Parts, and Country of Design on Hybrid Product Evaluations. *Journal of Advertising, 30*(4), 67-81.

Chau, P.Y.K.; Au, G. and Tam, K.Y. (2000). Impact of Information Presentation Modes on Online Shopping:

An Empirical Evaluation of a Broadband Interactive Shopping Service. *Journal of Organizational Computing and Electronic Commerce*, 10(1), 1-22.

Chen, H.; Wignad, R.T. and Nilan, M. (1998). Optimal Flow Experience in Web Navigation, Effective Utilization and Management of Emerging Information Technologies. In *Proceedings of the Ninth Information Resources Management Association International Conference*, Idea Group Publishing, Boston, MA.

Chen, L D. and Sukpanich, N. (1998). Assessing Consumers' Involvement in Internet Purchasing. In *Proceedings of the Fourth Americas Conference on Information Systems (AMCIS 1998)*. Baltimore, 281-283.

Chen, P.Y., & Hitt, L.M. (2002). Measuring switching costs and the determinants of customer retention in Internet-enabled businesses: A study of the online brokerage industry. *Information Systems Research*, 13, 3, 255-274.

Chen, Q, & Wells, W. D. (1999). Attitude toward the site. *Journal of Advertising Research*, 39 (5), 27-38.

Chen, Q. & Rodgers, S. (2006), Development of an instrument to measure Web site personality. *Journal of Interactive Advertising, 7(1)*. Retrieved Dec 12 2006, from http://www.jiad.org/vol7/no1/chen/index.htm

Chen, Q., & Chen, H. (2004). Exploring the success factors of eCRM strategies in practice. *Database Marketing & Customer Service Strategy Management, 11*, 333-343.

Chen, Q., Clifford,S., & Wells, W .D. (2002). Attitude toward the site II: New information. *Journal of Advertising Research*, 42 (2), 33-45.

Chernatony, L. d., Harris, F. J., & Christodoulides, G. (2004). Developing a Brand Performance Measure for Financial Services Brands. *The Service Industries Journal, 24*(2), 15.

Cheung, C.M.K. and Lee, M.K.O. (2001). Trust in Internet Shopping: Instrument Development and Validation Through Classical and Modern Approaches. *Journal of Global Information Management*, 9(3), 23-32.

Cheung, C.M.K. and Lee, M.K.O. (2001a). Trust in In-

ternet Shopping: A Proposed Model and Measurement Instrument. In *Proceedings of the Seventh Americas Conference on Information Systems (AMCIS 2001)*. Boston, 681-689.

Childers, T.L.; Carr, C.L.; Peck, J. and Carson, S. (2001). Hedonic and Utilitarian Motivations for Online Retail Shopping Behavior. *Journal of Retailing*, 77(4), 511-535.

Childers, Terry L., Christopher L. Carr, Joann Peck, and Stephen Carson (2001), "Hedonic and utilitarian motivations for online retail shopping behavior," *Journal of Retailing*, Vol. 77, pp. 511-535

Christy, R., Oliver, G. & Penn, J. (1996), "Relationship Marketing in Consumer Markets," Journal of Marketing Management, 12 (1), 175-88.

Chu, J., & Pike, T. (2002). *Integrated multichannel retailing (IMCR): A roadmap to the future.* IBM Institute for Business Value. Retrieved August 5, 2004, from http://www-1.ibm.com/services/strategy/e_strategy/integrated_multi_channel.html

Citrin, A.V.; Sprott, D.E.; Silverman, S.N. and Stem, D.E. (2000). Adoption of Internet Shopping: The Role of Consumer Innovativeness. *Industrial Management & Data Systems*, 100(7), 294-300.

Clark, T., Rajaratnam, D., & Smith, T. (1996). Toward a theory of international services: marketing insights in a world of nations. *Journal of International Marketing, 4*(2), 9-28.

Close, W. (2002). CRM at work: Eight characteristics of CRM winners. *Defying the Limits, 3*, 66-68.

Clott, C. B. (2004). Perspectives on Global Outsourcing and the Changing Nature of Work. *Business and Society Review, 109*(2), 153-170.

CMS Cameron McKenna LLP. (2000). *Meta-tagging on search engines*. London.

Collins, L. (1977) "A Name to Conjure With", European Journal of Marketing, Vol. 11, No. 4/5, pp.337-364.

Compeau, D., & Higgins, C. (1995). Computer self-efficacy: Development of a measure and initial test. *MIS Quarterly, 19*, 189-211.

Comscore (2006) Google sees its US search market share jump a full point in May, marking tenth consecutive monthly gain, Press Release, June 21.

comScore. (2004). Marketers take note: The elusive 18-34 year-old is habitually online. Retrieved April 18, 2006, from http://www.comscore.com/press/release. asp?press=445.

Corbett, M. F. (2002). Outsourcing's next wave. *Fortune*(July 15).

Cornell, C. (2004). Offshore Options: Outsourcing operations to overseas providers can save you money or cause you pain. The choice is yours. *Profit, 23*(4), 87-88.

COTHREL, J. & WILLIAMS, R.L. (1999) Online Communities: Helping them Form and Grow. *Journal of Knowledge Management* 3 (1), 54-60.

Cotte, June, Ratneswar R and Glen Mick David(2003), "The Times of their lives; Phenomenological and Metaphorical Characteristics of Consumer Timestyles", forthcoming article in Journal of Consumer Research, pp.2-4.

Cowen, T., & Tabarrok, A. (2000). "An Economic Theory of Avant-Garde and Popular Art, or High and Low Culture," Southern Economic Journal, Vol. 67, No. 2, pp. 232-253.

Coyles, Stephanie and Gokey C Timothy(2002), "Customer Retention is not enough", The McKinsey Quarterly, No.2, pp.1-6, www.mckinseyquarterly.com

Crié, D. (2003). Consumers' complaint behaviour. Taxonomy, typology and determinants: Towards a unified ontology. *Database Marketing & Customer Strategy Management, 11*(1), 60-79.

Cronin Jr., J. J., & Taylor, S. A. (1992). Measuring service quality: A reexamination and extension. *Journal of Marketing, 56*(55-68).

Cronin, J., Jr., Brady, M., & Hult, G. (2000). Assessing the effects of quality, value, and customer satisfaction on consumer behavioral intentions in service environments. *Journal of Retailing, 76,* 93-218.

Crosby, Lawrence A. and Nancy Stephens (1987), "Effects of relationship marketing on satisfaction, retention, and prices in the life insurance industry," *Journal of Marketing Research*, Vol. 24, pp. 404-411

Csikszentimihalyi, M. (1975). *Beyond boredom and anxiety.* San Francisco: Jossey-Bass.

Csikszentmihalyi, M. (1982). Towards a psychology of optimal experience. In L. Wheeler (Ed.), *Review of Personality and Social Psychology*, 2. Beverly Hills, CA: Sage.

Csikszentmihalyi, M. (1990). *Flow: The Psychology of Optimal Experience*, Harper & Row, New York, NY.

CULNAN, M.J. (1984) The dimensions of accessibility to online information: implications for implementing office information systems. *ACM Transactions on Office Information Systems* 2 (2), 141-150.

Czech Publishers Association (2006). Internetová reklama v roce 2005 přesáhla 1 miliardu Kč. Press release, Available: http://www.unievydavatelu.cz.

Czech Statistical Office (2006), *The survey on ICT usage in households and by individuals in the Czech Republic in 2006* (in Czech).

d'Astous, A. and Le´vesque, M. (2003). "A Scale for Measuring Store Personality". Psychology & Marketing. 20 (5), pp. 455-469.

d'Astous, A., Colbert, F., and d'Astous, E. (2006). "The Personality of Cultural Festivals: Scale Development and Applications". International Journal of Arts Management. 8 (2), pp. 14-23.

Dabholkar, P.A., Bobbitt, L.M., & Lee, E.J. (2003). Understanding consumer motivation and behavior related to self-scanning in retailing: implications for strategy and research on technology-based self-service. *International Journal of Service Industry Management, 14*(1), 59-95.

DAFT, R.L. & LENGEL, R.H. (1986) Organizational

information requirements media richness and structural design. *Management Science* 32 (5), 554-571.

DAFT, R.L., LENGEL, R.H., & TREVINO, L. K. (1987) Message equivocality media selection and manager performance: implications for information systems. *MIS Quarterly* 11 (3), 355-366.

Dahringer, L. D. (1991). Marketing services internationally: barriers and management strategies. *Journal of Services Marketing, 5*(3), 5-17.

Dailey, L. (2004), Navigational Web atmospherics: Explaining the influence of restrictive navigation cues. *Journal of Business Research,* 57, 795-803.

Dana, Mike(2001), " M Commerce will Outperform E Commerce", RCR Wireless News 20, No.2, 4

Darby, M. R. & Karni, E. (1973). Free competition and the optimal amount of fraud. Journal of Law and Economics 16 (April), 67-86.

Data-Monitor. (2004). Axa/Abbey: a passage to India. *3*(3), 16-17.

Daugherty, T. M., Li, H. & Biocca, F. (2001). Consumer learning and 3D e-commerce: The effects of sequential exposure of a virtual experience relative to indirect and direct product experience on product knowledge, brand attitude and purchase intention. In Frank Biocca, (Ed.), *Proceedings of the experiential e-commerce conference* (CD-ROM). East Lansing, Michigan: Michigan State University.

Daugherty, T., Matt, E., & Gangadharbatla, H. (2005). eCRM: Understanding Internet Confidence and the Implications on Customer Relationship Management. *Advances in Electronic Marketing.* Irvine Clarke & Theresa B. Flaherty (eds.), Idea Group Publishing, 67 – 82.

Daugherty,T., Li, H., & Biocca, F. (2005). Experiential E-commerce: A Summary of Research Investigating the Impact of Virtual Experience on Consumer Learning. In Curt Haugtvedt, Karen Machleit & Richard Yalch (Eds.), *Online Consumer Psychology: Understanding and Influencing Consumer Behavior in the Virtual World*

(pp. 457-490). Lawrence Erlbaum Associates.

Davis, F. D., Bagozzi, R. P., & Warsaw, P. R. (1989). User Acceptance of Computer Technology: A Comparison of Two Theoretical Models. *Management Science, 35*(8), 983-1003.

Davis, F.D. (1989). Perceived usefulness, perceived ease of use, and user acceptance of information technology. *MIS Quarterly,* 13(3), 319-340.

Davis, F.D. Bagozzi, R.P., & Warshaw, P.R. (1992). Extrinsic and intrinsic motivation to use computers in the workplace. *Journal of Applied Social Psychology,* 22(14), 1111-1132.

Davis, F.D.; Bagozzi, R.P.; & Warshaw, P.R. (1989). User acceptance of computer technology: a comparison of two theoretical models. *Management Science,* 35(8), 982-1003.

Dayal, S., Landesberg, H., & Zeisser, M. (2000). Building digital brands. *McKinsey Quarterly, 2,* 3.

de Chernatory, L. (2001). Succeeding with brands on the Internet. *Brand Management, 8*(3), 186–195.

De Mooij, M. (1998). *Global marketing and advertising: Understanding cultural paradox.* Sage Publications, Thousand Oaks, CA.

De Wulf, K., Odekerken-Schröder, G., & Iacobucci, D. (2001), "Investments in Consumer Relationships: A Cross-Country and Cross-Industry Exploration," Journal of Marketing, 65 (October), 33-50.

Deci, E.L. (1971). Effects of externally mediated rewards on intrinsic motivation. *Journal of Personality and Social Psychology,* 18, 105-115.

Degeratu, A.M.; Rangaswamy, A. and Wub, J. (2000). Consumer Choice Behavior in Online and Traditional Supermarkets: The Effects of Brand Name, Price, and other Search Attributes. *International Journal of Research in Marketing,* 17(1), 55-78.

Deleersnyder, B., Inge, G., Gielens, K. & Dekimpe, M.G. (2002), "How Cannibalistic is the Internet Channel? A Study of the Newspaper Industry in the United

Kingdom and The Netherlands," *International Journal of Research in Marketing*, 19 (4), 337-348.

DeLone W.H. & McLean, E.R. (1992). Information systems success: The quest for the dependent variable. *Information Systems Research*, 3(1), 61-95.

DeLone, William and Ephraim R. McLean (2004), "Measuring e-commerce success: applying the DeLone & McLean information systems success model," *International Journal of Electronic Commerce*, Vol. 9, No. 1, pp. 31-47

Dequech, D. (2000). Confidence and Action: A Comment on Barbalet. *Journal of Socio-Economics, 29*(6), 503-516.

Devaraj, Sarv, Fan, Ming, and Kohli, Rajive (2002), "Antecedents of B2C channel satisfaction and preference: validating e-commerce metrics," *Information Systems Research*, Vol. 13, No.3, pp. 316-333

Dholakia, U. R. & Bagozzi, P. (1999). Consumer behavior in digital environments. Working paper.

Dobie, K.; Grant, J. and Ready, K. (2001). Product Motivation and Purchasing Activity: An Exploratory Study of Consumers' Intention Purchasing Activity. *Journal of Promotion Management*, 6(1/2), 31-43.

Doll, W.J. & Torkzadeh, G. (1988). The measurement of end-user computing satisfaction. *MIS Quarterly*, 12(2), 259-274.

Doll, W.J.; Hendrickson, A.; & Deng, X. (1998). Using Davis's perceived usefulness and ease of use instruments for decision making: A confirmatory and multi-group invariance analysis. *Decision Sciences*, 29(4), 839-869.

Donthu, N. and A. Garcia (1999). The Internet Shopper. *Journal of Advertising Research* 39 (5), 52-58.

Dou, W., U.O. Nielsen, and C.M. Tan (2002). Using corporate websites for exporting marketing. *Journal of Advertising Research*, 42 (5), 105-115.

DoubleClick, (2005) Search Marketing: It's Not About Your Brand, It's About the Customer, Smart Marketing Report, Jan / Feb (Online), Retrieved 29 December,

2006

Douglas, M. & Isherwood, B. (1996). *The world of goods: Toward an anthropology of consumption.* New York: Routledge.

Douglas, S.P.; Morrin, M.A. and Craig, C.S. (1994). Cross-National Consumer Research Traditions. In G. Laurent, G. Lilien, and B. Bras, ed., *Research Traditions in Marketing*, Kluwer, Boston, MA.

Dowling, G. & Uncles, M. (1997), "Do Customer Loyalty Programs Really Work?" Sloan Management Review, 38 (Fall), 71-82.

Dowling, G., & Staelin, R. (1994). A model of perceived risk and intended risk-handling activity. *Journal of Consumer Research, 21,* 119-134.

Duncan, T. (2002) "IMC: Using Advertising and Promotion to Build Brands", McGraw Hill, 2002

Duncan, T. and Ramaprasad, J. (1995). Standardized multinational advertising: The influencing factors. *Journal of Advertising*, 24(3), 55-67.

Dwyer, F. Robert, Paul H. Schurr, and Sejo Oh (1987), "Developing buyer-seller relationships," *Journal of Marketing*, Vol. 51, 11-27

Eastin, M. S. (2002). Diffusion of E-commerce: An Analysis of the Adoption of Four e-commerce Activities. *Telematics and Informatics, 19*(3), 251-67.

Eastin, M. S. (2005). Teen Internet Use: Relating Social Perceptions and Cognitive Models to Behavior. *CyberPsychology & Behavior, 8*(1), 62-75.

Eastin, M. S., & LaRose, R. L. (2000). Internet Self-Efficacy and the Psychology of the Digital Divide. *Journal of Computer-Mediated Communication. 6.* Available [Online]: http://www.ascusc.org/jcmc/vol6/

Economist Intelligence Unit (2006), *The 2006 e-readiness rankings.*

Economist. (2001). Back office to the world. *359*(8220), 59-61.

Editors of Advertising Age. (1988). *Proctor & Gamble:*

The house that Ivory built. Lincolnwood, IL: NTC Business Books.

Eisenmann, T.E., G.G. Parker, M. Van Alstyne (2006). "Strategies for Two-Sided Markets." Harvard Business Review, October, 1-12 .

Elinder, E. (1961). How International Can Advertising Be?" in S. W. Dunn (ed.), *International Handbook of Advertising*, NY: McGraw-Hill, 59-71.

Elixir Systems. (2006). *Online Reputation Management: Protect your brand.* Scottsdale, AZ.

Elliot, Steve and Sue Fowell (2000), "Expectations versus reality: a snapshot of consumer experiences with internet retailing," *International Journal of Information Management*, Vol. 20, pp. 323-336

Engel, J.F.; Blackwell, R.D. and Miniard, P.W. (2001). *Consumer Behavior*, The Dryden Press Series in Marketing.

Erdem, T. & Swait, J. (1998), "Brand Equity as a Signaling Phenomenon," *Journal of Consumer Psychology,* 7(2), 131-157.

Ernst & Young. (2003). *Global online retailing.* Retrieved from http://www.ey.com/GLOBAL

Eroglu, S.A.; Machleit, K.A. and Davis, L.M. (2001). Atmospheric Qualities of Online Retailing - A Conceptual Model and Implications. *Journal of Business Research,* 54(2), 177-184.

Eurostat (2005), *Europe in figures: Eurostat yearbook 2005.*

Eurostat (2006), *Community survey on ICT usage in households and by individuals.*

FALK, J. (1995) The Meaning of the Web. Retrieved September 13 2005 from http://swissnetaimitedu/6805/articles/falk-meaning-of-the-webhtml

Fan, Y. (2000). Strategic outsourcing: evidence from British companies. *Marketing Intelligence & Planning, 18*(4), 213.

Fazio, R. H., & Towles-Schwenn, T. (1999). The MODE model of attitude-behavior processes. In S. Chaiken & Y. Trope (Eds.), *Dual process theories in social psychology* (pp. 97–116). New York: Guilford Press.

Featherman, M. S. & Pavlou, P. A. (2003). Predicting e-services adoption: a perceived risk facets perspective. *International Journal of Human-Computer Studies, 59,* 451-474.

Feinberg, R. (2001). Customer service and service quality. In G. Salvendy (Ed.), *Handbook of industrial engineering* (pp. 651-664). New York: John Wiley and Sons.

Feinberg, R., & Trotter, M. (2003). The customer access evolution: Leveraging touch points for customer acquisition, retention, and wallet share. *Defying the Limits, 2,* 30-35.

Feinberg, R., Trotter, M., & Anton, J. (2000). At any time- from anywhere- in any form. *Defying the Limits, 1,* 296-304.

FINHOLT, T. & SPROULL, S. (1990) Electronic groups at work. *Organization Science* 1 (1), 41-64

Fishbein, M. & Ajzen, I. (1975). *Belief, attitude, intentions and behavior: An introduction to theory and research.* Boston: Addison-Wesley.

Fishbein, M. (1967). Attitude and Prediction of Behavior. In M. Fishbein, ed., *Readings in Attitude Theory and Measurement*, New York: John Wiley, 477-492.

FISHER, B., MARGOLIS, M. & RESNICK, D. (1994) *A New Way of Talking Politics: Democracy on the Internet.* In Annual Meeting of the American Political Science Association, New York City,

Fisk, R. P., Grove, S. J., & John, J. (2004). *Interactive Service Marketing* (2nd ed.). Boston: Houghton Mifflin Co.

FLAVIÁN, C. & GUINALÍU, M. (2004) Virtual community: a model of successful business on the Internet. In *Advances in Electronic Marketing* (Clarke III I and Flaherty TB, Eds), pp 270-286, Idea Group Publishing Inc.

Flavian, C., Guinaliu, M., & Gurrea, R. (2006). The role

played by perceived usability, satisfaction and consumer trust on website loyalty. *Information & Management*, 43, 1, 1-14.

Fleming, J., & Courtney, B. E. (1984). The Dimensionality of Self-Esteem II: Hierarchical Facet Model for Revised Measurement Scales. *Journal of Personality and Social Psychology*, 46(February), 404-421.

Folkes, V.S. (1988). Recent Attribution Research in Consumer Behavior: A Review and New Directions. *Journal of Consumer Research*, 14, 548-565.

Fornell, C. & Bookstein, F.L. (1982). Two structural equation models: LISREL and PLS applied to consumer exit-voice theory, *Journal of Marketing Research*, 19(4), 440-452.

Fornell, C. (1982). *A second generation of multivariate analysis*. New York, NY: Praeger.

Fornell, C., & Larcker, D. (1981). Evaluating structural equation models with unobservable variables and measurement error. *Journal of Marketing Research*, 18, 39-50.

Fornell, C., Johnson, M. D., Anderson, E. W., Cha, J., & Bryant, B. E. (1996). The American customer satisfaction index: Nature, purpose, and findings. *Journal of Marketing, 60*, 7-18.

Forrester (2002), *Forrester's Global eCommerce Predictions For 2004*. Available: http://www.forrester.com/home/0,6092,1-0,FF.html

Forrester Report (2001) *Get ROI from design*. Forrester Research, Inc., Cambridge, MA.

Forrester Research (2005). Young consumers are the first "technology everywhere" generation. Retrieved April 18, 2006, from http://www.forrester.com/ER/Press/Release/0,1769,1051,00.html

Forunier, S. & Dolan, R. J. (1997), "Launching the BMW Z3 roadster," Harvard Business School Case, Harvard Business Online. Retrieved Dec 30, 2006, from http://harvardbusinessonline.hbsp.harvard.edu/b01/en/common/item_detail.jhtml;jsessionid=SH2Q0JDKFMVW4AKRGWCB5VQBKE0YOISW?id=597002

Fournier, S. (1998). Consumers and Their Brands: Developing Relationship Theory in Consumer Research. *Journal of Consumer Research, 24*(4), 343-373.

Francese, P. A., & Renaghan, L. M. (1990). Data-Base Marketing: Building Customer Profiles. *Cornell Hotel and Restaurant Administration Quarterly, 31*(1), 60-63.

Franz, C.R. & Robey, D. (1986). Organizational context, user involvement and the usefulness of information systems. *Decision Sciences*, 17(3), 329-356.

Freed, L. (2003). *The insiders view of e-retailing 2003*. Retrieved August 5, 2004, from, www.foreseereults.com

Freling, T. H. and Forbes, L. (2005). "An Empirical Analysis of the Brand Personality Effect". Journal of Product and Brand Management. 14 (7), pp. 404-413.

FRIEDLAND, L. (1996) Electronic democracy and the new citizenship. *Media culture and society* 18, 185-212.

Friedman, B.; Kahn, Jr P.H. and Howe, D.C. (2000). Trust Online. *Communication of the ACM*, 43(12), 34-40.

FUKUYAMA, F. (1999) *The Great Disruption: Human Nature and the Reconstitution of Social Order*. Free Press, New York.

Fung, R.K.K. and Lee, M.K.O. (1999). EC-Trust (Trust in Electronic Commerce): Exploring the Antecedent Factors. In *Proceedings of the Fifth Americas Conference on Information Systems (AMCIS 1999)*. Milwaukee, 517-519.

Gallafent, R. (2006) Branding: The demands of the client, the needs of society and the effect of the law. *Journal of Brand Management*, 13 (3), pp 201-205.

Ganesh, J., Arnold, M.J., & Reynolds, K.E. (2000). Understanding the customer base of service providers: An examination of the differences between switchers and stayers. *Journal of Marketing*, 64, 3, 65-87.

Garbarino, E. & Johnson, M.S. (1999), "The Different Roles of Satisfaction, Trust, and Commitment in

Customer Relationships," Journal of Marketing, 63 (April), 70-87.

Garbarino, E., & Johnson, M.S. (1999). The different roles of satisfaction, trust, and commitment in customer relationships. *Journal of Marketing, 63,* 2, 70-87.

Garbarino, Ellen and Mark S. Johnson (1999), "The different roles of satisfaction, trust, and commitment in customer relationships," *Journal of Marketing,* Vol. 63, 70-87

Garrity, E.J. & Sanders, G.L. (1998). Dimensions of information systems success measurement, in *Information Systems Success Measurement,* Garrity, E.J. & Sanders G.L (eds.), Hershey: Idea Group Publishing, 13-45.

Garrity, E.J.; Glassberg, B.; Kim, Y.J.; Sanders, G.L.; & Shin, S.K. (2005). An experimental investigation of web-based information systems success in the context of electronic commerce. *Decision Support Systems,* 39(3), 485-503.

Gauzente, Claire (2004), "Web merchants' privacy and security statement: How reassuring are they for customers? Two sided approach," *Journal of Electronic Commerce Research,* No. 5, No.3, pp.181-198

Gefen, D. (2000). E-Commerce: The Role of Familiarity and Trust. *Omega,* 28(6), 725-737.

Gefen, D. (2002). Customer Loyalty in E-Commerce. *Journal of the Association for Information Systems,* 3, 27-51.

Gefen, D. and Devine, P. (2001). Customer Loyalty to an Online Store: The Meaning of Online Service Quality. In *Proceedings of the Twenty-Second International Conference of Information Systems (ICIS 2001). New Orleans,* 613-618.

Gefen, D., & Straub, D. (2000). The relative importance of perceived ease-of-use in IS adoption: a study of e-commerce adoption. *Journal of Association for Information Systems, 1*(8), 1-20.

Gefen, D., Karahanna, E., & Straub, D. (2003). Trust and TAM in online shopping: An integrated model. *MIS Quarterly,* 27, 1, 51-90.

Geissler, U., Will, M. (2001) "Corporate Branding of E-Business Ventures", in: R. Sprague (ed.): Proceedings of the 34th Hawaii International Conference on System Science (HICSS), Maui, January 2001.

George, A. (2006) Brand rules: When branding lore meets trade mark law. *Journal of Brand Management,* 13 (3), pp 215-232.

Georgiadis, M., Singer, M., & Harding, D. (2003), *Online Customer Practice.* McKinsey Marketing Practice white paper.

GfK (2006). Increasingly more kids use the Internet. One in three Polish Internet users willing to buy music on the Internet. Press release, Available: http://www.gfk. pl/podstrona.php?page=/page.php?id=630&ltr=.

Ghani, J., & Deshpande, S. P. (1994). Task characteristics and the experience of optimal flow in human-computer interaction. *Journal of Psychology,* 128(4), 381-392.

Ghani, J.A., Supnick, R., & Rooney, P. (1991). The experience of flow in computer-mediated and in face-to-face groups. J.I. DeGross, I. Benbasat, G. DeSanctis, & C.M. Beath, (eds.) *Proceedings of the 12th International Conference on Information Systems,* New York, 229-237.

Ghose, S. and Dou, W. (1998). Interactive Functions and Their Impacts on the Appeal of Internet Presence Sites. *Journal of Advertising Research,* 38 (2), 29-43.

Gibson, J. J. (1977). The theory of affordances. In R. Shaw & J. Bransford, (Eds.) *Perceiving, acting and knowing: toward an ecological psychology* (pp. 67-82). Hillsdale, New Jersey: Lawrence Erlbaum Associates.

Gilbert, D., & Hewlett, J. (2003). A method for the assessment of relative brand strength: A UK tour operator example. *The Service Industries Journal, 23*(2), 166.

Gilmore H. James and Pine B. Joseph II, (2000), "Markets of One, Creating Customer - Unique Value through Customer", HBS, pp.62-65.

Glazer, R. (1991), "Marketing in an Information-Intensive Environment: Strategic Implications of Knowledge As An asset," *Journal of Marketing,* 55 (October), 1-19.

Glynn, W. J. (1997). Building Future Relationships. Marketing Management, Chicago: *American Marketing Association, 6* (Fall), 34-36.

Goldsmith, R.E. (2000). How Innovativeness Differentiates Online Buyers. *Quarterly Journal of Electronic Commerce,* 1(4), 323-333.

Goldsmith, R.E. (2001). Using the Domain Specific Innovativeness Scale to Identify Innovative Internet Consumers. *Internet Research: Electronic Networking Applications and Policy,* 11(2), 149-158.

Goldsmith, R.E. and Bridges, E. (2000). E-Tailing VS Retailing: Using Attitudes to Predict Online Buying Behavior. *Quarterly Journal of Electronic Commerce,* 1(3), 245-253.

Gollwitzer M. Peter (1996), "The Volitional Benefits of Planning". Gollwitzer P. Peter and John A. Bargh (Eds.), "The Psychology of Actions, Living Cognition and Motivation or Behavior", Guilford Press, pp.287-312.

Goodhue, D.L. (1990). Developing a theory-based measure of user satisfaction: The task systems fit questionnaire. *Working Paper, Information and Decision Sciences, University of Minnesota.*

Graeff, T. R. (1996). Image congruence effects on product evaluations: The role of self-monitoring and public/private consumption. *Psychology and Marketing,* 13(5), 481-499.

Grandon, E.E. and Ranganathan, C. (2001). The Impact of Content and Design of Web Sites on Online Sales. In *Proceedings of the Seventh Americas Conference on Information Systems (AMCIS 2001).* Boston, 920-926.

Greenspan, R. (2000). Be seen and get paid. http://Internet_com's Electronic Commerce Guide – EC Tips.

Griffith, D.A.; Krampf, R.F. and Palmer, J.W. (2001). The Role of Interface in Electronic Commerce: Consumer Involvement with Print Versus On-Line Catalogs. *International Journal of Electronic Commerce,* 5(4), 134-153.

Griffith, David A. and Robert F. Krampf, and Jonathan W. Palmer (2001), "The role of interface in electronic commerce: consumer involvement with print versus online catalogs," *International Journal of Electronic Commerce,* Vol. 5, No. 4, pp. 135-153

Gronhaug, K., & Gilly, M. C. (1991). A transaction cost approach to consumer dissatisfaction and complaint actions. *Journal of Economic Psychology, 12*(1), 156-183.

Gronroos, C. (1999). Internationalization strategies for services. *Journal of Services Marketing, 13*(4/5), 290-297.

Gronroos, Christian (1990), "Relationship Approach to Marketing in Service Contexts: The Marketing and Organizational Behavior Interface," *Journal Business Research,* Vol.20, pp.3-11

Gulli, A., & Signorini, A. (2005). *The indexable Web is more than 11.5 billion pages.* Poster proceedings of the 14th international conference on World Wide Web, Chiba, Japan.

Gupta, A., Su, B., & Walter, Z. (2004). An empirical study of consumer switching from traditional to electronic channels: A purchase-decision process perspective. *International Journal of Electronic Commerce,* 8, 3, 131-161.

Gupta, M., & Gramopadhye, A. (1995). **An evaluation of different navigational tools in   using hypertext.** *Computers & Industrial Engineering,* 29, 437-442.

Gupta, S. & Kim, H.W. (2007). Developing the commitment to virtual community: The balanced effects of cognition and affect. *Information Resources Management Journal,* 20(1), 28-45.

Gutzman, A. D. (2000). Unconventional wisdom: Traffic is overrated. Retrieved , from *http://ecommerce.Internet.com/solutions/tech_advisor/article/html*

Gwinner, Kevin P., Dwayne D. Gremmler, and Mary Jo Bitner (1998), "Relational benefits in services industries: The customer's perspective," *Journal of the Academy of Marketing Science,* Vol. 26, No.2, pp.101-114

Ha, L., & James, E. L. (1998). Interactivity Reexamined: A Baseline Analysis of Early Business Web Sites. *Journal of Broadcasting & Electronic Media, 42*(4), 457-474.

Hackbarth, G.; Grover, V.; & Yi, M.Y. (2003). Computer playfulness and anxiety: positive and negative mediators of the system experience effect on perceived ease of use. *Information and Management*, 40, 221-232.

Haig, M. (2001) The great search debate, e-volve, November 29, pp 47-51

Hair, J. F., Anderson, R. E., Tatham, R. L., & Black, W. C. (1998). *Multivariate Data Analysis* (5th ed.). Upper Saddle River, NJ: Prentice Hall.

Hair, J.F. Jr, Anderson, R.E., Tatham, R.L., & Black, W.C. (1995). *Multivariate data analysis* (4th ed.). New Jersey: Prentice-Hall.

Hair, J.F., Jr., R.E. Anderson, R.L. Tatham, and W.C. Black (1998), Multivariate Data Analysis, Fifth Edition, Upper Saddle River: Prentice-Hall, Inc.

Hall, E. T. (1969). *The hidden dimension.* Garden City, NY: Anchor Books.

Hall, J. (2007). "Google vs Yahoo vs MSN - What's the Difference?". Ecademy-Business Networking. Feb. 12, 2007. Available at: http://www.ecademy.com/node.php?id=80164&seen=1

Hallberg Garth, (1995), "All Consumers are Not Created Equal" John Wiley and Sons, 19.

Han, C. M., & Terpstra, V. (1988). Country-of-origin effects for uni-national and bi-national products. *Journal of International Business Studies, 19*(Summer), 235-255.

Han, H.J.; Ocker, R. and Fjermestad, J. (2001). An Investigation of University Students' On-Line Shopping Behavior. In *Proceedings of the Seventh Americas Conference on Information Systems (AMCIS 2001),* Boston, 930-933.

Hansell, S. (2006, 16/8/06). Seek (on the Web) and the advertisers shall find you. *International Herald Tribune,* p. 13.

Hanson, W. (2000). *Principles of Internet marketing.* Cincinnati, OH: Southwestern College Publishing.

Harris, G. (1994). International Advertising Standardization: What Do the Multinationals Actually Standardize?"

Journal of International Marketing, 2 (4), 13-30.

Harrison-Walker, L. J. (1995). The relative effects of national stereotype and advertising information on the selection of a service provider. *Journal of Services Marketing, 9*(1), 47-59.

Hart, P., & Carol, S. (1997). Power and trust: Critical factors in the adoption and use of electronic data interchange. *Organization Science,* 8, 1, 23-42.

Hatch, M., Schultz, M. (2001) "Are the strategic stars aligned for your corporate brand?" Harvard Business Review, February, pp.128-134.

Haubl, G. and Trifts, V. (2000). Consumer Decision Making in Online Shopping Environments: The Effects of Interactive Decision Aids. *Marketing Science,* 19(1), 4-21.

Hayward, M. (2004). I showed them the future and they ignored it. *Management Today*(Sep), 68-69.

Heaton, Jr., E. E. (1967) "Testing a New Corporate Name", Journal of Marketing Research Vol. 4, No. 3, pp. 279-285.

Heckman J., & Singer, B. (1984) "A Method for Minimizing the Impact of Distributional Assumptions in Econometric Models for Duration Data." Econometrica, Vol. 52, No. 2., pp. 271-320.

Heijden, H.v.d.; Verhagen, T. and Creemers, M. (2001). Predicting Online Purchase Behavior: Replications and Tests of Competing Models. In *Proceedings of the Thirty-Fourth Annual Hawaii International Conference on System Sciences*, Maui, HI, USA, IEEE Computer Society, Los Alamitos, CA.

Heilbronner, M., Heilbronner, S. & Estis Green, C. (2006) *Profits and Pitfalls of Online Marketing: A Legal Desk Reference for Travel Executives*, TIG Global LLC, New York.

Hellier, P. K., Geursen, G. M., Carr, R. A., & Rickard, J. A. (2003). Customer repurchase intention: A general structural equation model. *European Journal of Marketing, 37*(11/12), 1762-1800.

Hill, J. (1996). Keeping customers loyal at Liverpool Victoria Friendly Society. *Managing Service Quality, 6*(4), 27-31.

Hirschman, E. C. & Thompson, C. J. (1997). Why media matter: Toward a richer understanding of consumers' relationships with advertising and mass media. *Journal of Advertising*, 26 (1), 43-60.

Hitwise. (2006) *Best Practice for Search Engine Brand Management.* London.

Ho, C.-F. and Wu, W.-H. (1999). Antecedents of Customer Satisfaction on the Internet: An Empirical Study of Online Shopping. In *Proceedings of the Thirty-Second Annual Hawaii International Conference on Systems Sciences*, Maui, HI, USA, IEEE Computer Society, Los Alamitos, CA.

Hoch, S. J., & Deighton, J. (1989). Managing What Consumers Learn from Experience. *Journal of Marketing, 53* (April), 1-20.

Hocutt, Mary Ann (1998), "Relationship dissolution model: antecedents of relationship commitment and the likelihood of dissolving a relationship," *International Journal of Service Industry Managment*, Vol. 9, No. 2, pp.189-200

Hoffman, D. L., & Novak, T. P. (1996). Marketing in Hypermedia computer-mediated environments: Conceptual foundations. *Journal of Marketing*, 603, 50-69.

Hoffman, D. L., & Novak, T. P. (2000). Measuring the customer experience in online environments: A structural modeling approach. *Marketing Science*, 19(1), 22-24.

Hoffman, D. L., & Thomas P. N. (1996). Marketing in Hypermedia Computer-Based Environments: Conceptual Foundations. *Journal of Marketing, 60* (July), 50-68.

Hoffman, D. L., Novak, T. P., & Chatterjee, P. (1995). Commercial scenarios for the Web: Opportunities and challenges. *Journal of Computer Mediated Communication*, 1(3). Retrieved Dec 12, 1995, from shum.huji.ac.il/j cmc/voll/issue3/hoffman.html.

Hoffman, D.L. & Novak, T.P. (1996). Marketing in hypermedia computer-mediated environments: Conceptual foundations. *Journal of Marketing*, 60, 50-68.

Hoffman, D.L.; Novak, T.P. and Peralta, M. (1999). Building Consumer Trust Online. *Communications of the ACM*, 42(4). 80-85.

Hoffman, K. D., & Bateson, J. E. G. (1997). *Essentials of Service Marketing*. The Dryden Press, Fort Worth, TX.

Holt, D. B. (2004). *How brands become icons*. Boston: Harvard Business School Press.

Hong, J.W., Muderrisoglu, A. and Zinkhan, G.M. (1987). Cultural differences and advertising expression: a comparative content analysis of Japanese and U.S. magazine advertising. *Journal of Advertising*, 16 (1), 55-62, 68.

Hong, Weiyin, James Y. L. Thong, and Kar Yan Tam (2005), "The effects of information format and shopping task on consumers' online shopping behavior: a cognitive fit perspective," *Journal of Management Information Systems*, Vol. 21, No.3, pp. 149-184

Hoque, Abeer Y. and Gerald L. Lohse (1999), "An information search cost perspective for designing interfaces for electronic commerce," *Journal of Marketing Research*, Vol. 36, No.3, pp.387-394

Hosany, S., Ekinci Y., and Uysal, M. (2006). "Destination Image and Destination Personality: An Application of Branding Theories to Tourism Places". Journal of Business Research. 59, pp. 638-642.

Hsu, M. H., & Chiu, C. M. (2004). Internet Self-efficacy and Electronic Service Acceptance. *Decision Support Systems, 38* (3), 369-381.

Huang, M.-H. (2000). Information Load: Its Relationship to Online Exploratory and Shopping Behavior. *International Journal of Information Management*, 20(5), 337-347.

Huang, W.-Y., Schrank, H., & Dubinsky, A. J. (2004). Effect of brand name on consumers' risk perceptions of online shopping. *Journal of Consumer Behavior*, 4(1), 40-50.

Hugot, O. & Hugot, J. (2005) Preliminary Relief Granted Against Google France in Adwords Case", Juriscom.net, Feb 2, Retrieved 12 September, 2006

Hui, M. K., & Bateson, J. E. G. (1991). Perceived control and the effects of crowding and consumer choice on the service experience. *Journal of Consumer Research, 18* (September), 174-184.

Hwang, J.S., McMillan, S.J. and Lee, G. (2003). Corporate Web sites as advertising: An analysis of function, audience, and message strategy. *Journal of Interactive Advertising*, 3(2), Available: http://jiad.org/vol3/no2/mcmillan/index.htm

Ibeh, K.I.N., Luo, Y., Dinnie, K. (2005) E-branding strategies of internet companies: some preliminary insights from the UK", Brand Management, Vol.12, No.5, June 2005, pp.355-373.

IMD World Competitiveness Center Yearbook (2005), IMD Business School, Geneva, Switzerland.

Inman, J., Shankar, V., & Ferraro, R. (2004). The roles of channel-category associations and geodemographics in channel patronage. *Journal of Marketing, 68,* 51-71.

Internet Software Consortium (2001), *Distribution of Top-Level Domain Names by Host Count, Jul 2002.* Online: http://www.isc.org/ds/WWW-200207/dist-by-num.html.

IPDI (2004) Political Influentials Online in the 2004 Presidential Campaign. Retrieved September 13 2005 from http://wwwipdiorg/UploadedFiles/political%20influentialspdf

Iqbal, A., Verma, R., & Baran, R. (2003). Understanding consumer choices and preferences in transaction-based e-services. *Journal of Service Research, 6*(1), 51-65.

Jain, S. (1989). Standardization of international marketing strategy: Some research hypotheses. *Journal of Marketing*, 53(1), 70-79.

Janiszewski, C. (1998). The Influence of Display Characteristics on Visual Exploratory Search Behavior. *Journal of Consumer Research*, 25(3), 290-301.

Jarboe, G. R. and McDaniel, C. D.(1987). A Profile of Browsers in Regional Shopping Malls. *Journal of the Academy of Marketing Science*, 15(1), 46-53.

Jarvenpaa, S.L. (1999). Consumer Trust in an Internet Store: A Cross-Cultural Validation. *Journal of Computer-Mediated Communication*, 5(2).

Jarvenpaa, S.L. and Todd, P.A. (1996). Consumer Reactions to Electronic Shopping on the World Wide Web. *International Journal of Electronic Commerce*, 1(2), 59-88.

Jarvenpaa, S.L.; & Todd, P.A. (1997). Consumer reactions to electronic shopping on the World Wide Web. *International Journal of Electronic Commerce*, 1(2), 59-88.

Jarvenpaa, S.L.; & Todd, P.A. (1997). Is there a future for retailing on the Internet? R.A. Peterson, (ed.) *Electronic Marketing and the Consumer*. Thousand Oaks, CA: Sage.

Jarvenpaa, S.L.; Tractinsky, N. and Vitale, M. (2000). Consumer Trust in an Internet Store. *Information Technology & Management*, 1(1-2), 45-71.

Jarvenpaa, S.L.; Tractinsky, N.; Saarinen, L.; & Vitale, M. (1999). Consumer trust in an Internet store: A cross-cultural validation. *Journal of Computer Mediated Communications.* 5(2) 1-35.

Jarvenpaa, Sirrka L. and Peter A. Todd (1997), "Consumer reactions to electronic shopping on the World Wide Web," *International Journal of Electronic Commerce*, Vol.1, No.2, pp.59-88

Javalgi, R. G., Cutler, B., & Winans, W. A. (2001). At your service! Does country of origin research apply? *Journal of Services Marketing, 15*(6/7), 565-582.

Javalgi, R. G., Griffith, D. A., & White, D. S. (2003). An empirical examination of factors influencing the internationalization of service firms. *Journal of Services Marketing, 17*(2/3), 185-201.

Javed, N. (1997) "Naming for global power", Communication World 1997, Vol.14, No. 9, pp. 32-35.

Johansson K. Johny and Nonaka Ikujiro, (1996), "Relentless, The Japanese Way of Marketing", Harper Business, pp.143-148.

John, D. R., Loken, B., & Jointer, C. (1998), The negative impact of extensions: Can flagship products be diluted? *Journal of Marketing*, 62 (1), 19-33.

Johnson, C. (2004). *The growth of multichannel retailing*. A Forrester document prepared for the National Governor's Association and the National Conference of State Legislatures. Retrieved from www.nga.org/cda/files/0407MULTICHANNEL.PDF

Jones, J.M. and Vijayasarathy, L.R. (1998). Internet Consumer Catalog Shopping: Findings from an Exploratory Study and Directions for Future Research. *Internet Research: Electronic Networking Applications and Policy*, 8(4), 322-330.

Jones, Michael A. and Jaebeom Suh (2000), "Transaction-specific satisfaction and overall satisfaction: an empirical analysis," *Journal of Services Marketing*, Vol. 14, No. 2, pp. 147-159

Jungwon, L.; Jinwoo, K. and Jae, M.Y. (2000). What Makes Internet Users visit Cyber Stores Again? Key Design Factors for Customer Loyalty. In *Proceedings of the Conference on Human Factors in Computing Systems*, The Hague, Netherlands.

Ju-Pak, K.H. (1999). Content dimensions of Web advertising: a cross-national comparison. *International Journal of Advertising*, 18 (2), 207-231.

Jupiter Communications. (2000, August 29). *Multichannel shoppers buy more, but 76 percent of retailers unable to track then across channels*. Retrieved from http://retailindustry.about.com/library/bl/bl_jup0829.htm

Kamins, M. A. (1990). An investigation into the 'match-up' hypothesis in celebrity advertising: When beauty may be only skin deep. *Journal of Advertising*, 19 (1), 4-13.

Kania, D. (2000). *Branding.com: Online branding for marketing success*. Chicago: NTC Business Books, American Marketing Association.

Kania, D. (2001). Branding.Com. NTC Business Books, American Marketing Association (AMA).

Kannan, P.K. and Kopalle, P.K. (2001). Dynamic Pricing on the Internet: Importance and Implications for Consumer Behavior. *International Journal of Electronic Commerce*, 5(3), 63-83.

Kannan, P.K.,Wagner, J., & Velarde, C. (2002). Initiatives for Building e-Loyalty: A Framework and Research Issues. In Michael Shaw (ed.) *E-Business Management: State-of-the-Art Research, Management Strategy, and Best Business Practices*. New York: Kluwer.

Kanso, A. and Nelson, R.A. (2002). Advertising Localization Overshadows Standardization. *Journal of Advertising Research*, 42 (1), 79-89.

Kant, I. (1977). *Prolegomena to any future metaphysics*. (P. Carus, Trans., J. W. Ellington, Rev.). Indianapolis, Indiana: Hackett Publishing Company, Inc.

Kapferer, J.-N. (1992). *Strategic brand management*. London: Kogan-Page.

KATZ, J. (1997) The Digital Citizen. *Wired*. Retrieved September 13 2005 from http://wwwwiredcom/wired/archive/512/netizen_prhtml

Kaynak, E., Kucukemiroglu, O., & Kara, A. (1994). Consumer perceptions of airlines: a correspondence analysis approach in an airline industry. *Management International Review, 34*(3), 235-254.

Keaveney, S.M. (1995). Customer switching behavior in service industries: An exploratory study. *Journal of Marketing,* 59, April, 71-82.

Keaveney, S.M., & Parthasarathy, M. (2001). Customer switching behavior in online services: An exploratory study of the role of selected attitudinal, behavioral, and demographic factors. *Journal of the Academy of Marketing Science,* 29, 4, 374-390.

Keen, C., Wetzels, M., de Ruyter, K., & Feinberg, R. (2004). E-tailers versus retailers: Which factors determine consumer preferences. *Journal of Business Research, 57,* 685-695.

Keen, C.; Ruyter, K.D.; Wetzels, M. and Feinberg, R. (2000). An Empirical Analysis of Consumer Preferences Regarding Alternative Service Delivery Modes in

Emerging Electronic Service Markets. *Quarterly Journal of Electronic Commerce*, 1(1), 31-47.

KEETER, S. & CARPINI, D.M. (2002) The Internet and an Informed Citizenry. In *The Civic Web: Online Politics and Democratic Values* (ANDERSON, DM & CORNFIELD, M. Eds). Rowman & Littlefield

Keil, M.; Beranek, P.M.; & Konsynski, B.R. (1995). Usefulness and ease of use: Field study evidence regarding task considerations. *Decision Support Systems*, 13(1), 75-91.

Keller Lane Kevin, (2003), "Strategic Brand Management, Building, Measuring and Managing Brand Equity", Prentice Hall of India, pp.132-149.

Keller Lane Kevin, Sternthal Brian and Tybout Alice, (2002), "Three Questions You Need to Ask About Your Brand", Business Review, pp.3-8.

Keller, K. L. (2002). *Strategic brand management: Building, measuring, and managing brand equity* (2nd ed.). Upper Saddle River, NJ: Prentice Hall.

Keller, K. L. (2003). Strategic Brand Management: Building, Measuring and Managing Brand Equity. 2nd ed. Upper Saddle River (NJ): Prentice Hall.

Keller, K.L. (1993), "Conceptualizing, measuring, and managing customer-based brand equity," *Journal of Marketing*, 57(1), pp. 1–22.

Keller, K.L., Heckler, S.E., Houston, M.J. (1998) "The effects of brand name suggestiveness on advertising recall", Journal of Marketing, 63, pp.48-57.

Kennedy, C. (2002). Name and shame: If you outsource, beware. Your brand may be in tatters through appalling customer service - and you may never know it. *Director, 56*(5), 23.

Kenny, David A., "Mediation," 2001, (Accessed January 2002), [http://nw3.nai.net/~dakenny/mediate.htm]

Kerner, S.M. (2006). "Are Google Results More Relevant?". InternetNews.com. Available at: http://www.internetnews.com/dev-news/article.php/3601751

Kestnbaum, R.D., Kestnbaum, K.T., & Ames, P.W. (1998),

"**Building a Longitudinal Contact Strategy,**" *Journal of Interactive Marketing*, **12 (1), 56-62.**

Khalifa, M. and Liu, V. (2001). Satisfaction with Internet-Based Services: A Longitudinal Study. In *Proceedings of the Twenty-Second International Conference of Information Systems (ICIS 2001)*, New Orleans, 601-606.

Kim, C. K., Han, D., and Park, S. B. (2001). "The Effect of Brand Personality and Brand Identification on Brand Loyalty: Applying the Theory of Social Identification". Japanese Psychological Research. 43 (4), pp. 195-206.

Kim, D.J.; Cho, B. and Rao, H.R. (2000). Effects of Consumer Lifestyles on Purchasing Behavior on the Internet: A Conceptual Framework and Empirical Validation. In *Proceedings of the Sixth Americas Conference on Information Systems (AMCIS 2000)*, Long Beach, 688-695.

Kim, M.-K., Park, M.-C., & Jeong, D.-H. (2004). The effects of customer satisfaction and switching barrier on customer loyalty in Korean mobile telecommunication services. *Telecommunications Policy, 28*(2), 145.

Kim, S.Y. and Lim, Y.J. (2001). Consumers' Perceived Importance of and Satisfaction with Internet Shopping. *Electronic Markets*, 11(3), 148-154.

Kim, Y.J., E.J. Garrity, G.L. Sanders, and B.A. Sherman. (2004). A means-end model of IS success: Toward understanding the cognitive structure of IS users. *Working Paper State University of New York at Buffalo.*

Kimelfeld, Y.M. and Watt, J.H. (2001). The Pragmatic Value of On-Line Transactional Advertising: A Predictor of Purchase Intention. *Journal of Marketing Communications*, 7(3), 137-157.

King, S. (1991) "Brand-building in the 1990's", Journal of Marketing Management, 1991, 7, pp. 3-13.

Klemperer, P. (2004). "Auctions: Theory and Practice." Princeton University Press. Also available online at http://www.paulklemperer.org/index.htm.

Klink, R.R. (2000) "Creating Brand Names with Meaning: The Use of Sound Symbolism", Marketing Letters, 11(1), pp. 5-20.

KNSO (Korea National Survey Office), (2003), "The Annual Results of e-Commerce Transaction Survey in 2002," (Accessed July 2003) [http://www.nso.go.kr/eng/releases/e_suec0144.htm]

Kohli, C., LaBahn, D.W. (1997) "Observations: Creating Effective Brand Names: A Study of the Naming Process", Journal of Advertising Research, January/February 1997, pp. 67-75.

Koivumaki, T. (2001). Customer Satisfaction and Purchasing Behavior in a Web-based Shopping Environment. *Electronic Markets*, 11(3), 186-192.

Kolbe, R. H. and M. S. Burnett. 1991. "Content-Analysis Research: An Examination of Applications with Directives for Improving Research Reliability and Objectivity". *Journal of Consumer Research*, 18 (September), 243-250.

Kolesar, Mark B. and R. Wayne Galbraith (2000), "A services-marketing perspective on e-retailing: implications for e-retailers and directions for further research," *Internet Research*, Vol. 10, No.5, pp.424-438

Kollmann, T. (2006): "What is e-entrepreneurship? Fundamentals of company founding in the net economy", International Journal of Technology Management, Vol. 33, No. 4, pp. 322-340.

Kotabe, M., Murray, J. Y., & Javalgi, R. G. (1998). Global sourcing of services and market performance: an empirical evaluation. *Journal of International Marketing, 6*(4), 10-31.

Kotler Philip, "Marketing Management", 11ed. (2003), Pearson Education, 623.

Kotler, P. (2000). *Marketing Management: The Millennium Edition*, New Jersey: Prentice-Hall Inc.

Koudelova, R. and J. Whitelock (2001). A cross-cultural analysis of television advertising in the UK and the Czech Republic. *International Marketing Review*, 18 (3), 286-300.

Koufaris, M. (2002). Applying the Technology Acceptance Model and Flow Theory to Online Consumer Behavior. *Information System Research*, 13(2), 205-223.

Koufaris, M.; Kambil, A. and Labarbera, P.A. (2001). Consumer Behavior in Web-Based Commerce: An Empirical Study. *International Journal of Electronic Commerce*, 6(2), 115-138.

Koufaris, Marios (2002), "Applying the technology acceptance model and flow theory to online consumer behavior," Information Systems Review, Vol. 13, No. 2, pp.205-223

Kozinets, R.V. (1997), "E-Tribalized Marketing?: The Strategic Implications of Virtual Communities of Consumption," *European Management Journal*, 17(3), 252-264.

Krippendorff, K. (1980). *Content analysis: An introduction to its methodology.* Sage Publications, Newbury Park, CA.

Krishnan, B. C., & Hartline, M. D. (2001). Brand Equity: Is It More Important in Services? *Journal of Services Marketing, 15*(2), 328-342.

Krol, C. (2006, 16/1/06). Search engine marketing up 44% in 2005. *B to B, 91,* 3.

Kumar K and Mahadevan B, (2003), "Evolution of Business Models in B2C E Commerce; The Case of Fabmall", Management Review, Vol.15, No.4, pp.23-30.

Kumar S. Ramesh, (2002), "Managing Indian Brands", Vikas, pp.299-300.

Kumar S. Ramesh, (2002, Conceptual Issues in Consumer Behaviour – Indian Context", Pearson Education, pp.82-89.

Kumar, N. and Benbasat, I. (2001). Shopping as Experience and Web Site as a Social Actor: Web Interface Design and Para-Social Presence. In *Proceedings of the Twenty-Second International Conference on Information Systems (ICIS 2001)*, New Orleans, 449-454.

Laffont, J.J., & Martimort, D. "The Theory of Incentives: The Principal-Agent Model," Princeton University Press, 2002.

Landler, M., Schiller, Z., & Therrien, L. (1991) "What's in a name? less and less", Business Week, July 8, pp.66-

67.

Laroche, M., Kirpalani, V.H., Pens, F. and Zhou, L. (2001). A model of advertising standardization in multinational corporations. *Journal of International Business Studies*, 32(2), 250-65.

LaRose, R., & Eastin, M. S. (2002). Is Online Buying Out of Control? Electronic Commerce and Consumer self-regulation. *Journal of Broadcasting and Electronic Media, 46*(4), 549-564.

Lastowka, F. G. (2002). Search Engines Under Siege: Do Paid Placement Listings Infringe Trademarks. *Intellectual Property & Technology Law Journal, 14*(7), 1-7.

Lederer, A.L., Maupin, D.J., Sena, M.P., & Zhuang, Y. (2000). The technology acceptance model and the World Wide Web. *Decision Support Systems*, 29(3), 269-282.

Lee, D. and Park, J. (2001). On the Explanation of Factors Affecting E-Commerce Adoption. In *Proceedings of the Twenty-Second International Conference of Information Systems (ICIS 2001)*, New Orleans, pp. 109-120.

Lee, J.; Kim, J. and Moon, J.Y. (2000). What Makes Internet Users Visit Cyber Stores Again? Key Design Factors for Customer Loyalty. In *Proceedings of the Conference on Human Factors in Computing Systems*, The Hague, Netherlands, 305-312.

Lee, M.K.O. (1999). Comprehensive Model of Internet Consumer Satisfaction, *Unpublished Working Paper, City University of Hong Kong.*

Lee, M.K.O. and Turban, E. (2001). A Trust Model for Consumer Internet Shopping. *International Journal of Electronic Commerce*, 6(1), 75-91.

Lee, P.M. (2002). Behavioral Model of Online Purchasers in E-Commerce Environment. *Electronic Commerce Research*, 2(1-2), 75-85.

Lefcourt, H. M. (1981). *Research with the Locus of Control Construct. Volume 1: Assessment Methods*. New York: Academic Press.

Leitch, S., Richardson, N. (2003) "Corporate branding in the Net Economy", European Journal of Marketing,

Vol.37, No. 7/8 2003, pp. 1065-1079.

Leong, E.K.F., Huang, X. and Stanners, P.J. (1998). Comparing the Effectiveness of the Web site with Traditional Media. *Journal of Advertising Research*, 38 (5), 44-51.

Lerman, D., Garbarino, E. (2002) "Recall and Recognition of Brand Names: A Comparison of Word and Nonword Name Types", Psychology & Marketing, Vol. 19 (7-8), pp.621-639.

Levitt, T. (1983). The Globalization of Market. *Harvard Business Review*, 61(May/June), 92-102.

Levy, M., & Weitz, B. (2003). *Retail management* (5th ed.). New York: McGraw-Hill.

Levy, S. J. (1986). Meanings in advertising stimuli. In J. Olson & K. Sentis (Eds.), *Advertising and consumer psychology* (Vol. 3) (pp. 214-226). New York: Praeger Publishers.

Lewis, D., & Weigert, A. (1985). Trust as a social reality. *Social Forces*, 63, 967-985.

Li, H., Daugherty, T., & Biocca, F. (2001). Characteristics of Virtual Experience in Electronic Commerce: A Protocol Analysis. *Journal of Interactive Marketing, 15*(3), 13-30.

Li, H., Daugherty, T., & Biocca, F. (2002). Impact of 3-D advertising on product knowledge, brand attitude, and purchase intention: The mediating role of presence. *Journal of Advertising*, 31(3), 43-57.

Li, H., Daugherty, T., & Biocca, F. (2003). The Role of Virtual Experience in Consumer Learning. *Journal of Consumer Psychology, 13*(4), 395 – 405.

Li, H.; Kuo, C. and Russell, M.G. (1999). The Impact of Perceived Channel Utilities, Shopping Orientations, and Demographics on the Consumer's Online Buying Behavior. *Journal of Computer-Mediated Communication*, 5(2).

Li, Z.G., Murray, L. W., & Scott, D. (2000). Global Sourcing, Multiple Country-of-Origin Facets, and Consumer Reactions. *Journal of Business Research, 47*, 121-133.

Liang, T.P. and Huang, J.S. (1998). An Empirical Study

on Consumer Acceptance of Products in Electronic Markets: A Transaction Cost Model. *Decision Support Systems*, 24(1), 29-43.

Liang, T.P. and Lai, H.J. (2002). Effect of Store Design on Consumer Purchases: An Empirical Study of On-Line Bookstores. *Information & Management*, 39(6), 431-444.

Liao, Z. and Cheung, M. (2001). Internet-Based E-Shopping and Consumer Attitudes: An Empirical Study. *Information & Management*, 38(5), 299-306.

Liao, Ziqi and Michael Tow Cheung (2001), "Internet-based e-shopping and consumer attitudes: an empirical study," *Information and Management*, Vol. 38, pp. 299-306

Lieigh, J. H. (1992). Modality congruence, multiple resource theory and intermedia broadcast comparisons: An elaboration. *Journal of Advertising*, 21(2), 55-63.

Lightner, Nancy J. and Caroline Eastman (2002), "User preference for product information in remote purchase environment," Journal *of Electronic Commerce Research*, Vol.3, No.3, pp.174-186

Lilien, G.L.; Philip, K. and Sridhar, M.K. (1992). *Marketing Models*, New Jersey: Prentice Hall.

Limayem, M. and Khalifa, M. (2000). Business-to-Consumer Electronic Commerce: A Longitudinal Study. In *Proceedings of the Fifth IEEE Symposium on Computers and Communications*, 286-290.

Limayem, M.; Khalifa, M. and Frini, A. (2000). What Makes Consumers Buy from Internet? A Longitudinal Study of Online Shopping. *IEEE Transactions on Systems, Man & Cybernetics, Part A (Systems & Humans)*, 30(4), 421-432.

Lin, J.C.-C. and Lu, H. (2000). Towards an Understanding of the Behavioral Intention to Use a Web Site. *International Journal of Information Management*, 20(3), 197-208.

Linstrom Martin, Peppers Don and Rogers Martha, (2001), "Clicks, Bricks and Brands", Kogan, pp.24.

Lippman, W. (1965). *Public opinion*. New York: The Free Press.

Liu, C. and Arnett, K. (1999). Assessing the Customer Behavioral Intentions on the Web: A Research Model. In *Proceedings of the Fifth Americas Conference on Information Systems (AMCIS 1999)*, Milwaukee, WI, 307-309.

Liu, Chang and Kirk P. Arnett (2000), "Exploring the factors associated with web site success in the context of electronic commerce," *Information and Management*, Vol. 38, pp. 23-33

Liu, Chang, Jack T. Marchewka, Jun Lu, and Chun-Sheng Yu (2004), "Beyond concern: a privacy – trust- behavioral intention model of electronic commerce," *Information & Management*, Vol., 42, pp. 127-142

Lohse, Gerald L. and Peter Spiller (1998), "Electronic shopping," *Communications of ACM*, Vol. 41, No. 7, pp 81-89

Lovelock, C. H. (1999). Developing marketing strategies for transactional service operations. *Journal of Services Marketing, 13*(4/5), 278-289.

Loveman, G. (1998). Employee satisfaction, customer loyalty, and financial performance: An empirical examination of the service project chain in retail banking. *Journal of Service Research, 1,* 18-31.

Luna, D. and Gupta, S.F. (2001). An Integrative Framework for Cross-Cultural Consumer Behavior. *International Marketing Review*, 18(1), 45-69.

Lynch, P.D., Kent, R.J. and Srinivasan, S.S. (2001). The global Internet shopper: Evidence from shopping tasks in twelve countries. *Journal of Advertising Research*, 41(3), 15-22.

Lynd, R. S. (1939). *Knowledge for what? The place of the social sciences in American culture*. Princeton: Princeton University Press.

Mackay, S. (2004). Parliament Approves New Government. *Executive Perspectives: Poland, Price Waterhouse Coopers*. Available: http://www.pwcglobal.com/.

Madden, C.S., Caballero, M.J. and Matsukubo, S. (1986). Analysis of information content in U.S. and Japanese magazine advertising. *Journal of Advertising*, 15 (3), 38-45.

Malhotra, Naresh K., Sung S. Kim, and James Agarwal (2004), "Internet users' information privacy concerns(IUIPC): The construct, the scale, and a causal model," *Information Systems Research,* Vol. 15, No. 4, pp. 336-355

Manning Magid, J., Cox, A. & Cox, D. (2006) Quantifying Brand Image: Empirical Evidence of Trademark Dilution. *American Business Law Journal*, 43 (1) pp 1-42.

Markus, L. and Soh, C. (2002). Structural Influences on Global E-Commerce Activity. *Journal of Global Information Management*, 10(1), 5-12.

MARKUS, M. L. (1995) Electronic mail as a medium of managerial choice. *Organization Science* 5 (4), 502-527.

Marx, K. (1967). Commodities. In *Capital: A critique of political economy.: Vol 1. The process of capitalist production.* (S. Moore & E. Aveling, Trans.). New York: The International Publishers Co.

Maskin, E. & Riley, J.G. (1984) "Monopoly With Incomplete Information." Rand Journal of Economics, 15, Summer.

Mathieson, K. (1991). Predicting use intentions: Comparing the technology acceptance model with the theory of planned behavior. *Information Systems Research*, 2(3), 173-191.

Mayer, K. J., Bowen, J. T., & Moulton, M. R. (2003). A proposed model of the descriptors of service process. *The Journal of Services Marketing, 17*(6/7), 621.

Mayer, R. C., Davis, J. H., & Schoorman, F. D. (1995). An integrative model of organizational trust. *The Academy of Management Review*, 20(3), 709-734.

Mayer, R.C. & Davis, J.H. (1999). The effect of the performance appraisal system on trust for management: A field quasi-experiment. *Journal of Applied Psychology*, 84(1), 123-136.

McCartney, L. (2003). A shore thing. *CFO-IT Magazine*(Spring), 60–63.

McCaskey, D., & Symes, S. (2004). Travel Inn: everything you want for a good night's sleep - 100 per cent satisfaction guarantee or your money back. *International Journal of Contemporary Hospitality Management, 16*(3), 167.

McCracken, G. (1986). Culture and consumption: A theoretical account of the structure and movement of the cultural meaning of consumer goods. *Journal of Consumer Research,* 13 (June), 71-84.

McCracken, G. (1990). Culture and consumer behavior: An anthropological perspective. *Journal of the Market Research Society*, 32(1), 3-11.

McKinney, Vicki, Yoon, Kanghyun, and Zahedi, Fatemeh "Mariam" (2002), "The measurement of web-customer satisfaction: an expectation and disconfirmation approach," Information Systems Review, Vol. 13, No.3, pp. 296-315

McKnight, D. H., Choudhury, V., & Kacmar, C. (2002). Developing and validating trust measures for e-commerce: An integrative typology. *Information Systems Research*, 13(3), 334-359.

McMillan, S.J. (2000). The Microscope and The Moving Target: The Challenge of Applying Content Analysis to The World Wide Web. *Journalism and Mass Communication Quarterly*, 77 (1), 80-98.

McNeal, J.U., Zeren, L.M. (1981) "Brand Name Selection for Consumer Products", MSU Business Topics (1981), pp.35-39.

McWilliam, G. (2000). Building strong brands through online communities. *Sloan Management Review*, 41(3), 43-54.

Meeker, M. (1997). *The Internet Advertising Report.* New York, NY: Harper Business.

Mehrabian, A. & Russel. (1974). *An approach to environmental psychology.* Cambridge, MA.: MIT Press.

Meinert, D.B., Peterson, D.K., Criswell, J.R., & Crossland, M.D. (2006). Privacy policy statements and consumer willingness to provide personal information. *Journal of Electronic Commerce in Organizations,* 4, 1, 1-17.

Memmi, D. (2006). The nature of virtual communities. *AI & Society,* 20(3), 288-300.

Merkow, M. (2000). Inside the Platform for Privacy Preferences (P3P). http://Internet_com's Electronic Commerce Guide – EC Outlook.

Meuter, M. L., Ostrom, A. L., Roundtree, R. J., & Bitner, M. J. (2000). Self-Service Technologies: Understanding Consumer Satisfaction with Technology-Based Service Encounters. *Journal of Marketing, 64*(3), 50-64.

Meyer-Levy, J. & Tybout, A.M. (1989), "Schema congruity as a basis for product evaluation," *Journal of Consumer Research,* 16, pp. 39–54.

Meyers, H. and Gerstman, R. (2001). Branding @ the Digital Age. New York: Palgrave.

Mick, D. G. (1986). Consumer research and semiotics: Exploring the morphology of signs, symbols and significance. *Journal of Consumer Research* 13 (September), 196-213.

Mirchin, D. (2005). Google wins U.S. keyword case. *Information Today,* 22(9), 1-5.

MITCHELL, A. & KIRKUP, M. (2003) Retail development and urban regeneration: a case study of Castle Vale. *International Journal of Retail and Distribution Management* 31 (9), 451-458.

Miyazaki, A.D. and Fernandez, A. (2001). Consumer Perceptions of Privacy and Security Risks for Online Shopping. *The Journal of Consumer Affairs,* 35(1), 27-44.

Moe, W. W. and Fader, P. S. (2000). *Which Visits Lead to Purchase? Dynamic Conversion Behavior at E-Commerce Sites.* University of Texas.

Moe, W.W. and Fader, P.S. (2001). Uncovering Patterns in Cybershopping. *California Management Review,* 43(4), 106-117.

Molla, Alemayehu and Paul S. Licker (2001), "E-commerce systems success: an attempt to extend and re-specify the DeLone and McLean model of IS success," *Journal of Electronic Commerce Research,* Vol.2, No.4, pp.131-139

Moon, J. & Kim, Y. (2001). Extending the TAM for a world wide web context. *Information and Management,* 38, 217-230.

Moon, J., & Kim, Y. (2001). Extending the TAM for world-wide-web context. *Information and Management, 28,* 217-230.

Moon, Ji-Woon and Young-Gul Kim (2001), "Extending the TAM for a World-Wide-Web context," *Information and Management,* Vol.38, pp. 217-230

Moore, G.A. (1995) "Crossing the Chasm: Marketing and Selling High-tech Products to Mainstream Customers", New York, 1995

Moorman, Christine, Gerald Zaltman, and Rohit Deshpande (1992), "Relationships between providers and users of market research: the dynamics of trust within and between organizations," *Journal of Marketing Research,* Vol. 29, pp. 314-328

Morgan, R., & Hunt, S. (1994). The commitment-trust theory of relationship marketing. *Journal of Marketing, 58,* 20-38.

Morr, T. (1997). You can build it, but will they come back On The Highway. *SEMA News,* June. Specialty Equipment Market Association.

Mueller, B. (1991). An analysis of information content in standardized vs. specialized multinational advertisements. *Journal of International Business Studies,* First Quarter, 23-39.

Müller, B. and Chandon, J.L. (2003). "The Impact of Visiting a Brand Website on Brand Personality". Electronic Markets. 13 (3), pp. 210-21.

Muller, B., & Chandon, J.-L. (2003). The impact of visiting a brand website on brand personality. *Electronic Markets, 13,* 210–221.

MUNIZ, A. & O'GUINN, T.C. (2001) Brand Community. *Journal of Consumer Research* 27, 412-432

Murphy, J. (1999). Surfers and searchers: An examination of Web-site visitors' clicking behavior. *Cornell Hotel & Restaurant Administration Quarterly*. 40(2), 84.

Murphy, J., Raffa, L., & Mizerski, R. (2003). The use of domain names in e-branding by the world's top brands. *Electronic Markets, 13*(3), 30–40.

Murphy, T. (2000). *Web Rules: How the Internet is Changing the Way Consumers Make Choices*, Chicago, IL: Dearborn Financial Publishing, Inc.

Mussa, M., & Rosen, S. (1978) "Monopoly and product quality." Journal of Economic Theory 18, 301-317.

Muthitacharoen, A. (2000). Consumer's Preference Between the Internet and Conventional Stores (An Exploratory Study). In *Proceedings of the Sixth Americas Conference on Information Systems (AMCIS 2000)*, Long Beach, 1373-1379.

Nandan, S. (2005). "An Exploration of the Brand Identity-Brand Image Linkage: A Communications Perspective". Journal of Brand Management. 12 (4), pp. 264-278.

Nash, S. (2000). Online Catalogs Will Come to Life and You'll View Merchandise From Every Side. PC Magazine, January 2000. [Online available at] http://www.zdnet.com/pcmag/stories/trends/0,7607,2418240,00.html

Nel, D.; Niekerk, R.v.; Berthon, J.-P. and Davies, T. (1999). Going with the Flow: Web Sites and Customer Involvement. *Internet Research: Electronic Networking Applications and Policy*, 9(2), 109-116.

Nemes, J. (2000). Domain names have brand impact. *B to B Chicago, 85*(12), 20–22.

Ness, G. (2007). "And Some Still Think of Google As Just a Search Engine Company…". SUNDOG. April 11, 2007. Available at: http://www.sundog.net/index.php/sunblog/comments/and-some-still-think-of-google-as-just-a-search-engine/

Neviite, N. & Kanji, M. (1999). Orientations towards authority and congruency theory. *International Journal of Comparative Sociology*, 40(1), 160.

New Atlantis, (2004). "Gaga Over Google". 5 (Spring), pp. 99-101. A Journal of Technolgy & Society. Available at: http://www.thenewatlantis.com/archive/5/soa/google.htm

Nicoulaud, B. (1989). Problems and strategies in the international marketing of services. *European Journal of Marketing, 23*(6), 55-66.

NIDA (National Internet Development Agency of Korea) report (2004), "Survey on the computer and internet usage," www.nida.or.kr

Nielsen NetRatings. (2006). *MegaView Search Engine Ratings*. NewYork: Nielsen NetRatings.

Nielsen-NetRatings. (2003, February 20). Global Internet population grows an average of four percent year-over-year.

Nöth, W. (1988). The language of commodities: Groundwork for a semiotics of consumer goods. *International Journal of Research in Marketing*, 4(3), 173-186.

Novak, T. P., Hoffman, D. L., & Yung, Y. (2000). Measuring the customer experience in online environments: A structural modeling approach. *Marketing Science*, 19(1), 22-42.

Novak, T.P., Hoffman, D.L., & Duhachek, A. (2003). The influence of goal-directed and experiential activities on online flow experiences. *Journal of Consumer Psychology*, 13(1-2), 3-16.

O'Cass, Aron and Tino Fenech (2003), "Web retailing adoption: exploring the nature of internet users," *Journal of Retailing and Consumer Services*, Vol.10, pp. 81-94

O'Donnell, J.B.; Ferrin, D.L.; Glassberg, B.; & Sanders, G.L. (2004). The influence of web site characteristics on consumer trust and the purchase decision. *Working Paper, Canisius College.*

O'Keefe, R.M. & McEachern, T. (1998). Web-based customer decision support systems. *Communications of the ACM*, 41(3), 71-78.

OBP (2001). Advertising in Poland. Available: http://www.obp.pl/03-raport/2001/advertising_in_poland.htm

Oh, K.W., Cho, C.H. and Leckenby, J.D. (1999). A Comparative Analysis of Korean and U.S. Web Advertising. *Proceedings of the 1999 Conference of the American Academy of Advertising,* Gainesville: University of Florida, 73-77.

Okazaki, S. (2004). Do multinationals standardise or localise? The cross-cultural dimensionality of product-based Web sites. *Internet Research: Electronic Networking, Applications and Policy,* 14(1), 81-94.

Okazaki, S. (2005). "Excitement or Sophistication? A Preliminary Exploration of Online Brand Personality". International Marketing Review. 23 (3), pp. 279-303.

Okazaki, S. (2005). Searching the Web for global brands: How American brands standardise their websites in Europe. *European Journal of Marketing,* 39 (1/2), 87-109.

Okazaki, S. and Alonso, J. (2002). A content analysis of Web communication strategies: Cross-cultural research framework and pre-testing. *Internet Research: Electronic Networking, Applications and Policy,* 12 (5), 380-390.

Okazaki, S. and Alonso, J. (2003). Beyond the Net: Cultural Values Reflected in Japanese Multinationals' Web Communication Strategies. *Journal of International Consumer Marketing,* 16(1), 47-70.

Okazaki, S. and Alonso, J. (2003). Right messages at the right site: on-line creative strategies by Japanese multinational corporations. *Journal of Marketing Communications,* 9(4), 221-239.

Oliva, R. (2004). Playing the Search: So little time, so many sites. *Marketing Management* (April), 48-51.

Oliver, R. L. (1997). *Satisfaction: A behavioral perspective on the consumer.* New York, NY: McGraw-Hill.

Oliver, R.L. (1980). A Cognitive Model for the Antecedents and Consequences of Satisfaction. *Journal of Marketing Research,* 17, 460-469.

Olsen, S. (2004) *Google plans trademark gambit.* CNET News April 13th

OMD Czech (2005). Odhady reklamních výdajů. Available: http://www2.omd.com/OMDOffice/section/subsection.asp?CompanyID=9&SubSectionID=105.

Onkvisit, S. and Shaw, J.J. (1987). Standardized International Advertising: A Review and Critical Evaluation of the Theoretical and Empirical Evidence. *The Columbia Journal of World Business,* 22 (Fall), 43-55.

Onkvisit, S., & Shaw, J.J., (1989), "Service marketing: image, branding and competition", Business Horizons, 32 (1), 13-18

Osgood, C. E., & Tannenbaum, P. H. (1955). The Principle of Congruity in the Prediction of Attitude Change. *Psychological Review,* 62(1), 42-55.

Osgood, C. E., May, W. H. & Miron, M. S. (1975) *Cross-cultural universals of affective meaning.* Urbana, IL: University of Illinois Press.

Osgood, C., Suci, G., & Tannenbaum, P. (1957). *The measurement of meaning.* Urbana, IL: University of Illinois Press.

Pace, S. A grounded theory of the flow experiences of web users. (2004). *International Journal of Human-Computer Studies,* 60(3), 327-363.

Page, C. and Lepkowska-White, E. (2002). Web Equity: A Framework for Building Consumer Value in Online Companies. *Journal of Consumer Marketing,* 19(3), 231-248.

Palacio, A. B., Meneses, G. D., & Perez, P. J. (2002). The configuration of the university image and its relationship with the satisfaction of students. *Journal of Educational Administration,* 40(4/5), 486-505.

Parasuraman, A. (2000). Technology Readiness Index (TRI): A Multiple-Item Scale to Measure Readiness to Embrace New Technologies. *Journal of Service Research,* 2(4), 307-320.

Parasuraman, A., & Zinkham, G. (2002). Marketing and serving customers through the Internet: An overview and research agenda. *Journal of the Academy of Marketing Science,* 30, 286-295.

Parasuraman, A., Zeithaml, V. A., & Berry, L. L. (1988). SERVQUAL: A multiple-item scale for measuring consumer perceptions of service quality. *Journal of Retailing,* 64, 12-37.

Park C. Whan, Jaworski J. Bernard and MacInnis J. Deborah, (1996), "Strategic Brand Concept – Image Management", Journal of Marketing, pp.135-145.

Park, C., & Kim, Y. (2006). The effect of information satisfaction and relational benefit on consumers' online shopping site commitments. *Journal of Electronic Commerce in Organizations,* 4, 1, 70-90.

Park, C.W. & Lessig, P.F. (1981), "Familiarity and its impact on consumer decision biases and heuristics," *Journal of Consumer Research* 8, pp. 223–230.

PARKER, C., ANTHONY-WINTER, T. & TABER-NACLE, D. (2003) Learning by stealth: introducing smaller retailers to the benefits of training and education in Barnet. *International Journal of Retail and Distribution Management* 31 (9), 470-476.

Parthasarathy, M. and Bhattacherjee, A. (1998). Understanding Post-Adoption Behavior in the Behavior in the Context of Online Services. *Information Systems Research,* 9(4), 362-379.

Parthasarathy, M., & Bhattacherjee, A. (1998). Understanding post-adoption behavior in the context of online services. *Information Systems Research,* 9, 4, 362-379.

Pasternack, D. (2006). Good Organic Rankings Aren't Enough. In M. Alam Khan (Ed.), *Essential Guide to Search Engine Marketing.* New York, NY: Courtenay Communications Corporation.

Pastore, M. (2000). *Future of e-tail lies with multichannel retailers.* Retrieved August 5, 2004, from http://cyberat-las.internet.com/markets/retailing/article/0,1323,6061_417411,00.html

Patterson, Paul G. and Tasman Smith (2001), "Relationship benefits in service industries: a replication in a southeast asian context," *Journal of services marketing,* Vol. 15, No.6, pp. 425-443

Pattison, W. (2006, 9 March 2006). *Trademark Infringement Issues for Pay-per-Click (PPC) Advertisers.* Retrieved 25 August, 2006.

Pavlou, P. (2001). *Integrating trust in electronic commerce with the technology acceptance model: model development and validation.* AMCIS Proceedings, Boston, MA.

Pavlou, P.A. (2001). Integrating Trust in Electronic Commerce With The Technology Acceptance Model: Model Development And Validation. In *Proceedings of the Seventh Americas Conference on Information Systems (AMCIS 2001),* Boston, 816-822.

Pavlou, P.A. (2003). Consumer acceptance of electronic commerce: Integrating trust and risk with the technology acceptance model. *International Journal of Electronic Commerce,* 7, 3, 101-134.

Pavlou, P.A., & Gefen, D. (2004). Building effective online marketplaces with institution-based trust. *Information Systems Research,* 15, 1, 37-59.

Pedhazur, E.J. (1997). *Multiple regression in behavioral research: Explanation and prediction.* Fort Worth: Harcourt Brace College Publishers.

Pennington, R. (2000). Brands as the language of consumer culture. *Journal of Global Competitiveness,* 8(1), 318-329.

Pennington, R. (2000). The theory is the press: A view of the press as developer of informal theory. Phoenix: Association for Education in Journalism and Mass Communication Annual Convention (Communication Theory and Methodology Division).

Pennington, R. (2001). Signs of marketing in virtual reality. *Journal of Interactive Advertising,* 2(1), <http://jiad.org/vol2/no1/pennington>.

Pennington, R. (2001). The conceptual definition of culture in advertising, marketing and consumer research literature. In M. Roberts & R. L. King (Eds.), *Proceedings of the 2001 Special Asia-Pacific Conference of the American Academy of Advertising* (pp. 34-40). Gainesville, FL: The University of Florida.

Pennington, R. (2004). Brands, culture and semiotics (revisited) in creative strategy development. In P. Ribeiro Cardoso & S. Nora Gaio (Eds.), *Publicidade e Comunicação Empresarial: Perspectivas e Contributos* (pp. 29043). Porto, Portugal: Edições Universidade

Fernando Pessoa.

Pennington, R. (2004). Revising a psycho-linguistic application of information theory for the consumer psychology of brands. In J. D. Williams, W.-N. Lee & C. P. Haugtvedt (Eds.), *Diversity in Advertising* (pp. 201-214). Hilldale, NJ: Lawrence Erlbaum Associates, Inc.

Pennington, R. (2005). Affording cultural and social presence in e-marketing. In Y. Gao (Ed.), *Web Systems Design and Online Consumer Behavior* (pp. 305-318). Hershey, PA: The Idea Group Inc..

Pennington, R. (2006). A cultural framework for studying youth, brands, and lifestyles. In P. Ribeiro Cardoso, S. Nora Gaio & J. Pérez Seoane (Eds.), *Jovens, Marcas e Estilos de Vida* (pp. 15-24). Porto, Portugal: Edições Universidade Fernando Pessoa.

Peppers, D. & Rogers, M. (1999), Enterprise One-to-One: Tools for Competing in the Interactive Age. New York: Doubleday.

Pereira, R.E. (1998). Factors Influencing Consumer Purchasing Behavior in Electronic Commerce. In *Proceedings of the Fourth Americas Conference on Information Systems (AMCIS 1998)*, Baltimore, 450-452.

Perreault, W.D. and L.E. Leigh (1989). Reliability of nominal data based on qualitative judgments. *Journal of Marketing Research*, 26 (May), 135-148.

Peterson, Robert A., Sridhar Balasubramanian, and Bart J. Bronnenberg (1997), "Exploring the implications of the internet for consumer marketing," *Journal of the Academy of Management Science*, Vol. 25, No.4, pp.329-346

Phau, I. and Poon, S.M. (2000). An Exploratory Study of Cybershopping in Singapore. *Quarterly Journal of Electronic Commerce*, 1(1), 61-75.

Phau, I. and Poon, S.M. (2000). Factors Influencing the Types of Products and Services Purchased over the Internet. *Internet Research: Electronic Networking Applications And Policy*, 10(2), 102-113.

Philport, J.C. and J. Arbittier (1997). Advertising: Brand communications styles in established media and the Internet. *Journal of Advertising Research*, 37 (2), 68-76.

Pine, B. J., & Gilmore, J. H. (1999). *The Experience Economy.* Boston: Harvard Business School Press.

Pinker, S. (1994). *The language instinct.* New York: William Morrow and Company, Inc.

Plave, L. (2005) *E-Business Legal Survival Kit*, DLA Piper Rudnick Gray Cary, Washington DC

Plummer, J.T. (1984). "How Personality Makes a Difference?". Journal of Advertising Research. 24 (6), pp. 27-31.

Popov, A. (2005) The extraterritorial reach of the Lanham Act over trademarks on the Internet: Adapting the Lanham Act to global e-commerce or an unjustified extension of US laws? Journal of Internet Law, May, pp 19-28

Porra, J & Parks, M. S. (2006). Sustainable virtual communities: Suggestions from the colonial model. *Information Systems and eBusiness Management*, 4(4), 309-341.

Prahalad and C K Ramaswamy Venkat, (2004), "Future of Competition - Co-Creating Unique Value with Customers", HBS, pp.83-85.

Preece, J. (2000). *Online communities: Designing usability, supporting sociability.* New York: John Wiley & Sons.

PRELL, C. (2003) Community Networking and Social Capital: Early Investigations. *Journal of Computer Mediated Communications* 8 (3). Retrieved September 13 2005 from http://wwwascuscorg/jcmc/vol8/issue3/prellhtml

Princeton Research Associates. (2002). *A Matter of Trust: What Users Want From Web Sites - A Report on Consumer Concerns About Credibility of Web Sites.* Yonkers, New York: Consumer Reports WebWatch.

Pritchard, Mark P., Mark E. Havitz, and Dennis R. Howard (1999), "Analyzing the commitment-loyalty link in service contexts," *Journal of the Academy of Management Science*, Vol. 27, No. 3, pp. 333-348

PUTNAM, R.D. (2000) *Bowling Alone: The Collapse and Revival of American Community.* Simon & Schuster, New York.

Quelch, J.A. and Klein, L.R. (1996). The Internet and International Marketing. *Sloan Management Review*, 38 (Spring), 60-75.

Quester, P., & Lim, A. L. (2003). Product involvement/ brand loyalty: is there a link? *Journal of Product & Brand Management, 12*(1), 22-38.

Quinn, J. B. (1997). *Innovation Explosion: Using Intellect and Software to Revolutionize Growth Strategies*. New York: Free Press.

RAFAELI, S. & SUDWEEKS, F. (1994) Interactivity on the nets. In *Information Systems and Human Communication Technology Divisions ICA Annual Conference*, Sydney, Australia.

Rafaeli, S., & Sudweeks, F. (1997). Networked Interactivity. *Journal of Computer-Mediated Communication, 2*(4), [On-line] Retrieved June 10, 2002, from http:// www. http://www.ascusc.org/jcmc/vol2/issue4/rafaeli. sudweeks.html.

Raijas, A. and Tuunainen, V.K. (2001). Critical Factors in Electronic Grocery Shopping. *International Review of Retail, Distribution and Consumer Research*, 11(3), 255-265.

Rajani R. & Rosenberg D. (1999) "Usable?...or not?...factors affecting the usability of web sites. *CMC Magazine*, 1-5 (January).

Ramaswami, S.N.; Strader, T.J. and Brett, K. (2000). Determinants of On-Line Channel Use for Purchasing Financial Products. *International Journal of Electronic Commerce*, 5(2), 95-118.

Randall, T., Ulrich, K., & Reibstein, D. (1998). Brand equity and vertical product line extension. *Marketing Science, 12*, 356-379.

Ranganathan, C. and Ganapathy, S. (2002). Key Dimensions of Business-to-Consumer Web Sites. *Information & Management*, 39(6), 457-465.

Rathmell, J. M. (1966).What Is Meant by Services? *Journal of Marketing*, 30 (4), 32-36.

Ravald, Annika and Christian Gronroos (1996), "The value concept and relationship marketing," *European Journal of Marketing*, Vol. 30, No. 2, pp. 19-30

Reda, S. (2002). Active multi-channel shoppers may be a liability, less loyal than other on-line shoppers. *Stores Magazine, 84*(9), 78-82.

Reibstein, D. (2002). What attracts customers to online stores and what keeps them coming back. *Journal of the Academy of Marketing Science, 30*, 465-473.

Reichheld, F., & Schefter, P. (2000). E-loyalty your secret weapon. *Harvard Business Review*, July-August, 105-13.

Reichheld, F.F., & Schefter, P. (2000). E-loyalty: Your secret weapon on the web. *Harvard Business Review,* 78, 4, 105-113.

Reilly, P. (1997). Outsourcing: employers becoming cautious. *Management Services, 41*(6), 9-11.

Reinartz, W.J. & Kumar, V. (2002), "The Mismanagement of Customer Loyalty," Harvard Business Review, 80 (July), 86-94.

Reinatz W, Thomas J and Kumar V, (2003), "Linking Acquisition and Retention to Maximize Profitability", Working paper, University of Connecticut.

Rettie, R. (2001). An Exploration of Flow During Internet Use. *Internet Research: Electronic Networking Applications and Policy.* 11(2), 103-113.

Reynolds J. Thomas and Gutman Jonathan, (Feb/Mar 1988), "Laddering Theory; Method, Analysis and Interpretation", Journal of Advertising Research, pp.11-23.

Reynolds, Jonathan (2000), "eCommerce: a critical review," *International Journal of Retail & Distribution Management,* Vol. 28, No.10, pp. 417-444

RICE, R.E. & AYDIN, C. (1991) Attitudes toward new organizational technology: network proximity as a mechanism for social information processing. *Administrative Science Quarterly* 36 (June), 219-244.

RICE, R.E. (1993) Media appropriateness: using social presence theory to compare traditional and new organizational media. *Human Communication Research* 19

(4), 451-484.

RIDINGS, C.M., GEFEN, D., & ARINZE, B. (2002) Some antecedents and effects of trust in virtual communities. *Journal of Strategic Information Systems* 11, 271-295.

Ries Al and Laura Ries, (2000), "Immutable Laws of Internet Branding", Harper Collins.

Ries Al and Trout Jack, (1987), "Brand Positioning; The battle in the Mind", Tata McGraw Hill, pp.1-5.

Ries, A., & Ries, L. (2000). *The 11 immutable laws of Internet branding.* New York: HarperCollins.

Ripin, P. (2003) Hotel Internet Marketers Beware: Pop-up and Keyword Advertising Threaten Your On-Line Brand. American Hotel & Lodging Association Knowledge Base. Retrieved 12 September, 2006

Ritson, M. & Elliott, R. (1999). The social uses of advertising: An ethnographic study of adolescent advertising audiences. *Journal of Consumer Research,* 26(December), 260-277.

Roberts, M. L. (2003). *Internet marketing: Integrating online and offline strategies.* New York: McGraw-Hill Irwin.

Roberts, M.L. & Berger, P.D. (1999), Direct Marketing Management. Englewood Cliffs, NJ: Prentice Hall.

Roberts, M.S. and Ko, H. (2001). Global Interactive Advertising: Defining What We Mean and Using What We Have Learned. *Journal of Interactive Advertising,* 1 (2), Online: http://www.jiad.org/vol1/no2/roberts/index. html.

Rochet, J.J., & Tirole, J. (2005) "Two-Sided Markets: A Progress Report." The Rand Journal of Economics, forthcoming.

Rode, V., Vallaster, C. (2005) "Corporate Branding for Start-ups: The Crucial Role of Entrepreneurs", Corporate Reputation Review, Vol.8, No.2, pp.121-135.

Rodgers, S. & Thorson, E. (2000). The interactive advertising model: How users perceive and process online ads. *Journal of Interactive advertising,* 1(1). Retrieved

Dec 12 2006, from http://www.jiad.org

Roehm, H. A., & Curtis P. H. (1999). Understanding Interactivity of Cyberspace Advertising. In David W. Schumann & Esther Thorson (Eds.) *Advertising and the World Wide Web,* 27-39.

ROMM, C., PLISKIN, N., & CLARKE, R. (1997) Virtual Communities and Society: Toward an Integrative Three Phase Model. *International Journal of Information Management* 17 (4), 261-270.

ROMM, CT (1999) *Virtual Politicking: Playing Politics in Electronically Linked Organizations.* Hampton Press, Cresskill NJ.

Root, F.R. (1994), *Entry Strategies for International Markets.* Heath, Washington DC: Lexington.

Rousseau, D.M.; Sitkin, S.B.; Burt, R.S.; & Camerer, C. (1998), Not so different after all: A cross-disciplined view of trust. *Academy of Management Review,* 23(3), 393-404.

Rowley, J. (2004). "Online Branding: The Case of McDonald's". British Food Journal. 106 (2/3), pp. 228-237.

Rowley, J. (2004). Online Branding. *Online Information Review, 28* (2), 131-138.

Rowley, J. (2006). An analysis of the e-service literature: towards a research agenda. *Internet Research, 16*(3), 339-359.

Roy, M. (2003). Outsourced call centres damage long-term effort. *Precision Marketing*(Nov 7), 14.

Rusbult, C.E., Martz, J.M., & Agnew, C.R. (1998). The investment model scale: Measuring commitment level, satisfaction level, quality of alternatives, and investment size. *Personal Relationships,* 5, 4, 357-391.

Rusch, R. (2001). "Google: The Infinite Quest". Brandchannel.com, Aug. 13, 2001. Available at: http://www.brandchannel.com/features_profile.asp?pr_id=30

Rust Roland J, Zeithmal Valarie A and Lemon N. Katherine, (2000), "Driving Customer Equity, How Customer Lifetime Value is Reshaping Corporate Strategy", The Free Press, pp.223-241.

Rust, R. T. (1997). The dawn of computer behavior: Interactive service marketers will find their customer is not human. *Marketing Management, 6* (fall), 31-34.

Rust, R. T., & Lemon, K. N. (2001). E-service and the Consumer. *International Journal of Electronic Commerce, 5*(3), 85-101.

Rust, R., & Zahorik, A. (1993). Customer satisfaction, customer retention, and market share. *Journal of Retailing, 69,* 193-215.

Rust, R., Zeithaml, V., & Lemon, K. (2000). *Driving customer equity: How customer lifetime value is reshaping corporate strategy.* New York: The Free Press.

Rust, R.T,, & Kannan, P. K. (2002). Preface. *E-service: New Directions in Theory and Prac*tice. Roland Rust & P. K. Kannan (eds.), New York, NY: M.E. Sharpe.

Rust, R.T., Zeithaml,V.A., & Lemon, K.N. (2000), Driving Customer Equity: How Customer Lifetime Value Is Reshaping Corporate Strategy. New York: The Free Press.

Ruyter, K. d., Birgelen, M. v., & Wetzels, M. (1998). Consumer ethnocentrism in international services marketing. *International Business Review, 7,* 185-202.

Ruyter, K.d.; Wetzels, M. and Kleijnen, M. (2001). Customer Adoption of E-Service: An Experimental Study. *International Journal of Service Industry Management,* 12(2), 184-207.

Sanders, G.L. (1984). MIS/DSS success measure. *Systems, Objectives, Solutions,* 4, 29-34.

Sauer, P. L., Young, M. A., & Unnava, H. R. (1991). An Experimental Investigation of the Processes Behind the Country-of-Origin Effects. *Journal of International Consumer Marketing, 3*(2), 29-59.

Schiffman G. Leon and Kanuk, Lazer Leslie(2002), "Consumer Behavior", Pearson Education, pp.141-153.

Schloss, I. (1981) "Chickens and Pickles", Journal of Advertising Research, Vol. 21, No.6, pp. 47-49.

Schlosser, A. E. & Kanfer, A. (2001, May). *Impact of product interactivity on searchers' and browsers' judg-*ments: Implications for commercial Web site effectiveness. Paper presented at the Advertising and Consumer Psychology Conference on "Online Consumer Psychology: Understanding How to Interact with Consumers in the Virtual World," Seattle, WA.

Schmitt H. Bernd(1999), "Entrepreneurial Marketing", The Free Press, pp.71.

Schoenbachler, D.D. and Gordon, G.L. Multi-Channel Shopping: Understanding What Drives Channel Choice. *Journal of Consumer Marketing,* 19(1), 42-53.

SCHULER, D. (1996) *New community networks: Wired for change.* Addison-Wesley Reading, MA.

Schultz, D. E. & Barnes, B. E. (1995). *Strategic advertising campaigns* (4th ed.). Lincolnwood, IL: NTC Business Books.

Schultz, D.E. & Bailey, S. (2000), "Customer/Brand Loyalty in an Interactive Marketplace," *Journal of Advertising Research,* May/Jun2000, Vol. 40 Issue 3, 41-53.

Schultze, U. (2003). Complementing self-serve technology with service relationships: the customer perspective. *E-service Journal, 3*(1), 7-31.

Schwartz, E. I. (1996). Advertising webonimics 101. *Wired,* 4.02 Electrosphere section, February.

Scott, W.E., Farh, J., & Podaskoff, P.M. (1988). The effects of intrinsic and extrinsic reinforcement contingencies on task behavior. *Organizational Behavior and Human Decision Processes,* 41, 405-425.

Sealy, P. (1999). How e-commerce will trump brand management. *Harvard Business Review, July–August,* 171–176.

Seda, C. (2004). *Search Engine Advertising.* Indianopolis, IN: New Riders.

Selnes, F. (1993). An examination of the effect of product performance on brand reputation, satisfaction and loyalty. *European Journal of Marketing, 27*(9), 19-35.

Selnes, F. (1998). Antecedents and consequences of trust and satisfaction on buyer-seller relationships. *European Journal of Marketing, 3,* 305-322.

Sen, R. (2005). Optimal Search Engine Marketing Strategy. *International Journal of Electronic Commerce, 10*(1), 9-25.

Sen, S. (1999) "The Effects of Brand Name Suggestiveness and Decision Goal on the Development of Brand Knowledge", Journal of Consumer Psychology, Vol.8, No.4, pp. 431-455.

Senecal, S. (2000). Stopping Variables in Online Buying Processes: An Innovation Diffusion Approach. In *Proceedings of the Sixth Americas Conference on Information Systems (AMCIS 2000)*, Long Beach, 1380-1385.

Sewell, C., & Brown, P. (2002). *Customers for life: How to turn that one buyer into a customer for life*. New York: Doubleday.

Seybold Patricia and Marshak T. Ronni(2000), "Customers.com", Times Business, pp.99-102.

Shapiro, C. & Varian, H. (1999), *Information Rules*. Cambridge, MA: Harvard Business School Press.

Sharma, S., Shimp, T. A., & Shin, J. (1995). Consumer ethnocentrism: A test of antecedents and moderators. *Journal of the Academy of Marketing Science, 23*(1), 26-37.

Shemwell, Donald J., Ugur Yavas, and Zeynep Bilgin (1998), "Customer-service provider relationships: an empirical test of a model of service quality, satisfaction, and relationship-oriented outcomes," *International Journal of Service Industry Management*, Vol. 9, No.2, pp. 155-168

Sheram, Katherine, and Tatyana P. Soubbotina (2000), *Beyond Economic Growth: Meeting the Challenges of Global Development*, Washington D.C.: World Bank.

Sheth, Jagdish N. and Atul Parvatiyar (1995), " Relationship marketing in Consumer Markets: Antecedents and Consequences," *Journal of the Academy of Marketing Science*, Vol. 23, No. 4, pp. 255-271

Shim, S.; Eastlick, M.A.; Lotz, S.L. and Warrington, P. (2001). An Online Prepurchase Intentions Model: The Role of Intention to Search. *Journal of retailing, 77*(3), 397-416.

Shimp, T. A. (1984). Consumer ethnocentrism: The concept and a preliminary empirical test. *Advances in Consumer Research, 11*, 285-290.

Shimp, T. A., & Sharma, S. (1987). Consumer ethnocentrism: Construction and validation of the CETSCALE. *Journal of Consumer Research, 24*(August), 280-289.

Shipley, D. (1985) "Marketing Objectives in UK and US manufacturing companies", European Journal of Marketing, Vol.19, No.3, pp. 48-56.

Shipley, D., Hooley, G.J., Wallace, S. (1988) "The Brand Name Development Process", International Journal of Advertising, 1988, Vol.7, pp. 253-266.

Siems, T. F., & Ratner, A. S. (2003). Do What You Do Best, Outsource the Rest. *Southwest Economy*(Nov/Dec).

Siguaw, J., Mattila, A., and Austin, J.R. (1999). "The Brand Personality Scale: An Application for Restaurants". Cornell Hotel and Restaurant Administration Quarterly. 40 (3), pp. 48-55.

Singh, J. (1988). Consumer Complaint Intentions and Behavior: Definitional and Taxonomical Issues. *Journal of Marketing, 52*(January 1988), 93-107.

Singh, J., & Pandya, S. (1991). Exploring the Effects of Consumers' Dissatisfaction Level on Complaint Behaviours. *European Journal of Marketing, 25*(9), 7-21.

Singh, J., & Wilkes, R. E. (1996). When consumers complain: a path analysis of the key antecedents of consumer complaint response estimates. *Journal of the Academy of Marketing Science, 24*(4), 350-365.

Sirgy, J. (1982). "Self-concept in Consumer Behavior: A Critical Review". Journal of Consumer Research. 9, pp. 287-301.

Siu, N.Y.M. and Cheng, M.M.-S. (2001). A Study of the Expected Adoption of Online Shopping – The Case of Hong Kong. *Journal of International Consumer Marketing, 13*(3), 87-106.

Skibell, R. & Kazemi, N. (2005) The Unanticipated Consequences of the Trademark Dilution Revision Act for Search engine Advertising. *Journal of Internet* Law, 9 (5), pp 1, 6-16.

Skinner, B.F. (1938). *The Behavior of Organisms: An Experimental Analysis*, New York: Appleton Century Crofts.

Slywotsky, A.J. (2000), "The Age of the Choiceboard," *Harvard Business Review*, 78/1 (January/ February), 40-41.

Smith, A.C.T., Graetz, B.R., and Westerbeek, H.M. (2006). "Brand Personality in a Membership-based Organization". International Journal of Nonprofit and Voluntary Sector Marketing. 11 (3), pp. 251-266.

Smith, S. (2005). The Emerging Search Economy. *e-content* (Jan / Feb), 31.

Sohn, C. (1999). The Properties of Internet-based Markets and Customers' Behavior. In *Proceedings of the Fifth Americas Conference on Information Systems (AMCIS 1999)*, Milwaukee.

Solomon Michael(2003), "Conquering the Consumer Mindspace", Amcom 10, pp.151-153.

Solomon, M. R., Ashmore, R. D., & Longo, L. C. (1992). The beauty match-up hypothesis: Congruence between types of beauty and product images in advertising. *Journal of Advertising*, 21, 23-34.

Solomon, M. R., Suprenant, C., Czepiel, J. A, & Gutman, E. G. (1985). A role theory perspective on dyadic interactions: the service encounter. *Journal of Marketing, 48*, 99-111.

Song, J. and Zahedi, F.M. (2001). Web Design in E-Commerce: A Theory And Empirical Analysis. In *Proceedings of the Twenty-Second International Conference of Information Systems (ICIS 2001)*, New Orleans, 205-220.

Speer, L. (2005) (French Translation) French Trademark Ruling Against Google Keyword Advertising Upheld on Appeal (French Translation), Commerce & Law Report, pp 296-297.

Spiller, P. and Lohse, G. L. (1998). A Classification of Internet Retail Stores. *International Journal of Electronic Commerce*, 2(2), 29-56.

Spinello, R. (2006) Online brands and trademark conflicts: A Hegelian perspective. *Business Ethics Quarterly*, 16 (3), pp 343-367.

Spiteri, L.F. (2001). Information Architecture of Business-to-Consumer E-Commerce Websites. Part I: The Online Catalogue of Selected Video Retailers. *Journal of Information Science*, 27(4), 239-248.

SPROULL, R. & KIESLER, S. (1991) *Connections: New Ways of Working in the Networked Organization*. MIT Press, Cambridge.

Srinivasan, Srini S., Rolph Anderson, and Kishore Ponnavolu (2002), "Customer loyalty in e-commerce: an exploration of its antecedents and consequences," *Journal of Retailing*, Vol. 78, pp.41-50

Stafford, M. R. (1998). Advertising sex-typed services: The effects of sex, service type, and employee type on consumer attitude. *Journal of Advertising*, 27(2), 65-82.

Staples, D. S., Hulland, J. S., & Higgins, C. A. (1998). A self-efficacy theory explanation for the management of remote workers in virtual organizations. *Journal of Computer Mediated Communication, 3*, 1-38. Available online at www.ascusc.org/jcmc/vo3/

Steenkamp, J.-B. E. M. (1990). Conceptual Model of the Quality Perception Process. *Journal of Business Research, 21*(4), 309-333.

Steinfield, C., & Whitten, P. (2000). Community level socioeconomic impacts of electronic commerce, Journal of Computer Mediated Communication, 5(2). Available online at http://www.ascusc.org/jcmc/vol5/issue2/steinfield.html

Steuer, J. (1992). Defining virtual reality: Dimensions determining tele-presence. Journal of Communication, 42(2), 73-93.

Steuer, J. (1992). Defining Virtual Reality Dimensions Determining Telepresence, *Journal of Communication*, 42 (4), 73-93.

Straub, D.; Limayem, M.; & Karahanna-Evaristo, E. (1995). Measuring system usage: Implications for IS theory and testing. *Management Science.* 41(8), 1328-1342.

Straub, D.W. (1989), "Validating instruments in MIS research" *MIS Quarterly*, Vol. 13, No. 2, pp. 147-169.

Strebinger, A., Treiblmaier, H. (2004) "E-Adequate Branding: Building Offline and Online Brand Structure within a Polygon of Interdependent Forces", Electronic Markets, Vol. 14(2), pp.153-164.

Stringer, K. (2004, September 3). Shoppers who blend store, catalog, Web spend more. *The Wall Street Journal*, p. A7.

Sukpanich, N. and Chen, L. (1999). Antecedents of Desirable Consumer Behaviors in Electronic Commerce. In *Proceedings of the Fifth Americas Conference on Information Systems (AMCIS 1999)*, Milwaukee, 550-552.

Sullivan, D. (2002, 2 July). *FTC Recommends Disclosure to Search Engines.* Retrieved 3 September, 2006

Sullivan, D. (2004). Buying Your Way In: Search Engine Advertising Chart. Available at: http://searchenginewatch.com/showPage.html?page=2167941

Sullivan, D. (2004). Major Search Engines and Directories. Available at: http://searchenginewatch.com/show-Page.html?page=2156221.

Sullivan, D. (2004). *Search Engine Wars V Erupts.* Retrieved 27 August, 2005

Sullivan, D. (2004, 13 Aug). *Pay Per Click Search Engine.* Retrieved 2 September 2006

Sullivan, D. (2004, 5 July). *Submitting via Paid Listings: Overture & Google Adwords.* Retrieved 2 September 2006

Sullivan, D. (2004a, 22 November). *Buying your way in: Search Engine Advertising Chart.* Retrieved 2 September, 2006

Susman, W. I. (1985). *Culture as history: The transformation of American society in the twentieth century.* New York: Pantheon Books.

Swartz, N. (2004a). Much More Than Jobs Being Outsourced. *Information Management Journal, 38*(3), 3.

Swartz, N. (2004b). Offshoring Privacy. *Information Management Journal, 38*(5), 24-26.

Sweeney, J. and Brandon, C. (2006). "Brand Personality: Exploring the Potential to Move From Factorial Analytical to Circumplex Models". Psychology & Marketing. 23 (8), pp. 639-663.

Synodinos, N., Keown, C. and Jacobs, L. (1989) Transitional Advertising Practices: A Survey of Leading Brand Advertisers. *Journal of Advertising Research*, 29 (2), 43-50.

Szymanski, D.M, Bharadwaj, S.G. and Varadarajan, P.R. (1993). Standardization versus Adaptation of International Marketing Strategy: An Empirical Investigation. *Journal of Marketing*, 57 (October), 1-17.

Szymanski, David M. and Richard T. Hise (2000), "e-satisfaction: an initial examination," *Journal of Retailing*, Vol. 76, No. 3, pp.309-322

Talukder, M. & Yeow, P. H. P. (2007). A comparative study of virtual communities in Bangladesh and the USA. *The Journal of Computer Information Systems*, 47(4), 82-90.

Taylor, C.R. and Johnson, C.M. (2002). Standardized vs. specialized international advertising campaigns: What we have learned from academic research in the 1990s. *New Directions in International Advertising Research*, 12, 45-66.

Taylor, Charles R., P. Greg Bonner and Michael Dolezal (2002). Advertising in the Czech Republic: Czech perceptions of effective advertising and advertising clutter. In Charles R. Taylor (ed.), *New direction in International Advertising Research* (Vol 12, pp. 137-149), San Diego, CA: Elsevier.

Tchong, M. (1998). ICONOCAST. *Imagine Media, Inc.* Retrieved on Dec 12 2006 from http://www.iconocast.com/

Teo, S., Lim, V., & Lai, R. (1999). Intrinsic and extrinsic motivation in Internet usage. *Omega International*

Journal of Management Studies, 27, 25-37.

Tharp, M. and Jeong, J. (2001). Executive insights: The global network communications agency. *Journal of International Marketing,* 9(4), 111-131.

Thompson, B. (2003). *Multi-channel service: Boosting customer value and loyalty.* RightNow Technologies. Retrieved from http://www.rightnow.com/resource/crm-whitepapers.html

Thompson, C. (2004). Search Engines Invite New Problems. *Marketing Management* (April), 52-53.

Tirole, J. (1988) "The Theory of Industrial Organization." The MIT press.

TNS Factum (2004). Firemní weby a marketing. Available: http://www.factum.cz/tz93.html.

TNS Factum (2005). Češi a reklama v roce 2004. Available: http:// www.factum.cz/tz124.html.

Tobias, R.D. (1999). *An introduction to partial least squares regression.* SAS Institute, Inc., 1-8.

Tönnies, F. (1957). *Gemeinschaft and Gesellschaft.* (C. P. Loomis, Ed. And Trans.). East Lansing, MI: Michigan State University Press.

Trapp, R. (1999). Blunder Boss. *The British Journal of Administrative Management*(Jul/Aug), 12-16.

Travis, D. (2001). Branding in the digital age. *Journal of Business Strategy, 22*(3), 14–18.

Trevino, L.K. & Webster, J. (1992). Flow in computer-mediated communication: Electronic mail and voice mail evaluation and impacts. *Communication Research,* 19(5), 539-573.

Trevino, L.K. and Webster, J. (1992). Flow in Computer-Mediated Communication. *Communication Research,* 19(5), 539-73.

Trout Jack and Rivkin Steve(1999), "The Power of Simplicity", Tata McGraw Hill, 55.

Tse, D. K., & Lee, W.-N. (1993). Removing Negative Country Images: Effects of Decomposition, Branding and Product Experience. *Journal of International Mar-*

keting, 1(1), 57-75.

Turley, L.W., Moore, P.A. (1995) "Brand name strategies in the service sector", Journal of Consumer Marketing, Vol. 12, No. 4, 1995 pp.42-50.

Tysver, D. (2005) Trademark Dilution, www.bitlaw.com/trademark/dilution.html. Retrieved 3 September 2006

UCLA (2004) Surveying the Digital Future UCLA University. Retrieved September 13 2005 from http://wwwccpuclaedu/pdf/UCLA-Internet-Report-Year-Threepdf

Unie vydavatelů (2005). Internetová reklama v roce 2004 dosáhla 760 milionů Kč. Available: http://www.uvdt.cz/download.aspx?id_file=209.

UsabilityNet (2006). The business case for usability. Article available at http://www.usabilitynet.org/management/c_business.htm

Van Rekom, J., Jacobs, G., and Verlegh, P.W.J. (2006). "Measuring and Managing the Essence of a Brand Personality". Marketing Letters. 17, pp. 181-192.

van REPEN, Erica, Rik Pieters, Jana Fidrmucova and Peter Roosenboom (2000). The Information Content of Magazine Advertising in Market and Transition Economies. *Journal of Consumer Policy*, 23, 257–283.

Varadarajan, R., & Yadav, M. (2002). Marketing strategy and the Internet: An organizing framework. *Journal of the Academy of Marketing Science, 30,* 296-312.

Vellido, A.; Lisboa, P.J.G. and Meehan, K. (2000). Quantitative Characterization and Prediction of On-Line Purchasing Behavior: A Latent Variable Approach. *International Journal of Electronic Commerce,* 4(4), 83-104.

Venable, B.T., Rose, G.M., Bush, V.D., and Gilbert, F.W. (2005). "The Role of Brand Personality in Charitable Giving: An Assessment and Validation". Journal of the Academy of Marketing Science. 33 (3), pp. 295-312.

Venkatesh, V. & Davis, F. D. (2000). Theoretical extension of the technology acceptance model: Four longitudinal field studies. *Management Science,* 46 (2), 186-204.

Venkatesh, V. (2000). Determinants of perceived ease of

use: Integrating control, intrinsic motivation, and emotion into the technology acceptance model. *Information Systems Research*, 11(4), 342-365.

Verhoef, P. (2003), "*Understanding the Effect of Customer Relationship Management Efforts on Customer Retention and Customer Share Development," Journal of Marketing*, 0022-2429, October 1, 2003, Vol. 67, Issue 4

Vijayasarathy, L.R. (2001). The Impact of Shopping Orientations, Product Types, and Shopping Aids on Attitude and Intention to Use Online Shopping. *Quarterly Journal of Electronic Commerce*, 2(2), 99-113.

Vijayasarathy, L.R. and Jones, J.M. (2000). Intentions to Shop Using Internet Catalogues: Exploring the Effects of Product Types, Shopping Orientations, and Attitudes towards Computers. *Electronic Markets*, 10(1), 29-38.

Vijayasarathy, L.R. and Jones, J.M. (2000). Print and Internet Catalog Shopping: Assessing Attitudes and Intentions. *Internet Research: Electronic Networking Applications and Policy*, 10(3), 191-202.

Vijayasarathy, L.R. and Jones, J.M. (2001). Do Internet shopping Aids Make a Difference? An Empirical Investigation. *Electronic Markets*, 11(1), 75-83.

Vividence, Corp. (2001) Moving on up: Move.com improves customer experience. Article available at: http://www.vividence.com/public/solutions/our+clients/success+stories/movecom.htm.

Vrechopoulos, A.P.; Siomkos, G.J. and Doukidis, G.I. (2001). Internet Shopping Adoption by Greek Consumers. *European Journal of Innovation Management*, 4(3), 142-153.

Wagner, T. (2002). Multichannel customer interaction. *Defying the Limits, 1,* 277-280.

Wang, Richard Y. and Diane M. Strong (1996), "Beyond accuracy: What data quality means to data consumers." *Journal of Management Information Systems*, Vol. 12, No.4, pp.5-34

Ward, M.R. and Lee, M.J. (2000). Internet Shopping, Consumer Search and Product Branding. *Journal of Product & Brand Management*, 9(1), 6-20.

Warden, C.A., Lai, M. and Wu, W.Y. (2003). How worldwide is marketing communication on the World Wide Web? *Journal of Advertising Research*, 43(5), 72-84.

Warrington, T.B.; Abgrab, N.J. and Caldwell, H.M. (2000). Building Trust to Develop Competitive Advantage in E-Business Relationships. *Competitiveness Review*, 10(2), 160-168.

Watzlawick, P., Bavelas, J. B. & Jackson, D. D. (1967). *Pragmatics of Human Communication*. New York: W. W. Norton & Company.

Weber, J. (1999). The bottom line. *The Industry Standard*, 5, 2-9.

Webster, J. and Watson, R.T. (2002). Analyzing the Past to Prepare for the Future: Writing a Literature Review. *MIS Quarterly*, 26(2), xiii-xxiii (13-23).

Webster, J., & Martocchio, J.J. (1992). Microcomputer playfulness: Development of a measure with workplace implications. *MIS Quarterly*, 16(2), 201-226.

Wee, Tan T.T. (2004). "Extending Human Personality to Brands: The Stability Factor". Journal of Brand Management. 11 (4), pp. 317-330.

Wehr, L. (2005, 10 May). *Thieves, Scallywags and Scoundrels: Combating Trademark Infringement in Search*. Retrieved 28 August, 2006

Werts, C.E.; Linn, R.L.; & Joreskog, K.G. (1974). Interclass reliability estimates: Testing structural assumptions. *Educational and Psychological Measurement*, 34(1), 25-33.

West, Douglas C. and Stanley J. Paliwoda (1996). Advertising adoption in a developing market economy: The case of Poland. *International Marketing Review*, 13 (4), 82-101.

Westbrook, Robert A. et al. (1983), "Value-percept disparity: An alternative to the disconfirmation of expectations theory of consumer satisfaction," *Advances in consumer research*, Vol. 10, pp. 256-261

Whitaker, L. A. (1998). Human navigation. In Forsythe, C., Grose, E. & Ratner, J. (Eds.) *Human Factors and Web*

Development. Lawrence Erlbaum Associations.

White, G.K. and Manning, B.J. (1998). Commercial WWW Site Appeal: How Does it Affect Online Food and Drink Consumers' Purchasing Behavior? *Internet Research: Electronic Networking Applications and Policy*, 8(1), 32-38.

White, T.B. (2004). Consumer disclosure and disclosure avoidance: A motivational framework. *Journal of Consumer Psychology*, 14, 1&2, 41-52.

Wickens, C. D. (1992*). Engineering psychology and human performance*. New York: Harper Collins.

Williamson, J. (1978). *Decoding advertisements: Ideology and meaning in advertising*. London: Marion Boyars.

Wilson, D.T. (1995). An integrated model of buyer-seller relationships. *Journal of the Academy of Marketing Science*, 23, 4, 335-345.

Wilson, P. (2000, July 4). Canadians hot for net but slow to buy online. Retrieved , from www.ottawacitizen.com

Wind Yoram and Mahajan Vijay(2001), "Digital Marketing", John Wiley and Sons, pp.210-320.

Winer, R.S. (2001), "A Framework for Customer Relationship Management," California Management Review, 43 (Summer), 89-108.

Wold, H. (1974). Causal flows with latent variables, *European Economic Review*, 5, 67-86.

Wold, H. (1985). Partial least squares, in *Encyclopedia of Statistical Sciences*, Kotz, S. & Johnson, N.L. (eds.), 6, New York: Wiley, 581-591.

Wolfinbarger, M. and Gilly, M. (2000). Consumer Motivations for Online Shopping. In *Proceedings of the Sixth Americas Conference on Information Systems (AMCIS 2000)*, Long Beach, 1362-1366.

Wolfinbarger, M. and Gilly, M.C. (2001). Shopping Online for Freedom, Control, And Fun. *California Management Review*, 43(2), 34-55.

Wolfingbarger, Mary and Mary C. Gilly (2001), "Shopping Online for freedom, control, and fun," *California Management Review*, Vol. 43, No.2, pp. 34-55

Wong, A. (2004). The role of emotional satisfaction in service encounters. *Managing Service Quality*, 14(5), 365.

Wong, A., & Sohal, A. (2003). Service quality and customer loyalty perspectives on two levels of retail relationships. *The Journal of Services Marketing*, 17(4/5), 495-511.

Woodruff, R.B. (1997), "Customer Value: The Next Source for Competitive Advantage," Journal of the Academy of Marketing Science, 25 (Spring), 139-53.

Woodside, A.G. & Walser, M.G. (2007), "Building strong brands in retailing," *Journal of Business Research*, Volume 60, Issue 1, January, 1-10.

World Advertising Resource Center (WARC) (2004). *European Marketing Pocket Book*.

Wright, A. A. & Lynch, Jr., J.G (1995), "Communication Effects of Advertising vs. Direct Experience When Both Search and Experience Attributes Are Present," *Journal of Consumer Research*, 21(4), 708-718.

Wu, F., Mahajan, V., & Balasubramanian, S. (2003). An analysis of e-business adoption and its impact on business performance. *Journal of the Academy of Marketing Science*, 31, 425-447.

Zahay, D., Peltier, J.W., Schultz, D., & Griffin, A. (2004), "The Role of Transactional versus Relational Data in IMC Programs: Bringing Customer Data Together," *Journal of Advertising Research*, March, 3-16.

Zajonc, R.(1978), "Feeling and thinking: Preferences need no inferences," *American Psychologist*, 35, 151-175

Zaltman Gerald(2003), "How Consumers Think Insights into the Mind of the Market", HBS, pp.80-90.

Zandpour, F., Campos, V., Catalano, J., Chang, C., Cho, Y.D., Hoobyar, R., Jiang, H.F., Lin, M.C., Madrid, S., Scheideler, P. and Osborn, S.T. (1994). Global Reach and

Local Touch: Achieving Cultural Fitness in TV Advertising. *Journal of Advertising Research*, 34 (5), 35-63.

Zauberman, G. (2003), "The Intertemporal Dynamics of Consumer Lock-In," *Journal of Consumer Research*, 30 (3), 405-419.

Zeithaml, V., Parasuraman, A., & Malholtra, A. (2002). Service quality delivery through Web sites: A critical review of extant knowledge. *Journal of the Academy of Marketing Sciences, 30*, 362-375.

Zeithaml, Valarie A. and Mary Jo Bitner (1997), *Services Marketing,* Singapore, p.114, McGraw-Hill.

Zenith Optimedia (2004). Poland's advertising market in 2004. Available: http://www.eniro.com/AR/EN/2004/filter.asp?filename=eniro04_016.html

Zetlin M and Pfleging, (Oct 2001), "Creators of Online Community", Computer World 29, 34.

Zhang, X., & Prybutok, V. R. (2005). A consumer perspective of e-service quality. *IEEE Transactions on Engineering Management, 52*(4), 461-77.

Zhang, Xiaoni, Kellie B. Keeling, and Robert J. Pavur (2000), "Information quality of commercial web site home pages: an explorative analysis," *in Proceedings of the Twenty First International Conference on Information Systems*, Brisbane, Australia, pp.164-175

Zmud, R.W. (1979). Individual Differences and MIS Success: A Review of the Empirical Literature. *Management Science*, 25(10), 966-979.

Zumpano, A. (2007). "Similar Search Results:Google Wins". Brandchannel.com, Jan. 29, 2007. Available at: http://www.brandchannel.com/features_effect.asp?pf_id=352

Zyman, S. (2002). The end of advertising as we know it. Hoboken, NJ: John Wiley & Sons.

About the Contributors

Subir Bandyopadhyay is a professor of marketing at the School of Business and Economics, Indiana University Northwest. He has also taught previously at McGill University, the University of Cincinnati, and the University of Iowa. He obtained his PhD in marketing from the University of Cincinnati in 1994. He also holds an MBA and a BS in mechanical engineering. He has research interests in e-marketing, retailing, brand management, and global marketing. One of his papers titled "Beyond Country-of-Origin Effects: Introducing the Concept of Place-Origin" won the Best Paper award at the 5th International Society of Marketing and Development conference in June 1995 in Beijing. He has published extensively in many reputed marketing journals including *Marketing Science, Marketing Management, Journal of Retailing and Consumer Services, Journal of Product and Brand Management, Quarterly Journal of Electronic Commerce, Journal of Segmentation in Marketing, Journal of International Consumer Marketing,* and *International Journal of Advertising.* His research has been funded by the Research and University Grants of Indiana University, The Center for Sustaining Regional Vitality, and the Center for Cultural Discovery and Learning, both at IUN, and by many government agencies and NGOs such as SSHRC, CIDA, the Lilly Endowment, the McArthur Foundation, and by private corporations such as Procter & Gamble, Kraft, and the Kroger Co. Dr. Bandyopadhyay has taught many courses including marketing strategy, consumer behavior, marketing management, advertising, e-marketing, and international marketing at the BBA, MBA and PhD levels. Dr. Bandyopadhyay won the Trustee's Teaching Award, Teaching Advancement Grant and the CIBER grant at Indiana University, and Royal Bank Teaching Innovation Grant as well as the Distinguished Teaching Award at McGill University in recognition of his teaching excellence. Recently, he has been inducted in the Faculty Colloquium of Teaching Excellence at Indiana University. Besides North America, Dr. Bandyopadhyay has taught in many countries such as China, Croatia, Singapore, India and Malaysia. In recognition of his contribution to teaching management in China, he was awarded Honorary Professorship in 1995 by the Xi'an Statistical Institute in Xi'an, and in 1998 by Renmin University in Beijing.

* * *

Jose J. Canals-Cerda is an economist working at the Federal Reserve Bank of Philadelphia. He received a PhD in economics from the University of Virginia and was honored with the Tipton R. Snavely Dissertation Award for the best dissertation over a three year period. His research interest is in the area of applied econometrics with applications to industrial organization, Internet markets, development economics, labor economics and risk analysis. His work has been published in *The International Journal of Game Theory, Economic Letters, Econometric Theory* and *The Econometrics Journal* among others.

Luis Casaló is assistant professor at the University of Zaragoza (Spain). His main research line is focused in the analysis of online consumer behaviour in the context of virtual communities. His work has been presented in national and international conferences, and has been published in several journals, such as *Journal of Marketing Communications, Computers in Human Behaviour, Online Information Review*, and books, such as *Mobile Government: An Emerging Direction in E-Government* and *Encyclopedia of Networked and Virtual Organizations*.

Patrali Chatterjee is associate professor of marketing at the School of Business, Montclair State University. Prior to joining Montclair State University, Dr. Chatterjee was assistant professor of marketing and vice chair, Department of Marketing at Rutgers Business School, Rutgers University. She holds a PhD in marketing from Owen School of Management, Vanderbilt University. Prof. Chatterjee's research interests include modeling online consumer behavior using clickstream data, customer equity management and the leveraging technology in sustaining online businesses and nonprofits. Dr. Chatterjee's research has appeared in several books and academic journals including *Advances in Consumer Research, Journal of Business Research, Journal of Computer-Mediated Communication, Journal of Electronic Commerce Research, Journal of Non-Profit and Public Sector Marketing, Marketing Science*, and *Review of Economics and Statistics*. Her research has been featured in business journals like *The Wall Street Journal, Stanford Innovation Review* among others.

Terry Daugherty (PhD, Michigan State University) is an assistant professor in the Department of Advertising and co-director of the Media Research Lab at the University of Texas at Austin. His research focuses on exploring strategic, social, and technological issues involving the mass media with his work appearing in the *Journal of Advertising, Journal of Consumer Psychology, Journal of Computer-Mediated Communication, Journal of Interactive Advertising, Journal of Interactive Marketing, International Journal of Internet Marketing and Advertising*, and is co-editor of the forthcoming *Handbook of Research on Digital Media and Advertising*.

Matthew S. Eastin (PhD, Michigan State University) is an associate professor in the Department of Advertising and co-director of the Media Research Lab, University of Texas at Austin. Dr. Eastin's research focuses on new media behavior and has appeared in the *Journal of Communication, Communication Research, Human Communication Research, Journal of Broadcasting & Electronic Media, CyberPsychology & Behavior, Journal of Computer-Mediated Communication, Computers in Human Behavior* and is Co-Editor of the forthcoming *Handbook of Research on Digital Media and Advertising*.

Carlos Flavián holds a PhD in business administration and is professor of marketing in the Faculty of Economics and Business Studies at the University of Zaragoza (Spain). His research in strategic marketing has been published in several academic journals, such as the *European Journal of Marketing, Journal of Consumer Marketing, Journal of Strategic Marketing, International Review of Retail, Distribution and Consumer Research, Journal of Retailing and Consumer Services*, and different books such as *The Current State of Business Disciplines or Building Society Through e-Commerce*. He is in charge of several competitive research projects being developed on the topic of e-marketing. He is a member of the editorial board of the *Journal of Retailing and Consumer Services*, the *Industrial Marketing Management* and the *Journal of Marketing Communications*.

Harsha Gangadharbatla (PhD, The University of Texas at Austin) is an assistant professor in the Department of Advertising at Texas Tech University. His research interests include, but are not limited to, interactive advertising, social and economic effects of advertising, and alternative media strategies. His work has appeared in the *Journal of Interactive Advertising, the International Journal of Advertising, and the Journal of Computer Mediated Communication* among others.

Miguel Guinalíu holds a PhD in business administration and is assistant professor in the Faculty of Economics and Business Studies (University of Zaragoza, Spain). Previously, he worked as an e-business consultant. His main research line is online consumer behaviour, particularly the analysis of online consumer trust and virtual communities. His work has been presented in national and international conferences, and has been published in several journals, such as *Journal of Marketing Communications, Information & Management, Industrial Management & Data Systems, Internet Research, Journal of Retail & Consumer Services, International Journal of Bank Marketing* or *International Journal of Retail & Distribution Management,* and books, such *as Advances in Electronic Marketing, Mobile Government: An Emerging Direction in E-Government, Encyclopedia Of Networked And Virtual Organizations and Encyclopedia of E-Commerce, E-Government and Mobile Commerce.*

Tobias Kollmann is a professor of business administration at the University of Duisburg-Essen, Germany. He received his doctoral degree in 1997 at the University of Trier, Germany. From 2001, he held the chair for e-business at the University of Kiel/Multimedia Campus Kiel, Germany. Since 2005, he holds the chair for e-business and e-entrepreneurship at the University of Duisburg-Essen, where he focuses particularly on questions of business development in the field of net economy. He published articles in the *International Journal of E-Business Research, Electronic Markets, International Journal of Technology Management,* and books about e-business, online marketing and Web 2.0.

Ning Nan is an assistant professor of management information systems at Price College of Business, University of Oklahoma. She received her PhD from the Ross School of Business at University of Michigan. Her research interests focus on behavioral and economic factors in management information systems. Her work has been published in peer-reviewed journals such as *Journal of Knowledge Management* and *Computational and Mathematical Organization Theory* and presented at numerous national and international conferences such as ICIS, AMCIS, Academy of Management, CSCW and CHI. She has a Master of Art in journalism and mass communication from the University of Minnesota and a Bachelor of Art in advertising from Peking University, China.

V. Aslıhan Nasır received her bachelor's degree in economics and PhD in marketing. In 2004, she joined the Department of Management Information Systems, Bogazici University as assistant professor of marketing. She is currently associate professor at Bogazici University, Turkey. Her research and publications focus on brand management, consumer behaviour and business ethics. Nasır is the author of several articles and research reports that are published in prominent journals and conference proceedings.

Süphan Nasır holds a bachelor's degree in sociology and a master's degree in business administration. In 2005, she got marketing PhD. She is currently assistant professor at the Economics Faculty of

Istanbul University, Turkey. Customer relationship management, consumer behaviour and brand management are the scope of her interest area. She is the author of several articles published in prestigious international journals and international conference proceedings.

Peter O'Connor, PhD, is professor of information systems at Essec Business School France, where he also serves as academic director of Institute de Management Hotelier International (IMHI), Europe's leading MBA program in international hospitality management. His research, teaching and consulting interests focus on distribution, e-commerce and electronic marketing in hospitality and tourism. He has authored two leading textbooks: *Using Computers in Hospitality* (Cassell, UK - now in its third edition) and *Electronic Information Distribution in Hospitality and Tourism Industries* (CABI, UK) as well as countless articles in both the academic and trade press. He is widely sought after to teach seminars on technology management, distribution and electronic marketing by both international hospitality companies and industry associations.

Robert Pennington earned his PhD in mass communication research at the University of Wisconsin. He is on the faculty of the Graduate Institute of Technology & Innovation Management at National Chung Hsing University in Taichung, Taiwan. Within the institute, he specializes in the market realization of technology and innovation. In general he specializes in consumption and marketing communication as cultural processes. He has written previously about marketing communication development, Marketing in virtual reality, advertising and brands within consumer culture, the meanings of consumer brands and psycho-linguistic methodology.

Rosemary Serjak is a graduate student at the Faculty of Administration, University of Ottawa in Canada.

Malcolm Smith received his PhD from the University of Oregon. His research has been presented at numerous national and international conferences, and published in various texts and such journals as the *Journal of Gerontology: Psychological Sciences, Journal of Business Research, Psychology and Marketing, Journal of Tourism Research, and the Annals of Tourism*. He has been a visiting professor at the L'viv Institute of Management (Ukraine), University of Oregon, Thammasat University in Bangkok, Thailand, and also for the University of Victoria's (British Columbia) IEMBA.

Christina Suckow graduated in 2004 with a Master of Science in international management at the University of Maastricht, The Netherlands. Since 2005, she has worked as a researcher at the chair for E-Business and E-Entrepreneurship, completing her doctorate degree in the area of marketing. Her academic interests are primarily located in the areas of online marketing and e-branding. She published articles in the *Qualitative Market Research Journal* and the *International Journal of Business Environment*. She is currently completing her dissertation.

Fang Wan is an assistant professor in marketing at the I. H. Asper School of Business, University of Manitoba, Canada. Her research deals with advertising effects, branding, e-commerce and cross-cultural consumer psychology. Dr. Wan has published articles in *Asia Pacific Journal of Marketing and Logistics, American Behavioral Scientist, Advances in Consumer Research* and *European Advances in Consumer Research, Journal of Interactive Advertising and Journal of Marketing Channels*. She has also presented her work at the conferences of the *Association for Consumer Research, American Marketing Associations, Society for Consumer Psychology* and *American Academy of Advertising.*

Index

W

Web site, and consumer experience 78
Web site success, and consumer shopping 241–261
word-of-mouth communication 1, 297

Y

Yahoo 7, 31, 32, 33, 35, 36, 37, 41, 42, 44, 45, 138,
        141, 150, 155, 157